Dictionary of Literary Biography
Yearbook: 1987

Dictionary of Literary Biography Yearbook: 1987

୮୫୲୦

Edited by
J. M. Brook

A Bruccoli Clark Layman Book
Gale Research Company · Book Tower · Detroit, Michigan 48226

Copyright © 1988
GALE RESEARCH COMPANY

Manufactured by Edwards Brothers, Inc.
Ann Arbor, Michigan
Printed in the United States of America

Library of Congress Catalog Card Number 82-645187
ISSN 0731-7867
ISBN 0-8103-1835-0

Contents

Obituaries

Updated Entries

Plan of the Series

The advisory board, the editors, and the publisher of the *Dictionary of Literary Biography* are joined in endorsing Mark Twain's declaration. The literature of a nation provides an inexhaustible resource of permanent worth. We intend to make literature and its creators better understood and more accessible to students and the reading public, while satisfying the standards of teachers and scholars.

To meet these requirements, *literary biography* has been construed in terms of the author's achievement. The most important thing about a writer is his writing. Accordingly, the entries in *DLB* are career biographies, tracing the development of the author's canon and the evolution of his reputation.

The purpose of *DLB* is not only to provide reliable information in a convenient format but also to place the figures in the larger perspective of literary history and to offer appraisals of their accomplishments by qualified scholars.

The publication plan for *DLB* resulted from two years of preparation. The project was proposed to Bruccoli Clark by Frederick G. Ruffner, president of the Gale Research Company, in November 1975. After specimen entries were prepared and typeset, an advisory board was formed to refine the entry format and develop the series rationale. In meetings held during 1976, the publisher, series editors, and advisory board approved the scheme for a comprehensive biographical dictionary of persons who contributed to North American literature. Editorial work on the first volume began in January 1977, and it was published in 1978. In order to make *DLB* more than a reference tool and to compile volumes that individually have claim to status as literary history, it was decided to organize volumes by topic, period, or genre. Each of these freestanding volumes provides a biographical-bibliographical guide and overview for a particular area of literature. We are convinced that this organization–as opposed to a single alphabet method–constitutes a valuable innovation in the presentation of reference material. The volume plan necessarily requires many decisions for the placement and treatment of authors who might properly be included in two or three volumes. In some instances a major figure will be included in separate volumes, but with different entries emphasizing the aspect of his career appropriate to each volume. Ernest Hemingway, for example, is represented in *American Writers in Paris, 1920-1939* by an entry focusing on his expatriate apprenticeship; he is also in *American Novelists, 1910-1945* with an entry surveying his entire career. Each volume includes a cumulative index of subject authors and articles. Comprehensive indexes to the entire series are planned.

With volume ten in 1982 it was decided to enlarge the scope of *DLB*. By the end of 1986 twenty-one volumes treating British literature had been published, and volumes for Commonwealth and Modern European literature were in progress. The series has been further augmented by the *DLB Yearbooks* (since 1981) which update published entries and add new entries to keep the *DLB* current with contemporary activity. There have also been *DLB Documentary Series* volumes which provide biographical and critical source materials for figures whose work is judged to have particular interest for students. One of these companion volumes is entirely devoted to Tennessee Williams.

We define literature as the *intellectual commerce of a nation:* not merely as belles lettres but as that ample and complex process by which ideas are generated, shaped, and transmitted. *DLB* entries are not limited to "creative writers" but extend to other figures who in their time and in their way influenced the mind of a people. Thus the series encompasses historians, journalists, publishers, and screenwriters. By this means readers of *DLB* may be aided to perceive literature not as cult scripture in the keeping of intellectual high priests but firmly positioned at the center of a nation's life.

DLB includes the major writers appropriate to each volume and those standing in the ranks immediately behind them. Scholarly and critical counsel has been sought in deciding which minor figures to include and how full their entries should be. Wherever possible, useful references are made to figures who do not warrant separate entries.

Each *DLB* volume has a volume editor responsible for planning the volume, selecting the figures for inclusion, and assigning the entries. Volume editors are also responsible for preparing, where appropriate, appendices surveying the major periodicals and literary and intellectual movements for their volumes, as well as lists of further readings. Work on the series as a whole is coordinated at the Bruccoli Clark Layman editorial center in Columbia, South Carolina, where the editorial staff is responsible for accuracy of the published volumes.

One feature that distinguishes *DLB* is the illustration policy—its concern with the iconography of literature. Just as an author is influenced by his surroundings, so is the reader's understanding of the author enhanced by a knowledge of his environment. Therefore *DLB* volumes include not only drawings, paintings, and photographs of authors, often depicting them at various stages in their careers, but also illustrations of their families and places where they lived. Title pages are regularly reproduced in facsimile along with dust jackets for modern authors. The dust jackets are a special feature of *DLB* because they often document better than anything else the way in which an author's work was perceived in its own time. Specimens of the writers' manuscripts are included when feasible.

Samuel Johnson rightly decreed that "The chief glory of every people arises from its authors." The purpose of the *Dictionary of Literary Biography* is to compile literary history in the surest way available to us—by accurate and comprehensive treatment of the lives and work of those who contributed to it.

The *DLB* Advisory Board

Foreword

The *Dictionary of Literary Biography Yearbook* is guided by the same principles that have provided the basic rationale for the entire *DLB* series: 1) the literature of a nation represents an inexhaustible resource of permanent worth; 2) the surest way to trace the outlines of literary history is by a comprehensive treatment of the lives and works of those who contributed to it; and 3) the greatest service the series can provide is to make literary achievement better understood and more accessible to students and the literate public, while serving the needs of scholars. In keeping with those principles, the *Yearbook* has been planned to augment *DLB* by reflecting the vitality of contemporary literature and summarizing current literary activity. The librarian, scholar, or student attempting to stay informed of literary developments is faced with an endless task. The purpose of *DLB Yearbook* is to serve these readers while at the same time enlarging the scope of *DLB*.

DLB Yearbook is divided into four sections: articles about the past year's literary events or topics; obituaries and tributes; updates of published *DLB* entries; and new author entries. The articles section features essays which discuss the year's work in fiction, poetry, drama, and literary biography. The *Yearbook* also endeavors to cover major awards and prizes. This volume covers the 1987 Nobel Prize in Literature (including Joseph Brodsky's Nobel Lecture). There is also an entry on the Elmer Holmes Bobst Awards in Arts and Letters. Each year a literary research archive is described; the 1987 *Yearbook* features Washington University's Special Collections. In "Literary Documents II" the *Yearbook* presents statements and questionnaires from first novelists solicited by *Library Journal* for use in their survey of new creative writers. The 1987 *Yearbook* marks the beginning of two new surveys that will continue in subsequent volumes: "Book Reviewing in America" and "New Literary Periodicals." Special features of the first section include a description of Columbia University's holdings of papers of prom-

inent American publishers and literary agents and an interview with a distinguished practicing biographer–this year David Herbert Donald.

The death of a literary figure prompts an assessment of his achievement and reputation. The Obituaries section marks the passing of three authors in 1987.

The third section, Updated Entries, is designed to supplement the *DLB* series with current information about the literary activities of authors who have entries in previously published *DLB* volumes. An Updated Entry takes as its point of departure an already published *DLB* entry, augmenting primary and secondary bibliographical information, providing descriptions and assessments of new works, and, when necessary, reassessing an author's reputation. The form of entry is similar to that in the standard *DLB* series, and an Updated Entry is preceded by a reference to the *DLB* volume in which the basic entry on the subject appears. Readers seeking information about an author's entire career should consult the basic entry along with the Updated Entry for complete biographical and bibliographical information.

The fourth section is devoted to New Entries on figures not previously included in *DLB*. These entries follow the established format for the series: emphasis is placed on biography and summaries of the critical reception of the author's works; primary bibliographies precede each entry, and a list of references follows the entry.

Each *Yearbook* includes a list of literary prizes and awards, a necrology, and a checklist of books about literary history and biography published during the year.

From the outset, the *DLB* series has undertaken to compile literary history as it is revealed in the lives and works of authors. The *Yearbook* supports that commitment, providing a useful and necessary current record. The march of literature does not halt.

Acknowledgments

This book was produced by Bruccoli Clark Layman, Inc. Karen L. Rood is senior editor for the *Dictionary of Literary Biography* series.

Production coordinator is Kimberly Casey. Art supervisor is Cheryl Crombie. Copyediting supervisor is Patricia Coate. Typesetting supervisor is Kathleen M. Flanagan. Michael D. Senecal is the editorial associate. The production staff includes Rowena Betts, Charles Brower, Joseph Matthew Bruccoli, Mary Colborn, Mary S. Dye, Sarah A. Estes, Cynthia Hallman, Judith K. Ingle, Maria Ling, Warren McInnis, Kathy S. Merlette, Sheri Neal, Joycelyn R. Smith, and Virginia Smith. Jean W. Ross is permissions editor. Joseph Caldwell, photography editor, and Gabrielle Elliott did photographic copy work for the volume.

Walter W. Ross and Rhonda Marshall did the library research with the assistance of the staff at the Thomas Cooper Library of the University of South Carolina: Daniel Boice, Kathy Eckman, Gary Geer, Cathie Gottlieb, David L. Haggard, Jens Holley, Dennis Isbell, Jackie Kinder, Marcia Martin, Jean Rhyne, Beverley Steele, Ellen Tillett, Carole Tobin, and Virginia Weathers.

Special thanks are due Robert Moore and the John Dixon Library at the Lawrenceville School for their help in preparing the entry on Owen Johnson.

Dictionary of Literary Biography
Yearbook: 1987

Dictionary of Literary Biography

The 1987 Nobel Prize in Literature
Joseph Brodsky
(24 May 1940-   )

George L. Kline
Bryn Mawr College

BOOKS*: *Stikhotvoreniia i poemy* (New York & Washington: Inter-Language Literary Associates, 1965);

Elegy to John Donne and Other Poems, selected and translated, with an introduction, by Nicholas Bethell (London: Longmans, Green, 1967);

Ostanovka v pustyne [edited by Max Hayward and George L. Kline] (New York: Chekhov, 1970);

Selected Poems, translated, with an introduction, by Kline, foreword by W. H. Auden (Harmondsworth, U.K.: Penguin, 1973; New York: Harper & Row, 1973);

Konets prekrasnoi epokhi: stikhotvoreniia 1964-1971 (Ann Arbor, Mich.: Ardis, 1977);

Chast' rechi: stikhotvoreniia 1972-1976 (Ann Arbor, Mich.: Ardis, 1977);

V Anglii (Ann Arbor, Mich.: Ardis, 1977);

Einem alten Architekten in Rom: Ausgewählte Gedichte, translated by Karl Dedecius, Rolf Fieguth, and Sylvia List (Munich: Piper, 1978);

A Part of Speech, various translators (New York: Farrar, Straus & Giroux, 1980);

Verses on the Winter Campaign (London: Anvil Press Poetry, 1981);

Novye stansy k Avguste (Ann Arbor, Mich.: Ardis, 1983);

Mramor (Ann Arbor, Mich.: Ardis, 1984); translated by Alan Myers and Brodsky as *Marbles,* in *Comparative Criticism: An Annual Journal,* 7 (1985): 199-245;

Less than One (New York: Farrar, Straus & Giroux, 1986);

Poesie, translated by Giovanni Buttafava (Milan: Biblioteca Adelphi, 1986);

Uraniia (Ann Arbor, Mich.: Ardis, 1987);

Poèmes 1961-1987, various translators (Paris: Gallimard, 1987).

Joseph Brodsky is a traditionalist both in his adherence to strict poetic forms and in his attachment to the historical sources of the fundamental values–mythological, cultural, moral, and religious–of Western civilization. In his poetry sources and origins, whether Greek, Christian, or Old Testament, tend to be characterized by wholeness, the presence of love and miracle, and a sense of the sacredness of life. The break with such origins, in the "imperial" stages of Byzantium and Rome, is marked by fragmentation and dividedness: the opposition of the individual, especially the artist, to the political order, and the corollary themes of betrayal, coercion, and banishment–themes clangorously repeated in our own "imperial" age.

---

*Except for *Mramor,* a play, and *Less than One,* a collection of essays, all of the titles here listed are books of poetry.

Joseph Brodsky in London following the announcement that he had won the Nobel Prize for Literature
(AP/Wide World Photos)

Brodsky employs the traditional forms of Russian prosody in strikingly untraditional ways, displaying impressive technical virtuosity. His language is robust and unsentimental, by turns bookish and colloquial. He is a master of poetic ambiguity and an accomplished ironist, although his irony tends to be playful or gentle rather than harsh or bitter. Some of his most powerful poems evoke an "existentialist" and even "absurdist" vision of the "horrors and atrocities" of human existence. Poetry, for Brodsky, is a revelation of "what time does to the existing individual"–as manifested in loss, separation, deformity, madness, old age, and death. Yet it is poetry which offers a way, in the end perhaps the *only* way, of enduring these horrors. Consciously alluding to his illustrious predecessors in exile–Ovid, Martial, Dante, Osip Mandel'shtam, Marina Tsvetaeva–Brodsky expresses in haunting images, untinged by self-pity, the searing sense of loss

and isolation which comes with banishment from one's native city and native tongue. But Brodsky is above all a moralist, for whom the absurd and the death-in-life of enforced silence are not the whole or final story. "[E]ven after the Absurd," he has written, "one has to live, to eat, drink, . . . betray or not betray one's neighbor."

Joseph Brodsky (in Russian: Iosif Aleksandrovich Brodskii) was born in Leningrad on 24 May 1940 of Russian-Jewish parents. His father served in the Soviet Navy during World War II and later worked as a photojournalist when anti-Semitic regulations cut short his career as a naval officer. His mother worked as a German-Russian interpreter in Soviet prisoner-of-war camps and later as a clerk and bookkeeper. (Vivid details of Brodsky's early life and moving reminiscences of his parents are provided in the first and last essays of *Less than One,* 1986.) The infant Brodsky lived through the German blockade of his city, largely in the care of his grandparents. His mother taught him to read at age four and by age five he was reading Pushkin aloud to her.

Brodsky attended public schools in Leningrad through the eighth grade, but by that year (1955) he had become increasingly impatient with the pervasive indoctrination and the ubiquity of the icons of Lenin and Stalin in every schoolroom. He abruptly quit school, but actively pursued his education on his own. He learned a great deal from other poets, writers, scholars, and translators, many of them much his senior (Victor Zhirmunsky, Boris Tomashevsky, and Efim G. Etkind); and he read widely and deeply in Russian and Western literature, in Russian religious and philosophical thought, in Greek mythology, Roman history, and the poets of the classical world. It was only in 1963–for he was brought up in an entirely secular environment–that he discovered the Old and New Testaments. There is doubtless much truth, despite the hyperbole, in Brodsky's claim in *Less than One* that, as a schoolboy, repeatedly walking past the "magnificent pockmarked façades" of St. Petersburg, with their "porticoes–classical, modern, eclectic, with their columns, pilasters, and plastered heads of mythic animals or people," he "learned more about the history of our world than I subsequently have from any book. Greece, Rome, Egypt–all of them were there. . . ."

Brodsky has said that the "first cry" of his generation was an expression of pain, shock, and shame at the Soviet crushing of the Hungarian uprising of 1956. One consequence of the events of 1956 was the lively cultural ferment of the "Polish October"; under its impetus, and with the help of a young Polish woman who was studying at Leningrad University and who brought him books when she returned from her vacations in Poland, Brodsky mastered the language. This brought him two immediate benefits: acquaintance with some of the leading modern Polish poets (Cyprian Norwid, Zbigniew Herbert, Czeslaw Milosz, Konstanty Galczynski–several of whom he later rendered expertly into Russian), and access to major Western writers then unavailable in Russian translation but widely translated into Polish, among them Joseph Conrad, Marcel Proust, Franz Kafka, William Faulkner, Virginia Woolf, and Eugene Ionesco.

Brodsky worked at various jobs in Leningrad factories and laboratories, and even briefly in a morgue. He joined geological expeditions to the Far North (White Sea region, 1957), the Far East (1958), and the South (Caspian Sea region,

1959 or 1960). It was during one of these expeditions that he experienced something of the horror of the Gulag at first hand: he had to shoot starving, half-crazed bears which had been deprived, by the closing of a slave-labor camp, of their copious supply of human corpses.

It was in 1958 that Brodsky began to write poetry and in January 1959 that he gave his first poetry reading. Over the next two or three years he completed a number of verse translations, from Polish, which he knew, and also from Spanish and Serbo-Croatian, which he did not. In the latter cases he followed a distinguished tradition of Russian poets who have translated from unfamiliar languages (Boris Pasternak from Georgian, Anna Akhmatova from Korean), making use of literal Russian versions prepared by linguists. Professor Etkind, an outstanding theoretician and practitioner of poetic translation (since 1974 a professor at the University of Paris), welcomed Brodsky to his informal translation workshops.

The most momentous event in the young poet's life at the beginning of the 1960s was his meeting with Akhmatova (1889-1966). He was personally close to her during the last half-dozen years of her life and has called her "the best human being I have ever met." He had a similarly close relationship with W. H. Auden (from June 1972 until Auden's death in September 1973). For Brodsky the two older poets served not as direct literary models but rather as vivid exemplars of what it means to be a great poet, and a great human being, living with courage and dignity in desperate times. Akhmatova was the first major literary figure to recognize Brodsky's talent. In December 1963, at a time when he was being hounded by the Soviet authorities, she dedicated a volume of her poetry to him with the inscription: "To Joseph Brodsky, whose poems seem to me to be magical."

Akhmatova was a living link with the great tradition of Russian lyric poetry that stretches back to Gavrila Derzhavin in the eighteenth century. She also knew something of English and American poetry and encouraged Brodsky's already awakened interest in it. Finally, her special love and esteem for Dante, parallel to Mandel'shtam's, found a powerful response in the young poet.

Brodsky had been arrested twice before the arrest in January 1964 which led to his trial for "social parasitism." He has said in an interview with Giovanni Buttafava (*L'Espresso*, 6 December 1987)

that the first arrest is dreadful, the second less so, while the third seems almost a matter of course. It is still not clear why Brodsky was chosen for repressive measures; perhaps the authorities recognized his talent, his energy, and, above all, his independence of mind. Brodsky's was the first trial since the 1930s of a writer simply for the crime of writing, not for any alleged political offense. But the Leningrad crackdown was part of a more general campaign carried out by Nikita Khrushchev between 1958 and 1964 to harness all the energies of Soviet society to socially useful work—as he and the Party defined it. The most brutal of Khrushchev's measures was the introduction in 1961 of capital punishment for a range of large-scale crimes against (state and public) property, a Draconian edict which is still on the Soviet lawbooks.

Brodsky's trial was conducted in February and March 1964 and ended with a sentence of five years at hard labor in the Far North, and this despite support from such prominent Soviet intellectual and cultural figures as Akhmatova and Etkind, Kornei Chukovsky and Dmitri Shostakovich. If Khrushchev had not been toppled in September 1964, Brodsky would most probably have served the entire five-year term. In fact he was released after only twenty months, mostly spent working on a state farm in the tiny, isolated village of Norinskaia in the Archangel region, near the Arctic Circle.

In response to a question as to what had been the most difficult time for him in the Soviet Union, Brodsky said that during his trial he was confined in a psychiatric prison hospital where he was given dreadful "tranquilizing" shots, wakened in the middle of the night, plunged into a cold bath, wrapped in a wet towel, and placed next to a heater. When the heat dried the towel, it tightened, cutting painfully into his flesh.

For Brodsky hard labor—cleaning stables, hauling manure, digging up large stones to clear fields for cultivation—was a drastic change for a city boy, though he had been partly prepared for it by his work on geological expeditions. But he was well treated by the villagers, who were devout and charitable; and because of the harsh climate and long winter nights, he had a great deal of time for reading and writing. He recalls it as one of the most productive periods of his life.

It was also in exile that Brodsky mastered literary English. He had studied the language during the last four years of his enrollment in the Leningrad schools; but foreign languages were taught in a formal and theoretical way—by incompetent and inexperienced teachers using inadequate texts—and the results were meager. In Norinskaia Brodsky had Louis Untermeyer's anthology of English and American poetry. Using a Russian-English dictionary he made literal translations of the first and last stanzas of poems by Dylan Thomas, Auden, T. S. Eliot, William Butler Yeats, and Wallace Stevens, and then tried to "imagine" what, poetically speaking, should come in between.

When Eliot died (on 4 January 1965) the news reached Brodsky within a week, and he had, within twenty-four hours, completed his powerful and moving poem "Verses on the Death of T. S. Eliot," the formal model of which was Auden's 1939 poem "In Memory of W. B. Yeats."

By the time Brodsky returned to Leningrad (in November 1965), a book of his poetry had been published, in Russian, in the United States. Brodsky, needless to say, had no part in its preparation and was dissatisfied both with the selection (too many of his juvenilia from the period 1958-1960, which he did not wish to have published) and with the large number of misprints, some of which distorted his meaning. It is now generally known that the Russian-American editor and introducer of the volume was the late Gleb Struve, writing under the pseudonym "Georgi Stukov"; the texts he used were the often unreliable samizdat versions, the only ones then available. On the other hand, the 1965 volume did contain two of Brodsky's major poems of 1963, "Elegy for John Donne" and the still untranslated "Isaac and Abraham."

In June 1966, on the occasion of the Day of Victory, Evgeni Evtushenko, already a celebrated and widely traveled Soviet poet, invited Brodsky to join Bella Akhmadulina and Bulat Okudzhava in a public reading at Moscow University. The other poets read their war poems, and Brodsky had none, which left him in a rather awkward position. But Brodsky recognizes that Evtushenko was taking a considerable risk in including him. On the other hand, Evtushenko stubbornly refused to include the poem "A Prophecy" (1965) in a selection of Brodsky's verse that he was planning to publish in the journal *Iunost'*—he found it "too metaphysical," and, since Brodsky insisted on its inclusion, the entire publishing project was dropped. In fact, between 1961 and 1987 only four of Brodsky's poems appeared in Soviet print, in *Molodoi Leningrad* (1966) and *Den' poezii* (1967). After the announcement of Brodsky's

Nobel Prize, several of his poems appeared in *Novyi mir* (Moscow) for December 1987.

The first volume of Brodsky's poetry in which he was actively involved was *Ostanovka v pustyne* (A Halt in the Wilderness, 1970). Beginning in 1967 and 1968 Brodsky put together a table of contents for the book, stipulating not only which poems should be included, but in what order.

On 10 May 1972 Soviet security officials "invited" Brodsky to leave, to accept an "invitation to Israel." They made it clear that things would go badly for him if he refused. He managed to get an extension so that he could spend his thirty-second birthday with his parents, then flew to Vienna on 4 June.

He was met in Vienna by the late Carl R. Proffer, a publisher (he and his wife Ellendea founded Ardis Publishing Company) and professor of Russian language and literature at the University of Michigan. Proffer arranged for Brodsky to be named poet in residence and special lecturer at his campus and introduced him to Auden, then spending his summers at Kirchstetten, near Vienna. Auden took Brodsky to London and introduced him to several literary figures, including Stephen Spender. Brodsky became a U.S. citizen on 11 October 1977, in Detroit. (In responding to questions inspired by his receipt of the Nobel Prize, he has identified himself as "A Russian poet, an English essayist, and an American citizen.")

He is currently a professor at the Five Colleges (Amherst, Smith, Mt. Holyoke, Hampshire, and the University of Massachusetts), where he regularly teaches during the Spring Semester courses both in Russian poetry and in contemporary world poetry. Brodsky has also taught at Queens College, Columbia University, and New York University. He maintains an apartment in Greenwich Village, New York. He has held a Guggenheim Fellowship in poetry and a five-year McArthur Fellowship; in May 1978 Yale University conferred on him the honorary degree of Doctor of Letters. He is a member of the Bavarian Academy of Fine Arts and was a member of the American Academy of Arts and Letters until he resigned in protest in 1987 at the naming of Evtushenko as an honorary member. He has given numerous poetry readings in the United States, Canada, Western Europe, Iceland, and the Caribbean. His works have been translated into more than a dozen languages. *Less than One*

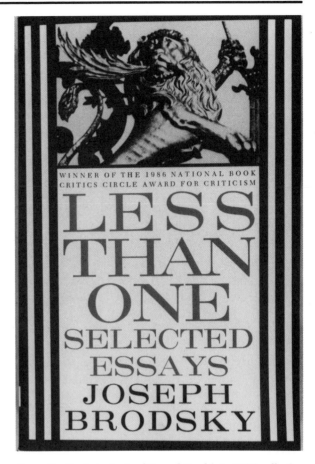

Cover for the paperback edition of Brodsky's 1986 collection of essays

won the National Book Critics Circle award for 1986.

Brodsky has recalled that at age sixteen he was fascinated by the poetry of Robert Burns, which he read in the Russian translations of Samuel Marshak. Another early influence was that of Boris Slutsky, a poet insufficiently appreciated, according to Brodsky. But the main influences upon Brodsky's writings of his mature period are Russian, English, and Polish poetry. In the Russian tradition it is Derzhavin of the eighteenth century, Evgeni Baratynsky of the early nineteenth century, and the three twentieth-century giants: Mandel'shtam, Tsvetaeva, and Pasternak. Equally powerful has been the influence of the English "metaphysical poets" John Donne and Andrew Marvell (both of whom Brodsky has brilliantly translated into Russian), and the twentieth-century English and American poets Robert Frost, Dylan Thomas, Eliot, and Auden. Finally, there is the influence of certain twentieth-century Polish poets, in particular Nobel Laureate Czeslaw Milosz (whom Brodsky has also rendered into Russian verse).

Brodsky has said: "Perhaps exile is the poet's natural condition. . . . I felt a certain privilege in the coincidence of my existential condition with my profession." There are, in Brodsky's work, three distinguishable cycles of "poems of exile": (1) those written during his temporary internal exile in Norinskaia; these poems date from between May 1964 and October 1965; (2) those poems—including several major ones—written in February and March of 1972 in anticipation of the permanent foreign exile which in fact began three months later; (3) those poems written during the early years of his permanent exile, beginning in November 1972, and continuing, with special emphasis, in the period 1974-1976 and 1980.

That the banishment from his native country was much more traumatic than his earlier internal exile is evidenced by two circumstances: (1) the "dry period" during which he was unable to write was twice as long (eight months as against four) in the second case as in the first; (2) to the sense of loss, suffering, and isolation expressed in the first two cycles there is added, in the third cycle, the poignant themes of growing old and dying, of lapsing into the silence of "nonspeaking" (*molchanie*), the loss of that total control of his language which is essential to the poet. At the beginning of the first cycle Brodsky was just twenty-four; at the beginning of the third cycle he was thirty-two. The concern in the latter with growing old and growing silent is not a function of biological age so much as of the finality and irreversibility of his banishment from his country, culture, and language.

In the poems of the first cycle the poet feels "somewhere overboard," "buried alive," "without memories, with only an inner noise." He fears the loss of his five senses and the loss of his mind:

> What does it matter that a shadow of mindlessness
> has crossed my eyes . . . ?
> ....
> But my heart pounds suddenly when I discover
> that somewhere I am torn.
>
> ....
> Here I stand, my coat thrown open,
> letting the world flow into my eyes
> through a sieve of incomprehension.
> I'm nearly deaf. O God, I'm nearly blind.
> ("New Stanzas to Augusta," *Selected Poems;* unless otherwise indicated all translations are by George L. Kline)

In the second cycle of poems of exile a historical and mythological dimension becomes prominent. "Letters to a Roman Friend" (March 1972) evokes the fate of Martial, the Spanish-born Latin poet who, following a brilliant literary career in Rome, was banished to his native Spain where he spent the last years of his life. Here the message is that if one is fated to live out one's life in a great empire, it is best to live as quietly and inconspicuously as possible, remote from the centers of power and intrigue, where—in contrast to one's friends in the metropolis—one will have no need to "hurry, flatter, play the coward."

Mythology is used in another poem of the second cycle to make the painful and personal point—but one presented without self-pity—that a father has been permanently separated from his young son. Odysseus, midway on the long return voyage from Troy, pauses to address his son Telemachus:

> I can't remember how the war came out;
> even how old you are—I can't remember.
>
> Grow up, then, my Telemachus, grow strong.
> Only the gods know if we'll see each other
> again. You've long since ceased to be that babe
> before whom I reined in the pawing bullocks.
> ("Odysseus to Telemachus," *Selected Poems*)

When Brodsky left Leningrad his son Andrei, born on 9 October 1967, was four-and-a-half. (Brodsky was never married to Andrei's mother, the "M.B." to whom the sixty poems in the collection *Novye stansy k Avguste* are dedicated.) And in fact, he has not seen his son, now a twenty-year-old husband and father, during the intervening fifteen years.

The urgent sense of the impending end, of irrecoverable loss, of growing old and lapsing into silence, powerfully expressed in the first major poem of the third cycle—"1972," written in November-December of that year—echoes the parallel between life/speech and death/silence put forward in *Gorbunov and Gorchakov* (1965-1968), an extraordinary, very long poem written between the end of the first and the beginning of the second cycle of poems of exile. There we read:

> And silence is the future of all days
> that roll toward speech; yes, silence is the presence
> of farewells in our greetings as we touch.
> Indeed, the future of our words is silence—
> ....
> And silence is the present fate of those who
> have lived before us. . . .

Life is but talk hurled in the face of silence.
(Gorbunov and Gorchakov, Selected Poems)

In "1972" Brodsky declares: "to grow old is to lose the use of the organ/of hearing, an organ directed toward silence," in other words, the increasing deafness of the old is a preparation for the silence of death, the silence of eternity. Elsewhere in the same poem Brodsky offers a stark list of the things he is losing, things both physical and cultural or spiritual: "Here I shall end my days, losing/my teeth and hair, my verbs and endings," in other words, the total control of the poet's language to which we have already referred.

The sense of loss is movingly expressed in Brodsky's "Christmas" poem "Lagoon" (1973), set in Venice:

And a nameless lodger, a nobody, boards the boat,
a bottle of grappa concealed in his raincoat
    as he gains his shadowy room, bereaved
of memory, homeland, son. . . .
(A Part of Speech, translated by Anthony Hecht)

In three poems of the third cycle, dating from 1974 to 1976, a new theme appears: the poet's identification, or at least close association, with three historical figures: Dante, Mary Queen of Scots, and Marshal Georgi Zhukov. Different as these three historical figures are, they share a common fate: each of them was abused (imprisoned, exiled, or executed) by the city or country which eventually came to pay them high honor. This "rehabilitation" is clearest in the case of Dante, least clear—or at least not yet complete—in the case of Zhukov.

"On the Death of Zhukov" (1974) draws an anology between the "gift" which a great military leader brings to his people (the gift of victory, of freedom) and the gift which a poet brings. The ingratitude with which both are treated is also analogous: disgrace and banishment. The opening lines depict a military funeral:

Splendid regalia deck out the corpse:
thundering Zhukov rolls toward death's mansion.

Following a description of Zhukov's great victories in World War II, his fall from grace is evoked:

    And his last days
found him, like Pompey, fallen and humbled—
like Belisarius banned and disgraced.

The name of Hannibal is added to those of Belisarius and Pompey–generals who had brilliantly served their respective countries, but then suffered disgrace and exile. Finally, the parallel between soldier and poet is made explicit:

Marshal! These words will be swallowed by Lethe,
utterly lost, like your rough soldier's boots.
Still, take this tribute, though it is little [.]
(A Part of Speech)

Both the form and certain key terms of Brodsky's poem evoke the memory of Derzhavin's poem "The Bullfinch" (1800), written on the death of Marshal Alexander Suvorov. The meter of Brodsky's poem, with a caesura in each line, like that of Derzhavin's poem, suggests the slow interrupted beat of a military funeral march.

In the "Twenty Sonnets to Mary Queen of Scots" (1974) the parallel between the fate of Mary Stuart and the poet is clearly drawn. In Sonnet eight Brodsky, or his poetic persona, pictures himself as living in the time of, and indeed living with, Mary Stuart:

Your Scottish shires would serve as lovers' beds.
I'd show you off to my proud Slavs, Mary.

....

We'd face our death together; and the headsman's blade would turn out to be blunt and
    wooden.

The executioner's axe is "wooden," presumably, not in the sense of "make-believe" or "harmless" but in the quite different sense of "blunt," causing a slow and painful death, in contrast to the quick death which a sharp metal blade would cause.

In the Dante poem–"December in Florence" (1976)–although Dante's name is not mentioned, numerous parallels between the lives and fates of the two exiled poets are formulated in the closing stanza:

There are cities in this world to which one can't
    return.
....
Rivers in those cities always flow beneath six
    bridges.
There the crowds besieging trolley stops are
    speaking
in the language of a man who has been written off
    as dead.

("December in Florence," *Shearsman*, translated by Maurice English and George L. Kline; another translation, by Brodsky, appears in *A Part of Speech*)

In Dante's time there were six bridges in Florence (there are now seven), the same number as in Brodsky's native St. Petersburg/Leningrad. The final lines assert a bold parallel between the way Dante shaped the Italian language–now spoken by the ordinary people of his native Florence– and the way Brodsky has shaped the contemporary Russian literary language. Perhaps an overstatement, but the basic point is that both exiled poets have made permanent contributions to their respective languages and cultures despite their condition of banishment.

The description of the abused poet is even more personal in "Plato Elaborated," written in February 1977, thirteen years to the month after the beginning of Brodsky's trial. The title refers to Plato's proposal (in the *Republic*) that poets be banished from the ideal city. Brodsky is imagining what would have happened to him if he had stayed in, or returned to, the Soviet Union.

> And when they would finally arrest me for
>   espionage,
> for subversive activity, vagrancy, for *ménage*
>   *à trois*, and the crowd, boiling around me,
>   would bellow,
> poking me with their work-roughened forefingers,
>   "Outsider, we'll settle your hash!"–
>
> then I would secretly smile, and say to myself, "See,
> this is your chance to find out, in Act Three,
>   how it looks from the inside–you've stared long
>   enough at the outside–
> so take note of every detail as you shout, '*Vive la
>   patrie!*'"
>
> (A Part of Speech)

Despite Brodsky's searing depictions of loss and suffering there is a kind of serenity about his work. Related to this is his sense of gratitude for the gift of life, a theme which remains constant from his earliest to his most recent poems of exile. His first Christmas poem of exile–"1 January 1965"–opens with a sharp sense of loss and loneliness:

> The Wise Men will unlearn your name.
> Above your head no star will flame.
> ....
> You glare in silence at the wall.
> Your stocking gapes: no gifts at all.

But it continues:

> Let it sound in my hour of death–
> as gratefulness of eyes and lips
> for that which sometimes makes us lift
> our gaze to the far sky.

And it ends:

> –But suddenly, lifting your eyes
> to heaven's light, you realize:
> your *life* is a sheer gift.
>
> (Selected Poems)

Fifteen years later, in a memorable poem written on his fortieth birthday, Brodsky reiterated this theme. After cataloging the disasters that have filled his life–"I've abandoned the country that nourished me./ . . . /I've eaten the bread of banishment and left no crusts."–he goes on to declare in the closing lines: "Until my mouth is wholly stopped up with clay,/nothing but gratitude will issue from it."

As a poet in exile Brodsky stands in the tradition of Conrad rather than in that of Ovid. Rather than wasting himself in nostalgia for his lost homeland (like Ovid in the Crimea), he has thrown himself with notable energy and imagination into the language, literature, and culture of his adopted country. Like Goethe, and in sharp contrast to his fellow exiles among Russian writers, Andrei Siniavsky and Alexander Solzhenitsyn (the latter, like Brodsky, a Nobel Laureate), he is, and indeed always has been, a "good European."

At his trial in Leningrad, when asked by the judge why he had not attended a Soviet university in order to learn how to be a poet, Brodsky answered that he did not think that was the way poets are made. "How, then are poets made?" demanded the judge. "I think . . . by God" was Brodsky's response. Not only the calling of the poet, but poetry as such, has for him a spiritual, religious foundation and core. One can discern at least six explicitly religious themes in his poetry: (1) the theme of suffering and sacrifice; (2) the theme of the transition from the Old Testament to the New; (3) the Nativity theme; (4) the theme of the loss or absence of miracle; (5) the Easter theme; and (6) the theme of religion and (modern, secular) culture.

The principal text of the first theme is the untranslated, and in part untranslatable, long poem "Isaac and Abraham," which Brodsky composed within a matter of days after first reading *Genesis*.

Publisher's advertisement in the 28 October 1987 New York Times

This is a meditation on the meaning and value of sacrifice, a series of variations on the theme of sacrifice. Its untranslatability stems in part from the way that words interact with things. Thus, there is a stunning transformation of the word *kust* ("bush") into the word *krest* ("cross"), a process which takes place (in Isaac's dream) painfully, letter by letter, symbolizing the conversion of a part of nature into the altar upon which Isaac is to be sacrificed. The very name "Isaac" becomes a kind of acronym, formed from the first, the last, or the first and last letters of several key words:

> I Snov̲A̲ zhertv̲A̲ na ogne K̲richit:
> Vot to, chto "ISAAK" po-russki znachit.
> (The victim wr̲I̲the̲S̲ upon the fl̲A̲me A̲nd s̲C̲reams:
> This is what "ISAAC" comes to mean in Russian.)
> 　　　　　　　　　　　　　(*Ostanovka v pustyne*)

St. Simeon, in the poem *"Nunc dimittis"* (February-March 1972), serves as bridge from the Old to the New Testament. His death is the "first Christian death in history"; he dies–as had been foretold–as soon as he has seen the Christ child. Here are the last two stanzas:

> The rustle of time ebbed away in his ears.
> And Simeon's soul held the form of the Child–
> its feathery crown now enveloped in glory–

> aloft, like a torch, pressing back the black
> 　shadows,

> to light up the path that leads into death's realm,
> where never before until this present hour
> had any man managed to lighten his pathway.
> 　The old man's torch glowed and the pathway
> 　grew wider.
> 　　　　　　　　　　　　　(*A Part of Speech*)

Brodsky has written more than a score of poems on the Nativity theme, beginning with "A Christmas Ballad" (1962), with its haunting refrain "In anguish unaccountable." One of them, which has already been quoted, expresses the joy in life and gratitude for the gift of existence, something close to what Siniavsky saw in Pasternak: "astonishment at the miracle of existence."

In some of his later Christmas poems, such as "Lagoon," from the third cycle of poems of exile, there is a sense of loss or absence of miracle and mystery.

The Easter theme–passion, crucifixion, suffering, death, and resurrection–is expressed most clearly in *"Adieu, Mademoiselle Véronique"* (1967) and *Gorbunov and Gorchakov* (1965-1968). In the former poem we read:

> In some twenty years I shall fetch the armchair
> that you sat on, facing me, on Good Friday
> when, for Christ's body, the cross's torments

at last were ended. . . .

....

The total of all of today's embraces
gives far less of love than the outstretched arms of
Christ on the cross. . . .

....

(for death can have variants, and it's valor
in men to foreknow them), alas, my fate is
to be worthy of being denounced and sentenced
to a term in a work-camp, and dysentery–
but if only it isn't a lie they've told me,
and old Lazarus rose from the dead in truth, then
I too shall rise, rushing for that armchair.

(Selected Poems)

Gorbunov and Gorchakov is a formal tour de force. It is a sustained Dostoevskian dialogue between two inmates of a psychiatric hospital. The name "Gorbunov" suggests the Russian word for "hunchback" (*gorbun*); Gorbunov is a kind of spiritual and emotional cripple, beaten down and tormented by the world. "Gorchakov" suggests the Russian word for "bitterness" (*gorech'*); Gorchakov is a bitter man who embitters the lives of others, especially that of Gorbunov. He reports to the hospital authorities the unorthodox dreams which Gorbunov had related to him in confidence and is rewarded with a promise of "release at Easter time." Gorchakov thus emerges as a Judas figure and Gorbunov as a Christ figure, betrayed and crucified.

The Easter theme is sounded again in "*Nature Morte*" (1971), the final section of which reads as follows:

Mary now speaks to Christ:
"Are you my son?–or God?
You are nailed to the cross.
Where lies my homeward road?

How can I close my eyes,
uncertain and afraid?
Are you dead?–or alive?
Are you my son?–or God?"

Christ speaks to her in turn:
"Whether dead or alive,
woman, it's all the same–
son or God, I am thine."

(Selected Poems)

The theme of the opposition between the values of religious tradition and the values of contemporary secular culture is most clearly expressed in the poem "Ostanovka v pustyne" (1966, A Halt in the Wilderness [or Desert]). It involves as well the opposition of life ("the spirit") to dead matter, especially that of machines. A Greek-Orthodox church has been razed to make room for a glass and steel concert hall; this in fact happened, not far from Brodsky's home in Leningrad in the mid 1960s. The church is a living thing. The neighborhood dogs, at least, are faithful to its memory; for them "the church still stands." But the machines that batter down the church's walls are quite insensitive to the miracle of its life:

Moreover, the power shovel may have thought
the wall a dead and soulless thing and thus,
to a degree, like its own self.

....

So, in the end, I sat–late that same night–
among fresh ruins in the church's apse.
Night yawned behind the altar's gaping holes.
And through these open altar wounds I watched
retreating streetcars as they slowly swam
past phalanxes of deathly pale streetlamps.

....

Some day, when we who now live are no more,
or rather after we have been, there will
spring up in what was once our space
a thing of such a kind as will bring fear,
a panic fear, to those who knew us best.
But those who knew us will be very few.

(Selected Poems)

Brodsky maintains that poetry stands between intuition (or "intuitive synthesis") and what in biblical terms is called "revelation." He also insists that the poet is the instrument of language, rather than vice versa.

His prose is a poet's prose, full of imagery, startling insights, and provocative (sometimes extreme) claims. Since 1976 he has been writing essays directly in English. *Less than One* contains, in addition to the memoirs of his Leningrad childhood already mentioned, brilliant explorations of the work of such Russian poets as Akhmatova, Mandel'shtam, and Tsvetaeva; of such English-language poets as Auden and Derek Walcott; of Cavafy and Eugenio Montale; and (in "Flight from Byzantium") of the moral and spiritual contrast between East and West. This prompts a few concluding remarks about Brodsky as a moralist and political thinker.

Brodsky insists that the writer's only duty to society is to write well, adding that "No form of government can save people from death or from evil." As he had declared in "To Lycomedes on Scyros" (1967):

When all is said and done, a murder is
a murder. And we mortals have a duty

to take up arms against all monsters. Who
maintains that monsters are immortal?

(Selected Poems)

Although Brodsky's is a private, not a public
muse, and he had written only one political
poem before 1972, the untranslated and uneven
"Rech' o prolitom moloke" (1967, Discourse
about Spilt Milk), he greeted the Soviet invasion
of Afghanistan with a powerful denunciatory
poem, "Verses on the Winter Campaign of 1980"
(1980), reminiscent of Auden's powerful short
poem "August 1968" on the Soviet invasion of
Czechoslovakia ("The Ogre does what ogres
can"). Brodsky has recalled his experience of the
three Soviet invasions of the past thirty-odd
years: "The invasion of Afghanistan [in 1979]
was worse for me than the invasion of Hungary
[in 1956] or the invasion of Czechoslovakia. First,
because, of course, I didn't see those invasions on
television [as he did that of Afghanistan]. Second, because, after all, the Hungarians and the
Czechs had voted for the Communists. But in Afghanistan a people was attacked which had not
had the least connection with the Soviet Union.
Even worse for me is the thought that my own
son might in a few years be among the twenty-year-
old Red Army troops invading a foreign
country."

Brodsky's moral and political position is admirable, especially when—as is often the case—it
goes against the received wisdom of the hour, particularly the received wisdom of Western intellectuals. However, as Brodsky himself has pointed
out, the critical acclaim which he has received, including the 1987 Nobel Prize for Literature,
came as a response to his literary work, not his political perspicacity.

Interviews:

George L. Kline, "A Poet's Map of his Poem" [on
Nunc Dimittis], *Vogue,* 162 (September 1973):
(228, 230);

Sven Birkerts, "The Arts of Poetry XXVIII: Joseph Brodsky," *Paris Review,* no. 83 (Spring
1982): 82-126;

Bella Ezerskaia, "Esli khochesh' poniat' poeta," in
Mastera (Ann Arbor, Mich.: Hermitage,
1982), pp. 103-112;

Solomon Volkov, "Vspominaia Annu Akhmatovu;
Razgovor s Iosifom Brodskim," *Kontinent,*
no. 53 (1987): 337-382;

Giovanni Buttafava, "Iosif Alexandrovic Brod-
skij," *L'Espresso,* 6 December 1987, pp.
152-162;

Anna Husarska, "A Talk with Joseph Brodsky,"
New Leader, 14 December 1987, pp. 8-11.

Bibliography:

George L. Kline, "A Bibliography of the Pub-
lished Works of Iosif Aleksandrovich
Brodsky," in *Ten Bibliographies of Twentieth
Century Russian Literature,* edited by Fred
Moody (Ann Arbor, Mich.: Ardis, 1977),
pp. 159-175.

References:

George L. Kline, "Iosif Brodsky," in *Columbia Dictionary of Modern European Literature,* edited
by Jean-Albert Bédé and William B.
Edgerton (New York: Columbia University
Press, 1980), pp. 121-122;

Kline and Richard D. Sylvester, "Iosif
Aleksandrovich Brodskii," in *Modern Encyclo-
pedia of Russian and Soviet Literature,* 3
(1979): 129-137;

L. V. Losev, "Niotkuda s liubov'iu: zametki o
stikhakh Iosifa Brodskogo," *Kontinent,* no.
14 (1977): 307-331;

Losev, ed., *Poetika Brodskogo* (Tenafly, N.J.: Hermitage, 1986);

Michael Kreps, *O poezii Iosifa Brodskogo* (Ann
Arbor, Mich.: Ardis, 1984);

Carl R. Proffer, "A Stop in the Madhouse:
Brodsky's *Gorbunov and Gorchakov,*" *Russian
Literature TriQuarterly,* no. 1 (1971): 342-351;

Richard D. Sylvester, "The Poem as Scapegoat:
An Introduction to Joseph Brodsky's *Halt in
the Wilderness,*" *Texas Studies in Literature and
Language,* 17 (1975): 303-325;

Kees Verheul, "Iosif Brodsky's 'Aeneas and
Dido,'" *Russian Literature TriQuarterly,* no. 6
(1973): 490-501.

NOBEL LECTURE 1987
Delivered by Joseph Brodsky

Translated from the Russian
by Barry Rubin

I

For someone rather private, for someone who all
his life has preferred his private condition to any

role of social significance, and who went in this preference rather far–far from his motherland to say the least, for it is better to be a total failure in democracy than a martyr or crème de la crème in tyranny–for such a person to find himself all of a sudden on this rostrum is a somewhat uncomfortable and trying experience.

This sensation is aggravated not so much by the thought of those who stood here before me as by the memory of those who have been bypassed by this honor, who were not given this chance to address 'urbi et orbi,' as they say, from this rostrum and whose cumulative silence is sort of searching, to no avail, for release through this speaker.

The only thing that can reconcile one to this sort of situation is the simple realization that–for stylistic reasons, in the first place–one writer cannot speak for another writer, one poet for another poet especially; that had Osip Mandelstam, or Marina Tsvetaeva, or Robert Frost, or Anna Akhmatova, or Wystan Auden stood here, they couldn't have helped but speak precisely for themselves, and they, too, might have felt somewhat uncomfortable.

These shades disturb me constantly, they are disturbing me today as well. In any case, they do not spur one to eloquence. In my better moments, I deem myself their sum total, though invariably inferior to any one of them individually. For it is not possible to better them on the page; nor is it possible to better them in actual life. And it is precisely their lives, no matter how tragic or bitter they were, that often moves me–more often perhaps than the case should be–to regret the passage of time. If the next life exists–and I can no more deny them the possibility of eternal life than I can forget their existence in this one–if the next world does exist, they will, I hope, forgive me and the quality of what I am about to utter: after all, it is not one's conduct on the podium which dignity in our profession is measured by.

I have mentioned only five of them–those whose deeds and whose lot matter so much to me–if only because if it were not for them, I, both as a man and a writer, would amount to much less: in any case, I wouldn't be standing here today. There were more of them, those shades, better still, sources of light–lamps? stars?–more, of course, than just five. And each one is capable of rendering me absolutely mute. The number of those is substantial in the life of any conscious man of letters; in my case, it's dou-

bling, thanks to the two cultures to which fate has willed me to belong. Matters are not made easier by thoughts about contemporaries and fellow writers in both cultures, poets and fiction writers whose gifts I rank above my own and who, had they found themselves on this rostrum, would have already come to the point long ago, for surely they have more to tell the world than I do.

Therefore, I will allow myself to make a number of remarks here–disjointed, perhaps stumbling, and perhaps even perplexing in their randomness. However, the amount of time allotted to me to collect my thoughts, as well as my very occupation, will or may, I hope, shield me, at least partially, against charges of being chaotic. A man of my occupation seldom claims a systematic mode of thinking; at worst, he claims to having a system, but even that in his case is borrowing from a milieu, a social order, or from the pursuit of philosophy at a tender age. Nothing convinces an artist more of the arbitrariness of the means he resorts to to attain a goal–however permanent it may be–than the creative process itself, than the process of composition. Verse really does, in Akhmatova's words, grow from rubbish; the roots of prose are no more honorable.

II

If art teaches anything (to the artist, in the first place), it is the privateness of the human condition. Being the most ancient as well as the most literal form of private enterprise, it fosters in a man, knowingly or unwittingly, a sense of his uniqueness, of individuality, of separateness–thus turning him from a social animal into a perceptible "I." Lots of things can be shared: a bed, a piece of bread, convictions, a mistress, but not a poem by, say, Rainer Maria Rilke. A work of art, of literature especially, and a poem, in particular, addresses a man tête-à-tête, entering with him into direct–free of any go-betweens–relations. It is for this reason that art in general, literature especially, and poetry in particular, is not exactly favored by the champions of the common good, masters of the masses, heralds of historical necessity. For there, where art has stepped, where a poem has been read, they discover, in place of anticipated consent and unanimity, indifference and polyphony; in place of the resolve to act, inattention and fastidiousness. In other words, into the little zeros with which the champions of the common good and the rulers of the masses tend to operate, art introduces a "period, period, comma, and a minus," transforming each zero into a tiny human, albeit not always pretty, face.

The great Baratynsky, speaking of his Muse, characterized her as possessing an "uncommon visage." It's in acquiring this "uncommon visage" that the meaning of human existence seems to lie, since it is for this uncommonness that we are, as it were, prepared genetically. Regardless of whether one is a writer or a reader, his task consists first of all in mastering a life that is his own, not one imposed or prescribed from without, no matter how noble its appearance may be. For each of us is issued with but one life, and we know full well how it all ends. It would be regrettable to squander this one chance on someone else's appearance, someone else's experience, on a tautology—regrettable all the more because the heralds of historical necessity, at whose urging, a man may be prepared to agree to this tautology, will not go to the grave with him or give him so much as a thank-you.

Language and, presumably, literature are things that are more ancient and inevitable, more durable than any form of social organization. The revulsion, irony, or indifference often expressed by literature towards the state is essentially the reaction of the permanent—better yet, the infinite—against the temporary, against the finite. To say the least, as long as the state permits itself to interfere with the affairs of literature, literature has the right to interfere with the affairs of the state. A political system, a form of social organization, as any system in general, is by definition a form of the past tense that aspires to impose itself upon the present (and often on the future as well), and a man whose profession is language is the last one who can afford to forget this. The real danger for a writer is not so much the possibility of finding oneself mesmerized by the state's features; be they monstrous or undergoing changes for the better, they are always temporary.

The philosophy of the state, its ethics—not to mention its aesthetics—are always "yesterday"; language, literature are always "today," and often—particularly in the case where a political system is orthodox—they may even constitute "tomorrow." One of literature's merits is precisely that it helps a person to make the time of his existence more specific, to distinguish himself from the crowd of his predecessors as well as his like numbers, to

avoid tautology—that is, the fate otherwise known by the honorific term, "victim of history." What makes art in general and literature in particular remarkable, what distinguishes them from life, is precisely that they abhor repetition. In everyday life you can tell the same joke three times and, having elicited laughter each time, become the life of the party. In art, though, this sort of conduct is called "cliché." Art is an unrecoiling weapon, and its development is determined not by the individuality of the artist but by the dynamics and the logic of the material itself, by the previous fate of the means that each time demand (or suggest) a qualitatively new aesthetic solution. Possessing its own genealogy, dynamics, logic, and future, art is not synonymous with, but, at best, parallel to history; and the manner by which it exists continually reinvents aesthetic reality. That is why it is often found "ahead of progress," ahead of history whose main instrument is—should we not, once more, improve upon Marx—precisely the cliché.

Nowadays, there exists a rather widely held assertion, postulating that in his work a writer, in particular a poet, should make use of the language of the street, the language of the crowd. For all its democratic appearance, and its palpable advantages for a writer, this assertion is quite absurd and represents an attempt to subordinate art, in this case, literature, to history. It is only if we have resolved that it is time for Homo sapiens to come to a halt in his development that literature should speak the language of the people. Otherwise, it is the people who should speak the language of literature. On the whole, every new aesthetic reality makes man's ethical reality more precise. For aesthetics is the mother of ethics; the categories of "good" and "bad" are, first and foremost, aesthetic ones, at least etymologically preceding the categories of "good" and "evil." If in ethics not "all is permitted," it is precisely because not "all is permitted" in aesthetics, because the number of colors in the spectrum is limited. The tender babe who cries and rejects the stranger or who, on the contrary, reaches out to him, does so instinctively, making an aesthetic choice, not a moral one.

Aesthetic choice is a highly individual matter and aesthetic experience is always a private one. Every new aesthetic reality makes one's experience even more private, and this kind of privacy, assuming at times the guise of literary (or some other) taste, can in itself turn out to be, if not a guarantee, then a form of defense against enslavement. For, a man with taste, particularly literary taste, is less susceptible to the refrains and rhythmical incantations peculiar to any version of political demagogy. The point is not so much that virtue does not constitute a guarantee for producing a masterpiece, as that evil, especially political evil, is always a bad stylist. The more substantial an individual's aesthetic experience is, the sounder his taste, the sharper his moral focus, the freer–though not necessarily the happier–he is.

It is certainly in this applied, rather than Platonic, sense that we should understand Dostoevsky's remark that beauty will save the world, or Matthew Arnold's belief that we shall be saved by poetry. It is probably too late for the world, but for the individual man, there always remains a chance. An aesthetic instinct develops in man rather rapidly, for, even without fully realizing who he is and what he actually requires, a person instinctively knows what he doesn't like and what doesn't suit him. In an anthropological respect, let me reiterate, a human being is an aesthetic creature before he is an ethical one. Therefore, it is not that art–particularly literature–is a by-product of our species' development, but just the reverse. If what distinguishes us from other members of the animal kingdom is speech, then literature–and poetry in particular, being the highest form of locution–is, to put it bluntly, the goal of our species.

I am far from suggesting the idea of compulsory training in verse composition; nevertheless, the subdivision of society into intelligentsia and all the rest seems to me unacceptable. In moral terms, this situation is comparable to the subdivision of society into the poor and the rich; but if for the existence of social inequality it is still possible to find some purely physical or material grounds, for intellectual inequality these are inconceivable. Unlike anything else, in this respect equality has been guaranteed to us by nature. I am speaking not of education, but of the education in speech, the slightest imprecision in which may trigger the intrusion of false choice into one's life. The existence of literature prefigures existence on literature's plane of regard–and not only in the moral sense, but lexically as well. If a piece of music still allows a person the possibility of choosing between the passive role of a listener and the active one of performer, a work of literature–of the art which is, to use Montale's phrase, hopelessly semantic–enlists him in the role of performer only.

In this role, it would seem to me, a person should appear more often than in any other. Moreover, it seems to me that, as a result of the population explosion and the attendant, ever-increasing automations of society (i.e., the ever-increasing isolation of the individual), this role becomes more and more inevitable for a person. I don't suppose that I know more about living than anyone of my age, but it seems to me that, in the capacity of an interlocutor, a book is more reliable than a friend or a beloved. A novel or a poem is not a monologue, but the conversation of a writer with a reader, a conversation, I repeat, which is very private, excluding all others, if you will, mutually misanthropic. And in the moment of this conversation a writer is equal to a reader, as well as the other way around, regardless of whether this writer is a great one or not. This equality is the equality of consciousness, and it remains with a person for the rest of his life in the form of memory, foggy or distinct, and, sooner or later, appropriately or not, it conditions a person's conduct. It's precisely this that I have in mind, in speaking of the role of the performer, all the more natural for one because a novel or a poem is the product of mutual loneliness–of a writer or a reader.

In the history of our species, in the history of Homo sapiens, the book is anthropological development, similar essentially to the invention of the wheel. Having emerged in order to give us some idea, not so much of our origins as of what this sapien is capable of, a book constitutes a means of transportation through the space of experience, at the speed of a turning page. This movement, like every movement, becomes a flight from the common denominator, from an attempt to elevate this denominator's line, previously never reaching higher than the groin, to our heart, our consciousness, our imagination. This flight is the flight in the direction of "uncommon visage," in the direction of the numerator, in the direction of individuality, in the direction of privacy. Regardless of whose image we are created in, we already number five billion, and there is no other future for a human being save that outlined by art. Otherwise, what lies ahead is the past–the political one, first of all, with all its mass police entertainments.

In any event, the condition of society in which art in general, and literature in particular, are the prerogative of a minority appears to me unhealthy and dangerous. I don't appeal for the replacement of the state with a library–although this thought has been visited upon me frequently—but there is no doubt in my mind that, should we have been choosing our leaders on the basis of their reading experience and not their political programs, there would be much less grief on earth. It seems to me that a potential master of our fates should be asked first of all, not about how he imagines the course of his foreign policy, but about his attitude toward Stendhal, Dickens, Dostoevsky. If only because the lock and stock of literature is indeed human diversity and perversity, it turns out to be a reliable antidote for any attempt—whether familiar or yet to be invented—toward a total mass solution to the problems of human existence. As a form of moral insurance, at least, literature is much more dependable than a system of beliefs or a philosophical doctrine.

Since no laws can protect us from ourselves, no criminal code is capable of preventing a true crime against literature: though we can condemn the material suppression of literature—the persecution of writers, acts of censorship, the burning of books—we are powerless when it comes to its worst violation, that of not reading the books. For that crime, a person pays with his whole life; if the offender is a nation, it pays with its history. Living in the country I live in, I would be the first prepared to believe that there is a set dependency between a person's material well-being and his literary ignorance; what keeps me from doing so is the history of that country in which I was born and grew up. For, reduced to a cause-and-effect minimum, to a crude formula, the Russian tragedy is precisely the tragedy of a society in which literature turned out to be the prerogative of the minority: of the celebrated Russian intelligentsia.

I have no wish to enlarge upon the subject, no wish to darken this evening with thoughts of the tens of millions of human lives destroyed by other millions, since what occurred in Russia in the first half of the twentieth century occurred before the introduction of automatic small weapons—in the name of the triumph of a political doctrine whose unsoundness is already manifested in the fact that it requires human sacrifice for its realization. I'll just say that I believe—not empirically, alas, but only theoretically—that, for someone who has read a lot of Dickens, to shoot his like in the name of some idea is more problematic than for someone who has read no Dickens. And I am speaking precisely about reading Dickens, Sterne, Stendhal, Dostoevsky, Flaubert, Balzac, Melville, Proust, Musil, and so forth; that is,

about literature, not literacy or education. A literate, educated person, to be sure, is fully capable, after reading this or that political treatise or tract, of killing his like, and even of experiencing, at that, a rapture of conviction. Lenin was literate, Stalin was literate, so was Hitler; as for Mao Tse-tung—he even wrote verse. What all these men had in common, though, was that their hit list was longer than their reading list.

However, before I move on to poetry, I would like to add that it would make sense to regard the Russian experience as a warning, if for no other reason than that the social structure of the West up till now is, on the whole, analogous to what existed in Russia prior to 1917. (This, by the way, is what explains the popularity in the West of the nineteenth-century Russian psychological novel, and the relative lack of success of contemporary Russian prose. The social relations that emerged in Russia in the twentieth century apparently seem no less exotic to the reader than do the names of the characters, which prevent him from identifying with them.) For example, the number of political parties alone, on the eve of the October coup in 1917, was in no way fewer than we find today in the United States or Britain. In other words, a dispassionate observer might remark that, in a certain sense, the nineteenth century is still going on in the West, while in Russia it came to an end; and if I say, it ended in tragedy, this is, in the first place, because of the course of that social—or chronological—change. For in a real tragedy, it is not the hero who perishes; it is the chorus.

III

Although, for a man whose mother tongue is Russian, to speak about political evil is as natural as digestion, I would like to change the subject now. What's wrong with discourses about the obvious is that they corrupt conscience with their easiness, with their quickness, with which they provide one with moral comfort, with the sensation of being right. Herein lies their temptation, similar in its nature to the temptation of a social reformer, who begets this evil. The realization or, rather, comprehension of this temptation and rejection of it are, perhaps, responsible to a certain extent for the destinies of many of my contemporaries, responsible for the literature that emerged from under their pens. It, that literature, was neither a flight from history nor the muffling of memory, as it may seem from the outside. "How can one write music after Auschwitz?" inquires Adorno, and one familiar with Russian history can repeat the same question by merely changing the name of the camp–and repeat it perhaps with even greater justification, since the number of people who perished in Stalin's camps surpasses by far the number of German prison-camp victims. "And how can you eat lunch?" the American poet Mark Strand once retorted. In any case, the generation to which I belong has proven capable of writing that music.

That generation–the generation born precisely at the time when the Auschwitz crematoria were working full blast, when Stalin was at the zenith of his God-like, absolute power, which seemed sponsored by Mother Nature herself–that generation came into the world, it appears, in order to continue what, theoretically, was supposed to be interrupted in those crematoria, and in the anonymous common graves of Stalin's archipelago. The fact that not everything got interrupted, at least not in Russia, can in no small degree be credited to my generation, and I am no less proud of belonging to it than I am of standing here today. And the fact that I am standing here is a recognition of the services that generation has rendered to culture; recalling a phrase from Mandelstam, I would add, to world culture. Looking back, I can say again that we were beginning in an empty–indeed, a terrifyingly wasted–place, and that rather intuitively than consciously, we aspired precisely to the recreation of the effect of culture's continuity, to the reconstruction of its forms and tropes, toward filling its few surviving, and often totally compromised, forms, with our own new, or appearing to us as such, contemporary content.

There presumably existed another path: the path of further deformation, the poetics of ruins and debris, of minimalism, of choked breath. If we rejected it, it was not at all because we thought that it was the path of self-dramatization, or because we were extremely animated by the idea of preserving the hereditary nobility of the forms of culture we knew, the forms that were equivalent, in our consciousness, to forms of human dignity. We rejected it because in reality the choice wasn't actually ours, but that of culture it seems–and this choice, again, was not moral but rather aesthetic. To be sure, it is natural for a person to perceive himself not as an instrument of culture, but, on the contrary, as its creator and custodian. But if today I assert the opposite, it's not because toward the close of the

twentieth century there is a certain charm in paraphrasing Plotinos, Lord Shaftesbury, Schelling, or Novalis, but because, unlike anyone else, a poet always knows that what in the vernacular is called the voice of the Muse is, in reality, the dictate of the language; that it's not that the language happens to be his instrument, but that he is the means of language toward the continuation of its existence. Language, however, even if one imagines it as a certain animate creature (which would only be just), is not capable of ethical choice.

A person sets out to write a poem for a variety of reasons: to win the heart of his beloved; to express his attitude toward the reality surrounding him, be it a landscape or a state; to capture his state of mind at a given instant; to leave–as he thinks at that moment–a trace on the earth. He resorts to this form–the poem–most likely for unconsciously mimetic reasons: the black vertical clot of words amidst the white sheet of paper presumably reminds him of his own situation in the world, of the balance between space and his body. But regardless of the reasons for which he takes up the pen, and regardless of the effect produced by what emerges from beneath that pen on his audience–however great or small it may be–the immediate consequence of this enterprise is the sensation of coming into direct contact with language or, more precisely, the sensation of immediately falling into dependence on it, on everything that has already been uttered, written, and accomplished in it.

This dependence is absolute, despotic; but it unshackles as well. For, while always older than the writer, language still possesses the colossal centrifugal energy imparted to it by its temporal potential–that is by all time lying ahead. And this potential is determined not so much by the quantitative body of the nation that speaks it (though by that, too), as by the quality of the poem written in it. It will suffice to recall Dante. And that which is being created today in Russian or in English, for instance, secures the existence of these languages in the course of the next millennium also. The poet, I wish to repeat, is language's means for existence–or, as my beloved Auden said, he is the one by whom it lives. I who write these lines will cease to be, as will you who read them. But the language in which they are written and in which you read them will remain not merely because language is more lasting than man, but because it is more capable of mutation.

One who writes a poem, however, writes it not because he courts fame with posterity, although often he hopes that a poem will outlive him, at least briefly. One who writes a poem writes it because the language prompts, or simply dictates, the next line. Beginning a poem, the poet as a rule doesn't know the way it's going to end, and at times he is very surprised by the way it turns out, since often it turns out better than he expected, often his thought carries further than he reckoned. And that is the moment when the future of language invades its present. There are, as we know, three modes of cognition: analytical, intuitive, and the mode that was known to the Biblical prophets, revelation. The distinction of poetry from other forms of literature lies in that it uses all three of them at once (gravitating primarily toward the second and the third). For all three of them are given in the language; and there are times when, by means of a single word, a single rhyme, the writer of a poem manages to find himself where no one has ever been before him, further, perhaps, than he himself would have wished for. The one who writes a poem writes it above all because verse writing is an extraordinary accelerator of conscience, of thinking, of comprehending the universe. Having experienced this acceleration once, one is no longer capable of abandoning the chance to repeat this experience; one falls into dependency on this process, the way others fall into dependence on drugs or on alcohol. One who finds himself in this sort of dependency on language is, I guess, what they call a poet.

Book Reviewing in America: I

George Garrett
University of Virginia

and

David R. Slavitt

"It's all sour grapes. Jay [McInerney] could have written the St. James Bible [sic] and people would have panned it."

—Gary Fisketjon, *Editorial Director of Atlantic Monthly Press,*
quoted in the International Herald Tribune,
19-20 September 1987

George Garrett and David Slavitt–
How Do You Do?

Consider this as only a beginning, the first show-and-tell arising out of our ongoing research and examination of the business of book reviewing in America. It is, then, the first part of an enterprise which will, we hope, become a feature of the *DLB Yearbook* as regularly as we, or others, are able to acquire more information and as the constantly changing literary scene in America changes significantly enough to merit investigation. Presumably, the biblical promise that there is no end to the making of books includes the corollary idea that somebody will always be reviewing at least some of those books. As readers all our lives we have been aware of and have depended on the credibility, if not the kindness of book reviewers. And, of course, as professional writers for a good many years we have been at once observers of the scene and living in the midst of it, in this case often depending on the kindness of strangers. Both of us have also been writing and publishing book reviews during most of our adult lives. David Slavitt was, for some years, associate editor of *Newsweek* and regularly reviewed books for that influential magazine. For thirty years George Garrett has been a teacher of contemporary literature (among other things) and, for better and for worse and probably for poorer, he has had to try to keep up with what has been happening, not merely the arrival and departure of books and writers, new and old, but also the fortunes of both, their fate at the hands of various kinds of reviewers. All this is asserted here to make the point that we came to this examination with some experience of at least aspects of the subject and some earned opinions, as well. Clearly we are not either innocent or entirely objective, neutral, of and about book reviewing. On the other hand, like reporters (and both of us have done some of that, reporting, also), we have tried to control our own, separate but equal, prejudices and points of view by examining whatever pertinent texts we could lay hands on and by talking and listening to as many people who are actively involved in the business of book reviewing as we possibly could, as many as would give us the time of day. The time of day is precious to all these people, and we are most grateful to those, both named and anonymous, who were willing to talk with us and to deal with our questions. Nobody ever really works all alone, and so it is a pleasure as well as a duty to acknowledge that we have gained both insight and information (both hard to come by) from others who have recently examined the same scene and some of the same problems and questions, albeit usually from a somewhat different point of view and with a different focus.

Finally, funny as it may seem, we owe each other a good deal. In a sense this piece is the result and reflection of conversations, sometimes debates (for we are both old debaters) between each other. It seemed logical, then, to present examples of our individual views as well as offering what might be called some mutually accepted positions.

David Slavitt: Book Reviewers–
Notes and Observations

Jack Miles of the *Los Angeles Times* is neither a villain nor a Philistine. He is an educated person who spent ten years as a Jesuit seminarian, was educated in Rome, Germany, and Israel, and received a Ph.D. in Near Eastern languages from Harvard (in 1971). He taught at Loyola University of Chicago and at the University of Montana and was a postdoctoral fellow at the University of Chicago before moving to New York where he was an editor for Doubleday and Company. From Doubleday, he went out to be executive editor of the University of California Press at UCLA, and it was from that post that he moved over to the *Los Angeles Times,* to which he had been a frequent contributor, writing some forty reviews and articles before being named book editor of that paper. He is the author of *Retroversion and Text Criticism* (Scholars Press, 1985).

Miles's decision in the spring of 1987 to take the *Times* out of the poetry reviewing business was not altogether crazy. There had not been a very heavy investment in poetry anyway. A very few books got noticed, and everyone understood that, given the severely limited space for which so many books compete week after week, there was never much chance for any book to get reviewed in which the lines did not come out to the right-hand side of the page. And Miles wasn't ignoring poetry altogether. He decided that it might be better for poetry and for his paper's readers to print a short poem every week from some recently published book with a few words about the author and the new collection. Those people who liked what they read there could figure out how to get hold of the book–which was almost the same thing as if he'd run a favorable short review, wasn't it?

The poets weren't happy, though. Thirty-five poets and their friends picketed the *Times* building. People wrote letters, two hundred of them, nearly all critical. Worse yet, Miles's colleagues expressed their disapproval. The most powerful book-review editor in the country, Mitchel Levitas of the *New York Times,* called the *Los Angeles Times* decision "regrettable." Dianne Donovan, book-review editor of the *Chicago Tribune,* said, "We don't in any way correlate the books we review to the popularity they receive." In the *Washington Post* Jonathan Yardley came to Miles's defense with a tepid endorsement, saying he could understand the reasons for the Angeleno's decision and admitting that the decision to stop running reviews of poetry was "something that newspaper book review editors have for years yearned, in their innermost hearts, to do." Yardley pointed out that the names of the leading poets of the nation are virtually unknown in the general culture. "I don't think we owe a thing to poets and poetry," he said.

Yardley was not exactly trashing poetry. He was being honest. And the great secret of book reviewing is that taste and judgment and even writing ability are not so hard to find, it's honesty that is the rarity. The book reviewer's desk is an ethical wringer, and after only a few months, the books become the assaults of an enemy, a huge pile, a barrage aimed at your head. The editors to whom the book reviewer reports are unsympathetic. They want to turn the space over to reviews of videocassettes, rock albums, restaurants–areas where the readers are still interested and lively, and numerous enough to attract advertisers! Yardley is a graduate, in English, of UNC/Chapel Hill, was a Nieman Fellow, has contributed reviews and articles to the *New Republic, Life,* the *New York Times Book Review, Saturday Review, Sewanee Review, Partisan Review, Sports Illustrated,* and *Esquire,* as well as the *Los Angeles Times Book Review* and the *Washington Post Book World.* He has won a Pulitzer Prize for criticism and has an honorary doctorate of letters (1987) from George Washington University. He wasn't opposed to poetry, or to quality literature of any genre. He was just pointing out that the newspaper business is a business. There are readers and advertisers and managing editors and publishers, all of whom are in one way or another breathing down the necks of book reviewers. The poets themselves are listless at best about buying the works of their fellow poets. A thousand copies is a respectable sale for a collection of poetry (in hard and soft cover, combined). And ten thousand is a runaway best-seller!

When a newspaper or a magazine has a circulation up in the millions, there is a real disproportion between its numbers and those of all but very few of the books up for consideration. And the honest reviewer admits that the circumstances are not at all propitious for the activity he or she thought would be the real satisfactions of the job–the celebration of excellence and the promotion from obscurity of deserving beginners or those who, for one reason or another, have been slogging away meritoriously for years or

Peter Prescott (photo by Martha Kaplan)

even decades without adequate recognition or reward.

Peter Prescott, *Newsweek*'s book review editor, is perfectly clear-eyed about how things are. "Readers of book reviews are perhaps not aware that the editors of the publications they read aren't particularly concerned with the skills of this or that reviewer, nor do they agonize greatly over which books shall be reviewed and which ignored; they think book reviews irrelevant altogether. Who worries about how well a job is done when the job itself is thought not worth doing at all?" He is candid enough to follow this observation to the consequences he sees all around him, and he says that "New authors like Kate Hepburn, Bruce Springsteen, and Bill Cosby will never be ignored, but a good new author will rarely be reviewed until he has published two or three books—and of course the likelihood is that publishers won't carry him that long. Full-time reviewers will never be aware of all the new and worthy authors who should be reviewed, but they shouldn't miss many. Editors don't care: we're a news organization, they say, and this isn't news. I've always claimed it is. What

we get here is a classic debate: is news what is new and worth noticing, or is it what people are waiting for, what they already know something about? Is it our job to get people engaged or to follow their engagement?"

Prescott is a graduate of Choate and Harvard and studied at the University of Paris, has won the George Polk Award for Criticism and a Guggenheim Fellowship, and he puts the "Golden Age of Reviewing" at somewhat between 1885 and 1915, which is before his father's time (his father is Orville Prescott, who, with Charles Poore, did the daily reviews in the *New York Times* a generation ago). "Bernard Shaw's idea that a review was itself worth reading, quite apart from the worth of its subject, is shared by fewer editors every year," Prescott says. "This is in part due to the leveling times in which we live. Editors are no longer the headstrong entrepreneurs of 50 and 100 years ago; today they are basically very cautious men, far more nervous than their best writers."

As if in attempt to provide a dramatic illustration of Prescott's gloomy point, the editors of the *Philadelphia Inquirer* cut back their freestanding book review section, gave a raise in pay and a cut in duties to their book review editor, Carlin Romano, and came out in December of 1987 with a new section called "View" which combines books (with Romano as chief critic, though reviews are no longer assigned by him), art, architecture, design, antiques, video, and "collectibles" as well as the chess, coins, bridge, stamps, pets and gardening columns, a cryptogram, and the *New York Times Magazine* crossword puzzle—all in eight pages. Book reviews still run, but there is less space given to books than in the earlier "Books/Leisure" section, and the ukase from the management is that they want no more "professors" writing reviews. The emphasis is to be more commercial, more marketplace (or less intellectual and boring).

One can't blame Romano. He had the choice of arguing and getting fired, or taking the money and not running. (He chose 2 or B.)

Prescott does see a ray of sunshine in the introduction in recent years by *Time*, *Newsweek*, and the London *Times Literary Supplement* of signed reviews, the bylines being a way to "encourage . . . critics to take responsibility for what they wrote," he says.

As a matter of fact, David Slavitt was the one who kept *Newsweek* from introducing signatures for a couple of years when he was the Newspaper Guild unit chairman and *Newsweek*'s movie reviewer in the middle 1960s. "I was willing to put my name to the backs of their checks," he says, "but not to anything else they wrote. Or rewrote. And there was always a lot of rewriting. Not more than at the *New Yorker*, maybe, but enough so that one no longer had the proprietary sense of responsibility that Prescott is talking about. Maybe they have it now. Maybe it is better, with an art critic like John Ashberry and a book reviewer like Prescott–both of whom are grown-ups with their own clout and, presumably, a willingness, if the argument gets hot enough, to walk out of the room or even the building; but I doubt it. I knew that across the street at *Time* there were editors who assigned a book to two or three different reviewers and then created a collage, snipping and pasting the best paragraphs from each man's effort to produce the confection that finally appeared. I knew about reviews that were written to order. And that was okay, if it was their magazine and my name wasn't on the copy. It still happens. John Leonard got eased out of *The New York Times* for panning a book that had been dedicated to A. H. Rosenthal–and everybody knew about it. And the fact that Leonard had a byline didn't help him at all. It only made the pain of the situation more exquisite. It was still Rosenthal's paper, as Leonard found out."

On the other hand, Prescott reports that there is an unwritten understanding that "one can always demand that his name be removed from a piece. I've only seen that done once in the book department–by a writer who shortly resigned."

Slavitt finds that reassuring but says that resignations don't help literature much either. "Unless they are like my resignation in 1965," he jokes, adding after a slight pause, "which is forty books ago."

George Garrett: My Turn in the Barrel

"I didn't want the assistant professor of whales to review 'Moby Dick' anymore. I wanted novelists reviewing fiction for us."

–John Leonard, quoted in the *Los Angeles Times* (13 December 1985)

That Slavitt always had *cojones*, plenty of *chutzpah*, too. Imagine that! To open up talking about poets. Last shall be least, and right up

front, too. What happened at the *Los Angeles Times* when Jack Miles took his paper out of the poetry reviewing business was sure enough news around the country, caused a minor tempest in a tired old teapot, and gave some book and cultural affairs editors something to write about, to wise off about. The most serious reaction, at once general and specific, came from David Lehman of *Newsweek*. A poet of distinction, himself, he was quoted by the London *Times Literary Supplement* (11-17 December 1987) as making a strong statement to his fellow members in the National Book Critics Circle: "A book review's pages are meant to perform critical discrimination for us–otherwise, what are they but publicity sheets?–and the way to make critical discriminations, with poetry as with any other serious form of literature, is by getting the best possible reviewers to write the best possible reviews. To print poems from a new book is fine and dandy. But to print a snippet of verse from a book in lieu of a review of that book seems to me to patronize poetry." None of it changed anything much. Miles's plan to publish poems would have been a significant change and, in theory, a change for the better for poets. But otherwise it was more like a paper loss of imaginary money in some board game than a real blow to the fragile economy of literary art.

But it is a good jumping-off point, because it leads directly to some of the problems I ran into along the way. And these are general things which should be dealt with here and now.

First: Book reviews and practicality.

Everybody I talked with, publishers and agents and writers and even most reviewers, agreed on one thing: with very rare exceptions, good reviews cannot help a good book very much. Jane Gelfman, who heads up the John Farquharson literary agency, didn't allow that reviews had much effect on sales, one way or the other, except maybe on the writers who might be encouraged or demoralized by reviews. "I don't think book reviews sell books," she said. "Publicity can and does sell books, but that is a different thing." She cited examples from among her clients. "James McConkey's *Court of Memory* (Dutton, 1983) got well-placed rave reviews everywhere." McConkey's book arrived with a garland of truly impressive blurbs–Annie Dillard, Wright Morris, May Sarton, Maxine Kumin–and, from beginning to end of its brief season, picked up splendid reviews the way Third World generals pick up medals and decorations–until they are topheavy with honors. *Publishers Weekly,* in the crucial "Forecasts" notice (26 November 1982), set the tone which other reviewers across the nation seemed to have accepted and followed: "McConkey is one of our best writers; the gracefulness of his prose, the depth and clarity of his perceptions are often profoundly moving. . . . His brilliant synthesis of recollections and intuitions, in which he finds connections between moments of desolation and moments of joy, produces an affirmation of the kind that the best literature can give to us." Can't do a whole lot better than that; though, in fact, he did. But, according to Gelfman, none of it sold copies of *Court of Memory.* On the other hand, Gelfman cites the fortune of another distinguished and original book by a client–Carolyn Chute's *The Beans of Egypt Maine* (Ticknor and Fields, 1985). Chute received nothing like the critical response or praise which greet McConkey; indeed, many of the notices she received, while not unfavorable, did not describe the book accurately and were often . . . well, kind of *odd.* But Chute's own life and life-style, together with her subject of implacable rural poverty in Maine, gained her and the book a great deal of conventional publicity–interviews, TV talk shows, magazine pieces. And the book sold wonderfully well.

A brief digression about publicity. In every article I have seen (including this one) book editors complain that they are forced to contend and compete with the more transient world of "news." Books aren't "hard news," usually, and neither are their creators, most of the time. Unless they stab their wives or something. In a printed letter addressed to "Los Angeles Times Book Reviewers and other friends" of 27 December 1985, Jack Miles argued that books ought to be considered "news of the mind," saying: "News of the mind is news, in short, even when it leads to no purchase." In any event, a good deal of literary news, which by no sleight of hand could be called "news of the mind," captured attention and filled up space in literary and cultural sections of the nation's newspapers and magazines in 1987. Much ink was used up to describe the fall from power at Random House of Howard Kaminsky and then, a little later, his return to work for Hearst. There was the matter of Joni Evans who had already departed from Simon and Schuster and her boss and husband there, Richard Snyder, and replaced Kaminsky at Random House. This series of events was widely covered. Even by *People* magazine. And then there was the outcry and counterattack of critics when Larry Heinemann upset the odds and some of the pundits by winning the National Book Award for *Paco's Story* (Farrar, Straus and Giroux). The lawsuits of J. D. Salinger and of William Blatty were seriously considered. Rust Hills raised a few jaded eyebrows with his "Esquire's Guide to the Literary Universe" (*Esquire,* 27 August 1987, pp. 51-61), where in addition to certain predictable if arguable choices among the writers, he chose to celebrate the likes of editor Gary Fisketjon, "the only young editor in the business who has the power–and the inclination–to publish his contemporaries," critic Michiko Kakutani, "the only one who serious people take at all seriously," Gordon Lish, "the Man Who Mistook His Career for Too Many Hats," and Amanda ("Binky") Urban, a literary agent. The takeover as editor of the *New Yorker* by Knopf's Robert Gottlieb was front-page news in some places and table talk at many others. Gottlieb was also in the news when he was attacked, in print, by British author Frederic Raphael, who was his classmate at Cambridge University. Raphael was quoted in the press: "All his (Gottlieb's) authors include gushing preambles, testifying to his amazing insight and fruitful editorial expertise, but most of the texts I have read are entirely lacking in the genius he is supposed to possess and foster." Other publicized literary quarrels included a battle at the highly intellectual *Partisan Review* between editor William Phillips and writer Michael Ledeen; and ("Big Fight Among the Little Magazines," *New York Post,* 22 June 1987, p. 6) "a battle royal" between little magazine editors–Robert Fogarty of *Antioch Review,* Gordon Lish of *The Quarterly,* and Ben Sonnenberg of *Grand Street.*

It is somewhat more difficult to explain or excuse the amount of time, energy, and space which was wasted in 1987 on three writers from the so-called Brat Pack. Magazines, newspapers, even television gave them the full benefit of pitiless attention, and the subject seems to have obsessed many book editors and cultural journalists, in some cases waking them to their best efforts of the year. Two pieces of genuine literary merit were Nikki Finke's "Literary Brat Pack: Young, Brash, Rich," *International Herald Tribune,* 19-20 November 1987; and Jonathan Yardley's "Bad Times for the Literary Brat Pack," *Washington Post,* 12 October 1987. "The ironic of it," as my old Army First Sergeant used to say, is

Larry Heinemann accepting the 1987 National Book Award for fiction for his novel Paco's Story *(photograph by Lori Grinker/NYT Pictures)*

that the novels of Bret Ellis, Tama Janowitz, and Jill Eisenstadt (see "The Year in the Novel") were almost universally panned and were not selling well even in New York City until all this cumulative publicity seems to have turned things around.

I found next to no one who would really make the claim that good reviews have the practical value of selling books. (A possible exception is *Time* reviewer Stefan Kanfer, who, in *Publishers Weekly*, 10 April 1987, asserts that his *Time* reviews sell a lot of books. Thing is, though, Kanfer is something of a kidder. He told an audience at the 1987 Wesleyan Writers Conference that no good books get lost in the shuffle of reviewing. "Nothing gets by us," he said.) Novelist Hilary Masters (*Cooper*, St. Martin's, 1987) can be legitimately taken as expressing the consensus view of most serious and professional writers. He opened, as most of us usually do, with a firm disclaimer—"I can't complain." Went on to argue, "I don't think it [sales/success] has anything to do with reviews." As for the market itself, he added this comment: "The market is New York City. I

think when things start moving in New York City, they start happening elsewhere." The most affirmative statement by a publisher concerning the potential value of book reviews came from Herman Gollob, editor in chief at Doubleday. "Book reviews can mean a hell of a lot," he said. "There was an era when one great review, a front page review in the *Times*, could make a book. Now it takes a lot more—a consensus in the key places."

In a significant article about the marketplace ("Publish and Perish: On the death of the modern book business and why I'm happy about it," *Philadelphia*, August 1987, pp. 57-61) David Slavitt discussed one important recent change in the book marketplace and how it changes everything else more than a little; namely, the power of the bookstore chains—B. Dalton, Waldenbooks, Barnes and Noble, Encore, Crown Books, Doubleday, etc., and the ways and means, between mergers with each other and foreign and domestic conglomerates, by which they select the books which they choose to market. Which books constitute the overwhelming percentage of all trade books sold in this country. Reviews have next to nothing to do with it all. It is much simpler than that. As Slavitt described the process: "They punch up the author's name on their microcomputers. All these chains are computerized now and they have database programs, and they can see how many of Author X's books they sold last time around. And the order for X's new book will be that of the old number plus or minus a little bit if the salesman from the publishing house has been extremely persuasive (or hasn't been persuasive at all)." Opinion-makers and trendsetters don't contribute a lot to this process, though, as indicated, publicity—*any kind of publicity* these days, almost—can help.

After a lot of hemming and hawing (and pleas for anonymity), publishers tend to agree with each other that while good reviews can help keep "in-house" interest and enthusiasm alive and can keep the author happy, their real value is as a kind of limited form of advertising, a very modest form of needed publicity.

If publishers and agents don't care a lot, if the chief bookstores don't pay much or any attention to reviews (and, in a sense, with a shelf time of six or eight weeks for everything except bestsellers, they *can't* wait around for reviews), what is in it, in a practical way at least, for the book reviewers themselves? Of course, for the top national reviewers, as well as the city book editors from all around the country, it is a living. Sometimes not bad. "We have about 25 people on the editorial staff," says Mitchel Levitas. "And they make a good living." Not all book editors make anything like a good living for their labors, and, to be truthful, the rewards for the labors of the actual book reviewers, where the reviews are assigned rather than directly handled by editorial staff, are more in the nature of honoraria than earnings. Poet and professor Jay Parini is reported to have told friends and students at Breadloaf, in the summer of 1987, that he had managed over the past year to earn about $20,000 from book reviewing; though he added that the largest part of this windfall, which he acknowledged was very unusual, came not directly from book reviewing, itself, but from related articles and interviews and lectures, etc. Still, even allowing for that and for some exaggeration, it is a figure which astounds other free-lance reviewers. In one of a series of excellent articles on book reviewing published in the *Los Angeles Times*, 11-13 December 1985, *Times* staff writer David Shaw wrote that "at most papers—with the notable excep-

tion of *The New York Times* and, to a much lesser degree, the *Washington Post*—book reviews are a neglected stepchild; most reviews are written by free-lance reviewers who are underpaid, assigned and edited by editors who are overworked and understaffed, and published in sections with little or no financial support from book advertising." For those few who make a living at it, the primary and inescapable obligation is to the institution they are employed by and to the advertisers, if any. Next come the larger, if more impractical obligations, the traditional ancient and honorable duties of the critic. It may be fortunate for everyone involved, especially book editors and reviewers, that the institutional powers-that-be, in Mr. Prescott's words, "think book reviews irrelevant altogether."

Irrelevancy leaves the reviewers of books free not so much to say whatever they may please as to pick and choose freely which book to pay attention to and which to ignore. Seen from the limits of their own point of view, this is the most significant job of book review editors. They have to decide, and quickly, and on the basis of very little information, and of limited time even for good guesswork, which books to review. According to the best recent statistics roughly 50,000 books are published annually in America. The three leading newspapers—the *New York Times*, the *Washington Post*, and the *Los Angeles Times*—each review something between 1,500 and 2,000 books a year. Except for *Publishers Weekly*, which manages brief advance notices of more, nobody else even comes close. No wonder that the subject of how books get picked to be reviewed is one that seems to interest book editors, as well as reporters, most of all. Most of the published pieces about book reviewing in America are concerned with just this issue. A first-rate recent article on this subject is Howard Eisenberg's "So Many Books So Little Space: What makes a book review editor pick up a book?" (*Publishers Weekly*, 10 April 1987, pp. 25-30). Eisenberg interviewed some of the outstanding book editors in the country, including Walter Berkov of the *Cleveland Plain Dealer*, Mark Feeney of the *Boston Globe*, Ruth Coughlin of the *Detroit News*, Shirley Williams of the *Louisville Courier-Journal*, Steve Paul of the *Kansas City Star*, Bill Robertson of the *Miami Herald*, Carlin Romano of the *Philadelphia Inquirer*, Dianne Donovan of the *Chicago Tribune*, Jack Miles of the *Los Angeles Times*, Clarus Backes of the *Denver Post*, *Time* magazine's Stefan Kanfer, and others. The interested reader is invited, with strong recommendations, to seek out this article. Perhaps it was the nature and form of the Eisenberg interviews, but it seemed that the editors were uniformly defensive about the complex process of how they go about making their choices, all the variable factors involved. They aren't really able to address the skepticism of the interested outsider (writer or publisher, for example) who points out the enormous statistical improbability that they all manage to overcome–that, come what may, they all seem to review pretty much the same books, coming from the same pool. Some of this remarkable coincidence comes from what Feeney of the *Boston Globe* calls "professional scuttlebutt" and Coughlin is quoted as calling "grassroots word of mouth." "But," as Eisenberg writes, "all that follows religious reading of the trade early warning system: *PW*'s 'Forecasts,' *Kirkus Reviews*, *Library Journal*, and the catalogues." The numbers and the exercise of choice are perhaps more clearly explained in David Shaw's *Los Angeles Times* pieces. He points out that the initial screening is fairly easy, because most of the editors are not interested in reviewing "science fiction, Westerns, romances, mysteries, and children's books. . . . " After the easy screening, the editor still must deal with a ratio of about one book out of fifty that can be reviewed. Next come books which are "obvious choices": books by or about major writers or public figures, books of particular local or regional interest, books which "illuminate a current or recent controversy," books published by (no kidding) Knopf. The delightful Dianne Donovan of the *Chicago Tribune* is all alone in admitting that "a book's cover sometimes does influence her decision about whether a book is worth a review." After the serious choices and considerations, most of the editors are likely to invoke mysticism and the spirit world together with Michael Dirda of the *Washington Post*: "You pick up a book and hold it to your forehead and wait for it to buzz. It's almost a psychic experience. . . . You just know it should be reviewed." Presumably the psychic buzz power is fairly uniform since they all review pretty much the same books and with roughly the same ranking.

In an excellent and tough-minded article, "Inside Book Reviewing" (*Boston Review*, August 1987, pp. 8-10), Gail Pool pointed out the part that reviewers play in shaping editorial choices. "Most of the books that will end up discussed in newspapers and magazines are the lead books of major trade publishers. These are the books read-

ers may expect to see reviewed–because they will have seen them advertised, because they are familiar with the authors. These are the books reviewers are most eager to be assigned–because they think they will be interesting or important."

The pride and the power of America's book editors and book reviewers, at least on a national or fairly widespread regional basis, is that though they may not, in truth, be engaged in serious *commerce* or may not deal with serious *news*, they are, in a serious sense, the guardians and custodians (notice I never said *janitors*) of American literary culture. They are in a position to support what they feel to be genuinely worthy and (yes, indeed) socially worthwhile. Just so they are charged to separate "bad books" from the good. As Jack Miles writes in his open letter, each book review and each book, whether it be panned or praised, is part of a much larger, more ambitious and admirable process: "And the prize at the end of that kind of labor is not just the truth of a particular book, it is the reinforcement of the same engendering attitude, the same rejection of the facile and the fake in every area of national life." Alan Cheuse, who reviews books regularly for several million listeners on National Public Radio, has an equal, if somewhat less exalted awareness of his own power, seeing his function as more a matter of public service than pedagogical leadership. "People don't have the time to read everything that is published. They tend to find reviewers whose opinions they trust, then use the reviews as a guide in deciding whether a particular book is important enough to spend time with." He adds that his responsibility is to the work itself. "A reviewer is not in the book publishing business and has no obligation to publishers or authors, only to the work being reviewed." Somewhere in between these two views of stewardship, and perhaps closer to the views of most reviewers, is the position taken by Stefan Kanfer, in the 10 April 1987 *Publishers Weekly* piece, who honestly acknowledges that he has a duty to give serious attention, if not necessarily support, to the work of certain authors, come what may. "When it's a tough call," he says, "I wait to see the reviewer's prose and how it reflects the book's importance. Occasionally, pictorial possibilities tip the scales, but a new Bellow or Updike is our lead, no matter what."

What all of this adds up to is, among other things, a system whose chief practical function is not subject to the sales it may or may not influence, but, in a broader and most serious sense, works, as if so designed, to maintain and pre-serve the literary status quo, the Establishment. Only the stated rigor of Alan Cheuse–the value of the work itself, nothing more and nothing less–theoretically allows for the flexibility of discovery and rediscovery. But, except for his frequent news-paper reviews, he has a greater time problem, on radio, than most of his peers in print. He must sell the unknown much more strongly than the known to give the unknown an equal billing.

There is nothing shameful in this. Most edi-tors spend far more time rejecting than accepting manuscripts for publication. That is their pri-mary job–rejecting things. Similarly, book review-ers, like haughty doormen at the club's front door, have a primary duty to do honor to the members-in-good-standing and to distinguish the new member from the gate-crashers. The very na-ture of book reviewing in America, at the highest level at least, is conservative and defensive. The Es-tablishment, which therefore *includes* these promi-nent reviewers, owes its custodians a great deal. Since every society is a seamless whole, every dis-tinct part of which (like the human body) has the same chills and fever or good health, it is fair to quote from Solzhenitsyn's 1987 Baccalaureate Ad-dress at Harvard where, speaking of the media (which can be said to contain the book review-ers), he said: "Without any censorship, in the West, fashionable trends of thought are carefully separated from those that are not fashionable. Nothing is forbidden, but what is not fashionable will hardly ever find its way into periodicals or books or be heard in colleges."

In that sense, and, let us be honest, in the laudatory as well as the perjorative senses of the word, our book reviewers are front-rank intellec-tual censors of our times.

But there are two more things to be said, both of which, inevitably, modify that judgment.

Second: What reviews mean to writers.

This can be said quickly. Book reviews can have immediate practical effects for writers, in-deed *do* have almost immediate practical results. Which, as far as I can tell, neither the publishing industry nor the reviewers have fully or openly considered. At this late date of our century we find ourselves in a situation in which the over-whelming majority of our literary writers, almost all of the poets, and the great majority of our liter-ary novelists and story writers are, one way and an-other, full-time or part-time, sinecure or hard labor, attached to or associated with educational institutions. Now then: the key to getting and keep-ing any kind of a job, as writer, in any of our insti-tutions, is *reputation*. Only a very few academics, as overworked as everyone else, have time, en-ergy, or inclination to read and judge the work of the writers on their staff, or the larger num-ber of those who are applying for positions. Like Cheuse's customers they depend on the credible good judgment of others–i.e., book reviews. The writers who are or wish to be on college and uni-versity faculties must publish (or perish) and must earn some visibility. These are almost purely practical matters. Book reviews are a nor-mal part of the writer's dossier which is passed around to committees and deans for purposes of hiring and promotion. We are talking money. It is the money that keeps most writers alive and kick-ing, enabling them to get on with writing the next book. The universities are supporting hun-dreds of writers, but they don't want to support losers. With the universities supporting writers, the publishers don't really have to; which is why advances against royalties, except for exceptional cases, have remained almost the same (*less*, in real terms) since World War II. Thus publishers, reviewers, and institutional writers are closely linked, symbiotic. But there is more. Consider that many writers, especially the better known, add considerably to their salaried income by giv-ing public readings and lectures at other institu-tions. Their own institutions encourage them in this enterprise. It "shows the flag," is good adver-tising and publicity for the home school, and the extra money keeps the writer happy on the job. It ought to. Not a few, but a goodly number of well-known poets and fiction writers make a good deal more than Parini's 20K in additional in-come from their annual readings. For the more fa-mous, the highly visible, this can add up to real money. In 1987 Margaret Atwood was asking for $7,500 per lecture appearance. Toni Morrison was reported to receive $10,000 or more. Reputa-tion, in the long term, is a significant factor; but reputation without "visibility," that by-product of advertising and publicity, is now all but meaning-less. Colleges and universities don't mind paying dearly, sometimes an entire year's speakers' bud-get, for one well-known speaker or visitor; but the same places are unwilling to spend money on "unknowns," including those among them whose work has long since earned recognition as repre-senting the highest standards of literary excel-lence. An actual example is of value here.

Recently at a major institution (call it Nameless University) a donor offered money to bring in a writer of distinction for a brief residence period. The writing staff recommended Shelby Foote, one of the most honored and distinguished of living American writers. The English chairman was cautious. "We have this money on a one-year trial basis," he wrote in a memo. "The donor is a very status-conscious person, and if he thinks we are not trying to bring in the best and the brightest, he will probably not continue the program." The chairman argued that "it would be wise to get the program established by bringing in big names for the first couple of years, before turning to those equally (or even more) deserving who are, for whatever reason, less well and less widely known." The chairman then suggested Ann Beattie as a good choice. It is important to realize that the chairman, in this case, was both honest and realistic. In our world Beattie has more glitter than Foote.

Reviews don't sell books, but they can buy and sell writers. Publishers and book-review editors may not be fully aware of all this, but most *book reviewers* are. Most book reviewers are writers. John Leonard has replaced the assistant professor of whales with the associate professor of creative writing. In many ways it may not have been a change for the better. One of the three articles on book reviewing in the *Los Angeles Times*, "Fear, Power of N.Y. Times Book Review," 12 December 1985, dealt mainly with the problems of possible conflict of interest and of ordinary street-level corruption when writers review each other and when it matters, in plain dollars and cents, how it all comes out. The truth of it, not really touched in that piece or anywhere else I have found (except, occasionally, in some fiction), is that the literary scene is no more corrupt and dishonest than any other part of our society. It is up to the mature reader to decide if that is a curse or a compliment.

Slavitt began with the poets. For whom, ironically, there are special problems and temptations. Poets—and it should be understood that both David Slavitt and George Garrett have written and published a good deal of poetry in their time—have a tiny public. They don't even read each other very much. There is a much better public for poetry readings. Since the middle years of this century the situation for some poets has significantly changed. Thanks to Dylan Thomas, and many others, the poetry reading is now a fixture of campus life. And there are grants and fellow-ships and prizes. There are endowed chairs to sit in or on. But there are not enough of these good things to go around. For the fortunate and "visible" few there are rich rewards, almost on the junior executive level. For the others there is a fierce barnyard pecking order. And it is in the poetry world that one can see most clearly the essentially conservative nature of book reviewing. During the course of interviews it was apparent that, in general, no poets felt that contemporary poetry received enough critical attention. Nobody was happy with the situation. But the most influential among them, those high in the hierarchy, while deploring the situation, would not move to change anything much. That is, having achieved a certain eminence and even security, in part *because of good reviews* at some point in their careers, they do not now seem to favor the kind of scrutiny or competition that widespread and regular reviewing of their poetry would force upon them. The risks are too much. Moreover, the fewer the number of places which review poetry, the easier it is for these poets to exercise some measure of control. The major means of exercising critical control, in the absence of much serious reviewing, has proved to be through consultantships and editorships for the various commercial and university presses which publish poetry. In the absence of the corrective scrutiny of honest criticism, it is possible to exercise considerable power by determining which books of poems are published and which are not. And—no one denies it—this has been happening. Poet and editor (University of Iowa Press) Paul Zimmer says that more than five hundred book-length manuscripts were submitted to his press last year to fill two publication slots. What is especially significant in this case is that it was *not* a contest for first books. First books were ineligible. These manuscripts came from poets with at least one published book of poems already behind them. Nobody has any idea how many poetry manuscripts, including first books, are looking for publishers. Poet Brendan Galvin, who has judged several contests, says: "There is a vast cloud of manuscripts out there shambling around from book contest to book contest. Or maybe it's less like a cloud than a battalion of bag ladies. Or a Xerox avalanche...." Thus Jack Miles, in all his innocence and good will, backed into a hornet's nest (more like a hive of killer bees) when he decided to replace highly uneven poetry reviews with representative poems. Nobody in the poetry world could be happy with a plan like that.

Those on the outside need at least the chance of being reviewed somewhere, anywhere.... Those on the inside might go along tacitly if they were allowed to pick and choose the poems to be published. Meantime, in point of fact and without (so far) any notice or praise for it, Mitchel Levitas has published more poetry reviews, more regularly than any of his immediate predecessors on the job, including the poet Harvey Shapiro. In interviews with poets Garrett found a distinctly negative reaction to Levitas's editorship at the *New York Times Book Review*. They professed surprise to learn that there are more poetry reviews there now than in recent memory. Others, who at least were aware of the facts, complained about the uneven quality of the reviews and the choice of reviewers.

It would all be funny if there were not so many very good American poets–in Garrett's view some of the best among the living poets–being studiously ignored. Also being ignored are some serious critical questions and controversies which, even as recently as a decade ago, would have been widely aired, if not settled in book reviews.

Third: Other Kinds of Book Reviewing and Book Reviewers

One of the enduring myths, strongly entrenched at the national level of the literary scene, is that local and regional reviews are distinctly and unquestionably inferior, in style and content, to the book reviews being published in the major magazines and the big-city newspapers. It's a convenient notion since barring some methodical, exhaustive, and exhausting study, it remains quite impossible to prove or to disprove. And it has this much basis in fact–it remains at least doubtful that the good (often, but not always, volunteer) reviewers of hometown dailies, large and small, and weeklies and local magazines could produce work of the quality and professionalism that is regularly demonstrated by the *New York Times* staff of paid reviewers: Michiko Kakutani, Christopher Lehmann-Haupt, and John Gross. These are all highly educated people, with wide interests and knowledge, who are first-rate writers as well. Lehmann-Haupt, for example, holds an M.F.A. degree from the Yale University School of Drama; he has expertise (enough to merit writing articles and lecturing) in bluegrass banjo picking, chess, and fly-fishing.

Since 1969 he has been senior daily book reviewer for the *New York Times*, and he has published more than 2,000 book reviews in the *Times*. There aren't a lot of people like that wandering around like mute, inglorious Miltons in the boonies. But there are some first-rate reviewers who know their stuff and write with admirable skill and grace, far from the national limelight. The "Membership Directory" of the National Book Critics Circle lists more than 500 members, and they come from everywhere. Garrett has been observing local and regional book reviewing, not systematically but with genuine interest, for more than the thirty-odd years of his professional writing career. He argues that there were good reviewers in local papers thirty years ago; but, it's true, they seemed to be exceptions to the rule of mediocrity. Not so today. The country has changed greatly in a generation. On the whole it is a much more sophisticated country than it was, certainly prior to World War II. And there are good, well-educated writers of all kinds everywhere, many of whom regularly write solid, well-executed book reviews. There are excellent book editors all over the country. The whole situation, with all its faults and flaws, is much better than it used to be. Of course, it remains an uneven enterprise for a great many reasons; but, nevertheless, some of the most interesting and best-written book reviews being written in America are being produced for local publications. And these reviews do often tend to have a practical effect. Because so many bookstores, independents as well as chains, are computerized and able to handle special orders promptly and efficiently, a good local review can lead to good local sales. It seems likely that in the near future, thanks to technology among other things, local book reviews will begin to exert an increasing influence on the publishing scene.

Nobody in the publishing business–not publishers, agents, national reviewers–takes the book reviewing and criticism in the quarterlies and literary magazines very seriously. For one thing, reviews appearing in the quarterlies are usually months, sometimes even years, after publication date. And in this time, when the life of a book is as brief as a butterfly, there cannot even be a pretense that there is any connection with the commerce of literature. It is also believed that, because of the very modest circulation of even the best-known quarterlies, their reviews cannot exercise much influence for good or for ill. The people in publishing whom Garrett has talked to seem to think of the quarterlies and literary magazines as minor-league teams at most. There was a time before and soon after World War II when (it is said) some quarterlies exercised a real influence on the literary scene. There were the *Hudson Review* and the *Partisan Review* like the Upper East Side and Greenwich Village. There, like Lee's Lieutenants, stood the *Southern Review*, the *Sewanee Review*, the *Georgia Review*, the *Virginia Quarterly Review*, and (yes, even way up there) the *Kenyon Review*. For a while–a time of critical giants– they made things happen. So, whatever happened to *them*, anyway? Truth is, they endured. In a much-changed world they are still there, together with a good many others, under new and sometimes improved management, and still very influential in more (and different) ways than have been considered. True, many aspiring American poets and fiction writers would probably kill to be published in one of the major quarterlies, but we are concerned with criticism, book reviewing. The big quarterlies publish fiction and poetry but are significantly different from the purely literary magazines and the little magazines. One difference is that the quarterlies do a lot more reviewing. My estimate, a guess but close enough, is that the *Virginia Quarterly Review* actually reviews about seventy-five books per issue. George Core, editor of the *Sewanee Review*, uses a somewhat different system and format, but, in my guess, averages about thirty-five or forty book reviews per issue. Give or take. What is special about the quarterlies is that they have easy access to the assistant professor of whales, or of anything else. They can and do assign their books for review to the best, often most influential, critics in America. They may or may not sell books; they are far removed from the pressures and pleasures of publicity; but they do, finally, deal in one commodity which is of great importance to the whole literary system in America. They create and preserve or break ... *reputations*. Like a sort of Supreme Court, they can right wrongs, correct or modify injustices, overrule the judgments of the popular media. The quarterlies sit on the shelves in the periodical sections of good libraries for months and months. They have an old-fashioned shelf life. They may well be the closest facsimile in the contemporary scene to the invisible and metaphorical "word of mouth."

Can these magazines sometimes exert a more immediate influence? Yes. Example? Years ago, in 1966, the *Hollins Critic*, a magazine which

offered a single 5,000-word essay review, together with a couple or three poems, appearing five times a year, published an essay by critic Robert Scholes–" 'Mithridates, he died old': Black Humor and Kurt Vonnegut, Jr." Scholes broke the basic rule at the *Hollins Critic*–that the essay-review of an author's work should begin on the occasion of the publication of a new book. There was no new book. At the time Scholes wrote the article, most, if not all of Vonnegut's books, were out of print; he had no publisher; he had no book in progress. Scholes's piece was one of the things used by Vonnegut's friends to catch the attention of a publisher. Two years later, with *Welcome to the Monkey House* (Delacorte), a collection of previously published stories, Vonnegut was back and on the way to finishing his first "breakthrough" book–*Slaughterhouse-Five*. It is, of course, *possible* that a literary journalist or book reviewer might have rediscovered Vonnegut and written about him and helped to change his luck. But the fact is that none did. It took an interested critic (a professor of whales?) to review the man's work in a quiet, but quietly influential publication to do the job.

David Slavitt–An Interview with Terrence Rafferty

The apartment is small, tiny in fact–as Manhattan apartments often are. Terrence Rafferty works in a corner of the living room. There is a framed poster on the wall above his desk for *Long Day's Journey into Night* showing Laurence Olivier's profile. On the opposite wall, Olivier and Maggie Smith are about to become corpses at the end of *Othello*. In the bookcase on the other side of Rafferty's carrel arrangement, there is a framed note from William Shawn, the former editor of the *New Yorker*. The note is dated 22 November 1984 and says: "A check for your fine piece on Truffaut. Thank you for writing it." It is, in a sense, Rafferty's diploma as a critic.

He has written for other magazines, of course. He has written for anyone who would publish him. For the *New Yorker*, he has done a few other pieces, a couple of which appeared while Shawn was there–one on an anthology of writings from *Cahiers du Cinema*. Then, when Gottlieb came on, as Rafferty remembers it, "We got in touch. He had heard of me through Pauline Kael who is a friend of mine. And he started giving me assignments. I'd done something on Walker Percy and Larry McMurtry–that was the first thing I did for the new *New Yorker*. And then a piece on Bellow. And then the Capote piece."

He has actually been trying to do what few men or women have even imagined as a possibility at any time since the 1950s–which is to be a critic who wasn't primarily an academic. And who wasn't a novelist or poet or short story writer who, from time to time, wrote a review. It was his essay in the 26 October 1987 issue of the *New Yorker* that caused what was perhaps the greatest stir of any book review of the year. It was mentioned in the news columns of the *New York Times*. People talked about it at cocktail parties. Rafferty was delighted and surprised to get letters from strangers, some of whom he admired–Edna O'Brien and Norman Rosten and Vance Bourjaily among them–as well as editors of magazines and book publishing companies and agents, looking to recruit him and congratulating him for what he had done.

And what was it that he had done? He'd written about Bret Easton Ellis's and Tama Janowitz's books, *The Rules of Attraction* and *A Cannibal in Manhattan*. This piece hadn't represented any particular effort on Rafferty's part. He'd done it on assignment, and he'd done it fast, scribbling it out before catching a plane to London. But he'd said the necessary thing, pronounced the needed deflation of two enlarged reputations that seemed more a matter of hype than literature. Janowitz had made her mark with her hairdo as much as her prose style, and she'd parlayed a promotional appearance on the David Letterman show into a demi-celebrity that was getting her writing assignments for the *New York Times Magazine* and temporary teaching jobs at such prestigious places as Princeton–where she appeared for a term as part of a feminist double bill with poet Carolyn Kizer. Ellis was a kid from Bennington who was an equivalent success partly because of the sheer shock value of such youthful cynicism. He was a corrupted, modernized, American version of a Raymond Radiguet or Françoise Sagan.

None of this is in Rafferty's eight-column piece. He confined himself mostly to the books at hand. Much of the credit for the éclat of the review properly belongs to Gottlieb, who sensed that it was time for the Newtonian reaction that invariably sets in with these inflated reputations. For no particular reason, the enthusiasm turns to boredom and even disgust. And the public begins to resent the object of its flighty attention, as though that writer, or painter, or rock star, or pure and inert celebrity (What, exactly, does Vanna White *do?*) had been the cunning artificer of the mass hysteria, as if it weren't a delusion in which the public had itself been at least a coconspirator.

Still, having said that, it was a nice little piece, modest, graceful, and above all, given the occasion, balanced. It was not unfair, admitting at the very start that "bad art isn't such a crime against humanity that it requires show trials and public executions as deterrents," and allowing that Janowitz at least has shown "evidence of a real–if not very rigorously applied–talent: moments of sharp, unforced humor, some dead-on observations of artistic types caught with their attitude down." But the balance and grace and the barbs of critical wit–Rafferty speaks of how these books drop like "anomic bombs into the book stores"–had little to do with the cheering. It was mostly that enough people were sick and tired of hearing about these midgets as if they were N.B.A. candidates.

"I was shocked by how much reaction I got," Rafferty declared, in what was neither real nor affected modesty but evidence of the clinical interest that is his stock in trade. "It was the sort of thing where I thought it was so obvious how bad these writers are. It was almost not worth my time to dump on them. But Gottlieb convinced me that I should do it. I guess there were just a lot of people out there who had succumbed to the hype and put down their six bucks for the paperbacks of *Less than Zero* [Ellis's first novel] or *Slaves of New York* [Janowitz's first book, a collection of short stories], and really felt burned."

I suggested that that couldn't, alone, account for the cheers. More people, after all, had been burned by James Clavell's dreary *Whirlwind*. Rafferty's piece was more an unmasking, a declaration that the emperor was standing there bucknaked. But still Rafferty doesn't enjoy hatchet jobs. He prefers to do what most critics imagine themselves doing, which is pointing out the virtues of this ignored book or that undervalued film. What he says he finds attractive is "what is ambitious or interesting, whether they work or not–and sometimes the failures are more interesting. The things that stimulate you are the reasons to write. The *Nation* has been a good place for me to write about movies because I don't have to deal with every piece of crap that comes out. The most deadening thing is all those movies that it's almost not worth having any opinion about at all."

Similarly, the Ellis and Janowitz books were almost not worth writing about. "I read the novels," Rafferty remembered, "and I thought these books are so bad, and so obviously bad. . . . Is it worth it?" But he also realized that the bubbles of success that magnified the achievements of Janowitz and Ellis were "puzzling in literary terms but make perfect sense in movie terms or pop-culture terms." Rafferty said, "The standards are not the same. Somebody can project a tremendous amount of personality, can seem to embody something in some immediate way without necessarily having been trained in the arcane arts, the skills that are necessary for writing. In some ways, the book publishers are looking for some way to tap into that pop-culture noble-savage possibility."

Rafferty has never been comfortable about the exploitation upon which these pop phenomena are based and which can sometimes manifest itself in the more serious realms of the arts. After he graduated from Cornell, he got a job at Doubleday, first as an editorial assistant and then an assistant editor. "But I was in a little backwater there of the category books—you know, mysteries, science fiction, westerns. It was like working on B movies. Nobody paid much attention to what you were doing. All you had to do was just put out the best books within these limitations that you possibly could. You didn't have to get involved in advertising budgets. There was so little money that nobody cared. I stayed there because I just didn't want to get involved in that marketing machinery. I was quite happy there."

He blinked behind the wire-rimmed glasses he wears that make him look a little like one of Edward Koren's cartoon gnomes and said, "I don't think of myself as particularly conservative. I'm certainly not conservative politically. I don't think I'm particularly conservative aesthetically either. But these books [i.e. Ellis's and Janowitz's] made me feel like a raving reactionary. Why can't people just tell a damned story any more? Why can't anybody write a sentence? I found myself feeling older and more entrenched than I feel comfortable feeling. And for some reason, I found myself pulling out Forster and that most lucid exposition of traditional values. My favorite teacher from Cornell is a novelist, not very well known, James McConkey, who is one of the great Forsterians. He's a very solid, honorable, decent man. He's interested in the traditional virtues of fiction—opening out windows on the world and understanding people's lives and all the good things

about traditional fiction. And he's probably my favorite teacher ever, a big influence on me. And so when it came to writing this piece, I thought of Forster. I realized that this was one of the reasons that these novels made me angry. They were being promoted in such a way, and they themselves purport to represent something new in literature. And they're using my terms of reference—rock music and movies. . . ." He shook his head. "They infuriated me. I mean, there are writers who are doing the things that they intended to do, but better. With enough wit and craft so that you understand something about this generation. I think of Martin Amis, who has very much the same rather savage point of view, but he's a real writer. He's illuminating things. He's questioning himself and his own implication in that with-it world that they [Ellis and Janowitz] seem to be describing. There's the discipline of genuine satire, of real craft."

Aside from McConkey, Rafferty's other great teacher was Pauline Kael, whose "fabulous vernacular style" he encountered when he was a high-school student. "It sounded like . . . it sounded like a person thinking!" he recalled excitedly.

"The thing I'm curious about in all this," Rafferty said, having been nudged back to the subject of his book review, "is how they themselves, how Ellis and Janowitz and their agents and editors are going to react. Are they in fact immune to literary criticism of a traditional sort and the kind of standards I was applying? One of the infuriating things is that they seem to have positioned themselves so that they are."

That would perhaps be asking too much. Indeed, before Rafferty's performance and its resulting noise, few observers of the literary scene would even have allowed the possibility that any book review could have any kind of consequence at all. Rafferty himself said, "All the assumptions of literary culture now just seem stupid to me, when it comes right down to it. I don't understand how the *Times Book Review* works, or how people become pop novelists, or are called novelists, or are dismissed entirely. I mean, it all seems to be based on something that precedes the actual reading of a book. Maybe it is all marketing. Maybe it is the sheer volume of things that are published. All book review editors can do is to be more dependent on publicity handouts and sales figures and whatever sort of buzz is created. I don't know. You just don't get the impression that there's a lot of very serious reading going on."

His lack of understanding may be his greatest asset, however. A cannier fellow might never have attempted his kind of career, or not in the 1980s anyway. That canny operator would never have wondered, as Rafferty wonders, "how few book reviewers are actual literary critics and not novelists who are doing literary criticism as something extra." But that canny fellow would never have found himself being offered–as Rafferty now has been–a continuing connection with the *New Yorker.* The current arrangement with Robert Gottlieb, who must be pleased with the results of their labors together, is that Rafferty will do ten book pieces a year. It is a position a lot of other writers and critics would kill for. He also has a Guggenheim to do film criticism. The lovely thing is that for a variety of reasons, partly talent, partly innocence, partly moral fervor, and partly just luck, Rafferty richly deserves his success.

As the admiring butler says to Walter Matthau in Elaine May's movie of a few years back, *A New Leaf:* "Sir, you are maintaining a way of life that was dead before you were born."

George Garrett Talks With William Tazewell

Staige Blackford, editor of the *Virginia Quarterly Review,* had this to say about Tazewell's book reviewing: "William Tazewell is giving Virginians book reviews of the quality worthy of the most distinguished English language journals." Tazewell smiles and shakes his head at the claim. "I'm working with and for a *newspaper* readership," he says. "I am writing for general readers who read my column for entertainment." He goes on to explain that these days he has "a fortunate franchise," working for Ruth Warren, book editor of the *Norfolk Virginian Pilot* and, as it happens, being published by three other area papers as well–the *Charlottesville Daily Progress,* the *Roanoke Times,* and the *Greensboro News Record.* Those years of training as an editorial writer, working under the Pulitzer Prize-winning Lenoir Chambers, whom Tazewell describes as one of the last of the old gentleman-scholar editors, like Douglas Freeman, have taught him to write easily and close to deadline. His column, always roughly 1,000 words, give or take a little, is published every Sunday. He stresses that it is a column. He reviews books, true; only very rarely writes a column that does not begin and end with a book. "But it can be a

William Tazewell

point of departure for talking about something else, too. Often–it's often the case with biography, my favorite genre–it becomes a kind of feature story."

Column or not, he does, in fact, review a lot of books, about 300 in the four years since, "more or less by accident," he began doing the column. "I know it doesn't make any real economic sense," he says, "but what I have here is an indulgence. It legitimizes my habit of reading."

He is not a speed reader, but he reads quickly and all the time. He can pick and choose what he wants to write about. He does not deal with any criticism, poetry, westerns, science fiction. He will very rarely review short stories. He does review detective stories. "The detective story is my favorite form of trash or leisure literature. And, of course, I try to do various kinds of nonfiction, especially history and biography, and a good deal of fiction." He will read and review "popular" fiction when he feels like it. "I am happiest when I can tell people about a good book they ought to read," he says. "When I get a book that disappoints me, I am likely to discard it, not to review it. Space is best used to talk about good books. If all I can say is don't waste your time, I don't review it."

Because his column is written close to deadline, just like an editorial, it is timely. He doesn't get to wait and see what the general national consensus is. He is usually coterminous with the first reviews after publication date. It wouldn't matter. He reads very few reviews and will ignore any review of a book he knows he is planning to review himself. He has neither time nor interest in seeing how his judgments compared with others. He is interested in literary awards and prizes. "They always seem to lead me to good new writers that I may have missed. Especially the P.E.N.-Faulkner awards which are judged by writers and already have a tradition of finding good books that aren't as well known as they might be."

His columns are, then, almost always 1,000-word reviews of worthy books, written and published on time. Almost always the reviews focus on a single book. But every once in a while he will put two books together in interesting, even odd juxtapositions. Would you believe Joan Didion and John D. MacDonald, Edgar Rice Burroughs and Roger Shattuck, Tama Janowitz and Kurt Vonnegut, Jr.? Tazewell notices and makes interesting connections and his readers look for that quality on Sundays. Virginia bookstores report a noticeable response to his columns. He tends to doubt his influence in that way. "Only if there is already a predisposition toward your book, can you give it a real push."

"I don't write criticism," he continues. "I write book reviews. I am trying to write 1,000 entertaining words. I'm getting better at it. I am a constant reader. I have read a lot by now. There are so often resonances. . . .

"Besides," he adds, "I am not so intimidated any more. I'm married to a writer [Mary Lee Settle], and through Mary Lee I've gotten to know a lot of them. And I have lived around academics."

Is he intimidated by the Big Boys in New York City?

He smiles at that.

"Some of them are very good and very smart," he says. "But there are plenty of smart people outside the boundaries of New York."

Finally: Odds and Ends and Inklings . . .

. . . One of the best book sections in any of the big city papers is that of the *Washington Times*, edited by Colin Walters. His reviews include many of the best writers around and therefore the literary quality of the reviews is uniformly high. Somehow this paper and its worthy book editor don't get mentioned in any of the articles about the state of book reviewing in America.

. . . On 12 January 1988 the National Book Critics Circle presented its annual citation for the best book reviewing of the past year to Josh Rubins, who writes for the *New York Review of Books* and the *Nation*.

. . . For funniest book review of 1987, in the face of all the sport at the expense of the Brat Pack, we nominate "Between the Sheets in Mo Town," by Diana McLellan (the *Wall Street Journal*, 20 November 1987, p. 27), a review of Maureen Dean's *Washington Wives* (Arbor House). Incidentally, the reviews of the *Wall Street Journal* are first-rate.

. . . Second funniest book review. Review of Allan Bloom's *The Closing of the American Mind*, by Robert Paul Wolff in *Academe* (September-October 1987, pp. 64-65), in which Wolff treats the book as if it were a meta-fiction by Saul Bellow and Bloom were one of Bellow's nutcase professors.

. . . Mutual Assured Destruction Award. One Georgian living in Florida (Gainesville) reviews the first novel of another good ole boy from Georgia living in Florida (Tallahassee). "The Poet Out of Rhyme: David Bottoms In Over His Head" (review of *Any Cold Jordan*, Peachtree, by David Bottoms), *Washington Post*, 21 May 1987, p. D4. Harry Crews comes out swinging ("It reads, in fact, rather like the thesis for a master of fine arts in creative writing from an inferior university.") and pulls no punches. Writes that Bottoms's performance is "mechanical, arbitrary and unbelievable," "repetitive," "interminable," "Impossibly contrived and not believable for a moment." Enough of that kind of thing could hurt a writer's feelings.

Publishers and Agents: The Columbia Connection

Kenneth A. Lohf

Butler Library, Columbia University

During the early decades of this century Columbia University sent many young graduates into book publishing in New York, perhaps more than any other educational institution. Several of the country's most prominent publishing houses still bear their names, among them, Alfred Harcourt, Donald Brace, Alfred A. Knopf, M. Lincoln Schuster, Richard Simon, George Delacorte, Ian Ballantine, George Macy, and Robert Giroux. Their taste and daring, their enterprise and imagination have made them part of the history of publishing in America. Because of the Columbia connections and the university's location in the city where most of the publishing activity of the country centers, it was only natural that its libraries collect the literary and editorial papers, letters, manuscripts, contract files, and publicity records of these publishers and preserve them for future research into the history of publishing and printing, the growth of authorship, the marketing of books, and, occasionally, the freedom of the press.

The active collecting of publishers' files began during the mid 1960s when initial contacts were made and discussions held with several editors and publishers. Preliminary discussions with Bennett Cerf and Donald Klopfer began in 1964, and the Random House papers were formally presented in 1970. During the six-year hiatus I visited the offices of Random House several times to search the papers, identify author and editorial files that were to comprise the collection, and prepare the files for shipment to the Rare Book and Manuscript Library.

The Random House files, now numbering more than one million letters and manuscripts, as well as 6,180 volumes of their imprints, contain the publishing history of many of the acclaimed writers of this century. The firm was founded in 1925 when Bennett Cerf and Donald Klopfer joined forces to buy the Modern Library Series from Boni and Liveright, and during the following six decades Random House reflected, and oftentimes was in the forefront of, the changing literary taste of the country and the revolu-

tions in sales and production techniques. In 1936 they acquired the firm of Smith and Haas, and consequently both Robert K. Haas and Harrison Smith were made members of the firm, bringing with them a list of established authors. During the 1930s Random House issued fiction by Erskine Caldwell, Isak Dinesen (Baroness Karen Blixen), William Faulkner, Sinclair Lewis, André Malraux, William Saroyan, and Gertrude Stein, all of whose novels are documented in the archives. New names appeared during the war years and the period following, including Paul Bowles, Truman Capote, John Cheever, Christopher Isherwood, James Michener, Wright Morris, John O'Hara, Budd Schulberg, Irwin Shaw, William Styron, and Eudora Welty; many of these authors still form the mainstay of the Random House list.

The firm is well known for a series of distinguished books, the most notable being the first American edition of James Joyce's *Ulysses*, the publication of which in 1933 marked the end of one of the most famous trials in the history of publishing, "the United States District Court, Southern District v. One Book Called Ulysses." The landmark decision by Judge John Munro Woolsey affected the course of censorship in America from that time forward. Joyce's congratulatory cablegram to Cerf, sent on 7 December 1933, at the conclusion of the trial–THANKS CONGRATULATIONS TO YOU COLLEAGUES COUNSEL SUCCESSFUL CASE JAMES JOYCE– is present in the files, along with the actual copy of *Ulysses* imported by Cerf, seized by customs officials at the New York docks, marked by the district attorney to indicate "offensive" passages, and used as primary evidence at the trial.

Contemporary poetry has always been prominent on the Random House list, and the archives contain lengthy series of letters by and about such notable poets as Conrad Aiken, W. H. Auden, Robert Creeley, Kenneth Fearing, Robert Graves, Randall Jarrell, Robinson Jeffers, Robert Lowell, Archibald MacLeish, Louis MacNeice, Thomas Merton, Marianne Moore, John Crowe

Contract for Augustus S. Doane's Midwifery Illustrated, *dated 24 September 1834, signed by the four Harper brothers (Harper Papers, Rare Book & Manuscript Library, Butler Library, courtesy of Columbia University Libraries)*

Ransom, Stephen Spender, Robert Penn Warren, Richard Wilbur, and William Carlos Williams. The house also emphasized drama and the theater, perhaps reflecting Cerf's own interest in the Broadway stage. The playwrights and composers on its list have included George Axelrod, S. N. Berman, Russell Crouse, George and Ira Gershwin, Moss Hart, Lillian Hellman, William Inge, George S. Kaufman, Howard Lindsay, Clifford Odets, Eugene O'Neill, Richard Rodgers, and Tennessee Williams.

The publisher's archive of the production files of the Modern Library and the Illustrated Modern Library are also included, as well as the manuscripts and corrected proofs of *The American College Dictionary.* There are also separate and

extensive files of Random House's major editors, such as Saxe Commins, Jason Epstein, Albert Erskine, and James H. Silberman; these contain important data on the preparation of texts for publication, and on negotiations with authors and their agents, paperback publishers, and television and film producers.

Random House also donated the editorial and production files of its subsidiary, Pantheon Books, covering the years 1944 to 1967. Numbering more than 12,000 letters and manuscripts, the files document the publication of volumes of poetry, fiction, and critical writings by such authors and artists as A. Alvarez, Georges Bernanos, Herman Broch, Winifred Bryher, Albert Camus, Eugene Ionesco, Karl Jaspers, Jacques Ma-

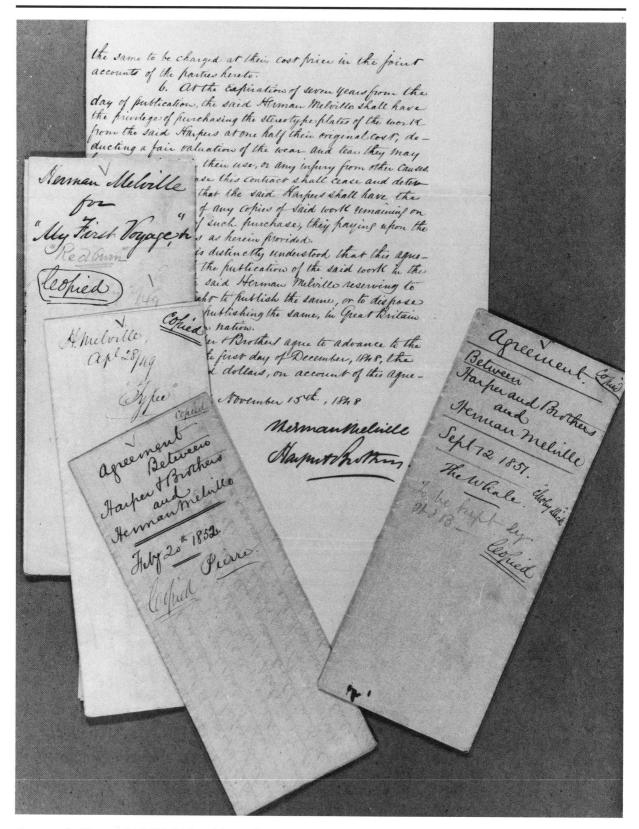

Contracts for Herman Melville's Moby-Dick, Redburn, Typee, Mardi, *and* Pierre; Or, The Ambiguities *(Harper Papers, Rare Book & Manuscript Library, Butler Library, courtesy of Columbia University Libraries)*

ritain, Isamu Noguchi, José Ortega y Gasset, Pier Paolo Pasolini, Sir Herbert Read, and Ben Shahn. Many of the letters are written to Kurt and Helen Wolff, Jacques Schiffrin, and André Schiffrin, all of whom have headed Pantheon Books at various times since its founding in 1942.

The W. W. Norton and Company papers arrived at the library in 1968 and established the second major publishers collection. The files of correspondence, manuscripts, galley and page proofs, and illustrations and artwork numbered more than 165,000 pieces and date from the founding of the firm in 1923 by William Warder Norton through 1967, a period when W. W. Norton developed into a leading publisher of books in the fields of psychology, music, philosophy, literature, and public affairs. Norton's frequent trips to Europe and his contacts with British and Continental publishing houses led to the firm's early publication in America of such notable authors as José Ortega y Gasset, C. K. Ogden, John Cowper Powys, Henry Handel Richardson, Rainer Maria Rilke, and Bertrand Russell; filed in the Norton papers are the editorial files for the novels, poetry, and nonfiction by these writers issued by the firm over more than forty years.

In addition to the files relating to the above-mentioned nonfiction authors, the Norton archives contain extensive correspondence of Ruth Benedict, Bernard Berenson, Pablo Casals, Carlos Chavez, Aaron Copland, Jo Davidson, John Dewey, Irwin Edman, Dwight D. Eisenhower, Erich Fromm, Karen Horney, Paul Henry Lang, Margaret Mead, Karl Menninger, Ashley Montagu, Douglas Moore, Frances Perkins, Herbert Read, Margaret Sanger, and Arnold Schoenberg. Other poets and fiction writers represented in the literary files include Sylvia Beach, T. S. Eliot, H. L. Mencken, James Purdy, John Crowe Ransom, Muriel Rukeyser, Robert Sherwood, and Mark Van Doren.

Archives of Harper & Brothers and Harper and Row were received at the library in 1972 and 1974, adding to the growing publishing resource the documents of one of New York's most imaginative publishers during the early decades of the nineteenth century. From the founding of the firm in 1817, when it issued its first work, an edition of Seneca's *Morals*, the four brothers vied, most successfully, with their competitors in selecting for their lists the writings of the best-known American authors and soon became the largest and most influential publishing house of the cen-

tury. One can derive a sense of the growth of American literature in the nineteenth century by a mere tally of its leading authors–R. H. Dana, William H. Prescott, Herman Melville, Henry James, William Dean Howells, and Mark Twain; the contracts for their books, and related correspondence and publishing ephemera, form the core of the Harper & Brothers papers.

The 13,250 contracts and agreements and supporting letters, document the firm's publishing history from 1817 to the 1920s. (Additional Harper correspondence files are at the Pierpont Morgan Library, Princeton University Library, and the Humanities Research Center at the University of Texas at Austin; the files of Harper periodicals are at the Library of Congress.) Several thousand novelists, poets, and historians are represented in the Columbia collection, including Jacob Abbott, James Lane Allen, John Kendrick Bangs, George Bancroft, Henry Ward Beecher, Richard Harding Davis, Mary Wilkins Freeman, Henry Blake Fuller, Ellen Glasgow, Lafcadio Hearn, Benson J. Lossing, Frederic Remington, Lydia Sigourney, Lew Wallace, and Owen Wister. The publication of some of the most notable books of the nineteenth century are documented in the papers by contracts, signed by their authors: Melville's *Moby-Dick, Redburn, Typee, Mardi,* and *Pierre; or, The Ambiguities;* Prescott's *History of the Conquest of Mexico* and *History of the Conquest of Peru;* and Henry James's *An International Episode, Daisy Miller, The Private Life, The Awkward Age,* and *The Ambassadors.* Harper & Brothers also published the work of noted English authors Arthur Conan Doyle, George du Maurier, Thomas Hardy, H. Rider Haggard, and Israel Zangwill; their contract files and receipts for payments of royalties are also present.

Of special bibliographical interest are the 2,760 volumes bearing the Harper imprint, and the following historical records: William H. Demarest's handwritten catalog of Harper books published from 1817 to 1879; the set of "Contract Books," containing file copies of agreements with authors, 1832 to 1916; and the "Memorandum Books," dating from 1857 to 1939, in which were recorded book announcements, advertisements, works in preparation, number of copies printed, and other bibliographical data.

The Harper and Row papers cover a more recent period of the firm's publishing history, 1935 to 1965. In addition to author files, the approximately 23,750 manuscripts and pieces of correspondence also contain files pertaining to three

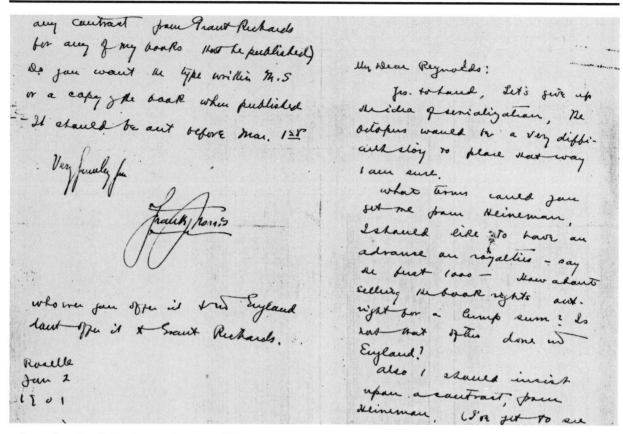

Letter from Frank Norris to Paul R. Reynolds, 2 January 1901, concerning serialization and publication in England of The Octopus *(Paul R. Reynolds Papers, courtesy of the Rare Book & Manuscript Library, Butler Library, Columbia University Libraries)*

important series published by the house, *The New American Nation,* edited by Richard B. Morris and Henry S. Commager, *The Rise of Modern Europe,* edited by William B. Langer, and *World Perspectives,* edited by Ruth Nanda Anshen. Several hundred authors are covered in the Harper and Row papers, including Nelson Algren, Jacques Barzun, Rachel Carson, Janet Flanner, Erich Fromm, Julian Huxley, Margaret Leech, Alan Moorehead, Lewis Mumford, A. L. Rowse, Ignazio Silone, Lillian Smith, and Sloan Wilson.

The papers of Simon and Schuster, cofounded in 1925 by M. Lincoln Schuster and Richard Simon, came to the library from several sources: the estate of M. Lincoln Schuster, Mrs. Ray Schuster and various other members of the Schuster family, and Mrs. Andrea Simon. Dating from the year of founding to 1970, the combined files number approximately 125,000 pieces of correspondence, manuscripts and proofs, production and sales records, and editorial reports, not only for Simon and Schuster, but also for its subsidiary, Pocket Books, Inc.

A general trade publisher, Simon and Schuster's list is particularly strong in American and English literature, religion, philosophy, psychology, and art. The firm published the highly successful series of volumes of philosophy and history by Will and Ariel Durant, several philosophical and mathematical works by Bertrand Russell, and the writings of the American art connoisseur Bernard Berenson, which have become classics in the history of art and collecting. In the field of literature the firm was equally successful in issuing books by Max Beerbohm, Max Eastman, Laura Hobson, Nikos Kazantzakis, Groucho Marx, H. L. Mencken, Henry Miller, John Cowper Powys, Upton Sinclair, Louis Untermeyer, and Hendrik Van Loon.

All of these authors and their works are represented in M. Lincoln Schuster's files, along with a fascinating piece of realia, the copper cornerstone box from Schuster's home, Green Laurels, in Sea Cliff, Long Island, constructed in 1936, in which he placed statements and letters solicited from close and famous friends, and which was to be opened a thousand years hence. When the Schusters moved to a new home in 1948, the library wing at Green Laurels was demolished and the box removed for safekeeping; Mrs. Schuster presented the copper box and its contents to the library in 1972, and among the treasures that came to light were letters and statements from Albert Einstein, Will Durant, Theodore Dreiser, Christopher Morley, Lewis Mumford, Donald Culross Peattie, Charles A. Beard, and H. L. Mencken, among numerous others, along with a fourteen-page essay by Schuster entitled "To an Unknown Mortal of 2936 A. D."

The papers of Richard L. Simon comprise 14,000 letters, memoranda, manuscripts, photographs, and documents relating to the editorial and business affairs of the house. Reflecting his special interests, there are extensive files on authors and publishers, including Bennett Cerf, Max Eastman, Edna Ferber, Erich Fromm, Joseph Heller, Dan Longwell, Kenneth Roberts, Arthur Schnitzler, Jerome Weidman, and Sloan Wilson. There is also an important file of 66 letters written to Simon by Schuster, dating from 1923 to Simon's death in 1960 (complementing the series of letters from Simon to Schuster in the Schuster portion of the papers), regarding all aspects of the firm's publishing activities. Simon's special interest in art, photography, and music are reflected in his correspondence with Irving Berlin, Margaret Bourke-White, Henri Cartier-Bresson, Philippe Halsman, Oscar Hammerstein II, Jerome Kern, Cole Porter, and Richard Rodgers.

Several other collections of publishers' papers of a more specialized nature are worthy of mention: Chilmark Press (1960-1976), 9,100 letters and manuscripts, primarily the files of Louis G. Cowan, including correspondence with David Jones, Frank Kermode, J. B. Priestley, John Sparrow, and Stephen Spender; Columbia University Press (1893-1960), comprising some 160,000 items in the editorial files documenting the publication of such authors as Ruth Benedict, John Dewey, John Erskine, Ashley Montagu, Allan Nevins, George Odell, and James T. Shotwell; Greenberg: Publisher (1924-1958), 49,000 letters and related editorial material of the house founded in 1924 by Jacob W. and David B. Greenberg to publish "how to" books, westerns, and books on health, cooking, police techniques, agriculture, and theater by Louis Bromfield, Theodore Dreiser, Alfred Kinsey, Karl Menninger, Deems Taylor, and others; House of Books, Ltd.,

Crown Octavo Series (1932-1969), edited by Louis Henry and Marguerite Cohn, comprising letters and manuscripts of John Galsworthy, William Saroyan, Booth Tarkington, James T. Farrell, Robert Frost, T. S. Eliot, Eudora Welty, Marianne Moore, and Robert Duncan, among others; George Macy (1916-1960), 2,500 items covering his career as publisher of Heritage Press and his work with the Nonesuch Press; George Haven Putnam (1900-1930), 750 letters from authors and publishers, such as William Beebe, Lady Augusta Gregory, and T. Fisher Unwin, and copies of replies from Putnam; and Roberts Brothers, Boston (1841-1932), 1,500 letters from English and American writers and publishers, including T. Fisher Unwin and John Lane.

Related to the publishers' files are the papers of the cofounder and one-time chairman of the board of the Book-of-the-Month Club, Harry Scherman. Forming the core of the collection of approximately 19,500 letters, manuscripts, and readers' reports are large groups of Scherman's correspondence with members of the editorial board, Henry Seidel Canby, Clifton Fadiman, Dorothy Canfield Fisher, Gilbert Highet, John P. Marquand, Christopher Morley, and William Allen White. There are numerous additional letters from writers, publishers, agents, and book-related organizations, as well as Scherman's personal papers as writer, economist, and philanthropist.

As the publishers' archives were being acquired and cataloged it became apparent that, in the more recent decades, the writing and marketing of books had changed dramatically. The publishing of books involved a greater risk in an increasingly commercial world, and central to the process was the role of the literary agent, who acted as adviser to the author and as his advocate before the publisher. A. P. Watt is considered the first professional literary agent, having begun his business in London in 1875. English agent William Morris Colles founded the Authors' Syndicate in 1890, and a collection of his papers in the library, 2,300 items dating from 1890 to 1928, includes correspondence with several hundred minor nineteenth-century British authors, among them, Helen Allingham, Algernon Blackwood, James Bryce, T. Hall Caine, Alfred Perceval Graves, Frederic Harrison, Marie Belloc Lowndes, and Mrs. Humphry Ward.

America's first literary agent, Paul Revere Reynolds, founded his agency in New York in 1893 after having served as an American repre-

690

relaxation of the thing done : the fallaciously inferred debility of the female the muscularity of the male : the variations of ethical codes : the natural grammatical transition by inversion involving no alteration of sense of an aorist preterite proposition (parsed as masculine subject, monosyllabic onomatopœic transitive verb with direct feminine object) from the active voice into its correlative aorist preterite proposition (parsed as feminine subject, auxiliary verb and quasimonosyllabic onomatopœic past participle with complementary masculine agent) in the passive voice : the continued product of seminators by generation : the continual production of semen by distillation : the futility of triumph or protest or vindication : the inanity of extolled virtue : the lethargy of nescient matter : the apathy of the stars.

In what final satisfaction did these antagonistic sentiments and reflections reduced to their simplest forms, converge ?

Satisfaction at the ubiquity in eastern and western terrestrial hemispheres, in all habitable lands and islands explored or unexplored (the land of the midnight sun, the islands of the blessed, the isles of Greece, the land of promise) of adipose posterior female hemispheres, redolent of milk and honey and of excretory sanguine and seminal warmth, reminiscent of secular families of curves of amplitude, insusceptible of moods of impression or of contrarieties of expression, expressive of mute immutable mature animality.

The visible signs of antesatisfaction ?

An approximate erection : a solicitous adversion : a gradual elevation : a tentative revelation ; a silent contemplation.

Then ?

He kissed the plump mellow yellow smellow melons of her rump, on each plump melonous hemisphere, in their mellow yellow furrow, with obscure prolonged provocative melonsmellonous osculation.

The visible signs of postsatisfaction ?

A silent contemplation : a tentative velation : a gradual abasement : a solicitous aversion : a proximate erection.

What followed this silent action ?

Somnolent invocation, less somnolent recognition, incipient excitation catechetical interrogation.

Page from the district attorney's marked copy of James Joyce's Ulysses, *1930 (Gift of Bennett Cerf, courtesy of Rare Book & Manuscript Library, Butler Library, Columbia University Libraries)*

sentative for Cassell and Company marketing English books to New York publishers. Reynolds handled some of the most prominent British and American writers of the late nineteenth and early twentieth centuries, numbering among his clients Gertrude Atherton, Arnold Bennett, Robert Bridges, James Branch Cabell, Willa Cather, Winston Churchill, Richard Harding Davis, Margaret Deland, Theodore Dreiser, Zona Gale, John Galsworthy, Hamlin Garland, Ellen Glasgow, Jack London, John Masefield, George Moore, Frank Norris, Booth Tarkington, Sidney and Beatrice Webb, H. G. Wells, and Israel Zangwill. Reynolds's son joined the firm in 1923, and later additions to the collection included his correspondence with a wide range of publishers, editors, and other agents, as well as authors Margery Allingham, Howard Fast, Edna Ferber, MacKinlay Kantor, W. Somerset Maugham, Ogden Nash, Conrad Richter, George Bernard Shaw, Upton Sinclair, Lincoln Steffens, Lytton Strachey, Kurt Vonnegut, Jr., Thornton Wilder, and P. G. Wodehouse. Also preserved among the papers are the firm's account books for the period, 1902 to 1939, a valuable source for information on royalty payments and the economics of an author's representative during the first third of this century.

Covering a period of more than sixty years, 1927 to 1987, the papers of James Oliver Brown begin with the files of George T. Bye, whose agency Brown acquired in 1958. Bye founded his firm in January 1927 and represented popular American and English writers who were prominent in the 1920s, such as George Ade, Louis Bromfield, Gelett Burgess, Erskine Caldwell, John Erskine, Ford Madox Ford, Zane Grey, Richard Hughes, Fannie Hurst, Manuel Komroff, Don Marquis, Christopher Morley, John Cowper Powys, Mary Renault, Albert Payson Terhune, Rebecca West, and Alexander Woollcott. When Brown acquired Bye's business in 1958 he added other authors who were to gain status as important writers in the decades following–Louis Auchincloss, Cecil Beaton, Lonnie Coleman, Herbert Gold, Richard Lockridge, Alberto Moravia, Katherine Anne Porter, John Selby, Jean Stafford, and Harvey Swados. The significance of the agent's files, numbering approximately 210,000 items, become readily apparent when one considers the extent of the individual authors' correspondence, such as 2,011 letters from Erskine Caldwell and 2,424 letters from Herbert Gold to Brown, series that any future biographer

or critic will deem essential to their researches.

In 1978 James Brown Associates absorbed the literary agency of John Cushman Associates, comprising 72,000 letters and documents dating from 1965, including letters from A. Alvarez, Randolph S. Churchill, Lawrence Durrell, Nicolas Freeling, H. Montgomery Hyde, Doris Lessing, Mary Renault, C. P. Snow, Julian Symons, Honor Tracy, John Wain, Patrick White, and Angus Wilson. James Brown Associates merged with Curtis Brown, Ltd., in 1981; however, that New York agency, through its president Perry H. Knowlton, had established a collection of the firm's papers in 1976 and has continued to develop the resource which now numbers nearly two million letters, manuscripts, and contracts, and covers more than seventy years as one of the leading and largest agencies in New York.

Containing primarily correspondence with leading English and American authors, the Curtis Brown papers are comprised of files pertaining to the editing and publishing of trade books and textbooks, serial rights, reprints, dramatic rights, translations and foreign rights, publicity and promotion, and copyright registration. Represented by lengthy files of letters are poets W. H. Auden, Robert Graves, Thomas Merton, Ogden Nash; novelists and short story writers Kingsley Amis, Saul Bellow, Elizabeth Bowen, Joyce Cary, John Cheever, Frederic Dannay, Lawrence Durrell, Ian Fleming, Erle Stanley Gardner, William Goyen, Christopher Isherwood, Sinclair Lewis, Richard Llewellyn, Helen MacInnes, Robert Nathan, Sean O'Faolain, James Purdy, Mary Renault, C. P. Snow, Eudora Welty, and Sloan Wilson; and nonfiction writers Eve Curie, Frieda Lawrence, Samuel Eliot Morison, Vincent Sheean, Susan Sontag, and Angus Wilson.

The agency of Ann Watkins was founded in 1910 and continued under her management until she retired in 1957, after which time the firm was operated by her son, Armitage Watkins. The 101,500 letters, manuscripts, contracts, and account books acquired by the library date from the founding of the firm to 1981 and deal with editorial, financial, and legal aspects of book, magazine, theatrical, and film rights of the firm's notable list of American and English clients, who have included Michael Arlen, Frances Hodgson Burnett, Roald Dahl, Peter DeVries, Theodore Dreiser, Ernest Hemingway, Sinclair Lewis, Carson McCullers, Ezra Pound, Ayn Rand, Dorothy Sayers, Gertrude Stein, and Dylan Thomas.

AN INQUIRY INTO MEANING AND TRUTH.

This book is concerned with the foundations of knowledge, which it approaches first from the standpoint of language. " Meaning", as applied to words, is shown to be different for words of different kinds - object-words, proper names, logical words, and dictionary words. In regard to sentences, we have to consider first the relation of an experience to the various sentences that partially describe it, then the distinction between significant and nonsensical sentences, then the state of the speaker that they express and the state of affairs that (when true) they indicate. We pass next to a discussion of the observational premisses of empirical knowledge, and thence to the relation between a belief and a sentence in which it is expressed. These discussions enable us to consider the definition of "knowledge" and of "truth", involving the relation of truth to experience, and the question whether we can know that there are unknowable truths. After a discussion of analysis, the book ends with an investigation of the structure of language and the structure of the world, with a suggestion that the former permits some inferences as to the latter, though these inferences are fewer than was assumed to be the case in traditional philosophy, which was largely based on a crude object-ification of vocabulary and rules of syntax.

A feature of the book is an attempt to build a bridge between psychology and modern logic, by giving psychological interpretations of logical ideas which make it possible to see how the most refined intellectual processes have developed from pre-linguistic sources such as are exemplified in animal behaviour.

Jacket text by Bertrand Russell for his An Inquiry into Meaning and Truth *(W. W. Norton Papers, courtesy of Rare Book Manuscript Library, Butler Library, Columbia University Libraries)*

Two collections, the papers of Leah Salisbury and Annie Laurie Williams, added nearly 300,000 letters and manuscripts to the library's holdings relating to the theater and cinema. Consisting of correspondence, contracts, playscripts, and financial records, the papers of Leah Salisbury, dating from 1925 to 1975, contain files relating to dramatists, composers, directors, and actors, such as Edward Albee, Maxwell Anderson, Jean Anouilh, S. N. Behrman, Guy Bolton, Albert Camus, Marc Connelly, Russell Crouse, Howard Dietz, Maurice Evans, Christopher Fry, William Gibson, Alec Guinness, Moss Hart, Katharine Hepburn, Langston Hughes, Eugene Ionesco, Jerome Kern, Christopher Morley, Ogden Nash, S. J. Perelman, Mary Pickford, Richard Rodgers, Robert E. Sherwood, Margaret Webster, Kurt Weill, Thornton Wilder, and Stark Young.

New York drama and motion picture agent Annie Laurie Williams founded her agency in 1929 at the time the "talkies" were being established as a major entertainment art, and her collection documents the negotiations that resulted in some of the most celebrated motion pictures of the following four decades. Williams acquired the rights to Margaret Mitchell's *Gone With the Wind*, Alice Tisdale Hobart's *Oil For the Lamps of China*, Lloyd C. Douglas's *The Robe* and *Magnificent Obsession*, John Hersey's *A Bell for Adano*, Alan Paton's *Cry, the Beloved Country*, Lillian Smith's *Strange Fruit*, Patrick Dennis's *Auntie Mame*, Kathleen Winsor's *Forever Amber*, and John Steinbeck's *The Grapes of Wrath* and *Of Mice and Men*. In addition to these authors, the collection of approximately 100,000 letters and manuscripts includes correspondence by, and relating to, Truman Capote, John Dos Passos, Paul Horgan, William Humphrey, Frances Parkinson Keyes, Kenneth Roberts, George R. Stewart, and Ben Ames Williams. The author whose writings are documented most completely is John Steinbeck, whose file numbers more than 200 letters, dating from 1933, the year of his *To a God Unknown*, through the publication of his last major work, *Travels With Charley*, in 1962. The papers of Williams's husband, Maurice Crain, agent for numerous novelists and short story writers, are also part of the archives.

Before Harold Matson founded his agency in 1937 he had served as manager of McClure's Syndicate and had run his own syndicate feeding news and features to radio stations; almost immediately after founding his literary agency, Harold Matson Company, Inc., he attracted such writers

as Phil Stong, H. Allen Smith, James Street, James Ramsay Ullman, Wilbur Daniel Steele, and William Saroyan. During the next three decades, largely because of his skill at forceful negotiation, Matson arranged the sale of such bestsellers as Ullman's *The White Tower*, Herman Wouk's *The Caine Mutiny*, Robert Ruark's *Something of Value*, William Manchester's *The Death of a President*, and Ray Bradbury's *The Martian Chronicles*. Comprising some 75,000 letters, manuscripts, contracts, and publicity materials, the Matson papers cover the period from the firm's founding to 1980. Among the novelists and short-story writers, in addition to the above, represented by extensive files are William S. Burroughs, John Collier, Arthur Koestler, Malcolm Lowry, Flannery O'Connor, and William Styron. Playwrights and poets include Lillian Hellman, John Mortimer, Charles Norman, and Stephen Spender; prominent among literary critics and prose writers are Frank Kermode, J. B. Priestley, V. S. Pritchett, and William L. Shirer.

The correspondence and financial records of agent John Schaffner, dating from 1947 to 1980, contain nearly 100,000 letters and manuscripts of essayists, novelists, and short-story writers. During the nearly thirty-five-year period Schaffner represented Winifred Bryher, Sheilah Graham, Barbara Howes, Marianne Moore, Frederic Prokosch, Santha Rama Rau, and Alice B. Toklas, as well as numerous writers for American magazines and television.

The archive also contains specialized files of several agents. Of interest among the 18,250 letters, memoranda, contracts, and royalty statements of authors' representative Toni Strassman, covering the period 1937 to 1976, are files concerning the publication of books, short stories, and articles by Gina Berriault, Allen Churchill, William Goyen, Joseph Hayes, and Harry Mark Petrakis. The correspondence between Harold Ober Associates and fiction writer, sports columnist, and newspaperman Paul Gallico, dating from 1933 to 1977, comprises 7,250 letters that discuss literary works in progress, plans for future articles and books, contracts and financial agreements, and screenplays of his novels, including *The Snow Goose, Thomasina*, and *Mrs. 'Arris Goes to Paris*. Among the letters presented by the literary agent Blanche Gregory are 76 from the novelist and travel writer Paul Theroux, dated 1966 to 1980, and 269 long and detailed letters from Joyce Carol Oates, a series that begins in 1963 when the young author was writing and publish-

Envelope addressed by Hendrik Willem Van Loon to Simon and Schuster with a drawing of an elephant (M. L. Schuster Papers, courtesy of Rare Book & Manuscript Library, Butler Library, Columbia University Libraries)

ing her first short stories, to 1982, a twenty-year period during which Oates published more than forty novels, collections of short stories, and volumes of poetry.

The most recent collection of agent's papers received is that of the firm of Georges and Anne Borchardt, who began representing French publishing firms in New York during the early 1950s and later acted for individual French authors who were seeking American publication; they formed their agency in 1968, and, in addition to French authors, they began to represent American and English writers as well. The files, which date from 1952 to 1982 and comprise 110,000 items, contain correspondence with authors, publishers, and other agents, including Mme. Guillaume Apollinaire, Hervé Bazin, Laurent de Brunhoff, Michel Butor, Albert Camus, Marguerite Duras, Jean Giraudoux, Julian Green, Henri Michaux, Henri Troyat, and Marguerite Yourcenar. Among English and American authors represented by the Borchardts are John Ashberry, Eric Bentley, Paul Carroll, Caresse Crosby, Lawrence Ferlinghetti, John Gardner, Meyer Levin, Mary McCarthy, Anaïs Nin, William Plomer, Alan Sillitoe, Ruth Rendell, and Harvey Swados.

This combined resource of nearly five mil-

lion papers of New York publishers and literary agents has been developed over little more than two decades. Nearly all of these files came from basements, warehouses, garages, barns, attics, storage rooms, and closets, where they had been stored in bulging cardboard boxes, sagging transfiles, or dusty bundles wrapped in brown paper. Some of them were damp-stained, many had been nibbled at their edges by mice, others had become browned with acidity and were dry and crumbling, and virtually all were inaccessible to the writers and researchers who had need of them to complete their biographies, bibliographies, histories, and critical studies. Storing them in proper archival boxes and acid-free folders in a temperature- and humidity-controlled environment, processing and inventorying the vast files in a logical and retrievable order, cataloguing the most important letters and documents to achieve maximum security, making the files available to scholars and researchers in a research library setting–these have been the aims in establishing and developing this resource which is important not only to the history of publishing in New York but also to the preservation of the record of human endeavor in the advancement of thought and imagination during this century.

Small Presses III: Pushcart Press

Bill Henderson

Pushcart Press started in hurt and frustration and has evolved into joy and inspiration. The hurt and frustration are familiar to most writers. I wrote a novel I believed in, and nobody wanted to publish it. This was back in 1971, when it seemed that if the commercial people in New York didn't want your fiction you had only the vanity presses to turn to. And even my Aunt Gertrude knew that vanity presses brought shame to the author "published" by them.

Like most authors, I had no idea what publishing was all about. And there were no books around to tell me. The commercial folks knew all the great mysteries, and it was up to me to find out what they were if I was to avoid the vanity disaster.

I had a big-hearted uncle (Aunt Gertrude's brother) who offered to help out. We created a small publishing house called Nautilus Books with his money (I paid for the printing of my novel–titled *The Galapagos Kid* and authored by one "Luke Walton"), and off we ventured into the mists, determined to start another Doubleday, or McGraw-Hill. We hired a group of independent sales representatives who worked on a commission-only basis and signed up five other titles besides Luke Walton's novel. In total we invested about $75,000.

Most of that went for printing and advertising. It seemed that part of the publishing mystery was letting people know you were serious, and that required big ads in *Publishers Weekly* and the *New York Times Book Review*. It also seemed that publishing was divided into seasons. You had to have at least two lists, Summer-Fall/Winter-Spring. By the end of our first Summer-Fall season we were broke and exhausted. My uncle sold his house and moved to the West Coast. I joined Doubleday for a stint and on weekends started Pushcart Press with the one book I knew people needed: *The Publish-It-Yourself Handbook–Literary Tradition and How-To* (1973).

This time I knew at least a few things besides that fact that it is impossible to sell literary first novels in any great quantity. I realized that to start a publishing business you need only one

good idea–not big ads, not a string of sales reps, not seasons of selling, not even a catalog or an office. You need a good idea and a good printer. The *Handbook* was such an idea.

During lunch hours at Doubleday I visited the Fifth Avenue Public Library and investigated the claims of vanity houses that many authors had paid to have their books published–implying that they had gone to vanity houses–people like Thomas Paine, Edgar Allan Poe, Walt Whitman, Stephen Crane, Upton Sinclair, and Anaïs Nin. Not *one* had used a vanity house. They all did their books themselves. A whole tradition of do-it-yourself publishing was buried here.

I started by asking "Walton" to write a chapter, and I contributed an introduction about the do-it-yourself history I had turned up, plus a few how-to tips. I had a beginning, chapter one, and an end, but I wasn't confident that anybody else would get excited about the idea of the *Handbook*. I tried it out on editors at various firms but received only dull stares. The editors did not understand that writers would need such a book; weren't there all the commercial publishers listed in *Literary Market Place?* Every good book would find a home, they remarked. I realized that if this title ever got off the ground, it would have to be without a commercial publisher. At best it would be boring to such a publisher; at worst it would be insulting.

I asked a few other do-it-yourself publishers to join me with contributions to the *Handbook*. One of the first people I wrote to was Anaïs Nin, who had published all her own work during the 1940s, when she was a commercial outcast. She wrote back: "I'm too busy, but this summer I may not be and I will let you know." I took that for a no and shelved the project to concentrate on the Doubleday slush pile and coaching the softball team.

I don't think there would have been a *Publish-It-Yourself Handbook* without the late Anaïs Nin. One day in summer, completely unannounced and unexpected, without a request for payment of any kind, and without any knowledge of who I was or if I knew a thing about publishing a

Bill Henderson

book, her chapter arrived, with a letter saying, "Your book is certainly needed."

The rest was easy. I wrote to thank her and she wrote back suggesting several other people who might be interested in contributing a chapter about their own publishing. It seemed that everybody I contacted had a friend (who in turn had a friend) who had self-published or published someone else's book. An editor at Knopf suggested a sailor, Patrick Royce, who had published his own how-to sailing books, and a tailor-poet, Clarence Poulin, in New Hampshire, who issued his own poetry and also instruction books on tailoring. Stewart Brand gave me permission to reprint his afterword to the *Whole Earth Catalog* (a catalog how-to). Barbara Garson, author-publisher of *MacBird,* consented to an interview about her play publishing–but only after I argued with her agent, who thought the whole project sounded anticommercial and might be bad for Garson's career with commercial publishers. I picked up a chapter from Leonard Woolf's autobiography about the start of Hogarth Press–first publishers of T. S. Eliot, E. M. Forster, and others–and one by Alan Swallow on the history of Swallow Press. And so it went, as the Yonkers edition of the *Handbook* assembled itself. There was even a pseudonymous author, Oliver Lange, who then had a novel on the *New York Times* best-seller list. Lange admitted that his favorite among his own

books was one which he had published twenty-five copies of at his kitchen table. The commercial people were more enthusiastic than I had first expected. A literary agent, Alex Jackinson, contributed a chapter. Martin Baron, an ex-vanity editor, slammed vanity publishing. And *Esquire*'s Gordon Lish knocked out his humorous piece about why the whole idea of the book was ridiculous–something about having lunch with Gordon Lish at fine New York restaurants and how, if you self-published, you didn't get to do that. A veteran of lunches with Lish, I admit that missing a lunch with him is a drawback to do-it-yourselfing.

When I knew what I had to do–publish this book with my wife's help from our studio apartment–I told Doubleday what I was up to and prepared to say goodbye to the corporation. Several editors there supported the book with suggestions, and two gentlemen, Sam Vaughan and Ken McCormick, were particularly helpful. *Publishers Weekly* gave the book a four-page send-off with an excerpt from my history of do-it-yourself publishing. *PW* later reviewed the book so well that I went reeling off to the Italian Pavilion restaurant, half in irony, half seriously, because that was where publishers often dined and I suddenly knew I was a publisher. (*PW* had said my Pushcart Press was "delightfully named," and for that I give credit to George Plimpton and others.

Their Project Pushcart down Fifth Avenue, to protest publishers' ineptitude in getting books around, inspired the naming of Pushcart Press in 1973.)

I was determined to be cautious no matter what the prepublication fireworks might be. The first printing of the *Handbook* was a mere 1,000 copies–100 in cloth and 900 in paperback. I spent almost our entire savings on printing.

More than 100 newspapers and magazines serenaded the book. (Many reviewers are frustrated writers, as are lots of editors–rejected by New York and bound to be sympathetic.) Orders piled up faster than we could reprint. One mention in the *New York Times Book Review* by Victor Navasky, a paragraph buried in a longer article, brought in 400 prepublication orders. To date the *Publish-It-Yourself Handbook* has sold over 40,000 copies. Pushcart Press is now on something approximating a financial footing, and I am able to publish full-time, typing my own letters and hauling my own mailbags. The bad news is that I suspect many authors, while quite ready to buy a book about how to publish their own stuff, are far too reluctant to buy the works of other authors.

In order to give some sort of recognition to the more outstanding authors encouraged by the *Handbook* and by today's small-press movement, in 1975 I asked several distinguished editors to help me start an annual prize anthology: the Pushcart Prize series. Again Anaïs Nin was one of the first to respond to Pushcart's appeal. Buckminster Fuller, Charles Newman, Daniel Halpern, Gordon Lish, H. L. Van Brunt, Harry Smith, Hugh Fox, Ishmael Reed, Joyce Carol Oates, Len Fulton, Leonard Randolph, Leslie Fiedler, Nona Balakian, Paul Bowles, Paul Engle, Ralph Ellison, Reynolds Price, Rhoda Schwartz, Richard Morris, Tom Montag, and William Phillips also joined the founding staff. In the first eleven Pushcart Prize collections we have promoted the short stories, poems, essays, and literary whatnots of more than 650 small-press authors as they appeared in over 275 presses.

The Pushcart Prize series is, first of all, publication and recognition for small presses and their authors who have done outstanding work in the previous calendar year. The series is only an attempt–but an attempt that receives more than 4,000 nominations every year from small-press editors. Even with the help of 150 contributing editors and a constant influx of new editors each

Dust jacket for a revised edition of Pushcart Press's how-to manual of self-publishing

year, the prize can be thought of as inclusive only if it is seen as a continuity of many volumes.

The Pushcart Prize is also a cooperation between a small press and commercial publishers. The first nine volumes were published in paperback by Avon Books, and the series is now published for a paperback audience by Penguin Books. Finally, the Pushcart Prize is a promotional event, a celebration by hundreds of small presses that says we seek meaning and excellence and are willing to take chances with the new and with young authors. Looking back over these eleven years, I am pleased to note that many of our authors have achieved national recognition–John Irving, Mary Gordon, Jayne Ann Phillips, Andre Dubus, Tim O'Brien, Raymond Carver, and most recently, Mona Simpson–to name but a few from a long list.

In all of this I have remained something of a cross between a cheerleader and a secretary. Every fall we invite nominations from over 2,000

Dust jacket for the latest installment in the Pushcart Prize series, which seeks to provide recognition for small presses and their authors by republishing outstanding work from the previous calendar year

presses listed in Len Fulton's *International Directory of Little Magazines and Small Presses*. We also ask our evolving board of contributing editors (you get on the board by having work published in a previous *Pushcart Prize* volume) to suggest work and/or authors they have admired from the previous year's small press-little magazine output.

When my Wainscott, New York, garage is filled with boxes of tear sheets, we begin to read. I read the fiction; Anthony Brandt is first reader for the essays; and we invite new poetry editors to judge the poetry nominations each year. In recent years we have been honored by the poetry selections of editors Stanley Plumly and William Stafford (volume X); Philip Levine and David Wojahn (XI); Jorie Graham and Robert Hass (XII); and Philip Booth and Jay Meek for volume XIII, to be published in August 1988.

I have also invited guest introductions to recent volumes: Gail Godwin (VIII); Jayne Anne Phillips (XI); George Plimpton (X); Cynthia Ozick (XI); and Frank Conroy (XII). Writing introductions turned out to be the most difficult chore of each volume, and I was rather tired of my own voice after introductions for the first seven.

The Pushcart Prize series has been a joyous and exhausting project. Financially it has done little better than break even despite terrific reviews each year and other glories: *Publishers Weekly* gave it the Carey-Thomas Award for "creative publishing" in 1978, and the *New York Times Book Review* named it an "Outstanding Book of the Year" several years in a row.

Now and then a little money has been left over–and a little time too–to publish other books. In order to keep track of these projects I prefer to establish publications in series. Back in 1978 Pushcart started a copublishing series with outstanding literary journals by joining *TriQuarterly* in its 800-page work, *The Little Magazine In America: A Modern Documentary History*. *TQ*'s Elliott Anderson and Mary Kinzie did the magazine version and Pushcart issued the book edition simultaneously.

This series was continued with four copublished volumes: *Shenandoah: An Anthology*, edited by James Boatwright; *The Ploughshares Reader: New Fiction for the Eighties*, edited by DeWitt Henry; *TQ20: Twenty Years of the Best Contemporary Writing and Graphics from TriQuarterly Magazine*, edited by Reginald Gibbons and Susan Hahn; and *The Writing Business*, edited by the staff of *Coda: Poets & Writers Newsletter*.

In 1983 Pushcart started another series–this one dedicated to overlooked manuscripts. To quote our catalog, "The Editors' Book award series publishes important and unusual book manuscripts that have been overlooked by today's high pressure, bottom-line commercial firms. The purpose of the Award is to encourage the writing of distinguished books of uncertain financial value and to support the enthusiasms of editors without regard to concerns other than literary merit." Sponsoring editors for this award are Simon Michael Bessie, James Charlton, Peter Davison, Jonathan Galassi, David Godine, Daniel Halpern, James Laughlin, Seymour Lawrence, Starling Lawrence, Robie Macauley, Joyce Carol Oates, Nan A. Talese, Faith Sale, Ted Solotaroff, Pat Strachan, and Thomas Wallace. Each manuscript must be nominated by an editor who, for one reason or the other, could not publish it commercially.

When Pushcart started this award for the best rejected manuscript of the year, I expected we would turn up one work every five years or so. Instead, we have published a new title every year since our first announcement. *Saul's Book* (1983) by Paul Rogers is an autobiographical novel about the rough underside of New York's 42nd Street; *The Tale of the Ring* (1984) is an account of survival in the death camps of Treblinka and Auschwitz by Frank Stiffel, which had been rejected for over forty years and is one of the most important books I have ever read; *The Adventures of Jeremiah Dimon* (1985) by Everett Rattray is a first novel rejected over the author's lifetime and published to general acclaim by Pushcart five years after his death; and, published in 1986, *From My Father Singing* by David Bosworth is a first novel by a young writer who also won the Drue Heinz Award for his first short story collection. Soon to be published is our 1987 winner, *Eyestone* by D. R. MacDonald, a brilliant collection of short stories set in Cape Breton. The Editors' Book Award receives from sixty to eighty manuscripts each year and has proven that many manuscripts are unjustly overlooked.

A final series, one published for fun, is the Literary Companion series. Many of our books have been rather large. These books are slim–about 100 pages and 5 x 7–and the contents seri-

ous but lighthearted. *The Writer's Quotation Book,* edited by James Charlton; *The Lover's Quotation Book,* edited by Helen Handley; and *The Cook's Quotation Book,* edited by Maria Bolushkin Robbins contain about 300 entries each of a literary sort.

Late in 1986 I edited another volume for the Literary Companion series–*Rotten Reviews*–a compilation of 175 ghastly reviews of books that became classics. Like Pushcart Press itself, this sly little collection had its start in my reaction to the few mean-spirited reviews of books that I published with love. It was the happy outcome of anger and frustration. It was followed in 1987 by *Rotten Reviews II,* a collection of contemporary mean mentions, many selected by the attacked authors themselves.

Pushcart Press has been on an interesting roll since my uncle and I dreamed the impossible–and luckily failed–in 1971. I would like to thank hundreds of people–and have tried to do so in this article. But a final thank-you belongs to George Brockway, president of W. W. Norton, who encouraged me at the very start and later distributed Pushcart's modest list through Norton. Before him, publisher David Godine helped to get the titles around. Before him, my hat is off to the post office and an old Chevy that drove from store to store.

Literary Documents II: *Library Journal*–Statements and Questionnaires from First Novelists

The well-known *Library Journal* series of articles based on questionnaires and responses solicited from first novelists was originated in 1951 by the late Margaret Cooley, who for many years was a seminal force within the Bowker organization, where she edited, with great integrity, the "New Books Appraised" section of the journal. The first survey, which appeared under the heading "New Creative Writers" in the issue for 1 October 1951, dealt with fourteen writers. Of that group only Hortense Calisher seems to have had any lasting success. Calisher was featured for her first collection of short stories, *In the Absence of Angels,* and she reappeared in the series in 1961, on the appearance of *False Entry,* her first novel. Cooley prepared the initial survey on her own, and later other members of the "Books Appraised" staff took it over, including Anne Woods, Judith Margoshes, Susan Sacher, Judith Serebnick, Irene Stokvis Land, and, in recent years, Anne Burns. The surveys, always a notable feature of the *Library Journal,* generally appeared in February, June, and October through 1969, and then a bit more erratically each year until 1984, when the journal switched to an annual compilation appearing 1 October of each year, covering the fall and winter crop. The series initially depended for its copy on an awkward question-answer form which was superseded in the mid 1960s by a request for a short autobiographical essay. The essay, with modifications, continues to be the format. A selected group of the first novelists was allowed a rather generous amount of close-set typespace in which to express themselves. The latest appearance of the survey (October 1987) is more streamlined with shorter quotes and full-color dust jacket reproductions which crowd the author's words a bit.

In 1967 and 1968, thanks to the kindness of Margaret Cooley and her successor as editor of "New Books Appraised," Judith Serebnick, and to the generosity of Daniel Melcher, Bowker's publisher, the Penn State Library was given a considerable selection of the first-novel files then remaining in the *Library Journal* offices. They comprise biographical and literary responses from about 900 authors, a more than representative gathering drawn for the most part from the period from 1958 to 1968. Peggy Humphreys drew upon the *Library Journal* files in an article, "First Novels, The State of the Art" (*Library Journal,* 97 [1 September 1972] 2696-2699), and tabulated 1,072 first novels published from 1962 to 1971 by eighty-four publishers. The rate of production varied from ninety to 125 such novels a year. It is evident that the 1960s was a fertile period for new writers; otherwise this voluminous record would be of major interest only to those interested in the sociology of publishing rather than literature. However, one does not wish to imply that sociology is not a legitimate or even fascinating approach to the documents. There was always the odd convict writing from a cell, or Alice Denham, the Playmate of the Month for July 1956, rubbing shoulders with Mary Astor or Jules Feiffer. Such people stood out, but the initial impact of the surveys was always one of bemusement as to how to choose from among the many unfamiliar faces and novels those which might count in the future. It was easier to notice the celebrities and the writers already established in other genres who carried something of their fame into the new area of fiction. Such people were often rather generous with their words, and often revealingly uncomfortable about their temerity in taking on a difficult and unfamiliar line of work.

Art Buchwald (columnist), Ernie Kovacs (humorist), John Kenneth Galbraith (economist), Robert Goulet (director), Leslie Fiedler (critic), and Jules Feiffer (cartoonist) all had a go at the novel in the 1960s; yet Elia Kazan (director) and Mary Astor (actress) perhaps had a better knack for the form than they did. No matter how well known they were, these writers didn't depend on their agents to fill out the forms and noted their professions as well as their hopes for success at novel writing.

New authors, not yet shunning publicity, were willing, consciously or unconsciously, to open up a bit, to talk of their work in a promotional and confessional way. Ken Kesey, James Purdy, Joan Didion, and Hortense Calisher offered personal responses; but Philip Roth characteristically gave but little away, responding "yes and no" to a few questions and nothing at all to most of the others. Kesey, on the other hand, was quite willing to say how he had come upon the title for *One Flew Over the Cuckoo's Nest.* Others responded not at all; Donald Barthelme, Robert Kelly, and Ishmael Reed kept their own counsel.

Time tends to sort out the files, and most of the names remain obscure. The Humphreys survey noted that backing first novels is a near hopeless business for all concerned; for many writers a first novel is also the last, and the verities of publishing deal harshly with new writing. But the files do contain many original responses from writers with staying power. John A. Williams, the Pulitzer Prize-winning N. Scott Momaday, the versatile Thomas Berger, and Richard Condon offer insight into their plans and practice. A short list of names does provide some idea of the scope of the collection. Walker Percy, Mary Ellin Barrett, Hilary Masters, Thomas Rogers, Paul Theroux, Evan S. Connell, Jr., Allen Drury, Elaine Dundy, Sumner Locke Elliot, Fereidoun Esfandiary, Bruce Jay Friedman, William Goldman, Shirley Ann Grau, James Leo Herlihy, John Irving, Jim Kirkwood, Alison Lurie, Larry McMurtry, Gordon Parks, John Rechy, and Wilfrid Sheed are all names which help brighten the archival file.

The *DLB Yearbook* intends to publish the more notable of these letters and questionnaires. It will never get around to all 900 authors. However, for those who would like to prospect for some novelists to revive, a complete list is available from the Rare Books Room, Fred Lewis Pattee Library, University Park, PA. 16802. The following letters and questionniares are reprinted from *Library Journal,* © in the year of first publication by Reed Publishers U.S.A., Division of Reed Holdings, Inc.

–Charles W. Mann
Chief, Rare Books and Special Collections
Pennsylvania State University Libraries

EDITED BY KATE McQUADE

FIRST NOVELISTS

Thirty-Six new writers—Spring 1967
discuss their first published novels

roles: the beautiful and sexually-oriented Eloise, the witty and intellectual Rebecca, and the earth-directed and maternal Lila. In each role, the heroine, who is married to a man she calls Gus, has a child. When the final role fails because, as maternal woman, she is responsible for the death of her child, she abandons feminine roles altogether and calls herself Gus, i.e., she takes on a male role and sets herself up as the father of the remaining children. This section has Greenwich Village as its locale (the earlier identities were ⸻ in Houston) "Gus" ⸻⸻ fur⸻

dry exotics, all of them in one way or another unfitted to cope with life, to whom she gave sanctuary. *Esperie* has, I think, three underlying themes. 1) It's not what we are, but how we are it, that really matters. 2) How does gentleness of heart survive in an ungentle world? 3) Letting go—no less than cherishing—at the right moment can be a valuable legacy from one human being to another. These themes have b⸻ my mind for so⸻ ⸻ fi⸻ pertinent and

CHESTER AARON
BOUT US"

Portion of a series article in the 1 February 1967 issue of Library Journal

Piermont, New York
23 April 1958

Miss Judith Serebnick
Library Journal
62 West 45th Street
New York 36, N.Y.

Dear Miss Serebnick:

Thank you for sending me your questionnaire. I started to fill it out in ink and thus soon defaced it. Therefore I made a typed copy, which I trust is acceptable.

Let me know if there's anything else I can say. I some frequently go to New York, but am seldom there early enough for lunch.

May I have a copy of the issue of LJ which mentions me?

Thank you for your good wishes. The book is written, anyway-- and God, there were times when I never thought it would be!

Yours very truly,

Thomas Berger

QUESTIONNAIRE FOR NEW CREATIVE WRITERS

NAME: Thomas Berger

ADDRESS: Piermont, New York

BIRTHPLACE AND BIRTHDATE: Cincinnati, Ohio; July 20, 1924

EDUCATION: BA with honors in English, Univ. of Cincinnati, 1948.
          Columbia graduate school, no degree.

IS A COLLEGE EDUCATION A GREAT ASSET IN WRITING?

    Not unless one learns to read in college, which few people do.
Grammar school, with emphasis on grammar, the old-fashioned kind,
would probably be more useful for serious writing.

PRESENT OCCUPATION BESIDES WRITING

    Free-lance copy editor, etc., for book publishers.

FAMILY: My wife, Jeanne Redpath, is a ceramist. We have no children.
       My father is business manager of a suburban public-school
       system near Cincinnati.

PREVIOUS PUBLISHED WORK:

    Fiction in literary magazines such as New World Writing and
    The Western Review.

DO YOU CONSIDER WRITING A VOCATION OR AN AVOCATION?

    A vocation, in the a nun's sense of the word.

WHAT CIRCUMSTANCES GAVE YOU THE IMPETUS FOR YOUR NOVEL? AND WHICH
    CAME FIRST: PLOT, THEME, OR CHARACTERS?

    I was a corporal with the first American troops in the occupation
of Berlin, summer 1945.

    Theme came first: a German-American in Germany.

FOR HOW LONG HAVE YOU CONSIDERED WRITING A SERIOUS PART OF YOUR LIFE?

    Since about the age of sixteen.

WHAT WRITERS OR SCHOOLS OF THOUGHT ABOUT WRITING DO YOU FEEL HAVE
    INFLUENCED YOUR WORK OR YOUR DESIRE TO BE A WRITER?

    I have been influenced by every piece of printed matter I have
    ever read, from King Lear to the labels on cans. I always
    yearned for some kind of power, and that of language seemed
    most appropriate for a fellow who read such a fanatical   5

page 2/ questionnaire/ T/ Berger

hunger.

WORK HABITS

How many hours a day did you devote to writing?

Usually about four.

How long did it take you to complete the novel?

Four years/ two months of writing; twelve years
of thinking.

Do you enjoy writing while you're doing it?

It is the greatest joy when I can do it, and the greatest
horror when I cannot. Fortunately, during the ~~the~~
writing of Crazy in Berlin the ~~joyxprevailedxprevailedvx~~
~~Xutvxxxvxxxxrvxxxxx~~ joy prevailed. One never
knows how long it will last, however; already I have had
Horrors over the second novel.

Did you rewrite much? How many drafts?

I never have understood what a 'draft' is: in whatever
stage, my manuscript is intended to be the final one.
Writing quickly and sloppily, on purpose, I could never
do. And I should have contempt for myself if I wrote
something which editors and advisors had to put together
for publication. Writing is a personal affair.

Nevertheless, in whatever stage (except, I hope, the final
one)/ my work is, to me, embarrassingly bad, and I spend
far more time on revision than on the original composition.
I remind myself of Flaubert, except in talent. For Crazy
in Berlin I wrote and threw away about 100,000 words and
revised the remaining 150,000 about eight times. But pride
in this is a mistake. Only the final product matters. One
wishes he were good the first time out.

What aspects did you find most difficult? (objectivizing
experience? plot? characterization? etc.?)

Description of Nature, which bores me to do, so I don't
do it.

WHAT DO YOU THINK SHOULD BE THE FUNCTION OF LITERATURE AT ITS
VERY BEST? AND WHAT ASPECTS ARE MOST IMPORTANT? THEME? USE OF
LANGUAGE? ENTERTAINMENT VALUE?

The function of serious literature ~~isviexx~~ is to compete
with life. In a work of artistic merit, theme and ~~use of~~
style should be inseparable, I think--if they are not, it
is deficient in art. As to entertainment, one man's meat
is another's ~~pix~~ poison.

page 3/ questionnaire/ T. Berger

WHAT DO YOU THINK SHOULD BE THE FUNCTION OF THE POPULAR NOVEL?

To divert from life. And nothing wrong with that.
                          DO
WHAT WERE YOU TRYING TO/IN YOUR NOVEL?

To compete with life. To make some laughter where in life
there was, quite properly, weeping; and vice versa. To
beat life. I have lost--quite properly,life, I hope, will
always **kx** win over art--but perhaps I made a few points.

That of course is my public aim; my private one was to pla-
cate my personal demon, but that is nobody else's business.

IN YOUR FUTURE WORKS:

Do you feel you are much better equipped now than when you
began your first novel? Do you feel that you learned much
from your first?

Oh yes, much. But at the cost of literary virginity.

Are you working on a second novel?

Yes. I began it one minute after finishing the first.

Do you think you will try any other fictional form: plays,
short stories, poetry?

Probably not plays, certainly not poetry.

MISCELLANY:

Three cheers for librarians! I have been one, twice in a
checkered career. They, and writers, should get more honor
and money. Particularly money. My personal library is arranged
according to the Dewey Decimal System (but that is now out-
moded, no?).

7

Reprinted from Library Journal, *83 (1 June 1958): 1767*

Harry, the Rat with Women.

April 4, 1963

Dear Mrs Serebnick :

My novel, "Harry, the Rat
with Woman" was begun two years
ago on Fire Island as an idea
for a short story that would
occupy my summer hours and
thereby fill the time that inadequate
television reception had left
open to me. Somewhere in the
middle of my outline of the story
I realized that this work, unlike
my past work, was inappropriate
for illustration. At a point just

past that I realized that it was not a short story at all but a novel. All in all, with time off for deep depressions, the book took a little over two years to finish.

At the time I began I could have given cogent lectures, had anyone asked, on what my book was about. By the time I finished I wasn't at all sure. I do know that I have long been bothered by our glib acceptance of certain psychological truisms: the individuals need to relate meaningfully, to _communicate_, to _make_ _contact_. So I created a hero who did none of these things and was quite healthy — until society got after him.

My previous books have all been collections of cartoons: "Sick, Sick, Sick"; "Passionella," "The Explainers"; "Boy, Girl. Boy, Girl." and, most recently, "Hold Me!"

In answer to the question of why I decided to write a novel I can only answer that in this world all people with imagination, perception and sensitivity dream of becoming either one of two things — a movie star or a novelist. I guess I'm stuck with novels.

Sincerely,

Jules Feiffer

Reprinted from Library Journal, *88 (1 June 1963): 2278-2279*

General Delivery
Damariscotta,
Maine 04543

July 26, 1968

(Mrs.) Irene Stokvis Land
Assistant Editor
The Book Review

Dear Mrs. Land:

My agent forwarded me your letter, asking for biographical data,
etc., and a 300-500 word statement about myself and my writing. I very
much appreciate your saying that whatever I say about myself you will
try to publish "verbatim," although I must confess that I'm caught at
a bad moment to be doing this -- and consequently, I can't promise the
time I should give it; therefore, I'd certainly understand if you did
not publish what I say "verbatim." I'll make things up as I go along,
which is perhaps the sum-total of what I could honestly say is the way
I write, generally. Feel free, then -- in your publication -- to cut.

I was born in Exeter, New Hampshire, March 2, 1942. My grandmother,
with whom I lived for some years, is a member of The Society of Colonial
Dames(of whom I know nothing about). Of my childhood reading, I remember
very little. Certainly all of Winnie The Pooh(I have never forgotten the
night of the heffalump), and certainly The Wind in the Willows. Very
traditional, I suppose(but I hated Walt Disney's Toad of Toad Hall --
except for the weasels and the skulking music). Also, when I was a little
older, I remember liking Penrod, but I don't like Penrod anymore, and
I still like Wind in the Willows and Winnie the Pooh. Also, a book called
My Father's Dragon(I don't know who wrote it), and a poem my uncle could
recite from memory, called the Ginat Thunder Bones, by Stella Doughty.
Actually, having a three-year-old son, I feel much more influenced by
children's books today than I think I ever was as a child. Sendak stuff
is very good(Where the Wild Things Are), and a book I just read called
Drummer Hoff, by Barbara Emberley, is beautiful. I think a lot of good
children's books are probably more for adults, but my son loves Drummer
Hoff too.

Since what I had to say about childhood-influences was so short,
I'm sorry I forgot to put it on a separate sheet, as you asked.

Presently, and until this summer's end, I'm living in Damariscotta,
Maine. But my home town is Exeter, New Hampshire; there are two libraries
there. The Town Library of Exeter, where I remember going to read but
don't remember what I read and the Davis Library of the Phillips Exeter
Academy, where my father still teaches, and where I went to prep school,
graduating in 1961(my only distinction being that I was Captain of the
wrestling team; although I did a lot of writing at Exeter, and certain
few on that faculty were instrumental in encouraging me to do more).

I went to the University of Pittsburgh, where I did little else
but wrestle and didn't do that very well. I left. I went to the University of New Hampshire(Durham, New Hampshire), where a writer-in-residence,
John Yount, did a great many beginning things for me; another writer there
Thomas Williams was responsible for getting me an agent. But I left
the University of New Hampshire, too, and went to the University of Vienna,
in Austria attending both the University and an English-speaking school,
called the Institute of European Studies. I liked Vienna very much. I was
met there in June of 1964 by a girl from back in the States, named Shyla
Leary, whom I took to Greece and married in Athens. At the end of that

summer, Shyla and I came back to America. I graduated from the University of New Hampshire the next year, B.A., English Literature, Cum Laude. I was offered a Fellowship in Writing at the Writers Workshop at the University of Iowa. I held that Fellowship for two years, teaching at the university my second year in Graduate School, and leaving Iowa in June of '67 with an M.F.A. in Creative Writing. Iowa was an important place for time. I had a lot of it. And Vance Bourjaily was a good father to me; Kurt Vonnegut, Jr., was one of the first writers I'd ever met whose writing I idolized — for sure. Vonnegut's work influences me. I can think of no other American's writing that influences me, at all. Unless, possibly, J.P. Donleavy. But I am certainly under the wing of Germany's Günter Grass, who is, I think, the greatest greatest living novelist today. I am not in the habit of making absolute statements of any kind, either. Grass is genius, and I don't use that word, either.

I left Iowa and took a job at Windham College in Putney, Vermont. I'll be there again next year, too; an Assistant Professor of English, and very fond of Vermont. The Putney Town Library would be another sort of hometown library for me; as would the Windham College Library, also in Putney.

Of my writing, I can really tell you very little. Prose matters a lot to me; I write aloud. That is not to say that I shout before I type, or even babble a little over the electricity of my Smith-Corona. But I mean that I have to be able to hear the language of prose, just as you hear a poem. I work slowly, go ahead slowly, and I rarely rewrite — not on any principle against rewriting, but simply for finding that I don't have to. That's just because I never think of first-drafts as such. I don't let myself go on with something until I am, at the moment, perfectly satisfied with what I've just said. Naturally, given a piece time to sit awhile, I will go back and make slight prose-changes. But I don't revise.

Vienna is surely the setting, not only of SETTING FREE THE BEARS, the first novel, but of FOR NO ONE, the second book, in-progress now, and a "setting" for all my thinking about writing, too. I can't explain this. I don't know Vienna especially well; there are places I certainly know better. I don't speak German fluently, either; I speak it all right. But it is part of the fact that I don't know Vienna that well, that enables me to have some respect for it — some awe in its people, and some general attraction for being something of a "stranger" in a place. That seems when the observation is keenest, and also — most peculiar, distortive, strangely shaded. I don't, in other words, believe that the novelist's job is a sociological one. There are better, non-fictional media available for the would-be novelist whose concern is to "tell it like it is" — "show what it's really like to be this sort of an American in America today." I don't need to be shown that, frankly. And if I'm interested in being taught such sociology, there are better places to look than in novels. I believe one should put a little fiction back in fiction. I don't want to meet, in a novel, the sort of person I meet every day; that he is "real" is no real creation, to me. I want to be introduced, in a novel, to someone or some situation I could no where else have met; fantasy, maybe, non-real fiction, to be sure — but, I hope, with a thread of some truth about men in general, of course (as everyone has always said), and some truth too about our "history" and where it leads (a vision); but all these real things put into metaphor and character and situation that are fiction; o.k., symbols, I guess. I can't say it better than that. I just write it as it comes along.

Above all, I've always thought that the "seriousness" or "difficulty" of a novel is no justification to be boring. There is no justification for being boring. If books are boring — with all the other, less taxing media that we have available to us today — why on earth should anyone read anymore? When he can get his information less painlessly watching a movie. If information is all that's there, then, a reader might well be better off going back to school, watching TV newscasts and specials, and becoming an avid cinema buff. I am an avid film-goer; I see twice as many movies as I read books — probably as much out of laziness as any other thing. And surely movies are more of an influence on the construction of my books than books are. A movie needn't pay heed to such strictly informative demands as chronology; books don't have to, either; they can be as selective as to what they show as a film is. I think I pick at scenes and visions in a novel's imagery and 'plot' or sense, the way a camera does; that can suggest the man's mood by the focus on his hand, or his surroundings. I am probably, for all of Vienna and the Old World that occurs in my writing, a genuine American at heart — in that I am a believer in inventions. Books should not only change through the influences of other books; they should keep a-pace of all our growing media, and, while not stripping bare their own medium's capability for in-depth focus, they should follow as many new movements of forms(devices or gimmicks, if you'd rather) as our films and magazine ads and rock songs show us. These things surely must hit a novelist as hard as other books. We build, after all, certain immunities to other writers — especially the ones we envy. But we can at least stay open to the other-media explosions around us. And use those. I use them a lot. Ads, songs, jingles, (skirts,) camera lap-dissolves, zoom-lensing, suchlike and on — influences me far more than books.

Because I'm a writer, though, I feel that a good book can be a far richer, certainly more personal experience, than a good film, photo, light-show, splash or whathaveyou. But books must go back to ~~xxxxxxxxxxx~~ remembering an early father(Aristotle), who quipped that art imitates life. Art does not imitate art. Books do too much of that. There are more substantial things to ~~imitate~~ imitate — not to make real, notice, but to imitate. Which, I'd like to see happen, means to leave literary 'realism' to the fields of non-fiction.

I hope, Mrs. Land, this is something of what you meant. I can't even promise you that it's much of what I meant. But I am at work on a book now, and have a few weeks to look at the galleys for the first one -- and find a house for my family to live in next fall, and move out of Maine and back to Vermont. Little things like that. Please, if this is unsatisfactory, drop me a curt note and I will try to find some time. I don't like having to rush. (although, it's my fault.)

Sincerely,

John Irving

~~P.S. Some further biography?~~ — I've been a motorcyclist, bartender, waiter, orchardman, dictionary-researcher, translator, football pennant ~~xxxxxxx~~ salesman, highschool wrestling referee, and assorted other odd-jobber type, both in summers and to work through school. My wife is a painter; she currently runs the Putney Community Nursery School. My son's name is Colin, after my father, and I have a yellow, female, Labrador Retriever(two-thirds) and Siberian Husky(one-third) whose name alternates between Zero and Xerox.

Reprinted from Library Journal, *93 (1 October 1968): 3587-3588*

*One Flew Over the   Kesey
Cuckoo's Nest*

Rt. 1 Box 76
Springfield, Ore.
August 24, 1961

Judith Serenbnick
Library Journal
62 West 45th St.
New York 36

Dear Miss Serenbnick:

I had discarded a number of titles for my novel about a mental institution because none of the names seemed to reflect the tone of the setting, and I was just on the verge of giving up and settling for a pedestrian The-Naked-And-The-Crazy type of title, when the phrase I finally used, ONE FLEW OVER THE CUCKOO'S NEST, came to me in this rather dramatic fashion:

I had one scene left to write, not the last scene in the book but the one I had put off doing until the rest of the book was complete, just in case I didn't survive the research the scene entailed--the scene where the Chief and McMurphy receive their Electroshock Treatment as a punishment for their fight with the two colored aides. The scene was enormously important to the book because the reader needed to understand why the Big Nurse's continual threat of shock treatment kept the patients on her word under her control so tightly, and I wasn't even certain that I understood. In the ten months I had been working as a aide in a government hospital I had learned that this threat is very real to all of the patients. Some of the men I met feared shock much more than death. Yet, when the patients tried to explain the treatment to me--a little jolt of electricity through the brain, then painless oblivion-- it didn't sound so fearsome. Finally, to understand this fear, I helped an electrician friend rig the apperatus, and I submitted myself to an Electro-shock Treatment.

And during the terrifying silent explosion set off by the shock, as a debre emotions and pictures and memories swirled around me, a rhyme, taught me years ago by my grandmother, kept re-occuring: "...one flew east, one flew west, one flew over the cuckoo's nest...." When I was clear enough to resume writing I recalled this child's rhyme and decided it might also have gone through the torn mind of my Indian narrator as he fought his way from the wierd mental hell that follows EST, and that the phrase from the rhyme, ONE FLEW OVER THE CUCKOO'S NEST, would make a fine title for a book in which one man, one brawling, laughing, roaring redheaded Irish gambler and con-man named McMurphy, fakes mental illness to get transfered from a workfarm to what he thinks will be a comparitively "easy life in the nuthouse," and finds instead of the easy life a strange, pathetic world where only his own destruction and self-sacrifice will save the half-men half-robot patients from the relentless power of the Big Nurse, who rules her ward to rigidly enforce conformity, and to cruelly castrate any individuality the men have left.

About the author: I am 25, married, two kids and two dogs, was an undergrad at the U of Oregon and attended Standford Graduate School to study writing on a Woodrow Wilson. There I was awarded a Saxton prize for early work on a novel. I'm no living in Oregon, on the banks of the McKenzie river, and working in a creamery. My second novel is in progress.

Ken Kesey

Reprinted from Library Journal, 87 (1 February 1962): 582-583

173

December 21st,

Larry McMurtry
2735 Clay St.
Apt. #3
San Francisco 15,
California

Miss Judith Serebnick
Library Journal
62 West 45th Street
New York 36, New York

Dear Miss Serebnick:

Thank you for your letter of inquiry. I hope you won't think me too gung-ho if I write a short reply in addition to, rather than in lieu of, the questionnaire. Actually, I rather enjoy answering specific questions about my views on writing; I seldom consider my views except when asked specific questions, and I have a certain narcissistic curiousity about my own responses. I don't think it behooves a young writer togo around making ͙͙͙͙ ͙͙͙͙͙͙͙͙͙ grandiloquent pronouncements about writing, or even about his writing; but neither do I subscribe to the Hemingway-Dorothy Parker-Philip Roth position that a fiction writer should clam up completely except when writing fiction. The Paris Review interviews demonstrate clearly enough that writers can be prompted to produce very valuable writing on the subjects of themselves and their work. I think the currently popular idea that a writer is his own worst critic is absurd; he may very well be his best.

Personally, as yet, I have no very coherent conception of what an artist should ideally be; nor do I have any working theory of the

2.

174

novel, though I've written two of them. I started writing because
I loved to read, and because I admired the people who could write
such good reading. I wanted to imitate them, and did---several of
them, at least. At that time I had of course had no experience with
editors, and I looked on writing as a way of being entirely my own
boss. I still do.

At the moment, as I said, I have few views on the end of art.
I know that xxxxx writing fiction is the kind of work I enjoy most,
and that I am most satisfied when I am writing. I think perhaps
my greatest asset as a fiction writer is my xxxxxxx feeling for my
home country---the shortgrass ranching country of North Central
Texas. I believe that one of the best things a writer can have---
or that fiction can convey---is a sense of place, xx of how a region
is; and I think it is a considerable advantage to come from a region
that had not been much written about. My area is fairly crude and
ugly and violent, yet from a fiction writer's point of view it is
virgin country, it's resources have not been worked over time and
time again; it has not been encompassed in fiction the way Mississippi
has been encompassed by Faulkner. There is much that is attractive
and much that is dramatic about an area such as this: for one thing,
it is possible to see here, with a good deal of clarity, the changing
xxxx structures of social life. I don't like to talk much about
themes---I myself am never conscious of writing on a given theme---
but the theme which will be most conspicious in fiction attempting
to deal with this area is the loss-of-the-homeplace, the destruction
of one tradition and the development of another. I think in the
increasing xx xxxxxx urban xxxx and suburbanization which is so
evident here (as xxxxxxxx elsewhere) one can witness the breakdown
of one of the xxxxxxxxxxxx most valuable relationships a people

3. 175

can have: the closeness of a man to his land and his kin. I think
the destruction of this relationship is a terrible, uprooting kind
of thing, but I have no doubt that it x will be the source of tensions
and conflicts which nourish good fiction, and I expect to see more and
more good writing come out of Texas and the West in future years.
I know I have gone well beyond the prescribed number of words, and
will close. I do x feel however that the change from a religious,
family-rooted, essentially rural way of life, to an irreligious,
existential, essentially urban way of life, is a subject which will
occupy me as a fiction writer for as long as I care to write. Rm I
don't doubt that the change was inevitable, and possibly it will
contain some renewals which I have not yet seen; but good or bad,
it gives rise to a great many poignant, compelling human situations,
and those are what a fiction-writer needs.

                                        Sincerely,

                                        Larry M McMurtry

                                        Larry McMurtry

p.s. The name of the first novel is <u>Horseman, Pass Ryk By.</u>

174

QUESTIONNAIRE FOR FIRST NOVELISTS

NAME: Larry McMurtry

PRESENT ADDRESS:

          2735 Clay St., Apt. #3, San Francisco 15, Calif.

BIRTHPLACE AND BIRTHDATE:

          Wichita Falls, Texas, June 3, 1936

EDUCATION:

     B.A. North Texas State Teachers College

     M.A. (in English) The Rice University

IF YOU HAVE A COLLEGE EDUCATION, DO YOU FEEL THAT THIS IS A GREAT ASSET IN YOUR
     WRITING?

Yes, I think college has been a great help to me, ~~xxxxx~~ although

I don't feel ~~xx~~ it was essential in making me a writer.

PRESENT OCCUPATION BESIDES WRITING, IF ANY:

 None besides writing at present; I now hold a Fiction Fellowship at Stanford University.

FAMILY:

     My parents, two sisters and a brother, live in Archer
     City, Texas.
     I am married, but have no children.

PREVIOUS PUBLISHED WORK OF ANY KIND:

 Have published one poem in the Southwest Review, and
 nothing else, except in ~~xxx~~ collegemagazines.

DO YOU CONSIDER WRITING A VOCATION OR AN AVOCATION?

     A vocation.

WHAT CIRCUMSTANCES GAVE YOU THE IMPETUS FOR YOUR NOVEL?

I started the novel at the end of a very ~~xxxxx xxxx~~ yeasty
semester at North Texas State. A more important impetus
was the fact that the fifty or more short stories I had written
were all lousy. The ones that ~~xxx~~ dealt with ranch life ~~xxxx~~
had some good material, but as short stories they ~~xxxxx~~ were
bad. I was entering graduate school and was half afraid
scholarship would strangle my creative impulses---a silly
fear, but one which carried me through a 550 page first
draft ~~xxx~~ of Horseman, Pass By. I knew what I thought was a
good story and went at it hammer and tong until I got it
roughly down.

177

WHAT WRITERS OR SCHOOLS OF THOUGHT ABOUT WRITING DO YOU FEEL HAVE INFLUENCED
    YOUR WORK OR YOUR DESIRE TO BE A WRITER?

Too many to name. I have been enthusiastic and excited, for
varying periods of time by almost every writer imaginable.
Growing up where I did, there's little doubt that the three most
pervasive influences on my work were Western movies, hillbilly
in music, and paperback fiction good and bad. Those three
mediums probably account for the element of melodrama in my
work. The fact is, I like melodrama. The contemporary writers
whom I admire most are Styron, Mailer, Agee, Algren, and Jones and
Kerouac. The American writer I admire most is Faulkner; the
critics I admire most are men like Cowley and Wilson, who
pre-eminently like and appreciate literature.

YOUR WORK HABITS WHILE WRITING THIS NOVEL:

    How many hours a day did you devote to writing?   on the average 3

    How long did it take you to complete the novel? to complete it 5 months,
                                                        to finish it, 2 years
    Do you enjoy writing while you're doing it?
                                        for the most part
    Did you rewrite much? About how many drafts?
                                            four to six
    What aspects did you find most difficult? (plot?   characterization?
        style?   etc.)
                            structure is devilish hard for
    me.

WHAT DO YOU THINK ARE THE CHARACTERISTICS OF LITERATURE AT ITS VERY BEST?   AND
    WHAT ASPECTS ARE MOST IMPORTANT: THEME?   USE OF LANGUAGE?   ENTERTAINMENT
    VALUE?
                            should
At its best I think it be aware and a little in awe of the
incredible complexity of life, and it should render that
complexity as fully as possible; it oughtn't to oversimplify
any more than it naturally has to. I think a feel for
language is very important---I find myself responding most
immediately to the writer who has some quality of the
lyric in his style---but not supremely so: I think an
intense sense of life, of character and of story, can often
over-ride stylistic deficiencies. As I said in the letter, I
that that a sense of milieu, of place, is also very important.
I believe in literary particularity: first,
I want a person in a place: if he turns out to be everyman and
place a microcosm, fine, but unless I'm convinced he's real and
there I don't care if he is everyman.

178

QUESTIONNAIRE   Page three

(here it is)   WHAT WERE YOU TRYING TO DO OR SHOW IN YOUR NOVEL?

I was trying to capture in words something of the texture
of life in my region, the sensual as well as the emotional
context of Lonnie Bannon, the novel's (sic)hero. In addition,
I was attempting to deal accurately with a series of
human relationships, in order to determine what the relationships
meant to the characters involved in them, and further, to
discover what the coordinate relationships would mean to me.
I was exploring a situation which was very real to me,to
see what emotional or dramatic harvests it would yield.

IN YOUR FUTURE WORKS:

        Do you feel that you are much better equipped now than when you began your
first novel?   In other words, do you feel that you learned much from your first?

Yes, a good deal. It made me a good deal more sensitive to to

problems of structure.

Are you working on a second novel?

I have finished a second and am working on a third.

Do you think you will try any other fictional form: plays, short stories, poetry?

  No plays, and only a poem every year or so. I hope to write

  a good many short stories.

MISCELLANY: anything else you care to discuss, plus biographical material such as
              interests, hobbies, etc.

Reprinted from Library Journal, *86 (1 February 1961): 603*

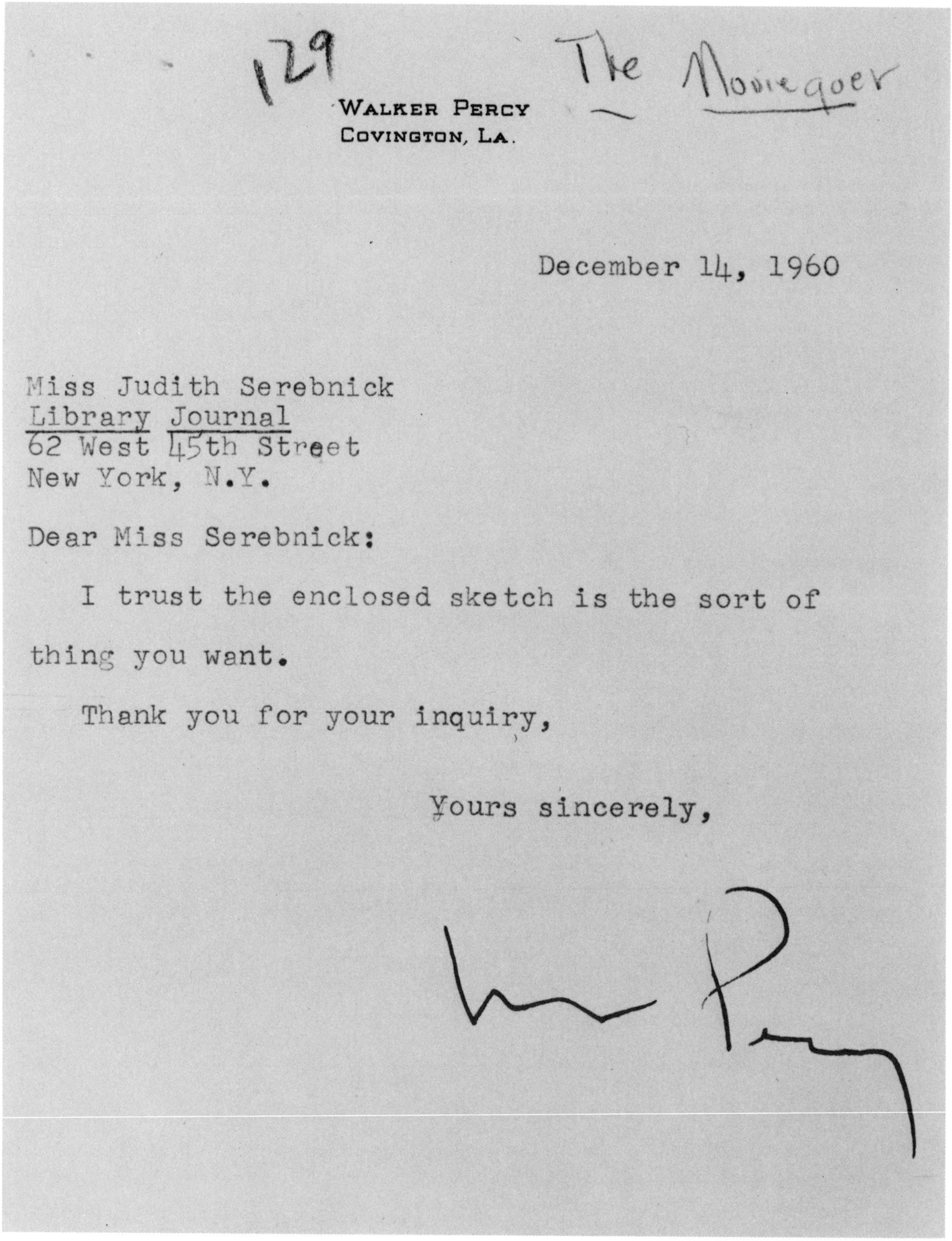

129   The Moviegoer

WALKER PERCY
COVINGTON, LA.

December 14, 1960

Miss Judith Serebnick
Library Journal
62 West 45th Street
New York, N.Y.

Dear Miss Serebnick:

    I trust the enclosed sketch is the sort of

thing you want.

    Thank you for your inquiry,

                    Yours sincerely,

130

Walker Percy
Covington, La

Born: Birmingham, Ala, May 28, 1916.

Education: B.A. University of North Carolina
           M.D. Columbia University

   My writing is a consequence of an illness which forced
me to abandon my medical career. The years of education were
by no means wasted, however, since my first writings were on
scientific subjects and were published in scholarly journals.
Later my interest veered toward the existentialist movement
in European thought and articles on the subject were published
in literary quarterlies like Partisan Review and Thought. Oddly
enough, it was precisely this interest in philosophy which led
directly to the writing of a novel (The Moviegoer, Knopf).

   Let me explain. Although philosophy is usually regarded
in this country as a dry and abstract subject, it is one of
the features of modern European thought that it focusses on
concrete life-situations rather than abstractions. In particular, of course, it is mainly interested in the predicament
                                          feelings of
of modern man, afflicted as he is with/uprootedness, estrangement,
anxiety and the like. It is quite natural, therefore, for phil-
sophers like Sartre and Marcel to write plays and novels. It also
seemed natural to me to express my ideas in a novel. And, to
give a more practical reason, people would rather read a novel
than an article.

   My novel is an attempt to portray the rebellion of two
young people against the shallowness and tastlessness of modern
life. The rebellion takes different forms. In Kate, it manifests
itself through psychiatric symptoms: anxiety, suicidal tendencies
and the like. In Binx it is a "metaphysical" rebellion-- a search

131

for meaning which is the occasion of a rather antic life in
a suburb of New Orleans (the action spans one week, Mardi Gras
week, in New Orleans). The antecedents of this book are
European rather than American: Dostoevski, Rilke, and especially
Albert Camus.

To answer your practical questions: I find the writing
of fiction a great deal more difficult than the writing of
expository articles. I rewrite a great deal, take a long
time at it, and am thankful to my editors. The most difficult
task to me is to write of a simple everyday action-- a man
walking down the street-- with both freshness and simplicity.
My greatest pleasure and, to me, the highest function of literature, is to express a facet of the contemporary consciousness
which has not yet found expression-- to hit on an everyday
mood or experience which we all feel but which has not yet
been formulated. I don't say I have succeeded

Work in progress: a second novel, a semi-popular philosophical work on modern alienation, a life work on the nature
of human communication.

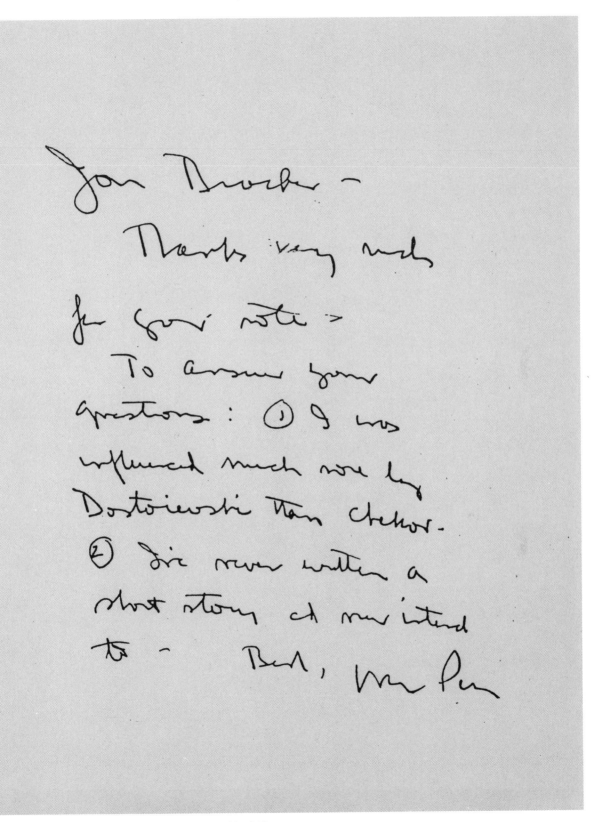

QUESTIONNAIRE FOR FIRST NOVELISTS

NAME:

Donald E. Westlake

PRESENT ADDRESS:

701 E 101 St, Brooklyn 36

BIRTHPLACE AND BIRTHDATE:

Brooklyn, N. Y., July 12th, 1933

EDUCATION:

Sophomore in three colleges: Champlain C., Plattsburg, N. Y.
Russell Sage C. (night division) Albany, N. Y.
Harpur C., Endicott, N. Y.

IF YOU HAVE A COLLEGE EDUCATION, DO YOU FEEL THAT THIS IS A GREAT ASSET IN YOUR
WRITING?
To a point, but then there's the onset of Academic Diminishing Returns, when the
academic methodology and outlook become an end instead of a means. Thereafter, one
writes "for posterity", and no one ever wrote for posterity on purpose, successfully.

PRESENT OCCUPATION BESIDES WRITING, IF ANY:

None, nein, no, never

FAMILY:

Wife, one each, black-haired, sympathetic, call letters 'Nedra'
Son, one each, blond-haired, irresponsible, age 10 months, call letters 'Sean'

PREVIOUS PUBLISHED WORK OF ANY KIND:

Lots of short stories, under my own name and pen-names, plus paperback books under
pen-names. Also article on how not to plot in Writer's Digest.

DO YOU CONSIDER WRITING A VOCATION OR AN AVOCATION?

A pleasure for which I get paid.

WHAT CIRCUMSTANCES GAVE YOU THE IMPETUS FOR YOUR NOVEL?

God knows.

QUESTIONNAIRE   Page two

WHAT WRITERS OR SCHOOLS OF THOUGHT ABOUT WRITING DO YOU FEEL HAVE INFLUENCED
        YOUR WORK OR YOUR DESIRE TO BE A WRITER?

Practically everybody. If I may quote from Benjamin DeMott in The Dead Writers,
New Directions 13 (an otherwise undistinguished volume): "I am not interested in
dealing with any of you who wish to be writers. For you and me, desire is a dangerous
thing. I want only those among you who feel that they are writers, that the thing is
done and over and that they are helpless before it." I ran across this about 1951,
while a college freshman. It still seems like the best summing-up of the whole thing.

YOUR WORK HABITS WHILE WRITING THIS NOVEL:
        How many hours a day did you devote to writing?
                                                        Three to eight.

        How long did it take you to complete the novel?
                                                        About two months

        Do you enjoy writing while you're doing it?
                                                        Certainly.

        Did you rewrite much? About how many drafts?
                Yes, dammit.   Two, complete.
        What aspects did you find most difficult? (plot?   characterization?
                style? etc.)
                                Either plot or pace. Probably pace. It's a mystery-crime
                                book, where my emphasis was on character, and the reader's
                                emphasis will be on events. It had to move fast enough to
                                keep the reader interested in the events, but slow enough
                                for me to insert some characterization here and there,
                                when nobody was looking.

WHAT DO YOU THINK ARE THE CHARACTERISTICS OF LITERATURE AT ITS VERY BEST? AND
        WHAT ASPECTS ARE MOST IMPORTANT: THEME? USE OF LANGUAGE? ENTERTAINMENT
        VALUE?

        Literature at its best does such a good job of entertaining the people of its
own time (that is, letting them 'escape' or forget their time for a while), that people
of later eras———— The hell with that sentence. I'm sorry, this is first-draftsmanship
all the way. Entertainment value, of course, is most important. Any and every theme
is usable, limited only by the interests of the author. And any style from the most
rococo to the most stark is useful at one time or another. But if a book doesn't
entertain, if it isn't read in its own time, it will never be read. And if it does
entertain the writer's contemporaries, what more can he ask? He'll never know whether
he'll be remembered or not, so it isn't worth worrying about.

QUESTIONNAIRE   Page three

(here it is) WHAT WERE YOU TRYING TO DO OR SHOW IN YOUR NOVEL?

It's a mystery-crime novel. The lead is a syndicate gangster. But he is not the
Mafia stereotype. I began with the idea that a crime syndicate is a <u>business</u>. The
syndicate doesn't rob banks, or hold up stagecoaches. It sells or rents <u>goods</u> (girls,
narcotics, liquor) to the consumer, to the public. The lead is a kind of vice-president,
who looks and acts and dresses and lives like an organization man, like any corporate
executive in his early thirties. It is where the business analogy misses that the lead
has trouble. There is a murder mystery, but the important things to me were the
character of the lead and his relationships to the syndicate and the rest of the world.

IN YOUR FUTURE WORKS:

        Do you feel that you are much better equipped now than when you began your
first novel? In other words, do you feel that you learned much from your first?

            Apparently not. I'm having even more trouble with the second. Each
novel is a separate entity, a new life. I could write the first one a lot easier
now. The second one, unfortunately, no.

Are you working on a second novel?

            Aren't I, though.

Do you think you will try any other fictional form: plays, short stories, poetry?

    I've fooled around with plays, and I've sold short stories, and I've played at
rhymes. Song lyrics are a fun hobby, when I have nothing else to do, but poetry, I'm
afraid, leaves me cold. I still do short stories, though less than before, and after
a number of plays, I'm finished with that kind of thing. Aside from the fact that the
American theater is an economic shambles and I prefer to eat regularly, there just isn't
any autonomy there. I'm not about to collaborate with a bunch of actors and directors, etc
MISCELLANY: anything else you care to discuss, plus biographical material such as
    interests, hobbies, etc.

I am a category writer. That is, most of my work is in the mystery field or the
science fiction field, and so on. I am also a commercial writer. That is, writing
is the only source of my income, so that I have written almost anything you can think
of, from non-fiction magazine pieces and confession stories (fictional, since I never
<u>really</u> bore an illegitimate child) through paperback books and bloody crime-pulp stories
to THE MERCENARIES and a science-fiction novel I've been doing, on and off, for about
a year now. I enjoy writing, no matter what. I usually enjoy the writing more than
the product. Whatever the level of my best work may be, it will probably still be in
category fiction somewhere. And now I must go back to work. Baby needs a new pair
of shoes.

44

Reprinted from Library Journal, 85 (1 June 1960): 2205

Eudora Welty: Eye of the Storyteller

(17-19 September 1987)

Dawn Trouard
University of Akron

When Eudora Welty talked about her literary beginnings for *Comment Magazine* in 1965, she credited John Rood's *Manuscript* of Akron, Ohio, with her first acceptance. This first story was "Death of a Traveling Salesman" and the year was 1936; but the actual site was Athens, Ohio, not Akron. In order to pay homage to Miss Welty the University of Akron hosted a national conference to bring southern literature scholars together and to offer continued proof of her own belief that her work "has always landed safely and among friends."

While Welty has been honored at assorted conferences in the South and has accepted awards and given readings outside of the region, this three-day event was the first national conference outside the South devoted exclusively to Welty scholarship. Bringing together approximately ninety scholars, the call for participation announced the event as "a celebration of 51 years of literary power." By accenting the asymmetry of a fifty-first-year anniversary and by focusing on artistic power, speakers addressed themes in Welty's fiction and gave critical readings of her work that avoided the worn path of regionalism. To underscore the centrality of artistic power to the conference John Sokol created a "word portrait" of Welty out of her short story "Powerhouse," an early work she regards as "completely outside" her "usual orbit."

The opening talk of the conference on Thursday afternoon was Barbara Harrell Carson's "Inside the Labyrinth: Eudora Welty's *The Eye of the Story*." Carson presented evidence that Welty's nonfiction provides explicit insights into the connection between her artistic theory, her vision of reality, and the mystery and wonder of relationships in art and life. Welty's consistent urge to unify contraries "discourages the passing of judgments on others because it acknowledges the intimate links between what is outside of us and what is within us."

Ruth Weston's "American Folk Art, Fine Art, and Eudora Welty" puts the methods of folk and fine art in the service of narrative theory. Weston demonstrates that "Lily Daw and the Three Ladies" and other Welty stories are "linguistic equivalents of 'collages,' combinations of the elements of painting, sculpture, drama, and dance, exhibiting a spatial form well suited to express her important theme of cultural confinement," especially "for women in her fiction."

Daniele Pitavy-Souques of the University of Dijon presented a paper on the image of the artist in Welty's fiction. She explored the dialectical nexus emergent in "Powerhouse" where grief ("the experience of Death and the Sacred") shatters artistic self-image and becomes an occasion to journey toward other ("the hidden Self"). This theoretical portrait of the artist was then applied to stories from *The Bride of the Innesfallen*.

William U. McDonald, editor of the *Eudora Welty Newsletter*, introduced the final speaker on Thursday's program, Noel Polk of the University of Southern Mississippi. A prodigious Faulkner scholar and assistant editor of the *Eudora Welty Newsletter*, Polk's talk, " 'Going to Naples' and Other Places in Fiction," challenged the traditional role of place in regional fiction and Welty's work in particular. He argued that the fanatical sway "place" holds on the southern imagination is at best a sentimentalization of the South and oftentimes a critical distortion of artistic intention–particularly in Welty's work. The presentation provoked a heated discussion, and Polk fielded charges that he was again salvaging and justifying "weaker" works of fiction. Polk deflected most assaults and remained steadfast in his position that readers are habituated to "place" arguments in southern fiction to the point of nonsense, invoking "A Visit of Charity" as a "no-southern features" story that is critically ignored in order to fulfill the fantasy that Welty always creates a sense of southern place in her fiction.

Friday's program commenced with Suzanne Ferguson's "The 'Assault of Hope': Style's Substance in Welty's 'The Demonstrators.' " This close look at "contrasting syntactical strategies" ac-

Eudora Welty as "Powerhouse"   John Sokol ©1986

EUDORA WELTY
EYE OF THE STORYTELLER
THE UNIVERSITY OF AKRON CELEBRATES
51 YEARS OF LITERARY POWER
A CONFERENCE SPONSORED BY BUCHTEL COLLEGE OF ARTS AND SCIENCES
AKRON, OHIO · SEPTEMBER 17th-19th, 1987

*Poster for the first national conference outside the South devoted
exclusively to Welty scholarship*

counted for Welty's ambivalent thematic and emotional effects in this story. Ferguson identified a range of cognitive dissonances that are created by the cumulative clashing of Welty's descriptions against her subjects.

Nancy Butterworth's analysis took issue with recent revisionist readings of Welty's treatment of race relations. Focusing on "A Worn Path," Butterworth views the character Phoenix as a racial avatar and the story as an allegory of black progress, spanning the years from the Civil War to pre-civil rights.

In her paper "Love and Separateness" Pearl McHaney found in "A Still Moment" Welty's artistic credo: imposed isolation and loneliness are revisioned as the necessary measures the artist takes "to see, to feel and to create." Audubon transcends his egotistical alienation and, like other characters in *The Wide Net*, accommodates himself as an artist must–lovingly to the world.

Daun Kendig's use of principles of frame analysis brought fine resolution to the provokingly enigmatic "Sir Rabbit." Kendig contends that "Welty creates *multiple realities* that interact to evoke an experience that is simultaneously comic, mysterious, and deeply moving." Moreover, the ambiguities of perception generated by Mattie will lead the reader to a more intense involvement with the story.

Michael Kreyling of Vanderbilt University is the author of *Eudora Welty's Achievement of Order* (1980), and his presentation gave a strong sense of Welty's career as revealed by literary correspondence. Excerpts illuminated the author's personal character and imagination. Kreyling's "The Benevolent Intermediary: Diarmuid Russell and the

Role of the Literary Agent" tracked the "set backs" and "hardships" of Welty's publishing career from the 1940s. Part of a scholarly edition on which Kreyling is currently at work, this talk shifted the emphasis from analysis of the interior world of Welty's fiction to the "world of circumstance" revealed by the correspondence between the dauntless author and her agent.

A crucial concern in feminist criticism has been the mother/daughter relationship, a controversial topic in recent Welty criticism. Focusing on *The Golden Apples* and *The Optimist's Daughter*, Elizabeth Evans examined the cost exacted from daughters who are compelled to dutiful behavior despite neglectful and diminishing responses from their mothers. Evans's talk sparked audience debate regarding Welty's conflicting attitudes about her own mother. Audience members made reference to remarks by Welty herself and evidence from *One Writer's Beginnings* to argue Welty's personal degree of ambivalence in her autobiographical role as a dutiful daughter.

In "Cycles in *The Golden Apples*" Thomas McHaney of Georgia State University explored the long-standing genre problem of Welty's experimental 1949 collection. Arguing that Welty has employed cycles in a rich and complicated way, McHaney demonstrated a range of subtle techniques by which she deepens the initial organizing strategy of *The Golden Apples* as a cycle of tales. Varying discussions of style and structure, he maintained that Welty's Morgana's cycle is studded with connections to other cycles in Western art and myth. Furthermore, language in the text is structured in such a way as to suggest song cycles and the book is deeply textured by musical references. At every turn seasons, tides, games, and literal "making the rounds" serve to reinforce Welty's central design.

In a daring cultural analysis Carey Wall utilizes anthropologist Victor Turner's "deep knowledge" theory to demystify "June Recital." Wall argues in "Virgie Rainey Saved" that the "empty" house "next door" is employed by the community "to turn the rules of organized social life 'upside down,'" in order to free Virgie from Miss Eckhart. In the process Miss Eckhart will be replaced in the scheme of the community. The "spontaneous" house burning counters the ritual of piano recital as the community asserts itself in the completion of social actions that, in Turner's terms, create "the opening to the future."

The final day of the program began with a discussion by Jan Nordby Gretlund of Odense

Universitet on Welty's affinities to Chekhov. Gretlund centered his argument on both authors' mastery of "compression," the trivial detail that conveys extraordinary emotion. Welty, like Chekhov, allows the minor detail to reflect her realistic and psychologically authentic visioning.

Isolating textual junctures where violent and strange tropes clash with the surrounding language, Peter Schmidt of Swarthmore College analyzed the crucial role of sibyl figures in short stories such as "Powerhouse," "Music from Spain," and "The Wanderers." Schmidt demonstrated that Welty's use of sibyl images is key to understanding the stories, and he feels that her use of sibyls places her in a feminist tradition where the prophetic powers of the sibyls serve as "complex" metaphors of the women artists who use them. This talk included slides of Domenichino's paintings of sibyls, works Schmidt maintains Welty had specifically in mind as sources for her fictional descriptions.

Ann Romines's "How *Not* to Tell a Story: Eudora Welty's First Person Tales" examined a technical and feminist strain in Welty's fiction. Working with "Circe" and "Why I Live at the P.O.," Romines demonstrated why these atypical first-person voices are necessary for characters who chafe at the constrictions of others' versions of experience and conventional plots. In order for Circe and Sister to satisfy their "lust for the satisfying finality of a 'last word,'" Romines maintained that "cyclical time, traditionally female, must confront heroic time, traditionally male." By using the audacious "first person" the storyteller fails so that the stories' outraged comedy might succeed.

Welty's view of herself as an artist was treated in Cheryll Burgess's analysis of failed artist figures in *A Curtain of Green*. Contrasted with Powerhouse, who "transcends self-absorption, glorying in and exploiting the strangeness of life," the failed artist figures are deficient in the "overbrimming love" that Welty insists is central to great art.

Marilyn Arnold of Brigham Young University offered a winning solution to the identity of the stranger-auditor in *The Ponder Heart*. In "The Strategy of Edna Earle Ponder" Arnold developed a case that Edna Earle is sizing up the stranger to see if she will be the fitting next bride for Uncle Daniel.

In "'Where is the Voice Coming From?': Teaching Eudora Welty" Ruth Vande Kieft, author of *Eudora Welty* (1962), the first full critical

Participants in the conference (left to right): Daniele Pitavy-Soques, Jane Reid-Petty, Noel Polk, and Dawn Trouard (photograph by Melissa Berry)

work on the author, provided deliberations on the state of Welty scholarship and the obligations of Welty's scholars. Vande Kieft defended the strategy of "lyric perception" as the most effective and appropriate approach for critics and teachers of Welty's work. Preferring a method that harmonizes with Welty's own, Vande Kieft argued that many "ideological critical structures" interfere with students' understanding of "the path between reality and the human soul" that Welty charts.

The final speaker of the program was Albert Devlin, author of *Eudora Welty's Chronicle* (1983). In his presentation, "Meeting the World in *Delta Wedding*," Devlin worked with manuscript evidence, a recent interview with the author, and the antecedent fiction that culminated in the 1946 publication of *Delta Wedding*. He claimed that this novel marks a career watershed for Welty. The key word for the text and the argument is "maturity" and how Welty transforms that word from "literary abstraction" to a method that gives meaning to her world view.

Over the three days four panel sessions were held. Each group had been asked to con-

sider certain texts and questions in order that the panel sessions would be focused. The first session, "Welty and Style: 'I associate happiness and getting something right with hot summer,'" began with "At the Landing" and *Eye of the Story* as the shared texts. Panelists explored how Welty transformed passive/descriptive fact into motion/living change; how Welty's interviews and reviews helped stylistic analysis of her work; and what problems attend acts of communication. The "Welty and Women" session worked with a quotation from "Kin": "the wildness of the world behind the ladies' view." The panel had as its anchor texts "No Place for You, My Love," "Ladies in Spring," and *The Golden Apples* and panelists were asked to explore expectation differences for male and female readers; the question of Welty's subversion of female stereotypes; and how anger fits into her vision. The third session, "Tradition and Influence: 'Everybody to their own visioning,'" looked at "Powerhouse" and *Delta Wedding*. Panelists probed Welty's relation to the modern tradition and regionalism; they also considered Welty's transformation of traditional sources and appropriations. "Love was just as arbitrary and one-sided as music teaching" served as the theme for the final session, "Welty in the Classroom." Looking at *One Writer's Beginnings*, "Why I Live at the P.O.," and "Death of a Traveling Salesman," the panel considered strategies for and obstacles to bringing out the best appreciation of Welty's fiction in the classroom. Problems of the "too familiar" text, coping with Welty's sophisticated style and the average student, and which of her works were best suited to be anthologized were some of the issues addressed.

The final act of the conference was a performance of Jane Reid-Petty's one-woman show, "An Evening of Welty with Edna Earle Ponder." Reid-Petty is founder and artistic director of New Stage Theatre in Jackson, Mississippi. Welty serves on the theater's board of directors.

With nineteen papers, four panels, a ban-quet, a luncheon, a cocktail party, and a lot of un-chaperoned discussion, most of the conferees, at the end of the intense three days, were referring to the mystical quality of the conference experience and felt they were closer to understanding Welty's "confluence." Perhaps Michael Kreyling captured the final effect best in his description of the event as a WELT-DOWN. In the end what emerged from the conference is the deep regard the scholarly community accords Miss Welty and her work. What she says of her creation Power-house can serve as tribute to Welty too: she "is so monstrous she sends everybody into oblivion. When any group, any performers, come to town, don't people always come out and hover near, leaning inward about them, to learn what it is? What is it? Listen."

The Practice of Biography VI

AN INTERVIEW————————————
with DAVID HERBERT DONALD

David Herbert Donald is Charles Warren Professor of History and Professor of American Civilization at Howard University. He has taught at Columbia University, Princeton University, the Johns Hopkins University, and Oxford University and has served as president of the Southern Historical Association. His biography *Charles Sumner and the Coming of the Civil War* (1960) received a Pulitzer Prize. His other works include *Lincoln's Herndon* (1948), *Lincoln Reconsidered* (1956), *Divided We Fought* (1952), *The Politics of Reconstruction* (1965), and his most recent publication, *Look Homeward: A Life of Thomas Wolfe* (1987).

DLB: You've written three full-scale biographies, the first on William Henry Herndon, then one on Charles Sumner, and now *Look Homeward*, a biography of Thomas Wolfe. You've also followed the calling of historian. Has your knowledge of history been very helpful to you as a biographer?

DONALD: Very much so. I regard the two forms as each strengthening and enlightening the other. If you look over my list of publications, you will see that I seem to go from one to the other and back again. This isn't any kind of deliberate oscillation, but when I work on an individual, I then become concerned about the background; if I'm working on a more general problem, I begin worrying about the individual who is connected with that movement.

DLB: Some critics have wondered why you, as a historian, chose Thomas Wolfe, a literary figure, to write about.

DONALD: First of all, I don't think these disciplinary lines are all that important. I had never felt that I must be essentially a historian or essentially a literary critic or whatever. My own training, such as it is, was as much in sociology and

David Herbert Donald (photograph © Jerry Bauer)

psychology as in history, and in general I have tried to work in interdisciplinary kinds of fields all my life. So I haven't thought of myself as now deserting the field of history and approaching somebody else's turf. If I wanted to be pretentious about it, I could make a reasonable case that my first book, *Lincoln's Herndon*, combined history and anthropology and folklore; it was a study of myth and legend. My second book, *Divided We Fought*, a pictorial history of the Civil War, was an attempt to connect visual images with the historical narrative. The third book, *Lincoln Reconsidered*, was primarily an attempt to interrelate sociological techniques with historical materials. *Charles Sumner and the Coming of the Civil War* was an attempt to use and connect history and psychoanalysis. *The Politics of Reconstruction* tried to combine history and quantitative political science. The most recent book, *Look Homeward*, was an attempt to do history and literary theory and literary criticism together. So I have thought of all my books as being interdisciplinary.

While I think it's right for the historian who writes biography to use the tools of other disciplines, I think it ought to be a two-way street: other people who write biography ought to know something about the tools of history and the texture of history. Too many biographies written by people who are not historians are devoid of context. And too many of them lack the precision and accuracy that a historian's training enables him to give to a story.

DLB: What do you consider the most important qualities of a good biography?

DONALD: I think there are many different kinds of good biographies. From time to time I have tried in my own mind to define what the ideal biography ought to be. But I've never come up with a satisfactory solution, because I think there are many different good kinds. Having said all of that, though, I think the first and essential thing is that a biography ought to be a work of art; it ought to create a self. It must not simply be a chronicle of happenings in a life. As in writing a novel, the author has to say to himself, I have in mind a pretty clear picture of a character, its development, its motivation, its drive; these are the things that I am going to present. *How* he presents them may vary considerably. I used to take great pleasure in making scornful remarks about the old life-and-letters technique; by and large those books are pretty dull, though they're sometimes useful. But I think even that kind of biography, if very skillfully done, could be a work of art. A book like Henry James's *William Wetmore Story and his Friends* (1903), in a very traditional mode, is a creative feat. This is rare, however.

But generally I prefer biographies that have a psychological approach. This does not necessarily mean that they must be an explicit psychoanalytical probing. For instance, I think Henry Commager's *Theodore Parker* remains not merely a beautiful book, but a very perceptive and insightful book, though Commager, if asked about it, would almost certainly say that *he* didn't have anything to do with psychoanalysis; he didn't believe in any part of it and considered it all a mistake. But what he does is enter Parker's psyche so well that he re-creates the kind of personality and the kind of man that Parker was.

Other people don't have that degree of empathy or skill, and for them it's probably more important to try to have some kind of theoretical basis. From that point of view, I think of Leon Edel's *Henry James* as being a superlative psychoanalytical biography, the first volume in particular. The latter volumes seem to be a bit out of hand in terms of length, but the first volume, I think, is a model of what the biographer can and should do.

DLB: You said in the preface to *Look Homeward* that you had "tried not to stress an interpretive structure that would reduce Wolfe to a case study, whether psychological, literary, or sociological." Would you elaborate on that remark and how it applies to what you feel the biographer should do?

DONALD: My disclaimer here had to do with the question of littering one's text with technical psychoanalytical jargon, which seems to me more suitable to clinical work and treatment than to the empathetic re-creation of a personality. I think it's absolutely essential that a biographer come up with a characterization of a personality. It does not necessarily have to be a clinical analysis, which would be more suited for treatment of psychological problems. But he needs in his own mind to understand how his character works and what his strengths and weaknesses and problems are. Whether it's desirable or necessary to present these to his reader in a kind of overt, flat, explicit form seems to me much more questionable. This is my essential point. In the present-day novel, rarely does the writer say as he goes along that his hero has an oedipal complex, or he's an anal-regressive type. It would throw readers off, it would add very little to their understanding, and it would make his work of fiction a kind of clinical case study. I think that's most undesirable. Similarly, it seems to me that as far as biography is concerned, the writer ought to know what he's doing. He presents a picture that allows the reader to see the psychological makeup of the subject in his mind and make his own connections. The sophisticated and perhaps technically knowledgeable reader might say, "Aha! Oedipal conflict"–or penis envy, or whatever. The more general reader, though he doesn't have that kind of technical knowledge, ought to be able to read the story and say, "Yes, I know people like that. I can understand how this person works."

DLB: You told Sam Staggs for *Publishers Weekly* (30 January 1987) that two of your literary heroes are Allan Nevins and Samuel Eliot Morison. Did you learn much about biography from them?

DONALD: I'm not sure that I did, in any kind of formal way. Allan Nevins was my office mate at Columbia many years ago when I started teaching there as a very junior instructor, in my first teaching job. One Saturday Allan Nevins came into the little office that, believe it or not, five of us shared. He looked at the small room with its row of desks and said, "This is impossible." Pointing at me, he said, "*You* are my office mate from now on." So he brought me down to his wonderful corner office with lots of room and installed me there, which was a remarkably generous thing. There I watched him work. I saw him operate with students, I watched him work on his own manuscripts, and we talked a good deal as he worked. I learned a lot from him by osmosis rather than anything else.

As far as Morison is concerned, I came to know him rather late in his life, after he had retired. I didn't know him at all while I was working on my Sumner book, but after it was published, quite out of the blue I got a wonderful and really warm note, surprising from a frosty old New Englander, saying that he had read the book, that he liked it, that he wished I would come up to Boston; he would take me on a drive and show me some of those places I'd been writing about. When I did move up here, it turned out that a neighbor of ours was Sam's favorite niece. He often came out here on Sundays, and she very generously invited us over most of those Sundays. So there were many times that we all got together to talk history. But my admiration for Morison is not merely personal, though he was always very friendly and generous and kind in those talks. Long before that, it was a literary admiration. The skill with which he writes and creates his subjects, the absence of the kind of cumbersome scaffolding that so many historian-biographers find it necessary to erect–those are the things that truly impressed me about him.

DLB: What biographies have particularly impressed you besides the ones you mentioned earlier?

DONALD: There are so many different kinds of biographies. Of quite recent books, for example, I am much impressed by Kenneth Lynn's new biog-

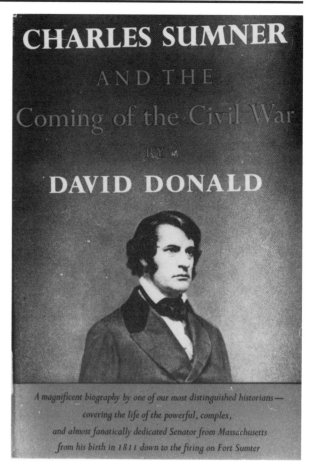

Dust jacket for Donald's 1961 Pulitzer Prize-winning biography

raphy of Hemingway. It is a brilliant psychoanalytical treatment of Hemingway that manages at once to probe without being reductive. I continue to be most moved and impressed by the biography by my former professor J. G. Randall, his *Lincoln the President*. It certainly is not psychoanalytically probing, but there is a degree of understanding, a degree of empathy, and a degree of judgment about very difficult matters. You can hear this man's calm and thoughtful voice as he writes. This is what it seems to me is missing in mediocre biographies: there's no distinct, powerful voice. You don't leave the book feeling, I would like to know that person, I would like to talk to that person. There's a feeling that it's sort of mechanically done, just putting one fact after another.

DLB: Researching your books, must you sometimes stop and remind yourself that this part of the process can't go on forever, that you have to begin writing?

DONALD: Yes. But research does go on forever! But it always seems to me that research goes into different stages, and you're aware when you pass from one stage to another. The first is what I think of as the dragnet stage, where you simply collect everything you can about your character. The little individual pieces perhaps don't add up to much; they're interesting, but you keep putting them together and saying, "I wonder if I'm ever going to make any sense out of this?" Then suddenly there comes a time when, as you continue your research, you say, "I already know this; I've passed this road before." At that point you shift into what I think of as ad hoc research. That doesn't mean you're finished, but it does mean that you know pretty well how a major issue is shaped, though you may need further research on the details of it.

I can demonstrate this through an example from Professor Randall, my teacher and friend, whom I served as a research assistant for a number of years while he was writing his Lincoln biography. The first two volumes of that biography were written before the Robert Todd Lincoln Papers in the Library of Congress were opened; they'd been under seal for many, many years and were about to be opened. Mr. Randall finished his manuscript for his first two volumes and sent it out to the publisher, who wrote back saying it was very brilliant and perceptive, but that he did wonder, since the Lincoln Papers were going to be opened that summer, if there wasn't a chance that Professor Randall might find materials there that would refute his conclusions, that would raise interesting points he hadn't raised, and if the book shouldn't be postponed. Mr. Randall wrote back a long letter–he dictated it to me while I sat at the typewriter and typed it out for him–saying, "I've been working on this subject for a long time. I have not seen the Robert Todd Lincoln Papers; nobody living has seen those papers. But let me tell you what's going to be in those papers relating to the subject I have covered here." He proceeded to say, "This is what you'd find in those papers concerning the Ann Rutledge affair; this is what you'd find in those papers concerning Lincoln's relationship with his wife; this is what you'll find in those papers about Lincoln's connection with Abolitionists in the Legislature. "

When those papers were opened, Mr. Randall's predictions proved to be a hundred percent right. He was not psychic, but when you know a subject that well, you know. It often hap-

pens that somebody gets in touch with me to say, "I just got a wonderful new Thomas Wolfe letter; I came upon something at the University of Montana Library that you really ought to go out to see, or get a Xerox of." I say to myself, "Sure, I want to get a Xerox of it, I want to see everything that there is"; but in my mind I know what it's going to say. That, I think, is what happens in that second stage of the research.

DLB: The charge of dull prose has never been leveled against you, as it has against many historians and biographers. You apparently have always striven to write your books in an entertaining and readable style.

DONALD: I don't think of myself as particularly entertaining, but I would like to think I'm readable. I have certain techniques that I follow that may not make any sense for anybody else, but basically I think that good reading ought to be good listening, so I compose aloud. As I formulate sentences, I talk them out. I can tell you a story about that. When we first moved up here, our house needed some repair–new windows and that kind of thing–so we had a couple of carpenters who were here pretty much every day, working around the place. I was writing downstairs in my study. One day I passed them as I was going out for lunch. They were having coffee out behind the house and didn't see me. They were talking to each other, and one of them was saying, "You know, I hope he's all right, but he sits there and talks to himself all day long." It does help. You tend to avoid complicated sentence structure. You tend to avoid heavy-handed use of language. You tend to avoid highly abstract words that you just would not use in everyday discourse.

DLB: So you compose everything aloud right from the beginning of a work?

DONALD: Yes, I do. I do it sentence by sentence. I try it out three or four times maybe, and when I finally get something I think is alright, I usually put it on my word processor. Then of course I rewrite and revise and all of that. But what you try to do, I think, is get that sense of communicating to somebody rather than just putting dead words on paper.

DLB: Do you think growing up in Mississippi put you in a better position to understand Thomas

Wolfe than someone from another part of the country?

DONALD: I do think so, for a number of different reasons. For one thing, small-town life in the South (and I grew up in a much smaller town than Thomas Wolfe) has now virtually disappeared. It's become so homogenized that it's like everything else. But in those days small-town life in the South was very different from life in Boston or life in San Francisco—or, for that matter, life in Peoria, Illinois. It was a very different kind of world in which there was great importance in social roles, family status, and the knowledge that everybody had of everybody else's family, past and present—the intricate relationships, that so-and-so was whoever's third cousin twice removed. That kind of thing, I think, would be very difficult for somebody who was not a Southerner to understand, yet it's very important in the Wolfe story.

DLB: Long before the idea of writing a biography of Thomas Wolfe came to you, you had read some of his fiction as a fairly young boy and had liked his writing very much.

DONALD: That's right. I think many adolescents then and even now discover Wolfe and find that degree of empathy. They feel, I am another artist who is not properly understood by his friends and family and relatives, and I really have within me the power to reshape everything. Most young people have that kind of fantasy, and they identify rather easily with Wolfe's heroes.

When I came back to Wolfe's writing many years later, in the 1970s, I responded to it on a very different level. This time I was impressed first of all that Wolfe wrote a kind of social history of the first three decades of the twentieth century seen from a particular point of view. Simply as a historian, I felt that there were things to learn from Wolfe's books. But more important, I was struck, even on a first rereading, by a degree of artistry that I had not previously been aware of. My earliest reading of Wolfe—I think like most people's—gave me a sense of a young genius who simply poured out his original inspiration. On rereading, I noticed more and more echoes of other writers, a decidedly literary bent—in fact, I think Wolfe was probably one of the most literary of our novelists. (Not always is that a good thing, by the way.) These were things that had escaped me on the first reading.

Dust jacket for Donald's 1987 biography of Wolfe, his first attempt at a literary subject

DLB: In the preface to *Look Homeward* you say that back in the 1950s many of the critics "condemned Wolfe's gigantism, his rhetorical extravagance, and his lack of form." In the 1980s, do the critics still say those things about Wolfe?

DONALD: Some do. Harold Bloom, for instance, in a rather nasty review in the *New York Times Book Review,* simply says that Wolfe has no literary merit, that we can't read him. In the *New York Review of Books,* Monroe K. Spears made a similar charge. Something of that same supercilious disdain appeared in reviews of my book that came out in *Newsweek* and *Time.* On the other hand, quite a number of critics said that it's time to rethink Wolfe. Some of them went back and reread Wolfe and came back with rather different impressions. The front-page review in the *Chicago Tribune* was one; another was a lovely review in the *Philadelphia Inquirer* by Carole Klein. Jonathan Yardley in the *Washington Post* was still another.

These were some of the critics who said, "There really is a lot to be said about Wolfe that we hadn't thought of before." Hugh Kenner in the *Times Literary Supplement* had very interesting things to say about Wolfe as a writer.

DLB: You've said you feel Wolfe belongs in the same high critical esteem as Faulkner, Fitzgerald, and Hemingway. Why do you think he isn't generally read as much as those writers are?

DONALD: I can offer two suggestions. First, remember that most of us became acquainted with these great twentieth-century American novelists in high school or college classes; their novels are relatively short and almost any one of them can be easily read in a week. But the size of Wolfe's novels effectively prevents their use in most classes. There is probably no high school class in the country where the students would read the 626 pages of *Look Homeward, Angel,* much less the 912 pages of *Of Time and the River* in a week.

Second, we have for more than a generation been under the influence of literary critics whose specialty has been the analysis of form and structure in the novel. Wolfe's loosely written, sprawling novels have no form in any conventional sense, and their structure is often imperfect because of the extensive editing to which his manuscripts were subjected. Consequently they have found it easy to dismiss Wolfe. And many teachers of literature, on the high school or college level, who generally follow blindly whatever they think is critically fashionable, have accepted that verdict.

DLB: Most of Wolfe's immediate family was already dead when you began working on the biography. Did that work in some ways as an advantage, perhaps allowing you to say certain things about your subject that hadn't been said before?

DONALD: Yes. There were not any skeletons to bring out of the closet, but the surviving Wolfe brother and sister who lived on many years after Wolfe was dead had some notions of family reputability. They liked to think of their parents as mildly eccentric but highly respected residents of Asheville. The family, they would grant, had its ups and downs but was really an upper-middle-class, solid, stable family of good industrious roots. It might have been quite difficult had those children still been alive to try to impose

that point of view on a biography. When I was about a year into the book, I saw but never had a chance to interview the brother Fred. I heard numerous interviews with Fred on tape recordings and a videocassette, and I don't think I missed a lot, because Fred tended to repeat the same stereotype time after time after time. I learned something from them, but I was just as glad that he was not there to look over my shoulder.

DLB: Some previously unused source material was available to you for the Wolfe biography. Did it provide any surprises?

DONALD: Yes, a number of them. On the lowest level, as I worked through those literally thousands and maybe even a million pages of Wolfe's manuscripts, I became increasingly impressed by the fact that he *did* revise; he did not just dash things off and let them stay in that form forever. He didn't tend to revise particularly on a line-by-line basis, but would write the same page over four, five, ten, twenty times–until he got it right. That was not a revision process that I would have expected.

On another level, there are in the Wolfe papers quite a number of adventurous and experimental attempts at different prose forms, the best embodiment of which is the "Hound of Darkness" sequence, those prose poems that capture vignettes of American life that occurred simultaneously on a given day, usually in the summer of either 1916 or sometimes 1913. These extensive extracts of plans for this book suggest a different type of writer from anything I had ever known, much more experimental and influenced in this case by cinema, the newsreel technique, by the attempt to produce the nonlinear, nonsynchronous novel.

DLB: Do you think Maxwell Perkins acted properly in editing Wolfe's work so heavily?

DONALD: That's such a hard thing to answer; one necessarily straddles the question. First of all, one is tempted almost to say that without a Maxwell Perkins there wouldn't have been a Thomas Wolfe. After all, Wolfe hadn't been able to get his big book published. He was defeated and discouraged. Without Perkins to help shape it properly, *Look Homeward, Angel* might never have been published, and there wouldn't have been anything else. Beyond that, there is the degree of encouragement, the faith, confidence, loyalty that Perkins gave to all his authors, but particularly to Wolfe, with whom he closely identified.

At the same time, increasingly over the years as he grew older and became more important, Perkins became more conservative in his political and literary tastes. He tended more and more to want his authors to do the things they'd already done and proved themselves successful at doing. Added to this was the fact that dealing with Wolfe must have been an impossible task for anybody. Perkins knew that working with Wolfe on a new book was going to require an endless amount of time and energy. His time and energy were fading. He was getting old, getting very gray, lacking energy. He was also drinking too much. He had other very responsible duties. One can imagine Perkins saying to himself, "My God! Can I face up to hour after hour, day after day, seven days a week, every evening working with Thomas Wolfe?" On the conscious level his answer would be, "Yes; it's the most rewarding thing I've ever done." On an unconscious level there was more reluctance: "At least," he would think, "let's do something that's fairly conventional, that we know the rules for; then we can go on with it as we've done in the past."

DLB: Would you like to see *Look Homeward, Angel* published as it was originally written?

DONALD: We have the full text, and I hope one of these days it will be published under its original title, "O Lost." The manuscript version is in Houghton Library, in the ledger books Wolfe wrote it in, and we also have the typescript, which then was edited down. That book ought to be published. *Look Homeward, Angel* was 626 pages. The published version of "O Lost," I would guess, would not run more than 900 pages. But it would be in many ways a significantly different book. Just as we are beginning to get authentic texts of other great American writers—such as Dreiser, for example—I think we ought now to get the legitimate text of "O Lost." One can perhaps do that also for *Of Time and the River.* The last books you can't because there is no authentic text.

DLB: Your discussions of Wolfe's sexual life are quite open and direct. Do you feel today's relative lack of censorship gave you much freer rein in this area than you'd have had if you'd written the book a few years earlier?

DONALD: I think that's true, both in terms of people—relatives, as we've talked about—and also in terms of the general climate of opinion. Twenty years ago, would one have written about Wolfe and masturbation? Probably not, at least not explicitly. But now I don't think most people are particularly shocked about masturbation. There were one or two quite minor reviews that said maybe it wasn't necessary to go into this sort of thing in such detail, but even they didn't seem terribly offended by it. There was one, in the *Wall Street Journal,* that was really a very nice review but gave the impression, as my friends here said, that David Donald was a dirty old man.

DLB: Why do you think Wolfe showed so much anti-Semitism in his work? When he was growing up in Asheville, there were very few Jewish families even living there.

DONALD: I think it often happens that when a person is himself an outcast, not well regarded, he vents his feelings of animosity and injustice on someone else who is even less well regarded. The Wolfe family, at least Thomas Wolfe's branch of the family, were not held in good repute in Asheville. The boy was sneered at. His father was a drunk who frequented prostitutes. The older brother was always in trouble for passing bad checks; the mother was known for running the stingiest boardinghouse in all of Asheville. A boy like that really needs somebody to pick on. He probably didn't know any blacks. In the South that he grew up in, blacks tended to become stereotyped blurs, not individuals that you could attack. But there was a handful of Jews who were highly visible in Asheville; they had distinctive names, and their religious ceremonies were held on Saturdays. Wolfe joined with other little boys in taunting these people, in making fun of them, getting under their houses and making obscene noises—this sort of thing. I think this is how it got started. Then you do have the family influence. Mrs. Wolfe was virulently anti-Semitic. Her reaction to Aline Bernstein was very much a case in point: she worried that Aline Bernstein was older than Wolfe and that she was already married, but mostly because she was a Jew.

DLB: It's interesting that he fell in love with Aline Bernstein in the first place, given his anti-Semitism.

DONALD: I think that was very necessary for his psychological makeup. Up to the time that he slept with Aline Bernstein, he had, I believe, never had "free" sex. He had frequented prostitutes; he'd paid for sexual encounters. But he'd never been able to have a sexual, much less affectionate, relationship with any woman of his own status. The fact that Aline Bernstein first of all was older (and Wolfe did indeed have a kind of mother fixation) was one thing. The fact that she was already well-to-do and married and therefore not interested in marrying Wolfe gave him a degree of freedom that he might not have had if she had been some young woman. In those days, before contraception, you worried about matters like getting somebody pregnant and having to support her. He didn't have that worry with Aline Bernstein. Third, there was the fact that she was Jewish. He could sleep with her because she was, in his mind, a person of a degraded race. Not *completely* degraded in the sense that blacks were, because Jews after all were supposed to have rich, exotic tastes, high intellect, a love for luxury and voluptuousness, all of which would have rather rich sexual overtones. At the same time, you thought they were not really your equals. Wolfe had been able to have sex with those who were not his equals before. Now there was this woman who had these other traits but who, because of her Jewishness, Wolfe thought inferior. I think that made it possible.

DLB: Do you think Wolfe's anti-Semitism has brought many critics down on him?

DONALD: I'm sure this is the case. There is something of a feeling–and I understand it–that if a man is that misguided, he couldn't have been a great writer. I think it quite unconsciously does influence a lot of critics.

DLB: Do you have another biography planned?

DONALD: I'm not sure what I'm going to do next. I'm torn between a desire to go on with the broad cultural history of the South that I interrupted to do the Wolfe biography. As I said at the very beginning of our talk, I tend to oscillate between biography and general history. But at the same time I must confess that I have in mind, at least at some point, writing a biography of Abraham Lincoln. That would be a challenge.

–Walter W. Ross

Callaloo

Kimberly Rae Chambers
University of Virginia

In 1986 *Callaloo*, a journal of Afro-American and African arts and letters, celebrated its tenth anniversary of continuous publication. When *Callaloo* was first published in December 1976, it was a triannual journal devoted to publishing works by black southern writers. Since that time, the journal has expanded its scope and has grown into a quarterly magazine of international importance, devoted to publishing creative works by black writers in the Americas and Africa, as well as scholarly and critical studies of their works. Studies of life and culture in the black world, visual arts, interviews, and literary bibliographies are also published in *Callaloo*. In its ten-year history, *Callaloo* has become what Henry Louis Gates, Jr., professor of English at Cornell University, describes as "the journal that Wallace Thurman, Langston Hughes, and Zora Neale Hurston envisioned when they published *Fire!!!*"

Because of its longevity, scope of interest, and influence, *Callaloo* occupies a unique position in the tradition of Afro-American publishing. *Callaloo* serves the dual function of Afro-American periodicals described by Abby Arthur Johnson and Ronald Mayberry Johnson in their book, *Propaganda and Aesthetics: The Literary Politics of the Afro-American Magazine* (1979). The authors detect, in this study of the evolution of Afro-American publishing, a pattern of dual emphasis in the aims of black writers and editors. Simply put, black journals have moved between two notions of the function of Afro-American literature: whether it should serve the aesthetic tastes of the individual or whether it should advance the interests of Afro-Americans as a group. The Johnsons show how this degree of emphasis has varied, or rather fluctuated, ever since the first Afro-American journals, such as the *Crisis, Colored American Magazine*, and *Opportunity*, established their goals in the first quarter of the twentieth century. As conditions in society evolved, so too did approaches toward black literature. In the beginning of the century black intellectuals and artists in the protest tradition moved away from the compromising efforts of Booker

Charles H. Rowell, founder and editor of Callaloo

T. Washington's accommodationism and into the more radical strains of W. E. B. Du Bois's philosophy and the struggle for fundamental liberties. At the end of World War I, a sense of freedom found its voice in the New Negro movement, and black writers and editors set about developing black little magazines which talked of universal concerns in literature, challenging the politics and aesthetics of the previous generation. With the Depression black periodicals renewed the protest theme, placing emphasis on the needs of both black and white workers. But at the end of World War II, universal themes again became prominent and stayed that way until the 1960s. Like the 1920s (the era of the Harlem Renaissance), the 1960s was a period of great radicalism as Afro-American journals rejected the concerns of their immediate predecessors and turned their backs on Western culture in general. In establishing the Black Arts Movement, the journals of this decade were responsible for drawing the attention of a wider literary community and providing fertile ground for the growth of a black aesthetic.

Thus, compared to journals created by more culturally dominant groups, Afro-American publications have been more committed to social and political expression. These journals continue to provide an essential platform for the needs of a minority and a historically oppressed people. Editors of Afro-American journals have provided this platform by allowing for a variety of expression in their publications, from scholarly articles to essays of persuasion to creative literature and art of many genres. Three editors in general were prominent in establishing the conditions for the growth of Afro-American culture. W. E. B. Du Bois (*Moon,* founded 1905; *Horizon,* 1907; the *Crisis,* 1910; *Phylon,* 1940) did so by being the first black editor to emphasize with consistency the richness of the Afro-American heritage and the worldwide unity of black people. Charles S. Johnson, who in *Opportunity* (1923) sponsored literary contests, increased the number of outlets for black writing and promoted the careers of many new writers. Finally, Wallace Thurman, with *Fire!!!,* which ran for only one issue (November 1926), challenged accepted notions of art and propaganda and offered another approach to aesthetics.

Taken as a whole, the tradition of Afro-American periodicals can be seen as serving the double function of providing black writers with an outlet for their work, thereby shaping black literature and culture, and of providing a record of the dominant political concerns of a minority people and their efforts to articulate their culture and its aims. Although the degree of emphasis on each function varied with the climate of the times, both aims have remained constant, and *Callaloo* sees itself as occupying an important position in this rich heritage by attempting to unite these claims.

Like *Fire!!!, Callaloo* promotes the notion of a black aesthetic by publishing scholarly articles and essays on black literature; like *Opportunity,* it creates a forum for black writers by offering awards, sponsoring contests, and by actively seeking and promoting new writers, placing their works alongside established writers in each issue; and, like the *Crisis, Callaloo* seeks to promote the unity of black culture worldwide by including features on black writers in the Americas, Africa, and the Caribbean.

The success of *Callaloo* owes much to the influence and devotion of its founder and editor, Charles H. Rowell. *Callaloo* began publication in 1976 when Rowell obtained financial support from several of his colleagues at Southern University in Baton Rouge, Louisiana, where he was an associate professor of English. Rowell sought, as Tom Dent says in the preface to *Callaloo* no. 1, "to give expression to the new writers in the Deep South area." Through the publication of the first four issues, this was the essential focus of *Callaloo* and its editors, who were witnessing the demise of many community-based literary magazines which had emerged in the 1960s and early 1970s. Though *Callaloo* encountered the inevitable problem of inadequate financial resources, it remained committed to the notion of being an independent organ of the southern black community. This goal was made possible in part by generous contributions from individuals. The future of *Callaloo* was made more secure when Professor Rowell accepted a teaching position in 1977 at the University of Kentucky, where the department of English pledged its support to the project. Thus between 1978 and March 1986 *Callaloo* was published at the University of Kentucky, where it remained faithful to its aims of publishing creative and critical works by black southerners.

A particularly interesting feature of *Callaloo* is its name. Rowell wanted a name that communicated the idea of Afro-American culture, particularly the culture that developed in the South. He thought of the gumbo, which slaves created (gumbo is the African word for okra). But, as he recounts: "One morning, before I decided on a title, I was talking with a friend, Lelia Taylor, about what we call gumbo in east Alabama. She said our gumbo sounded a lot like callaloo, a West-Indian word for a gumbo-like stew. When I first heard the word 'callaloo' I thought it was a very musical and intriguing word. This Afro-American dish, which contains various ingredients–a great mixture of things–I thought of as being like black culture itself." Thus this kind of potpourri is represented in the journal.

The naming of *Callaloo,* while appropriate for a black South journal, also hinted at the future direction *Callaloo* was to take. It quickly became more than a regional journal. In 1980 it began to publish works of black writers and visual artists from regions other than the South, and from outside the United States. *Callaloo* soon became the only international journal of its kind

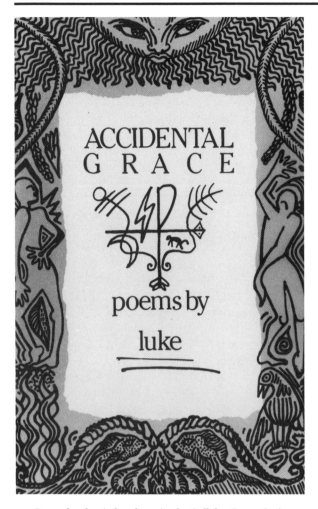

Cover for the sixth volume in the Callaloo Poetry Series

and attracted many writers and critics who had no other existing outlet in which to publish their works.

Like its historical predecessors, *Callaloo* had a political mission. Rowell strongly believed that just as previously blacks were threatened with the destruction of their lives and property, in recent history blacks have been threatened with the extinction of their culture and heritage. Rowell saw a new threat coming from editors and academicians who were ignoring black writers, "rendering black people invisible. Academic institutions have been trying for years to edit the black writer out of existence." Hence an ongoing mission of *Callaloo* is to address the needs of young black writers and make sure that their work gets considered. The problem, as Rowell sees it, is "not so much racism as cultural imperialism. When an editor is reading a manuscript he may not know the writer is black, but he may find themes and techniques contradictory to his own

culture and dismiss the work. It's really a matter of education."

Thus, Rowell insists that a journal like *Callaloo* is necessary and essential in order to compensate for the great lack of publishing opportunities for black writers in the literary establishment. While *Callaloo* serves this function, it does not take an overtly political stance. Nor do its editors use political viewpoints as a critical measure by which to evaluate works submitted for publication. In the 1960s it was the fashion to write about politics and for black journals to publish works whose primary mission was to convey a political point, but Rowell emphasizes that, while black writers have not "outgrown their politics, they can now write about self, about beauty, and about humanity."

In other words, Rowell hopes that *Callaloo*, and the writers it publishes, will convey the impression that black artists can unite political and aesthetic goals and thereby create works which possess their own literary integrity. Moreover, *Callaloo* can become a central forum for black writing and can help create international dialogue and communication. As Rowell states: "Through *Callaloo*, writers in Chicago will get some idea of what's happening in Senegal, black writers in Brazil or South Africa can see what's being written in New York, and they will all discover the literary activities in Jamaica and Martinique."

Callaloo flourished at the University of Kentucky, where its innovations enlarged its goals. Financial support grew as contributions came from the Coordinating Council of Literary Magazines and the National Endowment for the Arts. With these new funds *Callaloo* did two important things: it instituted writing awards, and it began to publish books of fiction and poetry by young black writers.

The first *Callaloo* awards were given in 1981 to Beth Brown for poetry and to Colleen McElroy for fiction. Since then awards have been given to Clyde Taylor, Audre Lorde, and Charles Johnson in 1982; Gerald Barrax, Cyrus Cassells, and Hal Bennett in 1983; Jay Wright, Rita Dove, and Sherley Anne Williams in 1986; and Albert Murray in 1987. The awards, like *Callaloo* itself, serve both to encourage young, new writers like Beth Brown, and to honor those who, like Albert Murray, have made long-standing contributions to Afro-American culture.

The Writers Series established by *Callaloo* serves to advance Walt Whitman's idea that "without great audiences, there can be no great litera-

Volume 9, Number 1   Lady at the Piano © by James Van Der Zee

Cover for Callaloo *no. 26, a comprehensive collection of contemporary Afro-American poetry*

ture." Providing literature to a knowledgeable, appreciative, and critical readership is the aim of *Callaloo* and its Writers Series. The Callaloo Poetry Series has published six volumes since 1983: *Change of Territory,* by Melvin Dixon; *Ceremony for Minneconjoux,* by Brenda Marie Osbey; *Explications/Interpretations,* by Jay Wright; *The Deaths of Animals and Lesser Gods,* by Gerald Barrax; *Water Song,* by Michael Weaver; and *Accidental Grace,* by luke (Joseph A. Brown, S. J.). The Callaloo Fiction Series, begun in 1985, has published two volumes: *Fifth Sunday,* by Rita Dove, and *Bedouin Hornbook,* by Nathaniel Mackey. *Callaloo* also has plans for a drama series and a series on contemporary literary criticism.

In 1986 Rowell accepted a faculty position at the University of Virginia in Charlottesville.

He chose to move and bring *Callaloo* with him to Virginia because the university pledged strong financial and moral support. *Callaloo* was seen by the university as a valuable addition to its growing Black Studies program. As of May 1986, the University of Virginia became the sponsor of the journal, although it is published and distributed by the Johns Hopkins University Press. Moreover, the University Press of Virginia is the publisher of the books in the Callaloo series.

The best description of what *Callaloo* was, is, and has become can be given by highlighting some of its twenty-eight issues published over the last ten years. Each issue is usually a blend of fiction, poetry, and criticism with a balance of contributions from new and established writers. Among those who have published in *Callaloo* are Jay Wright, Rita Dove, Ernest Gaines, Michael Harper, June Jordan, Audre Lorde, Alice Walker, and John Edgar Wideman. Visual artists whose works have been represented in *Callaloo* include Romare Beardon, John Biggers, Roland Freeman, Ed Hamilton, Richard Powell, and James Van Der Zee.

Some of the more noteworthy issues of *Callaloo* are those specifically devoted to one writer or topic. *Callaloo* no. 3 studied the works of Ernest Gaines; *Callaloo* no. 5 was a special issue on women poets, including a color reproduction of the mural "Contribution of the Negro Woman to American Life and Education" by John Biggers; *Callaloo* nos. 8, 9, and 10 were dedicated to works by writers from Africa, Latin America, and the Caribbean; *Callaloo* nos. 14 and 15 featured the poet Sterling Brown; *Callaloo* no. 16 presented Gayl Jones; *Callaloo* no. 17 drew attention to the architect of the Negritude Movement, Aime Cesaire of Martinique; *Callaloo* no. 18 featured the fiction of Paule Marshall; *Callaloo* no. 19 concentrated on Jay Wright; *Callaloo* no. 22 was a special issue devoted to fiction; *Callaloo* no. 23 dealt with Larry Neal and the Black Arts Movement; *Callaloo* no. 25 published essays from Europe on Afro-American literature; *Callaloo* no. 26 was a comprehensive collection of the best in contemporary Afro-American poetry; and *Callaloo* no. 28 examined the works of Richard Wright. *Callaloo* no. 31 introduced Nicolas Guillen, the Cuban poet.

Callaloo's scope is made possible in part by the contributions of its editorial staff. In 1984 Rowell established associate editorships for poetry, fiction, literary criticism, and book reviews. Assistant editors help with editorial tasks, and a board of advisory and contributing editors lend their reputation and support to *Callaloo*. Also, scholars have taken on the role of "special guest editor," assuming responsibility for an entire issue devoted to their area of expertise. Among those who have served as guest editors are Vera Kutzinski, Robert Stepto, Paul Carter Harrison, and Henry Louis Gates, Jr.

In addition to editors, *Callaloo* relies on a staff of contributing bibliographers in order to provide annual bibliographies, the only ones in the field, devoted to black literature in the Americas, Africa, and the Caribbean. The fall issue of each year is devoted to publishing these annual bibliographies.

Callaloo has achieved much since its early days, when it began as a Black South journal, to today, when it is known as an Afro-American and African journal of arts and letters. That *Callaloo* should exist at all is noteworthy, echoing the sentiments of J. Max Barber, editor of the *Voice of the Negro,* who, in his first editorial published in January 1904, said: "To the casual observer, there is nothing interesting in the launching of a Negro magazine; but to the careful observer, to the philosopher of history, to him who is a reader of the signs of the times it means much. It means that culture is taking a deep hold upon our people. It is an indication that our people are becoming an educated, a reading people, and this is a thing of which to be proud."

Callaloo is proud of the position it occupies in the history of Afro-American publishing–and American publishing in general–and it intends to continue in the spirit of improvisation and discipline. As Charles Rowell says: "While *Callaloo* has undergone many changes during the past ten years, two of its purposes have remained the same: to provide a long-needed forum for black writers, and to celebrate a rich and vital cultural heritage, whose literary component is presently witnessing a quiet but exciting renaissance. *Callaloo* is in the forefront, recording and encouraging writers, helping to keep alive a literary tradition."

New Literary Periodicals: A Report for 1987

Richard R. Centing
Ohio State University

The following report on new literary periodicals, the first in a series of annual surveys scheduled to appear in the *Dictionary of Literary Biography Yearbook,* documents scholarly journals, newsletters, reviews, and indexes launched in 1987. A few titles begun in 1985/1986 that completed their volume year in 1987 or which relate to another title in the survey are also included. Any titles that have not come to our attention by press time will be covered in the 1988 *Yearbook.*

These descriptions are not meant to be evaluative. The intention of the survey is to provide a brief analysis of the major points of each serial as an alerting service for librarians and scholars. In many cases the survey will be based on the first issue or two, a fact that precludes any final judgment. The examples in each descriptive annotation of particular poems, critical essays, or reviews attempt to serve as a yardstick of that publication's main features. Following the first discussion of a new title the publisher's address is provided in parentheses after the title.

The report serves as an indicator to persons involved in library collection development of potential new subscriptions; provides vital facts to reference librarians; alerts scholars to the burgeoning growth of serials; and notifies indexing services of the need for the inclusion of new titles in their core lists. Please contact the author with any comments on the report for 1987, and with suggestions for inclusion in the 1988 report.

Restoration and 18th Century Theatre Research (Loyola University of Chicago, 6525 North Sheridan Road, Chicago, IL 60626) has been restored to currency in a second series beginning July 1986. Scheduled to appear twice a year, it continues a journal of the same name published from 1962-1977. As the editor's note explains, the articles published in the first issue "were accepted for publication between 1975 and 1979," and those in the second issue (with the exception of a short note) were accepted between 1975 and 1981. The first issue of the second volume (Summer 1987) contains new articles on the casts of early-eighteenth-century operas, William Wych-

Cover for the journal edited by Douglas H. White

erley's *The Plain Dealer,* the acting of Sarah Siddons versus Ann Crawford, and Thomas Otway's work for Thomas Betterton's Duke's Theatre. The authors are from such establishments as the United States Naval Academy, York University, Marquette University, and the University of Arkansas. The editor, Douglas H. White, has published numerous articles in the field in such journals as *Modern Philology.* Presumably the *MLA International Bibliography* will continue to index this unique journal as it has done in the past.

The advent of the semiannual *Journal of Dramatic Theory and Criticism* (University of Kansas, Department of Theatre and Media Arts, Murphy Hall, Lawrence, KS 66045) establishes a primary vehicle for theoretical research on world theater from the Greeks to the present. The first three issues (Fall 1986; Spring 1987; Fall 1987) combine over four hundred pages of scholarly articles on subjects such as the application of Aristotle's *Poetics*; the ghost in *Hamlet*; the psychodynamics of theatrical spectatorship; the Irish playwright Brian Friel; modern productions of *King Lear*; an analysis of Samuel Beckett's *Not I* by Edith Kern, a major voice in Beckett criticism; and a definitional comparison between camp and burlesque treatments. The editor, John Gronbeck-Tedesco, expresses an interest in publishing primary source material, and "An Interview with Peter Barnes" by Yvonne Shafer is an admirable contribution to that goal. Dr. Shafer, currently a professor of theater at Florida State University, was a distinguished visiting professor at Nanjing University in the People's Republic of China during Fall 1987. She has produced noted research on Simon Gray, Eugene O'Neill, and on Restoration heroines in the above-reviewed *Restoration and 18th Century Theatre Research*. The ability to attract talents such as Dr. Shafer is one sign of Gronbeck-Tedesco's editorial acumen. The interview with Barnes casts new light on his "non-naturalistic, experimental, and explosive" plays. The journal's currentness is indicated by its publication of two articles on Caryl Churchill's infamous 1979 play, *Cloud Nine*. The journal concludes with a short section called "Plays in Performance" that provides signed commentary on various productions of Ibsen, Shakespeare, et al. in England and America.

Studies in American Drama, 1945-Present (The Behrend College, Humanities Division, Pennsylvania State University, Erie, PA 16563) has been awarded the Conference of Editors of Learned Journals Award for the best new learned journal of 1986. The first two annuals (1986 and 1987) have published fifteen essays, including a reassessment of Arthur Miller's *After the Fall* in which the play is called an "undervalued drama which has yet to find its audience"; an interview with David Mamet along with an extensive classified bibliography of primary and secondary sources; an analysis of the treatment of men and women in Sam Shepard's plays; an account of the influence of Clifford Odets's *Awake and Sing!*; an appraisal of Charles Fuller's *A Soldier's Play* and its reception

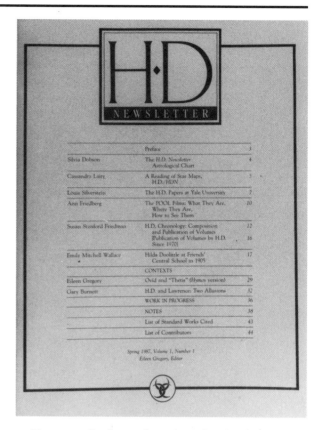

Front page for the newsletter devoted to American poet Hilda Doolittle

by the black American community; and additional evaluations of Tennessee Williams, Ed Bullins, Albert Innaurato, and others who have shaped American drama since World War II. The journal has a few illustrations of productions. *Studies in American Drama, 1945-Present* includes a "Theatre Reviews" section (like the "Plays in Performance" section of the *Journal of Dramatic Theory and Criticism*) that reviews several productions worldwide. It seems to be an important element of the journal, as it seeks to define trends in American drama exemplified in William Hoffman's *As Is* and a Paris staging of Shepard's *Buried Child* as *L'Enfant Enfoui* (the French have "discovered" Shepard). The journal is coedited by Philip C. Kolin (Department of English, University of Southern Mississippi) and Colby H. Kullman (Department of English, University of Mississippi).

Of the quartet of theater journals covered in this report, *Theater Three* (Carnegie Mellon University, Department of Drama, Schenley Park, Pittsburgh, PA 15213) covers the broadest spectrum. Addressing itself to theory, interpretation, criticism and performance of international drama since 1789 (the French Revolution appeals to *Theater Three* as the starting point of the modern era), it has erected an all-inclusive stage that is "receptive to heterogeneous approaches, Hegelian or Marxist, existential or religious, humanist or deconstructionist, Freudian or feminist." The 128-page inaugural issue (Fall 1986) honors Eric Bentley and includes numerous articles on Ibsen by noted scholars. The focus of number two (Spring 1987) is Bertolt Brecht. Ibsen and Brecht were chosen as foundation stones of modern drama. The names recruited to write for *Theater Three* include a Who's Who of modern criticism—Richard Gilman, Rolf Fjelde, Martin Esslin, and Eric Bentley, and other directors, editors, and dramaturges. There is a section devoted to documents in modern drama that reprints master statements from such authors as Maurice Maeterlinck. The "Classic Revisited" column has well-known writers on modern drama drawing attention to core titles in theater history, such as Bentley's *The Playwright as Thinker* (1946). There is a four-page review of a production of *John Gabriel Borkman* directed by Ingmar Bergman, who "falls short, largely due to a pedestrian biographical interpretation of Ibsen's work." The text in the theater is announced as the special theme of *Theater Three*, number three.

The Joyce industry continues to be served by a variety of publications. The new *James Joyce Literary Supplement* (University of Miami, Department of English, Coral Gables, FL 33124) is a tabloid edited by Bernard Benstock. The first twenty-four-page semiannual issue (May 1987) promises to review all new books on Joyce within six months of publication. Although created as a reviewing service, the first issue does include special features, such as a tribute to Maria Jolas and various brief commentaries. The *Times Literary Supplement* (21 August 1987) points out in its review that Joyce is already receiving adequate coverage in the *James Joyce Quarterly* (1963-) and the *James Joyce Broadsheet* (1980-); and it fails to mention the existence of another competitor, the *James Joyce Foundation Newsletter* (1969-).

Another new Joyce-oriented journal is *A Finnegans Wake Circular* (edited by Vincent Deane, 100 Congleton Road, Sandbach, Cheshire, England CW11 ODQ), a quarterly that fills the gap left by the demise of *A Wake Newslitter* (1962-1980). It is worth mentioning even though it was created Autumn 1985, as the contributors are recognized Joyce scholars such as Roland McHugh, Danis Rose, and Fritz Senn. The circu-

lar consists of short notes and queries on specialized facets of *Finnegans Wake*, such as Joyce's use of Armenian and the meaning of the book's concluding word ("the").

Essays in Graham Greene (Penkevill Publishing Company, Box 212, Greenwood, FL 32443) is an annual review that began in 1987. Ten knowledgeable critics contribute ten essays to the first 221-page hardbound compilation. The subjects covered range from discussions of sex in Greene's work to the impact of his conversion to Roman Catholicism in 1926. "Film Critic Versus Film Maker: Greene's Criticism of Hitchcock's Films," by Gene D. Phillips, S.J., discusses Greene's faultfinding with Hitchcock's films. Bernard F. Dick (Fairleigh Dickinson University) examines the film treatment of *The Confidential Agent* that appeared in 1945, based on Greene's 1939 novel. Dick clearly outlines the conflicting ideologies of the Spanish Civil War and how they would relate to a reader and/or audience in 1945 in the aftermath of the Allied victory in World War II. A textual study of *Brighton Rock* and a look at Greene's experiments in drama are also included in this annual that should help solidify the critical reputation of British novelist, short-story writer, journalist, and essayist Greene. It concludes with a section of signed book reviews of books by and about Greene.

Two single-author newsletters, the *H. D. Newsletter* and the *Jean Rhys Review*, are more informal than *Essays in Graham Greene* but are serious sounding-boards for scholars interested in the works of these women. There has been a renaissance of interest in the American poet and novelist H. D. (Hilda Doolittle), and the *H. D. Newsletter* (Dallas Institute of Humanities, 2719 Routh Street, Dallas, TX 75201), founded Spring 1987, should advance her cause. Louis Silverstein (Yale University Library) describes the H. D. papers at Yale University and the fortunate friendship between Norman Holmes Pearson (who held a chair in the American Studies Department at Yale when he met H. D. in 1937) and H. D. that resulted in the large collection of personal papers at Yale. Cassandra Laity (English and Women's Studies, Vanderbilt University) submitted an astrological chart on the *H. D. Newsletter*, which was "born September 13, 1986 at the H. D. Centennial Symposium in H. D.'s birthplace, Bethlehem, Pennsylvania." One article documents H. D.'s support of and appearance in "The POOL Films," an enterprise formed by Bryher and Robert Macpherson, circa 1927-1930. Also included is an im-

FALL 1987 $4.50

BOULEVARD

JOURNAL
OF CONTEMPORARY
WRITING

A PREVIOUSLY UNPUBLISHED STORY

DELMORE SCHWARTZ

CONVERSATIONS WITH

JOHN CHEEVER

FRANK STELLA

POETRY BY

JOHN ASHBERY

TOM DISCH

MOLLY PEACOCK

Louis Armstrong and ''Furniture Music''

#6

Cover for the multi-arts review edited by Richard Burgin

portant bibliographic chronology comparing the composition and publication dates of H. D.'s books, showing that some works of the 1920s were not published until the 1980s. The last five pages of the first, attractively printed semiannual contains informative announcements, queries, and notes on special journal issues devoted to H. D.'s centennial.

Also a semiannual, the *Jean Rhys Review* (edited by Nora Gaines, Columbia University, Department of Chemistry, Box 568 Havemeyer Hall, New York, NY 10027) was released early in 1987. The first article compares Rhys's short story "The Sound of the River" with Ernest Hemingway's "Hills Like White Elephants." This eleven-page article explores Rhys's narrative technique and her style that is partly "Hemingwayesque." Both stories deal with a couple in crisis and offer insights into the woman's point of view. A memoir of a visit to Jean Rhys's cottage just before her death is included, along with the first of an ongoing bibliography of primary and

secondary works. There are announcements of forthcoming papers to be given at the MLA conference and short biographies of the two members of the editorial board, Martien Kappers (University of Amsterdam) and Thomas Staley (University of Tulsa, where he also edits the *James Joyce Quarterly*).

Boulevard (Opojaz, Inc., 4 Washington Square Village, New York, N.Y. 10012), a multi-arts review edited by Richard Burgin (Department of English, Drexel University), is distributed nationally by Bernhard DeBoer, Inc. The list of patrons for this *Paris Review*-like triquarterly includes the NEA, McGraw-Hill Foundation, numerous arts councils, and personal donors. The result of this support network is a "journal of contemporary writing" that publishes fiction, nonfiction, and poetry by names like John Ashbery, Joyce Carol Oates, Alice Adams, Tess Gallagher, and Daniel Hoffman, along with upcoming talents like Tom Disch and Sharon Sheehe Starke. Critical essays have studied Kafka, Dos Passos, and Montale. Of particular interest to literary scholars are interviews with John Cheever and John Fowles. Music seems to be an art of continuing interest to *Boulevard*, with an article on "Glenn Gould as a Radio Composer" by Richard Kostelanetz, and interviews with such notable composers as John Cage and Philip Glass.

As a reporter of events and issues in the arts, *Arrival* (48 Shattuck Square, Suite 194, Berkeley, CA 94704) is worthy of national attention. Oversized and heavily illustrated, its first cover story (Spring 1987) was an interview with movie critic Pauline Kael which garnered her low opinion of television movie critics. Bruce Bawer's article, "Taking on the Literary Brat Pack," is an investigative dissection of a group of young writers, including David Leavitt and Susan Minot, who have published primarily in the *New Yorker* or been students of writer/editor Gordon Lish. Weakness of motif and style seem endemic to their work, according to Bawer, and right or wrong, these quarrels among the literati add a tonic to standard literary exchange, a vibrant alternative to the *PMLA*. In Summer 1987 the quarterly *Arrival* followed with Bawer's "Notes on being a Critic," an invited article wherein he defends harsh criticism and promotes the role of the critic. Other articles are political/social, dealing with the economic woes of Alaska or the icons of advertising. But each issue also includes good fiction and poetry.

Balcones (P.O. Box 50247, Austin, TX 78763) calls itself "a multi-partisan review with the sole purpose of promoting excellence in literature and in expanding the horizons of literary craft." The title evokes the Spanish for balcony or vantage point and the geographical area known as the Balcones Escarpment. *Balcones* has the glossy appearance of a regional *Atlantic*, with high-quality graphics and layout. The common reader will find a diversity of topics and genres in the table of contents: a new look at the darker side of Thoreau's *Walden*; fiction by Robert Coover, Jack Matthews, and Gordon Lish; poetry by Naomi Shihab Nye, a distinguished younger poet; and a long interview with Mary Robison, author of *An Amateur's Guide to the Night* (1983) and a teacher at Harvard, on the subject of "minimalism" and the pervasive influence of Gordon Lish. There is also an article by Noam Chomsky on media manipulation and one on the treatment of women in Busby Berkeley musicals. Lantz Miller is the editor.

Another powerful statement of Gordon Lish's omnipresence is the quarterly magazine of new American writing which he edits, simply called *The Quarterly* (Vintage Books, 201 East 50th Street, New York, NY 10022). Vintage is a division of Random House, where some of Lish's protégés have been published; others have been published at Knopf where Lish is a senior editor. The 312-page Spring 1987 anthology includes short stories by Amy Hempel and poetry by Linda Gregg, sharing space with lesser-known beginners. There is an informal commentary section at the back of each issue, with each letter-to-the-editor or mini-essay entitled " . . . to *Q* ," preceded by the respondent's name. This section is continually amusing and informative for readers wanting to know who has been thrown to the dogs or saved from the lions. *The Quarterly* is not to be missed.

City Lights bookstore has been a literary meeting place and beat publisher since 1953. Located in San Francisco, it is as much a tourist attraction as the nearby Coit Tower. Along with the Gotham Book Mart in New York City it forms a bicoastal link for traveling writers and book buyers. The annual *City Lights Review* (City Lights Books, 261 Columbus Avenue, San Francisco, CA 94133), edited by Lawrence Ferlinghetti and Nancy J. Peters, is the most recent journal from this avant-garde bastion. The first annual, for 1987, is an attractively printed 210-page issue that looks light years beyond the mimeographed

Cover for the oversized and heavily illustrated journal which presents coverage of events and issues in the arts

texts of the 1950s. The editorial states the publication's dedication to "live poetry, engaged literature, radical politics, and deep ecology." And almost as a challenge to Gordon Lish, without mentioning his name, they claim to support "a maximalist rather than a minimalist view of life and art in which the artist and poet are the divining rods or antennae on the frontiers of new consciousness." *City Lights Review* is quite a miscellany, with a heavy dosage of translations of poems by Michaux (France), Pavese (Italy), Lorca (Spain), and Tsvetayeva (U.S.S.R.). A love of internationalism in the world of poetry has always been an admirable trait of West Coast poets. Ivan Arguelles, a librarian at the University of California, Berkeley, submits "H-Bomb," an apocalyptic vision of "blank consuming amnesia," a rhetorical poem representative of the urge toward protest in verse that characterizes many previous beat poets, poets of tender compassion as well as passionate anger. A speech broadcast by Noam Chomsky on Pacifica radio in Berkeley is published as "The Global Drift Towards Nuclear War," a dread-producing blast that somehow fits in the review's environment. There are also quieter poems by New Directions founder, James Laughlin, and Charles Henri Ford. Finally, Allen Ginsberg's "Cosmopolitan Greetings" opens with the line, "Stand up against governments, against God," which could serve as the slogan of the *City Lights Review*.

New American Writing (Oink! Press, Inc., 1446 West Jarvis, Chicago, IL 60626) is a replacement for *Oink!* (1971-1985). Under the new name, which should give it a little more respect, it continues to publish a finely edited potpourri of stories, plays, and poems. The first annual for 1987 begins with Alice Notley's play, "Anne's White Glove," and ends with four chapters from *Ghost Waves* by James McManus. One defect is the lack of a contributor's page: it is always enlightening to browse the credits of authors, and learn about their small press history and forthcoming work. The editors, Paul Hoover and Maxine Chernoff, are recognized names among the writers to have emerged in the 1980s, and their national contacts have given *New American Writing* an enviable roster: Kenward Elmslie, Charles Bernstein, Anne Waldman, Rosmarie Waldrop, Ron Silliman, George Butterick, and Ann Lauterbach, among others. Number two features Clark Coolidge's lengthy narrative *At Egypt* and James Laughlin writing about Ezra Pound and Paul Blackburn.

The Spring 1987 premier issue of *Witness* (31000 Northwestern Highway, Suite 200, Farmington Hills, MI 48018) is a special issue on the Holocaust. Sponsored by the Center for the Study of the Child, a nonprofit corporation located in Detroit, *Witness* exhibits first-class production values. The quarterly combines original poetry and fiction with literary essays in a confrontation on the theme of the Holocaust. The editor, Peter Stine (Lecturer, University of Michigan), contributes a major piece, "Franz Kafka, Metamorphosis, and the Holocaust," a twenty-two-page essay with fifty-five bibliographic notes that explores turn-of-the-century anti-Semitism and Kafka's exile into writing. There is poetry by David Ignatow responding to the concentration camps; Alvin H. Rosenfeld (Director of Jewish Studies, Indiana University) on the Italian author Primo Levi's postulation of constant war against evil; and a short story about Jewish children in the Amsterdam ghetto from Clara Asscher-Pinkhof 's *Star Children*. The Fall 1987 *Witness* is also a special issue, "Writings from Prison," guest edited by Fielding Dawson, "a writer who lives in New York City and is complet-

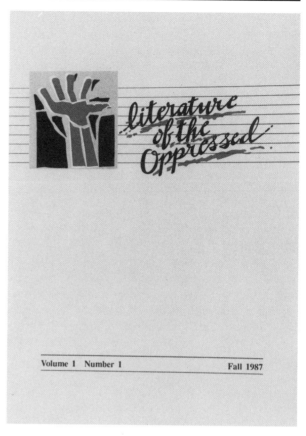

Volume 1   Number 1   Fall 1987

Cover for the journal devoted to the writings of victimized peoples

ing a novel about teaching in prison." The majority of the contributors are inmates or parolees, along with writers who teach in prisons or are otherwise committed to prison justice. Twelve poems, four fictional works, reproductions of art and photography, and twelve essays all provide a progressive interpretation of prison problems. Many of the pieces were submissions to the P.E.N. Prison Committee's annual writing contest. The editorial board includes Leslie Fiedler, Christopher Lasch, and Alice Fulton.

Literature of the Oppressed (1605 Lake Johanna Blvd., St. Paul, MN 55112) incorporates the spirit of *Witness* in a more modest format. The first forty-four-page semiannual issue (Fall 1987) promises "a journal devoted to the literature that arises from the experience of oppression, especially as written by the oppressed themselves." The first essay, "Literature and the Nonliterate," is by author Richard Rodrigues, from an address to the conference on Literature of the Oppressed held at Bethel College, in St. Paul, Minnesota, in October 1986. It provides thoughtful insights into the portrayal of the nonliterate in great works of literature. June Hagen re-

reads *Jane Eyre* from a feminist perspective and questions the usefulness of prefeminist criticism. Some stories, poems, and a drawing entitled *Auschwitz* (Poland, 1946) complete this independent excursion that "proposes to be a forum for helping to define this field of study."

Gothic (Gary William Crawford, P.O. Box 80051, Baton Rouge, LA 70898) is a new series annual replacing a previous *Gothic* (1979 and 1980). Its scope is defined as the genre originating with the eighteenth-century Gothic novel up to modern manifestations in literature and film. The first annual (1986) only runs twenty-two pages, and includes two essays: one on the artist as demon in the writings of Mary Shelley, Robert Louis Stevenson, Horace Walpole, Bram Stoker, and Stephen King; and a second on "Stephen King and the Tradition of American Gothic," showing the influences of Poe and Melville. There are three signed book reviews of considerable length that encapsulate recent scholarship on the genre.

Published by the Institute for Historical Study, *The Independent Scholar* (105 Vincente Road, Berkeley, CA 94705) was inspired by a conference on independent scholarship held 25 October 1986 in San Diego. The twelve-page newsletter was issued Winter 1987, edited by Georgia Wright. Dr. Wright holds a Ph.D. in art history, and she is affiliated with the Institute for Historical Study, described as "a group of academics and independent scholars." The newsletter hopes to be a communications station for numerous organizations such as the Center for Independent Study (New Haven) and the San Diego Independent Scholars. It contains announcements of forthcoming events, a call for a national coalition of independent scholars, suggestions on how to best utilize local libraries and archives, and grant information. The editorial board consists of Judith Ruderman (Independent Scholars Association of the North Carolina Triangle), Nancy Zumwalt (Alliance of Independent Scholars of Cambridge), Ronald Gross (Independent Scholarship National Program), and James Bennett (*The Chicago reSearcher*). The newsletter has no stated frequency.

A very informal publication is the tabloid *Diarist's Journal* (Gazette Publications, Inc., 102 W. Water Street, Lansford, PA 18232), a popular monthly conceived as an outlet for unpublished contemporary diary excerpts and letters. The first issue (predated January 1988) was released November 1987. The editor, Ed Gildea, is a former newspaperman. Having received considerable attention in the national media, it seems to have tapped the mother lode of amateur autobiography. Popular culture scholars should eventually find a wealth of material in these primary reflections on the killing of John Lennon, a Polish émigré party, and the experience of first solo flight. Books about diary writing are also reviewed.

Another tabloid that has a disposable, difficult-to-preserve look is *New Letters Review of Books* (University of Missouri-Kansas City, 5216 Rockhill Road, Kansas City, MO 64110), a free supplement to subscribers to the distinguished quarterly review, *New Letters*. Issues for Spring 1987 and Autumn 1987 have been distributed, with highly informed, signed reviews of major new works of poetry, short stories, novels, and scholarly editions. The important new poet Stephen Dobyns (*Cemetery Nights*, 1987) is interviewed about this latest book of his productive last decade. *New Letters Review of Books* is a very literate reviewing service that may be missed because of its method of distribution and may be lost because of its acid-rich paper stock.

Antipodes: A North American Journal of Australian Literature is the official semiannual publication of the American Association of Australian Studies (190 Sixth Avenue, Brooklyn, NY 11217). The editor, Robert Ross (Southern Methodist University), works with an editorial group that attempts to inform Americans about Australian literature. The journal uses an attractive typeface and has excellent illustrations. The contents of this eye-catching package include original fiction and poetry by Australian writers, long essays, and other departments, including book reviews. An interview with Sydney-born Shirley Hazzard garners her opinions on "bad literary criticism," Nobel Prize winner Patrick White, and on her novel *Transit of Venus* (1980). Her national identity is discussed, as she lived most of her life abroad, and maintains a home in New York City. Thoughtful pieces on teaching Australian literature and a history of Australian/American literary connections round out the inaugural issue (March 1987).

While *Antipodes* is clarifying Australian literature, the *Canadian Literature Index* (ECW Press, 307 Coxwell Avenue, Toronto, Ontario, Canada M4L 3B5) is a major effort to index all literary material about Canadian literature. The first index was a hardbound 404-page annual for 1985 that was published in 1987. Future subscriptions will

Cover for the semiannual publication of the American Association of Australian Studies

include quarterly supplements prior to the issuance of the hardbound annual. The editor, Janet Fraser, has both an M.L.S. and an M.A. in English, and she is compiling the index on a microcomputer-based system. Primary and secondary materials found in some 100 periodicals and newspapers are indexed, mostly Canadian sources, with some exceptional non-Canadian sources, such as *Yale French Studies*. An unusual appendix is a union list of Canadian libraries holding the source list titles, which will assist interlibrary loan applications. There is an author index and a detailed subject index where general subjects such as "Acadian Writing" or specific subjects such as the names of theater companies can be located. The thoroughness extends to the inclusion of book reviews, letters to the editor, and literary cartoons.

Published with the assistance of the British Comparative Literature Association, *New Comparison* (University of Warwick, Graduate School of Comparative Literature, Coventry, England CV4 7AL) is a semiannual that is subtitled "A Journal of Comparative and General Literary Studies." The first number (Summer 1986) is devoted to

"Literary Translation and Literary Systems." The editor, Theo Hermans, is a professor of Dutch at University College, London. *New Comparison* is the successor to *Comparison*, edited by Susan Bassnett at the University of Warwick (1975-1982). An editorial says that *New Comparison* "seeks to promote and re-invigorate comparative literary studies in Britain after the recession and retrenchment of the early 1980s," to "transcend narrow subject boundaries and national frontiers." The papers published in the first issue were presented at an International Comparative Literature Association congress (Paris, 1985). Written by specialists from Europe and North America, the papers cover such topics as translation in the Netherlands (1750-1800), in Spain (1834-1844), and France in the twelfth century; contemporary, bilingual Canada; and some theoretical articles on the field of translation.

Nineteenth-Century Studies (The Citadel, Department of English, Charleston, SC 29409) is an annual sponsored by the Southeastern Nineteenth-Century Studies Association. It is the intention of the journal to publish the most distinguished papers from their annual conference. The first ninety-page annual for 1987 is devoted to "Entertainment, Amusement, and Diversion in the Nineteenth Century." It seems to be an interdisciplinary chalkboard that focuses scholarly attention on such topics as gambling and Byron, the text of Oscar Wilde's "The Importance of Being Earnest," America's national image as reflected in pictorial works, and a visit to Venice by Goethe in 1786. Another article on nineteenth-century Chinese gardens is illustrated with sixteen views that add to the discussion. The editor is Suzanne O. Edwards (The Citadel).

Cultural Critique is published three times a year by Telos Press (431 East 12th Street, New York, NY 10009), the publishers of the political science journal *Telos*. From the first issue (Fall 1985) to the fifth issue (Winter 1986-1987), *Cultural Critique* has been an ambitious journal of advanced theoretical thinking, "dedicated to the critique not only of culture, but also of the categories by which it is constituted and transformed." It is "committed to those kinds of dialectical strategies–interdisciplinary, historicizing, cross-cultural–by virtue of which cultural phenomena become intelligible as partial constituents of larger constructs." Although this journal may find heavy use in nonliterary humanistic disciplines, it includes enough scholarly analysis of literary works to be included in this survey. The special issue

Cover for the annual sponsored by the Southeastern Nineteenth-Century Studies Association

(number three, Spring 1986) "American Representations of Vietnam" included lengthy discussions of David Rabe's Vietnam plays and Tom O'Brien's novel, *Going After Cacciato* (1978). Issue five (Winter 1986-1987) is a special issue on "Modernity and Modernism, Postmodernity and Postmodernism," that relates the ideas of Adorno to white South African literature. The importance of William James to American literary humanists and the dilemma of black intellectuals are two other examples of special features that pertain to debates that are refashioning the climate of American literary criticism.

The Library of Congress subject heading for *Cultural Critique* is "Culture–Periodicals," an all-encompassing term that could be applied to the three journals of culture studies that are currently being heavily promoted by Methuen (London): *Cultural Studies*, *New Formations*, and *Textual Practice*. *Cultural Studies* (Methuen & Co. Ltd., 11 New Fetter Lane, London, England EC4P 4EE) was established in 1987 as an expansion of *Austra-*

lian Journal of Cultural Studies (1983-1986) into an international journal. It is a triquarterly edited by John Fiske (Western Australian Institute of Technology) that advocates a study of "power and meaning in contemporary culture" through a "discussion of social practices, texts, and cultural domains." The editorial collective guiding this ambitious journal is still dominated by Australian academics. The first issue (January 1987) includes theoretical articles on the discourse of political cartoons, a stylistic analysis of the pop-song soundtrack of television's *Miami Vice*, photographs of the working classes, an examination of Pierre Bourdieu's sociology of culture, a postmodern glance at urban commercial culture and subculture, and a report on public cultural policy.

Methuen also released another triquarterly in 1987, *New Formations*, edited by James Donald. The introduction to the first issue (Spring 1987) calls for "sustained critical engagement with the regimes of representation that have been a characteristic and peculiarly pervasive feature of the way power is exercised in contemporary societies." *New Formations* hopes to avoid "a defection of the (post-'68) intelligentsia into a stylish and knowing pessimism" and to promote "the *pre*figuring of new formations." The contributors are filmmakers, poets, professors of literature and literary theory, philosophers, and teachers of cultural studies. Their contributions discuss cultural policies in London, 1981-1986; recent autobiographical writing; fashion and orientalism; the history of feminism and the definition of "women"; aesthetics and the sociology of the sublime; the role of art historians; and a remembrance of Frantz Fanon (*The Wretched of the Earth*, 1961).

The last journal in the triad from Methuen is *Textual Practice*, edited by Terence Hawkes (Department of English, University College, Cardiff). The "study of literary texts will be a central concern" of *Textual Practice*, that is, "textuality," informed by advanced theories of social, historical and political analysis, including "semiotic systems" and media studies. The first two issues (Spring and Summer 1987) include essays by Terry Eagleton on "The End of English," Christopher Norris on "The Rhetoric of Remembrance: Derrida on de Man," Simon During on "Postmodernism or Post-Colonialism Today," and Thomas Docherty on "Theory, Enlightenment and Violence: Postmodernist Hermeneutic as a Comedy of Errors," and some twenty other articles and reviews. The first few sentences of

Hawkes's editorial sets the tone: "It is never a good time to start a new journal. Even so, 1987 seems unpropitious to a remarkable degree. The academic world in general feels itself to be under attack. The Humanities in particular feel marginalized and underfunded. Outwardly querulous, inwardly riven, they sense themselves to be hopelessly at odds with a culture which has long abandoned any recognition of the value of their role." The entire Methuen trio may require closer scrutiny, especially in the light of their apparent overlapping of the subjects of discourse, and blurring of disciplinary lines: it would even appear that many of the articles could be moved from journal to journal with little discernible effect on their argument. The buzzwords in the advertisements for all three–"cultural studies," "post-structuralism," "post-modernism," "feminism," "textuality," "modernity," "social practices," "cultural domains," "cultural difference"–likewise seem interchangeable. Library practitioners who are used to traditional departmentalizations of budgets and priorities may be baffled as to the evaluation and disposition of such interdisciplinary materials.

The Elmer Holmes Bobst Awards in Arts and Letters

Rhonda Zangwill
Elmer Holmes Bobst Library

The first Elmer Holmes Bobst Awards in Arts and Letters were presented in 1983 at the tenth anniversary celebration of New York University's Elmer Holmes Bobst Library and Study Center. Gathered that evening were more than 500 distinguished guests including writers, editors, publishers, literary agents, and of course, librarians.

Rather than honor a single book, the Bobst Awards were designed to honor the sustained lifetime achievements of prominent American literary figures. More important, they were created to celebrate the unique bond between writers and libraries. And it is that connection that sets the Bobst Awards apart from most other literary honors.

The underlying philosophy of the Bobst Awards is grounded in several principles. Of all the arts, writing is perhaps the most personal, the most individual. And libraries are among the few establishments designed primarily to serve the individual. It is at libraries that any and everyone is free to pursue their interests, at their own pace, privately and anonymously. Libraries and writers are also particularly sensitive to any attempts at censorship. Together they have formed a natural alliance to pursue and defend free expression and to protect the individual right to open inquiry.

The Bobst Awards carry a cash prize of $2,000. Winners also receive a New York University citation and a medal which features a likeness of Bobst on one side and a rendering of the Bobst Library on the other.

Funded by the Elmer and Mamdouha Bobst Foundation, the Bobst Awards are a natural extension of the late Elmer Bobst's dedication to libraries and education. Bobst was the guiding force behind the construction of New York University's central research library on Washington Square. A self-educated man, Bobst built an impressive career in pharmaceuticals and later in life pursued wide-ranging philanthropic work. But libraries were always his first love. At the dedication of the Elmer Holmes Bobst Library and Study Center in 1973, Bobst said, "this is the most extraordinary occasion of my life" and that his contribution to the library building was his way of "paying back a lifelong debt to libraries." In his autobiography Bobst further reflected on the library: "the name on the building is not what thrills me. For me, the partial payment that I have made on my debt to mankind by my gift to the Library will live on after the building crumbles, in the minds of those who will learn from

James Merrill, President John Brademas, Eudora Welty, Harold Pinter, Mrs. Elmer Holmes Bobst, and Malcolm Cowley at the 1984 Bobst Awards ceremony (courtesy NYU/Phil Berkum photo)

the books it contains and who will pass their learning on to future generations."

The Bobst Awards are a magnificent tribute to Bobst's vision and serve as a lasting symbol of his and his wife's commitment to literature and letters. For the last eighteen years of his life Bobst shared his ideas and dreams with his wife Mamdouha, who after his death in 1978 dedicated herself to carrying on his legacy. Mrs. Bobst's commitment to the Elmer Holmes Bobst Awards in Arts and Letters, while just one of many activities at the library, is her most public expression of support.

The Bobst Awards are presented in six possible categories, including, but not limited to, publishing, literary criticism, poetry, fiction, nonfiction, and drama. The Bobst Awards were designed to be flexible. Not every category is necessarily represented every year and twice special awards have been presented to particularly distinguished non-American writers. Additional categories such as biography may be added in future years at the discretion of the selection committee. The composition of the committee varies from

year to year but is always comprised of scholars, writers, and librarians involved with American letters from the faculty of New York University. Over the years the selection committee has included distinguished poets, novelists, publishers, editors, and critics, including Pulitzer Prize-winner Galway Kinnell, Robert Giroux, M. L. Rosenthal, Denis Donoghue, Josephine Hendin, Philip Schultz, Lucy Rosenthal, Richard Sennett, and Aileen Ward.

At that first awards ceremony on 25 October 1983 awards were presented in all six original categories. Perhaps most poignant was the award given in publishing to Alfred Knopf. In his citation New York University President John Brademas said of Knopf, "We are proud to honor you as a distinguished publisher whose tastes and values have set a standard of uncompromising excellence . . . in the cultural and creative life of America in this century." Commenting on Knopf's legendary attention to detail, President Brademas added, "books with the Knopf imprint are tributes to your own independent taste and judgment. Indeed, your books are themselves works of art." The Bobst Award was Knopf's last public honor. Less than a year later, Alfred Knopf, dean of American publishing, died at the age of ninety-one.

But Knopf was in very good company that evening. In the fiction category the Bobst Award was presented to Bernard Malamud, cited by President Brademas as a man whose "writings have revealed with haunting clarity and humor the paradoxical encounter of American optimism with the Jewish immigrant's understanding of guilt and despair." He added, "you create a magic barrel in which anything might be possible, were it not for the lessons of convention, fidelity, assimilation and persecution that bind us to a simpler reality and a deeper moral awareness."

For literary criticism Kenneth Burke was presented with the Bobst Award for the "extraordinary scope of his critical writings and the plenitude of his perception." Burke was cited as the principal exponent of the proposition that language itself constitutes one of the crucial forms of our creative life, and his work was cited for its transcendence of the orthodox limits of disciplines.

Also honored at the 1983 ceremony were Arthur Miller for drama, Denise Levertov for poetry, and Russell Baker for nonfiction. Of Miller, President Brademas specifically cited the playwright's "deep commitment to political justice and the rights of individuals" as well as his ability to "dramatize disturbing aspects of our experience that too many of us neither see or choose not to see." Levertov was recognized for her "sense of the connections among poetry, morality and common experience which enable us to use the imagination as means of opening up reality," and Mr. Baker for his irreverent wit which "revealed the passions, frustrations and absurdities of our times."

The elegance of the first Bobst Awards celebration dinner, held in the library's soaring twelve-story atrium, not only provided a glamorous setting in which to honor such accomplished writers but also served as a fitting backdrop for a very special announcement. To underscore the historical affinity between libraries and writers symbolized by the awards, that evening Mrs. Bobst established the Mamdouha S. Bobst Book Endowment for the library and pledged $500,000 toward its eventual goal of $5 million. In the years since its creation the Bobst Book Endowment has become the cornerstone of the library's efforts to build its research collections and allowed it to offer increased avenues for scholarship and discovery. In 1987 Mrs. Bobst pledged an additional $500,000 to the endowment, thus renewing her commitment to the library and further extending her husband's lifelong passion for libraries and knowledge.

The second presentation of the Bobst Awards, in 1984, though somewhat more subtle, boasted a trio of writers easily on a literary par with the winners of the first awards. The categories that year were literary criticism, poetry, and fiction. Malcolm Cowley was honored for his "extraordinary contributions to American letters and to an understanding of our times." President Brademas then recalled the words of Alfred Kazin, who remarked that Mr. Cowley "represented the most dramatically satisfying confrontations of a new book by a gifted, uncompromising critical intelligence."

The 1984 Bobst Award in poetry was given to James Merrill, whose work was honored as "fusing the fine craftsmanship of the poet, the deep feeling for human relationships of the mature artist, and the apocryphal vision of the seer." Merrill accepted the award by reciting from his own poetry.

Citing her profound sensitivity and vivid imagination, President Brademas presented the 1984 Bobst Award for fiction to Eudora Welty. Quoting from the writer, President Brademas praised Welty for her ability "not to point the finger in judgment, but to part a curtain . . . the veil of indifference to each other's presence, each other's wonder, each other's human plight." Upon accepting the award Welty charmed the dinner guests by recounting the somewhat restrictive lending policies of the library she used as a child. "No matter what book I wanted to take out, the librarian would say, 'What do you mean by taking this book?' So I thought reading was something to do on the sneak and not for pleasure." In concluding, Welty further delighted her rapt audience. She said, with innocent irony, "Who would think that a library would give you an award—besides allowing you to take books out?"

In 1984 a special Elmer Holmes Bobst Award in Arts and Letters was presented. This award is given to distinguished non-American writers whose works nonetheless represent the same vital contributions to the world of letters as those of their American counterparts. This special award differs from the original in that it does not carry a cash prize.

The first recipient of the special Bobst Award was Harold Pinter, the eminent British dramatist whose works reassess the relationship between the playwright, the play, and the audience, and of the nature of truth and knowledge. Pinter accepted his special award by reading his own short piece called "Precisely." Its chilling dialogue exemplified Pinter's belief that "there are no hard distinctions between what is real and what is unreal, nor between what is true and what is false."

After a two-year hiatus the Bobst Awards were again presented in the spring of 1987. That year three categories were represented: nonfiction, fiction, and poetry. *New York Times* correspondent Flora Lewis was cited in nonfiction for her journalism that "transcends the mere reporting of facts to arrive at larger truths." President Brademas further saluted Lewis's "prudence, patience . . . good sense and wisdom," and her "rational voice in an often irrational world." Clearly moved by the honor, Lewis gracefully accepted her award while at the same time questioning whether she could claim nonfiction. She called fiction writing "the clearest truth," and poetry "that which comes the closest to a truth that can only be imagined." She concluded by saying, "we musn't be too afraid to ask questions that either don't have answers or don't have easy answers. It is better to put questions than it is to hide what we are asking." The 1987 Bobst Award for fiction was given to John Updike, cited as "a spectacular stylist" and "chief chronicler of the American middle class." Updike was further honored for his exploration of questions "that have preoccupied philosophers, theologians and ordinary people for centuries . . . and his ability to make a reader feel as if his mind has been read." Updike, in his acceptance speech, said, "this is not the first time New York University has given me the courage to go on." In 1949 Updike tested his then nascent literary ambitions by taking a battery of aptitude tests. Fortunately for us, Updike's less-than-dazzling test scores in accounting and spatial relations confirmed his belief that it was in writing that he "should persevere with a high heart and I did and here I am back for more reassurance." Updike also set forth his ideas on creativity. "Fiction or poetry or playwriting or history or

biography conceived as narrative arts is only partly a social act. An imitation of creation is afoot with some of the mysticism implied when that word is spelled with a capital C. For the moments of actual creation we are submitting to something beyond us. . . . Creative activity is to a degree childish and primitive and predates as it were the critical faculties. The solemn bliss of the process indeed is so keen and so faithful that one feels quite pleasantly sheepish accepting such additional award as the Elmer Holmes Bobst Award."

In poetry that year, the award was presented to Louis Simpson, recognized as "one of our greatest and most plain-spoken poets of war" who "devised a new poetic form . . . by combining the technique of characterization usually found in fiction with poetic narrative." In his remarks Simpson said, "We feel a truth in us that is difficult to express, for it involves our whole being. This truth has one thing to say at a time and only one way of saying it. An absolute language and form. Our task is to listen to it. Poetry isn't writing, not really. It is the art of listening."

Finally in 1987 a special Bobst Award was given to Sir Harold Acton. Although Acton was unable to attend, President Brademas traveled to Italy later that year to present him personally with his award. The president cited Acton's lifetime devotion to arts and letters and his prominent place in the Aesthetic Movement at Oxford University in the 1920s, and commended him for his self-professed lifelong avocation of "hunting the Philistines." Acton's award was accepted at the ceremony by Italy's consul-general in New York, Ambassador Francesco Corrias.

Although there are dozens of literary awards, each with its own particular focus, the Elmer Holmes Bobst Awards in Arts and Letters is the first such award from a library to honor a writer's lifetime achievement, rather than a single volume. It is thus freed from partisanship and even predictability that sometimes accompanies some of the other literary awards.

The next presentation of the Bobst Awards is scheduled to coincide with the fifteenth anniversary of the Bobst Library in the fall of 1988. Naturally, this celebration will be held in the library because, as Bobst Award-winner Arthur Miller commented back in 1983, the library was "the perfect place to salute writers."

Literary Research Archives VI: The Modern Literary Manuscripts Collection in the Special Collections of the Washington University Libraries

Anne Posega

Washington University Libraries, Special Collections

Washington University's Modern Literature Collection was begun in 1964 by William Matheson, who was the first Chief of Rare Books and Special Collections. Matheson and those who worked with him to develop a collecting policy knew they were faced with a difficult task. Many twentieth-century writers had already placed materials in other collections, and Washington University recognized the potential difficulty of acquiring complete collections of manuscripts and books from established writers. Competing for the materials of these writers could obviously be costly, and, in the long run, simply not worthwhile if their papers were scattered in various institutions. A different approach was necessary. Matheson enlisted the help of five authors, Mona Van Duyn, Donald Finkel, Constance Undang, Stanley Elkin, and Naomi Lebowitz, all associated with the university, to suggest writers who they thought would become important figures. Matheson requested that they keep in mind authors who were, "(1) to some degree neglected or underestimated, and/or (2) on the threshold of greater recognition, and (3) not to their knowledge extensively committed to another library." The last point was particularly important because the library wanted to "build a strong working collection of manuscripts and correspondence." These consultants made a list comprised of forty-six authors (thirty poets and sixteen novelists). All but two of the authors on the list were still living; five writers were British, one Canadian, and the majority American. It was feasible that manuscripts could be obtained from all those listed.

At the time the list was made, some observers were skeptical about many of the names, several of which were virtually unknown. But it is obvious that the choices made were good ones, as one "obscure" writer after another went on to win important critical acclaim, honored with prizes such as the National Book Award. The use of a jury of peers in compiling the list was clearly successful. Poet Mona Van Duyn, one of the authors consulted, edited the magazine *Perspective* with her husband Jarvis Thurston, and because she was acquainted with many of the authors on the list she agreed to write to all of them to solicit manuscripts for the library.

The library's top priority was to collect all published works by or about the authors, including first editions, variants, translations, and any other books to which they had in some way contributed (for example, anthologies). The library was able to establish good working relationships with varied British and American book dealers and was successful in obtaining most of the books it wanted. The clear collecting focus has allowed the library to keep closely to its list, and the holdings for the authors on the list (which has expanded to total 115) are for the most part near-complete collections of publications. Mona Van Duyn's solicitation of manuscripts was also quite successful. Some of the early acquisitions were papers of James Dickey, George P. Elliott, Isabella Gardner, James Merrill, May Swenson, and David Wagoner. One of the initial offers the library made to the writers on its list was a free appraisal for income tax purposes. Other writers, who indicated a desire to send the library their papers but were too busy to get them gathered, packed up, and sent off, were offered a $100 payment to do so. This payment became a standard offer to writers who were donating their papers. Some of the papers acquired in the early years of the department were those of writers who were affiliated with Washington University or, in the case of William Gass and Howard Nemerov, were later to join the Washington University faculty. Besides Gass and Nemerov were Stanley Elkin, Donald Finkel, Jarvis Thurston, Constance Urdang, and Mona Van Duyn. Also solicited for

Samuel Beckett manuscripts (courtesy of the Modern Literary Manuscripts Collection, Special Collections, Washington University Libraries; photograph by Jack Fisher)

the collection were manuscripts of Washington University alumni, including A. E. Hotchner, Fannie Hurst, Josephine Johnson, Shepherd Mead, and William Jay Smith. Special Collections was also able to obtain manuscripts through dealers and by the early 1970s had in hand manuscripts for Conrad Aiken, Samuel Beckett, Robert Creeley, Robert Duncan, William Everson, Elizabeth Jennings, David Meltzer, Muriel Spark, and Alexander Trocchi. Other acquisitions, while not strictly keeping to the original author list, nonetheless met the criteria originally set. Among these were collections relating to Tom Clark, Babette Deutsch, Erica Marx, George Marion O'Donnell, the Trigram Press, and Walter Lowenfels. Throughout the development of the collection, emphasis was placed on gathering *interesting* manuscripts and correspondence. It is inefficient to acquire large amounts of manuscripts if

the space needed to house them and the time required to process them are disproportionate to the interest of the manuscripts themselves, and out of necessity, *quantity* is secondary while *quality* is a prerequisite.

During the 1970s the manuscript collecting at Washington University decreased greatly, largely due to a change in tax law. The Tax Reform Act of 1969 made donations of self-created work ineligible for tax deduction. The tax deduction which formerly had been allowed was often sufficiently large to encourage writers to donate appraised papers, which was the case with more than twenty of the American authors whose papers Washington University was collecting. In the hopes that the former tax law would be reinstated, librarians suggested to writers that they put their papers on deposit, to be kept there permanently once the tax law changed and writers could once again take deductions for donated papers. Unfortunately the former law was not reinstated, and the university had to stop accepting papers on deposit. The likelihood that the library would be unable to purchase these deposited papers made the practice unwise, since it was not practical to do a thorough cataloging of materials that the library would not be able to purchase. The minimal cataloging done on many such collections frequently made access difficult for researchers, and because of this and the large amount of space these deposits often required, accepting papers on deposit is now generally avoided.

The policy of depositing papers caused concern in the early 1980s. Many writers whose papers were deposited at Washington University began receiving offers from other collecting institutions, and newer groups of papers were beginning to build up in the homes of the writers. Eager to deposit these papers, they began questioning the library on the department's intentions concerning their collections. It became clear that a decision could not be put off any longer or a large amount of manuscript material would be lost to the library, so Washington University applied for and received a Title II-C (Strengthening Research Library Resources) program grant from the United States Department of Education. In the introduction to the guide produced during the grant, Timothy Murray, the Curator of Manuscripts during the project, explained the project's three primary goals: "First, the Library wished to procure the funding necessary to acquire eight collections of literary papers in which it had already invested substantial acquisition and cataloging effort. Major portions of these collections were either on deposit in the Washington University Libraries or in the possession of the authors. Second, once these collections were acquired, the Library would fully catalog them and make their contents known and available to the research community. In addition, the Library proposed to catalog ten additional collections of literary manuscripts which it already owned but which had not yet been adequately cataloged. And third, Washington University proposed to prepare a guide to its entire Modern Literary Manuscript Collection and distribute it to the scholarly community." These tasks took two years to complete, and were well worth the efforts; the collections are well cataloged, and the information about them is highly accessible.

In addition to the books, manuscripts, and correspondence, a collection of little magazines was started. Many groups of materials acquired by the library contained a large variety of little magazines, particularly the John M. Bennett Papers, the Robert Creeley Papers, and the Robert Sward Papers. Broadsides and other printed ephemera are also collected and cataloged as printed holdings.

Once the collections of the authors on the original list began to build, the acquisition of related collections became inevitable. One good example of this is Robert Creeley; because of his close association with Charles Olson and Robert Duncan, it was a logical step to add their names to the collecting list. Other collections, such as those of Isabella Gardner and Lee Anderson, included large groups of correspondence from many well-known authors, such as the more than 300 letters of Allen Tate contained in the Gardner Papers. As the number of collections increases their contents become increasingly interrelated. The writers on the original list have recommended others and sometimes encouraged their friends to place their papers at Washington University, thus increasing the manuscript records of various literary circles.

One of the most important collections at Washington University is the Samuel Beckett Collection. The Irish author had been put on the original collecting list because although he was already widely known, he was not yet of worldwide repute, and thus it seemed that it would not yet be difficult or prohibitively expensive to acquire manuscripts of Beckett's works. However, most of Beckett's manuscripts up to 1965 had already been placed in other institutions, and William Matheson remarked in a 1964 letter to American bookseller Henry Wenning, "it seems clear that we will end up with little, if any, important manuscript material by Beckett." Wenning, with whom Matheson had developed a close working relationship, was eventually to play a major role in building up a large collection of Beckett manuscripts at Washington University. Through their business dealings together Beckett and Wenning had become friends, and when Beckett decided in the early 1960s to sell some of his manuscripts, it was Wenning that he asked to handle them. Wenning contacted Matheson, who had already been helping to build the library's collection of published Beckett material.

At the start of 1965 Washington University acquired its first Beckett manuscript, a typescript of the radio play *All That Fall*. Acquisitions of Beckett manuscripts continued for the next several

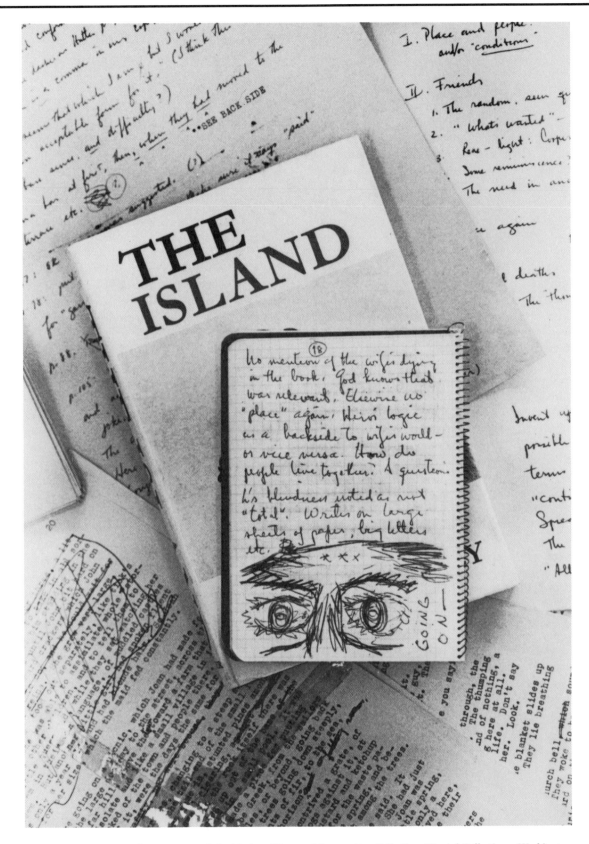

Robert Creeley manuscripts (courtesy of the Modern Literary Manuscripts Collection, Special Collections, Washington University Libraries; photograph by Herb Weitman)

years, and after five years the collection contained over 200 manuscript items and was one of the most important collections of Beckett manuscripts in the world. Beckett donated some of his manuscripts to other institutions in the 1970s, in particular to the University of Reading in England. Washington University and the University of Reading, in 1976, exchanged photocopies of portions of their Beckett manuscripts for deposit in each other's collections in an effort to make access easier for Beckett researchers on both sides of the Atlantic. In 1981 Ruby Cohn, a Beckett scholar and Washington University alumna, donated an additional group of manuscripts which included some of Beckett's more recent work. A guide to the Beckett Collection, produced in 1986 in conjunction with a special exhibition entitled "Beckett at 80," is an important catalog of a collection that the library once thought it would have little chance of acquiring.

Besides the collections of authors' papers the manuscript collection includes interesting holdings relating to the history of printing and the archives of several small presses and little magazines. The Isador Mendle Collection on the history of printing is made up of seven groupings, the first of which is the collection of James Moran Papers. Moran, a British author and historian of printing, wrote several books relating to printing, including a biography of British scholar and typographer Stanley Morison. Moran's papers consist primarily of material toward his books. The Ellic Howe Papers are another part of the collection. These consist of Howe's (a British printer) notes on the history of the printing trade, including varied documents relating to eighteenth- and nineteenth-century printing, and copies of lectures given by Howe. Correspondence makes up the bulk of the John G. Wilson materials. Wilson was a British book dealer, and his correspondence provides an inside view of the book trade. Two fine presses are also represented in the collection; the Alcuin Press and Gogmagog Press collections show book production at its various stages, and an album of designs by artist and historian of French bookbinding Leon Gruel shows another fascinating aspect of book production. Finally, there are ten groups of correspondence to and from various people in the book or printing trades; these letters, because of their variety, present a well-rounded view of the trades they discuss.

In addition to the Mendle History of Printing Collection, Special Collections houses several collections from small presses, which, because of the constant problems of trying to achieve high quality printing, frequently face an early demise. The Trigram Press, Ltd., faced such problems. Founded in 1965 in London by Asa and Penelope (Pip) Benveniste and Paul Vaughan, the press intended, according to Asa Benveniste, to "publish & print the most significant poetry/art being produced at this time, in a style which would clarify & illuminate the meaning of the text/image." Some of their publications were done in conjunction with other presses, and this led to problems; other printers had lower standards of quality, and the work they produced was frequently disappointing to the Benvenistes and Vaughan. The collection, covering 1965 to 1969 (the press lasted until 1975), contains manuscripts and correspondence from authors such as George Andrews, Lawrence Durrell, Jack Hirschman, Anselm Hollo, Christopher Logue, Edward Lucie-Smith, David Meltzer, Jeff Nuttall, Tom Raworth, Nathaniel Tarn, Jonathan Williams, and Louis Zukofsky.

The Release Press was founded in New York City in 1975 by Alan Ziegler, Larry Zirlin, and Harry Greenberg, who were also responsible for publishing *Some* magazine from 1972 to 1975. This press was interested in publishing first collections by emerging writers, good manuscripts which had not been picked up by larger publishers, and unique books, such as collaborative works, from established writers. The Release Press produced fifteen books and several broadsides during its eight-year run, including work by Jack Anderson, Philip Graham, Harry Greenberg, Karen Hubert, Bill Knott, John Love, Paul Oppedisano, B. Pelasi, Gay Phillipps, Steven Schrader, Terry Stokes, Ross Talarico, James Tate, John Yau, Alan Ziegler, Harry Zirlin, and Larry Zirlin. The collection is interesting because it is so complete; containing correspondence, manuscripts, editorial matter, business records, and ephemeral material, it gives a thorough view of all aspects of small-press operations.

Special Collections also holds the archives of *Perspective* magazine, whose twenty-eight-year run (1947-1975) was unusually long for a little magazine. *Perspective* was founded at the University of Louisville in 1947 by Jarvis Thurston and his wife, poet Mona Van Duyn. When Thurston joined the faculty at Washington University he brought the magazine with him to St. Louis in 1950. The magazine, which was produced quarterly, is notable for the quality of the work it published. Thurston, Van Duyn, and the other editors helped introduce work by such young writers as W. S. Merwin, Anthony Hecht, Douglas Woolf, Thomas McAfee, William Gass, Stanley Elkin, Donald Finkel, and Constance Urdang. The magazine's reputation as important also helped it attract contributions from many of the prominent literary figures of the time. *Perspective*'s archives contain correspondence, including two small groups of letters from Wallace Stevens and William Carlos Williams, manuscripts, editorial matter, and business records.

The collection and preservation of small-press and little-magazine archives are important because they illustrate various periods and trends in the history of literature. Many of the other archives in Special Collections offer even further detail on some of the movements that have occurred in the twentieth century, whether formally or informally organized, brief or lasting in their influence. The Progressive League Papers consist almost entirely of correspondence between league members; founded in the 1930s, the Progressive League was a London literary and political group which lasted through the early 1960s. The league, which grew from the Promethean Society, led in turn to the formation of the Contemporary Poetry and Music Circle which ran from 1957 to the early 1960s. The purpose of the Progressive League was to sponsor readings and lectures and to provide a forum for contemporary political and literary minds. The correspondence in the collection is generally made up of letters asking writers to give readings and are between the Progressive League secretaries and such writers as W. H. Auden, Robert Graves, Donald Hall, Elizabeth Jennings, V. S. Pritchett, Stevie Smith, and Enid Starkie.

The 1960s saw the start of another movement, the Sigma Project, a collaboration of international underground movements organized by Scottish author Alexander Trocchi. The Sigma Project was eclectic and amorphous and had no clear focus, but it drew a great deal of attention and was quite productive, with over thirty publications to its credit. The Trocchi Papers contain most of the manuscripts and correspondence concerning the Sigma Project, along with Trocchi's own manuscripts, material from projects Trocchi worked on in the 1960s, magazines and ephemera, and the existing archives of *Merlin* magazine. Seven issues of *Merlin* were produced from 1952 to 1955 and included such authors as Ionesco, Genet, Beckett, Creeley, Sartre, and Miller.

In the United States the 1950s and 1960s were heavily influenced by the Black Mountain movement. The Robert Creeley Papers, Washington University's largest manuscript collection, is one of the most important post-World War II literary archives. Creeley, whose writing career began in the 1940s, corresponded with several important Modernist writers who served as mentors for him, including Ezra Pound, William Carlos Williams, Louis Zukofsky, Basil Bunting, and Edward Dahlberg. Their correspondence with Creeley served to pass on the Modernist tradition. Creeley and Charles Olson inspired the Black Mountain School, named for the North Carolina college where Olson was rector and Creeley a faculty member. Over 600 letters from Olson to Creeley are contained in the Creeley Papers and show Creeley and Olson's experimentation with what Olson called "projective verse." As the Black Mountain movement grew, so did the number of people involved with it, and there is a great deal of correspondence between Creeley and other Black Mountain writers such as Robert Duncan, Denise Levertov, Ed Dorn, Paul Blackburn, Fielding Dawson, and Cid Corman. These letters, most of them written in the 1950s and 1960s, document the group's efforts to define a new poetics. The Creeley Papers also contain the existing archives of Creeley's Divers Press and the *Black Mountain Review*, two publications that were major outlets for the work of Black Mountain poets. Besides these groups of correspondence, there are also many letters from major writers outside of the Black Mountain movement, Creeley's own manuscripts and material for almost all of his published work, and a large number of runs and single issues of a variety of little magazines. Complementing Creeley's extensive Black Mountain material are the Robert Duncan Papers. In addition to his prominent role in the Black Mountain movement Duncan was a major figure in the San Francisco Bay Area movement in the 1950s and 1960s. The Duncan Papers contain correspondence with author LeRoi Jones from 1962 to 1964. These letters focus on such contemporary issues as black dada, current publishing, and other writers such as Creeley, Diane DiPrima, and Charles Olson. The remainder of the Duncan Papers consists of Duncan's correspondence and manuscripts relating to his books; the material for *A Book of Resemblances: Poems 1950-1953* is particularly notable.

During the 1970s several different movements sprang up. One of these, mail or correspondence art, is represented in the John M. Bennett Papers. Bennett, an American author and artist who is a significant figure in innovative poetry, founded Luna Bisonte Prods and produces *Lost and Found Times,* and is very active in the mail art movement. Mail art, a sort of visual literature made up of a combination of drawing, painting, stickers, rubber stamp prints, found objects, clippings, collage, and poetry, is created and then sent through the postal system. Much of the work of correspondence artists was sent to their peers, and the Bennett Papers contain hundreds of pieces by some of the most important correspondence artists from all over the world. Bennett is also involved in the use of mimeographic and xerographic techniques in producing his poetry, and his Luna Bisonte Prods (founded in 1976) publishes such works as broadsides, rubber stamp art, labels, and stickers. Besides the large quantity of mail art Bennett's papers include Bennett's own manuscripts, printed items from Luna Bisonte Prods, unusual small press publications, and Bennett's extensive correspondence with a variety of poets, artists, and small press editors.

In New York City the 1960s and 1970s saw a great deal of activity by avant-garde New York poets. These writers gave readings at Le Deux Magots, Le Metro Cafe, and St. Mark's Church, and among them was writer Carol Bergé. Bergé, whose papers from 1970 to the present are housed at Washington University, worked with poet Paul Blackburn and others to organize readings and workshops in New York City. In 1962 Bergé attended the important Vancouver poetry seminar at the University of British Columbia and wrote an account of the event entitled *The Vancouver Report* (1964). Bergé also founded *Center* magazine in 1970 and was the only editor during the magazine's ten-year run. The Bergé Papers contain an extensive collection of letters between Bergé and contemporary literary figures along with correspondence, manuscripts, and other publishing material toward most of her post-1970 books. The archives of *Center* magazine are included, and of special interest are the flyers, brochures, and announcements of "happenings" and readings Bergé was involved with in the 1970s in New York City.

Literary controversy is often difficult to document. Two collections at Washington University contain information about two very different controversies that have occurred in the twentieth century. Included in the William Jay Smith Papers

are manuscripts and materials toward Smith's book *Spectra Hoax,* tracing the "new school" of poetry created in 1916 by Witter Bynner and Arthur Davison Ficke under the pseudonyms Emanuel Morgan and Anne Knish. Morgan and Knish sent their volume *Spectra: New Poems* to a number of magazine editors and poetry reviewers. The preface to the book was Anne Knish's explanation of the book's purpose and a definition of Spectric poetry. Spectrism immediately gathered critics and proponents from some of literature's top ranks, and a third poet, Elijah Hay (Marjorie Allen Seiffert), joined Morgan and Knish's small Spectrist group. When several Emanuel Morgan poems were accepted by Harriet Monroe for *Poetry* it was clear that the Spectrist movement had arrived; even William Carlos Williams wrote to them about their work. The more Spectra fame spread, the more mysterious its poets became; while they corresponded with people, they were rarely seen, and rumors began that these three poets did not actually exist. In 1918 Bynner was giving a lecture in Detroit, part of which discussed Spectric poetry, when a young man in the audience stood up and asked Bynner if he were not really Emanuel Morgan, and poet Arthur Davison Ficke really Anne Knish. Bynner had to answer yes. This hoax is detailed in *Spectra Hoax.* Smith's papers relating to the book are extensive, consisting of correspondence, manuscripts, and editorial matter. Equally important are the materials in the Smith Papers which relate to his other work. Smith has produced more than thirty books of poetry, criticism, translations, and children's literature, and is highly regarded as a translator. He is responsible for bringing the work of many foreign authors to the United States, and his papers demonstrate his varied work. Included are hundreds of letters to literary figures, many from Eastern European writers, manuscripts, and editorial material toward all of his published work, manuscripts from other authors, and miscellaneous material relating to specific writing panels, academic work, literary awards panels, Smith's travel, and his personal life.

A more contemporary incident is what has become known as "The Great Naropa Poetry Wars," which also serves as the title to Tom Clark's book about the controversy. Clark investigated the Naropa Institute, a Buddhist studies center in Boulder, Colorado, where in 1975 a confrontation occurred between poet W. S. Merwin and the founder and director of the

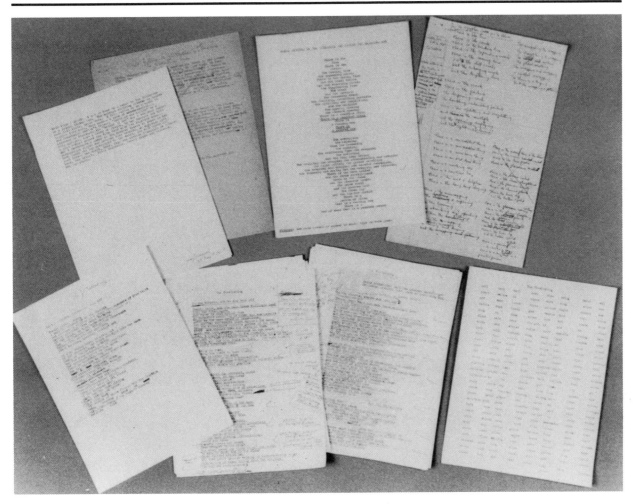

May Swenson and James Dickey manuscripts (courtesy of the Modern Literary Manuscripts Collection, Special Collections, Washington University Libraries; photograph by Jack Fisher)

Naropa Institute, Chogyam Trungpa. Clark's book focuses on this incident, which is controversial even today in the American poetry community. *The Great Naropa Poetry Wars,* published in 1980, was preceded by another controversial book by Clark, *The Master* (1979). *The Master* is a study of the influence of Naropa's poetics department, "The Jack Kerouac School of Disembodied Poetics," on American poetics. The Tom Clark Papers contain manuscripts, research notes, printed materials, correspondence, and miscellany relating to the books, an archive that will be an important source of information for this controversy. Also included in the Clark Papers are correspondence, manuscripts, and editorial material relating to Clark's second book, *The Sand Burg* (1966). The letters in this group discuss the poetry scene of the mid 1960s and offer a look at Clark's development as a poet.

Frequently the papers of a literary figure

are tremendously interesting in themselves, not only documenting movements or events but also thoroughly documenting that one person and his or her own work and friendships. The Conrad Aiken Papers are such a collection. Aiken, a somewhat neglected literary figure despite his important role in American Modernism, was a member of one of the famous 1910-1915 Harvard classes that included Robert Benchley, E. E. Cummings, T. S. Eliot, Walter Lippmann, and John Reed. In his senior year Aiken left Harvard to travel to Europe, where he met Ezra Pound and Amy Lowell. Aiken later graduated and moved to Europe, where he wrote and reviewed for several periodicals such as *Dial, New Republic,* and *Poetry;* by 1925 he had moved to Boston where he continued his productive writing career. Aiken's papers are made up primarily of his correspondence with Robert Linscott, an editor with Houghton

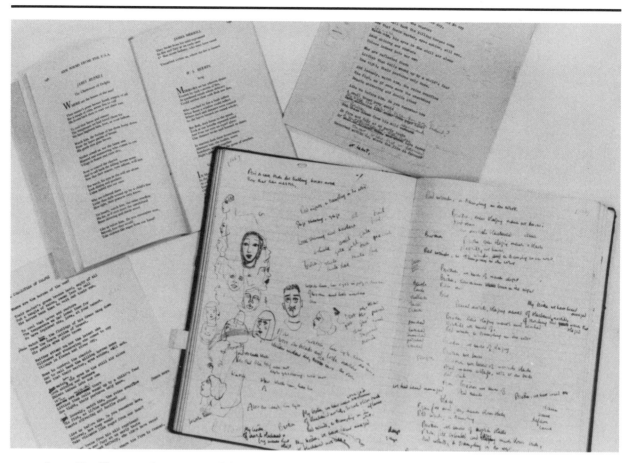

James Merrill manuscripts (courtesy of the Modern Literary Manuscripts Collection, Special Collections, Washington University Libraries; photograph by Cindy Ilges)

Mifflin and later Random House, whose friendship with Aiken started in 1917. These letters record Aiken's progress as a writer and his frustration at his lack of popular success. Many of the letters are very personal, discussing Aiken's two divorces, his friends, and his fellow writers, particularly T. S. Eliot and John Gould Fletcher. They offer a firsthand view of the literary 1920s, and the Aiken-Linscott correspondence serves as a memorial to their lengthy and honest friendship.

Also of interest as groups of long-term correspondence between two people are the Elizabeth Bishop Papers and the May Swenson Papers. Elizabeth Bishop was a popular and critically acclaimed poet, winning major awards for four of her five books. The Bishop Papers consist of correspondence between poet Anne Stevenson and Bishop between 1963 and 1970. During this time Stevenson was working on her critical biography, *Elizabeth Bishop* (1966), and the correspondence, which became a primary resource for Stevenson, is filled with Bishop's biographical information,

thoughts on her work, and comments on the current state of literature. The two writers became friends, and these letters show not only their relationship as friends but also Bishop's role as a mentor and her own reflections upon her life and her writing. The May Swenson Papers also contain a large number of Bishop letters. Swenson, a poet, playwright, critic, translator, and editor, was a close friend of Bishop's, and her papers contain 268 of their letters written from 1950 until Bishop's death in 1979. Also in the Swenson Papers are manuscripts and editorial material toward most of her books, and varied correspondence, including letters from editors John Hall Wheelock and Burroughs Mitchell.

The Isabella Gardner Papers are another collection important largely because of the correspondence included. Gardner, never a recipient of popular or critical acclaim, is nonetheless an important literary figure. She exerted a great deal of influence on younger poets and in 1951 became associate editor of *Poetry* magazine. While working on *Poetry* Gardner met several Chicago poets who were just emerging, including Karl Shapiro, John Logan, Reuel Denney, Wallace Fowlie, and later, Paul Carroll and Galway Kinnell. Gardner's many friendships with other writers are illustrated through her letters, and of special interest are the more than 300 letters between Allen Tate (Gardner's fourth husband) and Gardner. The collection also contains some of Gardner's own manuscripts and a great deal of ephemera from all periods of her life.

Yet another writer whose collection is important primarily for its correspondence is that of George Marion O'Donnell. O'Donnell, born in 1914 in Mississippi, became a follower of the Agrarian School while studying at Vanderbilt; he met John Crowe Ransom, Donald Davidson, and Allen Tate and maintained a steady correspondence with these three founders of Southern New Criticism. He also wrote to such authors as Ezra Pound, Basil Bunting, and Louis Zukofsky seeking advice, and they in turn offered encouragement. O'Donnell never reached his full potential as a poet and never produced a book. But he had a successful academic career, and his correspondence demonstrates the connections he had to many notable figures, including John Berryman, Truman Capote, William Inge, Flannery O'Connor, Robert Penn Warren, Wallace Stevens, Eudora Welty, and Delmore Schwartz.

Correspondence is also the main content of the Ivy Compton-Burnett Papers. Compton-Burnett, a prolific British novelist, was a reticent correspondent, and her letters provide a rare look into her life. Among the correspondence is a group of 167 letters from Compton-Burnett to English novelist and editor Kay Dick, and ninety-nine pieces of correspondence to Compton-Burnett's typist Cicely Grieg concerning the production of some of Compton-Burnett's manuscripts. Babette Deutsch, a versatile and productive American writer born in 1895, spent several decades in New York City where she met American literary figures, and her papers consist primarily of correspondence with these writers. Included are letters from William Carlos Williams, Marianne Moore, Elizabeth Bishop, Conrad Aiken, E. A. Robinson, Theodore Roethke, Thomas MacGreevy, and Dorothy Richardson. The Babette Deutsch Papers also contain a good deal of material relating to *The Collected Poems of Babette Deutsch* (1966).

The James Dickey Papers are significant for both correspondence and manuscripts in the collection. The correspondence in the Dickey Papers numbers over 1,000 letters covering the years 1954 to 1970. These letters are from editors, publishers, literary figures, and friends, and many of the letters from literary figures include manuscripts by these writers. The bulk of the collection is made up of Dickey's manuscript drafts of poems, reviews, essays, translations, and addresses. Dickey's manuscripts are very heavily revised, with the finished work often bearing little or no resemblance to the first draft. One can watch the progress of the work through each revised stage from first draft through proofs and the published version.

A collection which consists primarily of manuscripts and is one of the most important collections at Washington University is the James Merrill Papers. Merrill was one of the first authors selected for the Modern Literary Manuscripts Collection and one of the first to commit his manuscripts to Washington University. His papers, which have grown steadily, reflect Merrill's always-increasing literary reputation. Merrill, who has won several important literary awards, is widely read even beyond academic and literary circles despite the hermetic nature of his poetry. The collection includes thousands of pages of notebooks, typescripts, worksheets, and galleys. The drafts are meticulously reworked and show the progress of the work and the careful effort put into each piece. The Merrill collection is one of the best in the Modern Literary Manuscripts Collection to demonstrate the transformation of a poem. (James Merrill's written permission is required for access by researchers.)

The Modern Literary Manuscripts Collection also houses an extensive collection of the papers of poet Howard Nemerov, who received a 1987 National Medal of Arts. Nemerov, a professor at Washington University, is known mainly for his poetry but also writes novels, short stories, essays, and criticism. His large collection is varied, containing a great number of manuscripts and correspondence. Particularly interesting are the more than 800 letters from longtime Nemerov correspondents Kenneth Burke, Maxine Kumin, Kay Boyle, and Reed Whittemore. Completing the Nemerov Papers are business correspondence, photographs, and memorabilia.

While most of the collections in the Washington University manuscript department are modern, there are other valuable groups of manuscripts covering a wide period of time. Two of these collections are the William K. Bixby and the George N. Meissner Collections. Bixby and

Meissner, collectors during the late nineteenth and early twentieth centuries, donated to Washington University not only large rare-book collections but also extensive and varied autograph and manuscript collections. Bixby's autograph collection, numbering 891 items, includes such pieces as the original manuscript of Alexander Pope's *Windsor Forest*; holograph poems by Henry David Thoreau; letters and a manuscript of Robert Burns; a Washington Irving notebook; a number of American presidential letters and documents; 55 pieces of Emile Zola correspondence; and a large collection of Eugene Field materials. Meissner also acquired extensive autographs and manuscripts. Included in the Meissner Collection are ten Books of Hours; documents or letters of Americus Vespucci, Michelangelo, and Peter Paul Rubens; letters and documents of American presidents and political and military figures; a Robert Burns manuscript; Eugene Field manuscripts and letters; material relating to Washington Irving, James Whitcomb Riley, Oliver Wendell Holmes, and Walt Whitman; and over thirty letters and manuscripts by Mark Twain.

Special Collections has, since the mid 1960s, audiotape-recorded poetry readings, lectures, and other literary events of the faculty and visiting authors. Some individual authors have contributed recordings of their work so that the Washington University Audiotape Collection now includes recordings by over 125 literary figures, a number that continues to grow.

Certainly the variety and quality of the manuscript collections at Washington University demonstrate that William Matheson and the consultants who helped him begin the manuscript collection in 1964 did an exemplary job. The Modern Literary Manuscripts Collection represents a carefully thought-out and well-chosen list of important literary figures; the collections mesh and complement each other and serve as a significant research archive for scholars.

Materials in the Manuscript Collection are available for use by all qualified researchers between the hours of 8:30 A.M. and 5:00 P.M. Monday through Friday. Researchers are encouraged to contact the Curator of Manuscripts for further information before planning a visit, since certain collections have restricted access and others may require special permissions from donors or copyright holders. The *Guide to the Modern Literary Manuscripts Collection* is available free of charge; questions and guide requests should be addressed to: Curator of Manuscripts, Special Collections, Washington University Libraries, Campus Box 1061, St. Louis, Missouri 63130.

Publishing Fiction at LSU Press

Michael Pinkston
Louisiana State University Press

For nearly a century, university presses adhered, virtually without exception, to the principle that original contemporary fiction–and most especially novel-length fiction–was not appropriate to their publishing mission. For the most part, it was felt that university presses should stick to their lasts–namely the publication of specialized scholarly books. Fiction, as well as poetry, most conceded, should be left in the hands of commercial publishers.

However, in the early 1960s, changing conditions in the marketplace meant that many commercial houses had to cut back and in some cases even eliminate their poetry programs. Not long afterward, those same houses also began to publish fewer and fewer works of serious fiction. Hoping to help fill the void left by the commercial sector, a few university presses began to publish creative work–at first poetry and then fiction. Louisiana State University Press was one of the first university presses to make a commitment to the publication of contemporary poetry and fiction, and it remains today one of the leading university press publishers of creative work. While our poetry program, which began in 1964 and has seen the publication of more than seventy-five collections of poetry, is highly regarded, LSU Press is perhaps more noted for its fiction program.

In 1968 LSU Press, under the leadership of Richard L. Wentworth, now director of the University of Illinois Press, became the first university press to establish an ongoing program in the publication of contemporary fiction. Our first fiction title was *Night in Funland,* a collection of stories by the Missouri writer William Peden. For the next decade, we continued to publish short-story collections, albeit at a modest rate made necessary by the financial exigencies of the early 1970s. Among the story collections published during that period were *How They Chose the Dead* (1973) by Hollis Summers and *The Man Who Tried Out for Tarzan* (1973) by Harry H. Taylor.

However, the press increasingly received inquiries, first from authors and then from agents, about the publication of novels, and we began seriously to consider whether, in light of then-current conditions, we could justify the exclusion of full-length fiction from our program. The decision was by no means an easy one. The evaluation of fiction is quite different from that of scholarly writing, even with the assistance of specialists. More troublesome, however, was the realization that marketing such books was an even greater challenge. The audience for a specific scholarly book can usually be readily identified. The audience for a good novel, on the other hand, is often an elusive target; and, while one ostensible advantage of the purchase of independent publishing houses by conglomerates was to provide large infusions of cash to permit publishers to "fully exploit the property," no university press has ever received risk capital from its parent institution. Ultimately, we decided that to be published well, if modestly, was better than not to be published at all, and we took the leap into full-length fiction.

Correcting a publishing myth is about as easy as grabbing a handful of quicksilver, but nonetheless this seems an appropriate place to go on record that John Kennedy Toole's *A Confederacy of Dunces* was *not* the first novel published by LSU Press–or even the second. The first, published in 1978, was *Passage Through Gehenna* by Madison Jones. We had been concerned–probably too much so–that a novel published by a university press would immediately be assumed not to have been good enough to be published by a trade house. Madison Jones was, and is, an established writer with impeccable credentials. He had published five novels–among them the wonderfully well-received *A Cry of Absence*–but *Passage Through Gehenna* had been the victim of a policy decision to discontinue all fiction by the publisher with which it had been placed. Since he was aware of our short-story program, Jones inquired about our interest in his novel. He didn't know what he was starting. *Passage Through Gehenna* was published to excellent critical notices and modest but adequate sales. Virtually no one questioned why an established novelist would pub-

121

L. E. Phillabaum (left), director of LSU Press, and former directors Richard L. Wentworth and Charles East

lish with a university press, and certainly no one questioned the book's right to be published. We considered the novel program to be well launched.

Later in 1978 LSU Press published two works of fiction by Allen Wier, a native Texan. *Blanco,* Wier's first novel, was published concurrently with *Things About to Disappear,* a story collection. The simultaneous publication of two books by the same author—not a unique but nonetheless an unusual occurrence—helped to generate a good deal of press attention. It was "a significant debut in American fiction and an admirable achievement for LSU, which seems to be willing to move into the gap in our literature which is appearing as the New York houses become increasingly cautious and first-novel-shy," noted Garret Epps in the *New Republic.* Doris Grumbach, writing in the *Saturday Review,* described *Blanco* as "a deeply stirring novel about the large tragedies of lonely, empty, unrealized lives."

Blanco and *Things About to Disappear* were later published in a one-volume paperback edition by Avon Books. The warm reception accorded his first two books helped Wier secure a

trade publisher, Simon and Schuster, for his third, *Departing as Air,* published in 1983. It would be wise to mention here that LSU Press has never tried to usurp the place of commercial publishers in regard to the publication of fiction; we merely wish to be a home to quality work that, for whatever reason, has not found a place with a trade house. And while we cherish the relationships we have with all of our authors, we are pleased rather than saddened when a fiction writer whose career we have helped to launch subsequently moves on to a trade publisher, where the financial rewards may be greater.

One of the most talked-about publishing events in recent memory occurred in May 1980, with the appearance of *A Confederacy of Dunces* by John Kennedy Toole. While the story of the book's publication has by now become publishing legend, it nonetheless bears repeating.

John Kennedy Toole was born in New Orleans in December 1937. He attended Tulane University and Columbia University and taught for brief periods at Hunter College, in New York, the University of Southwestern Louisiana, in Lafayette, and Dominican College, in New Orleans.

Toole enlisted in the army for two years, during 1962 and 1963, most of which time he spent in Puerto Rico teaching English as a second language to inductees. It was during this period that he wrote the first draft of *A Confederacy of Dunces*. After his discharge he returned to New Orleans and attempted unsuccessfully to find a publisher for the novel while simultaneously revising and polishing the manuscript. In 1969 Toole committed suicide.

After Toole's death his mother, Thelma Ducoing Toole, continued to try to place *A Confederacy of Dunces* with a publisher. She sent the manuscript to "eight or nine" commercial houses in New York, but none were willing to invest in a lengthy comic novel about New Orleans by an author who was no longer living. Nearly eight years after her son's death Mrs. Toole approached Walker Percy, who was at the time teaching at Loyola University, in New Orleans. Mrs. Toole called him—several times, as he has said—in an effort to persuade him to read her son's manuscript. One day Percy found Mrs. Toole standing before him in his office with not just a manuscript but a bulky, badly smeared carbon at that. His hope was that it would be as bad as he expected, which he would know before the end of the first page. As subsequent events have shown, that did not prove to be the case. After his tentative initial probing, he was seized by the book and unable to lay it aside—an experience that has been repeated by thousands of readers since. Percy's commitment to the book was such that he encouraged the editors of the *New Orleans Review* to publish an excerpt from it. When the issue appeared he sent a copy to L. E. Phillabaum, who had become director of LSU Press in 1975, and asked if the press would like to look at the complete manuscript.

It is difficult to describe the enthusiasm with which the manuscript was greeted at LSU Press. Happily, the degree of the press's commitment to the book from the outset is recorded in a letter from Phillabaum to Percy, dated 26 February 1979: "We have completed our reading, and I'm completely stunned by the whole situation. The book is absolutely marvelous, but why is it still a manuscript? Hasn't anyone else seen it? It's wild, wacky, and brilliant—fantastic characterization, dialogue that keeps surprising from beginning to end. Obviously I need not tell you these things. But I have to wonder who this guy was, what else he did, and why haven't I heard about him before. In other words, yes, we want to do

the book. . . . The thing is just too darn good not to be published."

Our initial printing of 2,500 copies, which is what we had done on our earlier novels, was quickly sold out. The LSU Press edition has now gone through an additional eight printings, and there are now more than 59,000 copies of our hardcover edition in print. The book was on the *Washington Post Book World* best-seller list for five months in 1980. It was reviewed both widely and well, with critical notices appearing in almost every major publication, including the *New York Times Book Review*, *Time*, *Newsweek*, the *Boston Globe*, the *Chicago Sun-Times*, the *Los Angeles Times*, and many, many more. *A Confederacy of Dunces* was also the subject of numerous feature articles and stories on radio and television. The book was selected by both the Book-of-the-Month Club and the Quality Paperback Book Club. Paperback rights were licensed to Grove Press early on, and the Grove edition has sold about 750,000 copies. British rights were awarded to Penguin Books/Allen Lane in a transatlantic auction. Translation rights have been sold in France, West Germany, Spain (for translation into both Spanish and Catalan), Italy, Denmark, Finland, Sweden, the Netherlands, Norway, Brazil, Greece, Israel, and Czechoslovakia. Film rights were sold for $150,000. Even now, the book continues to generate interest. In 1986 radio dramatization rights were licensed to the British Broadcasting Corporation.

A Confederacy of Dunces was nominated for the Los Angeles Times Book Award for fiction and for the PEN/Faulkner Award. The book's highest achievement came in the spring of 1981 when it was awarded the Pulitzer Prize for fiction.

A Confederacy of Dunces served to give greater credibility to the press's fiction program and certainly brought it greater national visibility. But credit for the success of the fiction program at LSU Press cannot go exclusively to one book. The LSU Press fiction program prior to the publication of *A Confederacy of Dunces*, though fledgling, was already a healthy one, and the program has grown to its present stature because of the cumulative effect of all of the works we have published.

At one with the press's commitment to contemporary American fiction has been the belief that outstanding fictional works from other countries should be made available to American readers. One of the more notable achievements of

Dust jacket for LSU Press's acclaimed posthumous publication of Toole's only novel. The book was awarded the Pulitzer Prize in 1981.

LSU Press in this decade has been its association with the Pegasus Prize for Literature, an international award established in 1976 by Mobil Corporation to introduce into this country distinguished literary works from other nations. Presented on a country-by-country basis, the prize includes a monetary award, a medal depicting Pegasus, and publication (and, when necessary, translation) of the prizewinning work. Since 1980 LSU Press has been the publisher of the winning volumes.

The system established for selecting the award winners ensures that only works of quality are chosen. A five-member committee, which consists of three representatives from the worlds of literature and scholarship along with one representative each from Mobil and LSU Press, determines the countries in which the awards will be given. An independent selection committee in each nation chooses the winners. The three distinguished literary and scholarly representatives who have served on the committee to date are

Paul Engle, poet, novelist, and former head of the University of Iowa Writers' School; Jonathan Kistler, Professor Emeritus of English Literature at Colgate University; and William Jay Smith, poet, translator, and educator.

Thus far the partnership between Mobil and LSU Press has led to the publication of four widely acclaimed novels. The first was Kirsten Thorup's *Baby,* translated from the Danish by Nadia Christensen, which came out in 1980. The selection committee, headed by Thorkild Bjornvig, a leading Danish poet and cofounder of the Danish Academy of Literature, chose *Baby* as the best Danish novel of the 1970s. The *Los Angeles Times* named the translation one of the best books of 1980 and concluded: "Were it not for the Pegasus Prize for Literature *Baby* . . . would not now be available in English. One must wonder what other great works of European fiction we are missing."

The same might be said about books from Africa, and it was from the Ivory Coast that the next Pegasus Prize work came–Tidiane Dem's novel *Masseni,* published in 1982 in a translation by Frances Frenaye five years after its appearance in the original French. The selection committee chose *Masseni* as that country's best recent novel. Set in the Ivory Coast during the early years of the century, *Masseni* recalls a vanished society in all its color, drama, and humanity.

The third Pegasus Prize work published by LSU Press was Cees Nooteboom's *Rituals,* a novel from the Netherlands that appeared in 1983 in a translation by Adrienne Dixon. Written in 1980, the novel had earlier won the Netherlands' prestigious F. Bordewijk Prize. The chairman of the selection committee was Joost de Wit, director of the Foundation for the Promotion of the Translation of Dutch Literary Works. *Rituals,* which was selected by the Book-of-the-Month Club, is a spare, incisive work in three sections, each of which deals with the rituals that pervade the life of its hero, Inni Wintrop. The press has subsequently published two other novels by Nooteboom, *A Song of Truth and Semblance* (1984) and *In the Dutch Mountains* (1987), and has plans to publish more of his fiction.

In 1985 another Pegasus Prize-winner, *The Bone People,* by the New Zealand writer Keri Hulme, appeared. Although it has now enjoyed almost worldwide acclaim, *The Bone People,* like *A Confederacy of Dunces,* almost went unpublished. The novel, Hulme's first, was rejected by virtually every New Zealand publisher because it was

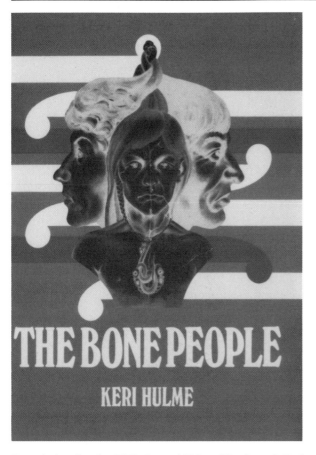

Dust jacket for the LSU Press 1985 publication of Keri Hulme's Pegasus Prize novel

deemed too large and unwieldy and too "different." The novel was finally published by Spiral, a small feminist collective. It became an immediate critical and commercial success. *The Bone People* went on to win the New Zealand Book Award for Fiction, not to mention Great Britain's Booker Prize as the best novel published in the British Commonwealth in 1985. The book's reception in the United States was gratifying. It was described in the *Washington Post Book World* as "an original, overwhelming, near-great work of literature." Sales of the LSU Press edition of the novel have been the second highest in the history of our fiction program. The book was an alternate selection of the Literary Guild. A paperback edition was recently issued by Penguin Books.

In the spring of 1987 the newest winner of the Pegasus Prize for Literature, *And the War Is Over*, by the Indonesian writer Ismal Marahimin, was published in a translation by John H. McGlynn. Set in Indonesia during the final days of World War II, this haunting novel about war and the fractured and ruined lives left in its wake

continues the high standards already established for this series.

Despite our interest in works in translation, the abiding concern of our fiction program remains original American work. Since *A Confederacy of Dunces* was published in the spring of 1980, LSU Press has published twenty-four books of new fiction–novels as well as story collections–by American authors. While some people assume that we publish only southern fiction–indeed, a good many of our works have been by southern writers, and we are proud to have published them– we do not seek out writers only from below the Mason-Dixon line. Our only criterion is that the books we publish be quality fiction of the highest order. A look at some of the books published in recent years readily reveals the diversity of our program.

Among our 1981 offerings was *Onliness*, a novel by Dave Smith. John Gardner noted that "*Onliness* has the startling vividness one expects– usually in vain–from a poet turned novelist. The storytelling is elegant and spare, rich in character and place, like the best of Erskine Caldwell, and the ear for real southern voices never misses."

The year 1982 saw the publication of *The Land that Drank the Rain*, a novel by the prolific Virginia writer William Hoffman. Hoffman is one of several writers (John William Corrington is another) who now move easily between the worlds of trade and university press publishing. Hoffman's most recent novel, *Godfires*, was published in hardcover by Viking in 1985 and in paperback by Penguin in 1986. A new story collection, "By Land, by Sea," is forthcoming from LSU Press in 1988.

Also published in 1982 were *First Wine*, Jack Dunphy's novel concerning a young boy's summertime coming of age, and the Acadian writer Chris Segura's *Marshland Brace*, described in the Philadelphia *Inquirer* as "exceptional stories by an exceptional writer, one who writes with economy and grace, emotion and understanding, sensitivity and exactness."

In 1983 and 1984 LSU Press published a number of fine novels, including John H. McCluskey, Jr.'s *Mr. America's Last Season Blues*, about a former black athlete trying to rebuild his life; R. H. W. Dillard's fanciful *First Man on the Sun; Vigil*, Elisabeth Young-Bruehl's evocative novel about two women who are the last surviving members of a once-prosperous Maryland family; and Harry H. Taylor's *The Divorce Sonnets*, which the *New York Times Book Review* called "a

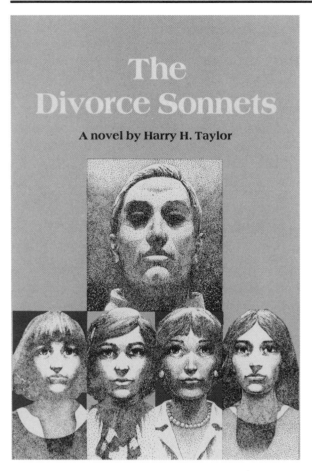

Dust jacket for one of the novels published by LSU Press in 1984. The book recounts one man's four unsuccessful attempts to bring order to his life through marriage.

haunting, elusive novel [that] unveils the thwarted passions, unfulfilled expectations and gradual disillusionment that presage the end of marriage."

Recent years have witnessed a strengthening of our fiction program both in terms of critical reception and sales. In the spring of 1985 we published *I Am One of You Forever,* a novel by the splendid North Carolina novelist Fred Chappell, who is also a gifted poet (he was cowinner of the 1985 Bollingen Prize in Poetry). Gene Lyons, writing in *Newsweek,* noted Chappell's "almost numinous gift for describing nature with a series of

interwoven rustic tall tales such as Twain (or Faulkner) might have written." *I Am One of You Forever,* which went through four hardcover printings, was the subject of an interesting and successful experiment in the fall of 1987, when we reprinted the novel in a trade paperback edition, a first for LSU Press.

Another writer published by LSU Press in the recent past whose reputation, along with sales of his books, has grown is James Lee Burke, a teacher of creative writing at Wichita State University. Burke published four novels with trade houses early in his career, but only with the publication of *The Convict,* a collection of stories brought out by LSU Press in fall 1985, and *The Lost Get-Back Boogie,* a novel set in Montana published in late 1986, has he begun to receive the recognition he deserves.

LSU Press has also recently published such accomplished writers–some seasoned, some new– as David R. Slavitt, Gordon Weaver, William Mills, and Lewis Nordan, who in two story collections, *Welcome to the Arrow-Catcher Fair* (1983) and *The All-Girl Football Team* (1986), has become one of the best living practitioners of the southern Gothic style.

The three most recent directors of LSU Press, Richard Wentworth, Charles East, and, especially, L. E. Phillabaum, have been largely responsible for guiding the LSU Press fiction program. But credit must also go to Martha Lacy Hall, who was the press's managing editor for a number of years and who became fiction editor in 1983. Hall is herself a writer, whose collection of stories, *Music Lesson,* was published by the University of Illinois Press in 1984.

Recent trends in the commercial sector of publishing indicate that serious, not necessarily commercial fiction is more welcome today than in years past. But while many trade houses now publish at least some serious fiction (and others, like Knopf, have lists filled with such titles), fiction programs such as those at LSU and other university presses are now firmly established. At LSU Press our fiction program will remain a small (generally only four titles a year) but vital part of the publishing scene.

The Society for Textual Scholarship and *TEXT*

D. C. Greetham
City University of New York

Founded by D. C. Greetham in 1979, the Society for Textual Scholarship (STS) is an organization devoted to providing a forum, in its biennial conferences and its yearbook *TEXT* (coedited by Greetham and W. Speed Hill), for the discussion of the interdisciplinary implications of current research into various aspects of contemporary textual work: the discovery, enumeration, description, bibliographical analysis, editing, and annotating of texts in disciplines such as literature (European, American, and Oriental), history, musicology, classical and biblical studies, philosophy, art history, legal history, history of science and technology, computer science, library science, lexicography, epigraphy, palaeography, codicology, cinema studies, and textual theory. All these, and several other fields, have been represented in conference or STS publication since the first gathering in New York in 1981, and the conference is now generally recognized as the most wide-ranging (and one of the most influential) of meetings of textual scholars in the world. In its first four conferences close to three hundred papers have been presented by speakers representing the disciplines listed above, with a chronological range of topics from early Egyptian and Mycenean inscriptions and pre-exilic biblical texts to computer concordances of still-living poets (Stephen Spender) and the examination of governmental and foundation funding for editing.

The first four presidents of the Society represent a similarly wide range of authority and discipline–beginning with G. Thomas Tanselle (John Simon Guggenheim Memorial Foundation, 1981-1983), to Paul Oskar Kristeller (Columbia University, 1983-1985), to Fredson Bowers (University of Virginia, 1985-1987), and Eugene Nida (American Bible Society, 1987-1989): from Anglo-American bibliography via Renaissance and neo-Latin scholarship to biblical studies and linguistics. The eighty-three members of the Society's Advisory Board (which evaluates contributions to *TEXT*) show a parallel range of interests, with large international component.

TEXT

Transactions of the Society
for Textual Scholarship

1

FOR 1981

Edited by

D. C. GREETHAM

and

W. SPEED HILL

AMS PRESS
NEW YORK

Title page for the collection of papers presented at the first annual meeting of the Society for Textual Scholarship

The range of editions represented by the advisers and officers of STS is very wide (from the *Anchor Bible* to the Garland James Joyce, from Old English to Chaucer and Wycliffe, Hoccleve, Wyatt, Shakespeare, Hooker, Donne, Milton, Dryden, Rochester, Johnson, Burns, Scott, Byron, Shelley, Keats, Cooper, Thackeray, Melville, Lewis Carroll, Morris, Howells, Henry Adams, Yeats, and Spender). The range of authors–both literary and nonliterary–represented in papers given at the Society's meetings and printed in *TEXT* is even wider.

Why was the Society for Textual Scholarship founded, and why is it necessary when there is already so much textual activity in this country and abroad? What is "textual scholarship" anyway?

Answers to both these questions were suggested in the presidential address given by Dr. Tanselle at the Society's inaugural meeting in 1981. While acknowledging the textual (and general scholarly) activity, Tanselle notes that the tendency is for both learned societies and journals to "focus on more and more specialized subjects and help to accelerate the fragmentation of scholarly endeavour" (*TEXT* 1). This, he suggested, is probably inevitable; but the purpose of STS is to move in the *opposite* direction–"it aims at nothing less than to bring together in fruitful discussion persons concerned with textual matters of all kinds. This goal encompasses, in effect, every conceivable field, since all fields involve communication of some sort; and where there is communication, there is a medium of communication, a means of transmission, the operation of which may produce distortions in what is communicated. Textual problems are not limited to literature, or even to all verbal communications in written or printed form. Problems of textual transmission arise in oral literature, in music, in sound recordings, in films, in engravings and etchings. The images of visual art, the sounds of aural art, are texts, just as the written and printed words and punctuation of manuscripts and books are texts. Investigating the relationships among versions of what purports to be the same work or among attempted reproductions of what purports to be the same version is the task of textual scholarship in all fields; and what this Society can usefully provide is a forum where common problems–and, at a basic level, there *are* common problems, however diverse their manifestation– can be discussed (indeed, perhaps, discovered) by persons representing a great diversity of experience in textual study" (*TEXT* 1). Incidentally, of the list of media for communication (and miscommunication) cited by Tanselle, only sound recordings have perhaps not yet received proper attention in conference or in publication.

Tanselle's recognition of the need for a common meeting ground to overcome disciplinary fragmentation has been exemplified by the typical structure of the STS conference sessions. While making some concessions to the familiar period or other taxonomies of research (by, for example, scheduling workshop panels on medieval,

Renaissance, or modern textual studies), the STS program organizers have typically arranged sessions under a theoretical rubric ("Can a Text Exist?," "The Relations of Text and Document: Literary and Historical Approaches," "The Authority of Authorial Intention," "The Meaning of the Text," "Visions and Revisions," "Transmission and Revision," "Editorial Ethics," "Problems in Attribution and Provenance," "Stemmatics and Contamination," "Transcription and the Question of Normalisation") with speakers from different disciplines, periods, and scholarly experience addressing the same issue. Another method of organization has been methodological or technical rather than conceptual (such as sessions on "Variorum Editing," "Manuals of Editing," "The Computer and Textual Scholarship," "The Production, Appearance, and Preservation of the Text," "The Discovery, Enumeration, and Description of Materials") or to hold interdisciplinary sessions on a particular genre or type of document (such as "The Dictionary as Text: Cross-Cultural Perspectives," "On Language, Translation, and Transliteration," "Words and Music," "Editing Letters: Quandaries and Queries," "Scholia and Commentaries, Marginalia and Annotation," "In the Margins: Scribal, Editorial, and Typographical Framing of the Text," "On Fragments and the Division of Labor: Bibliographical, Palaeographical, and Aesthetic Implications"). A recent feature of the conferences has been to encourage members of the Society to convene special workshop sessions examining particular problems within a genre or period, or even to hold meetings devoted to a single author or specific editorial project (such as "Editing Medieval Translations," "Ciné-Textual Scholarship," "Descriptive Bibliography and the Romance Languages," "Problems and Methods in Shakespeare Studies," "Policies and Procedures in Editing *The Manuscripts of the Younger Romantics*," "Editing the Manuscripts of W. B. Yeats"). In this way, STS hopes to preserve its basic interdisciplinary rationale, while providing facilities and a forum for concentrating on special problems. The theoretical and conceptual issues are discussed in plenary sessions, and the special issues in simultaneous workshop sessions. To date, all conferences have been held in New York City at the Graduate Center of The City University of New York on 42nd Street, with additional sessions at the New York Public Library.

The answer to the first question–why was STS founded–is therefore apparent most clearly in its conference programs. STS attempts to overcome the disciplinary short-sightedness that often results from typical research specialization by creating a series of open forums for the discussion of theoretical, conceptual, or methodological questions by representatives from different disciplines who might otherwise never meet professionally and therefore never have the opportunity to put their received principles and procedures to the test. As a recent review of the Society's publication *TEXT* put it: "this volume is refreshingly undogmatic. All editorial orthodoxies are useful and none is universal" (the *Library*, September 1986). And, as noted by the coverage of the 1985 conference in both the *New York Times* and the *Times Literary Supplement*, the STS conference organizers provided an equal opportunity to both sides of the debate on the authority of the new Gabler edition of Joyce's *Ulysses*. The conference forums on textual matters at other organizations tend either to focus each time on one major issue (the Toronto Conference on Editorial Problems), to be buried in general disciplinary gatherings (the Modern Language Association of America, the American Philological Association, the American Historical Association, the American Musicological Society), or to be limited by period (the Medieval Academy of America, the American Society for Eighteenth-Century Studies). In all such discipline-oriented organizations, textual scholarship tends to get short shrift. The only other conference which might have fulfilled an interdisciplinary need (the Association for Documentary Editing), while beginning–in Kansas and then in Princeton, 1979–with some promising cross-disciplinary concerns, has gradually become a professional organization (often with a very specific lobbying agenda) and is dominated by the projects and editors of American history. STS does not consider itself a professional or disciplinary organization, but a group responding to Tanselle's challenge for the open forum for common problems.

The initial answer to the second question–what is "textual scholarship" (as opposed, say, to "textual criticism," "editing," or "bibliography")–can also be found in the Tanselle presidential address. He notes: "a long tradition of what is usually called 'textual criticism' exists, concerned primarily with the texts of classical and biblical writings, and more recently, with medieval manuscripts. The word 'criticism' in 'textual criticism' suggests the important role that individual judgment plays in the process of evaluating textual authority and deciding on emendations. This

Society has chosen the term 'textual scholarship' rather than the term 'textual criticism' not in any sense as a rejection of the latter term but only because the former is the more encompassing term. The great tradition of classical and biblical criticism forms but one branch of textual scholarship as a whole" (*TEXT* 1).

There is another sense in which "textual scholarship" responds more accurately to the purposes of STS than would "textual criticism." While it is true that "textual criticism" (and particularly the stemmatic analysis and evaluation of variant readings) has a long tradition in classical and biblical studies, it has been taken up by "modern" editors to signify the stage of editing associated with such evaluation–and the subsequent production of "critical" editions. But "textual scholarship" is used–within STS anyway–with a signification that is not only (or even primarily) *editorial*. Most of the STS participants are indeed editors, but editing (and "textual criticism") is only one of the stages–and competencies–discussed at STS conferences under the aegis of "textual scholarship." As shown already, problems in the discovery of texts, in enumeration, bibliographical analysis, attribution, and annotation also form a considerable part of the STS curriculum, and the term "textual scholarship" has a wider reach–in part because it has a shorter history and currency–than the alternatives "textual criticism," "editing," or "bibliography."

There is one other problem in "textual" terminology that is reflected in the work of STS–and particularly in the organization of its yearbook *TEXT*. The word "TEXT" was chosen for the journal–actually, some time before the decision to adopt "textual scholarship" for the organization–not only because of its polyglottal currency (the word is part of the lexicon of many Western languages) and its simplicity but also because the "text" has become the focus for much theoretical speculation by critics who are not "textual" in *our* sense. The status of the *text(e)* is as much at stake in poststructuralist theory (indeed, there is a French-Canadian "critical" journal using this variant title) as it is in textual scholarship, and in part, the decision to adopt *TEXT* as the title for our journal was a recognition of the word's dual nature, but in addition, a tacit acknowledgment that there was a battle to be fought for the terminology, *and* (perhaps) some theoretical links to be made with textuists of a different water–critics who are most decidedly *not* editors.

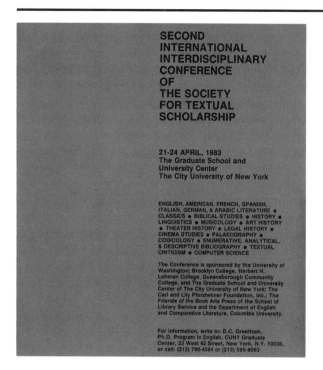

SECOND
INTERNATIONAL
INTERDISCIPLINARY
CONFERENCE
OF
THE SOCIETY
FOR TEXTUAL
SCHOLARSHIP

21-24 APRIL, 1983
The Graduate School and
University Center
The City University of New York

ENGLISH, AMERICAN, FRENCH, SPANISH,
ITALIAN, GERMAN, & ARABIC LITERATURE ●
CLASSICS ● BIBLICAL STUDIES ● HISTORY ●
LINGUISTICS ● MUSICOLOGY ● ART HISTORY
● THEATER HISTORY ● LEGAL HISTORY ●
CINEMA STUDIES ● PALAEOGRAPHY ●
CODICOLOGY ● ENUMERATIVE, ANALYTICAL,
& DESCRIPTIVE BIBLIOGRAPHY ● TEXTUAL
CRITICISM ● COMPUTER SCIENCE

The Conference is sponsored by the University of
Washington; Brooklyn College, Herbert H.
Lehman College, Queensborough Community
College, and The Graduate School and University
Center of The City University of New York; The
Carl and Lily Pforzheimer Foundation, Inc.; The
Friends of the Book Arts Press of the School of
Library Service and the Department of English
and Comparative Literature, Columbia University.

For information, write to: D.C. Greetham,
Ph.D. Program in English, CUNY Graduate
Center, 33 West 42 Street, New York, N.Y. 10036,
or call: (212) 790-4584 or (212) 595-8063

Program cover

This problem—and the challenge it represented—was noted in the first issue of *TEXT* by Jerome J. McGann, in an essay entitled "Shall These Bones Live?" In a defense of the historicity of the text, McGann notes the possibly ambivalent status of the movement represented by STS and *TEXT*. "A professional society launches itself in 1981 under the aegis of 'textual studies' and proposes to issue scholarly papers in a journal called *TEXT*. These are notable events, all the more so because their initial impression belies their actual significance. For such a society and such a journal, in an academic world currently dominated by structuralist and post-structuralist theory and practice, necessarily suggest an interest in the semiological and Derridean 'text' and in the entire critical enterprise which goes under the heading of 'textuality' " (*TEXT* 1). McGann goes on, as he does in several later essays (two of them published in subsequent volumes of *TEXT*), to suggest that there must be an accommodation between this "textuality" and the "textual scholarship" of "X'textual critics' in the traditional sense."

TEXT has therefore become not only an interdisciplinary journal of textual scholarship as defined above, but a forum for debating the validity of McGann's position with those who would use concepts more often associated with "textuality" in the elucidation of "textual" prob-

lems. Perhaps inevitably, essays co-opting "textuality" in "textual scholarship" tend to be written by younger scholars employing the concepts and terminologies of recent criticism: in *TEXT* 3 Robert F. Yeager has an essay on the Derridean concept of "marginalisation" as it affects the actual composition of the textual page in Gower's *Confessio Amantis*, and Gerald MacLean has an essay on the concept of "discourse" (rather than "poem") and how this affects the editing of Restoration verse. But *TEXT* also contains an essay by one of its presidents (and one of the founders of Anglo-American analytical bibliography and textual scholarship), Fredson Bowers, who declares that the McGann line of argument is spurious, since it uses "the language of literary criticism" not of "strict textual criticism"—and these two modes of criticism are simply different (Presidential Address: "Unfinished Business") (*TEXT* 4).

A different line of defense of the "text"—one based on the philological dispensation of nineteenth- and early-twentieth-century scholarship—occurs in two articles by Paul Oskar Kristeller, second president of STS and long associated with the value of careful historical research and discrimination. In his Presidential Address, *TEXT* 3, he observed that "textual scholarship, as I understand it, is now on the defensive, in the world at large which does not care for it or ignores it, and even in the academic world where it is often contemptuously dismissed as 'traditional' scholarship." But within the STS conference, Kristeller had been pleased to note a new generation of textual scholars and did not fear that the art and craft of such scholarship was being entirely lost: "I am not a literary scholar, as most of you are, but primarily an historian of philosophy and of learning, or if you wish, an intellectual historian (I trust we are all historians, and I hope we are all intellectuals)." His identification with the aims and tenor of STS bespeaks not only his sense that the interdisciplinary forum was salutary to the survival of textual scholarship as *he* understood it, but also testifies to the heterogeneity of STS itself, in publishing and promoting the diversity represented by Bowers, Kristeller, and McGann.

In publishing this range of opinion, the editors of *TEXT* aim to foster an open forum on the very nature of the *text* and scholarship thereon—just as the STS conferences are open to differing disciplines and differing textual scholars. The balance between theoretical issues and practical concerns is shown in the table of contents in each volume of *TEXT*. Typically, each volume is divided between essays on some general conceptual or theoretical problem (such as the series of essays presented at the 1983 conference on "The Meaning of the Text" which appear, as a group, in *TEXT* 3) and those more closely involved with a specific period, author, or text. The proliferation of theoretical articles reflects the serious debate now going on in the field of textual scholarship about the very nature–the ontology– of the text *and* the prerogatives of the editor. Four essays by European textual scholars illustrate the point rather nicely: Hans Walter Gabler debates "the text as *process*," Louis Hay discusses the concept of "genetic editing," Jean-Louis Lebrave challenges any uniformity in editing in his analysis of the rough draft, or *avant-texte*, and Klaus Hurlebusch uses the medium of the diary to illustrate the variable concepts–and differing editorial roles–based on the text as "relic" or "tradition."

However, while *TEXT* encourages such inter-

disciplinary and conceptual discussion of textual problems–largely because textual scholarship has not achieved, and may never, a synthesis or uniform methodology–the journal also welcomes articles with a more defined subject area. In addition to the theoretical articles mentioned above, *TEXT* 3 also contains essays by, for example, George Killough on Middle English verse punctuation, Elizabeth Aubrey on the transmission of troubadour melodies in a French manuscript, Gary Taylor on Shakespeare's revisions, Carl Woodring on editing Coleridge, Robert Rosenberg on Edison's technical drawings, and Edward Mendelson on W. H. Auden. Each of the essays–and the others in volume three and other similar articles in other volumes of *TEXT*–have interdisciplinary *implications*, but their focus is specific and limited, as opposed to the wide-ranging general issues discussed in the theoretical articles. *TEXT* (and the conferences of the Society for Textual Scholarship) welcomes contributions of both types.

The Year in the Novel

George Garrett
University of Virginia

"Every week on the New York Times *best-seller list there are thirty books, two of which are written in English."*

Andrew Wylie, literary agent, quoted in Vanity Fair

Best-sellers, blockbusters, are the essential bodily fluids which manage to keep the Frankenstein's monster of contemporary American trade book publishing, including fiction, more or less alive and croaking, if not very well. There were plenty of them in 1987. Here are some familiar names from among those which graced the year's various and sundry best-seller lists: Tom Clancy, Mary Higgins Clark, James Clavell, Michael Crichton, Thomas Fleming, Dick Francis, John Jakes, Louis L'Amour, Sidney Sheldon, and Danielle Steele. Names you see, not titles. Why? Because it is not titles, or indeed even the form and content of any given book, which leads to the necessary orders from the huge chain bookstores. Which chains account for at least three-fourths, maybe more, of all the trade books sold in America. Someone will surely have noticed that one important name is missing from the roster. The reason for that is that Stephen King belongs in a category by himself, having broken all records by having *four books* on the best-seller lists in a calendar year. This deserves attention and so do his titles: *It* (Viking), *Misery* (Viking), *The Eyes of the Dragon: A Fairy Tale* (Viking), and *The Tommyknockers* (Putnam's). Two of these, *Misery* and *The Tommyknockers,* are frankly "literary," at least to the extent that they involve writers as their central characters. No question that Stephen King is a phenomenon, a solid and successful storyteller, good and amazingly productive at what he does. If he can keep it up, he may yet become the Joyce Carol Oates of popular fiction.

More important, however, and a very pleasant surprise in any given year, are the writers of serious reputation who also somehow managed to have and to hold, sometimes but not always briefly, places on the best-seller lists. One book, a carryover from 1986, deserves some special recognition. Pat Conroy's *The Prince of Tides* (Houghton Mifflin), in spite of mixed reviews,

Dust jacket for Saul Bellow's tragicomic examination of the inability of intelligent people to make rational decisions about money and sex

was among the best-sellers for at least three-quarters of 1987, into October, a huge success. It should be remembered that even best-selling commercial authors must battle for time and shelf space in the bookstores. Other planned blockbusters are always coming along soon behind them, and to last beyond one season is extraordinary. Late in the year (30 November) the *Washington Post* book critic Jonathan Yardley took note that serious writers were also showing up on the best-seller lists. In "Finally, Best Sellers That Are Good Reads," he cited the 1987 success of four writers–Gail Godwin, Toni Morrison, and (both of these with first novels) Tom Wolfe and Scott

Turow. He did not mention writers whose books had earlier in the year been best-sellers–Philip Roth's *The Counterlife* (Farrar, Straus and Giroux), winner of the National Book Critics Circle Award for Fiction, Saul Bellow's *More Die of Heartbreak* (Morrow), William Safire's *Freedom* (Doubleday), Gore Vidal's *Empire* (Random House), John Gregory Dunne's *The Red White and Blue* (Simon and Schuster), Walker Percy's *The Thanatos Syndrome* (Farrar, Straus and Giroux), Elmore Leonard's *Touch* (Arbor House), Larry McMurtry's *Texasville* (Harper and Row), George V. Higgins's *Outlaws* (Holt), and Kurt Vonnegut's *Bluebeard* (Delacorte). None of these, except perhaps Toni Morrison's *Beloved* (Knopf) and Tom Wolfe's *The Bonfire of the Vanities* (Farrar, Straus and Giroux), is likely to have achieved a seriously competitive success compared to the standard blockbusters. But this year's relative success of "literary" books has at least challenged some cherished assumptions.

Simultaneously, maybe part and parcel of the whole changing scene, we have in 1987 the case of any number of books designed and tailored to be best-sellers, boldly advertised, heavily promoted works, often by previously successful popular writers, which somehow failed to make their mark, in sales at least. (Of course in many cases, the hardcover publishers had already earned the big money, paperback and movie sales, in advance, but nevertheless....) Among the list of sure things and shoo-ins which failed to rise to full glory were Andrew Greeley's *Patience of a Saint* (Geis), Robin Cook's *Outbreak* (Putnam's), William Goldman's *Brothers* (Warner), Celia Brayfield's *Pearls* (Morrow), Elizabeth Marshall's *Reindeer Moon* (Houghton Mifflin), Shirley Conran's *Savages* (Simon and Schuster), Howard Fast's *The Dinner Party* (Houghton Mifflin), and David Ignatius's *Agents of Innocence* (Norton). Each of these had a fresh angle on a tried-but-true (perhaps tired?) subject. Each was given the same basic trumpet fanfare announcing its claim to all the rights and privileges of best-sellerdom. Some did much better than others, but none achieved its full potential. All of which may mean any number of things. It may be good news that, even though, by and large, best-sellers must be manufactured and by means of some standardized moves, still many are called and few are chosen. Within certain limits the results are beyond fixing or arranging. Taken together with the surprising success of some literary artists, the message to publishers might be that

there is more wisdom in trying to sell books of good quality than investing in and depending on trash. To which the publishers could just as well reply with (the bad news) the examples of literary books by highly regarded serious writers who were given every possible chance, including best-seller support and treatment and advertising, and somehow failed to achieve "breakthrough" fully. You would have to acknowledge that even successful books like Dunne's *The Red White and Blue* and Vonnegut's *Bluebeard* do not appear to have lived entirely up to expectations. Meanwhile a fair number of other major works by major figures–for example, V. S. Naipaul's autobiographical *The Enigma of Arrival* (Knopf), James Dickey's massive and much-anticipated *Alnilam* (Doubleday), and Marge Piercy's even heftier *Gone to Soldiers* (Summit)–were, to an extent, disappointments both commercially and critically. Moreover, the thoughtful publisher would have to point out that it costs just as much to promote a failed best-seller as an actual one and that the intense difficulty of finding a way to keep the cash flowing by long-accepted ways and means is going to cause even more austerity and more trouble for books of high literary quality and doubtful commercial possibility.

Before capitulating, without conditions, you might offer the counterargument that one of the publishers' ploys, one not without some rational basis in the age of *People* magazine, the celebrity book, that is the book (in theory) created by a celebrity from some other field than serious literature, has not yet managed to achieve its goal. Probably hasn't really paid for itself. For celebrities don't come cheaply. Books of 1987 like Kinky Friedman's *A Case of Lone Star* (Morrow), Ilie Nastase's *The Net* (St. Martin's), or Maureen Dean's *Washington Wives* (Arbor House) do not appear to have done well at the marketplace. Nor do some better books by better writers from other fields, for example books by dramatists, such as the late Joe Orton's *Head To Toe* (St. Martin's) and Marsha Norman's *The Fortune Teller* (Random House). George Plimpton, who has done a little of everything else, came up with his first novel, *The Curious Case of Sidd Finch* (Macmillan), which began as an April Fool's joke for *Sports Illustrated*. It is the tale of a French horn-playing Buddhist monk from Tibet who can throw a baseball with some accuracy at 168 mph. Carrie Fisher, a young movie star who managed to break free from a siege of drug addiction, has given us *Postcards from the Edge* (Simon and Schuster), all about a young movie star with a serious drug problem. Highly fashionable in form and content, blessed by blurbs from the likes of Mike Nichols, Steve Martin, and Candice Bergen, the book and its author received plenty of public attention, if not significant sales. Two relatively successful celebrity books, done by intelligent and, by now, experienced celebrity writers were Margaret Truman's timely *Murder in the C.I.A.* (Random House), her eighth volume in her Capital Crime series, and William Buckley's latest–*Mongoose R.I.P.* (Random House).

Finally, in response, our idealized and honest publisher might be expected to point out that peculiar and peculiarly 1987 phenomenon–the sudden ascendancy of some writers, loosely to be classified as literary, and called the Brat Pack. The Pack usually includes Jay McInerney, who did not produce a new book this year; David Leavitt and Meg Wolitzer, neither of whom did either; Tama Janowitz, whose *A Cannibal in Manhattan* (Crown), the story of Mgungu Yabba Mgungu, straight from the South Pacific Island of Burnt Norton, and his adventures in the contemporary Big Apple, got lots of notice, very little of it even faintly favorable; Brett Ellis, author of *Less Than Zero* (1985), whose *The Rules of Attraction* (Simon and Schuster), a story of dope, sex, homework, and ennui at college, fared no better; and Jill Eisenstadt, Ellis's classmate at Bennington College, whose *From Rockaway* (Knopf) deals with (among other things) lifeguards, who, according to the jacket copy, have a hard life: "Winters they work shit jobs like unloading trucks at Mickey's Deli. At night, winter and summer, they drink." An interesting checklist of severely, often outrageously negative reviews for these books could be created and added to an even longer list of articles about the authors as personalities and as a group and as social symbols of something or other in every kind of magazine from *Commonweal* and the *Georgia Review* to *Vanity Fair*, *Gentleman's Quarterly*, *People*, and the *New Yorker*. It is easy to believe, and not worth the effort of proving one way or the other, that this group of writers has received more immediate and more extensive attention than any literary school or group in recorded history. Even the Beats, those old media masters, did not do so well. And even the camp followers, groupies, and corner crews, people like youngish editors Morgan Entrekin and Gary Fisketjon, are usually included in the limelight as self-proclaimed spokespersons for the era. Ellis, with a new book on the stands and

Dust jacket for John Barth's elaborate novel narrated by a couple sailing their yacht, Story, *on the Chesapeake Bay*

the critically savaged movie version of his first novel, *Less Than Zero*, dying out there somewhere, has been up front for months.

What our imaginary publisher (give him a few more years and books of experience than Entrekin and Fisketjon) would want to point out as indicated, if not yet proved, by the phenomenon of the Brat Pack is a two-fold observation. First, publicity, *literary* publicity, occupying precious space allotted for things literary, can be generated in the almost complete absence of any claims of or for quality. In the past at least somebody would have presented an argument that some kind of literary quality, perhaps yet to be defined, was involved. As far as I can tell only Campbell Geeslin of *People* (who called it "exceedingly effective") had any kind words about *The Rules of Attraction;* but his praise was, at best, measured. Nothing new or strange about publishers trying to hustle the books of celebrities. But in this case the celebrities had to be created from scratch, and their chief claim to fame had to be the writing of bad novels. Odd, isn't it? Even odder, however, and more ominous, at least for other writers, is that the huge weight and substance of publicity does not seem to have resulted in any consequent and significant difference in sales; that is, these writers probably sell more books than they would have without any publicity at all, but not enough to justify all the effort or, for that matter, the expensive fun and games.

Close study of the habits, ways, and means of the Brat Pack would probably prove nothing more than the validity of the combined worldly wisdom of Diogenes and P. T. Barnum and Leo Durocher.

Still, all in all, it was a good year in many ways for literary fiction in America.

There were books of all kinds, major and minor, from some of our most highly regarded novelists. There were new voices and rediscoveries. There were important translations and there were significant adventures in experimental fiction. And, as is altogether usual in our exceedingly careless and wasteful society, there were worthwhile novels, worthy of all serious attention, and sometimes of honor, which were either ignored or misrepresented or merely shoved aside amid the ceaseless rush and clamor of the present moment, its passing fancies. If a chronicle roundup like this one has no other value, it at least offers a second chance for some deserving books and authors.

There were special oddities of definition. For instance, Annie Dillard's autobiographical *An American Childhood* (Harper and Row) was at first announced as a novel, then published as a work of nonfiction. Conversely, Bruce Chatwin's well-praised *The Songlines* (Viking), an autobiographical accounting of his search to understand the worlds of the Australian Aborigines, appeared and was reviewed as nonfiction, but by year's end showed up in the *fiction* lists, including the "Notable Books of the Year" in the *New York Times Book Review.* Similarly *The Manzoni Family* (Seaver) by Italian author Natalia Ginzburg has been received and reviewed as nonfiction, a work of history and multiple biography, even though the book jacket itself proclaims it a novel and quotes the author's description of it as such. Slowly the distinctions between fiction and nonfiction break and blur away.

Something of this mild confusion between factual and fictive truth is offered in three 1987 novels about (of all things!) the literary life, each by someone with insider's experience. Richard Marek, president of E. P. Dutton, has produced in *Works of Genius* (Atheneum) the story of a good and decent literary agent. (improbable as that idea may seem to most writers), Tony Silver, and of his most successful and important client, Eric Meredith, a gifted writer who "writes like an angel and destroys the lives of those who love him most." At the end, after years of real trouble and ups and downs, Silver watches Meredith receive the American Book Award and a standing ovation from the Establishment. "Yet remarkably all anger vanished, and I felt calm, even euphoric." Watching Silver create, then outgrow his monster/writer is entertaining, and there is a lot of good information (what the Marines and the Navy used to call "good skinny") about the American publishing scene. It is a bit more reasonable and tidy than in real life, and there are more decent folk here than you will ever find listed in *The Literary Marketplace*, but it has a certain style. Charles Simmons, who won the William Faulkner Award years ago for his first novel, *Powdered Eggs* (1964), and who served for many years as an editor of the *New York Times Book Review*, published his third novel, *The Belles Lettres Papers* (Morrow). Which is all about a powerful literary organ and is wildly funny, slapstick, and crossover-beard stuff, maybe taking the edge off the really grotesque news he has to tell about how things there really are. Wilfrid Sheed's *The Boys of Winter* (Knopf) is satirical also, dealing with "art, life, and sex in a literary hamlet in the Hamptons," and centering around editor Jonathan Oglethorpe and novelist Waldo Spinks, together with a gang of almost-recognizable literati, and building to a climactic softball game among middle-aged and mostly inept jocks. Widely reviewed and widely declared to be hilarious, it all seemed to be a bit less than meets the eye. But maybe you just had to be there.

Books by established novelists, some of them solidly enough in the Establishment to be invited out to the Hamptons, are many and various. Both Amises, *pere et fils*, are represented, Kingsley Amis with *The Old Devils* (Summit), a wild and wooly story of some randy Welshmen in their sixties, which won back his shrugging critical audience who called it his funniest book since his first–*Lucky Jim* (1954). *The Old Devils* won Britain's prestigious Booker Prize in 1986. Martin Amis, whose sharp tongue and widespread publicity have earned him a reputation as Britain's one-man answer to the Brat Pack, was generally and negatively criticized ("nasty" seemed to be the word of choice) for his 1978 novel, *Success* (Harmony), which had never until now found an Amer-

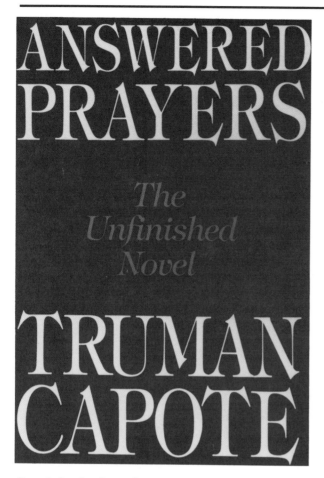

Dust jacket for the posthumous publication of chapters one, two, and seven, the only three known to exist, of Truman Capote's unfinished novel

ican publisher. Max Apple returned to the old themes of *The Oranging of America* (1976) with *The Propheteers* (Harper and Row), a novel starring wholly imaginary versions of Howard Johnson, Walt Disney, Charles Birdseye, inventor of frozen food, and others. "America is the subject of my book. Why not use grand Americans?," Apple told Charles Trueheart of the *Washington Post* ("Max Apple and the Well of Sorrows," 1 September 1987, pp. 1-2), adding that he had originally wanted to call it "The Disneyad." He also told Trueheart a great deal about his personal life, including some of the autobiographical details used in stories, especially "Bridging" in Apple's 1984 book *Free Agents*. The public account of how his wife, Debby Berman, developed multiple sclerosis, and how they were subsequently divorced, was heartbreaking, though unconfirmable in some details. For, as Trueheart wrote: "Reached by telephone in Grand Rapids, Faye Berman (Debby's mother) briefly expressed dismay that her former son-in-law is discussing Debby's illness for publication, speculating that he is 'trying to gain sympathy for his book.' " Presumably, in the age of publicity and public relations everyone's motives are always under suspicion.

John Barth blended together autobiographical and fanciful details in his elaborate and massive *The Tidewater Tales* (Putnam's), dealing with (among many other things) a sailing cruise taken by one Peter Sagamore and his pregnant wife Katherine on the Chesapeake Bay in their own good yacht *Story*. It is as wildly inventive as anything Barth has done. And more cheerful, more at ease with his literary habits. And the sailing scenes, in and of themselves, are splendid. Another native fabulist out of the 1960s, Peter Beagle, after some years of silence, returns with *The Folk of Air* (Ballantine), which, perhaps because it was published and marketed as *genre* fantasy, has not received much notice. Saul Bellow got plenty of attention if not an equivalent understanding for *More Die of Heartbreak*. The novel opens with a brief discussion of a Charles Addams cartoon, announcing thereby that it will be a comedy about some fairly darkly serious things. And so it is. The narrative is told, in a highly energetic and idiosyncratic style, by Kenneth Trachtenberg, a scholar of Russian literature and a classic Bellow intellectual whose exceptional mind is at odds with body and emotions. The central figure in a modestly complex plot is his uncle, world-famous botanist Benn Crader, who has serious romantic problems and to whom Kenneth looks for exemplary wisdom. The tone is familiar, yet exactly up to date: "Uncle made it his business in his steady scientific fashion to inform himself about herpes, AIDS and other venereal diseases. Assuming a purely clinical tone, he made horrific conversation about rectal and pharyngeal gonorrhea, cytomegalovirus, enterically transmitted protozoal infections. . . . He sometimes added that you might appraise an age by the nature of its sicknesses. . . . I mention this clinical interest because it foreshadows Uncle's later preoccupation with the demon of sexuality. He tried to take refuge from that in marriage." By the end, after many mishaps and misadventures, Uncle Benn has fled to far places to devote himself to Arctic and Antarctic research, telling his nephew: "It's a survival measure. I'm applying global masses of ice and hyperborean darkness. Thank God jet propulsion makes the remedy available, otherwise I'd have to go and drown myself right here, off Miami Beach." Some critics had problems getting at the fun of it all, perhaps confused by the apparent high-seriousness of the central characters. Thomas Berger's fourteenth novel, *Being Invisible* (Little, Brown), is also a dark comedy about men with "women troubles," chiefly one Fred Wagner, a would-be serious writer who has to earn his living writing ad copy for joke gifts. *His* joke gift turns out to be the power of invisibility which, like characters in the fiction of the late Marcel Aymé, he does not fully appreciate. It is a slapstick story of rage and revenge involving Wagner, his wife "Babe" (Carla), a megalomaniacal sculptor named Siv Zirko, and others, played out against the background of "a world in which some human beings casually killed others to gain possession of a piece of costume jewelry." Frederic Buechner, distinguished as theologian and preacher as well as a novelist (since 1950 and *A Long Day is Dying*), turned away from ours to an earlier world scene in his twelfth novel, *Brendan* (Atheneum). It is the story, part factual and part myth, of St. Brendan the Navigator, coming out of the mists of sixth-century Ireland and narrated by his friend and loyal follower, Finn. A beautiful stylistic tour de force, it is aptly described by poet James Merrill as having "the texture of shot silk" and as "a fine-spun irridescent book." William Burroughs turned to yet another kind of fable in *The Western Lands* (Viking), final volume of a trilogy also including *Cities of the Red Night* (1981) and *The Place of Dead Roads* (1984). Here, under the author's announced influence of Norman Mailer's *Ancient Evenings* (1983), we are exposed to such characters as Kim Carsons, Neferti, an Egyptian scribe, and the outlaw Joe the Dead. The experimental story was accurately described by the *New York Times*'s Michiko Kakutani as "a compendium of the author's preoccupations" and "a definitive summary of his distinctive and disturbing vision." Time was, not long ago, when publishers shuddered at the very idea of a trilogy. This year saw the announced ending of two in addition to Burroughs's—James Wilcox's *Miss Undine's Living Room* (Harper and Row), the final novel of the sequence set in the town of Tula Springs, Louisiana; and T. R. Pearson's *The Last of How It Was* (Simon and Schuster), which wraps up, in a family album of tall tales clothed in a unique and breathless prose style, the life and times of Neely, North Carolina—and the middle volume of another trilogy. In *Close Quarters* Nobel laureate William Golding continued the story, begun in *Rites of Passage* (1980), of a sea voyage to Australia during the Napole-

onic Wars, as told in the journal of Fitzhenry Talbot. Evidently to coincide with the publication of Gunter Grass's latest Teutonic fable, *The Rat* (Helen and Kurt Wolff/Harcourt Brace Jovanovich), described as the tale of "an impassioned and visionary She-rat," Pantheon released *The Danzig Trilogy*, offering Grass's *The Tin Drum*, *Cat and Mouse*, and *Dog Years*, all in one hefty two-handed volume. Another sizable addition to 1987's claim to be the Year of the Big Books was *A Capote Reader* (Random House), containing Truman Capote's *The Grass Harp*, *Breakfast at Tiffany's*, some short stories, and a fairly complete gathering of his travel sketches, portraits, and essays. This volume was designed to join *Answered Prayers: The Unfinished Novel* (Random House), edited by Capote's longtime editor, Joseph M. Fox, and presenting three chunks of Capote's much-discussed novel, all that can be found of it so far and perhaps all there is, satirizing New York and the Beautiful People, as witnessed by a kind of Capote shadow and surrogate, the writer and hustler P. B. Jones. Both the Big Apple and its best and brightest take a real beating even in this truncated version of the novel-in-progress. Tina Brown, editor-in-chief of glitzy *Vanity Fair*, reviewed it for the *New York Times Book Review* and called it "a socio-pornographic 'Ragtime' rife with the low crackle of camp." Another Reader, earned by a writer only recently discovered (with the Bollingen Prize, 1985), is *The Fred Chappell Reader* (St. Martin's). Chappell, poet and story writer as well as novelist, is represented by parts of four novels and all of *Dagon* (1968) as well as poems and stories and one of his essays—"A Pact with Faustus." Of Chappell and his work novelist Lee Smith has written: "Anybody who knows anything about Southern writing knows that Fred Chappell is our resident genius, our shining light, the one truly great writer we have among us."

One of the year's most publicized and widely reviewed novels, and by year's end one of its outstanding commercial successes, was also by a southerner, a skilled reporter with a sharp eye for the vulgar details of urban high life and a keen, hound's nose for the stinks and scents of hypocrisy. Tom Wolfe's *The Bonfire of the Vanities*, much revised since it earlier appeared in serial sequence in *Rolling Stone* magazine, takes on high and low life in contemporary New York City, black and white, and nobody emerges from these pages smelling much like a rose. In a rich and leisurely tapestry the story documents the decline

Dust jacket for Tom Wolfe's first novel, the story of investment-broker Sherman McCoy's fall from grace following a freak accident

and fall of one Sherman McCoy, wealthy young bond salesman. (McCoy was yet another *writer* in the *Rolling Stone* version.) But, as critic William Tazewell has written, the novel has a much larger subject than any of the many people in it: "The book's real subject is Manhattan's manipulated reality, and Tom Wolfe is unrivalled at exposing its hypocrisies and pretensions." Interesting that it took a couple of expatriate southerners to find New York City as a regional subject worth exploiting. And another southerner, this one only just thirty years old in late 1987, has been writing about New York, more seriously than satirically, in all his novels so far; and in his fifth work of fiction, *The Year of Silence* (Ticknor and Fields), Madison Smartt Bell has rung the bell with a major achievement, one which, in my best judgment, stands at a different and higher level of literary art than the visions and versions of Wolfe and Capote. Bell's story, gracefully accessible, yet complex in its depth and dimension, centers around a young woman who is dead, possibly a suicide, and a cast of characters whose lives have been

touched, one way or another, by her life and her death. Some knew her well and some only from a distance. What emerges is a sense of the *community* of the City which is closer than any single character can imagine. Bell knows New York from the gritty ground up, and what develops in his fiction is a place at once more dangerous and credible than the worlds of Wolfe and Capote. Its demons are real, not figures of fun. Longtime resident New Yorker, and an acknowledged master of what might be called experimental chic, Joseph McElroy took on the City in his sixth novel, *Women and Men* (Knopf), 1,600 pages of complicated story concerning James Mayn and Grace Kimball, who live in the same apartment building, but, it seems, never quite manage to meet. Not in this novel, anyway. One can't absolutely be sure of that, or of anything much; because the characters, themselves, have the greatest difficulty trying to keep fact and fiction straight and separate. Most reviewers seemed at least mildly annoyed at the problem of *describing* the novel to readers. Ivan Gold, writing for the *New York Times Book Review* (12 April 1987), was somewhat less than amused: "Mr. McElroy is said to speak to the preoccupations of our time; and he may well; there are simply too many preoccupations to have between covers–however wildly separated– of one novel."

Speaking of experimental fiction–and why not?, though it must here as always be a kind of digression–there was a surprising amount of the native product (foreigners have long been permitted to be as experimental as they please in translation) not only published, by commercial as well as small publishers, but also often reviewed here and there in mainstream publications. Gilbert Sorrentino and Ronald Sukenick, both of whom have earned their official Establishment cap and bells, were represented by *Rose Theatre* (Dalkey) and *Blown Away* (Sun and Moon) respectively. Toby Olson, once their peer, has moved up to Simon and Schuster for his latest, *Utah*, which was described by writer Charles Johnson for the *New York Times Book Review* as "a frequently beautiful meditation on the ambiguity of memory and the redemptive possibilities of art." Three more or less well-received experimental novels were brought out by commercial publishers. Jerome Charyn's twentieth book, *Paradise Man* (Donald I. Fine), proved to be a crime novel about S. Holden, a professional hit man. Emily Prager's earlier book of short stories, *A Visit From the Footbinder* (1984), had attracted attention, and she gained more of the same with her distinctly oddball creation–*Clea & Zeus Divorce* (Vintage), the story (more or less) of a pair of beautiful showbiz celebrities who, having been married for ten years, are about to be divorced on a national TV special. Clea and Zeus move about the world with their entourage of seven enormous bodyguards and an African witch doctor, plus a wide selection of pets. It is a world in which Clea's mother caught leprosy from an armadillo and Zeus's mother, a white Rhodesian, regularly dresses up in blackface. As to the style of the writing, Robert Plunket described it this way in the *New York Times Book Review:* "Is it a heavily ironic fable about a woman driven to madness, or a wicked parody of Joan Didion's writing at its most overwrought?" He describes her prose as a series of images lifted out of Calvin Klein advertisements and MTV. Prager was once a writer for *National Lampoon.* Poet and novelist Harry Matthews, on the other hand, is a member in good standing, and the *only* American member, of the Paris literary (and mathematical) group *Ouvroir de Litterature Potentielle.* His latest novel, his fourth, *Cigarettes* (Weidenfeld and Nicolson), is, in a relative sense, only mildly experimental, and, as described in the *Washington Post Book World* (20 December 1987), is "cloaked under a brilliant Jane Austen-like social comedy on the unfathomable nature of human relationships." Set in Greenwich Village and Saratoga Springs, it covers the years 1936-1963. Amid all this, there were in 1987 four genuinely first-rate experimental novels and a few others, these by well-known, more or less "mainstream" writers, worthy of the most serious attention. Bruce Duffy's *The World As I Found It* (Ticknor and Fields) is a virtuoso exercise disguised as an autobiographical work by Ludwig Wittgenstein, interpolating many of his own written words (including the title) and, in the best contemporary manner, including many historical characters and involving a subtle blending of fact and fiction. Poet Tom Clark's *The Exile of Celine* (Random House) is likewise a shotgun marriage of fact and fiction, concerned with the last years of Dr. Louis-Ferdinand DesTouches, who was, one way or another, a collaborator with the Nazis and, as Celine, wrote some of the most exciting and memorable experimental work of this century. Irwin's *The Arabian Nightmare* (Viking) puts a fifteenth-century pilgrim and spy, Balian of Norwich, into Cairo (arriving on 14 June 1486) where he promptly falls asleep and begins to dream. It presents an involuted series of stories,

tales within tales, each told by a different teller, the last of these being an ape. It is a tale about dreams told as a dream from which Balian finally wakes to find himself in hell. Irwin had to found his own publishing firm to first publish this book in England in 1983. Perhaps the most brilliant and moving of this year's overtly experimental novels is Thomas McGonigle's *The Corpse Dream of N. Petkov* (Dalkey), which treats the historical death of the courageous leader of the Bulgarian Agrarian Party who was tortured and hanged by the Communists in 1947. In a brief space (133 pages) McGonigle not only tells the story from several angles, but also introduces himself as a searcher for the truth and historical meaning of these events. This powerful novel was highly praised by Andrei Codrescu in the *New York Times Book Review.* Codrescu concluded: "One comes away from this little book with a bitter taste at the back of the throat, a taste that may very well be that of recent Eastern European history."

Turning to somewhat better-known writers, we find Robert Coover doing his lightly experimental number on Richard Nixon once again in *Whatever Happened To Gloomy Gus of the Chicago Bears?* (Simon and Schuster). This time it takes the form of a story narrated by a part-time union organizer and WPA sculptor named Meyer, dealing with "the rise and fall of the Chicago Bear who could not stay onside." Problem with this one is that Coover's satire is at once safe and entirely predictable. Another problem is that it was already published in a slightly shorter version, some years ago. Roughly the same size as Coover's little novel and McGonigle's is Russell Hoban's latest–*The Medusa Frequency* (Atlantic Monthly, 143 pages). This story reawakens the Orpheus myth in contemporary London. The central character is a blocked writer, Herman Orff, author of two unsuccessful novels, *Slopes of Hell* and *A World of Shadows.* He now works for Classic Comics, and his real life seems to consist in turning ancient myths upside down and inside out. Full of various kinds of homage and literary allusion, puns and jokes of every kind, it has a Persephone, here named Melanie Falsepercy, and Orff's Euridyce–Luise von Himmelbett. Orff has several lively encounters with the head of Orpheus–as itself in the mud near Putney Bridge, later as a ball, a grapefruit, and a cabbage. Hard to describe, but Hoban's publisher gives it a good try: "With comedy and wisdom and a vivid evocation of the London scene Rus-

Dust jacket for Russell Hoban's retelling of the Orpheus myth in a modern London setting

sell Hoban finds a mythic dimension for the modern world." Oh, well . . . *sure.* You mean like *that.* . . .

Cynthia Ozick is not generally classified as an "experimental" writer, but her work, from the earliest short stories until now, has been characterized by adventurous concept and execution. Her latest, *The Messiah of Stockholm* (Knopf), is no exception. It is the story of Lars Andemening, a book reviewer in Stockholm who believes himself to be the orphaned only child of the real (historical) Bruno Schulz, Polish Jew and author of *The Street of Crocodiles*, who was murdered by the SS in 1942. The story involves the discovery of a missing Schulz manuscript, *The Messiah;* and its layers of literary fact and fable are complicated by some autobiographical elements and concerns. It is at least plausible that the high jinks and derring-do of Erica Jong's newest, *Serenissima: A Novel of Venice* (Houghton Mifflin), could qualify as experimental also, if only because it has ghosts for characters, including the ghost of Shakespeare, with whom protagonist Jessica Pruitt manages a

physical affair, and some fancy time-warping between a contemporary film festival and sixteenth-century Venice where a "real" Shylock loans money and exacts his pound of flesh.

Other "mainstream" writers whose sometimes original habits and gestures serve now more as matters of identity and style than as experiments made a mark on the literary history of this year. Kurt Vonnegut received mixed notices all around and was chided for the predictability of his habits in *Bluebeard.* Abstract Expressionist and secret Realist, Rabo Karabekian (originally out of *Breakfast of Champions,* 1973) tells his own story while waiting for the end in enviable comfort out in East Hampton. The essential mystery and source of narrative suspense is in Karabekian's potato barn, which turns out to be "a gruesome Disneyland," containing a painting of an incredible multitude, ten per square foot, of World War II survivors of all kinds from all sides. Marge Piercy also tried to come to terms with the time of World War II in *Gone to Soldiers* (Summit), her ninth work of fiction, dealing with women (Bernice, Louise, Ruthie, etc.) at war. Heavily advertised as a possible blockbuster, it failed to earn critical support. Jonathan Yardley, reviewing it for the *Washington Post Book World,* faulted it for "leaden prose and lifeless dialogue" and called it "an unwitting parody of Second World War fiction." Korea is the war which casts long shadows over the present-day action of Barry Hannah's latest–*Hey Jack!* (Dutton), a rough and ready, good-ole-boys-in-the-New-South story, told in lively, jivey first person by a character named Homer, a Korean veteran who experienced some of the worst of it at Chosin Reservoir. *Hey Jack!* got mixed notices, but a full share of raves from a growing number of Hannah fans. Joyce Carol Oates (who also published another novel, *Lives of the Twins,* under another publisher's imprint, Simon and Schuster, and under the pseudonym of Rosamond Smith–she is, in fact, Mrs. Raymond Smith) dealt directly with the world of the 1950s, including the Korean War, in *You Must Remember This* (Dutton). This accounting of the outward and visible as well as the inward and spiritual lives of a Catholic family, the Stevicks, in upstate New York, centering around an incestuous love affair between young Stevick and her uncle Felix, a former prizefighter, has been acclaimed by reviewers as her finest fiction since the passionate novels of her early days. It is strongest in the obsessed visions and actions of her characters, weakest in the checklist quality of much of the revisited historical era. In a late essay review of this novel ("What You Deserve Is What You Get," *New Yorker*, 28 December 1987, pp. 119-123) John Updike gave it highest marks and had exceptional praise for the author: "Not since Faulkner has an American writer seemed so mesmerized by a field of imaginary material, and so headstrong in the cultivation of that field."

 Another large novel of roughly the same era is John Toland's *Occupation* (Doubleday), which continues the saga of the McGlynns of America and the Todas of Japan begun with *Gods of War* (1985). Literary generations follow quickly behind each other, and so it is no surprise to find Alice McDermott writing about *her* teenage years, in suburbia in the early 1960s, in her highly praised second novel–*That Night* (Farrar, Straus and Giroux). She was specially praised for her success, in this slim novel (184 pages), in transforming familiar materials into something freshly minted. Describing her own goals, she has said: "In 'That Night' I was sort of stubbornly trying to take very simple emotions and redeem them, to show that they are still serious, or can be."

 Closer at hand are the Vietnam novels which continue to appear. One of these, Larry Heinemann's *Paco's Story* (Farrar, Straus and Giroux), surprised many and outraged some (the *New York Times*'s Michiko Kakutani for one) by winning the year's National Book Award. Even the publisher must have been somewhat astonished; for, at the instant of the award, *Paco's Story* was only available in the Penguin paperback edition. Told to "James," who is the reader and anybody else out there listening, in an inventive and raggedly energetic style, by the ghostly plural voice(s) of Alpha Company which was wiped out, "wasted," at Fire Base Harriette, all except for one miraculous survivor, Paco, it alternates between Paco's impossible attempts to adjust to peacetime America and the retailing of the communal nightmare of Alpha Company. It is a remarkable novel which manages to put familiar materials into a new coat of many colors. Philip Caputo's *Indian Country* (Bantam), his third novel, puts a troubled Vietnam veteran, Chris Starkman, in Michigan's isolated Upper Peninsula, where he is somewhat soothed by the wisdom of Louis S. Germaine, an old Ojibwa Indian. Joseph Fernandino's *Firefight* (Soho) and Scott Ely's *Starlight* (Weidenfeld and Nicolson) are both combat novels. Bud Shrake's *Night Never Falls* (Random House) is set in Vietnam before

Dust jacket for Kurt Vonnegut, Jr.'s fictional memoir of Rabo Karabekian, a minor character in Breakfast of Champions *(1973), whom Vonnegut portrays as one of the originators of American Abstract Expressionism*

the Americans were involved, at the time of the battle of Dien Bien Phu. Perhaps the finest of the lot, not as stylish as *Paco's Story* but overwhelming in its gritty authority, is Kent Anderson's *Sympathy For the Devil* (Doubleday). Anderson, a former Special Forces officer, deals with a three-man Special Forces team (Hanson, Quinn, and Silver) working with Montagnard soldiers. Not widely noticed, *Sympathy For the Devil* nonetheless was called "a wonderful achievement" and "a very brave book" by the *Washington Post*.

 There were a number of books which, whether long or short in the telling, attempted to establish a larger and longer view of contemporary history and current events. Shortest (149 pages, including the verbatim text of the U.S. Constitution), and perhaps even the most ambitious, was James Michener's *Legacy* (Random House), which tells the story of the Starr family from the Declaration of Independence to the present. It was respectfully chided for lacking texture and story by most reviewers. Judith Martin ("Miss Manners") was an exception in the *New York Times Book Review,* dismissing it as "a book proposal." John Gregory Dunne's *The Red White and Blue,* covering, on a big scale, roughly twenty years of American life, and described by novelist and critic Anne Tyler in the *New York Times Book Review* as "a rambling rumination on the career of a radical lawyer named Leah Kaye" (and her former husband Jack Broderick), was expansively advertised and promoted and was, briefly, a best-seller. It earned a mixed response from reviewers. Anne Tyler complained that the time scheme seemed "stirred with a stick" and concluded that it is "not a very likeable book." T. Coraghessan Boyle's *World's End* (Viking) fared better at the hands of reviewers and ended up the year on the *New York Times Book Review*'s most selective list–"The Best Books of 1987." Set in an imaginary Peterskill, N.Y., in 1968, it leaps about in time and space as it follows several families– the Van Warts, the Van Brunts, the Cranes–from earliest Colonial days through the rebellious 1960s. Praising it as "a smashing good novel," the *New York Times* editors predict that "T. Coraghessan Boyle has no forseeable limits as a writer." Another novel of family and of time (in this instance a little over thirty years) is Wallace Stegner's *Crossing to Safety* (Random House). Quietly told, more conventional in the telling, but elegantly executed, as befits an American master who has won both the Pulitzer Prize and the National Book Award and has been publishing novels for fifty years, it is the story of two academic couples, the Morgans and the Langs, who became fast and true friends in Madison, Wisconsin, thirty-four years ago. Set in a single and dramatic day in New England, during August of 1972, *Crossing to Safety* tells the story of the two marriages, their likenesses and differences. It is a wise and mature book and has been, gratefully, so received.

The scenes of these timely novels were not always, by any means, American. Diane Johnson gave us, in *Persian Nights* (Knopf), Iran just before the 1979 revolution with the story of Chloe Fowler and her surgeon husband, Jeffrey, together with other Americans and Iranians, serving at Azami Hospital and living in Azami Compound. Johnson knows whereof she writes, for she is married to a doctor and together they lived in Iran, for a time, in 1979. Plenty of authenticity, though there is at least one false note in the character of Dick Rothblatt, who is identified

Cover for the paperback edition of Larry Heinemann's 1987 National Book Award-winning novel

as head of the dermatology department at Princeton. Princeton has no medical school and, of course, no department of dermatology. Lawrence Thornton presented a credible Argentina in *Imagining Argentina* (Doubleday), the story of Carlos Rueda, who has the gift of being able to imagine the fates of the "Disappeared." Although the Iron Curtain country is not named in Brian Moore's thriller *The Color of Blood* (Dutton), clearly and credibly it is an imaginary Poland (with, maybe, a little bit of Ireland added). Moore lived in Poland for a time as a journalist and once interviewed Cardinal Wyszynski. Here the protagonist is Cardinal Stephen Bem, caught (literally) in the middle between the totalitarian and Godless secular regime and the fanatics and fundamentalists of his own faith. Nadine Gordimer, not surprisingly, deals with the upheavals of contemporary Africa in *A Sport of Nature* (Knopf), which follows the life of a young South African woman as she changes (the title refers to "a spontaneous mutation") from "Kim" to "Hillela" to "Chiemeka," this latter meaning in Igbo–"God has done very well." Likewise she changes from privileged child to mistress of an African revolutionary leader to wife of an African statesman. Whether this represents upward or downward mobility is left for the reader to determine. A somewhat similar fate comes to pass for the rich American twins, Harriet and Michael Wishwell, who are captivated by the Fourth World Movement, a religious scam in India, and squander their inheritance on it in Ruth Prawer Jhabvala's *Three Continents* (Morrow). This is Jhabvala's tenth novel, though she is most widely known as the screenwriter for Merchant and Ivory. In what is a kind of ironic reversal of the thrust of *Three Continents*, V. S. Naipaul, who has divided his work with an approximate equality between fiction (eleven novels) and nonfiction (eight books), brings fact and fiction into an intimate fusion with *The Enigma of Arrival*. This is an autobiographical novel about a writer from Trinidad (himself in all known details) coming to England and eventually settling in the rural Salisbury Plain of Wiltshire. It is an extremely personal book, a witnessing to the immemorial yet ever-changing country life of Britain and the people there. It received mixed, but respectful notices. Not many reviewers seemed to notice that it is a book *about* the land we choose to inhabit, when we can, and how it gives back in kind some of what we bestow on it. Naipaul was nothing if not explicit about this: "Land is not land alone, something that is simply itself. Land partakes of what we breathe into it, touched by our moods and memories. And this end of a cycle, in my life of the manor, mixed up with the feeling of age which my illness was forcing on me, caused me grief." Somewhat different pictures, not altogether charming, of life in Margaret Thatcher's Britain come to us from Malcolm Bradbury in *Cuts* (Harper and Row) and Margaret Drabble in *The Radiant Way* (Knopf). *Cuts* is slighter and more simply satirical, being the story of Henry Babbacombe, writer, and his dealings with Lord Mellow of Eldorado T. V. *The Radiant Way*, Drabble's tenth novel and her first since *The Middle Ground* seven years ago, was widely reviewed and most seriously received. It is concerned with three intellectual women in London, all classmates at Cambridge in the 1950s. It begins with a 1979 New Year's Eve party, and goes on to cover five difficult years in the lives of these three interesting women, giving us (in the words of the publisher) "a sweeping, incisive view of England today and how, over the past quarter-century, it has changed, declined, and survived." Another novel set in Britain, present and future, is the almost indescribable *Staring at the Sun* (Knopf) by Julian Barnes, who also did some teasing and baffling with his last novel, the celebrated *Flaubert's Parrot* (1985). "Constantly surprising" is the epithet his publisher uses to describe the new book. That can be taken as understatement. Opening in June of 1941, when an R.A.F. night-fighter pilot named Prosser sees the sun rise twice, it shortly changes into a recollection of ninety years of living, and seeking for large and small truths, by Jean Serjeant, looking back from the year 2021. It ends with the old lady and her son Gregory in an airplane flying to stare at the sun a final time. In between there are events, voyages, and any number of interesting characters, not the least of which are the General Purposes Computer and its special program TAT–The Absolute Truth. Together with Bruce Chatwin, Peter Ackroyd, and some others, Barnes seems to be busily reinventing the British novel.

Not by any means ignored, though somewhat lost in the shuffle and hustle was Ward Just's excellent *The American Ambassador* (Houghton Mifflin). Here we have the life and times of Ambassador William North (stationed at Bonn), his wife Elinor, and his son William North, Jr. (code name Wolfgang), who is a terrorist with a rage against injustice. Formerly with the *Washington Post*, Just knows the world he writes about and with this book comes fully into his own.

The novel of family and family history, often bittersweet in its stylish mixture of humor and pathos, its blended language made rich and energetic with the living vernacular, and all set against a background of a constantly changing New South, has gradually become almost a genre in and of itself. And it has brought to the forefront of the literary scene a number of gifted southern women writers. This year they were well represented by the likes of Shelby Hearon's *Five Hundred Scorpions* (Atheneum), Laurel Godman's *The Part of Fortune* (Weidenfeld and Nicolson), Valerie Sayers's *Due East* (Doubleday), Beverly Lowry's *The Perfect Sonya* (Viking), and Kaye Gibbons's *Ellen Foster* (Algonquin). Susan Shreve's *Queen of Hearts* (Simon and Schuster) belongs

CROSSING TO SAFETY

A NOVEL BY THE AUTHOR OF ANGLE OF REPOSE AND THE SPECTATOR BIRD

WALLACE STEGNER

Dust jacket for Wallace Stegner's novel about the lifelong friendship between two couples

here, as well, though it is set in the port town of Bethany, Massachusetts, during the 1950s and early 1960s. Her protagonist, Francesca Woodbine, has the gift of prophecy. With the story built around a rape and two murders it is "gothic" enough to qualify as southern in spirit if not in fact. There were four more-than-moderately successful examples of the New South novel in 1987. Josephine Humphrey's second novel (her first, *Dreams of Sleep,* won the 1985 Ernest Hemingway Foundation Award), *Rich in Love* (Viking), focusing on the Odom family of Mount Pleasant, South Carolina, and especially the precocious seventeen-year-old narrator, Lucille, was widely advertised and reviewed. So was the third novel, *Tending to Virginia* (Algonquin), by Jill McCorkle, a generational novel about a North Carolina family, a compendium of stories about the men of the family as told to each other by the women. *Mother Love* (Farrar, Straus and Giroux) is also Candace Flynt's third novel, all about three sisters (who also tell stories

to each other) from Greensboro, North Carolina, who are seeking to come to terms with the recent death of their mother, a complex, passionate, difficult woman. How a family–the Quicks of a town in western North Carolina much like Gail Godwin's hometown of Asheville–deals with a sudden death is also the central subject of Godwin's best-selling *A Southern Family* (Morrow). This is a large and complex story of New and Old South with many characters and told from shifting multiple points of view. But at heart it is the story of Clare Camion, a novelist now living in New York who shares many autobiographical facts and details with the author.

Other New South novels, these told from a more assertively masculine angle, appeared in 1987. Among them mention should surely be made of Padgett Powell's *A Woman Named Drown* (Farrar, Straus and Giroux), a story which earned some credit for originality amid mostly negative reviews; John Logue's *Boats Against the Current* (Little, Brown), the story of a cynical newsman, Jack Harris, in Montgomery, Alabama, in 1967; Clyde Edgerton's second novel, *Walking Across Egypt* (Algonquin), following directly behind the surprisingly successful *Raney* (1985), and dealing mainly with seventy-eight-year-old Mattie Rigsbee of Listre, North Carolina; Robert Inman's *Home Fires Burning* (Little, Brown), all about a small-town newspaper editor, Jake Tibbets, and his trials and tribulations; and Harry Crews's latest example of the form he seems to have invented, call it Heavy Metal Southern Gothic, in *All We Need of Hell* (Harper and Row). Crews, by the way, was responsible for what must surely be high on the short list for "most complete hatchet job of 1987" in his *Washington Post* (21 May 1987) review of fellow southerner David Bottoms's first novel, *Any Cold Jordan* (Peachtree), which Crews greeted with comments like "mechanical, arbitrary and unbelievable," "thumping repetitiveness," and "simply boring."

Three major American novelists who happen to be southern by birth and choice, but who have transcended the strictly regional, published important novels in 1987. With *The Thanatos Syndrome,* Walker Percy brought back, from jail, Dr. Tom More of *Love in the Ruins* (1971), home to Feliciana Parish again where he and the indomitable Father Smith, and some others, have to deal with a secular plot to control mankind by putting heavy sodium in the drinking water. A funny and moving parable of and for our times. With *Texasville* Larry McMurtry turned back to the

Dust jacket for the American edition of Nadine Gordimer's novel which recounts the picaresque adventures of Hillela, a white South African woman whose life forms a paradigm for the paradoxes and brutalities of apartheid

town of Thalia, scene of *The Last Picture Show* (1966), and to some of the same characters, older if not a whole lot wiser, who have been up and down, boom and bust, with the oil business, "instant millionaires [who] are in the process of becoming dazed instant debtors." It is a very funny book, though a fair share of the reviewers seemed to have missed that. With *Alnilam*, the title coming from the name of the central star of the belt of the constellation Orion, his first novel since the hugely successful *Deliverance* (1970), James Dickey tells the story of blind Frank Cahill, who, together with his good dog Zack, goes searching for Frank's son, Joel, an heroic pilot who is missing and presumed dead after crashing in a training accident. Set during World War II, it is, though rich and full of specific, even mundane detail, a mythopoeic story, deeply symbolic and riddled with shadowy ambiguities. One reviewer called it "a mythical and sinister story." Former airman Dickey calls it "a novel of

the air." One technical innovation employed by Dickey is the use of double columns to offer simultaneously the point of view and perceptions of Cahill versus those of fully sighted narration. Ironically, this device renders large portions of the novel somewhat inaccessible to blind readers; for it cannot be accurately duplicated by braille or by sound recording.

Mythopoeic storytelling is essential to the experience of two novels by prominent black novelists—*Reuben* (Holt), by John Edgar Wideman, and *Beloved*, by Toni Morrison. *Reuben*, Wideman's first novel since he won the P.E.N./ Faulkner award for *Sent For You Yesterday*, is once again dealing with the Homewood section of Pittsburgh. Reuben is a tiny, slightly deformed, sixty-year-old black man who lives in a trailer and acts as a lawyer representing the various complex interests of his poor neighbors in their endless battle against Authority. It becomes a kind of slide show of stories, tales of every kind, told to and by Reuben in an unusual alloy of high literary rhetoric and jivey street language. *Beloved*, which is Toni Morrison's fifth novel and which has already received more rave reviews, more universal attention and acclaim than any American novel in recent memory, is intricate in the telling, as concentrated (a huge narrative compressed and condensed into less than 300 pages) as a poem. Its protagonist is Sethe, a former slave who once killed her own baby daughter to save her from the fate of slavery. Part ghost story, full of dreams and visions and living memories and many voices, it is a haunting, powerful, and disturbing story. Both books have the high polish of critical self-consciousness, a sheen and glitter of aesthetic achievement. But there are serious problems with both of these works. It is not precisely or entirely that both factual accuracy and authenticity have been often slighted in favor of poetic or purely emotional impact; for both writers are far more deeply concerned to exploit and explore myths than to try to replicate factual reality. A deeper and more serious problem is that these books are seething and boiling with an almost murderous sense of racial hatred, a subtext of stereotypical hatred which would be unacceptable almost anywhere, from any source, and ought to be so here. It is an ironic fact of the marketplace that for a black writer to succeed in America, he or she must write to and for an overwhelmingly white reading public. It is difficult to imagine what kind of real delight and truthful instruction, other than purely aesthetic pleasures, that same audience might possibly derive from the angry vilification of itself in these novels. Three other distinctive Afro-American novels of 1987 were Terry McMillan's *Mama* (Houghton Mifflin), a first novel following a black family through the tumultuous 1960s and into the 1970s; *Dessa Rose* (Berkeley), by Sherley Anne Williams, a slave story, much praised by Alice Walker, dealing chiefly with the relationship between Miss Rufel, a plantation owner, and Dessa Rose, a pregnant slave; and John A. Williams's latest, *Jacob's Ladder* (Thunder's Mouth), a story set in the imaginary African country of Pandemi in the 1960s.

Some superbly written and deeply humane novels have come to us this year from black writers who are neither American nor writing in terms of any contemporary Afro-American literary fashions. *Maps* (Pantheon), by Nuruddin Farah, comes out of Somalia, now torn, divided, and tormented, and, in an experimental mode, tells the story of an orphan boy, Askar, who can actually move backward and forward in time. Tribe, religion, nationality, and language are of enormous importance in this harsh world. *Search Sweet Country* (Morrow), by the British-educated poet from Ghana B. Kojo Laing, tells, in a freely experimental manner, both in form and content, and in an electric language, humming and sparkling, of a group of remarkable characters in the city of Accra in 1975. There are human beings of all kinds and races here, good and evil and altogether memorable. This has been called one of the finest novels ever written in Africa. Another quite wonderful work published this year is a first novel, *Clarise Cumberbatch Want To Go Home* (Ticknor and Fields), by Joan Cambridge, a native of Guyana. Split in setting between Guyana and New York, it is entirely composed in West Indian dialect and patois, a style as close to singing in prose as contemporary English can manage.

Even though the critical status and popular reputation of historical fiction have declined somewhat from their best days, plenty of good work in that demanding form is still being done. Of course, the genre of the historical romance is thriving, but, though widely advertised and available, is seldom reviewed or treated seriously. Some more serious historical fiction in 1987 managed to earn some success or critical appreciation or both. Among the well-received and more conventional historical novels were Gilliam Bradshaw's *The Bearkeeper's Daughter* (Houghton Mifflin—Constantinople in the sixth century A.D.), Nicho-

Dust jacket for Walker Percy's sequel to Love in the Ruins *(1971), a fantasy about a government experiment in mind control through contamination of a community's water supply*

las Guild's *The Assyrian* (Atheneum—sixth century B.C.), Gary Jennings's *Spangle* (Atheneum—nineteenth-century circus life), Stephen Marlowe's *The Memoirs of Christopher Columbus* (Scribners), Robert Somerlott's *Death of the Fifth Sun* (Viking—Cortez and the Aztecs), and Edward Rutherford's *Sarum* (Crown—England from Ice Age to here and now). At once more ambitious and successful in a literary sense were a number of other novels. Anthony Bailey's *Major Andre* (Farrar, Straus and Giroux) covers the last five days of the life of that charismatic British spy until Washington had him hanged on 2 October 1780. Maurice Shadbolt's *Season of the Jew* (Norton), despite its title, deals with a Maori revolt in New Zealand during 1868-1869. Another novel treating historical Down Under is Thomas Keneally's *The Playmaker* (Simon and Schuster). Keneally, whose distinctly original novels are set in past time, including *Confederates* (1979) and the remarkable *Gossip From the Forest* (1975), here presents the story of Lt. Ralph Clark of the Royal Marines who, in New South Wales in 1789, must produce and direct George Farquhar's *The Recruiting Offi-*

cer with a cast of and for an audience of "lags" (convicts). (Farquhar's play also figures in *Major Andre.*)

American history was the source of some of the best historical novels of the year. On the more popular side there were two large-scale books–William Safire's *Freedom* and Gore Vidal's latest revision of the American story–*Empire.* Large-scale? The research notes alone to Safire's book, a section he entitled "Underbook: Sources and Commentary," run to some 133 pages. Safire named his fiction of the life of Lincoln during the first twenty-one months of the Civil War, ending with the Emancipation Proclamation, a "docudrama." No less thorough, but more than a bit less rigidly factual was Vidal's vision of the age of McKinley and Teddy Roosevelt and the coming of "American imperialism." He tells his story in settings in England, New York, Washington, and Newport, Rhode Island, and includes among his large cast of characters well-executed, if somewhat fanciful versions of Henry James, Henry Adams, and, of course, William Randolph Hearst.

In her first novel, *Good King Harry* (1984), Denise Giardino had established herself as a gifted writer of the conventional historical novel. With her second, *Storming Heaven* (Norton), she begins again, as it were, with a powerful and gritty story of West Virginia coal miners in 1921, a time of strikes and armed rebellion. Four narrators cover the thirty years leading up to the revolt and follow it to its bitter end. This book, about an almost forgotten time and place in our history, comes with the highest praise of other young writers like Jayne Anne Phillips, Annie Dillard, Carolyn Chute, and Madison Smartt Bell. Probably the most widely discussed and praised novel of American history this year was Ivan Doig's *Dancing At the Rascal Fair* (Atheneum). The second volume in Doig's projected Montana trilogy, and Doig's fifth book since his first, a nonfiction memoir, *The House of Sky*, appeared in 1978, *Dancing At the Rascal Fair* begins in Scotland in 1889 and goes on to cover three decades of frontier life and times in Montana. A native of northern Montana, Doig has been writing with love and care of his own place and its people, the Scots immigrants and sheepherders. Celebrating his achievement, critic William Tazewell has written: "Doig's Montana saga, still unfolding, is one to which the adjective 'epic' can be applied without any embarrassment."

Dust jacket for James Dickey's "novel of the air" which attempts typographically to represent the perceptions of a blind man

Another mixed genre in American letters, sometimes treated with respect and other times relegated to the back of the literary bus, is the suspense thriller. Two of the most successful and respectable are first novels–Scott Turow's *Presumed Innocent* (Farrar, Straus and Giroux) and James W. Hall's *Under Cover of Daylight* (Norton). Turow's book, a tricky murder story combined with grainy and accurate courtroom drama (Turow worked as a U.S. attorney for eight years) and a texture of contemporary urban ethnicity, was one of the most widely publicized literary events of the year and quickly became a major best-seller. Poet and story writer James W. Hall's novel combines murder, sex, revenge, and high-level suspense in a firmly realized setting of the Florida Keys and is already scheduled to be translated into a feature film. Hall may very well be the best all-around *writer* working with the genre.

Two superbly gifted old-timers, masters of the trade, were also well represented this year.

The inimitable George V. Higgins produced his most involved and ambitious suspense novel so far with *Outlaws*. This one concerns political robbery and murder in Boston in the early 1970s, but covers a full fifty years and moves out of New England to New York, California, England, and Morocco. There is a larger and more various cast of characters than usual, and there is no falling off of Higgins's brightest gift–dialogue that hops, skips, jumps, and swings. Elmore Leonard, no slouch with the spoken lingo, himself, took pleasant advantage of his late-found fame to bring out a book, *Touch*, which had been written in 1977 and widely rejected by a string of publishers. It is not easy to see why they let it pass. Though the story of *Touch* is offbeat–it allows for the perhaps mystical and miraculous healing powers of a former Franciscan monk called Juvenal–it is firmly set in Leonard's home base of Detroit and is a novel of both suspense and crime, though it is a somewhat more subtle form of criminal behavior than we usually encounter in thrillers. In an introduction Leonard writes: "I had a good time writing *Touch*, imagining mystical things happening to an ordinary person in a contemporary setting. It's way off-trail compared to what I usually write, but it shouldn't be mystifying unless you look for symbols, hidden meanings."

In fairness, mention should be made of the latest and thirty-ninth book in the 87th Precinct series, *Tricks* (Arbor House), by Ed McBain (Evan Hunter), which is a crafty and professional entertainment of the first order.

Other thrillers which deserved and received more than casual notice include Stephen Dobyns's eighth novel, *A Boat Off the Coast* (Viking), John Katzenbach's latest, *The Traveler* (Putnam's), and Ruth Rendell's *Talking To Strange Men* (Pantheon). Rendell also published the mystery *A Fatal Inversion* (Bantam) under the pseudonym Barbara Vine. And here and now it can be revealed for the first time that P. J. Coyne, whose new Ned Spearbrooke novel, *Manuscript for Murder* (Dodd, Mead), was published in 1987, is, in fact, the pen name of novelist Hilary Masters. Ned Spearbrooke must surely be the only fictional detective who doubles as a literary agent.

The numbers are not in yet, but it is a good guess that there were not so many literary first novels as usual in 1987. Certainly fewer than usual managed to percolate up to notice in the major reviewing media. The year which began with great hoopla attending the publication of

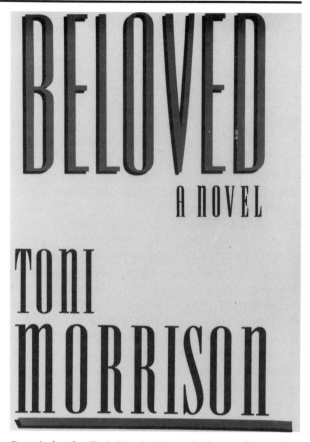

Dust jacket for Toni Morrison's novel about a former slave who killed her infant daughter to save her from slavery

first novel *Anywhere But Here* (Knopf) by Mona Simpson saw the publication of a few genuinely first-rate debuts. Among these were Gary Gildner's *The Second Bridge* (Algonquin), Ann Hood's *Somewhere Off the Coast of Maine* (Bantam), Robert Boswell's *Crooked Hearts* (Knopf), Stephen McCauley's *The Object of My Affection* (Simon and Schuster), Lionel Shriver's *The Female of the Species* (Farrar, Straus and Giroux), H. F. Saint's *Memoirs of an Invisible Man* (Atheneum), and Brett Lott's *The Man Who Owned Vermont* (Viking). And then there were those books which tried to do something more, something special, took real risks and aimed for real achievement. Here one would have to mention several (admitting that others could, no doubt did, slip easily through the net). Much attention was paid to story writer Charles Baxter's *First Light* (Viking), which, to make accounting of the lives of a sister and brother in Five Oaks, Michigan, starts at the end and works backward to the beginning. *Zion's Cause (1920-1950)* (Algonquin), by Jim Peyton, a comic novel of a small Kentucky town, captured the support of the *New Yorker* in its final issue of 1987. There it was called "a wonderful novel." Adding this encomium: "Jim Peyton's vision is akin to Buster Keaton's, blessed with ingenious clowning and erratic locomotion, and riddled with minor miracles you want to witness again and again." Also very funny, and a good deal more experimental (it ends in the middle of a sentence) than either of the above is David Foster Wallace's Pynchonesque romp in *The Broom of the System* (Penguin), oddly situated in the Cleveland of 1990.

Two of the best literary novels of 1987, first or otherwise, are *A Yellow Raft In Blue Water* (Holt), by Michael Dorris, and Sharon Sheehe Stark's *A Wrestling Season* (Morrow). Perhaps, in the strictest sense, Dorris's story (stories rather) of the lives of three Indian women doesn't qualify as a first novel, for he and his wife, Louise Erdrich, collaborate on all their works. And, indeed, in subject, form, and style, this is much like her novels. Never mind. It is at once bold and lyrical and honest in its picture of Native American life. Stark, who earlier published a highly praised collection of stories, *The Dealers' Yard*, here takes all kinds of chances in telling her story of a Pennsylvania family called Kleeves. She tried for new twists in style and tone and focus which some praised ("a beautiful sinewy way with words") and others faulted: "It's as if the author had set out to write a historical saga and got waylaid by four fast-talking and altogether charming individuals." Stark is a major talent and, given a little chance and encouragement, will go far.

It was an extraordinary year for the publication of foreign novels in translation, not only for the number and variety of translations, but also, in many cases, for the high quality and originality of the work. The latter encomium, to be sure, did not apply to Francoise Sagan's *A Reluctant Hero* (Dutton), for which the most common adjective used by reviewers was "trivial." But other French novels proved to be technically adventurous and interesting. Jean Levi's *The Chinese Emperor* (Harcourt Brace Jovanovich), a story set in China in the third century B.C., and George Perec's experimental literary games in *Life, A User's Manual* (Godine) attracted serious and extensive attention. Out of Morocco but written in French came *The Sand Child* (Harcourt Brace Jovanovich) by Tahar Ben Jelloun, an unusual mixture of myth and reality and a genuine surprise as an Islamic feminist novel. The Latin American boomlet continued. In a novel of Pinochet's Chile, Isabel Allende discarded some of the gestures of García Márquez and spoke

Dust jacket for the 1987 publication of Elmore Leonard's story about a Franciscan monk with a miraculous healing touch. The novel was written in 1977 but was rejected by several publishers.

more firmly in her own voice in *Of Love and Shadows* (Knopf). The productive Mario Vargas Llosa was represented by a suspense thriller set in Peru in the 1950s–*Who Killed Palomino Molero?* (Farrar, Straus and Giroux). From Spain came Juan Goytisolo's boldly experimental *Landscapes After the Battle* (Seaver). Equally experimental, though more so as a matter of wildly surreal content than form, was *Baltasar and Blimunda* (Harcourt Brace Jovanovich) by Portugal's José Saramago. From Italy we received new books by acknowledged masters–Albert Moravia's *The Voyeur* (Farrar, Straus and Giroux) and Natalia Ginsburg's epistolary novel, *The City and the House* (Seaver). Perhaps more interesting were three others: Anna Maria Ortese's surrealist *The Iguana* (McPherson), in which the protagonist falls in love with a maiden iguana on an island of exiled European nobility; Umberto Saba's explicitly sexual *Ernesto* (Carcanet), left unfinished when the great Triestine poet died in 1957; and Salvatore Satta's *The Day of Judgment* (Farrar, Straus and

Giroux), set in the Sardinian town of Nuoro during the last decades of the nineteenth century and the first years of our own. Satta is elegantly translated by the Irish poet Patrick Creagh. In addition to Gunter Grass's *The Rat*, the first translation from German into English of the late Herman Broch's "mountain novel," *The Spell* (Farrar, Straus and Giroux), aroused critical interest and created some controversy; for Broch, in his lifetime, had never considered it finished and ready for publication.

There were translations from contemporary writers in languages less often published in this country: from Norwegian, Knut Fadbakken's *The Honeymoon* (St. Martin's); from Indonesian author Ismail Marahimin was *And The War Is Over* (Louisiana State University Press). More rare than either, and much less known here, is the contemporary Albanian novelist Ismail Kadare. His *Chronicle In Stone* (Meredith) tells of the destruction of a Balkan city during World War II as witnessed and experienced by an extremely imaginative small boy. Poet Kadare is the author of nine novels which enjoy a considerable reputation in Europe. Polish writing is somewhat more familiar in the United States, and Tadeusz Konwicki had already earned some good repute for his work, especially *A Minor Apocalypse* (1983). But his latest, the complex autobiographical novel *Moonrise, Moonset* (Farrar, Straus and Giroux), surprised reviewers with both its freedom of form and by the openness of the content, considering the classically totalitarian character of the Polish government. Konwicki fought for Poland in the Home Army, first against the Nazis and later against the Communists. In the novel he writes about that time (1944-1945) as well as the troubled present times in Poland from autumn 1980 up through December of 1981. Finally, 1987 gave us a translation of *The Old Capital* (North Point) by Japan's Nobel Prize-winning (1968) Yasunari Kawabata. It is an elegant and evocative novel about the ancient city of Kyoto.

Even as more and more writers are seeing their earlier works brought out again in one or another of the trade paperback editions, hardcover and new editions of "old" books are becoming more familiar in the bookstores. For example, 1987 witnessed the publication of new hardcover editions of James Merrill's *The Seraglio* (Atheneum), Calder Willingham's *Eternal Fire* (Donald I. Fine), and Herbert Gold's *The Man Who Was Not With It* (Second Edition Books/Algonquin).

THE HUSSAR

A Novel by DAVID R. SLAVITT

Dust jacket for David R. Slavitt's attempt to re-create Prussian writer Theodor Fontane's novel Schach von Wuthenow *(1883)*

Atheneum brought out a twenty-fifth anniversary edition of Reynolds Price's *A Long and Happy Life*. The Book-of-the-Month Club published a fiftieth anniversary edition of J. R. R. Tolkien's *The Hobbit*. In a series entitled Book-of-the-Month Club Classics they also brought out new editions of novels, some of these with specially written introductions: Erich Maria Remarque's *All Quiet on the Western Front*, introduction by Mordecai Richler; Richard Wright's *Native Son*, introduction by David Bradley; James Agee's *A Death In The Family*, introduction by Alfred Kazin; Isak Dinesen's *Seven Gothic Tales*, introduction by John Updike; and Joseph Heller's *Catch-22*. Other slightly earlier books were reissued by various publishers. Among the more noteworthy examples: *Iola Leroy; Or, Shadows Uplifted*, 1892 (Beacon Press), by Frances E. W. Harper, a black woman's account of Reconstruction days; *The Fierce Dispute*, 1929 (St. Martin's), by Helen Hooven Santmyer; *Daughter of the Earth*, 1929 (Feminist Press), Agnes Smedley's autobiographical novel; *Siesta*, 1935 (Second Chance Press), by Berry Fleming.

The University of Georgia Press has begun to publish editions of earlier fiction of special interest. Among these are Humphrey Cobb's *Paths of Glory* (1935) and black writer Raymond Andrews's *Appalachee Red* (1929), with an afterword by novelist Richard Bausch.

Perhaps the most important part of this whole roundup of the year's novels has been left for the last. It is one thing to take due note of many of the books which were well noted during the year. It is another thing entirely—yet, perhaps, the best possible justification for a re-examination of the year's fiction—to cite books which are, in the best judgment of this reviewer, first-rate, fully deserving of honor and scrutiny, books which, though some were well and favorably reviewed (and others not), failed to capture the attention they deserve. It is too late for the marketplace, but never really too late for the interested reader. And so I salute these works here and now, recommending them with enthusiasm, without reservation: Stephen Becker, one of our finest novelists, in *A Rendezvous In Haiti* (Norton) evokes the Haiti of 1919, where the U.S. Marines were still on duty; *The Rabbi of Lud* (Scribners) by Stanley Elkin is an acquired taste to be sure, but who wouldn't delight in the gigs and gags of Rabbi Goldkorn, formerly Chief Rabbi of the Alaska Pipeline, now of Lud, not a dead city but a city of the dead in New Jersey; *Broken Ground* (Harper and Row) by John Keeble, his first since *Yellowfish*, this one a mythic story with strong (if predictable) political motives and implications; *Cooper* (St. Martin's) by Hilary Masters, a quiet and profoundly touching story which celebrates a triumph of the human spirit, by an author whose ceiling seems unlimited; *Catholic Girls* (Donald I. Fine) by Kit Reed, a lively and original version of what happened to four women who met twenty years ago at Mount Maria College, enthusiastically praised by Paul Horgan and Annie Dillard; *The Hussar* (Louisiana State University Press) by the prolific David R. Slavitt, a unique novel, a highly sophisticated version of a nineteenth-century Prussian novel which the author had only *read about*, but felt challenged to re-create in his own terms; Alexander Theroux's *An Adultery* (Simon and Schuster), his first since the autobiographical *Darconville's Cat* (1981), this one the complex and ironic confession of Christian Ford, recounting his adulterous relationship with a woman named Farol Colorado, a work of insight and "awesome linguistic virtuosity." At the other end of that particular technical spectrum stands novelist Theodore Weesner who, ever since his praised first book, *The Car Thief*, has been honored for his plain and transparent prose and his patient exploration of the depths and dimensions of his chosen subject. In *The True Detective* (Summit) he incorporates some of the characteristics of the suspense thriller to tell a story of Gil Dulac, a New Hampshire detective trying to solve a peculiarly contemporary sex crime. This is a good novel which fared badly in the hands of some prominent reviewers.

All in all, a surprising year. More so than many have yet realized. Perhaps 1987 cannot claim to have been a literary annus mirabilis, but the novels of this year, at the least, argue that our world is wider and deeper and wilder and stranger than we might have guessed.

The Year in Short Stories

David R. Slavitt

One begins with John Updike's collection, *Trust Me* (Knopf), or actually, one begins by wondering why this should be so inevitable a choice. Updike's stories are admirable, dextrous, often moving, and exactly what we might have expected from a *New Yorker* author whose reputation is so secure as to verge on the marmoreal. But if they had been published pseudonymously . . .

What a dizzying idea! It is hardly likely that Mr. Updike would risk so self-destructive an experiment. He was never one of Ken Kesey's Merry Pranksters—or even a Doris Lessing, whose shenanigans in London a while back proved what everyone knew anyway, that publishers are better at reading the names on the title pages than the manuscripts to which they may be attached. Or, more radically, that there is no distinction, that the reading of a manuscript is conditioned by the name on its title page. This is at the same time an obvious and breathtakingly bold assertion, and it takes the Yale deconstructionists (de Man, Hilles, Derrida, and that group) into new and scary territory. But if that's where the truth lives, that is where one must go.

For all their virtues, which are considerable, we read the stories in *Trust Me* in rather a different way because of its title page and the acknowledgments on the verso. At the very least, the temptation is to discover where the *New Yorker* editors were wrong, capricious, arbitrary, or stupid. We are eager to find among those few stories they rejected, the specially brave or insightful or daring pieces, the ones that were too good for that monument to conspicuous consumption and upper-middle-class taste. If that magazine is the only one left that pays well (other than the stroke magazines, the skin books) and runs serious fiction and even poetry, we ought to love it, right? We should be as solicitous of it as is a nature nut of the last California condors, right?

Wrong! The ecology is such that the one survivor is, like the inhabitant of Loch Ness, an absurd monster. It has prospered not because of its

Dust jacket for John Updike's latest collection of stories

virtue or shrewdness or adaptability, but out of perverse dumb luck. The magazine could very nearly maintain its circulation if it kept running the same editorial content week after week. All its editors really need to keep refreshing is the cartoons, the little jokes at the bottom of the pages, the movie and theater reviews, and the "Talk of the Town" items. The old guard knew this and liked to show off every now and then, running four- and six-part reminiscences by Ved Mehta of all the people who ever lived in India. And it hardly made any difference.

William Shawn is now gone as the editor, and Robert Gottlieb has taken his place (while Sonny Mehta–no relation to Ved, or even Zubin–has taken Gottlieb's old chair at Knopf). There may be a new day at the *New Yorker;* we shall see. Meanwhile, Updike bears both the laurel and the onus of his long and successful association with that publication. He is one of the few good writers in America to be making a living by his writing. He arouses, therefore, if not envy in the rest of us then at least a certain curiosity. How is what he does better than what other short-story writers are doing? How is he different, if not better? What is his knack or charm or special vision?

From the stories themselves, it would be difficult to make any sensible judgment. The stories are okay, or even better than that. But they are by no means head and shoulders above the crowd. Other efforts by less well-known writers, by newcomers, by provincials and rubes, either from "major" trade publishing houses or university presses or the small presses that have been springing up all around the country (like commuter airlines to service the traffic the major carriers can't figure out a way to exploit profitably), are distinguishable stylistically from Updike but by no means inferior in merit. And for persons who still entertain notions of fairness in life and art, this can be unsettling.

Updike, meanwhile, is no fool. He knows his position exactly and what its privileges are. He exploits his eminence, contriving little turns that call attention to his real gift for seizing upon the small detail in a way that is as flattering to his readers as it is actually useful or even justifiable in the fiction itself. He says of one character that he had "a full and fluffy head of hair gray in just the right places (temples, sideburns, a collielike frosting above the collar)" and the "collielike" is striking because of its effort, its reach. An authorial intrusion, it establishes, in case we've forgotten, that this is an Updike piece and that we, the readers, should sit up, pay attention, and appreciate! Similarly, he describes bushes that, beneath the snow "were bowed and splayed like bridesmaids overwhelmed by flowers." Well, yeah, okay. But it works too hard, is too elaborate.

Such gestures may go back to his earliest days at that peculiar magazine, when it was still considered vulgar pandering to have anything like a table of contents up in the front. You turned the slick pages and, with certain people, you just figured out that, hey, this must be Perelman (an easy call), or Cheever, or O'Hara,

Cover for Pinckney Benedict's first collection of stories, most of which deal with the Gothic quality of poverty in the South

or Irwin Shaw–or, a little later on, Updike. The glitzy gesture may have begun as a signature, but it got a kind of validation from the work of Nabokov, whom Updike much admired and from whom he learned the showy things, the outer flashiness if not the inner hardness. In fact, considered in its entirety, Updike's collection seems, in comparison to a number of others of this year, rather determined in its sentimentality. Beneath the bright surfaces there is a sameness in the limitation of his emotional and social range and the confinement of Updike's spirit to a group of characters who seem mostly to be spoiled brats of various ages. There are occasional exceptions. What gives the title story in the collection a little different timbre is that its protagonist at least has aspirations about how life ought to be lived and what relationships should be able to assume in the way of trust and honor. In few of the other stories do any of the characters even show remorse about their shortcomings, and it is Updike's habit to present remorse as if it were, in itself, the last shred of moral value anyone can be expected to take seriously.

Oddly enough, these same stories with another name on them might look different and better. As suppliants rather than bullies, they might have more charm. The crazy truth is that those editors who read title pages are in some sense correct. There is no logic or sense or order to the short-story scene except what the marketplace decrees, and there is hardly a marketplace anymore. The numbers are so small (of bookstores doing business, or of copies of short story collections that are sold) that any observation about relative market strength or weakness is distorted and partial. We have here what financial analysts call a "thin float."

To take another fix on the situation, we might consider *Town Smokes* by Pinckney Benedict (Ontario Review Press). Benedict is twenty-three years old, a kid, still in school for God's sake (well, anyway, he's in the graduate writing program at the University of Iowa). He is as different from Updike as he can be: rural rather than urban and urbane; a novice rather than an old hand (before the appearance of this book, only three of its pieces had appeared, one in the *Chicago Tribune* and two in the *Ontario Review*). And he comes out of nowhere, albeit with as much fanfare as Joyce Carol Oates, his former teacher, and Raymond Smith, Ms. Oates's husband and, with her, the coeditor of the *Ontario Review*, can muster for him (which is not negligible but still falls far short of the attention Updike can command). And how do his stories compare with Updike's? There are nine pieces in the Benedict collection, all of them accomplished, and at least four of them every bit as striking as Updike's work, but fresher, more generous in sympathy, and deeper in resonance than anything of Updike's since *The Poorhouse Fair* (1959). Benedict is expansive, perhaps because it just never crosses his mind not to be. He addresses the large themes of nature's savagery and man's, and how, in the long run, these two kinds of blind brutality may not be very much different.

There is no gainsaying that Benedict was dealt a fortunate hand. He writes of what he knows, which happens to be the rural poverty of the hill country of West Virginia. This isn't absolutely uncharted territory. Mary Lee Settle has been writing about it for years. And the North Carolina hill people in Fred Chappell's poems and stories are not-so-distant kinfolk to Benedict's

characters. But the terms of these lives are fresh and vivid. The town smokes of the title story are the store-bought Camels, cigarettes that haven't been rolled from the pages of a Gideon Bible. With an image like that–or never mind the image; with a piece of truth like that–a writer doesn't have to be so artful in the way he contrives to imply larger meanings. Those large meanings come gushing up like cold water from a spring.

One can argue that these country stories–Benedict's, Richard Ford's, and Jean R. Matthew's, to pick just a few from this year's crop–are easy, that they turn instantly into parable, that the trick these writers are using is almost as old as their hills and that Virgil and Theocritus rang all its changes a couple thousand years ago. And to some degree, there is a justice in such a judgment. The story is, after all, an artifact, a cultural adornment. And culture itself is urban, a by-product if not a direct consequence of city living. These kids like Benedict, who write about life up on the ridges and back in the hollows, don't stay there but come to the cities, or at least graduate faculties at places like Iowa, where there are town smokes and bookstores and libraries. And magazines. (Even, Lord help us, the *New Yorker*.)

The appearance of talent is probably random, but its gravitation to urban centers is not. And there, simplicity and honesty, the celebration of courage in the face of danger and ugliness (in "Boozer"), or the poignant assertion of personal pride on the part of poor people (in "The Sutton Pie Safe") seem, in comparison to what the city dwellers have been doing, nourishing.

Richard Ford made something of a splash this year with his stories of tattered machismo in the rugged sleaze of Montana, *Rock Springs* (Atlantic Monthly Press). Ford did not come out of nowhere. His third novel, *The Sportswriter*, was one of the successful books of 1986, both critically and commercially (even though those two favors of the Bitch Goddess are not necessarily doled out together). In some ways this collection stands between Updike's and Benedict's. Ford is shrewd, trendier than Benedict, not quite a Raymond Carver minimalist but verging in that direction, limited in emotional range as Updike chooses to limit himself. Ford's protagonists are mostly men, often loners, usually losers, people who are, whether they are bright enough to realize it or not, vessels of chagrin. On the other hand Ford shares with Benedict a kind of moral outrage at

Dust jacket for Richard Ford's collection of stories set in Montana

the meagerness of most of our experience which seems only the paltrier for the backdrop of huge mountains and expansive prairie. One needn't be a native of that Big Sky country to be struck by these incongruities. Norman Mailer got the sense of it with uncanny accuracy in *The Executioner's Song* (1979). Ford writes about the same weird discontinuity, and if his disasters and betrayals are on a smaller scale than what Mailer was addressing in Gary Gilmore's witless violence, the rhetorical effects are oddly similar. In a way it is the meanness of his characters that humanize the oppressive majesty of the landscape, bringing it down to something recognizable even if it is mostly loathsome. The pattern on which he works several variations is one involving a small-time malefactor who looks to be about to make an effort to get his act together but then, encountering some random and altogether trivial setback, relapses into an unspecified but indubitable hopelessness. It is sufficiently general to be effective in a variety of applications and, obviously, it is emotionally congenial. What Ford is able to do to keep the game going is to let his sufferers have a certain degree of humor about their predic-

aments and to not show them in moments of self-pity. Ford's narrators are sometimes young men, Hemingway novices, learning by observation what failure is like before they have to experience it at first hand, and the innocence of these narrators is a way to finesse the emotional swampiness that might otherwise be bothersome. It is a lively collection of stories, although not so dazzling as to make the first page notice of the *New York Times Book Review* an obvious or automatic reaction by the editors of that august organ. On the other hand there is a possible explanation. The success of any given book takes too long for the fidgety world of book reviewing and bookselling to adjust to. The shelf life of a new trade book is now six to eight weeks, and if it hasn't caught on in that cruelly brief span, it's dead. The players in the book business are already looking to the new titles with their fresher, or at least as yet undimmed, hopes. What this means is that the points an author picks up on one book, whether critical or commercial, are often cashed in with the next. Bernard Malamud's first great success was *The Assistant* (1957), but it wasn't until the following year, with his next publication, *The Magic Barrel*, a collection of short stories, that he cashed in, won prizes, and got to be a book club selection. I suspect that some similar set of forces may be operating here.

Elizabeth Tallent is another rural author whose collection of short stories, *Time with Children* (Knopf), attracted a fair amount of attention this year. Her jacket photo shows her on a park bench, curled up and looking winsome as she shows off her fancy western boots that are an advertisement for her current address "north of Sante Fe." Tallent is a *New Yorker* writer too, which is to say that most of the stories first appeared in that magazine. She is an admirer of Updike and has written a study of his fiction. She is also a novelist–*Museum Pieces* was published in 1985.

But the important thing is that the stories are *New Yorker* stories, not exactly in the O'Hara/Cheever/Updike line but close enough. Her settings are varied, ranging from the Southwest to London, but what distinguishes Tallent from these model practitioners isn't her locales so much as her use of children as pawns, or foils, or emblems. Her adults show no more discipline or self-control than her five-year-olds, which gives the children's roles an ironic edge that approaches as close to a judgment as the mode al-

Dust jacket for Elizabeth Tallent's second collection of stories, featuring two sets of interwoven tales

lows. Her characters are the same genteel folks we have always seen in the purview of Eustace Tilley's lorgnette, and their concerns are almost entirely those of sensibility, which is the fictional equivalent of the tasteful consumerism the advertisements are trying to promote. Her paradigmatic story is about a wife who is being unfaithful but not entirely enjoying her infidelity. She is having pangs of regret, or she has been drawing more or less imaginary lines to distinguish between what she is now doing and what she has, at least thus far, refrained from (what would compromise the feeling of primacy she has about her marriage). It's not at all heavyweight stuff, is hardly expansive, but it does allow for demonstrations of the same kind of hyperesthesia as her mentor has been showing off with for so many years.

No mistake, she performs in this limited arena with considerable grace and authority. She has an undeniable ability to assume a lot, or to imply the assumptions of her characters' lives.

Their choices are hardly even remarkable, she seems to be saying. It is deplorable, but this is just how things are. This is the moral weather. She reports it and then concentrates on how her people cope or fail to cope in whatever storms are breaking over their heads. In "Faux Pas," for instance, she describes a woman who lies to her lover and is curious about how it feels to lie, to be to some degree forced to lie, to be caught out in the lie, to be assumed by her lover to be a habitual liar, and to be accepted by him as such—which is, of course, insulting. These are interesting discoveries, and she makes them by considering her behavior with that distracted interest women show when they are trying on clothes and studying their images in mirrors.

Once more, to look at another kind of writer, less well connected but also less constricted, there are the stories of Jean Matthew, Cathryn Hankla, and Tom Alderson, this year's offerings in the University of Missouri Press's Breakthrough series. There are a great number of these university press publications of short fiction—Georgia, Pittsburgh, Indiana, and Iowa all come to mind, some of them with competitions, others just with programs that allow for the appearance of a certain number of short-story collections each year. The numbers of submissions are nothing less than awesome. For those who still think that publishing is an activity that goes on primarily in New York, they are also illuminating. Very few trade publishers do poetry anymore. So poems get sent to university presses—by the boxcar load. With short stories the situation is similar. The judge of the University of Missouri series reports that there were 775 manuscripts sent in, each of them a first book in that form. Half were poetry and half were short fiction. From this mountain his task was to select six titles for publication, and he chose three books of verse and three of short fiction. His opinion was that perhaps eighty of the submissions were perfectly publishable, books that could be "equally and honorably published," and he felt bad because all but six of these good writers had to be rejected.

The great difference between a judge in that competition and an editor at Knopf or Simon and Schuster or Farrar, Straus and Giroux is that the trade editor looks to the acknowledgment page for endorsements, for a Good Housekeeping Seal of Approval (although the magazines that hand them out are usually the *Atlantic, Esquire,* and one or two others, including, of course, the Beast of 43rd Street). These editors' acceptances are a kind of guarantee of a minimal quality–that any editor ought to be able to discern on his (or her) own. But they are also limiting, the tastes of this handful of competitors and rivals being not that various. It is as if the rules of college life were reversed and in the real world it were considered a violation of the honor code *not* to look at everyone else's exams.

In their freshness, diversity, and originality, the three Missouri selections are certainly impressive, however it was that they survived the cruel winnowing. The stories in Jean R. Matthew's *Testimony* are country stories. She writes about people who have only the meagerest resources, material or intellectual, with which they manage to scrape by. What seems extraordinary is the utter lack of sentimentality of these stories which is obviously the risk, given such a set of subjects. The poise Matthew demonstrates is all but Chekhovian. The title story, about a father and son who are trying to bury the woman who had been wife and mother to them, is awfully close to William Faulkner's *As I Lay Dying* except that Faulkner's novel was funny while Matthew plays it straight. (Many English teachers, who have been assigning the Faulkner work for years, have no idea that its author was unable to read aloud six consecutive sentences from that text without breaking out into chuckles, then guffaws, and finally gales of laughter.) Faulkner's dry humor was what kept his tale in balance, what gave him the ballast by which he kept the material from turning mawkish. Matthew just lets her characters have their heads and describes them, letting them cast whatever literary shadows they will. In another superb performance, "The Letters of Mrs. J. L. Hartle," she does an outrageous epistolary piece that lies somewhere between Nathanael West and Mark Harris. As in their work, her game here is flirting with the grotesque and the surrealist but never quite crossing the line beyond which we are willing to take her much-put-upon heroine seriously.

Tom Alderson's collection *Michelson in the Desert* is bright with Sunbelt glare and the desperation that bakes in a heat that his characters can't help but take personally, allegorically, emblematically, anagogically. They have little to fear of a Dantesque hell, which may be a little worse, a little hotter, but can't be all that much different from what they have been going through at the Dugway Proving Grounds in Utah or Fort Irwin out in the Mojave Desert. In the title story Michel-

Cover for Cathryn Hankla's first collection of stories, number fifty-three in the University of Missouri Press Breakthrough series

son is messing up (a talent with which many of Alderson's characters seem to have been abundantly endowed) and watching his life disintegrate. His wife has left him, his job is collapsing, and out in the compound are tanks full of nerve gas–or, as it turns out, perhaps not quite so full as they are supposed to be. Franz Kafka could not have dreamed up a more dismal psychoscape: "Heat waves warp the vistas beyond the warehouses. The disposal plant stands in the full blaze of the sun. He can see workers moving around, some wearing their protective suits, some not. There was a meeting about those suits a while back. Some kind of directive resulted from it. The men are all supposed to be wearing the suits. Smoke pours out of the two high stacks. Around the clock, three shifts, that plant functions, like some kind of organism."

It's a quick piece, a nineteen-page story, but it hangs in the mind—which is, no doubt, the touchstone of short fiction. To make a small series of moves that resonate, that echo, that bounce and live on, so that there is the illusion of having accomplished a larger kind of communication, by whatever combination of rhetorical ingenuity, spiritual strength, or linguistic dexterity, is to succeed in this Protean form.

Editors may have to decide what names are viable and whose books have some chance of getting onto the shelves of the chain stores that have acquired so large a share of the market. The reader is only partly limited by these constraints. Obviously, if you can't get hold of a book, or if you have no way of knowing that it exists, you aren't likely to read it. But with a little hustling and initiative, you can still find short fiction in however unsystematic and random a way. And once the books make it to a nightstand or bookcase, there is a rough kind of democracy—or at least its illusion—that obtains. *New Yorker* authors there rub spines with those who publish in *Artemis* or the *Chattahoochee Review*. These are, in fact, the real venues for a couple of the stories of Cathryn Hankla, who is a poet (*Phenomena*, University of Missouri Press, 1983) and assistant professor of English at Hollins College. She is also the author of the third of this year's Breakthrough Books from Missouri, *Learning the Mother Tongue*.

Without question, this is an extraordinary debut, a series of takes that are stories in the sense that they resonate outward. They are a series of small gestures that imply larger ones, and their surfaces are almost transparent and ingenuous, often with a voice addressing the reader directly and asking such impish questions as: "If we dream of things, are we then thinking of the things that really matter to us, or are we then indulging in things we don't have leisure to experience at any other time? Are dreams like vacations or like going to work?"

One reader has characterized this peculiar and wonderful book by suggesting that "If Italo Calvino had resided in William Goyen's house of breath, these are the stories he might have written there." What I take this to mean is that there is a folksy quality to the lives Hankla is describing that coexists somehow in tranquil harmony with a startling literary sophistication. The result of this conjunction is a commanding originality. Each of these little pieces could have been made into a more conventional story, but a better way of thinking of them is to say that each is what is

left when the superfluous furniture and machinery of conventional stories has been shipped elsewhere. The effects Hankla particularly prizes are linguistic; for her a linguistic event is a dramatic one. In the opening of "In Search of Literary Heroes," for example, she writes: "The Mother, it seemed, could read through anything. She read through the Harvard Classics, mysteries, romances, detective fictions, best sellers, biographies, cookbooks, partially condensed, digested novels by the scores. When she was a little girl it had been her recreation, having many older sisters to do the chores, to go to the library, biweekly, in the summertime, and struggle home with tall, two armfuls of books. Then, it had been her pleasure to sit, on an open porch at the front of the three-story white house, and dangle her feet while she read." The peculiar formality and bookishness of the capitalization of "The Mother" and of "it had been her recreation" and "it had been her pleasure" jostle with the little-girl awkwardness of "tall, two armfuls of books." This is the arena for much of Hankla's drama. Her characters write. A little girl whose father has disappeared at sea is keeping a journal in a diary he gave her for her birthday. Another young woman is writing stories for her English teacher and is exasperated by his dumbness when he confuses her fictional characters with her real life. For Hankla reading and writing are more interesting and more intimate than sex is in the work of Harold Robbins or Jackie Collins—and in any reasonable or intelligent universe, she'd have more readers than they ever did because she is right.

Because of the parlous economics of the publication of short fiction, one might expect some dwindling down, a certain languishing of the form, but the paradoxical truth is that by having been freed of commercial expectations, the short-story writers perform like poets, more freely, more independently, and with more diversity and energy than ever before. The odds against an appearance in the *New Yorker*'s pages are so long after all that one might as well ignore that remote possibility and just do what one wants. This is quite a different situation from that of the pre-television days in which Hemingway or Fitzgerald or Faulkner could turn to *Collier's* or the *Saturday Evening Post* for a quick if demeaning buck. The short story, no longer reliable in that way, has become high art. Its artists, quirky and recalcitrant, flourish. And they can come from anywhere, even performance art, as both Eric Bogosian and

Dust jacket for Madison Smartt Bell's collection of technically conservative but emotionally adventurous stories

Ron Carlson did this year. Bogosian's sketches from his one-man Off-Broadway show are collected in *Drinking in America* (Vintage), as Ron Carlson's theater pieces have been brought together in *The News of the World* (Norton). Carlson's titles are reasonably descriptive, and he has an eye for absurdity and extravagance that stands somewhere between cartoons (especially "The Far Side") and nonsense. "Bigfoot Stole My Wife" is one of his best pieces—about those checkout-counter newspapers. And "The Tablecloth of Turin" is a cheerful sacrilegious romp. Bogosian's work is grittier, angrier, and stands between Cathryn Hankla (in the sense that it's pared down and fragmentary) and Madison Bell (urban, almost crazed but trying to hang on). I mention these two authors and collections here not just for the grace of a transition but to suggest that what keeps fiction lively is its openness to other realms of experience, other art forms, other rhythms.

Madison Smartt Bell's *Zero db And Other Stories* (Ticknor and Fields) are technically conserva-

tive but emotionally adventurous. Bell might perhaps be best described as the high-brow end of the cyber-punk school, which is a term that was invented to characterize *Blade Runner, Max Headroom,* and that whole genre of science-fiction works. Bell is not writing science fiction but his present-day urban scenes have the same weird, all but surrealist quality those sci-fi writers are responding to. In "I♥NY" the first-person narrator recounts a series of outrages and absurdities that are characteristic of Bell's strange world. There is, early in the story, a mugging, which is commonplace enough. Bell's narrator is distinctive and quite uncommon, though, when he says, "It was offensive to me how slow he [the mugger] was walking. If you are going to rob someone you might have the politeness to run away afterward. . . . Opposite Stanton Street there is a parking lot enclosed in a storm fence. Guard dogs run behind the fence at night. They maul you first and ask questions later. By the time the mugger got to this parking lot he was through with the [victim's] coat, and he threw it over the fence and kept on walking at the same pace, whistling a little now, and swinging his arms. The muggee stopped by the parking lot and stood watching the dogs eat his coat." The story's turn involves the speaker's getting involved, however reluctantly, in one of these assaults, and through a misunderstanding he becomes, himself, the assaulter, joining the enemy.

In the title story the protagonist is a non-union sound man—who is, therefore, part outlaw and part victim. He has an expensive tape-recorder into which he is whispering and with which he is able to pick up other conversations in the bar where he hangs out, eavesdropping on the random violence of modern life that is at the same time fascinating and paralyzing. Bell's subject is the bizarre effect of these new stresses as they make themselves manifest in the character of this sound man, for instance, who, at the story's turn, calls his girlfriend to promise to amend his life. But it is a false promise, and he knows that and can't make it. He can't say anything at all, and by his inability to speak he becomes another outrage—a silent caller. Silence is, to a sound man, the "Zero db" of the title. And the peripety is a graceful variation of the reversal in "I♥NY".

James Purdy's stories in *The Candles of Your Eyes* (Weidenfeld and Nicolson) have certain similarities with Bell's in the grittiness of their urban settings and the way both writers try to convert

Dust jacket for a collection of James Purdy's stories written over a period of twenty years

wretchedness into something else. Purdy's images are deliberately ghastly and his conversions nothing less than spectacular. Thus, in "Sleep Tight" a little boy mistakes a wounded burglar in his room for the Sandman, is rather disappointed by the manner of the man's performance of dying when shot with a toy gun (he is not faking and is somewhat less energetic than what the child expects of him), but still manages to entertain himself with what he takes to be the red fingerpaint with which the intruder is so liberally covered. In the title story there is a crazed homosexual lover who keeps trying to persuade the police that he has committed a murder, having shot a whole clip full of bullets into his former companion and another man, unaware that they had both frozen to death in an unheated building where there are rats ice-stiff on the stairs and where ice hangs from the high ceilings "like it had grown chandeliers." What these bizarre scenes do in Purdy's pieces is carry a suggestion of the strength of the passions that are frequently blind to the grotesqueness around them. Purdy is a writer who has been around for years, working along in his slightly eccentric but altogether admi-

rable way and getting rather less attention than he deserves. He seems at last to be enjoying at least a small vogue, for his publishers have found it plausible to reissue some of his earlier novels and to bring out this collection of stories of the past twenty years.

Richard Bausch's *Spirits* (Linden Press/ Simon and Schuster) is quite distinctive in tone although it shares with the work of Hankla and Bell and Purdy a curious suspiciousness about the surfaces of everyday life. The commonplace, for which Bausch has a particularly keen eye, may be homey and homely but it is unreliable and, like thin ice, likely to give way at any time to horrors and marvels. In the title piece, for instance, a substantial story that is nearly a novella, a young writer is staying at a motel near the college where he has just been hired. He is befriended by the proprietor of the motel, probably because he is the same age as her son. During the course of the story, which is about something altogether different (or is it?), we learn that the proprietor's husband, Mr. Sweeney, has been arrested, that he is a pervert and mass murderer, that there are corpses he has planted all over the countryside. And the occasion by which Bausch introduces this catastrophic note is the protagonist's attempt to return to Mrs. Sweeney one of her husband's ties that she lent him so he could go to a faculty party. And having just seen her husband's image on the evening television news, she doesn't want it back. The small gesture— returning the tie—opens up a crevice that becomes a crevasse. There are other not-unrelated disasters surrounding the young writer, and what is most remarkable is how Bausch resists the temptations, fictional and philosophical, to melodrama and despair. He gets his young writer through these perils and chicanes unscathed, but he understands, as we do too, how great the risks are. It is a story, then, about growing up, a piece that is humane, generous, and, above all, artful. It is an optimistic story, but Bausch is clearly aware of the darknesses. They loom everywhere in "Spirits," and they can just as easily overwhelm—as in "All the Way in Flagstaff, Arizona," the powerful story of an alcoholic who remembers the moment when his last hope of keeping his family together and holding onto some semblance of an ordered life sputtered and died. In a rendition that is remarkable for its lack of frills and embellishment, Bausch writes about "how he walked out to the very edge of the lawn and turned to look upon the lighted windows of the house, thinking of the people inside, whom he had named and loved and called sons, daughters, wife. How he had stood there trembling, shaking as from a terrific chill, while the dark, the night, came." It is grief, of course, but in the presence of such clarity, such fidelity and honesty, one cannot but rejoice.

All three of the Barthelme brothers published collections of stories in 1987. Donald produced *Forty Stories* (Putnam's) and Frederick brought out *Chroma* (Simon and Schuster), while Steve's *And He Tells the Little Horse the Whole Story* appeared from Johns Hopkins University Press. Donald Barthelme is the best known of the three, and to his stories the reaction of readers is sharply divided. Some admire his postmodernist strategies, wild leaps, and daring juxtapositions of material in pieces that are collages as much as they are linear fictions; others dismiss these performances as nonstories, intellectual exercises, or, as one reviewer called them, "brain candy." I am of the latter persuasion.

Frederick Barthelme's stories are somewhat less unconventional, indeed are rather modish. One of the jacket blurbs claims that Frederick Barthelme "is doing for the '80s what Raymond Chandler did for the '30s. He does for the 7-Eleven what Edward Hopper did for the all-night diner." Perhaps so. He has a series of characters involved in curious situations to which one would expect a reaction and the expectation is frustrated. That is the typical strategy of the stories in this collection. In the title piece, for instance, the first-person narrator is consoling himself, while his wife, Alicia, dallies with someone named George—every other weekend plus odd nights in between. His consolation is a neighbor, Juliet, whose girlfriend, Heather, is understandably grumpy about this situation. The climactic moment is one in which Alicia, coming out of a bubble bath, almost affirms her commitment to the narrator but actually offers to make a cheese ball. "I am *dying* for cheese ball. I've been thinking about it all night long." "Cleo" also ends at tub-side, but this time the narrator's wife, Gretchen, has gone off on a trip to visit her family in Albuquerque, even though her husband has pleaded with her not to go—because he doesn't want to renew his affair with Cleo, Gretchen's old friend. Gretchen won't cancel the trip. She goes off. She calls from the airport. Cleo has already appeared and is, at that moment, in the bathtub, as the narrator inexplicably explains to his wife. "Gretchen says, 'Rock her

socks. It's O.K.'" And he goes into the bathroom to sit on the tub and watch Cleo wash.

Obviously it is difficult to feel for these people who refuse to feel, themselves. They all seem to be fugitives from some mental clinic for people who are lacking in affect. The physical settings of their lives are thrillingly ugly, which may be a coincidence or may be, in fact, Barthelme's point. I admire many of these stories but I can hardly say I like them.

Steve Barthelme's stories are concerned with the same kinds of issues as those of his brothers. Opacity and transparency of expression, or intimacy and distance, offer themselves over and over, either as contexts or as the actual subjects of these stories. "We used to fight all the time," one narrator says of himself and his sister, Tasha, "when we were children, but since my parents died, and since she got old enough that it no longer mattered whether I was older, Tasha's become very precious to me. She understands what I say."

In another piece, "Failing All Else," the narrator reads a story–a surrealist and extravagant and all but incoherent story–to a young woman in a restaurant. The young woman doesn't like the story, or anyway isn't tuned in, and she leaves. The narrator then strikes up a conversation with the waitress who asks what book he's reading, whereupon he asks her to read it to him and they sit down together. But if the concerns in Steve's work are related to those in the work of his brothers, he is not so devout or programmatic in his suspicion of character, motive, emotional connections, narrative, and all the usual machinery of traditional stories. In "Zorro" he can tell in a laconic but quite straightforward way of the sad predicament of a son who is helpless to intervene in his mother's drinking problem. The family's fascination with semiotics isn't abandoned but is, on the contrary, put to sensible use, as when he has the son say, "I can't fix it, Momma. Nobody ever fixes anything. Nobody ever ruins anything either. Patching is what you do." And then, in a lively stroke, Barthelme has the character add: "She's looking at me; I'm wondering whether I'm lying."

Less experimental, defiantly un-experimental, and therefore all the more bold in these peculiar times is a book that appeared too late in 1986 to be discussed in the fiction round-up of that year's volume, Wright Morris's *Collected Stories 1948-1986* (Harper and Row). Morris is an old master, the winner of an American Book Award and National Book Award. And his practice in fiction is conservative, for he still believes in narrative, the importance of stories, the fascination with what kinds of things happen to people, and just as surprising, what kinds of people have what kinds of things happen to them. He can, in sixteen pages, in "The Origin of Sadness," create the illusion of a whole novel's worth of information and experience, taking a man from childhood to the moment of his death and giving a sense of a life's duration and flavor. That it is not a novel but only the illusion is, in fact, enough to dazzle any alert reader, every bit as much as the Barthelme clan's showier tricks. And in "Drrdla," Morris is nothing if not an exponent of Parisian *symbolisme*. But the simple making of the connection between a strange stray cat and something larger–some general principle of female sexuality and ferocity–is only scaffolding, or even better foundation, for the telling of a story in which this happens, and then this, and then that, each turn and development interesting in itself but with the process of unfolding of events carrying its own weight of recognizable meaning. It is no more than reasonable, when all this prefatory work has been properly done, for Morris to write: "What it all came down to, in Walter's opinion, was the emergence of life from darkness. God knows where the creature had come from, or what had been the cause of its terror, but it now slowly squirmed its way from the primeval past into the present. It had managed to live, like a hibernating plant, on snatches of light. The very idea of a friendly gesture, or an upward look, had not emerged into its consciousness. What Walter found on his hands was a creature, like man, that had fallen from grace. Some blind or deliberate moment of terror had erased its mind of all experience. A *tabula rasa*. It had to

begin, once more, from scratch. Would it be possible to restore such a fallen creature to normal life? . . ."

It is an old-fashioned way of telling a story, but it is solid and admirable. There is a narrative, a history–which is still the root meaning of "story"–from which meanings emerge, or around which they agglomerate, in an organic process that invites the reader to collaborate but is never presumptuous or imposing.

There were other meritorious collections deserving at least of being mentioned here. In alphabetical order, they are: *The Age of Grief* by Jane Smiley (Knopf), a novella and five stories; *The Elizabeth Stories* by Isobel Huggan (Viking); *Fast Lanes* by Jayne Anne Phillips (Seymour Lawrence/ Delacorte); *Hard to Be Good* by Bill Barich (Farrar, Straus and Giroux); *High Ground* by John McGahern (Viking); *The Ideal Bakery* by Donald Hall (North Point); *Inventing the Abbotts and Other Stories* by Sue Miller (Harper and Row); *Lazar Malkin Enters Heaven* by Steve Stern (Viking); *Little Misunderstandings of No Importance* by Antonio Tabucchi (New Directions); *A Night at the Movies* by Robert Coover (Linden/Simon and Schuster); *The Old Left* by Daniel Menaker (Knopf); *Overhead in a Balloon* by Mavis Gallant (Random House); *The Pearlkillers* by Rachel Ingalls (Simon and Schuster); *A Scrap of Time* by Ida Fink (Pantheon); *Some Soul to Keep* by J. California Cooper (St. Martin's); *Spirit Seizures* by Melissa Pritchard (University of Georgia Press); *Stalin in the Bronx* by Suzanne Ruta (Grove); *Stories from the Warm Zone and Sidney Stories* by Jessica Anderson (Viking); *Tales from a Greek Island* by Alexandros Papadiamantis (Johns Hopkins); and *Temporary Shelter* by Mary Gordon (Random House). It is an impressively abundant, diverse, and accomplished crop. It was a good year.

The Year in Poetry

R. S. Gwynn
Lamar University

October 1987 marked the seventy-fifth anniversary of *Poetry*, and the editors celebrated the occasion with a special 266-page issue of the periodical Harriet Monroe subtitled "A Magazine of Verse" and T. S. Eliot dubbed "an American institution." There is little in the magazine nowadays that would pass for "verse," notwithstanding John Frederick Nims's openness to traditional forms during his tenure as editor (January 1978-February 1984), but there should be little doubt that *Poetry* is an institution, even if it may seem at times that the inmates are running it. Ezra Pound's constant hectoring of Miss Monroe led to the establishment of much of the canon of Modernism; Pound's influential review of Frost's *A Boy's Will* (1913), Eliot's "The Love Song of J. Alfred Prufrock," and important work by William Carlos Williams, Wallace Stevens, Marianne Moore, and Carl Sandburg appeared in early issues of the magazine. If much of the enthusiasm for the new has waned over seventy-five years and innovation has been largely replaced by the humdrum commonplaces of the creative writing workshop poem, publication in *Poetry* still remains the epitome of having arrived to most American poets, the attainment of what Gwendolyn Brooks refers to simply as "The Goal."

The work of 140 poets, alphabetically arranged from Abse to Wormser, is represented in the issue, and the diversity, by itself, speaks well for the art's state of health. Here is John Ashbery, blandly mandarin as ever: "And I mean what shall be saved/Of us as we live aimed at some near but unattainable mark on the wall?/ Not, one fears, a thing of hitherto unheard-of compacted density/That might relieve all the years with spaces in them, years of leggy growth,/ Too much foliage, the wrong light, the wrong taste to things." For the contrast of lucent clarity, attend to these lines from octogenarian Janet Lewis's "Sunday Morning at the Artist's House":

Small cat with the white lines of make-up
By your watchful eyes,

Dust jacket for W. D. Snodgrass's 1987 collection which consists of selections from his previous books as well as new and uncollected poems

You do not need to invent yourself
Each morning.
Each morning the hot bright sun
Sleeks your shoulders as it strokes
The tawn hillside, the tawny golden.

Your eyes are golden too.
You could not be improved upon
In grace, in poise, in clear intent
Of being. As for me,
Unrelated to the hill, and, for the moment,
Unrelated to my daily life, I ask,
How can I invent myself for this day?

163

Lewis, whose work first appeared in *Poetry* in 1920, clearly indicates that she knows the answer to her own rhetorical question.

Equally as interesting as the poems are the comments of some thirty poets on the lasting influence of the magazine. X. J. Kennedy recalls his first acceptance: "I was elated to have cracked *Poetry,* and brooded on my joy for days and nights. I brooded too much. I began toying with the accepted poem, rewrote the last lines, loused them up, but took a notion that my later inspiration was superior. Desperate lest a worse version appear in the great magazine–I couldn't blow this one shot at immortality!–I rushed the new draft to Mr. [Henry] Rago, begging him to substitute it." It is to Rago's credit that he successfully resisted Kennedy's second thoughts and printed the original version; the poem was the exquisite "Nude Descending a Staircase." Henry Taylor, recent winner of the Pulitzer Prize, recalls how, as an undergraduate at the University of Virginia in 1962, he traveled to Washington, D.C., to hear Robert Frost and others honor *Poetry*'s first fifty years: "It was as if I had suddenly disappeared into the pages of one of the books in my room back in Charlottesville–the Brinnin and Read anthology, say, with all its pictures–and the pictures had suddenly gotten up and started walking around and saying things, some of which I knew by heart already.... I still get a lump in my throat thinking of Frost's concluding remark on the second evening of the festival: 'But that's what we're celebrating, Harriet Monroe and her magazine. Mr. Rago is here, and he keeps it up, and I wish it everything.' " So, too, do many thousands of poets and readers.

It is, however, a sad irony to note that *Poetry* at one time quoted a remark of Walt Whitman's on its masthead: "To have great poets, there must be great audiences, too." One assumes that Whitman was referring to quality rather than quantity, for in an age of shopping-mall bookstores, MTV, and an appalling lack of what Professor E. D. Hirsch, in one of the year's nonfiction best-sellers, called "cultural literacy," the impact of poets on the life of the average citizen of the Republic continues to be almost negligible. Even Whitman, who dreamed of a copy of *Leaves of Grass* fitting neatly into the overalls hind pocket of every working man, must have eventually known, from the sickening success that made the mawkish "O Captain! My Captain!" his lifelong curtain-closer, that serious poetry would never be the chosen entertainment of the masses. Many

American poets, perhaps mistaking public relations pronouncements with genuine artistic merit, have confused popular approval of their work with widespread understanding of it. In the 1950s the Beats were indeed able to reach relatively large audiences, but outside of "Howl" how many of those "nuclear-espresso" dithyrambs are readable today? Similarly, many poets were so beguiled by the cheering crowds of young people at the anti-Vietnam War readings of the late 1960s and early 1970s that they stooped to the basest sort of propagandistic pandering, metaphorically taking the role, to cite one notable example, of a waitress at the "Inaugural Dinner" throwing a container of napalm "in Nixon's face," watching while "his crowd leapt back from the flames with crude/yells of horror." Mercifully, both the war and the reams of bad poetry it inspired are far behind us now, and even though most poets may, at some point, privately aspire to be among Shelley's "unacknowledged legislators," it may in fact be better for the art if they do their writing and performing in a relatively quiet decade that has grown to equate rhetorical posturing with bad taste. In such an age as the present one, where the big issues seem always removed from both the artist and the citizen, the more refined techniques of wit and satire may again flourish at their subversive best, even if the audience at the average reading is limited to six pimply adolescents, a blue-haired nun, two tweedy professors, and the ubiquitous lady in a turban.

That said, it is still something of a shock to read of the recent decision by Jack Miles, editor of the influential *Los Angeles Times Book Review*, to discontinue reviewing new books of poetry in that publication, substituting, instead, "one brief poem in each Sunday issue of the *Book Review* with just a word about its author and the new collection from which it had been taken." Blaming "the extremely fragmented character" of contemporary poetry and the fact that "writing well about poetry for a lay audience" is no longer within the grasp of most reviewers, Miles has relegated serious discussion of contemporary poetry to the status of end-of-column filler.

Even more disheartening, however, is the approving response of Jonathan Yardley, book review editor for the *Washington Post:* "Contemporary American poetry is read by poets, by writing students and by students of literature– and by almost no one else. Even more than 'literary' fiction, poetry has withdrawn into the confines of the campus and speaks almost en-

THE
MADE THING

AN ANTHOLOGY OF CONTEMPORARY SOUTHERN POETRY

EDITED BY LEON STOKESBURY

Dust jacket for the anthology that takes its name from a literal translation of poiēma, *the Greek word from which* poem *is derived*

tirely to itself; yet poets, and those who publish their work, continue to insist that they be given attention by the larger world that does not read them." According to Yardley, "the claims that contemporary poetry makes on [newspaper] space are at best, weak. The question Jack Miles asks is in no way frivolous: 'Is it not odd to publish comparative discussions of whole volumes of poetry for readers who rarely read even a single poem?' "

Fortunately we do have Fred Chappell, who continues to review poetry for the *Greensboro [N.C.] News & Record*. Says Chappell, "A book page that has exiled poetry is no longer a serious book page; it drops immediately into the literary bush leagues. Who cares what it says after that? A genuine haberdashery sells cravats; a genuine restaurant stocks a wine cellar; a genuine book page reviews poetry. It is a matter of good taste—and has nothing to do with a lot of macho hot gas about 'the facts of life.' " *Selah*.

In several prior installments of this yearly survey Lewis Turco has remarked the onset of a trend in contemporary American poetry which he calls "Neoformalism." I am a little uneasy with the term itself, since I can find nothing particularly "neo" (though a great deal that is *overdue*) about a return to the mainstream tradition of poetry in English. To give Turco his well-deserved due, however, one should attend to his definition: "One can tell the Neoformalists from the old by getting to know the names of the people who wrote formally twenty-five years ago, and the names of those who are currently struggling to throw off the anti-intellectual egocentrism of these last two decades and more." It is true that many poets of the post-World War II generation, schooled in the New Criticism and the then-current academic taste for the "well-wrought urn," favored a conservative approach to poetic form and also attempted Eliot's "escape from personality" in their verse. Think of the students of John Crowe Ransom—Randall Jarrell, Robert Lowell, James Wright—and then consider the multitude of other nascent poets who shaped their stanzas to fit the tony pages of the *Kenyon Review*. It was a time when a large number of poets wrote as if for one purpose: to have their work subjected to rigorous explication by objective critics who could not care less (and would never guess from the poems, anyway) if they beat their children, abused their spouses, and drank like fish.

But in the mid to late 1950s something began to happen to these well-scrubbed poets. Allen Ginsberg began to generate a great deal of publicity with work that was anything but tidy; Lowell himself found, on a West Coast reading tour, that "more and more I found that I was simplifying my poems. If I had a Latin quotation, I'd translate it into English. If adding a couple of syllables in a line made it clearer I'd add them, and I'd make little changes just impromptu as I read." At an obscure college outside of Asheville, North Carolina, a number of younger poets, led in that wilderness by a patriarch named Charles Olson, rediscovered Ezra Pound's notion of composition "in the manner of the musical phrase" and William Carlos Williams's "variable foot" and began to intone vatically about "fields" and "projective verse." W. D. Snodgrass's *Heart's Needle* (1959) happened (the pains of hell handled, to use Lowell's phrase, "in expert little stanzas"). Anne Sexton and Sylvia Plath happened, and the New Critical age of Eliot hegemony was forever shattered.

Ironically, the result has been, to lend some small credibility to Miles's arguments, that poetry is today rooted more firmly in academia than ever before. What university of the second or even third water does not boast of its graduate program in creative writing and its poet in residence? Yet there is reason to believe, despite the academic credentials (and crosses) that so many younger poets bear, that many of those who teach creative writing suffer from "metrical illiteracy," to borrow Brad Leithauser's phrase. Consequently, the work that one sees appearing from younger poets often seems music intended for a one-string guitar; by ignoring the resources of meter, rhythm, and rhyme, these poets curiously remove a whole level of understanding, what Turco calls in *The New Book of Forms* (1986) the "sonic level," from their work. The result has been to establish a new orthodoxy, that of plainsong clothed in the sheep's clothing of "honesty" or "spontaneity," that has made, to a large degree, the work of one younger poet sound indistinguishable from that of another.

When new work in formal patterns from poets under fifty does appear, one feels like Robinson Crusoe, at long last spotting a familiar sail. Thank God for Timothy Steele, Gjertrud Schnackenberg, Julia Alvarez, Leon Stokesbury, and, yes, even the omnipresent Mr. Leithauser. And while the thankful mood prevails we should all perhaps once more sing the praises of Richard Wilbur, who was named in April to succeed Robert Penn Warren as poet laureate of the United States. Few, if any, disparaged the justice of Warren's appointment as the nation's first laureate, for he is the elder statesman of American letters; and it is sad indeed to learn that he was forced by frail health to step down after only one year in the renewable position. But Warren is, by any sensible estimation, primarily known as a fictionist, author of *All the King's Men* (1946), greatest of our political novels. Although elaborate claims have been made for his poetry in recent years, such curious lines as "Under the fire/Of cannon buried howitzerwise, what else/But negotiation?" (this from his epic *Chief Joseph of the Nez Perce*, 1983) occur a bit too frequently in his poetry for me and, I suspect, many others to be entirely comfortable with his tenure in what is, after all, the *poet* laureateship. We honor his distinguished career and his immense contribution to American literature, but we likewise applaud his gentlemanly decision to step down in favor of a poet about whom one can have no reservations.

In naming Wilbur to the position, the librarian of Congress, Daniel J. Boorstin, said, "He is a poet for all of us, whose elegant words brim with wit and paradox. He is also a poet's poet, at home in the long tradition and traveled ways of the great poets of our language. And he is a cosmopolitan citizen of the world of letters, whose essays and translations help us to the poets of other languages. His poems are among the best our country has to offer." Since the publication of *The Beautiful Changes and Other Poems* in 1947, Wilbur has developed as a poet in a consistent manner that I tend to equate with *integrity*. He has resisted the temptations of the soapbox, the lure of the confessional box, and the open-form taunts from the batter's box to write the sort of poetry that the reader feels *he* must rise to. The elegance and wit which Boorstin mentions have not remained stable commodities over the last four decades, but Wilbur has managed to keep his head when all about were seemingly losing theirs. His Jeffersonian good sense, his boundless compassion for the "Things of This World," his intricate play with the language of the mind, which "is like some bat/That beats about in caverns all alone,/Contriving by a kind of senseless wit/Not to conclude against a wall of stone"–these are the qualities that make him a national treasure.

Concurrent with Wilbur's appointment, Cummington Press published *Lying and Other Poems*, a limited-edition chapbook of five recent poems that appeared originally in the *New Yorker*, *Ploughshares*, and a small booklet from the Deerfield and the Gallery Presses. Apparently the 160 copies of *Lying and Other Poems* were snapped up almost immediately by collectors, and the rest of us will have to wait until 1988, when a new collected edition will be released. If the five poems are representative of the work Wilbur has been doing in the last decade, we should be in for delicious surprises. Witness these brilliant stanzas from an uncollected poem, "The Catch," which appeared in the Fall 1983 number of the *Sewanee Review*. The poet has proved "once more the blindness of the male" by mentally noting that the new dress his wife has pulled from the box for his approval is "like a weird sort of fish//That she has somehow hooked and gaffed/And on the dock-end holds in air–/Limp, corrugated, lank, a catch too rare/Not to be photographed." Displeased with the "bright, discerning thing" that he says out loud, she stalks away and quickly returns, transformed:

IN OTHER
WORDS

NEW   POEMS

MAY
SWENSON

Dust jacket for May Swenson's first book since the publication of New & Selected Things Taking Place *(1978)*

The dress, now that she's in it,

Has changed appreciably, and gains
By lacy shoes, a light perfume
Whose subtle field electrifies the room,
And two slim golden chains.

With a fierce frown and hard-pursed lips
She twists a little on her stem
To test the even swirling of the hem,
Smooths down the waist and hips,

Plucks at the shoulder-straps a bit,
Then turns around and looks behind,
Her face transfigured now by peace of mind.
There is no question–it

Is wholly charming, it is she,
As I belatedly remark,
And may be hung now in the fragrant dark
Of her soft armory.

This may be light verse, but it says more to me than whole volumes I have read on marital relationships, the battle of the sexes, and the objective correlative.

Mention should also be made of three significant prizes awarded in 1987 to American poets, two of them for books published in 1986 and one for lifetime achievement. In January Edward Hirsch's *Wild Gratitude* (Knopf) was awarded the National Book Critics Circle prize for poetry. Reviewing Hirsch's book in the Fall 1986 issue of *New England Review and Bread Loaf Quarterly,* I said that he "gave one the impression of a young man so earnest he was apt to lose sleep over not being able to talk things over personally with Vallejo, Rimbaud, Lorca, Matisse, and Monet." Hirsch is a generally likable poet, but at times his work forces a sort of urgency on me that brings Budd Schulberg's Sammy Glick uncomfortably to mind. He is culturally adept and writes clear, understandable poetry containing a large measure of compassion for his subjects. Somewhat limited in technique and rather flat in idiom, he is a poet of the good news/bad news type: it is hard to dislike his poetry, but it is also difficult to derive any great excitement from it. Here are some closing lines from a poem on the painter Edward Hopper:

This man will paint other abandoned mansions,
And faded cafeteria windows, and poorly lettered
Storefronts on the edges of small towns.
Always they will have this same expression,

The utterly naked look of someone
Being stared at, someone American and gawky,
Someone who is about to be left alone
Again, and can no longer stand it.

In April Rita Dove was awarded the Pulitzer Prize in Poetry for *Thomas and Beulah* (Carnegie-Mellon University Press). A product of the Iowa Writers Workshop and current president of the Associated Writing Programs, Dove, one of the new generation of black poets who grew up and were educated during the troubled 1960s, is a competent craftsperson and, if the impression her poetry and occasional editorial statements in the *AWP Bulletin* give is accurate, the kind of humanitarian the Pulitzer Board (with Russell Baker the only member having credentials as a creative writer) often favors over the artist. *Thomas and Beulah* is the account of Dove's grandparents' migration northward in the early days of the century and of their long and often troubled marriage. Like Hirsch's poetry, it is marked by clarity and empathy but is hardly likely to generate much enthusiasm for style, use of language, or technique. Helen Vendler in the

New York Review of Books says that Dove has "planed away unnecessary matter; pure shapes, her poems exhibit the thrift that Yeats called the sign of a perfected manner." One notes in passing that Yeats had hardly perfected his own manner before expiring at seventy-three; Dove is thirty-five.

One award given to a poet in 1987 was universally applauded: Joseph Brodsky's receipt of the Nobel Prize for Literature. Brodsky, who has lived in this country since being "invited" to leave the Soviet Union in 1972, is a rare bird indeed, an exiled Russian Jew who is resolutely apolitical, so "defiantly so," as W. H. Auden noted in his foreword to Brodsky's *Selected Poems* (1973), that his stance "may explain why he has . . . failed to win official approval." In a year of *glasnost*, Mikhail and Raisa Gorbachev's visit to this country, and the American publication of Mr. Gorbachev's own book, Brodsky is a sobering reminder of the distances that still separate East and West, especially since his sins, unlike those of Solzhenitsyn, are in Soviet eyes mainly of omission. Labeled a "social parasite" and sentenced to five years of internal exile at hard labor, Brodsky passed the twenty months that he actually served by rigorously educating himself not only in Russian but also American and English poets, all this with a single paperback anthology and a Russian-English dictionary. "Verses on the Death of T. S. Eliot," one of his important early poems, was modeled on Auden's "In Memory of W. B. Yeats."

Brodsky must regularly awake to find himself trapped in one of those unenviable Nabokovian paradoxes: for two entirely different reasons, neither his old nor his new countrymen can read his poetry in the original. Thus, at least on these shores, he must rely on the skill of his translators to convey both the sense of his poems and the unique music that they must possess in Russian. He has been fortunate in finding, first, George L. Kline, translator of the 1973 collection, and later such eminent poet-translators as Wilbur and Anthony Hecht. Here are some of Brodsky's thoughts on his exile, lines taken from Hecht's version of "Cape Cod Lullaby":

> Like a snake charmer, like the Pied Piper of old,
> Playing my flute I passed the green janissaries,
> My testes sensing their pole axe's sinister cold,
> As when one wades into water. And then with the
>   brine
> Of sea-water sharpness filling, flooding the mouth,
> I crossed the line.

> And sailed into muttony clouds. Below me curled
> Serpentine rivers, roads bloomed with dust, ricks
>   yellowed,
> And everywhere in that diminished world,
> In formal opposition, near and far,
> Lined up like print in a book about to close,
> Armies rehearsed their games in balanced rows
> And cities all went dark as caviar.

And these, taken from the same source, describing the struggle to begin writing after the shock of involuntary expatriation:

> But now the giddy pen
> Points out resemblances, for after all,

> The device in your hand is the same old pen and
>   ink
> As before, the woodland plants exhibit no change
> Of leafage, and the same old bombers range
> The clouds toward who knows what
> Precisely chosen, carefully targeted spot.
> And what you really need now is a drink.

In view of the above, it seems a shame that Hecht has occasionally to write his own poems; this translation is masterful work. Indeed, one salivates at the thought of locking Brodsky up with several American metrical translators of note–Wilbur, Hecht, X. J. Kennedy–in a sort of benevolent *gulag* from which all four would not be released until a collaborative translation of Brodsky's collected works is completed.

While I am on the subject of translation, I should mention a couple of excellent versions of familiar poetry that have passed my desk this year. Christopher Logue's *War Music* (Farrar, Straus and Giroux) is a spirited paraphrase of Homer's best passages of what Logue insouciantly calls "*GBH* (Grievous Bodily Harm, an English legal term for serious forms of criminal assault)." Adroitly mixing pentameters and hexameters with linking passages of free verse and wisely deleting the epithets ("ten-second-miler-Achilles") that turn most literal renderings of Homer into leaden exercises in comparative linguistics, Logue has produced a lively fragment that strives for what Wilbur has called "equivalent effects in the key of English."

Antony Wood's *Mozart and Salieri* (Dufour) is even more to the point when discussing Brodsky, giving us a taste of Pushkin's "The Little Tragedies." The title piece, after the film *Amadeus*, will cover familiar ground for most readers, and "The Stone Guest" is a retelling of the Don Juan legend. Wood's blank-verse lines are

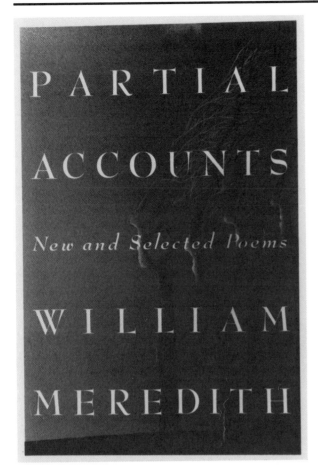

Dust jacket for William Meredith's collection of eleven new poems and selections from his previous seven books

flawless and, to my ear, eminently suited to recitation. (Both of the pieces mentioned were originally commissioned by the BBC.) It is interesting to note that both Logue and Wood are British; other than works by the three American poets commended above and by such past masters as Edwin Honig and the late Robert Fitzgerald, most translations of foreign poetry published in this country are so bad that, were nations inclined to honor their poets as much as their athletes, international incidents might well break out. There has been so much hot air expended by ersatz translators in defense of the illogical practice of translating what is rhymed, metrical poetry in the original tongue into English free verse that it hardly seems worthwhile to repeat it here. One has only to listen to a recording of Borges or Brodsky to understand that a horrible injustice is done when they are stripped of their music and left standing almost naked in the tattered unmentionables of what passes for a "literal rendering." "Poetry," as Robert Frost continues

to observe twenty-five years after his death, "is what is lost in translation." Granted that fully satisfactory translation of poetry is an impossible task, one still has to try, if only from the imperative that nations that understand each other rarely blow each other up. We should thus be grateful to those poets who interrupt their own work and submerge their egos in another's depths long enough to recover those "lost" treasures. Nothing is more doomed to failure than poetic translation; yet there is perhaps nothing more rewarding for a poet to attempt and, at least sporadically, to succeed at. As Dr. Johnson said, "We must try its effect as an English poem. That is the way to judge of the merit of a translation."

Briefly noted are several collections of translations that rise above the crowd. Marian Shore's *For Love of Laura: Poetry of Petrarch* (University of Arkansas Press) duplicates Petrarch's ABBAABBA octaves with little concession to slant rhyme or broken meter. The attempt is largely successful, reminding us once again that the whole tradition of the English lyric might have been radically different had it not been for the pioneering attempts of Thomas Wyatt and Henry Howard, Earl of Surrey, to translate his sonnets for their Tudor peers. Richard L. Predmore's *Solitudes, Galleries, and Other Poems* (Duke University Press) makes little attempt to follow the complicated meters and patterns of consonance and assonance of Antonio Machado's *Generación de 1898* symbolist verse, but the translations seem clear in diction and syntax, even if the meanings at times invoke Verlaine at his mistiest. Carlos Bauer's version of Federico García Lorca's first collection, *Poem of the Deep Song/Poema del cante jondo* (City Lights), contains numerous ironic foreshadowings of the poet's own fate: "Dead he was left in the street,/ with a dagger in his chest./Nobody knew who he was./How the lamppost was shaking!/Mother." What an immense lyric gift died with Lorca in the Falangist terrors of 1936! William Arrowsmith is one of the deans of American translators, best known to most readers for his spirited versions of Aristophanes. In *The Occasions* (Norton) he translates a 1939 collection by Eugenio Montale, winner of the 1975 Nobel Prize for Literature. A difficult work produced under repressive restrictions, it is widely considered, in Arrowsmith's phrase, "an act of courageous, if necessarily oblique, resistance to the Fascist regime." Finally, Mark Anderson's translation of Ingeborg Bachmann's *In the Storm of Roses* (Princeton University Press) presents a little-translated German woman poet who was of the same generation of Anne Sexton, Adrienne Rich, and Sylvia Plath. Bachmann was widely acclaimed as one of the leading lights of the postwar generation of German writers, but she drifted into near silence well before her tragic death by fire in 1973. Her poems are philosophically and rhetorically complex, marked by strong visual imagery. All of these collections are bilingual texts, a boon to the reader who is leery of taking the translator's word for accuracy of idiom and music.

"A well-chosen anthology," the late Robert Graves once observed, "is a complete dispensary of medicine for the more common mental disorders, and may be used as much for prevention as cure." Like many of Graves's gnomic pronouncements, this one sounds a bit less positive on second reading. Nevertheless, anthologies provide many portable moments of escape from the most pressing of life's difficulties; Paul Fussell, in *Siegfried Sassoon's Long Journey*, relates the story of how the soldier-poet, given up for dead by his companions on the Somme after a fearless one-man sortie, was discovered in an abandoned German trench, nonchalantly perusing the *Oxford Book of English Verse*. Certainly the recent anthology most relevant to these observations is W. D. Ehrhart's 1985 compendium of Vietnam War poetry, *Carrying the Darkness*, which probably gained new readers from the success of three of this year's films–*Platoon, Full Metal Jacket,* and *Hamburger Hill*–each of which exhibited considerable revisionism of attitudes toward America's unhappy misadventure in Indochina. The collection is extremely variable in quality, many of the selections either dated propaganda or obviously sincere expressions of outrage and loss that simply do not succeed as poems. But the book does contain much that is good, particularly work by Walter McDonald, John Balaban, Yusef Komunyakaa, and Bruce Weigl.

In 1985 Lewis Turco mentioned the appearance of Helen Vendler's *The Harvard Book of Contemporary Poetry*, which, observed Turco, was chiefly notable for the number of dead "contemporary" poets it contained and the "extremely subjective" nature of the editor's choices. Near the end of 1987 appeared Robert DiYanni's *Modern American Poets: Their Voices and Visions* and its hefty companion volume of biographical and critical essays, *Voices & Vision: The Poet in America* (both from Random House), edited by Vendler. Both volumes are geared to the eponymous

thirteen-part PBS series, which will begin airing in January 1988. All three should become standards for many introductory courses in modern poetry, and the television series, if it lives up to its impressive publicity, should help to steer the reading public and hordes of sophomores through some forbidding-looking poems, including *The Waste Land* (1922) and passages from Pound's *Cantos*. The poets selected for inclusion range from Walt Whitman and Emily Dickinson through Lowell and Plath, with Hart Crane, Langston Hughes, and Elizabeth Bishop the only choices that occasion even mild surprise.

Most regional anthologies attempt to make some claim for poetic commonality of experience or style; thus, it is curious to encounter Jim Moore and Cary Waterman's *Minnesota Writes: Poetry* (Milkweed/Nodin), especially in light of Moore's ingenuous admission that "other than certain subjects (hockey, for example) which would be less likely to appear in a similar anthology from Florida, there seem to me few, if any, common themes or subjects." Handsomely printed and illustrated, the book contains many poets who are unknown to me, though Philip Dacey and Robert Bly put in welcome appearances.

Leon Stokesbury, whose book of poems *The Drifting Away* was praised in these pages last year, has tackled a much more ambitious project with, it seems to me, a larger degree of success. *The Made Thing: An Anthology of Contemporary Southern Poetry* (University of Arkansas Press) is, I believe, the weightiest post-Fugitive collection of its type to date and provides impressive evidence that the South continues to be a wellspring of some of the best poetic talent in the country today. Fred Chappell's recent Bollingen Award (shared with John Ashbery) and Henry Taylor's 1985 Pulitzer Prize for Poetry, along with such praiseworthy poets as James Dickey, Donald Justice, Miller Williams, Vassar Miller, James Whitehead, Jim Hall, Ellen Bryant Voight, Alice Walker, David Bottoms, and George Garrett, should convince readers in any part of the country of the liveliness of the various writing centers of the region. Stokesbury, knowing that the red clay has been well trodden before by his lofty predecessors of the 1930s, wisely avoids any excessive claims, noting only that southern poets have unusually strong attachments to the past, to the natural world, and to traditional poetic form. The reader is left to make his own generalizations from over 300 pages of poems that demonstrate, if anything, Stokesbury's exceptional taste for poems

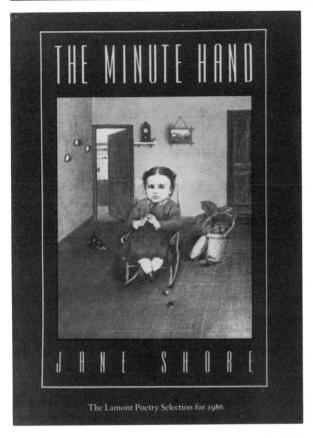

Dust jacket for the collection of twenty-five poems in which Jane Shore combines autobiography with myths, fairy tales, and biblical stories

that are consistently interesting and rewarding.

Proof, perhaps, that southern poets and editors are not parochial in the extreme comes from *Contemporary New England Poetry: A Sampler,* edited by Mississippian Paul Ruffin as a special release of the *Texas Review.* As X. J. Kennedy notes in his introduction, "Even if poets didn't have to compete with VCRs, today the map of American poetry has expanded hugely. Boston hardly dominates it anymore, and anyone who follows new poetry must look as well to Iowa City and Atlanta, Denver and Santa Barbara, . . . Seattle and Anchorage, not to ignore Edison, New Jersey. Indeed, I doubt that, right now, most present-day New Englanders sense any tremendous explosion of poetic energy in their neighborhoods. Still, without always calling attention to themselves, quiet explosions have been happening." Sixty-five poets are represented in 170 pages, and Ruffin explains that an equivalent number of poets and poems will appear in a second collection.

I must also mention two thematic anthologies. *This Sporting Life* (Milkweed), edited by

Emilie Buchwald and Ruth Roston, is a collection of "contemporary American poems about sports and games," arranged in such categories as "Life Is Water: Swimming, Diving, Canoeing, Sailing," "Blood Sports: Hunting, Fishing, Boxing, Wrestling," and "Coaches." As might be expected, such familiar but by no means unwelcome titles as Gary Gildner's "First Practice," Robert Francis's "The Base Stealer," and James Wright's "Autumn Begins in Martins Ferry, Ohio," appear. There is also excellent work by less well-known poets like David Allen Evans and Ronald Koertge. A stanza from Norman German's "New World in the Morning," about the surreal exploits of a Zen Buddhist basketball team in southeast Texas ("where you burn your neighbor's house/for revenge/and then your own for insurance money/to leave the county"), is worth quoting:

> Waiting underneath, docile as a doe,
> Sardria Char opens his hands
> like a baby bird's mouth, open in praise.
> Avoiding the karma-disturbing thuds of a dribble,
> he takes the ball and hands off to Krishna
> who passes to Gandhi sitting cross-legged
> and sleepy-eyed under the home town hoop.
> The ball rises in a perfect silent curve.
> Never touching the rim, it swishes through the net
> like a good soul coming into being.

In a year in which much of the news was dominated by Jim, Jessica, and Tammy and the Papal visit to the Superdome, Paul Ramsey's *Contemporary Religious Poetry* (Paulist Press) would seem inevitable, a timely updating of Samuel Hazo's *A Selection of Contemporary Religious Poetry,* which came from the same publisher in 1963. There are many fine poets here, though H. D., William Carlos Williams, and Edwin Muir, to mention a few, seem clearly antedated; similarly, the inclusion of such poems as Frank O'Hara's "To the Harbormaster" and Donald Justice's "An Elegy Is Preparing Itself," fine as they may be, stretches the definition of "religious poetry" almost to the point of meaninglessness. That the editorial placement of poems varies between thematic sections and alphabetical arrangement of authors seems to me another indication of Ramsey's vague intent. Nevertheless, a section of light verse and several poems by Karol Wojtyla (Pope John Paul II) make the occasional shortcomings of the anthology secondary to its many strengths.

The publication of a poet's selected or collected poems should be cause for celebration, giving his or her admirers a chance to look

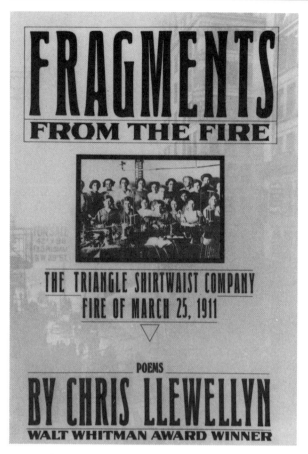

Dust jacket for Chris Llewellyn's 1986 poem cycle that recounts the story of immigrant women and children who died in the tragic fire that brought about demands for safe working conditions in U.S. factories

retrospectively over a whole career, or at least a significant portion of one, and chart the development of style and theme. *The Selected Poems* by A. R. Ammons (Norton), now in an "expanded edition," however, summons only Dr. Johnson's remark that "none would have wished it longer." A plodding and tedious poet of primitive technique (Ammons gained early notoriety for a book of poems written on adding machine tape), Ammons has been championed by Professor Harold Bloom of Yale University. There is not much indication of "visions of clarity and terror" in Ammons's poetry, but there are numerous hints at the Alphonse and Gaston routine that often goes on between poet and critic. Note, for example, the precision of phrasing and enjambment in this sample, taken from a poem appropriately entitled "For Harold Bloom":

> I went to the summit and stood in the high
>   nakedness:
> the wind tore about this

way and that in confusion and its speech could not get through to me nor could I address it:
still I said as if to the alien in myself
    I do not speak to the wind now:
for having been brought this far by nature I have
    been
brought out of nature
and nothing here shows me the image of
    myself. . . .

"Disembodied" is the first adjective that comes to my mind when attempting to describe Ammons's peculiar qualities.

A much more significant and lasting poet, in my opinion, is W. D. Snodgrass, whose *Selected Poems 1957-1987* (Soho) provides a chance to reexamine thirty years' development of the poet who, for all the wrong reasons, caused the unfortunate term "confessionalist" to be coined. Snodgrass's career is a fascinating case history in the cupidity of critics. Hard on the heels of the almost universal acclaim and the Pulitzer Prize that followed publication of his first collection, *Heart's Needle* (1959), came the widespread critical disapproval of the remarkable *After Experience* (1968), for which he was excoriated in some circles for not suffering extravagantly or publicly enough. Any book that contains such wonders as "The Examination," "Mementos, 1," "What We Said," " 'After Experience Taught Me . . . ,' " and the three remarkable poems on paintings by Monet, Van Gogh, and Manet should have more than satisfied even the most demanding tastes. I suspect that Snodgrass's candor was a bit too much for some reviewers; these lines from "The First Leaf," one of the poems that continue the "Heart's Needle" sequence, were widely cited as examples of his sour pessimism:

> Next year we'll hardly know you;
> Still, all the blame endures.
> This year you will live at our expense;
> We have a life at yours,
>
> Now I can earn a living
> By turning out elegant strophes.
> Your six-year teeth lie on my desk
> Like a soldier's trophies.

What other American poet, I wonder, has more accurately commented on the bitch-goddess of success?

It is remarkable to recall that Snodgrass, just emerging into prominence himself, was one of the first to promote and encourage Anne Sexton's work, when she was in attendance at the

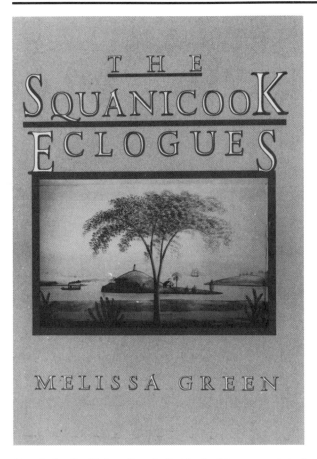

Dust jacket for Melissa Green's first book of poems, comprised of four long elegies

1958 Antioch Writers Workshop. Sexton's own development, from her first collection to her suicide, should prove a cautionary tale for those who would approach poetry as a therapeutic method of easing a troubled psyche. Spurred on by her eager audiences, what the Australian poet A. D. Hope has called "an adoring cannibal audience waiting for the next effusion of soul meat," Sexton began to substitute naked emotionalism for the skillful craftsmanship that was the saving grace of her early work. Witnessing at least one public display of tears was a standard inducement to attend one of Sexton's later readings.

Snodgrass, on the other hand, has not charted a predictable course. He has written a considerable amount of light verse, all the more remarkable when set beside his ten years' labor on the dramatic monologues of *The Fuehrer Bunker* (1977), which are anything but light. Consider Frau Magda Goebbels's lines, spoken while she is administering cyanide to her children:

> I set this spoon between your tight
> Teeth, as I gave you your first bite;

This satisfies your appetite
    For other nourishment.
Take this on your tongue; this do
Remembering your mother who
So loved her Leader she stayed true
    When all the others went,

When every friend proved false, in the
Delirium of treachery
On every hand, when even He
    Had turned His face aside.
He shut himself in with His whore;
Then, though I screamed outside His door,
Said He'd not see me anymore.
    They both took cyanide.

Snodgrass once again proves that he is a poet for all seasons, one who, like Heinrich Heine, can make exquisite songs from the deepest sorrows.

Speaking of unpredictable courses, I cannot help but observe that Karl Shapiro's *New & Selected Poems, 1940-1986* (University of Chicago Press) is 230 pages *shorter* than its predecessor, the *Selected Poems* of 1968, a diminution which implies a retrograde motion on the poet's part. Shapiro takes Emerson's warning about foolish consistencies to the extreme; he began as a poet who seemingly had sprung fully armed from the forehead of I. A. Richards, writing a formal poetry of wit and irony that the New Criticism seemed designed for, elegies with titles like "F. O. Mattheissen: An Anniversary," even editing *Poetry* during the height of the Eisenhower years. But as early as the 1945 *Essay on Rime* he began to exhibit restive uncertainties which came to fruition in the prose poems of his 1964 collection, *The Bourgeois Poet.* Now he has apparently returned to his roots, once more writing sonnets and quatrains. Even the epigraph to the whole collection, "To Sophie," reminds one more of John Greenleaf Whittier than of Shapiro's beloved Walt Whitman:

> Roses in late November
> Here where the skies begin
> Bring poetry back to love.
> Thank you for bringing them in.

At his best Shapiro is one of the finest poets of his generation; as an observer of the ironies of ordinary life his only peer is Howard Nemerov.

For over thirty years a seemingly endless fount of sane, practical advice has washed over and away would-be poets who have read Judson Jerome's column in *Writer's Digest. The Village:*

New and Selected Poems (Dolphin-Moon Press) could almost serve as a textbook on versification. Jerome, who is an unabashed friend, lover, and admirer of the fair sex, reminds us that a poet who works within the limits of traditional poetic form does not necessarily have to be a bluenose where subject matter is concerned. The sonnet sequence "Partita in Nothing Flat" is a candid and often charming depiction of a ménage à trois, and one of the more recent poems, "Licensed by Love," is a graphic life study of his wife:

> When Art's too close to Nature, all Art stops.
> Age has its fissures, but it has its points,
> among them reawakening of youth's rush.

> Disrobed to one another by the years,
> we mesh our wrinkles and arthritic joints.
> Let's kick up our heels and celebrate the bond
> that spirit animates and flesh coheres.

Ironically, Jerome writes some of his best verse when he works in freer forms; the title poem of the collection, a narrative of the hard leave-taking two parents experience when they leave their aphasiac daughter at a special boarding school, is the most powerful single poem in the book. Here is a representative section:

> Driving away, my mind plays tricks:
>
> Suppose there were
>
> a village
>
> just for people who lived in care
>
> of one
>
> another, where
>
> differences were expected.
>
> Judge
>
> not.
>
> With what one has, make do.
>
> I see a village
>
> spreading its cottages and economical gardens

> on the verdant hills,
>
> people sharing whatever,
>
> coming
>
> together to work, play, learn, worship, in joy.
>
> No last
>
> names.
>
> Ages all relative.
>
> The sexes mingling.
>
> The point
>
> of life being
>
> nurture, fulfillment, happiness.

The prosody here is derived from William Carlos Williams's variable foot, despite the fairly consistent fourteen-syllable-per-line meter. Jerome's poetry is full of such happy surprises.

I first remember reading Marvin Bell's poetry in Al Lee's 1971 anthology, *The Major Young Poets*. The eight poets included–Bell, Michael Benedikt, Wm Brown [sic], Charles Simic, Mark Strand, James Tate, C. K. Williams, and David P. Young–were all under thirty-five in 1970 and remain more or less visible presences on today's scene. At the time they represented the new breed of academic poets, slightly older role-models one might well aspire to. They wrote hip, surrealistic poetry, freshly inspired by such diverse sources as poets of the continent and of South America that captured the mood of the day well; and if their wares look a bit shopworn today it is only because so many even-younger poets imitated them. Bell, whose *New and Selected Poems* (Atheneum) provides a cultural junket through some interesting times, is that rarity, a serious meditative poet with a fine sense of mordant humor. An early poem, "Things We Dreamt We Died For," is a powerful evocation of the disillusioned mood of the children of the 1960s:

> Each time we dreamt we'd done
> the gentlemanly thing,
> covering our causes
> in closets full of bones

to remove ourselves forever
from dearest possibilities,
the old weapons re-injured us,
the old armies conscripted us,
and we gave in to getting even. . . .

Bell has unfortunately not grown much; the new poems in the collection sound like nostalgic evocations of the Age of Aquarius, as evidenced by the opening lines of a poem entitled "Classified":

I am no more stupid now than I ever was; I am the
    same.
The end of tomorrow is no further away than it
    ever was.

Three poets whom I have read for years without having registered strong impressions about their work also published collected or selected editions in 1987. Donald Finkel's *Selected Shorter Poems* (Atheneum) presents almost thirty years' work from a poet who has also published four book-length narrative poems. The first poem in the present collection is "An Esthetic of Imitation," and the title alone may provide a clue to my lack of interest in Finkel's work. In 209 pages he manages to sound like almost every poet of his generation, incorporating James Dickey's spatial cesurae, Robert Creeley's skinny meters, even Richard Howard's lengthy quoted passages from historical personages. Exploring, in historical and geographical terms, that is, is a constant motif here just as it was in Finkel's long poem *Answer Back* (1968). However, one eventually wishes more insight into the perpetrator of these expeditions.

From Princeton One Afternoon: Collected Poems of Theodore Weiss 1950-1986 (Atheneum), despite James Merrill's assertion that it "is among the most valuable work produced in our time," strikes me as the dreariest sort of academic/hermetic poetry imaginable. Much of Weiss's work sounds like Talmudic commentary on the poems of other authors, as witness the following:

One poet tells us
of blinded children beating
at their eyes, perhaps to strike
the sparks from them of light
burnt out.
        And another
is much moved to make a poem
out of a report that H. D.,
having a stroke, fiercely desires
to communicate. . . .

One gets the feeling of Weiss's having produced most of these poems while safely locked in his office in the Humanities Building, a queue of students seeking their research-paper grades gathering dust in the hallway outside.

William Meredith is the third of these poets, and I am quite willing to admit that my inability to appreciate his work fully is perhaps a defect of taste. He is gregarious and sociable, a poet who is most at home in the elegaic and dedicatory modes. Well-known names abound here–Robert Lowell, Robert Penn Warren, Richard and Charlee Wilbur, W. H. Auden–and one often gets the impression of poems written as thank-you notes for delightful house-parties. Meredith's self-characterization as "a mild-spoken citizen" is perhaps only too accurate; this mildness often leads to equivocation. Here is a section from a poem entitled "Examples of Created Systems":

        The homeless
Solzhenitsyn, looking at Russia,
saw a configuration of camps
spotting his homeland, 'ports' where men
and woman were forced to act out
the birth-throes of volcanic islands,
the coral patience of reefs, before
a 'ship,' a prison train, bore them down
that terrible archipelago
conceived and made by men like ourselves.

Although the paraphrase of Solzhenitsyn sounds as innocuous as a dust-jacket blurb, the last line seems simplistic, banal, and ultimately false. Though Meredith passes on advice to writers to "Keep your word-hoard dry," his own remains rather damp tinder unlikely to catch a spark. *Partial Accounts* (Knopf), which received the 1987 *Los Angeles Times* Book Prize, contains poems from seven previous books and a selection of new poems.

Dave Etter is a poet who has taken William Carlos Williams's notions about "local conditions" to heart, becoming an unapologetic regionalist (in this case Illinois) who has managed to publish in just about every quarterly imaginable. His background as a small-town newspaperman shows up in his short lines and anecdotal narratives of his *Selected Poems* (Spoon River Poetry Press). His work is full of what is best termed "human interest." Etter is not a particularly demanding poet, but he is a solid one who can be relied on to dispense with most of the formalities of technique to get to the heart of the matter. One stanza of

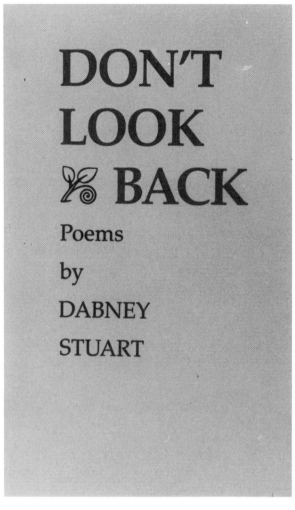

Dust jacket for Dabney Stuart's collection of autobiographical poetry that, according to his publisher, "recalls central people and emotions from his past and integrates them into a search for personal wholeness in the present"

There are some poets we learn from and others we simply enjoy. Etter is clearly one of the latter type.

Ruth Stone's *Second-Hand Coat: Poems New and Selected* (Godine) contains work that dates from as early as 1951. Stone, like many women poets of her generation, seems to have been detrimentally influenced by some of the feminist rhetoric of the 1970s. The landscape of "Laguna Beach," to twist John Ruskin's terminology a bit, seems pathetically phallic:

> The shingle roofs burgeon moss, green as tender
>   acacia.
> Under their eaves giant roses in cinemascope flash
> Over-developed boobs; huge green penises rise,
>   hairy,
> Bristling with impotence, into trees that hold them.
> Meanwhile the trees wait around on one foot for a
>   place
> To set the penises aside. It rains.
> The sun draws off all the water.
> Nature says yes to everything.

Stone is much more controlled in her character studies; mercifully, the book contains many of these. Here is the conclusion of "Mother's Picture":

> You stare from inside the picture
> wordless as the virgin oaks on Lake Kegonsa,
> though they cry in the ice storms
> with the voices of the waterfowl.
> The wild swans cross over
> That lake in late March.
> Your look is silent as their shadows
> flying on the reedy bottom.

"Aunt Alice Is Dead" is representative of his wry style; he has learned via a phone call from "Uncle Ulysses" that the elderly lady has "died this afternoon/while eating her/daily double dip/ ice cream cone." Here is the conclusion:

> I say nothing
> for twelve seconds,
> then cough twice,
> clear my throat.
> I always hated
> horrible Aunt Alice.
> "Ulysses," I say,
> "did Cousin Candace
> say what flavor?"

Two selected works by black authors with strong followings appeared in 1987, a year that also saw the death of James Baldwin, who endures, after two decades of relative neglect, as one of the most intelligent commentators on race that this country has produced. Jay Wright and Wanda Coleman could not be more different in their approach to the racial issue. Wright is a poet whom Professor Bloom elucidates in an afterword to *Selected Poems of Jay Wright* (Princeton University Press) by noting that the "*askesis* here [in "The Dead"] is Wright's characteristic apotropaic gesture toward tradition, toward all his traditions." In other words, according to Robert B. Stepto's introduction, "the predominating, Europhilic equations of comparative art and culture cannot fully calculate the figures of Wright's poetry." Clear as mud. I assume that what they are saying is that Wright does not write about race very much. He *does* write the type of poem in which a spectral first-person pronoun predominates:

> Inscrutable when I speak,
> I am learning how my body sounds.
> In the sand by the river's edge,
> my head is a moon's egg,
> my shell is a bell in my boat.
> My arms and legs are storms.
> I turn left, I turn right. . . .

Much ado about not much, it would seem. The organism describing itself here defies easy taxonomy.

Wanda Coleman's *Heavy Daughter Blues: Poems and Stories 1968-1986* (Black Sparrow) comes from the other end of the racial spectrum. Coleman alternates between bluesy doggerel and polemical rant. Herewith a sample of the former:

> hate came by romancin', gave me the evil eye
> got so hooked on his juju, thought i was gonna die
> that low down dirty dirty promised to be true
> then had me drinking all the misery he could
>   brew. . . .

And of the latter:

> i hated dolls. white dolls
> dolls with pasty flesh unlike my own
> and alien straight hair
> and stiff sticky crinoline dresses . . .
>
>
> i destroyed them with pleasure

Compared to the enervated Wright, Coleman is positively bracing. One wonders what Professor Bloom would make of her *askesis*.

Three final collections bear mention, though largely as curiosities. *The Collected Poems of Marsden Hartley 1904-1943* (Black Sparrow) proves that famous painters can write as poorly as any juvenile poet: "The cinnamon rose doth/ bloom so close to my/south window that bees/do rumble in and fill/my humble house with free/ and ever pleasant music." On the other hand, *The Poems of Lincoln Kirstein* (Atheneum), by the longtime director of the New York City Ballet, is a genuine treat. Kirstein credits Gerard Manley Hopkins and Rudyard Kipling as "two to whom I most often turn," and the wonderful British light verse poet Gavin Ewart (whose *The Gavin Ewart Show* appeared recently from Bits Press) is the dedicatee of the first half of the book. Living in

the very bowels of the avant-garde beast, Kirstein writes lively old-fashioned verse. Here are two stanzas describing a memorable childhood initiation:

> My mother's brother hauled me to the big-boys'
>   club,
>   Where they swam nude, drank beer, shared
>   secrecy.
> Males young and old held mystic privilege.
>   I was condemned to join their mystery.
>
>
> These men were hairy on belly and groin;
>   The boys were hairier at least than me,
> No boy, no man, a neuter in-between,
>   One hairless silly, neither he nor she.

No less a judge than W. H. Auden declared that Kirstein's book of war poems, *Rhymes of a PFC* (1964), was, as "a picture of the late war . . . by far the most convincing, moving, and impressive book I have come across," adding that "I cannot believe . . . that any poet, no matter how accomplished, will read these poems without admiration and envy." And finally, the third of these "curiosities" is *Wind Around the Moon: New and Collected Poems* (Dragon's Teeth Press) by Marcia Lee Masters, daughter of the Spoon River anthologist. Most of this is verse of the genteel type, but "One Evening at Mrs. William Vaughan Moody's" is a fascinating glimpse of a childhood spent on the lower slopes of Parnassus:

> When we came down, we raced up to the huge
>   square mattress
> That dangled from above on copper chains;
> We jumped on it and pushed and floated,
> Kicking our patent leathers as we would kick at
>   flames.
>
>
> And then we saw the poets—
> Countryfuls of poets;
> Some had the rumpled strength of shepherds
> With voices tousled by the wind;
> Others, shy and slim, were listening to the fire—
> Red and sapphire coals cupped in a wrought-iron
>   basket
> That matched the fences down the street.

The evening reaches an appropriate climax: "And then Tagore took us aside/To hear the seashells of his poems." Dazzled by such glamour, one wonders why there have been so few second-generation poets. Perhaps Masters's debut was happier than most.

Dust jacket for Ellen Bryant Voigt's collection of poems exploring the interrelationship of exile and nostalgia

It is impossible to make any sweeping statements about the many individual volumes of poetry published in 1987. Any large assertion could be quickly refuted on the evidence of four or five books. That said, a few cautious words may be in order. Following the trend Lewis Turco noted in previous years, I find more openness among publishers to poetry written in traditional forms or modifications thereof. Perhaps the widespread classroom use of Philip Dacey and David Jauss's *Strong Measures: Contemporary American Poetry in Traditional Forms* (1986), along with such other texts as Miller Williams's *Patterns of Poetry* (1986), and Turco's own *The New Book of Forms*, has rekindled interest in meter, rhyme, and stanza among younger poets. Another detectable trend is the decline of surrealism, particularly when it is attached to the poem of social comment so prevalent in the 1960s and 1970s. Poets today seem to be following the lead of the new generation of short-story writers in examining the realistic surfaces of the quotidian, what has been disparagingly labeled "K-Mart realism" in some

quarters. A third direction that might be noted is the increased prevalence of direct statement, as opposed to oblique epiphany, in American poetry. Perhaps the proliferation of poetry readings as the only real public forum for poets has affected their desires to make their meanings plain to their audiences. Beyond these observations I would venture no further generalization save that the best indicator of a nation's literary condition is its diversity, and that we have.

Peter Viereck's *Archer in the Marrow: The Applewood Cycles, 1967-1987* (Norton) was twenty years in the writing and, I fear, will be at least that much in the puzzling out. One of those vast designs (290 pages, with notes) that, at best, calls Blake or Pound to mind and, at worst, the Spasmodic poets of the high Victorian era, the poem unfolds as a dialogue among three archetypal characters: God the "father," the "son" of Man, and "you," a modern Everyman. This is yet another poem mislabeled as an "epic" by those who have forgotten that the essence of epic poetry is *narrative*. Fred Chappell's *Midquest* (1981), while epic in length, is essentially a collection of miscellaneous poems held together by a time-frame (the poet's thirty-fifth birthday) and an intricate numerological design. James Merrill's ouija-board poems consist largely of dramatic dialogue. Frederick Turner's *The New World* (1985), with its careful use of the classical "machinery," is perhaps as close as a contemporary poem can come to matching any generally approved definition of the epic. Viereck's poem, on the contrary, employs a complex structure of "parts," "transitions," and "cycles" to fence in a rather heterogenous menagerie of poems. Some parts, to be sure, are quite engaging, for example these lines, spoken by a potato:

In each Kiwanis Club on every plate,
So bland and health-exuding do I wait
That Indiana never, never knows
How much I envy stars and hate the rose.

You call me dull? A food and not a flower?
Wait! I'll outshine all roses in my hour.
Not wholesomeness but hubris bloats me so
In Indiana and in Idaho.

Viereck, it will be remembered, won the Pulitzer Prize for poetry in 1949, coincidentally the same year of the immense controversy that surrounded Ezra Pound's receipt of the Bollingen Award for *The Pisan Cantos*.

Twenty-five March 1911 is a date of special significance in the history of American labor. At 4:45 P.M., just as employees were receiving their paychecks, a fire broke out in New York's Asch Building, home of the Triangle Shirtwaist Company. Some of the 500 employees, mostly female Russian and Italian immigrants, were trapped on the ninth floor, where the doors had been locked to keep out union organizers. One hundred forty-six people died, many of them young women who leaped to their deaths to escape the flames. This is the subject of Chris Llewellyn's *Fragments from the Fire* (Viking), winner of the Walt Whitman Award, selected this year by Maxine Kumin. Llewellyn's method is to "write about *them*/yet not interfere, although I'm told/a poet's task is to create a little world." Her method of telling the story largely through the words of survivors and culprits brings to mind the "Objectivist" methods of Charles Reznikoff's *Testimony: The United States 1885-1890* (1934). Although at times Llewellyn's account of the tragedy seems simplistic the subject matter alone makes the poems compelling:

> "I could see them falling,"
> said Lena Goldman. "I was sweeping out
> front of my cafe. At first we thought
> it was bolts of cloth–till they opened
> with legs! I still see the day
> it rained children. Yes.
>   It was nearly Passover."

The book's accompanying photographs help to underscore the ironies of a time in which one generation of immigrants fed a younger one into the numbing and dangerous drudgery of the sweatshops.

Jane Shore's *The Minute Hand* (University of Massachusetts Press) was the 1986 Lamont Poetry Selection of the Academy of American Poets. The judges were Philip Booth, Louise Gluck, and Mary Oliver. Shore's poetic debts seem fairly clear. "The Other Woman" reprises the dramatic situation of Sylvia Plath's "The Rival"; "A Luna Moth," dedicated to Elizabeth Bishop, similarly reminds one of Bishop's "The Moose" and "The Armadillo." Here is its concluding stanza:

> This morning,
> a weekend guest sunbathing on the deck
> sun-blind, thought the wind had blown
> a five dollar bill against the screen.
> He grabbed the luna, gasped,
> and flung her to the ground.
> She lay a long moment in the grass,

> then fluttered slowly to the edge of the woods
> where, sometimes at dawn,
> deer nibble the wild raspberry bushes.

It is perhaps significant that throughout the poem Shore refers unhesitantly to the moth in the feminine gender.

I can't think of any contemporary poet who can be as versatile as May Swenson. In *In Other Words* (Knopf) she writes spatial poems, sometimes with contrapuntal stanzas facing each other from opposite sides of the page; a neo-Emersonian Harvard Phi Beta Kappa poem ("Get up, get out on the fresh edge/of things, away from the wow and the flutter. Stand alone./ Take a breath of your own. Choose the wide-angle/ view. That's something, maybe, you can begin to/learn to do, once you're *out* of college."); even a good occasional poem (possibly the *only* good poem) inspired by the *Challenger* disaster. Here are some lines from a light verse piece, "Fit":

> Let's do one of those long
> Narrow *New Yorker* poems to
> Fit between the ads on about

> Page 69. It should be fresh,
> Have color and panache and
> Make a few references to

> Mainstream name brands,
> Such as Sulka, Cuisinart or
> Baggies–to fit with the ads. . . .

The conclusion?

>   Still too
> Short? Three-line stanzas

> Instead of four may make it
> Fit. It's worth it. Here goes.
> Poetry pays better than prose.

Jo McDougall's *The Woman in the Next Booth* (BkMk Press) consists of poems laconic and ancedotal, sharp little observations of people and places of the American byways that expand to larger truths when pondered. Here is one example, "When the Buck or Two Steakhouse Changed Hands":

> They put plastic over the menus.
> They told the waitress to wear white shoes.
> They fired Rita.
> They threw out the unclaimed keys
> and the pelican with a toothpick

that bowed as you left.

That same anonymous, corporate "they," one suspects, is also responsible for putting Musak in public washrooms and removing the talking clowns from Jack-in-the-Box.

That the hirsute T. R. Hummer, photographed in denims and crew neck on the cover of *Lower-Class Heresy* (University of Illinois Press), should occupy John Crowe Ransom's old position at Kenyon College is an indication of how much the poet's academic image has changed over the years. Hummer has a good eye and ear for southern rural life, where "we are all good Methodists singing/About the weak and the heavy laden," but he seems incapable of compression; most of his poems ramble on for several pages. This, indeed, is not always to his detriment; a long, erotic poem entitled "Bluegrass Wasteland" must have steamed the ears of quite a few readers of the *Georgia Review* when it appeared there this year. Here are some telling lines from "Dogma: Pigmeat and Whiskey":

> What is it I'm trying to say here? I know I sound
> Like just another Southern storyteller telling
>
> Another Southern story about the war, that Dark
> 　and Bloody Ground,
> Family, memory, history, old men, time.
> Everyone's sick of that, me included. Once Pound
>
> Wrote, with characteristic wisdom
> And a dogmatic sneer *The narrative impulse is a*
> 　*product*
> *Of the village mentality.* I can't argue with him.

Hummer, like his contemporary Dave Smith, seems the latest embodiment of the portrait-of-the-artist-as-good-ol'-boy school of poetry.

David Bottoms is another unreconstructed southern poet, and his poems are filled with fishing, guitar picking, and all kinds of mayhem. He is also one of the best narrative poets in recent memory. *Under the Vulture-Tree* (Morrow) succeeds by the twin virtues of the storyteller's art, characterization and plot. "White Shrouds," a poem about a husband's attempts to heat his home during an unexpected Georgia cold snap, should get a special award for being the one memorable poem from a whole year's worth of the *New Yorker*. This is its conclusion:

> I listened all night to the fanatical ministry
> of the brain, the alarm

Dust jacket for Mark Halliday's first book of poems, which show the influence of Kenneth Koch and Frank O'Hara

it sounds to keep the body alert,

> which wasn't the ringing of bells over city shelters,
> or the sirens of ambulances spinning out of alleys
> but was only that breathing,
> the white easy breathing of sleepers curling
> in doorways, behind dumpsters, their ears
> slowly turning into stone, and no one
> to husband the small logs, two at a time, onto the
> 　fire.

Ray Gonzalez is perhaps best known as poetry editor of the *Bloomsbury Review*, one of the few magazines devoted to reviewing small-press books for a nationwide audience. *Twilights and Chants* (James Andrews) is his first collection of poetry. Unlike many younger Hispanic poets he avoids macaronics, writing poems of description reminiscent of Richard Hugo's work. In "Isleta

Pueblo" Gonzalez depicts an abandoned adobe ruin where he can imagine

> animals of habitation
> were hung to bleed,
> the crucifix torn off the wall,
> the dwelling where the strong ones
> copulated and screamed
> in the muddy dark.

Not unlike Hugo, Gonzalez's eye occasionally moves faster than his syntax. He is, nevertheless, a strong poet, well worth reading.

Charles Martin's *Steal the Bacon* (Johns Hopkins) is a book that I have looked forward to for several years, since reading his miraculous "Passages from Friday" in the *New England Review and Bread Loaf Quarterly*. In that poem, Friday decides that "I must learn to//write as my *Master* did & so set down/tho' withowt any Hope of Recovery" his own version of *Robinson Crusoe*. In the idiom of William Cowper's "The Castaway" Martin presents a perceptive lecture on civilization's encounter with the primitive that, in its moments of humor, is worthy of Evelyn Waugh. The best poem in *Steal the Bacon* is the delightful "E.S.L.":

> Tonight my students must
> *Agree or disagree*:
> *America is still a land of opportunity.*
>   The answer is always, uniformly, *Yes*—even
>   though
>   *"It has no doubt that here were to much free,"*
>   As Miss Torrico will insist.
>   She and I both know
>
>   That Language binds us fast,
>   And those of us without
> Are bound and gagged by those within.

Martin's formal control of these intricate stanzas, and of a variety of others, is truly remarkable.

Sydney Lea is the respected magazine editor who published Martin's "Passages from Friday." He is also a technically inventive poet who has tried a number of poetic modes successfully, most prominently the blank verse narrative. "The Light" recalls Robert Frost's "Directive":

> There is light. The darkness has not overcome it.
> Parents, children, brothers, sisters play
> within a house of yellow, white and gray,
> house candescent there upon its summit.
> House on a hill, my room forever my room,
> and ever light within to bring me home.

Of especial notice is how the spare rhymes help to bring this meditation to a tight conclusion. *No Sign* (University of Georgia Press) is a fine, thoughtful book. Like his great New England precursor, Lea is closely attuned to the seasons. The splendid "Annual Report," a twelve-sonnet sequence about a year, a wife, and children, closes the book. Here is part of its final section:

> Now, the year's full circle:
> cased blossoms bursting from the apple tree,
> the prostrate dog now grass, one son a man,
> a daughter who like you grows beautiful,
> an infant who has found a way to stand,
> the worm entombed as if beneath a mountain,
> this spot of ground a fête of resurrection,
> since what is hope if not futility
> for moments stood on end? My love, it's May,
> first month of our obscure divinity,
>
> creator, creature, riddle, lover, maid.

Using the word "beautiful" to describe poetry went out of fashion in the Gilded Age; however, I would not hesitate to use it here.

Peter Cooley's *The Van Gogh Notebook* (Carnegie-Mellon University Press) covers the same ground as Irving Stone's *Lust for Life* (1934) and his useful edition of Van Gogh's correspondence, *Dear Theo* (1937). Cooley, reviewing the major paintings with a knowledgeable eye and perhaps the unique envy poets often feel when confronted by masterpieces of another medium, attempts to get inside the painter's troubled psyche by examining his own:

> Vincent, this is where our stars part company.
> Your eyes here are taking down the thunderheads
> flooding another shore, a point of vanishing
> where the clouds break, the clouds break down
>   finally.
> Twice I have been there, I will not go back.
> I snap shut the book of graven images
> in which, time out of mind, your whitecaps wash
>   you up.
> With these words, brother, I set you straight beside
>   myself.

This is work which demands the reader's full attention; its high measure of achievement can be fully appreciated only with a set of reproductions of the paintings close at hand.

Dabney Stuart's *Don't Look Back* (Louisiana State University Press) is the poet's seventh collection, ironically titled in that poems like "My Mother Announces She Is Pregnant," "1943," and "Ex-Wife" do just what the poet advises against. Stuart is a poet of psychological processes; the question that repeatedly arises in his poems is "How did we get this way?" A poem about grammar school concludes in this manner: "their voices come/over the intercom system saying/*Good grades, good grades./*We live like this for years,/recess to recess, and nobody ever/ thinks to call it war." These "wars" take the sides of students vs. teachers, children vs. parents, and, most importantly, men vs. women.

Also from LSU Press comes Susan Ludvigson's *The Beautiful Noon of No Shadow*, a curiously restrained collection from a poet we have grown accustomed to for such energetic gifts as the bizarre "Man Arrested in Hacking Death Tells Police He Mistook Mother-in-Law for Raccoon." The high seriousness of Rainer Maria Rilke pervades these poems; this one is entitled " 'The Anonymous Multiple Rhythm of One's Blood' ":

> I sit on a rock, watching waves
> silvered by the mercurial
> Normandy sky, remembering how last night
> I couldn't find my heart's wash
> against any shore.
> Today the heart adjusted itself
> to an incoming tide in the right ear,
> Mozart in the left.
> Now I walk out to where,
> another Sunday, I saw a cathedral
> built of sand on sand.

I find Ludvigson more appealing in her earlier incarnations; "heart's wash" and sand cathedrals are enough to do any poem in.

The Lotus Flowers (Norton) is Ellen Bryant Voigt's third collection of poetry. There are many back-country Virginia customs ritualized here, most, like all-day prayer meetings and cemetery decoration days, centering on the rural churches and schools of the poet's childhood. Voigt does little that is unusual stylistically, but she does have a good eye for detail. Here is a description of a group of seventh grade children on "The Field Trip":

> A girl asks if she should also list
> the way she feels—she's the one
> who'll cite the shadow on the lake below.
> The others sprawl on gender-separate rocks
> except for the smart-ass, perched
> on the cliff-edge, inviting front-page photos—
> PICNIC MARRED BY TRAGEDY.

There is, of course, no overt tragedy to end the day, only a parting shot of "one/bad boy who carved a scorpion on his arm."

Pattiann Rogers's *Legendary Performance* (Ion Books/Raccoon) is a surprising departure for a poet best known for her detailed catalogs of natural phenomena. The present collection includes a repertory company–Kioka, Felicia, Eduard, Gordon–who intermingle in a series of poems reminiscent of films like *The Four Seasons* and *The Big Chill*. In apparently comfortable circumstances, the characters have adequate time to perfect their sensibilities. Here is a list given Felicia by her tutor, Eduard, in an attempt to improve her behavior:

> Somersaulting and leaping confuse clear-thinking.
> Running and bounding lead to chaos in the brain.
> No one can deny that shrieks destroy
> The most delicately balanced tedium.
>
> Strolling in moderation is tolerated.
> Twisting ribbons and twiddling by small
> Quiet fires is cultivated.
> Sighing is admired.

Taken in small doses these vignettes of social satire are mildly amusing; a whole book of them, however, ventures into the overly *précieux* and proves taxing of the reader's patience.

Above the Land (Yale University Press) by Julie Agoos is this year's winning volume in the Yale Series of Young Poets, selected by James Merrill. Knowing of Merrill's own globe-trotting sensibilities, one is not surprised to find titles like "Terzo Piano," "Porto Venere," and "Florence Interlude" in abundance–all examples of what critic Robert Peters has called "the Fulbright-year-abroad poem." Agoos occasionally gets down to a more mundane level in a poem like "Painting the Railing," but the broken meters of these janglingly rimed quatrains do not speak well for her technical skills:

> All afternoon, like a mixture of snow and rain,
> the old paint falls from the wooden railing.
> And the hot wind, lifting the shower of flakes
> carries them over the porch; the lawn is scaling.
>
> My arm is a plow, or a circling airplane.
> I am giving a grain to something soft and fraying.
> Powered by the faint wind as the knife scrapes,
> I kneel along the porch like someone praying.

One indeed wonders what is going on in the editorial offices of the Ivy League presses;

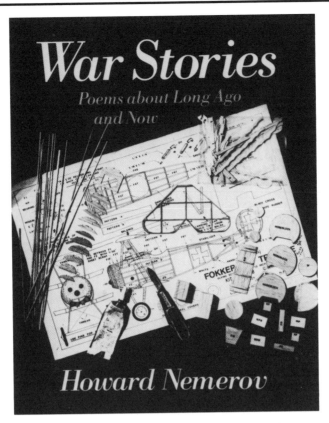

Dust jacket for Howard Nemerov's poems about a World War II flyer

books received this year from those quarters were undistinguished to say the least. David Lehman's *An Alternative to Speech* (Princeton University Press) seems one more needless addendum to the canon of the L=A=N=G=U=A=G=E poets. Here is a stanza from "The Evil Genius":

> Suddenly a voice: "You turn left at the stars."
> But I'm always hearing things wrong, hearing
> things rhyme:
> The Third Reich: the third rail: I like Ike: the Holy
> Grail.
> The marine had never seen so many shades of
> green.

Silence, in Mr. Lehman's case, would seem a more attractive "alternative to speech."

Restrictions of time, space, energy, and adjectives prevent me from giving more than briefest mention to other books published in 1987, all of them of some significance. The National Poetry Series was established in 1978 and sponsors publication of five volumes per year. This year's selections were John Engels's *Cardinals in the Ice Age* (Graywolf), selected by Philip Levine; Mark Halliday's *Little Star* (William Morrow), selected by Heather McHugh; Sylvia Moss's *Cities in Mo-*

tion (University of Illinois Press), selected by Derek Walcott; Charlie Smith's *Red Roads* (Dutton), selected by Stanley Kunitz; and Barbara Anderson's *Junk City* (Persea Books), selected by Robert Pinsky. Engels, with five previous collections to his credit, is primarily a poet of landscapes. Halliday writes garrulous autobiographical poems, full of dropped names, dates, literary gossip, and references to rock music. He seems much indebted to the late Frank O'Hara. Moss is another footloose traveler whose poems often begin with lines like "Once when we were in Bruges. . . . " Smith is yet another young poet of the Deep South whose lines abound with hymn-singing Freewill Baptists, tobacco fields, butterbeans and ham—another clone of Dave Smith.

A number of books also arrived from established poets or writers established in other genres. Robley Wilson, Jr.'s *Kingdom of the Ordinary* (Pitt Poetry Series) collects poems from the author of three volumes of short stories. The work is competent, but even a poem on the violence at Kent State and Jackson State fails to generate any real dramatic tension or revelation. Julia Randall's sixth collection, *Moving in Memory* (Louisiana State University Press), contains numerous fine nature poems, most with an ecological emphasis. Vern Rutsala's seventh collection, *Ruined Cities* (Carnegie-Mellon University Press), is a mixed bag, containing many mid-life poems from the "we" point-of-view that speak of reading "less/of the paper every day–headlines/and leads, enough of course/to make us want to cry, enough/to make us ravage the *TV Guide*/for Thirties movies when/no one settled for less.... " Former Yale Younger Poet David Wojahn contributes *Glass-works* (Pitt Poetry Series), which has an elegy to rock singer Jim Morrison and homages to painters Donald Evans, Thomas Eakins, and Mark Rothko. None of them seems to rise to the subject at hand. C. K. Williams's *Flesh and Blood* (Farrar, Straus and Giroux) is a sequence of long-meter octaves which can be read as separate poems on a variety of subjects–love, marriage, children, adultery, practically anything that catches Williams's probing eye. Most of these poems represent a direction counter to the surrealism of the poet's early work. Lawrence Rabb's *Other Children* (Carnegie-Mellon University Press) celebrates, among other things, marriage and fatherhood. Many of the poems verge on sentimentality. Tom Clark's *Disordered Ideas* (Black Sparrow) is the most fittingly titled collection of the year. Apparently Clark's poetic development was arrested shortly after 1965. He is still railing about "polyester lips," "word processor colleges," "plastic," and "synthetic turf." From the same publisher comes Robert Kelly's *Not This Island Music*. Kelly, one of the inheritors of the Black Mountain College torch, meanders through endless meditations, noting that "The poet's prime responsibility is to esteem nothing unworthy of notice, nothing too small or too large, too subtle or too obvious, to talk about." Those who believe that selectivity is the basis of art will perhaps disagree. Denis Johnson's *The Veil* (Knopf) uses works of art as points of departure for several poems; in others he seems to be observing the world from behind the passive "veil" of T. S. Eliot's Tiresias: "The man wants to make love to the crippled man's sister/because he loves the crippled man.... " BOA Editions publisher A. Poulin, Jr., collects some earlier work from his collections and pamphlets in *A Momentary Order* (Graywolf). Poulin employs many formal strategies, all with seeming ease. "A Nest of Sonnets" is a nicely observed piece of what might best be termed "suburban pastoral" poetry. Finally, two books from poet-teachers of long repute are worth noting. Robert Pack's *Clayfield Rejoices, Clayfield Laments* (Godine) details the exploits of an American Everyman about whom Pack says, "you'll see/Yourself in him, surmising him in me." The complications of the protagonist's life remind me of similar situations in fiction by Updike and Cheever. Peter Meinke's *Night Watch on the Chesapeake* (Pitt Poetry Series) comes up to Meinke's usual high level of achievement, offering poems about aging that are particularly worth singling out.

Four books by some of our most prolific poets should also be noted here. William Stafford's *An Oregon Message* (Harper and Row) contains little that will surprise anyone but much that will delight the many admirers of the poet named "The Greatest Living American Poet" in a recent poll of readers of *Writer's Digest*. Walter McDonald's *The Flying Dutchman* (Ohio State University Press) is the winner of the 1987 George Elliston Poetry Prize, following his 1985 collection *Witching on Hardscrabble* and preceding next year's *After the Noise of Saigon*, winner of the Juniper Prize for Poetry from the University of Massachusetts Press. McDonald, whose quiet idiom recalls Stafford's, is a skilled chronicler of life on the West Texas plains. Amy Clampitt's *Archaic Figure* (Knopf) is the third large collection in four years from a poet who was relatively unknown until well into her middle years. The poems focus on a number of literary and historical subjects, mostly relating to the experience of women, collectively and individually, through the centuries. The conclusion of a poem about Margaret Fuller, charter member of the Transcendental Club who died at sea while returning from Italy with her new husband and child, is worth quoting:

> Injustice. Ridicule. What did she *do?*
> it would be asked (as though that mattered).
> Gave birth. Lived through a revolution.
> Nursed its wounded. Saw it run aground.
> Published a book or two.
> And drowned.

Howard Nemerov's *War Stories* (University of Chicago Press) is made up of new work from a poet who has already published selected and collected editions. Nemerov remains one of the most trenchant satirists of the American scene, focusing, in this case, on "The Shopping Mall, the Moral Law":

> The mannequins, young visions of delight
> Outfitted all for sporting and for sports,
> Lean back a bit with breast and thigh outthrust

In lazily yielding postures that invite
Into their filmy designer's shirts and shorts.

To stabilize their stance and prop upright
These swooning figures of a plastic lust
And keep them coming to this pretty pass
Without arriving, a discipline of sorts
Makes sure each has a ramrod up her ass.

A few collections from poets with less well-established reputations seem to distinguish themselves and offer promise for the future. Robert Hill Long's *The Power to Die* (Cleveland State University Poetry Center) contains some slightly redactional poems on historical subjects, such as "A Photograph of Mr. Teach and Lord Cornwallis" and "The Death of Johnny Appleseed." This latter wonders "Whether he was meditating/on the serpent's fangs in the first apple/or a dipper-full of well water" and concludes with "Conestogas and Vistacruisers,/heading through a darkness lit/by nothing but falling apple blossoms." *People and Dog in the Sun* (Pitt Poetry Series) is Ronald Wallace's second book of poems. In "Poem Written Mostly by Fourth Graders" he says, "they're all here, exactly where we left them" and goes on to catalog: "Here's the girl with her pants snap open,/here's the boy excavating his nose,/here's the fat kid with bottle-thick/glasses, his shirt buttoned up to his neck,/gawking at nothing at all." Nancy Lagomarsino's *Sleep Handbook* (alicejamesbooks) contains surrealistic prose poems that begin with sentences like "The bathtub is glued to the wall, but it could tear itself free at any time. It stays because it loves human company, like any wild animal captured soon enough." Most of us thought that Russell Edson had cornered the market on this kind of poem. Barbara Chase-Riboud, author of two novels and one previous collection of poetry, offers *Portrait of a Nude Woman as Cleopatra* (Morrow), a series of short dramatic monologues inspired by the Rembrandt painting from which the book takes its title. Antony and Cleopatra alternate as speakers, but the only conclusion that one derives from the book is that Shakespeare is difficult to best. Michael Umphrey's *The Lit Window* (Cleveland State University Poetry Center) contains some good poems about working in the public schools. Not surprisingly, one of the best, about teaching the eternally controversial *The Grapes of Wrath*, originally appeared in *English Journal*. H. R. Coursen's *Rewriting the Book* (Cider Mill Press) has some careful work in syllabics, though at many moments the poet's counting seems at odds with the phra-

sal qualities of his lines: "Now and then, a day will stir the words. The/finches banked on the seedheads of long-dead/goldenrod, flicked like an eyelid closing/under the shadow of the silent spruce." Only the third line has an enjambment that does not call attention to itself. Frank Russell's *Dinner with Dr. Rocksteady* (Ion Books/Raccoon) is redolent of the late 1960s: "Watusi and twist/were all over. That frenzy made any shape./Gladly lost in sneaky feats, aesthetic lust" and so on. The book does contain a good poem about Hemingway, "Papa's Invisible Library," which perpetuates, I am afraid, the myth that the series of shock treatments at the Mayo Clinic was the sole cause of the novelist's suicide. David Spicer's work in *Everybody Has a Story* (St. Luke's Press) lives up to its title with a poem entitled "The Transsexual's Lament." A long poem called "This Poem Again" manages to embalm most of the clichés of contemporary magazine verse. Here are a few random items from the catalog:

This poem is not surreal as honey on a wienie, but
   real as the eyeball of your dead grandma.
This poem is self-indulgent.
This poem is awful, could ramble forever about
   itself, just might do it.
If you're an editor, this poem will scream at you to
   take it because it's clever.
This poem Edgar Allen [*sic*] Poe's muse
   commissioned me to write.
This poem refuses to kill its weak lines.

And so on.

In conclusion I want to note several prose collections of interest to poets. *The Peters Third Black and Blue Guide to Current Literary Journals* (Dustbooks Editions) will complement the two earlier entries in this series and *The Great American Poetry Bake-Off* collections of miscellaneous reviews. Robert Peters—partisan, outrageous, totally outspoken—is a fascinating critic to agree with or grind your teeth over. *Talking Poetry* (University of New Mexico Press), edited by Lee Bartlett, is a series of "conversations in the workshop" with thirteen contemporary poets. The presence of Clark Coolidge, Anne Waldman, and Diane Wakoski will give an indication of Bartlett's own taste. Thom Gunn, sensible as ever, is the odd man out in these proceedings. *Ecstatic Occasions, Expedient Forms* (Macmillan), edited by David Lehman, may be more useful to the reader looking for serious craft discussion. In this collection sixty-five poets comment on the genesis and formal strategies of their poems. Robert Lowell's *Collected Prose* (Farrar, Straus and Giroux), edited by Robert Giroux, consists of some familiar pieces like the *Paris Review* interview of 1961 and some autobiographical and critical fragments that have not been published before. Lowell was not a systematic critic by any means, but he was often very perceptive, particularly in his comments on his own psychological troubles and the poems that arose out of them. Finally, the December issue of *Poetry* contains a long review of David Perkins's *A History of Modern Poetry: Modernism and After* (The Belknap Press of Harvard University Press). According to the reviewer, Harold Fromm, this volume, like the first, is aimed at the general reader and shows no particular allegiance to one of the many "schools" that have fragmented and politicized much contemporary criticism.

In summary, 1987 was a year in American poetry marked by many significant events and publications. No one book or award dominated discussion, as has occurred in past years when works like Ezra Pound's *The Pisan Cantos* (1948) or Carolyn Forché's *The Country Between Us* (1981) were vaulted into the spotlight, largely for extra-literary reasons. The large number of meritorious books published in 1987 shows that American poets continue to value craftsmanship in a time when any kind of mass acceptance by readers grows increasingly remote. The coming year as well promises to be a full one. Poet Timothy Steele's long-awaited critical work on the origins of free verse is scheduled for publication in 1988, and new collected editions of poetry by Richard Wilbur, Louis Simpson, and Richard Eberhart have already been announced. All of these books should provide us with ample opportunities to review and once more to revise our conclusions about the course that American poetry has taken in the recent past.

The Year in Drama

Howard Kissel
New York Daily News

Surveying the New York theater for any length of time sometimes seems like training field glasses on a terrain that has long been barren in hopes of finding signs of vegetation.

Though many of the visible living things were imported from London, there were some hopeful signs in 1987. There were two modest but promising first plays, a major statement by a recognized playwright, and, among other things, a challenging entry by a distinguished novelist. In each case the voice was distinctly American, suggesting the theater may again become an attractive forum for writers with something to say.

It does seem worth noting that none of the new voices echoes any of the writers of the great postwar period. Unlike the English, many of whose writers are in conscious revolt against their predecessors, ours seem unconscious of models or mentors. It is as if the theater skipped a generation. The 1960s cut the thread, and the new writers are beginning as if there were no past, as if they had to start from scratch.

By all accounts the most important play of the year was August Wilson's *Fences,* which won the Pulitzer Prize and the New York Drama Critics Circle Award. *Fences,* part of an ongoing cycle of plays examining the life of blacks in America decade by decade, is set in 1957, three years after the Supreme Court decision on *Brown v. Board of Education.* That case was already having repercussions in the South, but in the large, unnamed midwestern city in which *Fences* takes place, the consequences are still uncertain. For the most part the mood is tranquil. None of these characters imagines the storm we know is on the horizon.

Unlike Wilson's *Ma Rainey's Black Bottom* (1984), in which there were several white characters, whose condescension toward and exasperation with the blacks provided a comic statement about relations between the races, all the characters in *Fences* are black. In fact all but one are members of the same family. It is very much a domestic drama, concerned more with how

Cover for a paperback edition of August Wilson's play which received the Pulitzer Prize and the New York Drama Critics Circle Award

blacks treat each other; their treatment by whites is inferred rather than delineated.

The focal character is Troy Maxson, a garbage man, a man with principles in a world where they don't matter, a man hedged in both when he lives up to his principles and when he violates them.

Maxson, a man whose disposition is generally expansive and agreeable, does harbor some bitterness about his brief, aborted career in baseball in the years when blacks had their own leagues. (Jackie Robinson's entry into major-

187

league ball had taken place less than a decade earlier.) Curiously he never seems bitter about having been imprisoned, perhaps because it was in prison that he discovered his athletic talent. It was also in prison that he met his closest friend, the only nonfamily member in the play.

Whatever misgivings he has about his failed career seem to manifest themselves in his complex relationship with his son. "I don't want him to be like me," he tells his friend. "I want him to move as far from me as he can." But his obstinacy defeats his aspirations for his son.

One of the key actions of the play is that he forbids the boy to play football. Ostensibly this is a punishment because the boy lied to him. But Maxson's decision seems unnecessarily harsh. He knows the boy might be seen by a professional scout. We suspect his refusal to allow the boy to play stems from some unspoken jealousy, or worse, some self-destructive mandate the system has planted within him. There is a powerful confrontation when the boy asks his father why he never liked him.

"Like you?" Maxson booms. "I go out of here every morning . . . bust my butt . . . putting up with them crackers everyday . . . cause I like you? You about the biggest fool I ever saw. (Pause) It's my job. It's my responsibility. A man got to take care of his family. You live in my house . . . sleep you behind on my bedclothes . . . fill you belly up with my food . . . cause you my son. You my flesh and blood. Not cause I like you! . . . I done give you everything I had to give you. I gave you your life! Me and your mama worked that out between us. And liking your black ass wasn't part of the bargain. Don't you try and go through life worrying if somebody likes you or not. You best be making sure they doing right by you. . . ."

This speech, delivered with ferocious disdain by James Earl Jones, is also indicative of the style of the play. The rhythms have a deeply musical quality. Unlike many plays about blacks, which are characterized by intense profanity, there is virtually none in *Fences*. Not only is the language believably poetic. So is the lovely character of Maxson's half-witted brother. So is Rose, his gentle, patient wife.

If *Fences* has a weakness, it is that the plot turns on an offstage situation that materializes suddenly in the second act. Maxson, we discover, has a mistress, and she has become pregnant. When she dies (a little too conveniently for credibility) Maxson must provide a home for his baby daughter. Rose agrees to take her in. "From right now . . . this child got a mother," she tells Maxson in a resigned, firm voice. "But you a womanless man." The moment is pungent. But it is hard to avoid feeling the extramarital affair weakens the more genuinely troubling conflict between his desire to do right by his son and his uncontrollable need to inflict his own misfortunes on his progeny.

The play ends with a poignant scene in 1965. Maxson is dead. His son, long estranged, has returned for the funeral. The boy is now a marine. He has fulfilled his father's best hopes for him. In many ways he has internalized his father's domineering spirit. For the mourners assembled in this quiet backyard the future seems hopeful. Maxson's friend tells the boy, "Stick with Uncle Sam. Retire early." None of them is aware (how many Americans were?) that their fates are intertwined with those of a small nation in Southeast Asia.

It is a play with deep reverberations, most of which center on the character of Maxson, which provided Jones with his best role in many years. Jones himself had ambiguous feelings about Maxson. If most people who see the play find Maxson a hero it may be because of the way Jones resolved his conflicts: "Troy is a mean man, but he has heroic energy."

Matters of race also played a part in another major play, Alfred Uhry's *Driving Miss Daisy*. Uhry's play covers the years 1948 to 1973, a tumultuous period in American racial relations. Rather than tackling the subject head-on Uhry focuses on an elderly, crotchety Atlanta Jewess, part of a curious, little-written-about southern elite, whose son insists she is too old to drive. He hires a black chauffeur for her.

The woman is annoyed on two counts. She does not like the implications about her insufficiency. And, though she protests she has no prejudices, she is resentful that she will now have to share a major part of her life with a black man. For his part the chauffeur represents an equally long southern tradition, that of the servant who deftly takes over his master's life without abandoning his subservient pose.

Part of the comedy is that both these members of the Old South are slightly disdainful of the woman's son, whose bustling energy is a symptom of Yankee tendencies they can no longer withstand.

The play is full of subtle humor. It never makes easy political points. All the comedy grows

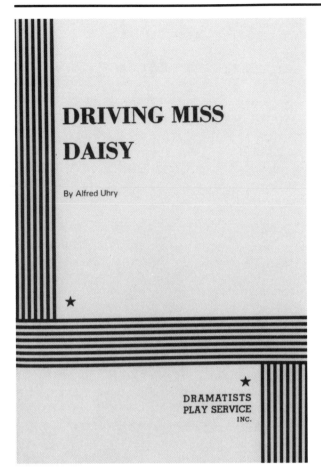

Cover for Alfred Uhry's first full-length play, a look at racial relations in America from 1948 through 1973 viewed through the relationship of an elderly Atlanta Jew and her black chauffeur

out of the beautifully, tenderly observed characters. Before *Driving Miss Daisy*, Uhry had written books for musicals, including the 1976 musical based on Eudora Welty's *The Robber Bridegroom* (1942). This was his first full-fledged play, an auspicious debut.

An equally welcome beginning was made by Robert Harling in *Steel Magnolias*. Set in a beauty parlor in a small Louisiana town, the play could easily have been a caricature of southern grandes dames. At first it seems an amiable comedy, full of hearty laughs about women very conscious of their positions on the social ladder. Toward the end the daughter of one of the women dies in surgery. That Harling manages the shift in tone so seamlessly is remarkable for a novice.

Though in England it is common for men of letters to try their hand at theater there is no similar tradition here. So it seems especially notable that the eminent novelist Don DeLillo should

have written as dazzling a first play as *The Day Room*.

The play opens in a hospital room with an elderly patient doing his t'ai chi exercises while his "roommate" buries his nose in the *Wall Street Journal*. When the martial artist has completed his exercises he tries to enlist his companion in conversational arts, delivering brilliant disquisition on how hospital conditions encourage the imagination and the tongue.

"Two people alone, a common history and anatomy, suitably dressed, in a semiprivate room. Mr. Wyatt, what better opportunity? We have all the essentials. Beds, chairs, regulated temperature. We don't have to go home to sleep, then come back here to talk. The beds are here and so are we. They bring in food. The food is on the premises. We don't have to interrupt our talk to go outside and hunt around for a decent restaurant, quiet, affordable, with unobtrusive waiters, subdued lighting, tables not too close together, where we can enjoy the free play of a mutual exchange, over a hearty and nourishing meal, without clashing utensils, on a sidestreet, with trees. It's all right here. Everything is arranged."

The two are visited by a succession of hospital staff, all of whom seem normal, then become uncontrolled and dotty. They have, we discover, escaped from the Arno Klein Wing, which is where psychiatric patients are kept. The tone in which all this transpires is droll, too restrained for out-and-out farce, but clearly surreal.

The second act opens in another room with two beds, this time a bland motel, where two trendies have come hoping to see a performance by an adventurous group of actors called the Arno Klein Theater. The troupe performs whether there's an audience or not. As one of the trendies puts it, "The idea has merit. They're out there, doing whatever they do, whether we show up or not."

The events in the motel room are full of references back to the conversation in the hospital room. The female trendy talks about searching for the Arno Klein Theater in Cairo. "I was told to find a cafe with a dirt floor, I took a taxi to the edge of the desert.... An old man with a broom was fifty yards up ahead, sweeping sand off the road. This is an actual job they do with brooms on a regular basis–keep the desert out." This giddy speech recalls one in the first act where the man obsessed with conversation extolls the virtues of dirt floors he remembers from an Egyptian café: "The chairs don't scrape as they do on wood floors or tile floors, interrupting the talk, when people get up. Plates and glasses break soundlessly, falling to the dirt, when waiters drop them. The talk swirls and eddies. . . . We came for the dirt but stayed for the talk."

One of the actors in the second act declares that acting is dangerous, echoing a nurse's remark in the first act that the room where the psychiatric patients are kept is full of perils: "In the day room, a speck of dust is charged with danger. A little mote dancing in the air gives off danger signals, weird static. People say things out of nowhere. The smallest word is packed with danger. . . ."

One of the characters in the second act is a mainstay of motel rooms, a TV set. The actor playing the TV sits in a corner and when characters aim the remote control device at him he begins uttering the inanities that make up the television day, changing from voice to voice as the device clicks channels.

Toward the end of the play, in the solemn voice of a scientific expert, he describes the safe way to watch an eclipse of the sun by catching its shadow through a small hole punched through a piece of cardboard.

The stage lighting changes and catches his head in silhouette against the wall. The stage has become a camera obscura, that Renaissance precursor of the camera, the movies, TV, any of those media, which, like the figures on the wall of Plato's cave, influence the way we perceive reality. The Renaissance image inevitably calls to mind another Renaissance convention, the commedia dell'arte. When, at the very end of the play, the leader of the Arno Klein troupe begins doing t'ai chi exercises in a hospital room, we have a sense of the whole play as a "perpetuum mobile," a series of variations on the theme of the great fugue at the end of Verdi's *Falstaff:* "Tutto nel mondo e burlo, l'uom e nato burlone" (Everyone is a clown, that's how men are born).

The night I saw the play an unusual number of people walked out during the second act, exhibiting more belligerence than confusion. It may have offered more wit than New York theatergoers are accustomed to sustaining in an evening.

Eric Bogosian is not exactly a new voice. He normally presents monologues about American life. In *Talk Radio* he has created a stunning piece about America's late-night verbal revels in which his own voice dominates but a host of others provides a jangling chorus.

Dust jacket for novelist Don DeLillo's first play, a surrealistic comedy

Bogosian plays Barry Champlain, the host of a late-night radio talk show that attracts the angry, the lonely, the crackpots. In their often neurotic, meaningless exchanges, it is as if Bogosian has filled the stage with exposed, live wires, full of frightening, potentially dangerous, unchanneled energy.

The voice Bogosian uses as Barry Champlain—rough and tangy as cheap bourbon—has the effect of a lion tamer's whip, rousing his charges to even more frenetic heights. It is a veritable circus of neurosis, with Champlain rarely missing an opportunity to display his own raw nerves in the center ring. Champlain presents himself as a moralist, a latter-day Savanarola, but he seems merely someone who knows how to merchandise outrage. In an anarchic time the bewildered feed on it, and he has a corner on the market.

There is a modicum of plot as a stoned kid invades the radio studio. The boy is mindless and hostile, his head filled only with media bilge like Champlain's. The confrontation between a media

PLAYBILL®
THE MUSIC BOX

Sweet Sue

Cover of the program for A. R. Gurney's play about a divorced woman who experiences a crisis of identity

master and his unwitting disciple recalls Scrooge's visit from the Ghost of Christmases yet to Come.

At times *Talk Radio* seems repetitive. On occasion it even seems as manipulative as its subject. Nevertheless it is a powerful look at one of those everyday phenomena we tend to dismiss but need to see more clearly. Though the tone of *Talk Radio* is wild and inflammatory it is a remarkably clearheaded, illuminating piece of theater.

Lanford Wilson, generally one of our more thoughtful playwrights, has written an eccentric piece, *Burn This*, which works best if one regards it as a flight of artifice rather than an instance of the realism for which Wilson is noted. A young woman dancer has shared a SoHo loft with a homosexual choreographer who has died in a freak accident. His straight brother arrives in the middle of the night and immediately launches into a profane speech.

This character calls himself Pale, as in the fourth word in the designation of good brandies ("Very Special Old Pale"). One doesn't necessarily believe the growing relationship between the sensitive dancer and the brutish Pale (his only fall from boorishness is a scene where he brews tea so impeccably he might be hired at Buckingham Palace). But one amusedly suspends one's disbelief because the play offers an abundance of wit, particularly in the character of a gay young man who also lives in the loft. Early in the play he describes the plot of Wagner's *Flying Dutchman*. Wilson seems to be parodying that story of an outcast's redemption, but with a sensibility closer to Noel Coward than anything as earnest or tragic as the nineteenth-century model.

Another play that was hard to believe but pleasurable to watch was Terence McNally's *Frankie and Johnny in the Clair de Lune*. At least Wilson set his romance in an artistic milieu. McNally's romantic duo are a waitress and hash slinger in a Manhattan greasy spoon. We watch their postcoital conversation in a Hell's Kitchen apartment. A lot of it is funny, and for one act you can accept it as a flip short story, a vignette.

But McNally insists on giving us another act. An even bigger mistake is that he insists we take his characters seriously. Though he provides details that suggest a fuller life for both of them, it is not really enough. Realism has never been part of McNally's sensibility. Why, one wonders, does he want to write about working-class characters in whose mouths his wit sounds false? Much of the dialogue in *Frankie and Johnnie in the Clair de Lune* is as vulgar as that of the foulmouthed Pale in *Burn This*. It is easier to accept it in the arch context of Wilson's play than the presumably natural setting of McNally's, where it seems a way of condescending to the characters.

Among the other new plays by established writers was *Sweet Sue* by A. R. Gurney, an uncharacteristically somber piece by the author of *The Dining Room* (1982). In some ways *Sweet Sue* almost seemed a piece commissioned by its star, Mary Tyler Moore, since the predicament of its central character paralleled her own. Moore played a divorced suburban woman who does greeting card design. Her trademark is a cheery character called *Sweet Sue*. She wants to break out of this trivial mode. She wants to be treated seriously.

The situation was not without possibilities, but Gurney developed it in an artificial way. The play chronicles the woman's affair with a young

Cover for Eric Overmyer's 1985 play featuring three time-traveling Victorian women explorers

man her son's age. Instead of treating it straightforwardly, Gurney has each character played by two actors (in Moore's case her counterpart was Lynn Redgrave). Nothing about the delineation of the characters made the doubling seem necessary. It only seemed to multiply—geometrically—the possibilities for characters bickering with each other and themselves. Moore herself was surprisingly unsympathetic. The brittle play seemed to underline a hardness in her voice, a coldness in her manner.

A bright note was provided by a play by Eric Overmyer, a playwright whose work is better known in the regional theater than it is in New York. His *On the Verge* follows three adventurous ladies, Victorian in dress and language, who set out to explore the unknown territory of the century ahead of them. They end their journey in 1955, when they have discovered such things as

early rock, barbecue, and the young Bebe Rebozo. "I have seen the future," one of the ladies declares. "And it is slang."

In many ways Overmyer's play is about language, contrasting the flexible, elegant, witty styles of the past with the flat vulgarity of the present. Parallel to his depiction of the descent of American civilization from the highmindedness of the Victorians to the emptyheadedness of the present, Overmyer is making a statement about American theater. He satirizes domestic realism and method acting. One sees the play as Overmyer's "manifesto" for a theater in which language and theatricality collaborate with the audience's imagination to create intellectually vigorous journeys like the one in *On the Verge*. If the play made a persuasive case for Overmyer's vision, it also betrayed his weakness. Overmyer is capable of wit, preciousness, cuteness, intellectual ambition, but rarely of recognizable emotion.

The British invasion has continued apace. The most dazzling of their contributions was Christopher Hampton's adaptation of Choderlos de Laclos's epistolary novel *Les Liaisons Dangereuses* (1782). Though Hampton's humor is sometimes crudely British and generally blunter than that in the book, he has done a remarkable job of transferring to the stage a sense of elegant surfaces, flippancy, and devotion to style that masks great cruelty and cynicism. He has added a scene at the very end in which the characters have a premonition of the revolution to come, which seems a tad melodramatic, but the overall feeling the play gives is of respect and fidelity to its powerful source.

The other major play from London was Hugh Whitemore's *Breaking the Code*, about the strange life and career of Alan Turing, who broke the German Enigma code during World War II, giving the English access to the commands issued to U-Boats. Turing was also the inventor of the modern computer. The title refers less to his wartime achievement than the fact he broke Britain's odd sexual code. Though homosexuality is hardly unknown there, the legal attitude toward it has not been liberal.

In the early 1950s, when the play is set, homosexual behavior was still classified legally as "gross indecency." For someone in a high-security position, like Turing, homosexuality was a particular risk in the wake of the defections of Guy Burgess and Kim Philby to the Soviet Union. Turing made no secret of his homosexuality, so he was not liable to blackmail. But Britain

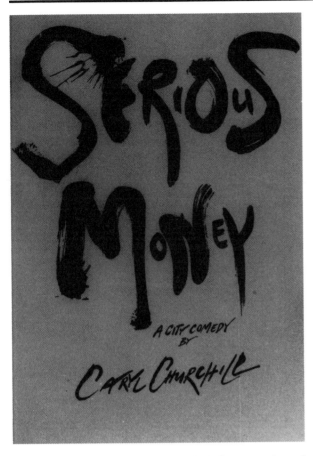

*Cover for Caryl Churchill's satire of high finance and greed
in the City of London*

was then very wary of its ally, the U.S., which
was engaged in a particularly virulent Red scare,
in which homosexuality had become a hot issue.

Consequently when Turing, in a foolish bit
of candor, revealed he had been engaged in a homosexual affair with a young man whose friend
had burgled his home, he was charged with
"gross indecency." Though the government was
well aware of his contributions during the war, it
made no effort to shield him. Turing was given a
choice–imprisonment or the ingestion of experimental drugs that would alter his sexual orientation. The upshot of the humiliation Turing
underwent was that he committed suicide.

His life has been chronicled in Alan
Hodges's excellent biography *Alan Turing: The
Enigma* (1983). Whitemore has done a beautiful
job of selecting images that tie these complicated
and unhappy events together. He focuses on
Turing's desire to give his computers a freedom
often denied their human creators, the freedom
to make errors.

Much of the play also reflects Turing's conviction that the mind is not subject to the follies and
indignities of the flesh. It is somehow eternal. As
a result when we sense that Turing is going to
kill himself our shock is somewhat mitigated by
the fact we know he feels he is freeing that part
of himself he most values rather than bringing a
brilliant career to an abrupt end.

The particular suicide Turing chose makes
an especially vivid theatrical moment. A great
fan of Disney's *Snow White and the Seven Dwarfs*,
Turing killed himself by eating an apple covered
with cyanide. The image abounds in ironies and
cruel meanings. It mocks Genesis quite sardoni-
cally. It also suggests a naive belief in some kind
of regeneration, depending, of course, on the
kiss of a handsome prince.

The actual Turing was a hopeless recluse
and eccentric who might have been dreadfully irritating if transferred to the stage with any semblance of reality. Again it is the heroic
performance of Derek Jacobi that makes Turing
vivid and unforgettable. Even Turing's stammer
takes on grand proportions in Jacobi's interpretation. It seems very much the failing of a mind constantly ahead of itself than the tic of someone
painfully insecure.

Another successful import was Caryl
Churchill's *Serious Money*, a not-very-subtle satire
on the cutthroat world of high finance by an author who has generally probed the constraints of
England's sexual and social codes (in *Cloud Nine*,
1979 and *Top Girls*, 1972). Churchill begins her
play with a witty excerpt from Thomas
Shadwell's seventeenth-century comedy *The Volunteers or The Stockjobbers*, which appears to have
chronicled a fever for speculation remarkably
like the one that has raged back and forth across
continents the last few years.

As in her other plays she deals in stereotypes. Here, however, she never provides any observation of these admittedly antipathetic
characters that suggests they are human beings
rather than textbook examples of capitalist vil-
lainy. Instead of realistic ballast to give her characters weight she provides a jaunty sort of verse
that gives them an Offenbachian flightiness.

One of the characters is a Peruvian copper
heiress who has chucked her mines, with their recalcitrant laborers, for the more lucrative growth
crop, cocaine. She quite understands what a British banker means when he says that third-world
countries:

Cover for Arthur Miller's two one-act plays about the convolutions of memory

"must accept restricted diets.
The governments must explain, if there are food riots,
That paying the western banks is the priority."

The Peruvian responds by explaining why her government pretends to destroy the airstrip from which planes bearing cocaine fly to the U.S. (and then secretly rebuilds it):

"To keep Reagan our friend
We have to pretend.
But the US pretends and we know it.
Who likes a coke buzz?
America does.
They stop using it, we won't grow it."

Profound it's not. Not even very witty. But in the uneasy wake of the stock market crash of 19 October 1987, it provided easy laughs and perhaps a kind of relief. If the system was still strong enough to laugh at, maybe it wasn't in as much trouble as it seemed.

It is always reassuring when the English send us garbage, lest we imagine we have a monopoly on it. Their major contribution in this area as *Women Beware Women,* a gloss on Thomas Middleton's play by the contemporary English playwright Howard Barker. Three pages in the program were devoted to a short biography of Middleton and a more complex introduction to Barker. In order to understand the latter one must be acquainted with Marcuse, Brecht, and Artaud. Does this sound like nostalgia for 1968? When was the last time you saw in print the word "relevance?"

As one might suspect, Barker's own reworking of the Middleton play was heavy on profanity and radical jargon. It was an attempt, as they used to say in 1968, to raise our consciousness. It all seemed very quaint, and even act one, which was a Reader's Digest condensation of Middleton's work, was not acted with enough proficiency to be enjoyable.

Well before Wole Soyenka was announced as the recipient of the 1986 Nobel Prize for Literature, his play *Death and the King's Horseman* (1975) was scheduled to be mounted by the Lincoln Center Theater, directed by the author. The prize may have raised audience expectations to an unwarranted level, for the production was a great disappointment.

The play itself presents fairly conventional themes, to wit, that the European colonialists' philosophical ideas were no more congenial to Africans than their political institutions. Set just after World War II, when colonial authority was beginning to break down, *Death and the King's Horseman* examined the unthinking way the British dealt with an ancient tribal custom they considered barbaric. According to that custom, when a king died, his righthand man had to kill himself so he could serve his master in the next world. In a benighted attempt at humanitarianism, the colonial administrators try to prevent the suicide, unaware that to do so called into question the religious understanding that had sustained the tribesmen for millennia.

Though much of the text seemed a kind of bloated poetry, the situation itself was certainly provocative. The production succeeded only in conveying a little visual atmosphere. None of the performances was on a grand enough level to convey the majesty or mystery of tribal life, let alone the intended sense of tragedy.

Among Lincoln Center's other well-intentioned efforts was the presentation of two recent one-acts by Arthur Miller, entitled *Danger: Memory!* The first, "I Can't Remember Anything," is a slight, somewhat congenial piece in which two aging friends argue over who more accurately remembers their shared past. The second, "Clara," centers on the murder of a young woman. Among the suspects is her father, whom we watch being questioned by a tough detective. Rather than a straightforward examination of why the father may have murdered his daughter, we are supposed to be caught up in the father's epistemological wrangling about whether or not he knows the truth. We see him dithering over his former ideas about politics and religion. Neither he nor Miller ever confronts the basic situation. The play becomes an exercise in self-absorption and Pinteresque elusiveness. The father becomes so involved in rehashing wrongs that have been done to him that he successfully evades the larger question of whether or not he murdered his daughter. The play is not sufficiently deep that we can regard this evasion as pointing to a greater truth. It is merely annoying.

Perhaps Lincoln Center's most useful contribution was a production of a modest, promising play by a young writer named Roger Hedden, called *Bodies, Rest and Motion*. Hedden has a good ear for dialogue, a sharp sense of character, but too little sense of what to do with them. His vignettes of young people leading confused, intense, and aimless lives is reminiscent of the work of Ann Beattie. In the literary world at large the news that there is yet another imitator of Beattie may not seem hopeful. It is a measure of the insularity of the theater that a Beattie-like voice is welcome because it is at least an attempt to capture contemporary reality, an effort that is depressingly uncommon.

The Broadway economy now seems to depend on the importation of at least one British musical a season. This season there were two, both mediocre, *Les Miserables* and *Starlight Express,* suggesting that lack of quality is no deterrent to theatergoers in search of entertainment. The most innovative show was a homegrown product, *Into The Woods,* by James Lapine and Stephen Sondheim.

The show was a witty reexamination of familiar Grimm fairy tales. Compared to some Sondheim scores, this one seemed relatively facile and straightforward. But from the first moment, when several of the characters sing, "I wish, more than anything," in music that is plaintive rather than hopeful, one is constantly aware of a disturbing counterpoint between the generally lighthearted material and the prickly, ironic score. Much of the time Sondheim takes musical themes as direct and spirited as children's rounds and uses them to build larger, more complex structures.

Although none of the new dramatic voices–Uhry, Harling, Hedden, Overmyer, or even Bogosian–reflects an older one, there is a sense of tradition, albeit an eccentric one, in American musicals. Sondheim is often seen as a trailblazer, which he is. But his aesthetic, rarefied though it may be, is clearly based on the ideas of Rodgers and Hammerstein. They applied their concepts to stories that reflected America at its healthiest, its most whole. Sondheim, using similar techniques, has focused on esoteric, even bizarre concerns. And virtually every serious young American composer now takes Sondheim as his model.

The most notable of the disciples this year was Douglas Cohen, who wrote a musical based on the odd film *No Way To Treat A Lady*. Though the music and lyrics were full of sophistication, the show seemed a curious exercise in futility. That considerable talent and energy (not to mention money and a production grant named after Richard Rodgers) went into musicalizing a story about a serial murderer with a mother fixation speaks volumes about the current state of the American theater.

The Year in Literary Biography

Mark Heberle
University of Hawaii

Reviewing last year's literary biographies in the 1986 *Yearbook*, Professor Gay Sibley pointed out how frequently literary geniuses are ignored or undervalued by society, while their personal relationships are marked by extraordinary intensity. The most common theme sounded by this year's biographers is that of personal failure or disappointment. Although nearly all of this year's subjects enjoyed public social validation–whether popular success or official recognition–most were also self-divided, self-estranged, or even self-destructive, their lives marked by frustration and unhappiness. Biographies of English and American writers in 1987 extend from the father of literature in English to a woman who is still expanding the scope of American writing while re-creating her past life. Fifteen biographies, along with autobiography, notebooks, and collections of letters and conversations are among this year's significant contributions to the art of life-writing.

As far back as the sixteenth century, English writers recognized Chaucer as the father of imaginative literature in our language–Spenser addresses him as his master in *The Faerie Queene*, as "a pure well of poesy." Donald Howard's panoramic biography, *Chaucer: His Life, His Works, His World*, completed just before the author's death in March of 1987, is a magisterial attempt to uncover and follow the sources of the wellhead itself. As its subtitle indicates, Howard's book traces the developing life history of the husband, father, and government bureaucrat; the writer; and the fourteenth-century Englishman.

The book begins by citing the first document related to Chaucer's life, an entry of 1357 from a household register recording the purchase of clothing for the teenaged Geoffrey, then serving as a page in the household of Elizabeth, Countess of Ulster and the wife of King Edward's second son, Prince Lionel. Comprehensive identification and discussion of the documentary record–surprisingly extensive due to Chaucer's long and varied public service–provide a credible foundation for detailing his personal circum-

Dust jacket for the first major study of Geoffrey Chaucer to combine biographical, historical, and critical elements

stances. From such sources we learn, among much else, that Chaucer was captured by the enemy and later ransomed during the English siege of Reims in 1360; rewarded by Edward III with a pitcher of wine a day for the rest of his life after successfully conducting negotiations with Genoa and Florence in 1372; granted an annuity of twenty marks in lieu of all that wine by Richard upon his accession in 1377; and robbed three times in four days in September 1391 while carrying large sums of money as the King's Clerk of the Works, an onerous and evidently dangerous job that he must have resigned with relief in

196

1391. Howard's use of such evidence brings Chaucer to life in ways that are often surprising: a royal payment in 1384 to a "Phillippus Chaucer" suggests that the father of English poetry was less well known at court than his wife Philippa, at least in the mind of the confused clerk who garbled his name.

The works, of course, have been a subject of discussion for centuries, and in *Chaucer* Howard sensibly provides general descriptions, while reflecting clearly and fairly the present critical consensus. The works are seen from the dual perspective of Chaucer's personal and social identity, and the result is a body of work that is more intimate and occasional than is usually recognized: for example, *The House of Fame* not only dramatizes Chaucer's own authorial anxieties but also ends with a gesture that may have been directed to the Vatican ambassador present at a reading sometime after 10 December 1379.

At its best, Howard's biography combines life, works, and world to present a picture of Chaucer that is profoundly illuminating. For example, the poet's residence over the Aldgate would have made him an eyewitness to the mobs streaming into London during the Peasant's Rebellion in 1381, and that haunting memory of civil chaos may have contributed to the dark vision of doomed Troy in *Troilus and Criseyde.* Chaucer's changing circumstances also affected the evolution of *The Canterbury Tales:* having resigned his official offices in 1386 to avoid possible prosecution during the hectic days preceding the Appellants' revolt against Richard II, Chaucer settled in Kent and not only changed his residence but also his audience, abandoning the troubled court society for a wider, more middle-class audience. During those terrible years in retirement, 1386-1389, when friends at court were being executed, planning and beginning the great comedy with its carnivalesque "Prologue" and initial tales provided solace and purpose. The second phase of writing, begun after Richard's reassumption of power in 1389 and centering upon the extensive discussion of marriage, involved the middle-aged poet's own questions and doubts about remarriage after the death of his own wife in 1387. And as Chaucer's own increasingly lonely pilgrimage came to an end in the 1390s, the third phase of writing brought both the poet and all of his pilgrims to their destination in the haunting figure of Death in "The Pardoner's Tale," the anticarnival lessons of "The Parson's Tale," and the final "Retraction," in which Chaucer speaks

to all his readers in his own voice, preparing for his death by renouncing his works of "worldly vanity" before God while freely cataloguing them for posterity. Such is the story Howard cogently suggests.

Despite all that it accomplishes, however, *Chaucer* is not an entirely satisfying biography. Chaucer's personal narrative is only sporadically interwoven with the works and background, making it difficult to sense a coherent development of the life, the "figure in the carpet" referred to in the preface. However, a superbly detailed chronology at the end of the book does provide guidance for the sometimes confused or forgetful reader. There is simply too much background information not directly related to interpreting Chaucer's life, even though many chapters, such as Howard's analysis of Boccaccio's creation of fiction, would be fine essays in their own right. But how do such subjects as the commercial history of Genoa or the bloody deeds of the brutal Visconti brothers really illuminate Geoffrey Chaucer? Finally, the book attempts both to be a popular history, like Barbara Tuchman's *A Distant Mirror,* and a scholarly biography, and the two purposes sometimes conflict. The direct quotations in Middle English are de rigueur for academics but may be troublesome and tiresome for other readers. The writing itself is colloquial and idiomatic, but Howard's ubiquitous contractions become irritating to me, and his inexact popular and contemporary analogies are unwittingly embarrassing. In his scholarly generosity and completeness, he details the arguments for and against on such intimate questions as whether Chaucer was cuckolded by John of Gaunt or happily married to Philippa but without coming to final judgments. As a result, the man who was Chaucer remains a very shadowy figure, although perhaps only a historical fiction or psychohistory would illuminate him.

Altogether, *Chaucer* is an impressive achievement, superseding all its predecessors as the standard study of the poet. The eighty pages of references alone provide a running annotated bibliography of significant criticism virtually up to the date of publication. As a sustained, readable, and entertaining biography, however, it is not as successful as the earlier works of John Gardner, Derek Brewer, or the outdated popular life by Marchette Chute.

Like *Chaucer,* Richard Ellmann's *Oscar Wilde* (Hamish Hamilton) is both a definitive critical biography and a splendid memorial to its author, who completed his final work before his death in May 1987. In it, Ellmann has extended his sovereignty over postromantic Irish literary biography, a dominion that began with two books on Yeats and most recently included *Four Dubliners* (Wilde, Yeats, Joyce, and Beckett). *Oscar Wilde* closely resembles Ellmann's superb biography of James Joyce, even in such details as the running headnotes that identify the year and subject's age on each page of the text. Like *Joyce*, this is a big book, but reader-friendly. The headnotes to text and documentation, chapter titles, and apt subtitles, punctuated throughout by memorable and appropriate epigraphs from Wilde's works, provide helpful orientation. Ellmann's prose is a model of clarity, grace, and sharp intelligence–continually delighting us with mots justes that Wilde himself would have appreciated, even if they are sometimes at the subject's expense: "A wife would save him from the moralists, and a rich one from the moneylenders" (describing Wilde's motivations for marriage); "Wilde appeared before the curtain and made a short speech, probably to say that the play was about passion rather than politics, or vice versa" (describing the playwright's attempt to salvage the New York premiere of *Vera*). The absorbing, well-crafted life narrative that Ellmann presents artfully assimilates the exhaustive, indefatigable research that supports it (including numerous previously unpublished letters, some of them purchased by Ellmann himself). Many years of preparation have gone into this work, but all that scholarly labor has been transmuted into great biography that is enjoyable to read.

While Chaucer seems to have cultivated reticence and self-withdrawal both as man and poet, Wilde's entire life was a self-consciously flamboyant performance. Ellmann claims that he moved from an aestheticism in which art was separated from life in order to grant it privileged status to a more complex perspective that dissolved boundaries between the two. His best works explore and realize in themselves the power of art to affect or infect life (for Wilde, Ellmann notes, "the function of art is to make a raid on predictability"), and his own life epitomized the interchangeability of the two. After his terrible fall Wilde was greeted by a fellow inmate of Reading Prison with the question, "What are you doing in this place, Dorian Gray?," and who went on to whisper, "I was at all your first nights and at all your trials."

Dust jacket for Richard Ellmann's posthumously published biography of Oscar Wilde, a sympathetic portrayal based on hitherto unused sources

Ellmann vividly portrays Wilde's successive performances throughout his life, detailing his dress, hairstyle, and furniture, as well as his changing aesthetic judgments, because, for Wilde, behind his shifting appearances lay successive manifestations of fuller identity: "Self-exfoliation might come through self-abandonment. He vaulted from stance to stance, putting on new selves as he put on new clothes." Initially, Wilde's theatricality might have been an attempt to gain recognition for himself in his own right, for, as Ellmann describes, his father was a world-famous surgeon and a noted Irish folklorist, his mother a famous national poet, and she initially favored Willie, his older brother. More mundane motives included the delights of self-promotion: Wilde loved being in the spotlight, and he brilliantly cultivated the art of usurping its attention. His successors crawl over each other in the age of *People* and Video-TV, but none have any of his grace, intelligence, or fortitude. Who but Wilde would have had the panache to bestow personally inscribed copies of his inaugural *Poems* (1881) upon such strangers as Algernon Swinburne, Robert Browning, and Matthew Arnold, the last of whom responded to Wilde's complimentary accompanying letter with one of his own. Even before he left the port of London Wilde had successfully solicited James Russell Lowell to introduce him to America by way of Oliver Wendell Holmes.

The year-long American-Canadian lecture tour of 1882 is perhaps the most exhilarating of Ellmann's many impressive reconstructions of Wilde's performances. Introducing North America to "The English Renaissance," "The Decorative Arts," and "The House Beautiful" in the stylishly dressed person of Oscar Wilde, he drew popular acclaim and journalistic abuse, a pattern to be repeated ad infinitum. In America his poems were pirated, and popular songs were published about him; during an improbable stop at Leadville, Colorado, he opened a new mine shaft named "The Oscar" in his honor with a silver drill presented to him by the miners. He responded to press attacks upon his lecture attire by musing, "Strange that a pair of silk stockings should so upset a nation." He also paid a call on Walt Whitman, and the old man was delighted with his visitor after Wilde introduced himself: Wilde—"I come as a poet to call upon a poet"; Whitman—"Go ahead."

The biography, organized in five sections, has the shape of a drama, a comic tragedy whose climax, "Exaltations," records the triumphs of *Dorian Gray, Salome,* and the three brilliant English comedies but also the passionate, disastrous love affair with Alfred Douglas. Just after the premiere of Wilde's masterpiece, *The Importance of Being Earnest,* Queensberry's charges of sodomy goaded the playwright into the fatal prosecution of Douglas's father that would result in the public revelation of Wilde's pederasty, criminal conviction, imprisonment, and public ignominy. Act four, "Disgrace," presents in excruciating detail the terrible peripeteia of the three trials which consigned Wilde to prison for two years and infamy in England for the rest of his life.

The last act, "Exile," initially discusses the last poem, "The Ballad of Reading Gaol," before descending into Ellmann's final chapter, hauntingly entitled "The Leftover Years." Ellmann portrays a once-great man slowly dying of life itself. A pariah to his friends and those who shared in his triumphs, unable or unwilling to write again, fruitlessly pursuing boys and still in love with the odious Douglas, Wilde wanders about the scenes of earlier triumphs, a ghost of himself, and often unrecognizable to former acquaintances. Some remained loyal—Yeats; his betrayed wife Constance; and two former lovers, Reggie Turner and Robert Ross, who attended him in the final days and witnessed the horrifying death throes detailed by Ellmann. *Requiescat in pace.*

Ellmann is an enthusiastic partisan of Wilde and critic of the hypocrites who prosecuted, persecuted, and abandoned him, but he reveals the whole truth, including Wilde's tacit prevarications during the trials. Among Wilde's other virtues, he reminds us that the man was a certifiable genius, blessed with a photographic memory; a brilliant classical scholar; a strong Irish nationalist; a positive influence on Yeats and Shaw; a kindly and generous man; and the most brilliant epigrammatist ever to grace the English language, as the humorous quotations of Wilde's conversation so wonderfully attest. Behind Wilde's epigrams is a mind that feasted on paradox, saw it as the human condition, and embodied it in his greatest works. Ellmann notes throughout his discussion of the literature that Wilde's work typically presents a division into contrary values that results neither in their reconciliation nor the triumph of one over the other, but the contemplation of both, a stance of ironic paradox.

Its ultimate source may be Wilde's contemplation of himself, for as Ellmann explains throughout, he was attracted to such contraries throughout his life: Ruskin and Pater, Freemasonry and Catholicism, Rome and Hellas, heterosexuality and homosexuality, respectability and criminality. Ellmann's discussions of the literature are everywhere revealing, with the exception of *The Importance of Being Earnest,* which is given a perfunctory glance. A more serious problem is his proposal that Wilde contracted syphilis while at Oxford and that it is central to interpreting his character. Wilde's syphilis is sometimes treated as a hypothesis, sometimes as a fact, and it actually receives very little emphasis. It may have prompted the cerebral meningitis that actually killed him, as Ross stated, but Ellmann makes no reference to it in detailing Wilde's final degeneration. Of course, to do so would have detracted from Ellmann's unforgettable account of the awful mystery of Wilde's final years, which seem to have been spent in passive suicide and the contemplation of a final paradox: the will to live coexisting with the desire to die.

Before Wilde nineteenth-century English drama had been a wasteland. His revitalization of

Dust jacket for the first comprehensive biography of Sherwood Anderson in more than thirty-five years

theater stimulated Yeats and Shaw in different ways, and another prominent successor was John Galsworthy, whose prolific career and distinguished life are illuminated in James Gindin's critical biography, *John Galsworthy's Life and Art: An Alien's Fortress* (Macmillan). Although he wrote almost thirty plays, more than twenty novels, and five collections of short stories before winning the Nobel Prize for Literature in 1932, Galsworthy is a relatively neglected writer, although the recent television dramatization of *The Forsyte Saga* novels, the first of Galsworthy's three trilogies, has reintroduced him to American audiences. Anyone interested in more of Galsworthy will find Gindin's long, definitive biography indispensable, and every reader will enjoy its clear, straightforward, and comprehensive reexamination of this transitional figure, whose life and works were suspended between a Victorian past and a modernist future.

As he traces Galsworthy's remarkably productive life, Gindin examines all of the works, pro-

viding concise, helpful précises of each drama closely tied to his critical analyses, evaluations, and descriptions of contemporary reaction, all of which are models of clarity and insight. Gindin is a forceful and convincing advocate for the enduring significance of Galsworthy's work, which he eloquently and authoritatively characterizes: "As a dramatist, he shaped two distinctive forms that account for all his best plays. One was a presentation of a contemporary social conflict locked finally in an irreconcilable and unresolvable silence, a form leading to dramatic stasis visible in *The Silver Box, Strife, The Skin Game,* and *Loyalties.* The other, more personal, was a relentless probing of a particular pain that was simultaneously social and psychological, visible intensely in *Justice* and somewhat randomly in *Escape.* His most significant novelistic form is best described as the chronicle, an extension of social, familial, and personal experience into history, shaped by a series of contrasts and continuities as public and private life intersect." Gindin shows us that successful and unsuccessful works alternated in Galsworthy's career, belying both the naive assumption that artists learn anything from their mistakes as well as the recent critical estimate that Galsworthy's work is marked by a decline into social complacency after the initial plays and the early satiric brilliance of *The Man of Property* (1906).

Galsworthy was born into a wealthy upper-middle-class family and remained socially and financially comfortable throughout his life, but Gindin shows that his dissatisfaction with that world and guilt over his own implication in it led to his choice of profession and was worked out in various manifestations throughout the body of his work. Simply becoming a writer constituted rebellion, but of a complex and ambiguous kind, as the pseudonym attached to his first four works indicates: John Sinjohn ("John, son of John"–his own father). Galsworthy's adulterous affair with Ada, the wife of his cousin Arthur, went on for ten years but was similarly muted: John Sr. never knew of it, and it was only after his father's death in 1905 that Galsworthy married her. He came to writing late, at the age of twenty-eight, went through a long and hesitant apprenticeship schooled by Edward Garnett, Ford Maddox Ford, and Joseph Conrad (whose vacant appreciations of his work, amusingly cited throughout by Gindin, are models of useless praise), and never felt comfortable about his elevated public reputation as a writer: he refused knighthood, and his Nobel Prize acceptance speech, composed one month before his death in 1933 and never delivered, makes nakedly clear his sense of being unworthy of the award.

Dissatisfied with himself and his society, Galsworthy dramatized his own conflicts in his works, most successfully and comprehensively in the massive novel trilogies that he composed up to the end of his life: *The Forsyte Saga* (1920), *A Modern Comedy* (1929), and *End of the Chapter* (1934). In them, Gindin shows us, Galsworthy defines himself so largely that they have seemed to readers to represent England itself. Although his earliest success was as a dramatist, Galsworthy himself felt that the novel afforded him the fullest and most reflective medium in which to examine the contradictions of himself and his society.

Galsworthy's discomforts produced direct action as well as literature. His play *Justice* brought about reform of the British jail system that had so crushed Oscar Wilde, whose protest in "Reading Gaol" had gone unheeded. A liberal in the best sense, Galsworthy tirelessly involved himself in humanitarian projects, working for five months in French hospitals during World War I, serving as first president of the International P.E.N. Club, which still protects writers around the world from political oppression, and to which he donated his Nobel Prize check, building cottages and investing money in Bury (Sussex), the village where he lived with Ada beginning in 1926.

To Rebecca West, speaking for her generation of writers, Galsworthy was one of the four massive post-Victorian "uncles," including Wells, Shaw, and Bennett: "All our youth they hung about the houses of our minds," she noted. In many significant ways, however, she very much resembled him: prolifically successful in a variety of genres (she wrote no plays, while he wrote no biographies or travel journalism); a classic liberal passionately devoted to social and political reform (she was present at the inaugural P.E.N. meeting in 1921 when Galsworthy was elected president); involved in a long adulterous love affair with the most significant other of her life; a public figure who came to personify the finest qualities of English thought and culture. In Victoria Glendinning's *Rebecca West: A Life* (Knopf) she is finally given a biographical treatment that is fitting for her remarkable life and career. Glendinning's is the "short" biography authorized by West in her will, and it anticipates the "full" life by Stanley Olson, to whom Glendinning's book is dedicated.

Rebecca West is nearly a perfect example of a short life. Glendinning concentrates on the early and middle years, eschews detailed literary criticism, and focuses instead on the intense and enduring relationships of this passionate woman who was intimately engaged in the literary, cultural, and political life of England and America for six decades. She has assimilated all the collected and uncollected papers, including letters from H. G. Wells and correspondence from her husband, Henry Andrews, that are quoted in Gordon Ray's *H. G. Wells and Rebecca West*, but currently sealed in the Yale Library until after the death of Anthony West. This life honors its subject convincingly, for Glendinning is justly critical where West falls short of herself: from aspects of her mothering and her prose style to the sense of persecution and recrimination that occasionally overcame her in her later years. Rebecca West would have admired Glendinning's honesty, and the story she tells, revealing previously undisclosed traumas and disappointments, is affecting.

One of West's "uncles" was also her lover, and the ten-year affair with H. G. Wells left West unmarried and responsible for a son, Anthony, who would become a successful writer himself but also a severe critic of his mother. Though West finally terminated Wells's adultery herself, Glendinning notes that he "was her first and only lover, mentor, prosecutor, enchanter." There were other lovers nearly as worthy of her–Lord Beaverbrook, John Gunther, Francis Biddle–but her marriage to Henry Andrews was childless, and she discovered only after his death that he had been unfaithful. It all seemed to start with her beloved father, who deserted his wife and three young daughters when West was ten. In her old age, she left poignant testimony of her father that seems to mean more than it says: "I had a glorious father. I had no father at all."

Glendinning shrewdly organizes her book in six chapters, each bearing a name that records the subject's accumulating identities. She was born Cicely Isabel Fairfield–"Cissy" to her family and friends–and first appeared as a girl wonder, producing brilliant feminist articles and reviews so alarming to her mother that she agreed to appear under the pseudonym by which she is known to us: "Rebecca West," heroine of Ibsen's *Rosmersholm*. "Panther" was the exquisitely erotic name H. G. Wells gave to his young mistress (she called him "Jaguar" and they named their son "Anthony Panther"); during the decade of their intense affair, she became a preeminent London

Dust jacket for the biography of Ezra Pound that offers an interpretative psychological study of Pound's artistic and emotional life

critic-reviewer and published her first two novels. "Sunflower" would have been the title of her uncompleted novel written to exorcise the frustrating affair with Beaverbrook, 1923-1927, years during which she wrote her classic study of Henry James and lectured in America. As "Mrs. Henry Andrews," happily married to a scholarly and wealthy English gentleman, she wrote her biography of Augustine; *The Strange Necessity*, her analysis of Joyce and modern art; and, after three trips to Yugoslavia on the eve of World War II, her flawed masterpiece of sociological meditation, *Black Lamb and Grey Falcon*. Firmly established as "Rebecca West," a preeminent English writer, she covered the trials of Lord Haw-Haw and the Nazi war criminals and wrote *The Meaning of Treason* as her political radicalism moved rightward from feminism to socialism to liberalism to militant anti-Communism. By the time she was officially honored as "Dame Rebecca," she had become an English institution, and when she died at the age of ninety-one, her story, as Victo-

ria Glendinning demonstrates, was "the story of twentieth-century women. She was both an agent for change and a victim of change."

Although Victoria Glendinning characterizes Rebecca West's life as "a sadder story than I expected," compared to the narratives presented in new biographies of four giants of modern American literature, it seems comparatively happy. The books in question are Kim Townsend's *Sherwood Anderson* (Houghton Mifflin), John Tytell's *Ezra Pound: The Solitary Volcano* (Doubleday), Stephen B. Oates's *William Faulkner: The Man and the Artist–A Biography* (Harper and Row), and Kenneth S. Lynn's *Hemingway* (Simon and Schuster). Like their subjects, each book is imperfect but important.

Anderson's career, though the least distinguished in such high company, was pregnant with significance for virtually every American postwar writer and critic: abandoning sterile commercial success in Elyria, Ohio, the thirty-eight-year-old company president became a writer and devoted his life to art. Such was the myth. Kim Townsend sets the story straighter, showing that when Anderson walked away from his American Merchants Company on 28 November 1912 he was undergoing a nervous breakdown and was abandoning his wife Cornelia and three children as well as business. The sources of his dissatisfaction are revealed on an envelope that he mailed during his crack-up addressed incoherently to "Cornelia L. Anderson, President, American Striving Co." Although he did become a writer after this incident, he had never been a fully successful businessman. He was an advertising genius, however, and in fact continued to work part-time at a major Chicago ad agency during the first ten years of his literary career. While he despised commercial success, Anderson reveled in his literary success and reputation throughout his life until it too would become burdensome and something to be resisted.

Townsend attributes Anderson's middle-age breakdown to a "fugue state" in which frustrating, contradictory strivings are replaced by a single activity. For Anderson that activity was writing itself, and the flight from any situation that could cripple it repeated itself throughout his life, largely accounting for his three failed marriages to women who truly loved him as well as for his nomadic existence: from Chicago to New York to Alabama, Paris, New Orleans, and his own estate in Virginia, St. Petersburg. Yet Anderson's true home was in his imagination, the

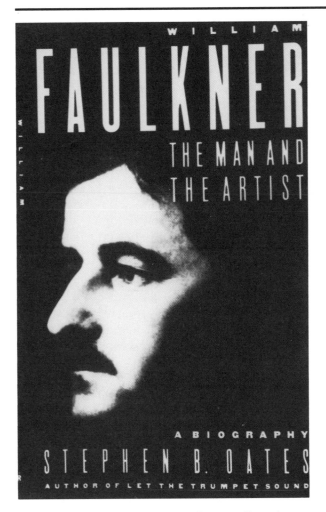

Dust jacket for the biography of William Faulkner that attempts "to compose that life as a work of art"

American small town of his youth, which he recreated repeatedly in his fiction and clung to in his mind as the genuine America. Theodore Dreiser was his great harbinger, Gertrude Stein his teacher, Ernest Hemingway and William Faulkner his pupils, but his true begetter was Walt Whitman, and Anderson aspired to celebrate America and himself as if the two were the same. Much of his work, like Whitman's, could be labeled "advertisements for myself" and like Whitman, his life embodied contradictions and ironies. His most popular novel, *Dark Laughter,* was also his worst. From the beginning he both realized and censured in himself the pursuit of the American dream: fame, fortune, and the love of women. He had little admiration of the American male, knowing that true manhood consists of questioning and then extending the manhood that has been achieved; yet he always remained something of an adolescent. He couldn't live or write with-

out the love of a woman and in *Perhaps Women* sensibly suggested that they alone could save the world from modern sterility; yet he took more than he gave, as in his correspondence with his patient muse, Marietta "Bab" Finley, and was irresponsible and unreliable as a husband. In his final marriage to the social reformer Eleanore Coperhaven, a woman with her own important project to realize, Anderson found personal happiness, renewed energy, and full manhood, turning his attention outward into social commentary and political involvement to further the New Deal, and proud of making his last novel, *Kit Brandon,* "much more objective" than the others (his words), with a woman as its hero. But by then his best fiction was long behind him, the stories of *Winesburg, The Triumph of the Egg,* the novel *Poor White,* and he and Eleanore traveled frequently through the late 1930s as an antidote to his occasional depression. En route to South America on a goodwill tour for the State Department in 1941 he swallowed a toothpick and died of the resulting peritonitis.

Kim Townsend relates this story nicely, fulfilling the interpretive assumption that lies behind his biography: "Anderson saved his life both *in* and *by* his writing, and we should expect to find him there." Fully researched and documented it also benefits from the author's interviews with Anderson's widow and children as well as the recently published correspondence between Anderson and his epistolary soulmate "Bab" Finley. Townsend also relies heavily upon Anderson's considerable autobiographical writing, which he uses frequently to construct a semidramatized interior narrative that brings out Anderson's feelings and reactions to life at the cost of occasional narrative confusion. Anderson's first three wives are given rather shadowy representation, and Townsend is rightfully so concerned with uncovering the author in his works that he provides little evaluation, though he indirectly glances at an important point: Anderson's power as a writer lay in sketches, while none of his novels, except perhaps *Poor White,* is very successful. Altogether, however, Townsend provides a presently definitive critical biography, superseding the earlier works by Irving Howe and James Schevill.

Both Sherwood Anderson and Ezra Pound were peripatetic, but while Anderson moved restlessly around America and reimagined it in his fiction, Pound fled from Indiana to Europe and sought to transcend any particular society in his poetry. Pound was the apostle of High Modernism, a movement characterized by experimental form, mythic or universal subject matter, and intellectual elitism. Anderson was a homespun romantic who wrote realistic stories for the people, and his two trips to Paris and lessons from Gertrude Stein merely made his prose even simpler. He did not even like to read very much, not to mention poems in strange languages. Both were giants of the 1920s, however; both have retained international reputations; and both failed to realize the full promise of their early careers.

In writing his biography of Pound, John Tytell intended to present the life fairly, to illuminate the circumstances behind the poetry, and to avoid a swollen "definitive" biography. In all these aims he has been successful. Unfortunately, Tytell's prose is often awkward and murky, particularly in covering the history of ideas. Pound is an artist who "makes of his life so exceptional a case that more mundane exigencies are exposed, and thus allows us to examine the very virtue and nature of our common behavior and governance." The troubadours "wrote their poetry to deny medieval asceticism of flesh and intelligence, and as the celebration of delight in beauty." The book needs tighter editing in general: Tytell claims that by the time of Pound's first Fascist radio broadcast to the West on 23 January 1941, the Germans were within thirty miles of Moscow and had taken half a million prisoners. In fact, Hitler attacked Russia on 22 June 1941 and by the time Operation Typhoon was stopped at the gates of Moscow the Germans had taken more than a million prisoners.

Tytell's subtitle, "The Solitary Volcano," taken from Yeats's characterization of his onetime secretary, appropriately suggests Pound's restless and angry energy, which was both fertilizing and destructive, especially self-destructive. Officially, Tytell would like to define Pound as an isolated tragic figure, but the fair and objective narrative that follows, with its wealth of outward details and paucity of psychological or spiritual reconstruction, works against such a view. In Tytell's account Pound seems to have been a remarkably unreflective and emotionally guarded person, supremely gifted and generous in inspiring and sharing literary and intellectual enthusiasms but not much interested in people otherwise—Tytell notes that he married Dorothy Shakespear partly because of her name, and when he had a son by her and a daughter by his mistress Olga Rudge, both children were farmed out to be raised by oth-

ers. Pound was fearlessly outspoken, prescriptive, and egomaniacal throughout his life. In the center of London and Paris literary life from 1908 to 1925, such qualities made him the proud father of literary modernism, although Pound's own work suffered from the time and effort he put into advancing the careers of others, as Hemingway noted. But in Rapallo from 1925 through World War II, his literary reputation surpassed by many of the writers he had promoted, Pound applied the same qualities to politics and economics and spectacularly exposed his ignorance and bigotry. If he was tragic, he most resembled Timon of Athens, the most ludicrous of Shakespeare's heroes—and a favorite of Pound's.

Tytell's treatment of the post-World War II years is the best section of the book. He has examined the U.S. Government files as well as those of St. Elizabeth's Hospital, where Pound was interned from 1945 to 1958 while facing treason charges for his broadcasts in behalf of Mussolini during the war, until the efforts of countless writers helped to free him. This is a sad story indeed, but Tytell's evidence shows that Pound was in fact an enthusiastic Fascist, a vicious anti-Semite and racist, and that he connived with his doctors' diagnosis of insanity in order to avoid trial even as he won the 1948 Bollingen Prize for the magnificent *Pisan Cantos,* composed during his horrendous caged imprisonment by the army at the end of the war. Finally released from the hospital and the treason charges, he returned to Italy for his final fourteen years, the angry voice gradually stilled, and Pound, who outlived all of the great modernists, finally seemed to rise to self-criticism and tragic self-awareness in his final interviews and the haunting last fragment of the *Cantos:*

> I have tried to write Paradise
> Do not move
>   Let the wind speak that is paradise
> Let the Gods forgive what I have made
> Let those I love try to forgive
>   what I have made.

Tytell compares Pound to Wilde, both flamboyantly eccentric exiles from societies that imprisoned them—but Pound lacked Wilde's personal gentleness and Wilde, Pound's anger. Tytell also notes that Pound began dating all his letters according to the Fascist calendar in 1931, when he was forty-six years old. Wilde died at that age, and Pound in later years may have wished that his life had ended then also.

In his first biography of a major writer and after his ambitious quartet of civil-rights biographies (Nat Turner, John Brown, Abraham Lincoln, Martin Luther King, Jr.), Stephen B. Oates reconstructs William Faulkner's life in what Paul Murray Kendall, citing Sir Harold Nicolson, calls a "pure biography"–here "the author, eschewing all extraneous purpose, writes the life of a man for its own sake, and though adhering to truth, attempts to compose that life as a work of art." Thus, Oates is a kind of novelist and Faulkner his hero, but the intimate, often dramatized narrative is firmly rooted in the facts of Faulkner's life. At every point Oates ties his re-creation of Faulkner to documented sources that are discretely itemized page by page at the back of the book. The result is an enjoyable popular biography that tells a story, darker than one had imagined, while avoiding the massive detail of Joseph Blotner's definitive life. But it also signifies, trivializes, and sentimentalizes the achievement. Here, for example, is an Oates reconstruction of the life that blends the great writer and the tragic post-middle-aged philanderer: "With *A Fable* done and in press, Faulkner plunged into an even deeper gloom. The book had been so difficult to write that he feared his life as an artist was really over now. At fifty-six, his life as a lover seemed over, too, for he was sure that he would never find another young woman, that he would never walk in April again. Ah, Joan, Joan. Not even the loss of Helen Baird had hurt so much as this." Fortunately, Oates is rarely quite so awkward.

In this novelistic reimagining of Faulkner's life the writing of the works becomes a part of the life story. Thus, Oates radically and inevitably dramatizes the primary assumption of all biographical criticism, that the works reflect the life. The results are often illuminating: for example, *Mosquitoes* affectionately caricatures Sherwood Anderson, an early mentor, and fictionalizes Faulkner's thwarted passion for Helen Baird, an early love; *Absalom, Absalom!* reflects his grief and guilt over the death of his beloved brother Dean in 1935. Oates everywhere presents Faulkner's characters as living people, since they *were* real and palpable in their creator's imagination.

Vivid, romantic characterizations, linked to Faulkner's family and personal history, together with convenient plot summaries, constitute Oates's discussion of the works. No literary critic, he describes the works without evaluation or criticism, although it is instructive to find that Faulk-

Dust jacket for the first part of Martin Stannard's two-volume biography that challenges accepted views of Evelyn Waugh as brilliant clown and conservative villain

ner considered *A Fable,* his ambitious but flawed World War I allegory, his greatest work–perhaps he needed to deny to himself in 1953 that his immortal novels had been written a decade and more earlier and remained forever rooted in the soil of Yoknapatawpha County. Oates's omission of critical evaluation extends to Faulkner himself as well as the works. In general, his method seems better suited to public figures, whose judgments stand in need of imaginative construction, than to writers, whose imaginative constructions need to be judged.

Oates suggests throughout that like Pound and, especially, Sherwood Anderson, Faulkner's fullest selfhood lay in writing itself, which drew its inspiration largely from his life, but constituted a life of its own. When he went into his study to write, Faulkner shut the door behind him and removed the doorknob. The life itself was unhappy, as Oates's narrative sadly demonstrates. Faulkner could generally live with his alcoholism, but it followed a chronic pattern: he was sober when writing but drunk soon after he had finished each work. Oates shows him carefully regulating his drinking before the Nobel Prize acceptance speech in 1950, emerging out of a week-long binge just in time to recover for the trip to New York and Stockholm. Estelle Faulkner was also an alcoholic, their marriage of thirty-two years a mutual misery most of the time. She had been his boyhood sweetheart, but she had unhappily married and then divorced a lawyer before returning to "Billy." Her initial rejection of him was the first of several romantic disappointments for Faulkner, whose tendency to idealize those he loved and covertly resent those who disappointed him helped contribute to the creation of powerfully realized female characters, whether nurturing like Lena Grove or destructive like Temple Drake. In his life, however, Faulkner always remained a romantic idealist, irresistibly drawn to far younger women. Much of Oates's biography details these love affairs, relying on the memoirs of Faulkner's mistresses–Meta Carpenter, Joan Williams, Else Jonsson, Jean Stein–since Faulkner suppressed information about himself. They provided his only happiness outside of writing but left no one satisfied, since he could not abandon Estelle–nor she him.

Finally, Oates reminds us of Faulkner's lack of popular acclaim and his financial insecurity during most of his life. In 1944, sixteen years after *The Sound and the Fury* and eight after *Absalom, Absalom!*, all seventeen of his books were out of print. Forced to make money writing for Hollywood in 1932, 1935, and 1942 and yoked to an absurd seven-year contract in the last case that literally constituted slave labor for Warner Brothers–he walked out in 1945–he was saved from drinking himself to death only by Meta's love and Howard Hawks's friendship and admiration. Three months before Malcolm Cowley's *Portable Faulkner* sealed his *succes d'estime* in 1946, Faulkner won $250–second prize!–in the *Ellery Queen Mystery Magazine* contest for a story written in his continual desperate attempt to stay alive and support Estelle. After MGM bought the movie rights to *Intruder in the Dust* in 1949 he was financially secure, yet even when he won the Nobel Prize in 1950, the *New York Times* and *Herald Tribune* groused about the Swedish Academy's decision to honor what they considered his pessimistic distortions of the American dream. Ironically, although Faulkner constantly complained during the 1920s and 1930s that poverty was preventing him from realizing his potential, his five greatest works were written between 1929 and 1936.

Like Sherwood Anderson as his creative powers receded, Faulkner nobly turned to public affairs and politics, speaking out on the problem of segregation, but even here he suffered the ignominy of public censure: friends and neighbors denounced him as a "nigger-lover," while northern white liberals dismissed him as hopelessly old-fashioned and timid. One is amazed that Faulkner survived at all, without even considering the magnitude of his achievement. After reading Oates's story of his life, the words of his Nobel Prize speech seem less a pious hope than a personal testimony: "I believe that man will not merely endure; he will prevail."

Kenneth Lynn's startling life of Ernest Hemingway is the boldest literary biography of 1987. Although he has written almost 600 pages on a writer already exhaustively covered in Carlos Baker's standard biography, not to mention the fine studies by Jeffrey Meyers, Michael Reynolds, and Bernice Kert, Lynn offers a fresh and powerful interpretation of his overworked subject that not only transforms our understanding of Hemingway the man but also reinterprets much of the literature in ways that are rich and strange. Whether one fully agrees with Lynn's view of Hemingway or not, this book must be carefully considered by anyone who will write on his subject in the future. Six years in the writing and originally envisioned as a "short" work, *Hemingway* is exhaustively researched and scrupulously documented; Lynn has mastered the available Hemingway commentary so well that he can convincingly refute much of it, both from idolaters and debunkers. Not least among the virtues of this work is its strong and clear rhetoric.

Lynn's fundamental thesis, extending previous critical assumptions to their limit, is that Hemingway's work is everywhere autobiographical, but that his self-revelation is guarded and limited to protect his own self-image: "Uncertain to the point of fear about himself, he was compelled to cope with the disorder of his inner world by creating fictional equivalents for it." A symptom of that disorder is the androgyny nakedly revealed in *The Garden of Eden*, Hemingway's massive uncompleted manuscript, published by Scribners in a drastically abridged and edited form in 1986. Lynn uncovers its source in Hemingway's troubled family life. The infant Ernest was raised as the "twin" of his older sister, Marcelline; his father was a resourceful outdoorsman, but alienated from his wife, who dominated him; and Grace, his mother, was a powerful and aggressive matriarch who enthusiastically encouraged and supported her boy's literary ambitions but confused his sexual identity and humiliated her husband. As a result, Ernest hated Marcelline, who revenged herself upon *him* in her memoirs; loved and was loved in turn by his younger sister, Ursula, who was devastated by his suicide in 1961 and killed herself five years later after being diagnosed for cancer; admired yet despised his father, who killed himself with his own father's Civil War pistol in 1928, and resolved to be a stronger man and father; hated his mother, "that bitch" as he called her to others, yet sought substitutes in her image all of his life.

Lynn convincingly illuminates this moving family tragedy and shows how Hemingway's life was twisted by it but his works empowered. His early stories "Up in Michigan" and *in our time* were scarcely veiled insults to the respectability of his parents and were recognized as such and resented. But in all his works, the ideal love relationships recapture the sexual ambiguity of his infancy, male and female assuming each other's identity as a culminating experience, as Lynn demonstrates. The "wounding" of the typical Hemingway hero, from Nick Adams and Jake Barnes onward, does not stem from Hemingway's experiences in World War I or his generation's spiritual malaise after the war—Hemingway enjoyed the war and lived quite nicely in Paris off his first wife's money until his own literary financial success—but from his own personal demons. Hemingway liked to present himself to the world as a man's (and woman's) man sexually. However, his constitutional infidelity stemmed from weakness, not strength. Hemingway was most comfortable with asexual forms of affection: paternal (he began calling himself "Papa" in his twenties); filial (he craved mothering from all his lovers, but deserted them, as he deserted Grace); and sibling love, which extended into androgyny.

The other half of the *machismo* myth that he cultivated was likewise only partly true. Lynn proves beyond any doubt that Hemingway was *not* critically wounded at Fossalta nor did he heroically risk his own life. Though he did not merely lie about his World War I experiences as Faulkner did, he exaggerated them and used the World War I hero image to advance his own career, unlike Faulkner, who simply wanted to gain the respect of his hometown. Thereafter, im-

pelled to advance the Hemingway myth, he became both its beneficiary and its victim, turning into a parody of himself as he sought U-boats off Cuba in his boat, "liberated" the Ritz when the Germans left Paris, and repeated earlier adventures as farce during his East Africa safari in 1953 and return to Spain in 1959. Unable to sustain the myth as a man–or as a writer, the real Ernest Hemingway–he fell into suicidal depression and terminated it with his shotgun.

Lynn grimly analyzes one particularly repellent feature of Hemingway's self-creation as hero-writer, his betrayal of mentors, friends, and acquaintances whose reputations had to be blackened in order for his own to shine all the brighter. Among many figures he attacked Gertrude Stein and F. Scott and Zelda Fitzgerald in words, actions, and/or his own fiction. In the case of Sherwood Anderson he killed two birds with one book. *The Torrents of Spring,* his savagely amusing parody of Anderson's *Dark Laughter,* had to be rejected by Horace Liveright, since he was Anderson's publisher as well as Hemingway's. Liveright's decision delighted Hemingway, for it allowed him to terminate his contract and complete a more attractive arrangement with Scribners. Hemingway had been signed by Liveright initially partly on Anderson's recommendation, so in writing the parody he was able to leave both Liveright and Anderson behind as well as helping to destroy the latter's reputation–just as he had planned it.

Lynn's biography reveals his great admiration for the writer, whose works seem to him more complex and richer than others have recognized. This life also presents a Hemingway who was a figure more troubled than either admirers or detractors have previously recognized. But though Lynn understands the man, he does not like him, and his continual, often ironic undercutting occasionally undermines his reliability. Lynn's biographical criticism of the works is often more successful at overturning earlier views than making his own case (his discussion of "Big Two-Hearted River" is an example).

Two of the most important and durable masters of recent English literature, one a poet and the other a novelist, are the subjects of definitive biographies whose first installments have now appeared in their American editions. Richard Perceval Graves, the writer's nephew, has begun his task with *Robert Graves: The Assault Heroic 1895-1926* (Viking). Martin Stannard, the editor of an anthology of Waugh criticism, has written

Evelyn Waugh: The Early Years 1903-1939, the first of a two-volume biography.

Ezra Pound eloquently fulminated against the Great War in *Hugh Selwyn Mauberley,* Faulkner pretended to have been shot down in it, Hemingway was wounded as a noncombatant, but the twenty-one-year-old Captain Robert Graves was wounded so badly during the Somme bloodbath in the summer of 1916 that his battalion commander initially informed Graves's mother of her son's death. Graves's mid-life memoir of that experience, the life that led up to it, and the life that followed, *Goodbye to All That* (1929), is one of the great English testaments of youth. Not least among the virtues of *The Assault Heroic* is his nephew's reconstruction of that material, which relies upon *Goodbye to All That* but presents a more truthful account, based on the biographer's assiduous search for the facts. As he explains, "Robert's terrible experiences during the 1914-1918 war, together with the considerable difficulties which he faced during subsequent years both in his private life and in his literary career combined, in my view, seriously to distort his memories of the past. This is no discredit to him, but a measure of the terrible ordeals through which he passed." The uncovering of facts is this biography's major accomplishment, its memorial the formidable *apparatus criticus* of the 1,132 reference and explanatory notes and annotated select Graves bibliography, in which the author also corrects the errors of the most recent Graves biographer, Martin Seymour-Smith, whose faulty or hypothetical account of the Graves antecedents is repaired in this work. In fact, *The Assault Heroic* is both an exhaustive life of the young Graves and a family chronicle, dedicated to the descendants of John Crosbie Graves and Helen Perceval, the eighteenth-century progenitors, including the author's children. The text is preceded by two massive and distinguished family trees–Graves and Ranke (Robert's German cousins)–and both minutely record the appalling carnage of World War I upon both sides. The entire first "book" of the biography presents biographical sketches of both the English and continental ancestors before we arrive at Robert's birth. The author's uniquely privileged access to family records, including his own father's unpublished life of Graves, *My Brother Robert,* his own intimate acquaintance with his famous uncle, "whom I have known since childhood," and his scholarly diligence and professional integrity as a biographer will make the completed biography definitive. This first install-

LINDA W. WAGNER-MARTIN

SYLVIA
A Biography
PLATH

Dust jacket for the second biography of Sylvia Plath, the first to make use of unpublished journals and letters recently made available to scholars

ment anticipates its sequel(s), ending with Graves's departure as the newly appointed professor of poetry at Cairo University, with his feminist wife Nancy Nicolson and his future muse Laura Riding, whose influence so affected his life and his writing.

Unfortunately, this is a very dull book. Its overwhelming accumulation of circumstantial details, effective in covering the war but mind-numbing in detailing Graves's domestic life, is suggested by the organization of the work: six 30-100 page books, divided into tiny chapters that fracture the life into discrete events with little overall pattern (for example, Nancy opens her poet's shop at Boar's Hill–the shop fails–Robert writes *On English Poetry*–the family discusses Charles Graves's problems at Oxford with him). Such mini-biography combined with chronicle unveils facts well, but to what purpose? This unenlightening circumstantiality extends to other matters. Graves is seen through actions, documents, and the testimony of others, but his inner life and motivations remain relatively unexplored territory. For example, we are told about his socialist convictions but given no explanation of why and little evidence to what end. Perhaps in an attempt to avoid idolatry of a beloved uncle, the author has made Graves uninteresting. Worst of all, although the author notes that the polymath Graves's fundamental interest was poetry and quotes poems extensively, his treatment is blankly descriptive and superficial, and the reader is left feeling that the younger Graves was a very minor poet indeed. The dullness of the work may be partly attributable to its subject, however, Robert Graves before he became a great writer, and we may hope for no fewer facts but more understanding in the next volume.

Martin Stannard is off to a better start. His first volume is very similar to Graves's in the problems it surmounts and its formal characteristics. Like *The Assault Heroic*, it announces itself as the definitive biography, clearing way for itself by referring to the recent spate of posthumous Waugh publications, such as *Diaries* (1976), *Letters* (1980), and *Essays, Articles, and Reviews* (1983), as well as the depository of Waugh's own library at the University of Texas at Austin. Thus it calls into question the conclusions of Christopher Sykes's 1975 life, the only previous biography, much as Richard Perceval Graves replaces Seymour-Smith. Both Stannard and Graves claim to be presenting fuller and more truthful accounts, and Stannard conveniently uses Sykes's disclaimers about the authoritativeness of his own account and references to interviews with his predecessor to establish his right to succession. Stannard begins, like Graves, with a lengthy chapter of antecedents, four generations of Waughs and Rabans, to ground his subject's history. He does not have the unique access to intimate family experience that distinguishes Graves's biographical resources, but he has interviewed all of Waugh's eminent friends, and, most significantly, his first wife, which gives his account authentic and specific detail often as precise as that in *The Assault Heroic*. In fact, this is an even bigger book, and anticipates at least 1,000 pages of text in the completed life. Like Graves, Stannard must present the truth about a writer who both covered up his tracks (Robert Graves ultimately repudiated his war poetry and omitted it from his collected poems, for example) and claimed to reveal himself. But though Waugh's *A Little Learning*, the autobiography of his youth

and his final work, is not deliberately untruthful, like *Goodbye to All That* it needs to be supplemented by the accounts of others to reveal what really happened, which is the most important purpose of each biographer.

But Stannard does much more than this. His biography uses both the life and the writings to trace Waugh's early intellectual movement from antibourgeois agnosticism to aestheticism to religious conversion, skepticism, and an idiosyncratic conservatism and explains how Catholicism and antihumanism were logical corollaries of a mind that had come to see the collective human race with Swiftian contempt and amusement. He superbly traces Waugh's complex development as an artist. Initially, no career appealed to him less than writing, which would have been to follow in his father's footsteps, and Waugh would rather have been an artisan. But his apprenticeship with the illustrator Francis Crease and others eventually revealed the limits of his considerable facility, and Waugh was forced to write in order to make the money necessary to support his extravagant lifestyle. Waugh threw himself enthusiastically into writing once he could define it as simply a means to an end–money, fame, social advancement–but craftsmanship remained one of its permanent features, as Stannard reminds us in his acute criticism of all the early works from reviews to travel journalism to the five brilliant pre-World War II novels, whose popular and critical reception, so important to Waugh's ambitions, he carefully defines. He details Waugh's movement from homoeroticism to failed marriage to heterosexual promiscuity as well, together with the development of his near-alcoholism. Above all, however, he captures the infinite variety of Waugh's troubled but brilliant young restlessness, tracing the sources of his voluminous writings through his intellectual, social, and geographical permutations. After the collapse of his marriage in 1929 Waugh traveled (usually on assignment) to Ethiopia, East Africa, British Guiana and the Amazon, the Mediterranean littoral, Morocco, Spitzbergen, and back to Ethiopia to cover the Italian invasion in 1935.

In sum, Stannard provides not only comprehensive factual detail but also explanation, analysis, and interpretation. Above all, he impresses us with Waugh's genius and literary preeminence, merely by revealing the truth. Although Richard Perceval Graves's task is certainly more difficult–poets are far more resistant than novelists to understanding and evaluation and Graves less

Dust jacket for the biography of the eccentric English poet Stevie Smith

self-promoting than Waugh–his uncle deserves no less than this in the next volume. As for Stannard's work, if the second volume is as good as the first, we can eagerly await the next 700 pages.

One poet whose life has excited intense controversy since her death is Sylvia Plath, whose suicide in London in 1963 remains a tragic puzzle. Linda Wagner-Martin's *Sylvia Plath: A Biography* (Simon and Schuster) is only the second book-length biography of Plath. It supersedes Edward Butscher's 1976 study which overstressed Plath's inner obsessions and was written before the appearance of previously unpublished stories and essays in 1979, Plath's *Collected Poems* (which won the 1982 Pulitzer Prize for Poetry and contained many new poems), and excerpts from her journals in the same year. But, as the author notes, no biography of Plath can claim to be definitive until all of her papers are released by Ted Hughes, the English poet who was Plath's husband and controls the rights to her work. In fact,

Wagner-Martin was unable to quote extensively from the writings because of Hughes's objections to the draft of her manuscript. Plath was estranged from Hughes at the time of her suicide, and, although he has brought out editions of her work and provided the collection of Plath's papers housed at Smith College, he destroyed one of the volumes of her journal after her death and other writings have disappeared, nor has he granted any interviews concerning his wife. The full documentary record of Plath's life and the story of her final years will probably never be known publicly.

Under the circumstance Wagner-Martin has written a sympathetic, perceptive biography. She has studied all of Plath's available writings, spoken with nearly everyone who knew her and was willing to be interviewed, and has constructed a detailed, straightforward narrative that both reflects Plath's view of herself and also provides an analytical and sometimes critical perspective. In fifteen well-defined chapters she traces Plath's life from her happy, all-American childhood in the 1930s through her achievements in high school and at Smith; the nervous breakdown, suicide attempt, and recovery before her senior year at college (fictionalized in her novel *The Bell Jar*); her year as an American "golden girl" at Cambridge and subsequent marriage to Ted Hughes. The marriage deeply satisfied both writers initially–"twentieth-century Brownings" friends called them–and was followed by *The Colossus and Other Poems* (1960) and Sylvia's motherhood but ended in rages against Ted, separation, a recurrence of Plath's desperate depression and her heartbreaking self-destruction at thirty-one, just at the height of her power as a poet.

Sometimes Wagner-Martin's interpretive narrative lapses into the banalities of American ego psychology and other clichés (for example, "For the Plath-Schober family–certainly for Sylvia– 1942 was the year of decision"), and the writing at its best is good journalism. The works elicit general observations rather than interpretation, but of course the author could hardly do more because she was not given permission for full quotation. But this biography provides a valuable corrective to earlier accounts of Plath's life. Wagner-Martin cogently describes and analyzes Plath's professionalism, perfectionism, and womanhood as fundamental to both her triumphs and sorrows. She emphasizes Plath's identity as an author above all, because "her life was shaped by her ambition to be a writer." From the very beginning Plath was productive, resourceful, eager, and determined to present her voice to the public. Her first poem was published in the *Boston Sunday Herald* when she was eight and a half, her own determination to publish was reinforced by her high-school English teacher, and her professional publications included journalism, criticism, romance, short stories, novels, and poetry—her métier—written for a wide variety of audiences and gaining her awards and prizes throughout her career. She was a writer's writer whose voice became stronger and more distinguished every year.

Wagner-Martin plausibly traces her perfectionism to childhood upbringing, but her desire to be the best was a component of her own genius as well. It made her acutely sensitive to being imperfect. When her summer apprentice work at *Mademoiselle* drew criticism from her supervising editor, it set off the anger and depression that resulted in her first suicide attempt. She admired Adrienne Rich, her only equal among young American women poets in the 1950s, but was envious of Rich's greater success in publishing, even though Plath was two years younger.

Finally, Wagner-Martin explains the personal, familial, and social pressures that impelled Plath to be the perfect 1950s all-American woman—wife, lover, mother, hostess, housekeeper, cook, educator—as well as the best poet of her generation. She worshipped Ted as the perfect man in whom fulfilling her own quest for perfection would be worth its emotional cost. She produced her greatest poetry as the marriage threatened to collapse, but it found no audience except herself until after her death. It was not enough to hold back the depression that overcame her in the terrible London winter of 1963 or to make her imperfect life worth living.

Wagner-Martin makes effective use of the unpublished writing, showing how Plath's outward demeanor and supreme competence in every aspect of her life masked an intense dissatisfaction with others and herself that is only recorded in her journals. She also shows that Plath's own plan of *Ariel*, her second book of poems, was intended not just to dramatize anger and despair but also to look forward with hope, like *The Bell Jar*. She suggests that the suicide was not an inevitable or logical outcome for the Sylvia Plath who completed her *Ariel* three months before her death, whatever the implications of the published version of that collection edited by her husband. The last, renunciatory

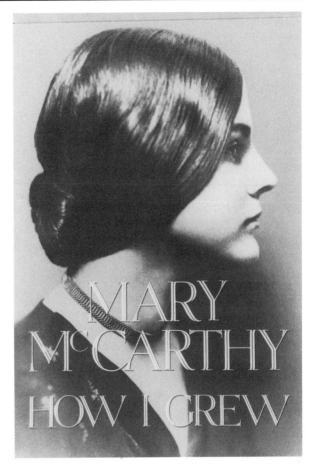

Dust jacket for Mary McCarthy's memoir of her intellectual development from age thirteen to age twenty-one

poems may have been preparations for her death, however, which we may see as a personal choice that satisfied her but has robbed the rest of us, as Anne Sexton noted in the comment that serves as epigraph to this biography: "the loss of it, the terrible loss of the more she could have done!"

Three months before her suicide, Sylvia Plath wrote a letter of inquiry to a longtime resident of London whose poetry she had come to admire greatly, inviting her to tea or coffee. The recipient, who replied with eccentric but grateful courtesy, is the subject of *Stevie: A Biography of Stevie Smith* (Oxford), by Jack Barbera and William McBrien, both great admirers of the writer and editors of a volume of her uncollected writings, *Me Again* (1982). They have been assiduous and untiring in their quest for information, both from everything ever written by or about Stevie Smith and from interviews with everyone who seems to have known her. Their text is followed by fifty-eight pages of reference notes documenting its sources page by page, and five pages of acknowledgements, testimony to the scope of their interviews and thoroughness of their research—as they note, citing Bernard Crick's characterization of biographers into "beavers" and "butterflies," they have been beavers.

The biography begins with the crowning moment of Smith's career, her Gold Medal for Poetry, presented to her by Queen Elizabeth II on 21 November 1969 at Buckingham Palace. Thereafter it traces chronologically her public and professional life year by year from her birth at Hull in 1902 to her death in London in 1971. As the authors note, an authorized biography is currently under preparation by Frances Spalding, but it is difficult to believe it could be much more detailed. This book makes little attempt at criticism, analysis, and interpretation of the works or the life, however, relying largely upon the testimony of Smith, her acquaintances, and reviewers of her books to present their factual narrative. There is little attempt to go below the surface of the life or Smith's relationship with others. For example, she lived alone with her "Lion aunt" Margaret Spear in their London residence for forty years until the aunt's death in 1968, but the authors provide only brief, descriptive references to the aunt, who must have been the most important person in Smith's emotional life, and they never explain precisely why she was called the "Lion of Hull," though they use the epithet continually to refer to her. Nonetheless, the book describes its subject's life and works thoroughly and should more than satisfy anyone interested in the writer.

Like Plath, Smith was a thoroughly professional writer, proficient in all sorts of work. She had to work as a secretary in a minor non-literary publishing house until 1953 in order to support herself and her aunt. But she turned to reviewing everything but poetry for the *Spectator* and *Observer* thereafter, was well known for her BBC broadcasts and *sprechstimme* public performances of her own poetry, and shrewdly retained the copyright of her first two novels and first collection, in effect having any sponsoring organization pay Stevie Smith in order to allow Stevie Smith to perform her own works. Like Plath, she was fundamentally a poet and later repudiated her semiautobiographical *Novel on Yellow Paper,* the work that gained her instant literary fame in 1936 and was so admired by Plath (the yellow paper was used for carbons in her secretarial work). Like Plath's, her life has

come to assume feminist significance, and a play and film, *Stevie,* have memorialized it for popular audiences, just as Plath's *Bell Jar* was made into a film. Finally, like Plath, she attempted to commit suicide, in 1953, after nearly a decade of neglect or rejections of her poetry and bored exhaustion in her secretarial job.

In more significant ways, however, Smith's life and career is a contrary of Plath's, deliberately narrowed and circumscribed, while Plath attempted to fulfill completely all the roles possible for a genius, a writer, and a woman. Smith never married, never even tried, and the authors are unable to define fully the extent of her sexual experience, though she liked men as friends and was flirtatious. (Her father, who deserted his family when she was three, did not provide a hopeful initial paradigm of manhood.) The authors note that "she liked children but was always thankful they belonged to someone else." She could have been an editor but chose to limit her responsibilities by remaining a secretary. And she remained in the same house in London for sixty-five years. In many ways, she was childlike, and she preferred childhood and old age, times of "instinctuality," to the "intellectuality" of the middle years, which she defined as from twenty to fifty.

Her poetry is likewise carefully and craftfully limited. Songlike, deriving its subjects and themes from everyday life and simple, almost childlike language, it most resembles the early lyrics of Blake without aspiring to go beyond them. Behind the best poems lies Smith's unique tone, a self-amused stoicism in contemplating the meaninglessness of life. This freshly original mixture of humor and bleakness is reinforced by the childlike yet grotesque drawings that Smith liked to append to her poems, which are nicely analyzed by the authors. She described herself as "a non-believer with a religious temperament," and something of the ironically comic and bitter tone of her work can be gauged from John Betjeman's comment, "She is a good girl and bites suddenly" and even from her titles: "The Necessity of not believing" (essay); "Is There Life Beyond the Gravy?" (story); *Some are More Human than Others* (drawings); and *Not Waving But Drowning* (collection). The latter, her most famous poem, written just before her suicide attempt, is almost a critique of her own adjustment to life's blankness—what seems to distant onlookers to be playful waving is a drowning person's doomed attempts to stay afloat. Although

Barbera and McBrien warmly trace Smith's deserved return to fame as a poet in the 1960s, her poetry never really developed or changed its narrow brilliance, and their biography honors nicely a very good minor poet. Stevie Smith revealed the painful source of her poetry in a 1969 essay written for *Vogue:* "I do not know how people can manage to have animals, wives, and children and also write. Of course isolation can be very painful. Many of my poems are about the pains of isolation, but once the poem is written, the happiness of being alone comes flooding back."

Three other important biographies of 1987 treat earlier women writers and should be noted in passing. Muriel Sparks's *Mary Shelley: A Biography* (Dutton) is an updated version of Sparks's first book, published only in England in 1951 and originally entitled *Child of Light.* The Brontë scholar Edward Chitham has brought out *A Life of Emily Brontë* (Blackwell), an investigative biography that reconstructs the life while analyzing earlier accounts of it. And Sharon O'Brien's *Willa Cather: The Emerging Voice* (Oxford) presents the early life and career of that writer, following the influences that helped Cather redefine her sexuality as a writer up to the emergence of her full authorial maturity in *O Pioneers!* (1913).

In a year with so many books dealing with tragic or painful narratives of important American writers it seems appropriate to mention the notebooks of Delmore Schwartz, published last year but omitted from the 1986 *Yearbook* survey. *Portrait of Delmore: Journals and Notes of Delmore Schwartz 1939-1959* (Farrar, Straus and Giroux) has been edited from 2,100 sheets of sometimes illegible writer's entries down to 645 chronologically ordered pages by Elizabeth Pollet, whose marriage to the writer lasted from 1949 to 1957. Schwartz began his journal the year after his multigenre book *In Dreams Begin Responsibilities* established him as a twenty-five-year-old wunderkind of American literature. According to the first entry, writing in the journal was intended to turn Schwartz *away* from "the long conversation of the soul with itself" and help produce more "objective observation" that might further his career as a writer; secondly, it was "intended for the insight and pleasure of an old man," something to look back on fondly as a reflection of his youth.

Appallingly, despite bits and even large chunks of the poems published by Schwartz during these twenty years and some scattered critical, political, or philosophical meanderings, it is the record of the writer's wounds as he struggles against his own self-destructiveness. The manic depression that characterized his emotional life, short-circuited his literary career, and led ultimately to his lonely and abysmal death in New York in 1966 is often explicitly addressed here and also recorded through its symptoms (insomnia, alcoholism, barbiturate addiction, despair, paranoia, hatred of others) as well as the repetitive mechanical activities enlisted to regain a sense of control: counting drinks taken daily–lists of books read–copying *Finnegans Wake* and *Ulysses* verbatim (the actual copied texts are sensibly omitted from this book). Occasionally, there are moments of terrible clarity: "Perhaps I am wrong to think that there is a reasonable explanation for the sterility and withdrawal in which I live. Don't think, as one says, don't think that it has not occurred to me that it may merely be a lack of talent and an unwillingness to accept one's limitations" (18 October 1945). Reading this material, it is difficult to believe that during these twenty years the writer taught at Harvard, NYU, Princeton, and Chicago; was editor of *Partisan Review* and poetry editor of the *New Republic;* and published five books of drama, prose, and poetry, winning the Bollingen Prize in 1959 for *Selected Poems.*

The book may be of some use to Delmore Schwartz scholars or people interested in psychopathology, but it is less than useful to anyone else due to the perversely inadequate identifications: some names of people referred to are provided, some are not; a chronology of Schwartz's life and works at the beginning of the volume provides some help, but not much; the index is huge but incomplete (where is "Rollins"?) and unhelpful without further identifications (who *was* Scowcroft?); references to the editor and her family are explained in the text–others, equally puzzling to those not already thoroughly familiar with Delmore Schwartz, are not. The editor stopped transcribing the notebooks in 1959 because later ones were indecipherable and her "judgment of their contents from scanning some of them are such that [she] did not want to proceed." But these are bad enough, and their publication seem to me to involve at least some poor taste if not bad faith. *Caveat lector.*

More discrete but more palatable self-revelations may be found in a series, "Literary Conversations," published by the University Press of Mississippi and under the general editorship of Peggy Whitman Prenshaw. This year's volumes deal with *Katherine Anne Porter* (edited by

Joan Givner); *John Cheever* (edited by Scott Donaldson); *Flannery O'Connor* (edited by Rosemary M. Magee); and *Peter Taylor* (edited by Hubert H. McAlexander). Attractively designed texts available in paperback editions, edited by an expert on each writer, each book presents a bibliography of the author's works (but only book-length publications), authoritative but brief introductions, a detailed biographical chronology, and reprints of fifteen to thirty interviews or conversations between the subject and journalists, writers, and critics. Well-detailed indices provide a guide to topics discussed by the writer. Although an interview is as much self-promotion as self-revelation, each collection allows the reader to appreciate, at the least, each writer's art of self-presentation, and taking all the interviews into consideration, gives a living portrait of the man or woman behind the works. Joan Givner, Porter's biographer, provides the longest and best of the introductions, alerting the reader to K.A.P.'s willingness to reveal everything, even if she has made some of it up, and she briefly characterizes the interviewers' performance as well. The series seems to be off to a good start, conveniently gathering materials scattered through numerous periodicals and journals, and should prove helpful for basic biographical information on each subject.

Among other significant collections, this year's publications include the sixth volume of *The Collected Letters of Thomas Hardy* (Oxford/ Clarendon), edited by Richard Little Purdy and Michael Millgate. Leon Edel and Lyall H. Powers have edited *The Complete Notebooks of Henry James* (Oxford). This edition, which includes James's pocket diaries and dictated notes, supersedes the 1947 edition by F. O. Matthiessen and Kenneth Murdock, for which Edel read proof and contributed suggestions. *Mencken and Sara. A Life in Letters: The Private Correspondence of H. L. Mencken and Sara Haardt* (McGraw-Hill), edited by Marion Elizabeth Rodgers, presents a love affair through the letters of Mencken and the woman who first wrote to him as an admirer in 1923, became his beloved wife in 1930, and died in 1935. It follows Thomas P. Riggio's publication last year of the Dreiser-Mencken letters.

While notebooks reveal the self to the self and letters, to one another, autobiography reveals the self to the whole world. Self-promotion along with confession is served up wittily in Mary McCarthy's *How I Grew* (Harcourt Brace Jovanovich), a personal memoir of the writer's

youth from childhood to her graduation from Vassar and first marriage, both in 1933. This period was covered in *Memoirs of a Catholic Girlhood*, but as a semifictional meditation, while the present book attempts to reimagine what really happened, in keeping with the credo that has energized McCarthy's richly miscellaneous career: "About truth I have always been monotheistic. It has always been an article of faith with me, going back to college days, that there is a truth and that it is knowable."

In nine chapters *How I Grew* narrates Mary McCarthy's development from early orphanhood, mistreatment by guardians and rescue by maternal grandparents in Seattle, public high school (one year) and sexual deflowering, followed by private schooling at Annie Wright Seminary in Tacoma and Vassar (three chapters each). But there is a more important organization of thought throughout as the now-famous author tries at seventy-seven to understand and interpret herself through reimagining the undefined, unreflective girl she once was. The real Mary McCarthy, the eloquent and acerbic guardian of truth, is only beginning to emerge at the end of this book. This movement between past and present occasionally locates real-life sources of the fiction, and it accounts for the digressiveness of the narrative, its apparent spontaneity (McCarthy will occasionally "remember" something else as she sets down her recollections or addresses the reader, à la Rousseau), and its truthfulness (the book wants to seem less an ordered life history than a discovery of the truth in the very act of narration). Through this double perspective, the earlier self, like nearly everyone else in these memoirs, is treated with detachment as an object of either inquiry or critical judgment–sometimes a puzzle, sometimes a fool.

The first sentence of the book sounds the keynote of the writer's life, her crisp intellectuality: "I was born as a mind during 1925, my bodily birth having taken place in 1912." Chapter one, childhood, ends with her entrance into public high school in 1925, where, she now realizes, her development as an intellectual began; the final episode recalls the momentous day when she received her first library card and checked out her first book–*The Nigger of the Narcissus:* "I remember the power conferred on me by the small, ruled piece of cardboard still empty except for my name typed at the top and my signature below." Intellectual virtue, signalized in this narrative by an interest in books of literature, distinguishes those who are worthy of admiration, whatever their faults, from those who are objects of satire, derision, and contempt. Thus, the young man who crudely ended her virginity is most bitingly dismissed by characterizing him as an illiterate who wrote her commonplace love letters, complete with misspellings and trite salutations: "My mind held itself apart, not finding him, to my surprise, very interesting. . . . Just as nothing can force us to *like* a hated vegetable, so I could never respond in depth to the man made manifest in those colorless letters. *Hasta la vista*." Even popular icons fall by the wayside: "It was not till I was much older, nearly thirty, that I developed a real sympathy for and interest in Lincoln. But it was his intellect, and above all, his melancholy that did it. Neither had a place, naturally, in the common Lincoln applesauce." The author's own intellect is constantly, automatically on display in its high literary allusiveness, dashing from discussions of Log Cabin Syrup and Del Monte Peaches to direct quotation of Proust, comparing the sexual tension of being entrapped in her first lover's roadster to Karl Jaspers's notion of a "boundary situation." Somewhat surprisingly, the real heroes within this narrative are her teachers, hardworking, underappreciated women whose influence helped to generate Mary McCarthy, intellectual, whose dispassionate voice dominates the text, briskly criticizing, judging, and evaluating everybody. It seems fitting, therefore, that she more closely identifies with the viewpoint of her teachers rather than that of her fellow students and that two of her Vassar English teachers are among her dedicatees.

OBITUARIES

James Baldwin

(2 August 1924-1 December 1987)

Fred L. Standley
Florida State University

See also the Baldwin entries in *DLB 2, American Novelists Since World War II; DLB 7, Twentieth-Century American Dramatists*; and *DLB 33, Afro-American Fiction Writers After 1955.*

James Baldwin died on Monday night 1 December 1987 at his home in Saint-Paul de Vence in southern France. He was sixty-three years old and had been in declining health for several months, especially after an operation for stomach cancer the previous spring; yet, he had resumed writing with the intention and hope of completing a book about Martin Luther King, Jr. On 8 December the author's family and friends gathered for his funeral in New York City at the Cathedral of St. John the Divine; and three fellow writers, Maya Angelou, Amiri Baraka, and Toni Morrison, presented tributes to him (as later reported in the 20 December 1987 *New York Times Book Review*). Angelou spoke of their personal relationship in which "brothers are hard to come by and are as necessary as air and as precious as love." James Baldwin knew that "black women in this desolate world, black women in this cruel time which had no soundness in it, have a crying need for brothers. He knew that a brother's love redeems a sister's pain." Baraka testified that Baldwin "was a man, spirit, voice–old and black and terrible as the first ancestor." As man he "traveled the earth like its history and its biographer . . . , reported, criticized, made beautiful, analyzed, cajoled, lyricized, attacked, sang, made us think, made us better, made us consciously human or perhaps more acidly pre-human." His was "the spirit of life thrilling to its own consciousness" which "made us feel good . . . that we could defend ourselves or define ourselves, that we were in the world not merely as animate slaves, but as terrifyingly sensitive measures of what is good or evil, beautiful or ugly." And his was the "voice" of a "consummate complete man of letters" who "will be remembered for his *word*" as "God's black revolutionary mouth . . . and elegant song the deepest and most fundamental commonplace of being alive." Morrison praised Baldwin for bestowing three gifts. First, he gave "a language to dwell in" and "made American English honest–genuinely international" by having "exposed its secrets and reshaped it until it was truly modern dialogic, representative, humane." Second, he embodied "the courage of one who could go as a stranger in the village and transform the distances between people into intimacy with the whole world" and "the courage to live life . . . and say what it was, to recognize and identify evil but never fear or stand in awe of it." Third, he expressed a "tenderness, of vulnerability, that asked everything, expected everything and like, the world's own Merlin, provided us with the ways and means to deliver."

For nearly four decades–from November 1948 to his death–Baldwin lived abroad in a mode of self-imposed exile, primarily in France, which he once described as a "refuge far from the American madness." However, he refused to consider himself an expatriate, retained his U.S. citizenship, and preferred to call himself a "transatlantic commuter." And the purpose of that commuting for Baldwin as a "maverick" man of letters–"a maverick in the sense" that he "depended on neither the white world nor the black world" for the enunciation of an "ideology"–was to fulfill the mission "to bear witness to the truth," especially to the maxim that "no society can smash the social contract and be exempt from the consequences" for "the consequences are chaos for everybody in the society."

From the age of twelve, when he published a short story on the Spanish revolution in a church newspaper, to the last few years of his life as revealed in interviews, Baldwin enunciated a conception and practice of literary art involving both personal and social dimensions.

"I consider that I have many responsibilities," he said, "but none greater than this: to last, as Hemingway says, and get my work done. I want to be an honest man and a good writer." To implement that personal function he recognized

219

James Baldwin (photograph copyright © 1982 by Layle Silbert)

that the author "cannot allow any consideration to supercede his responsibility to reveal all that he can possibly discover concerning the mystery of the human being"; and this meant for him the need to express to the audience the existential "states of birth, suffering, love and death . . . , extreme states–extreme, universal, and inescapable," for the "artist is present to correct the delusions to which we fall prey in our attempts to avoid this knowledge." An adequate perspective for the current technological era was possible only when the literary artist analyzes a man or woman as not "merely a member of a society or group or a deplorable conundrum to be explained by Science . . . but something resolutely indefinable, unpredictable." Thus, the writer in confronting "the disquieting complexity of ourselves" should be oriented primarily "to recreate out of the disorder of life that order which is art" and "to describe things which other people are too busy to describe." Baldwin is direct and distinct in declaring this "a special function" and

that "people who do it cannot by that token do many other things."

While the author's obligations include the personal necessity to avoid self-delusion by this "attempt to look on himself and the world as they are," that also implies that the writer is "responsible to and for the social order." Thus, in his essay "The Creative Dilemma" Baldwin emphasized the need to develop an ethical vision and a historical orientation; the artist is, after all, "an incorrigible disturber of the peace" who "cannot and must not take anything for granted" in the society but "must drive to the heart of every answer and expose that question the answer hides." He believed that every society and culture, and especially that in the United States, always determinedly attempts to restrict the artistic vision of human experience in which "one discovers that life is tragic, and therefore unutterably beautiful." Such a conception presupposes the validity of paradox as a means of exploring and explaining experience; nevertheless, America, as well as other nations, is "a country devoted to the death of paradox." Therefore, for Baldwin, the artist's inherent duty produces a condition of conflict with society; but, "the war of an artist with his society is a lover's war, and he does, at his best, what lovers do, which is to reveal the beloved to himself and, with that revelation, to make freedom real." This attitude was repeated late in his career in an interview entitled "Looking Toward the Eighties" in which he again stressed that the author's "function is very particular and so is his responsibility. After all, to write, if taken seriously, is to be subversive. To disturb the peace." Throughout a long career in which he examined a multitude of concerns and subjects Baldwin never wavered in this conviction that only two options are available to all writers: "to be immoral and uphold the *status quo* or to be moral and try to change the world." To the end of his life this sociocultural effort was in the forefront of his thinking and writing; and, in 1984 Baldwin told fellow writer Julius Lester that he was still in "the process of" finding "a new language. . . . I might say a new morality, which in my terms, comes to the same thing. And that's on all levels–the level of color, the level of identity, the level of sexual identity, what love means, especially in a consumer society, for example. Everything is in question, according to me. One has to forge a new language to deal with it."

Within this context of his role as a man of letters Baldwin worked prodigiously throughout forty years to explore a broad spectrum of themes and topics in his essays, dramas, novels, and poetry. Perhaps chief among those interests were the following: the responsibility of the writer to promote the evolution of the individual and society; the essential need to develop sexual and psychological consciousness and identity; the indivisibility of the private life and the public life; the past historical significance and the current potential explosiveness of color consciousness and the racial crisis; the need for demythologizing the prevailing ethos of American history, religion, and culture; and the intertwining of love and power in the universal scheme of existence as well as in society's structures.

From early teenage preacher in Harlem to activist in the civil rights movement, from book reviewer and essayist for New York periodicals to international celebration as literary artist, Baldwin's more than twenty books and dozens of smaller works attest to the manner in which autobiography becomes transformed into frequently unforgettable expressions of image and insight that transcend the specifics of personal experience to become the means for providing situations and statements of universal applicability that are then inferred to possess even more relevant individual significance. William Styron has called this "Baldwin's effect on the consciousness of the world," achieved through writing "which was flawed, like all writing, but which at its best had a burnished eloquence and devasting impact" and which "revealed to me the end of his soul's savage distress and thus helped me shape and define my own work and its moral contours." And in that regard several of his seminal works are worthy of further commentary: *Go Tell It on the Mountain* (1953), *Notes of a Native Son* (1955), *Nobody Knows My Name* (1961), *The Fire Next Time* (1963), *Blues for Mister Charlie* (1964), and *Just Above My Head* (1979).

Go Tell It on the Mountain was completed in France though its inception had predated Baldwin's exile in Paris in the late 1940s. This novel emerged from his days as a teenage preacher in a Harlem storefront church and from his ambivalent love-hate relationship with his stepfather. Later he would admit that it was "the book I had to write if I was ever going to write anything else. . . . I had to understand the forces, the experience, the life that shaped him before I could grow up myself, before I could become a writer." The novel focuses on the religious conversion of

John Grimes at the age of fourteen and is set in the storefront Temple of the Fire Baptized.

Replete with scriptural references and allusions, biblical names and church practices, *Go Tell It on the Mountain* is still fundamentally not a religious novel; instead, it is a book that draws on a major cultural concept of which religion is merely one facet. This is a sociopolitical novel that indicts the white-controlled society for its radical delimitations of the lives and hopes of blacks, whose skin color offers no hope better than "the back door, and the dark stairs, and the kitchen or basement." Escape seems available only through the options of drugs, drink, sex, or the church. John Grimes must learn to accept reality as recited in the lives of his relatives; and the only options appear to be either to leave the community of the faithful and accept disaster or to remain and reduce his possibilities by embracing a hopeless otherworldly religious experience divorced from reality. Therefore, Baldwin's novel indicts not only white racism but also that form of religious behavior by blacks that is illusory and irrelevant.

The basic means for demonstrating these points of condemnation is the use of irony. Despite his "religious" conversion, nothing is really changed for John Grimes at the end of this novel; "whom the son sets free is free indeed" is a scriptural illusion here. The ethical norm of the book is established and enforced by the community of saints, especially in their effort to be in the world but not of the world; yet each of the principal saints has his or her own secret code of behavior at variance with the so-called norm. John's mother Elizabeth's favorite scriptural passage is "everything works together for good for them that love the Lord," but loving the Lord has made no real change in the pain, suffering, and victimization of her family in the past or present. His stepfather Gabriel's favorite biblical text is "set this house in order," yet all of the households connected with him have been in disorder and his fanatical belief in structure is a rationalization for evading responsibility; the words of Gabriel as "God's messenger" are of despair, deceit, destruction, and disorder. *Go Tell It on the Mountain* thus became, as Baldwin's first book, a prefiguration of themes and motifs that its author would pursue in subsequent writings. Not only did he deride and derogate those who would oversimplify an authentic and effective mode of response to the dominance of the white society over the blacks' existence but also he revealed clearly that the endeavor for refuge in an otherworldly oriented religious experience, rationalized by a concept of God borrowed from the white society and its view of history, is an illusion and, consequently, damnation rather than salvation. It is not surprising, then, that a white critic, Granville Hicks, should note that as in much of the world's greatest literature, the theme of this book was "the strange fatal conflict between the ideal and the reality" or that a black critic, J. Saunders Redding, should suggest that the novel showed the influence of Faulkner, Wright, and Dostoyevski.

Two years later the publication of *Notes of a Native Son* marked the formal entry of Baldwin into the literary tradition of the personal essay. These ten essays, all of which had previously appeared singly in *Commentary, Partisan Review,* and other journals, were mainly autobiographical and impressionistic while offering penetrating and insightful comments on a variety of subjects that were to overlap with the material treated in Baldwin's fiction: the novel of protest, ghetto life in Harlem, black-white encounters in Europe, to specify only a few. The essay "Stranger in the Village" has been much anthologized; it reported on the author's unique experience of being the first black man encountered by a small Swiss village, and it became the instrument for expressing forcefully and cogently the basic premise of the racial revolution in the twentieth century: "the people who shut their eyes to reality simply invite their own destruction.... The world is white no longer and it will never be white again." Because for Baldwin it was the business of a writer to embark on the "journey toward a more vast reality which must take precedence over all other claims," a significant emphasis in this book was in the revelation of what it means to be black, especially in America–that is, to be regarded on the basis of skin color as inherently inferior and evil and thus "to live in a constant state of rage." The poet Langston Hughes contended that these essays were simultaneously "thought-provoking, tantalizing, irritating, advising and amusing" and that "few American writers handled words more effectively in the essay form than James Baldwin."

A few years later thirteen other journal pieces were collected and published under the title *Nobody Knows My Name: More Notes of a Native Son* (1961). The volume concerned predominately "the question of color" as well as the function and problem of being an artist in "the bottomless confusion which is both public and private of the American republic." Conjoining an intense personal honesty with touches of irreverent and extravagant opinion, he ranged over a vista of topics: William Faulkner, Richard Wright, Norman Mailer, the South, Harlem, Andre Gide, Ingmar Bergman, and others. The essay "East River Downtown" debunked the naive notion that local members of the Communist party had inspired the Negro riots at the United Nations following the death of African leader Patrice Lumumba in 1961 and asserted that any venture "to keep the Negro in his 'place' can only have the most extreme and unlucky repercussions." The often reprinted apologia entitled "The Discovery of What It Means to be an American" argues that travel to a foreign country can aid the American writer in gaining "a new sense of life's possibilities" and "unprecedented opportunities" in his own society as he learns that "there are no untroubled countries in this fearfully troubled world." Nick Aaron Ford proclaimed this volume as the "most significant literary work by or about Negroes" published that year and Baldwin as "the most distinguished contemporary Negro writer."

As the civil rights movement intensified during the early 1960s, Baldwin became an active participant. As various groups struggled to end racial discrimination and segregation Baldwin became an increasingly ardent spokesman, enunciating in essays and speeches the agony of being black in America. While the role was not new for him, the activities of the 1960s were undertaken because of his reputation. Whether with Medgar Evers or James Meredith in Mississippi, at a session with Robert Kennedy in New York, on a speaking tour for the Congress of Racial Equality, or helping in the voter registration drive in Selma, Alabama, Baldwin was committed "to end the racial nightmare of our country and change the history of the world." The culmination of his literary effort in this era was the publication of *The Fire Next Time*, a treatise which very likely helped "in restoring the personal essay to its place as a form of creative literature," as John Henrik Clarke has asserted. Additionally, a persuasive case can be made that with this treatise, as well as some other examples, Baldwin assumed a position among the most memorable American essayists: Ralph Waldo Emerson, Henry David Thoreau, Mark Twain, James Thurber, H. L. Mencken, E. B. White, and others.

The Fire Next Time consists of two essays in the form of letters, with the first as prefatory to the beliefs and concepts presented in the second. "My Dungeon Shook" contains advice to a young black male who is the author's nephew and is about to enter the domain of racial conflict on the 100th anniversary of the proclamation that is supposed to have set him free. It is a forthright assault upon the "impertinent assumption . . . that black men are inferior to white men" and an assertion of the black's inherent "unassailable and monumental dignity."

The second essay, "Down at the Cross," is an autobiographical account in three sections: recollections of growing up in Harlem, an evaluation of the Black Muslims, and a statement of personal credo. The Harlem section analyzes the psychological condition of learning to be black and "fighting the man" in a "white country, an Anglo-Teutonic, anti-sexual country," of experiencing the principles of "Blindness, Loneliness, and Terror" in the Christian church, and of recognizing that "if the concept of God has any validity or any use, it can only be to make us larger, freer, and loving." The Black Muslim portion evaluates Elijah Muhammad as a charismatic and disciplined leader who "refuses to accept the white world's definitions" and therefore threatens its power. The "personal credo" posits a series of ideas relevant to contemporary America: the fact that "life is tragic"; the need "to apprehend the nature of change, to be able and willing to change"; the importance of discarding "that collection of myths to which white Americans cling"; the reality that blacks may not rise to power "but they are very well placed indeed to precipitate chaos and ring down the curtain on the American dream." Finally, in a note of compelling alarm, Baldwin prophesies that "the relatively conscious" whites and blacks may be able "to end the racial nightmare, and achieve our country, and change the history of the world"; otherwise, "no more water the fire next time."

Although this book did not offer any easy solutions to the political, social, and psychological conditions of being black in America, it did suggest democracy as a means of promoting change and set forth what could be expected if such change were not forthcoming. Perhaps the greatest value of the essay's rhetorical flourishes of confession, anguish, quest, and warning was its dramatization of emotional conditions with the underlying design of evoking the emotional response of empathy. Critic Irving Howe said that

The Fire Next Time had reached "heights of passionate exhortation unmatched in modern American writing" and had thereby for the author "secured his place as one of these two or three greatest essayists this country has ever produced."

A year later Baldwin completed the drama *Blues for Mister Charlie* which enjoyed a run in New York of 150 performances. The play is an obvious reflection of the author's engagement in the civil rights movement and is based on the case of Emmett Till, a black youth from Chicago who was murdered in 1955 in Mississippi for supposedly flirting with a white woman. Two white men were indicted and subsequently acquitted of the crime by an all-white jury, though one of the alleged killers subsequently bragged about the murder and recounted the details. Some critics have dismissed the drama as propagandistic, bombastic, and melodramatic; others have lauded the manner in which it reveals the myths and stereotypes pertaining to black-white relations, a thematic concern that Baldwin had poignantly explored earlier in *The Fire Next Time*.

Blues for Mister Charlie is a complex drama that uses its dual settings for Whitetown (the courthouse) and Blacktown (the church) to present several stories and to explore several ideas simultaneously. Whereas Richard Henry, the young black entertainer who has returned home from New York after being hooked on dope, and the black student Juanita, who is friendly with the local white liberal newspaper editor, and Lyle Britten, the white store owner who kills Richard, play central roles in the unfolding story, the two major characters are Parnell James, the editor, and the Reverend Meridian Henry, local minister and father of Richard. These latter two figures embody the persistent motif of Baldwin's work at this point in his literary career: namely, the need for "the relatively conscious whites and the relatively conscious blacks, who must, like lovers, insist on, or create the consciousness of the others." Unfortunately, and rather tragically, *Blues for Mister Charlie* concludes with Parnell James, the white liberal, lacking the courage to testify at the trial that Jo Britten has lied about Richard, and with Meridian Henry, the embodiment of black moderation and nonviolence, conjoining "the Bible and the gun" in the pulpit "like the pilgrims of old." Darwin Turner has suggested in his essay "Visions of Love and Manliness in a Blackening World" that *Blues for Mister Charlie* was written for a white audience and belongs in the general category of that "traditional drama" which stresses the similarities between blacks and whites, examines the dilemma of middle-class blacks, and uses black characters who challenge whites verbally but passively reject physical confrontation.

In *Blues for Mister Charlie* as well as the later production *The Amen Corner* (1968), Baldwin uses motifs common to his fiction. His success as a playwright, however, remains even now a moot question. On one side is the typical contention, as voiced by Gerald Weales, that "despite the incidental virtues of both plays, they indicate that the dramatic form is not a congenial one for Baldwin." In stark contrast, however, Carlton Molette has reasoned in "James Baldwin as Playwright" that the author, being essentially a novelist and essayist, has shown as dramatist his trust of and reliance upon many other artists; that "the ability to accomplish that collaborative working relationship" may well account for his dramatic success when so many other novelists have failed; and that "given the present system of producing plays professionally in the United States, we are lucky indeed to get one play per decade from the likes of James Baldwin." Extraordinarily, Baldwin has been one of the few black playwrights who has had more than one production on Broadway.

Subsequent to *Blues for Mister Charlie* one work after another appeared over the years—short stories, essays, novels, dialogues. Nevertheless, Baldwin's most ambitious undertaking in fiction was perhaps *Just Above My Head*. Critical reactions to the novel were indeed mixed. Richard Gilman referred to "the disagreeable work of reviewing" the book and found it "a melancholy piece of creation," an "apologia for homosexuality" that alternates in dialogue between jive and street talk on the one hand and literary hyperbole on the other. Paul Darcy Boles, however, argued that "the power of love redeems the dead as well as the living" in this work which "continually discards outworn and shallow visions of existence" and rejects all pat religious or political answers to difficult human problems.

This novel is long (nearly 600 pages) and complex. Baldwin uses gospel music for purposes of structural organization, character development, and thematic emphasis; and common to those three uses is the aesthetic concept of music and its accompanying lyrics as "the verbalization of deeply felt feelings," feelings which in their totality of expression offer a sensitive statement about the meaning of being human. In the early essay "Many Thousands Gone" Baldwin had asserted that "it is only in his music, which Americans are able to admire because a protective sentimentality limits their understanding of it, that the Negro in America has been able to tell his story." Later, in *The Fire Next Time*, he was to attest that "there is no music like that music . . . and all those voices coming together and crying holy unto the Lord. . . . I have never seen anything equal to the fire and excitement that sometimes, without warning, fills a church, causing the church, as Leadbelly and so many others have testified, to 'rock.'" Again, in the same essay he described the crucial relationship between music, including gospel songs, and the concepts of freedom and survival: "In spite of everything there was in the life I fled a zest and a joy and a capacity for facing and surviving disaster that are very moving and very rare. . . . We sometimes achieved with each other freedom that was close to love. . . . This is the freedom that one hears in some gospel songs, for example, and in jazz. In all jazz, and especially in the blues, there is something tart and ironic, authoritative and double-edged."

Through its central focus on gospel music in the lives of brothers Hall and Arthur Montana, this novel explores such themes as the civil rights movement, the Korean War and the draft, the storefront church and religious passion, childhood preaching, incest, white racism, homosexuality, and the family.

Between this novel and Baldwin's death, four other books appeared. *The Price of the Ticket: Collected Nonfiction 1948-1985* (1985) was a compilation of fifty-one essays previously published and introduced by an autobiographical essay that is both confessional and revelatory. *The Evidence of Things Not Seen* (1985) was a polemic and meditation motivated by the infamous series of Atlanta, Georgia, child murders in late 1979 and the early 1980s. Using the arrest of Wayne Williams and the series of murders as basic subjects, Baldwin roamed over myriad subjects relevant to the general conditions of American society in the 1980s, with special attention to a familiar and often used leitmotiv: the problem of being black in white America. The most serious indictment, nevertheless, is focused on the coveted conception of the American Dream as "the final manifestation of the European/Western Christian dominance." Also published in 1985 was a small volume of verse: *Jimmy's Blues: Selected Poems*. The collection expresses numerous moods in its varying emphases and embodies emotions that are acute and intense and clothed in irony. An excursion through the poems confronts the commitment and the toughness of Baldwin's earlier essays, dramas, and novels. His last book, the novel *Harlem Quartet*, appeared in 1987.

A cursory glance at the various honors bestowed upon James Baldwin for literary attainments connotes the respect afforded him as a writer: Guggenheim Fellowship; National Conference of Christians and Jews Brotherhood Award; Foreign Drama Critics Award; National Institute of Arts and Letters membership; and the Legion of Honor (France). Both by the quantity and the quality of his endeavors his place is now secure in the mainstream of American literature. Louis Pratt has convincingly shown how Baldwin analyzed "the black experience for its universal dimensions" and used "that experience as a means of joining hands with humanity, with the universal brotherhood of mankind, and this effort may prove to be his ultimate triumph and distinction." As novelist, essayist, dramatist, and social critic, his corpus demonstrates unequivocably both a sustained productivity and a consistent and sensitive human perspective. At times alternately praised and damned by blacks and whites alike, he never lacked an audience. While the rationale for this public interest obviously consists of multiple factors, the principal elements would surely include his prophetic tone, moral concern, existential analysis, perceptive relevance, intense language, and poignant sincerity. In conclusion Benjamin De Mott's declaration seems irrefutable: "this author retains a place in an extremely select group: that comprised of the few genuinely indispensable American writers."

Jimmy was the only one of us who had magic in his style and his person both. So he paid twice as much for his talent, and had half as many good days as he needed, and probably deserved.

—Norman Mailer

Richard Ellmann

(15 March 1918-13 May 1987)

Steven Serafin
Hunter College of the City University of New York

"Quiet takes back her folded fields. Tranquille thanks. Adew."

—Finnegans Wake

"Biographies of men and women who have played a part in history emphasize the convergence of the individual with social forces, and do not often fasten on what they were like when alone. But a writer's life," as Richard Ellmann would characteristically remind us, "must necessarily be passed largely in seclusion, closeted with the implements of his profession, turned inward in order to turn outward." This is the legacy which at once entices and possesses the biographer in the intricate passage from "puzzle to portrait." Life writing is a unique form of literary expression, an art made possible by the combination of intuition and introspection. No longer merely a craft serving a useful purpose, biography has emerged as one of the major developments in twentieth-century literature, and the flowering of the genre is notably attributed to biographers of exceptional ability and vision, among them Leon Edel, Leslie Marchand, George Painter, and perhaps of most importance, Richard Ellmann.

The aim of modern biography is not to create but rather to re-create. "To live other people's lives is nothing," wrote Henry James, "unless we live over their perceptions, live over the growth, the change, the varying intensity of the same–since it was by these things they themselves lived." In essence, biography of distinction is often determined by the degree of intimacy which exists between subject and author. For this reason it is difficult to think of Henry James for instance without thinking of Edel, or Lord Byron without Marchand, or Marcel Proust without Painter. Similarly, it is difficult to think of the great writers of Irish literature–W. B. Yeats, James Joyce, or Oscar Wilde–without thinking of Ellmann. The subject of biography is essentially realized by the version of the subject offered by the biographer. Consequently, if we know Yeats, or Joyce, or Wilde, we know them as Ellmann

Richard Ellmann (photograph © Jerry Bauer)

wanted us to see them. It was this responsibility that he embraced with both conviction and reverence.

As a young man coming of age with an intense passion for learning, Ellmann early engaged in what would become a lifelong love affair with language and literature. His was a world peopled by those with whom he shared an infinite and often solitary pleasure. Eminently successful as a teacher, scholar, and author, he would provide a unique contribution as a man of letters. Known primarily for his biography of James Joyce, which is generally acknowledged as the definitive work on the novelist, Ellmann would be largely responsible for establishing a standard of excellence in the art of contemporary life writing. His academic career spanned nearly fifty years, and he remained a productive and influential literary personage despite the effects of a debilitating ailment at the end of his life. Shortly before his death at sixty-nine years of age, Ellmann completed his long-awaited biography of Oscar Wilde, a publication which has rekindled interest in both the subject and the biographer. Virtually assured a permanent position in the history of literary biography, Ellmann has given new and sustained meaning to an ancient art.

Born on 15 March 1918 in the "small and comparatively quiet enclave" of Highland Park, Michigan, Richard Ellmann was the son of James Irving Ellmann, a lawyer, and Jeanette Barsook Ellmann. Encouraged by his parents, Ellmann turned his affinity for the written word into an academic commitment and unlike his brothers who went into law made "the eccentric choice" of pursuing a career in teaching. Ellmann attended Yale University where he received his B.A. in 1939 and his M.A. in 1941. While at Yale he was first introduced to the poetry of Yeats, an author who would have a lasting and significant impression on his artistic sensibility. Although Yeats was "suspiciously and brazenly modern," Ellmann decided on the poet as the subject for literary analysis and was thoroughly immersed in the study of Irish literature while teaching at Harvard University when academic life was interrupted by military service. During World War II Ellmann served in the Navy and eventually in the Office of Strategic Services. Not one to bypass opportunity, while stationed in London Ellmann arranged a visit to Dublin where he met with Yeats's widow. Receptive to Ellmann's interest in writing her husband's biography, Mrs. Yeats offered him her complete cooperation and assistance in the project.

At the close of the war Ellmann received a fellowship in the humanities from the Rockefeller Foundation which allowed him the opportunity to return to both Ireland and England, where he spent thirteen months determined to unravel the web of the "immortal" Yeats. Ellmann considered Yeats one of the major literary figures of the age, an artist who "lived several lifetimes in one and made his development inseparable from that of modern verse and, to some extent, modern man." Attempting to bridge critical analysis with factual biography, Ellmann fashioned a lasting tribute to the poet, first in the form of his doctoral dissertation which was awarded the John

Addison Porter Prize in 1947 and then as a full-length biography published the following year as *Yeats: The Man and the Masks.*

Completed eight years after the poet's death, the biography was greatly enhanced by the involvement of Yeats's friends, acquaintances, and relations, above all by Mrs. Yeats, who proved an invaluable source of detail and creative insight. "I am grateful to her," wrote Ellmann, "not only for lending me manuscripts, a suitcaseful at a time, but for helping to interpret them." The manuscripts, which amassed nearly 50,000 pages of unpublished materials including "autobiographical notes, drafts of poems, letters, diaries, and other papers," allowed Ellmann access to the private life of the public persona. The result was a scholarly study praised as "thorough and precise" as well as "lively and entertaining," the qualities of biography which would ultimately define Ellmann's reputation.

Having simultaneously earned his Ph.D. from Yale and his B.Litt. from Trinity College, Dublin, Ellmann resumed his teaching career at Harvard where he was named Briggs-Copeland Assistant Professor of English Composition from 1948-1951. On 12 August 1949 Ellmann married Mary Donahue, who had also taken a doctoral degree from Yale and was herself an aspiring writer. The marriage would prove to be a resourceful bond. Ellmann shared with his wife the measure of his literary success, and she in turn became for him a source of critical perception, companionship, and sensitivity. In 1951 Ellmann's career was further enhanced by his translation of Henri Michaux's *L'Espace du dedans*, which was published under the title of *Selected Writings of Henri Michaux.* Briefly stationed in Paris during the war, Ellmann was introduced to the poems of Michaux and then to the poet himself. "Being subversive of all organized concepts, and unpretentious in the most ironical way," Michaux offered an interesting counter to Yeats and would provide Ellmann an opportunity for reflection.

In that same year Ellmann joined the faculty of Northwestern University, where he was named Franklin Bliss Snyder Professor of English from 1964-1968. While at Northwestern he completed his critical assessment of Yeats's poetry which was published in 1954 as *The Identity of Yeats*, an event which marked the beginning of Ellmann's literary association with Oxford University Press. Attempting to shed new light on the development of Yeats's thought and "the unending labour of the creative art," *The Identity of Yeats* at

Dust jacket for the first revision of Ellmann's most highly acclaimed work, incorporating nearly one hundred pages of new text and 117 illustrations, many never before published

once enhanced Ellmann's stature as a scholar and paved the way for his most significant achievement. During an interview with Yeats's widow, Ellmann asked Mrs. Yeats about "the notorious first meeting" between her husband and James Joyce, which occurred in 1902. In response she produced an unpublished document in which Yeats summarized the encounter. "Joyce's impudence with his distinguished and much older contemporary" suggested to Ellmann the possibility of exploring "the relations of the two writers." Instead he gradually turned his full attention to Joyce and twelve years later completed "the fascinating life story of one of the greatest creative writers of modern times." Published in 1959, *James Joyce* was acclaimed a major artistic achievement and pronounced by critical consensus as a biography "justified on every count as definitive." It has since become recognized as a model for literary scholarship and a contribution of lasting importance to the art of life writing.

James Joyce was a complex as well as intriguing subject for biography. "To his Irish contemporaries," remarked Ellmann, Joyce was considered "obscure and very likely mad." To the English, he was quite naturally "eccentric and 'Irish.'" To Ellmann, Joyce was at once enigma and genius. "Faithful to his own principle that random gestures might be as characteristic of the mind as its more formal behavior, I thought to present life with a little of the density of actual experience, yet always with at least covert reference to certain ruling passions and to his writings." Nearly eight years in preparation, during which time Ellmann seemingly interviewed every "surviving friend and relation" while retracing each step of Joyce's self-perpetuated odyssey, the finished product was acknowledged by Stuart Gilbert as "a masterpiece of scholarly objectivity and exact research." Assembled "with a mastery Joyce himself would have admired," the narrative amounted to "more than 300,000 words, ballasted with sixty pages of documentation and more than 2,000 citations of testimony." In celebrating "the fictional giant of our time" Ellmann presented both the man and the artist, "not only the puzzles, but the world in which they become valid, the creative mind of Joyce."

Absorbing the reader "like a great novel," *James Joyce* was indeed a literary phenomenon, a work of art, as noted by T. E. Cassidy, which would "stand with honor beside the work of the honored." Yet perhaps the most accurate description of Ellmann's contribution was provided by Cyril Connolly: "I do not know whether to be more impressed by the scholarship, patience, industry and devotion of such a biographer or to be appalled by the standard he sets. . . . If Joyce be a great writer, then this is a great book." *James Joyce* received the National Book Award for nonfiction in 1960. In that same year it also received the Friends of Literature Award in biography, the Thormond Monsen Award from the Society of Midland Authors, and the Carey-Thomas Award for creative book publishing to Oxford University Press. The biography of Joyce was unquestionably a professional as well as personal turning point for Ellmann. Shortly after its publication he ruminated about the future of his career: "There really aren't any other modern writers that measure up to Yeats or Joyce. I can't think of anyone else I'd want to work on the way I've worked on them." Having fixed "Joyce's image for a generation" Ellmann would essentially return to Yeats as a source for both inspiration and continuance. Upon the literary horizon, however, loomed the presence of yet another subject for Ellmann to engage. Taking his place at the same table with Yeats and Joyce would be Oscar Wilde, company Ellmann would keep for the remainder of his life.

Encouraged by the favorable reception of his biography of Joyce, Ellmann responded to his sudden preeminence with a markedly different pursuit, a joint venture with Charles Feidelson, Jr., investigating "the intellectual backgrounds of modern literature." Based on the conviction that "modern writers, for all their variety, were in some sense engaged in a communal enterprise of an imaginative kind," the pattern of modernism was thoroughly explored in *The Modern Tradition: Backgrounds of Modern Literature* which appeared in 1965. Fascinated with the nature and intricacy of literary "influence," Ellmann similarly offered both definition and clarity to Yeats's position in the scheme of modernism. Ellmann admired Yeats for his refusal "to subside, like some writers, into addled repetitiveness" and for his ability to extract from others what was necessary to advance his artistry. "Among poets he was one of the most generous," Ellmann observed, "not so generous however as to fail to take over what he needed." Published in 1967, *Eminent Domain: Yeats Among Wilde, Joyce, Pound, Eliot, and Auden* admirably juxtaposed the poet in relation to his illustrious contemporaries in the progression of literary history.

In 1968 Ellmann left Northwestern to become professor of English at Yale for a two-year period prior to becoming a fellow at New College, Oxford University, Oxford, England, as well as Goldsmiths' Professor of English Literature, the first American to be given the distinction. In his inaugural lecture Ellmann incorporated personal experience in order to address the responsibilities confronting the contemporary biographer. "More than anything else," he said, "we want in modern biography to see the character forming, its peculiarities taking shape." During his tenure at Oxford, Ellmann adhered to his own pronouncement in preparing his biography of Wilde while simultaneously continuing his exploration of the parameters of modern literature with such publications as *Ulysses on the Liffey* (1972), based on his 1971 Eliot Memorial Lectures at the University of Kent, *Golden Codgers: Biographical Speculations* (1973), and *The Consciousness of Joyce* (1977). In addition, he edited *The Norton Anthology of Modern Poetry* (1973),

Dust jacket for the American edition of Ellmann's definitive critical biography of Wilde

with Robert O'Clair, *The Selected Letters of James Joyce* (1975), and *The New Oxford Book of American Verse* (1976).

Prolific as well as demanding, Ellmann enjoyed a great reputation for scholarship and an academic career of diversification and distinction. He was a fellow of the American Academy and Institute of Arts and Letters, the British Academy, and the Royal Society of Literature. He was also a Guggenheim fellow in 1950, 1957-1958, and 1970 and a School of Letters fellow at Indiana University in 1956 and 1960 and a senior fellow from 1966 to 1972. He served as Frederick Ives Carpenter Visiting Professor at the University of Chicago in 1959, 1967, and from 1975 to 1977 and as visiting professor at Emory University from 1978 to 1981 where he was also named Woodruff Professor of English from 1982 to the time of his death. Ellmann held membership in the Modern Language Association of America, serving as the chairman of the English Institute from 1961 to 1962 and as a member of the executive council from 1961 to 1965, the United States/ United Kingdom Educational Commission, Phi Beta Kappa, Chi Delta Theta, and Signet. Ellmann received recognition for independent research from the American Philosophical Society, the *Kenyon Review,* and the National Endowment for the Humanities. Internationally recognized for his literary contribution, Ellmann received honorary degrees from various academic institutions both in the United States and abroad, including Northwestern, Emory, Boston College, the University of Rochester, Oxford, McGill University, the University of Gothenburg (Sweden), and the National University of Ireland.

Ellmann was an extraordinary individual of rare and exceptional talent. Among the vanguard of contemporary literary biographers emerging in the postwar decade he fulfilled "the ideal of sympathetic intuition" in re-creating and virtually reliving the lives of his subjects. It would be this attribute, as perceived by literary critic and fellow biographer Jeffrey Meyers, which would cast its shadow on "most subsequent literary biographies" of the age. Ellmann essentially redefined the art of biography. He loved language as he loved life and never failed in his work, as Anthony Burgess would astutely observe, "to stimulate, instruct, amuse and, for this writer, reawaken a sleeping belief in the glory of making literature."

Stricken in February 1986 with amyotrophic lateral sclerosis, a degenerative nerve condition commonly known as Lou Gehrig's disease, Ellmann completed in the last weeks of his life the final revisions of his biography of Oscar Wilde, published in 1987 by Hamish Hamilton in England and in January 1988 by Alfred A. Knopf in the United States. Richard Ellmann died 13 May 1987 in Oxford, England, survived by his wife and three children, Maud Esther, Lucy Elizabeth, and Stephen Jonathan.

Ironically, it was James Joyce who declared the biographer a "biografiend"; yet as Ellmann would remind us, "he also supplied the precedent for seeing his subject in all postures in order to know him." For this reason, "writers like Kafka, Eliot, Orwell and Auden vainly tried to protect their posthumous privacy by requesting that no biography be written about them." Joyce as well as his Irish compatriot Oscar Wilde might have agonized less in knowing Ellmann would write the story of his life. It was Wilde who professed every great man has his disciples, and it is usually Judas who writes the biography. Surely no Judas, Ellmann would neither deceive nor deny. Each writer leaves ajar the door of possibility, a door Ellmann opened for Wilde as he did Yeats and Joyce, with a sense of wonderment and grace.

Frederick A. Pottle
(3 August 1897-16 May 1987)

Irma S. Lustig
University of Pennsylvania

As editor, bibliographer, and biographer of James Boswell, Frederick Albert Pottle fulfilled both sides of his nature: he was research scholar and creative writer as well. Pottle was seriously committed to a career in chemistry when, in his senior year at Colby College, Maine (A.B. 1917), he came upon a volume of Shelley's poems, read through the night, and underwent, as he himself said, an almost instant conversion. He grew his hair long, affected a Byronic collar, defied authority, and boldly announced himself a poet. From 1918 to 1919, while on voluntary service in France as a surgical assistant with U.S. Army Evacuation Hospital No. 8, he devoured the volume of Browning he had borrowed from the embarkation library, wrote poems, and looked forward to the serious study of literature. In 1921 his war poems won honorable mention in the competition for the Cook Poetry Prize at Yale University, where he had begun graduate study (Ph.D. 1925), but (to paraphrase him again), within a month of entering Yale he fell passionately in love with literary scholarship, and like Congreve's Millamant, who consented to dwindle into a wife, he consented to dwindle into a scholar and teacher.

But he did not relinquish his ambition to be a man of letters. He vowed that in writing for specialists, which gave him the greatest pleasure in the doing, he would always be graceful, and that he would also write occasionally for the general reader, giving literary form to the product of research.

Pottle had planned in graduate school to make the Romantic poets his major subject; indeed, his first book, published in 1923, was *Shelley and Browning*. Throughout his career he also wrote occasionally on William Wordsworth and Sir Walter Scott; one of the disappointments of his later life was that he had not been able to make a major study of Scott. During Pottle's long and distinguished tenure at Yale University (1925-1966), he was as well known for his influential courses in nineteenth-century British litera-

Frederick Pottle in his office at work on the Boswell papers (photograph by William B. Carter, Alumni Communications and Public Information, Yale University)

ture as for his small class, "Special Studies in the Eighteenth Century" (if more than three students enrolled, he created a second section). Upon his approaching retirement from the faculty, his colleagues and former students recognized his interests by a festschrift entitled *From Sensibility to Romanticism* (1965).

Pottle's primary literary subject was determined, however, when Chauncey Brewster Tinker, father of eighteenth-century studies at Yale, suggested that he undertake as his thesis a bibliography of the works of James Boswell. Pottle wanted to work under Tinker; he was persuaded, moreover, by the extensive materials for original research and by the conviction that scientific bibliography was an essential preliminary to writing the life of a literary man. So he argued in the introduction to the expansion of his thesis, *The Literary Career of James Boswell, Esq.*, published by the Clarendon Press in 1929. By that date Pottle had realized that his chance of making an impact on contemporary literature was as Boswell's biographer.

The Literary Career set a new standard in an already exacting field of scholarship. It was reprinted, with a new introduction, in 1965 and 1967, and despite the cache of Boswellian materials discovered since 1929, remains to this day the standard resource of scholars, collectors, and booksellers because of its scope and accuracy, full collations, careful discrimination of variant issues, and many facsimiles. Pottle's deductions from the evidence then at hand were prophetic, and he advanced considerably the facts of Boswell's life and career. Over the years Pottle also provided researchers with updated information in a succession of catalogs and indexes, the most recent and accessible of them his fastidious entry on Boswell in the *New Cambridge Bibliography of English Literature,* volume 2 (1971).

The Literary Career proved to be a talisman at once. Pottle had had access in preparing it to the materials from Malahide Castle, Ireland, which had only recently become known and acquired by Lt. Col. Ralph Heyward Isham. Isham was printing Boswell's journal privately in an edition designed by Bruce Rogers and limited to 570 sets when his editor, Geoffrey Scott, died suddenly after completing the sixth volume. A day or two after his death an unsealed letter to Pottle found in one of Scott's pockets was brought to Isham. He took it as a message of guidance, for Scott had written to express his profound admiration—"amazement rather"—at the total achievement of *The Literary Career,* which he had just read. On 7 November 1929 Isham announced in a red-covered brochure matched to the Malahide volumes that Pottle had accepted appointment as Scott's successor, and in fact, was already at work. In 1931 he brought out with his wife, Marion Starbird Pottle, a catalog to Isham's papers, and by 1934 completed the twelve final volumes of Boswell's journal. In 1937 he published with the assistance of Joseph Foladare, John P. Kirby, and others an index to the edition

which is indispensable to eighteenth-century scholars of all kinds.

The Private Papers of James Boswell from Malahide Castle in the Collection of Lt-Colonel Ralph Heyward Isham preserves the spelling and capitalization of the manuscripts and furnishes only minimal annotation to the journal. At Isham's request Pottle prepared a trade edition with modernized text and extensive annotation, all the volumes to be published simultaneously by the Viking Press. But the work was outdated by the repeated discovery of Boswell materials, and Isham bought out the contract with Viking to clear the way for a new and final enterprise. In 1949 he sold the Malahide Papers with the successive finds he had acquired by purchase and litigation to Yale University, where he had been a student but taken no degree. Pottle, Sterling Professor of English since 1944, was named chairman of the editorial committee established to prepare the manuscripts for the press and see them through to bound books; he was also appointed general editor of both the trade and research volumes of the journal (his Viking manuscript became the foundation of the trade edition). Though he stepped down as chairman in 1979 he continued to work daily at his other duties until complications from a fall forced him to withdraw to his home in 1984.

Alone or in association with other scholars, Pottle brought out twelve volumes of the trade edition of the journal—all but the last volume—in the Yale editions of the private papers of James Boswell. He had a larger hand in two research volumes of Boswell's correspondence than he claimed and worked closely with two editors of the forthcoming research edition of the journal.

For fifty-five years Pottle worked with undiminished dedication at the scholarly task which gave him the most intense pleasure: editing unpublished manuscripts. Any unpublished manuscripts would have done, he told the Johnson Society of the Northwest in 1968, but Boswell furnished an extraordinary quantity and variety of documents. Moreover, he fulfilled Pottle's desire for literary creation because the journal had the prime qualities of twentieth-century writing. Its appeal was not limited to specialists, and it could be published competitively, without sacrifice of scholarship, in a trade edition.

The first volume in the Yale Boswell editions, *Boswell's London Journal, 1762-1763,* which was published in 1950, was adopted by book clubs and sold at least over half a million copies in all languages, in part, of course, because of its novelty and raciness, but also because Boswell's themes, his candor, and the clarity of his style engaged modern readers. By this volume alone the McGraw-Hill Book Company recovered the costs of the advance which enabled Yale University to buy the papers and gave the book company sole rights of publication in the United States. William Heinemann Ltd. secured the rights for Great Britain. Sales for successive volumes of the journal fell off drastically in numbers, but each publication has been acclaimed as a model of bookmaking and of scholarship, and an ardent following of readers and collectors is spread worldwide. Boswell's gregariousness, and his passion to live vividly and to record his experience, have preserved the eighteenth century in more intimate and comprehensive detail than any other work of the period. Bringing out his journal also greatly enlarged public knowledge of Boswell, who was famous as the author of the *Account of Corsica* (1768) by age twenty-eight but by the nineteenth century was known chiefly as Samuel Johnson's biographer and toady. Editing the trade edition of Boswell's journal did indeed satisfy Pottle's ambition as an author to add to the literature of our time. It is a remarkable coincidence that he died on 16 May in 1987, the date in 1763 that Boswell met Johnson.

Editing Boswell's journal was a creative achievement, as Pottle believed, not merely reflected glory, because aside from the *London Journal*, which he could print as a single, continuous manuscript, he and his collaborators had to compile the other volumes, give them shape as well as continuity. The journal suffers numerous lapses and losses, and completing the record chronologically, chiefly in Boswell's own words, requires artistry as well as research. Pottle's own favorite of the series was *Boswell in Holland, 1763-1764* (1952), which is virtually a substitute for a quarto manuscript of over five hundred pages lost in Boswell's lifetime. Pottle had to reconstruct the period from notes, memoranda, verses, letters, language exercises, and other miscellaneous papers.

He also rightly claimed that introductions and annotation (for the most part from primary sources) were a form of literary art. His certainly were, and he worked painstakingly with his associates to make all the notes harmonious and to place them exactly where needed. He was loath to relinquish a manuscript until he was satisfied that he could do no more. But when he did let

go, he began a new book at once with fresh vigor and joy.

Editing the journal chronologically and studying more than ten thousand Boswellian documents necessary to augment and annotate it–the correspondence, Register of Letters, Book of Company and Liquors, legal papers, periodical journalism, family charters, and so on–prepared Pottle uniquely for *his* magnum opus, his Rachel, as he said, during the many years that the journal was his Leah. *James Boswell: The Earlier Years, 1740-1769,* volume one of the two volumes Pottle projected, was published by McGraw-Hill in 1966 and recognized by many readers as one of the great biographies of the twentieth century. Here was the climactic demonstration of Pottle's mastery of the whole as well as of detail. Chiefly chronological in design, comprehensive and scrupulously factual (discreet back-notes reveal the extent of Pottle's investigation), *The Earlier Years* tells the story of Boswell's life to his marriage and first literary success with a fictional power that lures the reader from one chapter to the next. Pottle had always been an expressive stylist, with a large, precise vocabulary at his command, but comparing the biography with the more florid passages of the introductions to the Malahide Papers reveals that he had refined his style over the years.

No one could have been less like Boswell than Frederick Pottle, a gentle, soft-spoken man, reserved but firm in his own moral and religious convictions. It was typical of his penetrating mind and generous spirit, however, that he is both objective and sympathetic in illuminating Boswell's Manichaean character. Unlike Boswell himself, Pottle is seldom intrusive–no sidetracks or vendetta. He hews to his main structural principles, Boswell as a Scot of family, as lawyer, and writer, and fulfills the prime responsibility he assumed as Boswell's biographer, to define and assess Boswell's literary genius.

Pottle had intended to collaborate in writing the second volume of Boswell's life with the late Frank Brady (Distinguished Professor of English, City University of New York Graduate Center), his former student, co-editor of two volumes of the journal, and successor as chairman of the editorial committee of the Boswell editions. But late in the 1970s he turned the work over wholly to Brady, as Brady wished, and resumed what turned out to be his final individual project, the history of the Boswell Papers. Pottle had long ago extended and revised the version he had writ-

Dust jacket for the first volume of Pottle's projected two-volume biography of Boswell; Frank Brady completed the project.

ten for the *de luxe* edition of the *London Journal* published by Heinemann in 1951. But he had set his manuscript aside in deference to David Buchanan's *The Treasure of Auchinleck* (1974), a work to which Pottle made major contributions, as Buchanan later made contributions to Pottle's account. *Pride and Negligence: The History of the Boswell Papers,* published by McGraw-Hill in 1981, was therefore preempted; still, it discloses much that was hitherto unknown, presents another version of events, and brings the history of publication up to date. Though very detailed, the book is thoroughly engrossing, not least because of the autobiographical thread through which one glimpses the author's patience and integrity.

In addition to the two massive series of Boswell's journal, the bibliographies, and the biography, Pottle published other important books over the long course of his career. In 1927 he brought out with Professor Tinker *A New Portrait of James Boswell,* in which they established that this now well-known painting (it served as dust jacket of *The Earlier Years*) had been done by George Willison in Rome in 1765. They repro-

duced the painting for the first time and all other known portraits and sketches of Boswell. In 1929, the year of *The Literary Career,* Pottle also published *Stretchers,* the history of the army medical unit in which he had served. In 1936 he published, with Charles H. Bennett, the original manuscript of Boswell's *Journal of a Tour to the Hebrides* (reprinted with additions and an expanded index as volume eight in the Yale editions, 1963). In 1938 Pottle brought out *Boswell and the Girl from Botany Bay,* a slightly modified version of his presidential address to the Elizabethan Club of Yale University on 4 May 1932. Even in his last years Boswell sprang to the defense of the underdog, and Pottle writes movingly of his efforts to win freedom for five convicts, among them Mary Bryant, who escaped a penal colony and in a small boat made the treacherous voyage across the South Seas to England. In 1793 Boswell won a legal pardon for the woman and continued to press for the release of the four men, who were freed by proclamation late in the year.

In 1941 Pottle delivered the Messenger Lectures at Cornell University, published them that same year as the *Idiom of Poetry,* and again, in 1946, in a revised edition with additional essays. At the height of New Criticism he argued for critical relativism, basing his case on historical "shifts of sensibility." Martin Price, now Sterling Professor of English and Chairman of the Editorial Committee of the Yale Boswell Editions, says that for him as a student the book was intellectually liberating. It was characteristic of its author, whom Price found "open to ideas and personalities all together different from his own. . . . In his undergraduate lectures on Romantic poetry he deliberately presented a traditional historical approach in the early weeks, then gave equal time to a New Critical approach to the poems themselves. What was most remarkable in his teaching and his scholarship was the stretch of imagination that could see others in their own terms first of all."

It must be remembered that Pottle accomplished this prodigious feat of scholarship and literature, directed the Boswell project, and carefully read proof in all stages for every volume while also carrying a heavy load of professorial duties almost to the age of sixty-nine. He was chairman of the English department from 1932 through 1933, director of graduate studies in English from 1939 to 1945, and served on many graduate school committees throughout his tenure. He supervised innumerable doctoral dissertations in both eighteenth- and nineteenth-century literature. Outside the university he served his allegiances in many capacities, among them as a trustee of the General Theological Seminary for twenty-one years, 1947 to 1968, and of Colby College for thirty-nine years, 1932 to 1959, and 1966 to 1978, after which he was appointed honorary life trustee. Elected to the American Philosophical Society in 1960, he served on the research committee, which met in Philadelphia five times a year, from 1967 to 1979, and as a consultant thereafter to his death. In preparation for the meetings he read scrupulously the usual batch of 150 to 250 applications for grants.

How did he do so much? Not with the aid of a large and specialized staff, as the "Boswell Factory," the familiar but ironic name for the project, implies. That term was given affectionately to a moderate-sized room in a third-floor wing of Sterling Library where files and primary reference works were ranged around the walls and a motley assortment of desks and tables was crowded back-to-back and side-to-side. The door to the room was generally open in order to catch a cross-breeze from the hall and speed one's way to the stacks, the card catalog, or the small office next door which was shared with the Walpole Editions. In that room one could usually find Pottle bent over a library table (he had a remarkable scholar's hump) in one corner, his eyes, which were impaired by various disorders, shielded against the glare from the hall windows by a green eyeshade with a library card stuck in the band. In that corner, wearing the worn tweed jacket he had shed while working and his necktie pulled up, he received both famous and unknown admirers and beamed upon the former pupils, now themselves honored scholars, who shyly presented their newest volumes to him.

For almost twenty years Pottle carefully husbanded an initial grant from the university, repeated awards from the Old Dominion Foundation, and the gifts of Frederick W. Hilles, Bodman Professor of English at Yale and the first general editor of the research editions. From 1969 to 1975 the project was almost entirely supported by annual stipends from Hilles, but the staff was reduced to a bursary student and a part-time copy editor/typist/bookkeeper/file clerk/receptionist, on whose desk in the middle of the room sat the one telephone, sparingly used. Pottle ran the library stacks, which he knew thoroughly, and wrote many letters of inquiry by hand. After the Boswell editions won a substan-

Dust jacket for Pottle's account of the discovery and assembly of James Boswell's personal papers

tial grant from the National Endowment for the Humanities in 1975, he enjoyed the luxury of a regular research assistant and of an office shared only with the new managing editor. When the director of the division of research grants of the NEH first glimpsed the original office she observed quietly that no detractor of the foundation could accuse this project of applying its funds to Oriental carpets.

I furnish these details in order to emphasize the exceptional concentration, discipline, and method Pottle brought to his purpose. From the time that I met him, in 1966, when he had retired from teaching, until the age of eighty-five, he worked daily in the Boswell Office from 9 A.M. to 6 P.M. (5 P.M., to be accurate, in his last few years). He took a break at noon for a twenty-minute nap in a deep leather chair in the Brothers Library of Sterling Library and then went to lunch. When he arrived at the office in the morning he read his mail, generally composed the necessary responses at once, and picked up his work where he had left it the evening before. Quietly assured, he never procrastinated, never seemed to hurry, solving each problem, or writing a research query on a three-by-five slip, as it arose. Occasionally he raised his head to share a discovery, serious or humorous. "Let's make up a note," he cried out merrily one day. "Nobody will ever know the difference." He obviously enjoyed the camaraderie of his associates.

As even-paced as he was even-tempered, Pottle wrote confidently on one side of legal-sized yellow pads; when the copy had been typed and he had proofread it, he struck it through and used the blank side of the paper for other purposes. A model of Yankee thrift, he tore some of these sheets into strips about three inches long and on them recast sentences which were troubling him. Thus the copy he presented to the typist was always clean.

Pottle also practiced to a rare degree the principle of scholarly cooperation and gave as generously as he received. Unique in his combination of intellectual assurance and personal modesty, he exercised no territorial claims, rejoiced in the advancement of knowledge whatever the source, and welcomed every serious student and offer of assistance. For almost every manuscript on which his opinion was solicited, whether it be from the editor of a learned journal, a publisher, or a beginning scholar, he returned the famous legal-sized sheets, respectfully suggesting, page and line seriatim, revisions of fact and style and sources of additional information.

With an associate in the editing of a Boswell volume he repeated the procedure described above until both scholars were satisfied, though for him it might have been simpler at times to make the changes at once. Although he was exacting, the tone of his comments was always matter of fact and courteous; he was neither condescending nor effusive. His praise, even "an excellent note" or "hurrah! you found it," was immensely gratifying.

Despite Pottle's unquestionable authority, occasionally even the most deferential editor felt compelled to say, as Boswell did to Edmond Malone when they revised the *Journal of a Tour to the Hebrides,* "Stet. C'est *moi.*" Pottle argued stubbornly and yielded reluctantly but he also recognized and respected determined effort, cultural change, and pride of authorship. He could be autocratic, however, and complete the final copy alone or revise it in proofs if he thought it necessary.

From the time the Boswell Papers arrived at Yale, his most steadfast and trusted collaborator was his wife, his high school and college mate and a trained librarian. Until his illness she worked four days a week in her office at the Beinecke Rare Book and Manuscript Library at Yale, cataloging the Boswell Papers and answering queries both from its editors and from scholars worldwide. Mrs. Pottle has clear memory of every document, its contents, and its relationship to all the other documents. At the celebration of their eightieth birthdays at Davenport College, Pottle described their lives together: "We never run out of topics for conversation. Picture us at breakfast. I sit in sullen self-absorption turning over in my mind various annotative puzzles that I have been worrying all night just under the surface of consciousness. Then I open with questions. 'What was the name of that property in Fifeshire the superiority of which gave Boswell a vote in that county?' She knows. 'When did young Knockroon's grandmother die?' She knows." Regarding one speculation, "she thinks not, but will take a look at the manuscript. Whatever she reports I shall accept as beyond doubt."

This happy collaboration the Pottles continued at Highfields, the summer home in Maine which Mrs. Pottle had inherited from her godmother. Like his wife, Pottle was a native of rural Maine; he was born at Lovell, grew up on a farm in Otisfield, and for years did all the tasks expected of a Maine farm boy. He was probably the only professor at Yale who could drive a team of oxen (and probably the only one who had attended an ungraded one-room schoolhouse). Working close to nature–growing vegetables and flowers, pruning trees, scything the grass on the slopes–engrossed him to his very late years.

In early spring he went up to Highfields alone to plant peas. In mid June, when the Pottles left New Haven for the summer, their automobile was loaded with manuscripts and the dozens of seedlings he had started. In the morning he gardened; in the afternoon he wrote at a small desk, with books and documents piled on the bed behind him. Letters flowed to and from the Boswell Office, requesting and furnishing information.

The Pottles' work was almost their entire pleasure in New Haven; they rarely entertained guests outside the family. They were convivial, though shy, however, and he enjoyed conversing with his learned colleagues at luncheon at Daven-

from MARK HARRIS

port College and at the regular weekly meetings of the Fellows on Wednesday evening. Invariably one found him munching nuts and relaxing with a gin and tonic on the capacious leather sofa in the Fellows' Lounge before the group descended to the dining hall. At the joint celebration of the Pottles' eightieth birthday he quoted Psalm 16: "The lines are fallen unto me in pleasant places; yea, I have a goodly heritage." The verses applied to them both, he said, and the Boswell Papers were their goodly heritage.

Shortly afterwards, on 4 July 1979, they suffered the sudden death of their younger son, Sam, musician and composer, best known for his work on *Sesame Street*. Their eldest child, a daughter named Annette, had died when she was thirteen months old ("I think of her every day," he once told me). Pottle quietly endured in a life apparently serene and unblemished a human share of pain. He was fortified by his religious beliefs and drew much comfort from his surviving son, Christopher, professor of engineering at Cornell University, and Christopher's wife and three children.

Pottle won many honors in his lifetime, including honorary degrees from Colby College, Rutgers University, Northwestern University, and the University of Glasgow. He was twice a Guggenheim Fellow, Chancellor of the Academy of American Poets from 1951 to 1971, and a member to his death of the Provinciaal Utrechtsch Genootschap van Kunsten en Wetenschappen and the American Academy of Arts and Sciences. At Yale he was awarded the Wilbur Lucius Cross Medal in 1967 and the William Clyde DeVane Medal in 1969. He won the Lewis Prize of the American Philosophical Society in 1975 and the Distinguished Alumnus Award of Colby College in 1977.

All who knew Pottle remember him, in the words of one of his students, as a "Jovean figure." At the memorial service held at Dwight Chapel, Yale University, 11 November 1987, Harold Bloom said, "These days I quote Emerson on teaching to my students: 'That which I can gain from another is never instruction but only provocation.' Provocation, from Frederick A. Pottle, came very quietly, but has lasted me for half a lifetime. I read Wordsworth and Shelley and Samuel Johnson as Mr. Pottle provoked me into reading them. I have never done for any student what Mr. Pottle did for me, and I never shall. He was the best mind in my profession in my lifetime."

If I had a talent for drawing I would make a sketch of Mr. Pottle's eyeshade looped over the shoulder of his empty chair in his office at Yale. I saw it only once, for a moment, through an open door.

I had been reading the Boswell volumes for twenty years before I saw Mr. Pottle's eyeshade or Mr. Pottle himself. Always, in my readings of Boswell's journals as they came from Yale, and again in Mr. Pottle's biography, *Boswell: The Earlier Years,* at exactly the moment my curiosity was most aroused and least satisfied, Mr. Pottle, in a footnote or an editorial passage, answered the question my mind was asking.

Mr. Pottle's own life, I had innocently imagined, had been devoted only to this industry. Thus the vast literary work he achieved had been possible because he was free of distraction. But how could he have known so much without having lived his own life, too, neither in innocence nor in immunity to distraction?

I have heard lately of theories of the brain—how some minds seize the large idea, others focus upon detail. Everything I heard or knew about Mr. Pottle, everything I observed in him or in the enduring books which were his labor, impresses upon me the conviction of an immense and balanced mind poised between absolute loyalty to detail, and mastery of the whole. Under his supervision, the editors of the Boswell journals learned to give dramatic shape to an ordained body of material, designing each volume with a beginning, middle, and end, as if it were a story, as indeed it was to the rare man who simultaneously mastered detail and dramatic distance.

Mr. Pottle's style of writing was impeccably informative, economical, and unostentatious. Two books of his, perhaps less well-known than others, far apart in kind but equal in the level of their perfection, strike me as amazing proofs of his being. One is a slim work, *Boswell and the Girl from Botany Bay,* which follows Boswell to an obscure legal success in the case of a brave young woman bereft of resources who, having been transported for small cause to the South Seas, escapes, makes her way home across the sea in a frail boat, and undertakes her struggle legally to remain.

The other book is Mr. Pottle's *Pride And Negligence: The History of the Boswell Papers,* an account of Mr. Pottle's own struggle to restore and assemble Boswell whole: a scholar's journey through moral depths as hazardous in its way as the voyage of the girl from Botany Bay.

Viewing the matter selfishly, my own life would have been so much less rich, so much less satisfying had the Boswell volumes never so accessibly existed, or if they had been stodgily manufactured for our century only in the spirit of time-serving. Mr. Pottle's character and labor were one and triumphant.

UPDATED ENTRIES

Ernest Hemingway

(21 July 1899-2 July 1961)

Charles M. Oliver
Ohio Northern University

See also the Hemingway entries in *DLB 4, American Writers in Paris, 1920-1939; DLB 9, American Novelists, 1910-1945; DLB Yearbook 1981; DLB Yearbook 1985*; and *DLB Documentary Series 1*.

NEW BOOKS: *Complete Poems*, edited by Nicholas Gerogiannis (Lincoln: University of Nebraska Press, 1983);

Ernest Hemingway on Writing, edited by Larry W. Phillips (New York: Scribners, 1984; London: Granada, 1984);

Ernest Hemingway Dateline: Toronto: The Complete Toronto Star Dispatches, 1920-1924, edited by William White (New York: Scribners, 1985; London: Hamilton, 1985);

The Dangerous Summer, introduction by James A. Michener (New York: Scribners, 1985);

The Garden of Eden (New York: Scribners, 1986; London: Hamilton, 1987);

The Complete Short Stories of Ernest Hemingway, The Finca Vigía Edition (New York: Scribners, 1987).

PERIODICAL PUBLICATIONS: "The Art of the Short Story," *Paris Review*, 79 (Spring 1981): 85-102;

"Humanity Will Not Forgive This," *Los Angeles Times*, 28 November 1982, IV: 5;

"An African Betrayal," *Sports Illustrated* (5 May 1986): 58-72.

Hemingway studies have been extremely active during the past six years, producing rich opportunities for scholars, book publishers, and journal editors. More than fifty books about Hemingway and his works have been published, including thirteen biographical studies, plus more than one thousand articles; and the Hemingway Society, formed in 1980 and now with nearly four hundred members, has sponsored seven conferences during the past seven years, including international meetings in Spain and Italy.

At the 1976 University of Alabama Symposium, "Hemingway: A Revaluation," Jackson J.

Benson discussed the sixty-seven books written about Hemingway to that date, which marked the fiftieth anniversary of the publication of *The Sun Also Rises*. Benson spoke of the "Hemingway inflation," items "padded to articles," items that should have been articles "padded to books." It is clear that eleven years later the padding is worse and the inflation greater. The recent biographies might make three interesting books, one devoted to the women in Hemingway's life and fiction; and the thirty books of criticism might make three more books. On the other hand, the new biographies provide material that will force some changes in attitude toward Hemingway, especially toward his early development; and the wealth of new interpretations of the fiction will force changes in future readings, especially of the major works. Scholars no doubt feel it is better to have too much information than too little, but it will take some future scholar to produce the definitive biography, a work that would separate the life from the fiction and evaluate both more objectively.

The recent books on Hemingway (books published between 1982 and 1987) may be divided into the following loose categories: major biographies (6); minor biographies (7); general criticism (17); anthologies of criticism (13); comparative studies (4); and miscellaneous (10). There have also been six new posthumous publications of works by Hemingway. The final section of this essay is devoted to the recent work of the Hemingway Society.

Considering there were only six biographies before 1981 (not counting the family reports), one would expect a wealth of new material to warrant the surge of new books on Hemingway's life. Many new anecdotes have appeared, a few that even shed some light on the author's character, but there is little else that has not been said before, mainly by Carlos Baker in *Ernest Hemingway: A Life Story* (1969). Perhaps the only important revision to be made in the collective attitude toward Hemingway concerns the relation-

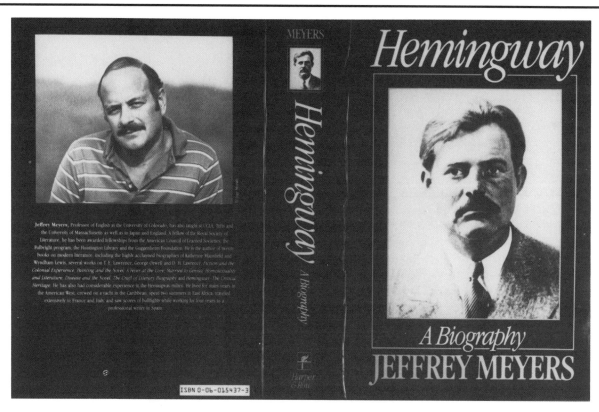

Dust jacket for Jeffrey Meyers's 1985 biography of Hemingway, the first major attempt at a full consideration of Hemingway's life since Carlos Baker's Ernest Hemingway: A Life Story *(1969)*

ship between his parents, Clarence and Grace Hall Hemingway.

Readers of Hemingway's life had been led to believe by Baker and other early biographers that Grace's domineering attitude was the prominent fact of family life. Particularly damaging was the report, with all its Freudian ramifications, that she had mailed to Ernest in Paris the gun Clarence used to commit suicide in 1928. But it is clear now that the story is untrue; that, in fact, as Bernice Kert reveals in *The Hemingway Women* (1983), Ernest wrote to his mother asking for the gun. The recent biographies, particularly those devoted to the writer's early years, make it clear that Clarence had a number of psychological problems, some because of his relationship with his wife but most because of illness and money, and these illnesses had an important if not crucial impact on the children. None of the new biographies, however, offers information that would change one's understanding of Ernest's own attitude toward his parents. Apparently he always blamed his mother for family problems, especially for his father's death.

Of the most important biographical works of the past six years, the most interesting are

Kenneth Lynn's *Hemingway* (1987) and Bernice Kert's *The Hemingway Women*; the best written is Michael Reynolds's *The Young Hemingway* (1986); and the most disappointing is Jeffrey Meyers's *Hemingway: A Biography* (1985). Peter Griffin's *Along With Youth: Hemingway, the Early Years* (1986) includes previously unpublished items, including five short stories; and Norberto Fuentes's *Hemingway in Cuba* (1984) has new and interesting material about Hemingway's Cuban connections and previously unpublished letters.

The Meyers book is disappointing because it is such a major undertaking, promising to supersede Baker's biography but failing in the attempt. Meyers seems incapable of separating Hemingway's life from his fiction, assuming as an almost automatic feature of the book that the fiction has its parallel in Hemingway's own life. Meyers says, for example, that "Hemingway's earliest memory describes the carefully preserved relics of his parents' lives. They are sexually suggestive and associated with birth, boyhood, marriage, home, family traditions and personal legacies. . . ." Meyers then quotes from a short story, "Now I Lay Me," as a way of proving the analysis. There is rarely any qualification of this merger of fiction and fact. Meyers says that Hemingway's sister Sunny, "a tomboy and an athlete," appeared in three of his stories: as the softball player Helen in "Soldier's Home," as Dorothy in "Fathers and Sons," and as "Littlest," who helps Nick run away from the game warden in "The Last Good Country."

There is no suggestion that Sunny might be a "prototype," a term that even the most ardent biographical critics will use occasionally; to Meyers she *is* each of the three characters. And Jane Mason, Hemingway's friend during his Cuban years, *is* Margot Macomber, "a beautiful but bitchy woman who sleeps with the white hunter and shoots her husband." Meyers seems unwilling to allow for Hemingway's creative imagination.

Second, Meyers makes it clear that Hemingway lied or exaggerated about nearly everything that happened to him, yet the biographer quotes statements in Hemingway's letters and articles as biographical facts; or, worse yet, he quotes others who quote Hemingway, and he sometimes quotes without citation. For example, where others have qualified information about Hemingway's first sexual encounter, Meyers is dogmatic: "At the end of the summer season Hemingway stayed in Michigan at the house of neighbors, the Dilworths, and slept with a woman for the first time." There is no citation given, except to quote "Up in Michigan," Hemingway's short story about a first sexual experience.

Less important, but nevertheless annoying in what should have been a good book, Meyers makes careless mistakes in his discussion of the fiction: he says, for example, that Catherine Barkley, in *A Farewell to Arms* (1929), dies in Montreux, Switzerland, when her death actually occurs in Lausanne. In addition, the material on the Cuban years is done without any reference to the Fuentes book, published two years before.

The Reynolds biography, on the other hand, is both more reliable and more readable. It is the first work to discuss with sensitivity Clarence's problems and to suggest that his "nervous condition" contributed to family troubles. His illness is handled piecemeal by Reynolds so that the reader only gradually becomes aware of the reasons for the eventual suicide. Reynolds is sympathetic toward Grace Hemingway, finding in her much to respect and even admire, and he suggests that in spite of what Ernest said about hating his mother, the reader should allow for Hemingway's "penchant for hyperbole" and re-

member "that love and hate are sometimes indistinguishable."

In discussing Grace Hall Hemingway, Reynolds makes it clear that "the more her husband retreated from the world into his private distress, the more she filled the vacuum." Reynolds states that "Hemingway found it far more convenient to accuse his mother. Mental problems were frightening and might be hereditary." Reynolds sums up better than anyone has the Hemingway family illnesses and their potential for mental disabilities. Ernest, Marcelline, and Ursula all suffered from insomnia; "Marcelline had low blood pressure, Ernest had high blood pressure"; Marcelline and Ernest "both suffered from diabetes, and both went through periods of severe depression."

Although the Hemingway family suicides have been well documented, Reynolds provides a summary of causes, implying that genetics played a larger role than other biographers have been willing to accept. Besides Clarence, three of the children—Ernest, Ursula, and Leicester—committed suicide, and Leicester, Reynolds writes, "suspected suicide" in the death of Marcelline. Reynolds also compares Ernest's ailments to Clarence's: "erratic high blood pressure, insomnia, paranoia, severe depression.... Like his father, he [Ernest] was caught in a biological trap not entirely of his own making.... Genetically, Ernest had inherited a time bomb which he carried unknowingly into his marriage [with Hadley]."

Further, Reynolds makes clearer than any other biographer the relationship of Ruth Arnold to the Hemingways. She moved into the Hemingway household in 1908, when she was thirteen, a "live-in [music] student and part-time baby sitter and cook." She became abnormally attracted to Grace, or at least Clarence thought so, for he fired her in 1919, apparently for that reason. And, although Reynolds says that by this time Clarence was "obsessed and erratic," he also says that none of the autobiographies of Leicester, Marcelline, or Sunny mentions Ruth, suggesting that the children, too, felt something of the abnormal relationship. "Oak Parkers all," Reynolds writes, "the children knew better than to rattle the closet bones."

Finally, Reynolds ignores the first law of Hemingway scholarship by imitating at the beginning of each chapter Hemingway's own familiar writing style. For the most part, the gamble pays off. He is able to shift in and out of Hemingway's style without condescension or cuteness. For example, chapter two begins, "Nothing in the Village seemed quite the same to him after the war. The houses were as large as he remembered them, the lawns as deep." And chapter three begins, "In the summer of every year the Hemingways lived in a house that looked across the lake to the farm." This imitative style continues for a paragraph or two and then shifts into Reynolds's own voice for the main body of the chapter. Reynolds makes at least one minor error in geography, writing that Hadley's train from Chicago to St. Louis goes "through the Indiana fields of corn stubble."

Griffin's biography, which includes a foreword by Hemingway's oldest son, Jack, has more details concerning Hemingway's early life than either Reynolds's or Meyers's books, although sometimes the details are more than most readers could possibly want. At the beginning of chapter four, for example, Griffin writes the following: "Ernest's train from Chicago to New York took the northern route: around the southern tip of Lake Michigan, across southern Michigan to Detroit, east into Canada at Windsor, along the north shore of Lake Erie to Buffalo, then through larger towns like Batavia and Geneva and smaller ones like Lockport and Seneca Falls. Finally, the train turned south at Albany and followed the Hudson River to New York City. Ernest rode in the second car, at the last window on the left side." One is more impressed with Griffin here than enlightened about Hemingway. Griffin also provides the titles of apparently all the songs Hadley played on the University Club piano one evening in "late February" of 1921. He does develop some new material from the six months Hemingway spent with the *Kansas City Star* that sheds light on his early development as a writer and person. The newspaper work provided Hemingway with his first touch with the violent death of people, and it helped him focus his thinking and writing, and, by implication, his life's work. Griffin's discussion of Hadley Richardson, Hemingway's first wife, is particularly good, making clear the nurturing quality of her influence on Hemingway's creative talent. He uses excerpts from Hadley's letters, which Jack Hemingway gave to the Hemingway collection at the Kennedy Library in the late spring of 1986.

Griffin sometimes quotes the fiction in support of the life, particularly when he discusses Hemingway's wound in northern Italy in the First World War. He uses the wounding of Frederic Henry in *A Farewell to Arms* to describe what happened to Hemingway–again, like Meyers, assuming that Hemingway could not have imagined details for the fiction that had not occurred in his own experience.

Although Griffin's "Sources and Notes" section lists new material and references, the citations to the notes are vague. The reader has to rely on incidents and scenes as keys rather than on the traditional endnote numbering system. The five previously unpublished short stories Griffin includes in the biography are "The Mercenaries," "Crossroads," "Portrait of the Idealist in Love," "The Ash Heel's Tendon," and "The Current." The first is the best, but none enhances Hemingway's reputation as a short-story writer.

The most interesting of all the biographical studies are Bernice Kert's *The Hemingway Women* and Kenneth Lynn's *Hemingway*. Kert's book is less important, perhaps, as a Hemingway biography; the Hemingway that readers see is filtered primarily through the eyes of Grace Hall Hemingway and Hemingway's four wives. But it is certainly a major work and of great importance to future Hemingway biographers. Kert's thesis is that the quality "most common to the women was resilience. Their composite story seemed to be a study in relinquishment. For no matter what their degree of commitment, Hemingway could never sustain a long-lived, wholly satisfying relationship with any one of them."

Although it is not difficult to infer from earlier biographers that Hemingway badly mistreated most of the women around him, Kert leaves no doubt. In stating that Ernest wrote to Grace asking for his father's gun, Kert says that the disclosure "ends the rumors, long circulated, that Grace shipped the revolver to Ernest for malign reasons of her own." Kert also reveals through a letter Hadley wrote to married friends in the late summer of 1929, a significant detail in her attitude toward her marriage to Ernest: "If Ernest had not been brought up in that damned stuffy Oak Park environment . . . he would not have thought that when you fall in love extramaritally you have to get a divorce and marry the girl."

What is often rather amazing about Kert's book is that so much detail about Hemingway's life has escaped previous biographers, apparently because they simply failed to research the women carefully enough. Even Alice Hunt Sokolof 's biography, *Hadley, The First Mrs. Hemingway* (1973), good as it is, includes only one of Hadley's letters written to someone other than a Hemingway family member. Kert uses the diary of Pauline Pfeiffer, Hemingway's second wife (rather than Hemingway's *Green Hills of Africa*, 1935), for the details of the couple's trip to East Africa in the winter of 1933 and 1934. There is no reason to believe, of course, that the women are any more reliable as sources of information about Hemingway than any of the men, but the approach is fresh and much of the information interesting enough so that *The Hemingway Women* has to be considered one of the most important books on Hemingway in the past six years.

Lynn's *Hemingway* is a psychological biography, explaining the effects of nearly all the important events in Hemingway's life on his mental and spiritual self. It is not too much of a simplification, in fact, to say that the book is a 593-page explanation of Hemingway's suicide. And Lynn makes it clear—without sentimentality—that one's sympathies should be with Hemingway.

Although Lynn occasionally reaches too far into the fiction for biographical connections, for the most part he concentrates on the life of the author, with interpretations of the fiction that are based on psychological responses to events in the life. He refutes the standard interpretation of "Big Two-Hearted River," for example, that Nick is reacting to some sort of recent trauma, perhaps war wounds, by reading it as Hemingway's reaction to the bitter split with his mother at Windemere. And both "The End of Something" and "The Three-Day Blow" are "veiled expression[s]" of Hemingway's ambiguous feelings about his marriage to Hadley.

The biographer calls "The Battler" the most "problematic" story, "biographically speaking," of all the short stories. "The marital break-up of Ad [Francis] and his ambiguously twinlike wife and manager is also a cause for wonder about the relationship of art to life. For their fatal disagreements, Bugs's yarn about the couple makes clear, grew out of the unpleasantness created by people who did not like it whether they were actually brother and sister or just rumored to be. In relating this strange tale of how a marriage failed, Hemingway may have been voicing his own dissatisfaction with Hadley and her ambiguous sister-wife-mother-manager role in their relationship."

The idea of twin relations and androgyny are major subtheses in Lynn's interpretations. He says, for another example, that "No other piece of his fiction . . . reveals as much about Hemingway's sexual duality as does *The Garden of Eden*."

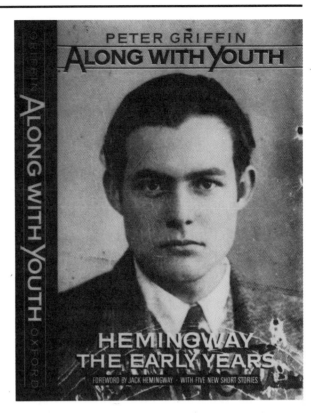

Dust jacket for Griffin's 1986 biography that uses previously unavailable archival material to describe Hemingway's development as a writer and a person

And there is a footnote that refers to the "striking resemblance" of the African part of Hemingway's story to Beryl Markham's *West With the Night* (1942), an autobiographical work about Africa that Hemingway praised highly. "That [Hemingway] could project his hero into Markham's girlhood is thus another instance of the sexual transmutations that characterize *The Garden of Eden*."

Lynn refers often to the effect on Hemingway of his mother's several reminders that he had "slept in her bed for half a year and lunched all night at her breast." He says of *A Farewell to Arms* that the novel allows Hemingway to fulfill a wish "to start talking–at long last!–about the remote origins of his emotional problems." The idea comes as a summary to his interpretation of *A Farewell to Arms*, where he makes the statement that "the portrait of Frederic Henry is a study in affective disorder, and retreat and desertion are functions of a larger disengagement from life."

Whatever one may think of these interpretations—and Lynn reads nearly every novel and short story as a psychological study of the author—at least Lynn avoids the trap of assuming a one-to-one relationship between fictional charac-

245

ters and real people. He uses terms such as "fictional counterpart" and "real-life counterparts," for example. And when he relates fictional events to biographical events, he makes it clear that it is *only* an interpretation, using terms such as "cause for wonder if," "may have been," and "could it be that" in order to avoid the biographical fallacy.

Lynn's book is certainly the most complete work so far on the growth and disintegration of Hemingway's mind, one which future biographers will no doubt make good use of in the continuing search for "truth."

Gabriel García Márquez says in his introduction to Fuentes's book that Hemingway biographers have not fully covered the nearly twenty-two years Hemingway spent in Cuba. It is no doubt true, but researchers have not had easy access to information, and, in fact, one of the difficulties about this biography is that one cannot be sure of its reliability. There are no footnotes and no documentation and no practical way to check any of the sources. Fuentes often includes more than one source for a particular anecdote, however, helping the reader feel a bit more comfortable.

In any case, *Hemingway in Cuba* is a good biography, portraying Hemingway's relations with the Cuban people, especially the people of San Francisco de Paula; and it is obvious that the relationship was one of love and mutual respect. Hemingway was generous in his gifts of money to various Cuban causes; he gave $2,000 for the construction of an aqueduct, and he outfitted two youth baseball teams (as a direct result of catching some boys throwing stones at his mango trees). Fuentes also says that, according to Roman Nicolan, the Cuban Communist party leader, Hemingway gave $20,000 to the Cuban Communists, more than any other foreigner. He defended Castro and the Cuban Revolution, declaring it to be necessary, saying that "Castro's government was bound to succeed if it remained free of foreign intervention." When false reports of Castro's death reached Hemingway in 1957, he said, according to Fuentes, "That is a lie! They say it in order to discredit the Movement. Fidel cannot die! Fidel has to make the Revolution."

Fuentes also provides a good, detailed explanation of how contemporary Cubans view Hemingway's relations with the Communists and with the Spanish Republicans. Nicolan says, for example, that although Hemingway was not a Communist, he was a humanist and so cooperated with the Communist cause in Cuba. There is a bronze bust of Hemingway in the "Plaza Hemingway" in Cojimar which was unveiled on 2 July 1962, one year to the day after Hemingway's suicide. The Cojimar fishermen not only raised the money needed to cast the bust, but they also melted down the bronze propellers of their boats in order to provide the material for it. Fuentes had an advantage on Baker and even on more recent biographers because he had access to all of Hemingway's Cuban papers, including bills and letters. The cost of upkeep on the Finca Vigía, for example, was $4,000 a month.

The most interesting new story discovered by Fuentes comes from an interview with Alexis Eisner in Moscow. Eisner had known Hemingway during the Spanish Civil War, and, according to Eisner, on parting, Hemingway gave him a blank check on a Paris bank. In April 1940 Eisner's home was searched by Soviet authorities, the check was found, and Eisner was sentenced to twenty-five years in Siberia "for receiving money from a capitalist." He was released in 1956.

There are also several important appendices included in the book: "the Finca Vigía papers" (love letters to Mary Welsh, Hemingway's fourth wife, and forty-five letters to Hemingway's son Gregory and to Adriana Ivancich), a chronology of the Cuban years, an inventory of the Hemingway museum, a bibliography, and notes and sources (without the American system of citation, however).

Besides these six biographies, there are seven others that have been published in the last six years which are somewhat less significant because of particular limits the authors have placed on their work. Keith Ferrell's book *Ernest Hemingway: The Search for Courage* (1984) has no documentation, making it impossible to check for accuracy. It includes biographical details, but no feeling, no life. It is an overly sympathetic book— the search for courage—even romantic, and, therefore, misleading for anyone new to Hemingway studies.

Arnold Samuelson wrote *With Hemingway: A Year in Key West and Cuba* (1984) as the result of spending part of 1934 with Hemingway. Samuelson was twenty-two at the time and wanted to learn how to write, so the book is full of conversation about fishing and writing, some of it good conversation, and including a fascinating description of an all-day trip aboard Hemingway's boat, the *Pilar,* in pursuit of sperm whales. Samuelson's daughter found the memoir after her father's death in 1981 and edited it for publication three years later. It is an interesting account of one person's seven-month sojourn with Hemingway.

A. E. Hotchner's *Papa Hemingway: The Ecstasy and Sorrow* (1983) needs to be included here because, although it is primarily a reprinting of his 1966 book, *Papa Hemingway: A Personal Memoir*, there is a new section, a "Postscript," that adds much to the already heated controversy over the first book. The new chapter is like a gossip column: Hotchner concentrates on the frequently public fights between Hemingway and Mary and then attacks Philip Young, one of Hemingway's early supporters. It is almost as if Hotchner were getting even with Mary for her attempt to stop publication of his earlier book and for some of her comments about him in her autobiography, *How It Was* (1976). In any case, the "Postscript" does not make for pleasant reading.

Jack Hemingway says in his book *Misadventures of a Fly Fisherman: My Life With and Without Papa* (1986) that he spent the first half of his life as the son of a famous father and the second half as the father of famous daughters (Muffet, a writer; Margeaux, a model; and Mariel, an actress). His book, which is really more autobiography than biography, is clearly a book about a man trying to find (and finding) his own way. However, what he says about his father is also probably the best biography by a member of the family available. In spite of what he says in his foreword to Griffin's biography about the new insight he has into his father's character, Jack Hemingway's book makes it clear that the father he knew best was not the Hemingway of the biographies. This is a warm and sensitive account by a man who loved his father and was loved by him in return.

Raymond S. Nelson's book *Ernest Hemingway: Life, Work and Criticism* (1984) is a forty-three-page handbook. It includes a biographical sketch, a list of Hemingway's works, a summary of the major works, an overview, and an annotated bibliography of criticism.

Gerald B. Nelson's *Hemingway: Life and Works* (1984) is a Facts on File publication, again a handbook of information that includes a year-by-year chronology of Hemingway's life and an index of names, places, and works. It is useful in part because at the beginning of each year in the chronology are listed the works published during that year.

An excellent short biography is a little-publicized book, *Hemingway in Toronto: A Post-Modern Tribute* (1982), written by David Donnell. It is an informative and interesting account of Hemingway's two stays in Toronto in 1920 and 1924, particularly the second, a four-month period just before he went back to Paris to produce *in our time* (1924) and *The Sun Also Rises* (1926). Donnell also discusses Hemingway's influence on the *Toronto Daily Star* writers, most of whom were willing to accept and take on a writing style that was to be called, "approximately 57 years later, the new journalism."

Of the thirty books of criticism published during the past six years, two attempt to cover most or all of Hemingway's fiction, four are on *The Sun Also Rises*, two are on Hemingway's women characters, one is on his popularity, ten are on other limited subjects, and eleven are anthologies of essays.

Gerry Brenner's *Concealments in Hemingway's Works* (1983) offers three theses, stated and defined in the introduction: that contrary to Faulkner's comment about Hemingway's "arrested" literary development, Hemingway was experimental until the 1950s; that "the aim of Hemingway's art . . . was to conceal both the artist and the art"; and that Hemingway "was fixated upon his father, the chief emotional object of his life."

Earl Rovit's fine Twayne Authors Series book (1963) has been reprinted (1986) with Gerry Brenner assisting in the revision. The most important difference is a new chapter on four posthumous works—*A Moveable Feast* (1964), *Islands in the Stream* (1970), *The Dangerous Summer* (1985), and "African Journal," published serially in *Sports Illustrated* in December 1971 and January 1972. There is also a new bibliography, reflecting the scholarship of the last thirty years and including a catalogue of audiovisual materials. The book is so well done it is unfortunate that a discussion of *The Garden of Eden* (1986), published after Rovit and Brenner had completed their work, is not included in the new chapter.

Wirt Williams's book *The Tragic Art of Ernest Hemingway* (1981) is outside the six-year limit set for this study but is included here because it is one of the best critical studies on Hemingway's works. Williams defines the idea of tragedy in Hemingway and presents one of the best discussions available of Hemingway's vision of the human condition. Williams says, in summary, that "when critical vision is no longer even par-

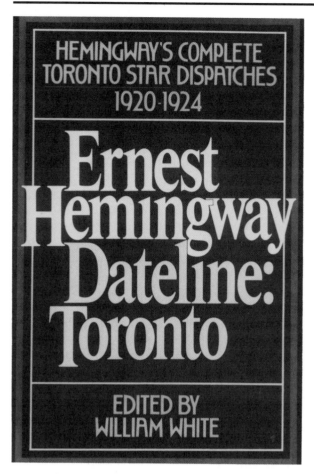

Dust jacket for the 1985 republication, in chronological order, of 143 previously uncollected Hemingway news dispatches, along with 29 from the earlier collection By-Line: Ernest Hemingway *(1947)*

tially blocked by his [Hemingway's] public persona, so awesome and yet so destructive of a cool appraisal of his authentic value, another generation may decide he was one of the century's greatest makers of tragedy."

Of the four books on *The Sun Also Rises,* two are anthologies, one is a manuscript study, and one is a critical study. *Ernest Hemingway's The Sun Also Rises* (1987) is part of the Modern Critical Interpretations series of books edited by Harold Bloom for Chelsea House; it includes eleven previously published articles, eight of which were written before 1972 and only two during the last six years. Linda Wagner-Martin's *New Essays on The Sun Also Rises* (1987), on the other hand, has six articles plus the editor's own "Introduction," all written especially for this book. It is only a slight exaggeration to say the essays present a revisionist point of view toward Hemingway's first novel; the writers have clearly turned away from the interpretative standards placed on the novel by

Philip Young and Carlos Baker in the early 1950s and by many of the writers reprinted in the Bloom anthology. Wendy Martin says, for example, in her essay "Brett Ashley as New Woman in *The Sun Also Rises,*" that Brett represents the "new woman's radical challenge to the traditional social structure." Brett has "stepped off the pedestal and now roams the world." The novel, according to Martin, "signals the possibility of new kinds of relationships for women and men in the twentieth century," a statement the early critics would not have thought of making.

Frederic Joseph Svoboda's *Hemingway and The Sun Also Rises: The Crafting of a Style* (1983) is a manuscript study; Bhim S. Dahiya's book *Hemingway's The Sun Also Rises: A Critical Introduction* (1986) classifies the novel as comedy in a genre with Joyce's *Ulysses* and the works of Henry Fielding.

Svoboda presents the step-by-step process by which Hemingway produced *The Sun Also Rises.* It is a careful study of the transformation of ideas into rough drafts and then into final book form, an excellent work of scholarship and use of the materials in the Kennedy Library. Svoboda examines Hemingway's scene-by-scene revision difficulties, including revisions for tone and pacing, and he discusses Hemingway's experiments with narrative stance and distance. The book includes three appendices: "the manuscript described," "the beginning cut from the galleys" (based on Fitzgerald's recommendations), and the letter from Fitzgerald to Hemingway recommending revisions. It is an extremely important addition to Hemingway studies.

Dahiya's book adds an interesting interpretation to what is already understood about *The Sun Also Rises,* one of the few studies of the novel as comedy. But the book is not very well written and is sometimes heavy with explanations, most of which would be familiar to most American scholars. It is an antibiographical approach to the novel, sometimes making long statements attempting to separate fact from fiction. One important conclusion, however, is that real people saw themselves as characters in the novel and rather liked it, Dahiya implying that early biographical criticism was encouraged by this factor.

The Fall 1986 issue of the *Hemingway Review* is also devoted to *The Sun Also Rises,* honoring the sixtieth anniversary of its publication. The journal carries seven new articles on the novel, including an essay that correlates the day-by-day work Hemingway did on the manuscript with the

Scribners published text and an essay that suggests textual changes for the next edition of the novel.

The two book-length studies of Hemingway's women characters add important new material to be considered in future perceptions of Hemingway's fictional treatment of women. Both Roger Whitlow in *Cassandra's Daughters: The Women in Hemingway* (1984) and Mimi Reisel Gladstein in *The Indestructible Woman in the Works of Faulkner, Hemingway, and Steinbeck* (1986) argue the positive value of most of the women characters.

Whitlow argues that Catherine Barkley (*A Farewell to Arms*) is more mature than Frederic Henry (Whitlow misspells the name as Frederick throughout); that Marie Morgan (*To Have and Have Not*) represents an "alternative vision" to the one offered by the men; that Maria (*For Whom the Bell Tolls*) has been through much that has made her stronger than Robert Jordan. Jordan, Frederic Henry, and Harry Morgan all opt for "duty," "courage," and "loyalty," whereas the three women are above those "petty ideas." Maria, who of all the women characters has been most often seen as a mere sex object, is seen by Whitlow as one who gives herself in love totally, in spite of all that has happened to her, perhaps the most capable of love of all the women characters. The important women, in other words, offer a "life-affirming vision of people and their relationships.... They try (like Cassandra, with notable lack of success) to share that vision with their men."

Gladstein's book is a revision of her 1973 study, but, as she says in her introduction, new biographical studies of all three authors require a revision of ideas. She cites Kert's *The Hemingway Women* and Scott Donaldson's *By Force of Will* (1977) as sources from which she has taken new ideas about Hemingway's attitude toward women. Although Gladstein is not as sympathetic toward the women as Whitlow, she sees them as positive forces. She classifies Hemingway's women, both real and fictional, according to their respective earth mother roles. The "terrible mothers" of the fiction are Brett Ashley, Margot Macomber, and Helen ("Snows of Kilimanjaro"); the nurturing mothers are Pilar, Maria, and Renata–Pilar considered by Gladstein to be "Hemingway's most fully drawn and interesting woman character."

John Raeburn's book *Fame Became of Him: Hemingway as Public Writer* (1984) is a study of Hemingway's popularity. Raeburn is interested in how Hemingway "became a celebrity." He says that the "literary achievement is tangential to understanding that public fame." His book, therefore, is a study of popular rather than of intellectual appeal, focusing particularly on Hemingway's appearances in *Time, Life, Esquire, Newsweek,* and *Cosmopolitan,* rather than in *Atlantic* or *Partisan Review.* Although the book is especially good on Hemingway in the late 1930s, when, according to Raeburn, he reached his peak in popularity, and on Hemingway's macho image, especially as developed by *Playboy,* there is not very much in the book that surprises.

Angel Capellán's book *Hemingway and the Hispanic World* (1985) attempts to "present a carefully balanced estimate of what the Hispanic world meant to Hemingway and his work." The author draws on Hemingway's fiction, letters, unpublished manuscripts, and "on numerous Spanish sources unknown to most American critics." Perhaps the most important section is on the influence of Spain in Hemingway's attitude toward death. The book includes an appendix listing details of Hemingway's trips to Spain.

Larry E. Grimes's book *The Religious Design of Hemingway's Early Fiction* (1985) is important as one of the few thorough studies of religious influences on Hemingway's works. Organized chronologically, it also provides a clear feeling for the growth of religious influences on the works–beginning with the influence of Oak Park's Protestant churches and of the Victorian morality of Hemingway's upbringing. One of the most interesting sections attempts to define Hemingway's concept of the "fifth dimension" as the "mystical-religious" center of both an aesthetic theory and a religious orientation. Grimes is careful with definitions, beginning with the word "religious" itself, an important point in such a book.

Joseph M. Flora, presenting another anti-biographical study, says in *Hemingway's Nick Adams* (1982) that Nick is "special" in American literature because he transcends the reader's interest in Hemingway himself. But the critic pulls his punches. Philip Young edited the Adams stories in 1972, according to Flora, as a psychobiography of Hemingway; Flora arranges the stories so they can be read as Nick's own biography as well as Hemingway's, a questionable improvement–although he treats the stories *primarily* as fiction. However, the book offers a thorough criticism of the Nick Adams stories and so is a valuable and reliable guide.

J. F. Kobler's book *Ernest Hemingway: Journalist as Artist* (1985) defines effectively Hemingway's journalism, nonfiction, and fiction in terms of content, ideas, and style, although he seems at times unwilling to allow for crossover examples. He includes tables that reflect stylistic differences among the three genres: "uses of certain words," "attributive words used with dialogue," "occurrences of questionable punctuation," "occurrences of *and* in descriptive-narrative passages."

Gregory S. Sojka discusses the role of fishing as "aesthetic of contest" in his book *Ernest Hemingway: The Angler as Artist* (1985). He works with the metaphor of "life as a game" in order to account for the idea of a "code hero" who must learn to do the best he can with what he has, playing life by the rules but as hard as he can–hardly a new idea. Bringing together fictional and nonfictional "origins" of Hemingway's theories about fishing is interesting, but concluding that "Big Two-Hearted River," *The Old Man and the Sea*, and *Islands in the Stream* are chiefly the result of ideas about fishing diminishes the very artistic value Sojka would have his readers see.

E. Nageswara Rao's book *Ernest Hemingway: A Study of His Rhetoric* (1983) also adds little to an understanding of the chosen topic. He uses no source more recent than 1975, effectively eliminating all of the recent studies, especially the vast amount of work on the manuscripts done since the opening of the Hemingway Room at the Kennedy Library in 1980.

The Hemingway Society has published three anthologies thus far, reflecting the proceedings of three of its national conferences. The papers from two earlier Hemingway conferences are also available: the Oregon Conference (1973) and the Alabama Conference (1976). The first book published by the Society was *Ernest Hemingway: The Papers of a Writer* (1981), edited by Bernard Oldsey. The book consists of selected papers given at the Thompson Island Conference in Boston during the official opening of the Hemingway Room at the Kennedy Library on 18 July 1980. The conference, and subsequently the book, offered Hemingway scholars their first official look at the Hemingway manuscripts.

James Nagel edited the second volume, *Ernest Hemingway: The Writer in Context* (1984), selected papers delivered in Boston at Northeastern University and at the Kennedy Library, 21 to 23 May 1982. The essays are organized into four parts: "personal comments and reminiscences" (by Charles Scribner, Jr., Patrick Hemingway,

and Tom Stoppard); "craft of composition"; "interpretations biographical and critical"; and "comparison studies." Nagel says in his introduction that the papers provide "interpretations of Hemingway's works in the context of an ever-developing wealth of information about his personal life," his creative process, and his attitudes toward other writers and friends.

The third anthology, *Up in Michigan: Proceedings of the First National Conference of the Hemingway Society* (1984), is edited by Joseph J. Waldmeir and Kenneth Marek from papers delivered at a conference in Traverse City, Michigan, between 20 and 22 October 1983. It includes a "Michigan Series" and a "General Series" with ten essays in each. Another book of conference essays is *Hemingway: A Revaluation* (1983), edited by Donald R. Noble, which includes eight of the papers delivered at the Alabama Conference in 1976–perhaps the most important of which is Jackson Benson's paper mentioned above–and five other essays. Benson, in "Hemingway Criticism: Getting at the Hard Questions," is harshly critical of much Hemingway criticism to that time and offers suggestions for future scholarship. He is particularly critical of those books and articles which continue the "contagious spread of the biographical fallacy," instead of getting "on with the difficult enough problems of the writing itself."

Another important collection is *Critical Essays on Ernest Hemingway's In Our Time* (1983), edited by Michael S. Reynolds. Besides ten reviews of the 1924 and 1925 publications of Hemingway's first stories, the book contains thirty articles of criticism, including source and manuscript studies, biographical and interpretive criticism. Reynolds says in an excellent introduction that the collection attempts "to wed the new scholarship and the once new criticism," to work our knowledge of the manuscripts into our understanding of the meaning of the stories.

Robert A. Lee edited a volume titled *Ernest Hemingway: New Critical Essays* (1983) in which he proposes to "help re-see, and to an extent re-site, Hemingway." But at least seven of the ten writers are British and show a 1960s prejudice toward Hemingway that sets the "re-seeing" through dark glasses. Faith Pullin, perhaps the best representative of the general attitude, argues in her essay "Hemingway and the Secret Language of Hate" that "Hemingway has no real interest in character and therefore no genuine comprehension of, or expertise in, the fictive treatment of human relationships." She says that Hemingway's

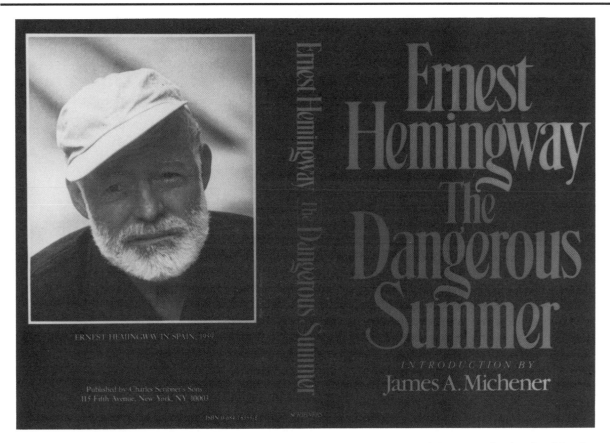

Dust jacket for the 1985 publication of Hemingway's nonfiction account of the 1959 bullfight season of Luis Miguel Dominguín and Antonio Ordóñez. The 45,000-word book was edited from Hemingway's 70,000-word final draft.

"work reveals a progressive repudiation of people in general and of women in particular."

The problem with Harold Bloom's *Modern Critical Views: Ernest Hemingway* (1985) is that of the twelve essays selected only two were written after 1979. Bloom calls it a "representative selection from the last forty-five years of Hemingway criticism," and one could not question the value of most of those early essays (by Lionel Trilling, Edmund Wilson, Robert Penn Warren, Harry Levin, Carlos Baker, Mark Spilka, George Plimpton, Reynolds Price, Malcolm Cowley, and Frederic Hoffman). But, as should be clear by now, the direction of Hemingway studies has changed considerably in the past six years, and so to weight an anthology to the pre-1980s attitude is to misrepresent "modern" critical views. In any case one of the editor's *post*-1980 selections is Alfred Kazin's essay "Hemingway the Painter" from his book *An American Procession* (1984). It is one of the best general essays on Hemingway ever published. Kazin makes three key points: "Hemingway's greatest gift was to identify his own capacity for pain with the destructiveness

at large in our time"; "Hemingway makes you feel in painfully distinct human detail how much the world merely echoes the endless turmoil in the human heart"; and truth is "at the heart of darkness that Hemingway unforgettably described: the sense of something irremediably *wrong*." On the other hand, John Hollander's essay "Hemingway's Extraordinary Reality" (written especially for this anthology) adds little new knowledge. Bloom's third anthology of essays on Hemingway—*Modern Critical Interpretations: A Farewell to Arms* (1987)—is a selection only a little more recent than the other two. Six of its nine essays were written before 1977, and the most recent one, Sandra Spanier's "Catherine Barkley and the Hemingway Code: Ritual and Survival in *A Farewell to Arms*," though presenting some new ideas, still relies too heavily on the idea of the "Hemingway code," a term not taken seriously in Hemingway studies for several years.

Kenneth G. Johnston's *The Tip of the Iceberg: Hemingway and the Short Story* (1987) includes essays Johnston had published previously on eighteen individual short stories, plus one on two of the fables, and three of a general nature. Not only are the essays generally good, some excellent, but at the end of each essay there is a bit of background information on the story, including publication data and Hemingway quotations about the story.

Linda Wagner's *Ernest Hemingway: Six Decades of Criticism* (1987) includes essays that are either previously unpublished or, as she says in her introduction, "taken from journal sources that might be difficult for the general reader to obtain." And there is no repetition of material from *Five Decades of Criticism* (1974). *Six Decades* is divided into four parts: biography, the early fiction, the later fiction, and the posthumous works. The book presents an excellent survey of the various critical points of view over the sixty or so years since the publication of *in our time*.

Finally, *Hemingway: The Critical Heritage* (1982), edited by Jeffrey Meyers, is a selection of 118 essays and reviews published in various newspapers and journals, all within two years of the publication of each of Hemingway's books to 1972. There are as many as eleven reviews of some works and a short biography of each reviewer, useful in determining credibility. The book is important for understanding the early critical response to the works.

There are two book-length studies comparing Hemingway to other writers: J. Bakker's *Fiction As Survival Strategy: A Comparative Study of the Major Works of Ernest Hemingway and Saul Bellow* (1983) and Robert E. Gajdusek's *Hemingway and Joyce: A Study in Debt and Payment* (1984). Bakker's thesis is rather naive: the fictional characters of Hemingway and Bellow have in common self-identity problems in a confused society that refused to offer up simple answers. Bakker's conclusion is that the essentials of human existence are the same from one historical era to the next (for Hemingway in the 1930s and 1940s; for Bellow in the 1950s and 1960s). Gajdusek's book, a monograph delivered as a paper to the Hemingway Society meeting in Boston in 1982, is more a study in influence and develops the idea that Hemingway learned from Joyce's "psychological symbol-building" (a term Gajdusek quotes from Carlos Baker) a structural similarity of character development.

A third book in comparative studies, *Ernest Hemingway in Holland, 1925-1981: A Comparative Analysis of the Contemporary Dutch and American Critical Reception of His Work* (1986), also by J. Bakker, compares, as the subtitle suggests, the contempo-rary Dutch and American reception of Hemingway's works. It is an interesting summary of Dutch reviews and criticism from *in our time* to *Islands in the Stream* and includes short biographies of the Dutch critics. Another comparison study is by Myler Wilkinson, *Hemingway and Turgenev: The Nature of Literary Influence* (1986) from UMI Research Press.

Eight other books and two journals need to be mentioned, even though four of the books were published in 1981, again slightly outside the definition of "recent." Two library catalogs have been printed, one of which is the *Catalog of the Ernest Hemingway Collection at the John F. Kennedy Library* (1982). This two-volume work is edited by Jo August, the first curator of the Hemingway Room at the library, and is an extremely valuable work, listing manuscripts, Hemingway's "incoming" correspondence, photographs, newspaper clippings, and so forth, everything in the largest collection of Hemingway manuscript materials anywhere in the world.

The second catalog is *The Ernest Hemingway Collection of Charles D. Field* (1985), a description of the 499 Hemingway items in the Stanford University Library collection. Two inventories of the books owned by Hemingway were published in 1981: *Hemingway's Library: A Composite Record*, a list of 7,700 books compiled by James D. Brasch and Joseph Sigman, "all the books that Hemingway is known to have owned . . . that can be proved to have been in his possession," and *Hemingway's Reading 1910-1940: An Inventory*, a list of what he "owned or borrowed" between 1910 and 1940, compiled by Michael S. Reynolds. The most important of the 1981 books is *Ernest Hemingway: Selected Letters, 1917-1961*, edited by Carlos Baker, including 600 of the 3,500 available letters, and discussed in detail in the 1981 *Dictionary of Literary Biography Yearbook*.

Another item of miscellany is the *Hemingway Review*, a semiannual journal of scholarship which began in the fall of 1981 and which is published at Ohio Northern University. The Spring 1986 issue includes a five-year index that also lists the articles published in its predecessor, *Hemingway Notes*. Of similar interest are the special issues on Hemingway published by the *Arizona Quarterly*, another journal of literary scholarship. A. F. Gegenheimer has edited five such special Hemingway issues: Winter 1970, Spring 1973, Summer 1977, Summer 1983, and Winter 1985. Another item, from University Press of Mississippi, is *Conversations With Hemingway* (1986), edited by Matthew J. Bruccoli as part of the publisher's conversations series.

Finally, with all the fascination with Hemingway, his life, and his fiction, it is not surprising that writers are beginning to produce novels based on Hemingway events. Vincent Cosgrove's *The Hemingway Papers: A Novel* (1983) and Bill Granger's *Hemingway's Notebook* (1986) are two such works. The first uses Hemingway's lost Paris manuscripts to build a story of intrigue and murder (even involving Anastasia, the lost princess of Russia). The second is a spy novel about a political war erupting in the Caribbean and centered on the main character's claim of having Hemingway's notebooks about the 1961 Bay of Pigs invasion of Cuba.

Of the six books by Hemingway published in the past six years, there is one new novel, *The Garden of Eden,* and seven new bits of short fiction. The other works are either largely reprints (*Ernest Hemingway Dateline: Toronto; The Dangerous Summer;* and *Complete Poems*) or excerpts (*Ernest Hemingway on Writing*).

The Garden of Eden (1986) has met with generally favorable reviews, a little surprising considering that before it was published few believed the novel could be any good. There is a lot happening in the novel that will take critics a long time to sort out, but one important thematic element is the "dark magic of change" that the protagonist, David Bourne, sees taking place in his new, young wife as she slowly moves from full female consciousness to male consciousness, this plot a metaphor for the dark change taking place in the world as a whole. One of the good reviews of the novel is by Allen Josephs (*Boston Review,* June 1986: 20-21). Josephs's tone is set in the opening sentence: "Reading *The Garden of Eden* . . . is like walking into the bar at the Palace Hotel in Madrid and finding an old friend you thought had been dead for twenty-five years sitting on one of the high stools drinking his customary glass of bone dry, straw-colored *manzanilla.* It is that exciting, that alive, and that unexpected." Whether the book will hold up as well in five years as it seems to now is another question, but both its characters and themes are different from any in previous Hemingway works, and that in itself will take awhile to interpret.

The Complete Short Stories of Ernest Hemingway, The Finca Vigía Edition (1987) has a misleading title and a badly edited text. (Not only is the book not "complete," but it no doubt sets back the publication of a serious work of complete stories by several years.) And three of the seven "new" stories are fragments from longer works, one a rejected section of *Islands in the Stream.* It seems clear that the book was rushed to print for its commercial value.

William White, who edited *By-Line: Ernest Hemingway* (1947), also edited *Ernest Hemingway Dateline: Toronto: The Complete Toronto Star Dispatches, 1920-1924* (1985). There are 172 dispatches included in the new book, 29 of which are reprinted from the 77 which comprised the 1947 publication. *By-Line* was organized for the most part by subject matter; *Dateline* is organized chronologically and so gives a clearer picture of the development of Hemingway's journalistic achievement in the years just before the early fiction. Much of the writing is excellent, and readers may wonder if enough has been said about Hemingway's early nonfiction.

An example of the late nonfiction, *The Dangerous Summer* (1985) has been edited to 45,000 words from Hemingway's 70,000-word final draft. The book is about one-third larger than the *Life* version which appeared in 1960. It is a chronicle of the 1959 bullfight season of Luis Miguel Dominguín and Antonio Ordóñez. Dominguín came out of retirement to try to regain some former glory, and Hemingway treated him unfairly, throwing objectivity aside by traveling with Ordóñez and his entourage. But the most embarrassing passages are those where Hemingway shows his unkindnesses toward his wife Mary. Against these, however, there is a marvelous description of the Málaga corrida in chapter eleven that reminds one of Hemingway at his very best.

In *The Garden of Eden* there is a series of marvelous African hunting scenes, remembered increasingly more often by David Bourne as he attempts to escape the tension building in his relationship with Catherine and Marita. The African experience took place when David was a boy, and the scenes allow the reader to see David's first experience with personal relationships and with hunting, and it ties in with his present situation. *Sports Illustrated* took the hunting scenes out of the novel's context and published them as "An African Betrayal" with some nice paintings by Walt Spitzmiller. Even out of context it is a better short story than any of the previously unpublished ones in *The Complete Short Stories,* although it still misses the larger framework provided by the novel.

Larry W. Phillips edited *Ernest Hemingway on Writing* (1984), a book of 200 Hemingway comments about writing. Phillips divided the excerpts into thirteen categories: what writing is, the qualities of a writer, advice to writers, titles, politics, the writer's life, and so forth. The material comes from letters, articles, *Green Hills of Africa*, and *Death in the Afternoon.*

Two other short works should also be mentioned. "The Art of the Short Story," written by Hemingway in 1959 as a preface for a book of short stories planned but canceled by Scribners, was finally published in *Paris Review* in the Spring 1981 issue. "Humanity Will Not Forgive This" is a Spanish Civil War article published in *Pravda* on 1 August 1938, about the "murder done in Spain by the fascist invaders," but not published in English until it was discovered by William B. Watson in the Kennedy Library collection and published by various U.S. newspapers in 1982 (for example, the *Los Angeles Times,* 28 November).

The Hemingway Society, which in late 1987 had nearly 400 members, has made a significant impact on Hemingway studies during the past six years. The Society was organized at the Thompson Island Conference in Boston in 1980 and became officially recognized by the Modern Language Association in December of that year. Since Thompson Island, there have been six conferences sponsored by the Society, two sponsored by other organizations (one a year-long series of meetings at Boise State University), plus Hemingway sessions at MLA each December and MLA regional conference sessions–a total of perhaps thirty meetings involving Hemingway studies. Two or three twenty-to-thirty-minute papers are generally read at each of these meetings, allowing for an important outlet for scholarly work, usually preparatory to publication. This proliferation of meetings has attracted to Hemingway studies not only young scholars but also older ones who had drifted into other academic interests. Two of the most important meetings were held in Madrid in 1984 and in Lignano, Italy, in 1986, with plans for such international meetings every two years. (See the list of conferences at the end of the bibliography.)

The Society also publishes *The Hemingway Newsletter,* a four-page, semiannual letter to members that includes information about conferences, book publications, and "notes and queries" about Hemingway studies.

One must feel ambivalence toward all that has been done during the past six years in Hemingway studies. A lot of nonsense has been pub-

lished, some biographical, some critical and interpretative. The quantity of material has more than doubled in the eleven years since Benson made his plea for sanity at the Alabama Conference, and yet the inflation rate has continued unabated. But those books that contribute the most are in the process of changing the very direction of Hemingway studies. Certainly, one must conclude that if the quantity of scholarly work about an author has anything to do with his popularity, then Hemingway is clearly more popular at the end of 1987 than ever before.

Letters:
Carlos Baker, ed., *Ernest Hemingway: Selected Letters, 1917-1961* (New York: Scribners, 1981).

Interviews:
Matthew J. Bruccoli, ed., *Conversations With Hemingway* (Jackson: University Press of Mississippi, 1986).

Bibliographies:
Jo August, *Catalog of the Ernest Hemingway Collection at the John F. Kennedy Library,* 2 volumes (Boston: G. K. Hall, 1982);

Bonnie D. Cherrin, *The Ernest Hemingway Collection of Charles D. Field* (Stanford, Cal.: Stanford University Libraries, 1985).

Biographies:
David Donnell, *Hemingway in Toronto: A Post-Modern Tribute* (Windsor: Black Moss Press, 1982);

Bernice Kert, *The Hemingway Women* (New York: Norton, 1983);

A. E. Hotchner, *Papa Hemingway: The Ecstasy and Sorrow* (New York: Quill, 1983);

Keith Ferrell, *Ernest Hemingway: The Search for Courage* (New York: Evans, 1984);

Arnold Samuelson, *With Hemingway: A Year in Key West and Cuba* (New York: Random House, 1984);

Raymond S. Nelson, *Ernest Hemingway: Life, Work and Criticism* (Fredericton, New Brunswick: York Press, 1984);

Gerald B. Nelson, *Hemingway: Life and Works* (New York: Facts on File, 1984);

Norberto Fuentes, *Hemingway in Cuba,* introduction by Gabriel García Márquez (Secaucus, N.J.: Lyle Stuart, 1984);

Jeffrey Meyers, *Hemingway: A Biography* (New York: Harper & Row, 1985);

Michael Reynolds, *The Young Hemingway* (New York: Basil Blackwell, 1986);

Peter Griffin, *Along With Youth: Hemingway, the Early Years* (New York: Oxford University Press, 1986);

Jack Hemingway, *Misadventures of a Fly Fisherman: My Life With and Without Papa* (Dallas: Taylor, 1986);

Kenneth Lynn, *Hemingway* (New York: Macmillan, 1987).

References:

Arizona Quarterly, five special Hemingway issues, edited by A. F. Gegenheimer, 26 (Winter 1970), 29 (Spring 1973), 33 (Summer 1977), 39 (Summer 1983), 41 (Winter 1985);

Jim Auer, *Ernest Hemingway's For Whom the Bell Tolls* (Woodbury, N.Y.: Barron's, 1986);

J. Bakker, *Ernest Hemingway in Holland, 1925-1981: A Comparative Analysis of the Contemporary Dutch and American Critical Reception of His Work* (Atlantic Highlands, N.J.: Humanities Press International, 1986);

Bakker, *Fiction As Survival Strategy: A Comparative Study of the Major Works of Ernest Hemingway and Saul Bellow* (Amsterdam: Editions Rodopi B. V., 1983);

Harold Bloom, ed., *Modern Critical Interpretations: A Farewell to Arms* (New York: Chelsea House, 1987);

Bloom, ed., *Modern Critical Interpretations: The Sun Also Rises* (New York: Chelsea House, 1987);

Bloom, ed., *Modern Critical Views: Ernest Hemingway* (New York: Chelsea House, 1985);

James D. Brasch and Joseph Sigman, *Hemingway's Library: A Composite Record* (New York: Garland, 1981);

Gerry Brenner, *Concealments in Hemingway's Works* (Columbus: Ohio State University Press, 1983);

Denis Brian, *The True Gen: An Intimate Portrait of Hemingway By Those Who Knew Him* (New York: Grove, forthcoming);

Angel Capellán, *Hemingway and the Hispanic World* (Ann Arbor: UMI Research Press, 1985);

Stephen Cooper, *The Politics of Ernest Hemingway* (Ann Arbor: UMI Research Press, 1987);

Vincent Cosgrove, *The Hemingway Papers: A Novel* (New York: Bantam, 1983);

Bhim S. Dahiya, *Hemingway's The Sun Also Rises: A Critical Introduction* (New Delhi: Lakeside, n.d. [1986]);

Harriet Fallner, *Hemingway as Playwright: "The Fifth Column"* (Ann Arbor: UMI Research Press, 1986);

Joseph M. Flora, *Hemingway's Nick Adams* (Baton Rouge: Louisiana State University Press, 1982);

Robert E. Gajdusek, *Hemingway and Joyce: A Study in Debt and Payment* (Corte Madera, Cal.: Square Circle Press, 1984);

Mimi Reisel Gladstein, *The Indestructible Woman in the Works of Faulkner, Hemingway, and Steinbeck* (Ann Arbor: UMI Research Press, 1986);

Bill Granger, *Hemingway's Notebook* (New York: Crown, 1986);

Larry E. Grimes, *The Religious Design of Hemingway's Early Fiction* (Ann Arbor: UMI Research Press, 1985);

Hemingway Review, edited by Charles M. Oliver, volume 1 (1981-);

Kenneth G. Johnston, *The Tip of the Iceberg: Hemingway and the Short Story* (Greenwood, Fla.: Penkevill, 1987);

J. F. Kobler, *Ernest Hemingway: Journalist as Artist* (Ann Arbor: UMI Research Press, 1985);

Robert A. Lee, ed., *Ernest Hemingway: New Critical Essays* (London: Vision, 1983);

Jeffrey Meyers, ed., *Hemingway: The Critical Heritage* (London: Routledge & Kegan Paul, 1982);

James Nagel, ed., *Ernest Hemingway: The Writer in Context* (Madison: University of Wisconsin Press, 1984);

Donald R. Noble, ed., *Hemingway: A Revaluation* (Troy, N.Y.: Whitston, 1983);

Bernard Oldsey, ed., *Ernest Hemingway: The Papers of a Writer* (New York: Garland, 1981);

John Raeburn, *Fame Became of Him: Hemingway as Public Writer* (Bloomington: Indiana University Press, 1984);

E. Nageswara Rao, *Ernest Hemingway: A Study of His Rhetoric* (Atlantic Highlands, N.J.: Humanities Press, 1983);

Michael Reynolds, *Hemingway's Reading 1910-1940: An Inventory* (Princeton, N.J.: Princeton University Press, 1981);

Reynolds, ed., *Critical Essays on Ernest Hemingway's In Our Time* (Boston: G. K. Hall, 1983);

Earl Rovit and Gerry Brenner, *Ernest Hemingway*, revised edition (Boston: G. K. Hall, 1986);

Gregory S. Sojka, *Ernest Hemingway: The Angler as Artist* (New York: Peter Lang, 1985);

Frederic Joseph Svoboda, *Hemingway and The Sun Also Rises: The Crafting of a Style* (Lawrence: University Press of Kansas, 1983);

Linda Wagner, ed., *Ernest Hemingway: Six Decades of Criticism* (East Lansing: Michigan State University Press, 1987);

Linda Wagner-Martin, ed., *New Essays on The Sun Also Rises* (New York: Cambridge University Press, 1987);

Joseph J. Waldmeir and Kenneth Marek, eds., *Up in Michigan: Proceedings of the First National Conference of the Hemingway Society* (East Lansing: Michigan State University Press, 1984);

Roger Whitlow, *Cassandra's Daughters: The Women in Hemingway* (Westport, Conn.: Greenwood Press, 1984);

Myler Wilkinson, *Hemingway and Turgenev: The Nature of Literary Influence* (Ann Arbor: UMI Research Press, 1986);

Wirt Williams, *The Tragic Art of Ernest Hemingway* (Baton Rouge: Louisiana State University Press, 1981).

Hemingway Society Conferences:
1980–Boston (Thompson Island and J. F. K. Library), "Ernest Hemingway: The Papers of a Writer";
1981–Boston (J. F. K. Library), "A Moving Picture Feast: The Filmgoer's Hemingway";
1982–Boston (Northeastern University and J. F. K. Library), "Ernest Hemingway: The Writer in Context";
1983–Traverse City, Michigan (Michigan State University and Northwestern Michigan College), "Hemingway: Up in Michigan";
1984–Madrid, Spain (Instituto de Cooperation Iberoamericana), "Hemingway in Spain";
1985–Key West, Florida (Florida Libraries Association), "Hemingway: A Moveable Feast";
1986–Lignano, Italy (City of Lignano Sabbiadoro), "Hemingway in Northern Italy."

Galway Kinnell
(1 February 1927-)

Nancy Lewis Tuten
University of South Carolina

See also the Kinnell entry in *DLB 5, American Poets Since World War II.*

NEW BOOKS: *Mortal Acts, Mortal Words* (Boston: Houghton Mifflin, 1980);

Angling, A Day, and Other Poems (Concord, N.H.: Ewert, 1980);

Black Light, revised edition (San Francisco: North Point Press, 1980);

Selected Poems (Boston: Houghton Mifflin, 1982; London: Secker & Warburg, 1984);

How the Alligator Missed Breakfast, illustrated by Lynn Munsinger (Boston: Houghton Mifflin, 1982);

Thoughts Occasioned by the Most Insignificant of All Human Events (Concord, N.H.: Ewert, 1982);

The Fundamental Project of Technology (Concord, N.H.: Ewert, 1983);

Remarks on Accepting the American Book Award (Concord, N.H.: Ewert, 1984);

The Past (Boston: Houghton Mifflin, 1985; London: Secker & Warburg, 1986).

OTHER: "The Permanence of Love," in *New World Writing,* no. 14 (New York: Mentor Books, 1958), pp. 203-209;

The Poems of Francois Villon, translated, with an introduction and notes, by Kinnell (Hanover, N.H.: University Press of New England, 1982);

The Essential Whitman, selected, with an introductory essay, by Kinnell (New York: Ecco, 1987).

PERIODICAL PUBLICATIONS: "Poetry, Personality, and Death," *Field,* 4 (Spring 1971): 56-77;

"The Poetics of the Physical World," *Iowa Review,* 2 (Summer 1971): 113-126;

"Whitman's Indicative Words," *American Poetry Review,* 2 (March-April 1973): 9-11; republished as the introduction to *Walt Whitman: Walt Whitman's Autograph Revision of the Analy-*

Galway Kinnell (photograph by Zdenek Kluzak)

sis of Leaves of Grass (for Dr. R. M. Bucke's Walt Whitman), edited by Quentin Anderson and Stephen Railton (New York: New York University Press, 1974).

In the survey of the year's work in American poetry which appeared in the 1982 *DLB Yearbook* Brian Swann saluted Galway Kinnell as one of America's leading poets. In 1983 the critical world echoed Swann by honoring Kinnell with both the Pulitzer Prize for Poetry and the American Book Award for his *Selected Poems* (1982). Culled from six previous volumes, the poetry in *Selected Poems* represents Kinnell's work from as early as 1946 to the poems gathered in 1980 as *Mortal Acts, Mortal Words.* In addition to important fellowships and grants–a list which includes, among other honors, a MacArthur Fellowship, a

Fulbright Professorship, a Rockefeller Foundation Grant, and two Guggenheim fellowships–Kinnell has been awarded the Shelley Prize by the Poetry Society of America (1974), the Medal of Merit by the National Institute of Arts and Letters (1975), and the Harold L. Landon Translation Prize (1979). He has served as a Fulbright lecturer at the University of Nice in 1978 and at Macquarie University in Sydney, Australia, in 1979; and in 1980 he was Citizen's Professor at the University of Hawaii, during which time he was elected a member of the National Academy and Institute of Arts and Letters. He is currently the Samuel F. B. Morse Professor of Arts and Letters at New York University, where he served as director of the creative writing program from 1981 to 1984. In 1987 he served during the winter term at the University of Michigan as a visiting DeRoy Honors Professor.

In 1958, upon learning that his first volume of poetry was accepted for publication, Kinnell wrote an essay entitled "Thoughts Occasioned by the Most Insignificant of All Human Events," which first appeared in *Pleasures in Learning*, a publication of New York University, in 1959 and was republished in a limited edition in 1982. Amazed that any book of poems is ever brought out in a culture overtly concerned with "inventing, and then serving, the devices that are supposed to work in our stead," Kinnell ruminates on the state of poetry in America: "We fail to read poetry because we are not able to meet the demands it puts upon our humanity." While human existence is threatened by bombs, he asserts, a more crucial concern should be "the gradual atrophy of man's moral nature–his sense of God, his openness to beauty, his dedication to principle, his power to love, and his capacity to enjoy the simple material things." Kinnell consistently emphasizes in both his poetry and prose the need for individuals to come to terms with both their humanity and their mortality. In an interview with Jack Crocker (collected in *Walking Down the Stairs: Selections from Interviews*, 1978), Kinnell asserts that eternity and other theories of personal immortality "very likely are results of wishful thinking." While he feels that "eternity" is "our word for some condition we don't understand," Kinnell believes that a sense of this unknown element allows one to come to terms with death: "In the greatest moments of our lives, we do grasp that there's an element beyond our reach, from which we came and into which we will dissolve. . . . Our happiness in this life–our capacity

to sense this element–makes us able, when the time comes, to die willingly, to return to it without bitterness or the feeling of having been betrayed." Almost thirty years after the publication of "Thoughts Occasioned by the Most Insignificant of All Human Events" Kinnell's poetry is still dedicated to the "exploration of the wonder and terror of being a man."

Robert Langbaum praised Kinnell's *The Book of Nightmares* (1971) as "one of the best long poems of recent years," noting that while the imagery and preoccupation with nature were certainly not new to Kinnell's work, none of his earlier poetry "extends man's spiritual dimensions so high and so low" or "extends the range of man's connections so far into biological and cosmic process." Despite such praise Kinnell conjectures in a 1972 interview with Wayne Dodd and Stanley Plumly (*Walking Down the Stairs*) that after *The Book of Nightmares* his work would be different. "A door has been closed on something," he explains; "It would be foolish to go on in the same way." True to his prediction, Kinnell's next volume moves in a new direction, containing poems that, if not entirely unique in subject matter and poetic theory, are varied in tone and approach. *Mortal Acts, Mortal Words* deals with the individual's struggle to overcome the fear of death and to find happiness in a life ridden with mundane experiences. As he explained in a 1979 interview with Thomas Gardner, in the ninth section of *The Book of Nightmares* "there's a decision to remain in and happily accept the imperfect condition." *Mortal Acts, Mortal Words* takes up the optimistic challenge made by Kinnell in the final line of *The Book of Nightmares* when he implores his newborn son to "find/the one flea which is laughing."

R. W. Flint has suggested that even the Rilkean *Book of Nightmares*, with its "elevation verging on chant, its angels and stars, its civilized egocentricity, its love affair with poetic negatives," is centered less in evil and suffering than in a "private celebration of birth and parenthood." This domestic quality becomes dominant in *Mortal Acts, Mortal Words*, with its focus on individual family members, a milk bottle, a sow, fishing, playing tennis, eating blackberries, and making love. The collection is framed by "Fergus Falling" and "Flying Home," an arrangement which outlines the thematic direction of the book as it progresses from a young boy's initial glimpse of mortality toward a grown man's understanding that even love is difficult, shifting as it does "from transcending union always forward into difficult day." The first poem finds Kinnell's son Fergus climbing a tree and seeing for the first time a pond in the valley below which for years was the scene for the daily cycle of men who are now dead. Fergus "for the first time/... saw its oldness down there," and "he became heavier suddenly/in his bones/the way fledglings do just before they fly." Growing from this initiation, the characters in the poems must learn not to seek transcendence in an effort to escape from their earthly lives but rather to find the value that exists within human experience. Kinnell writes that one must withstand "ten thousand acts which encumber/and engross all the days," for only "between the pages of the slow-going" can satisfaction be derived from living. The final lines in "Flying Home" describe an airplane beginning to land which, despite its ability to transcend the earth, "comes in almost lightly" since "all its tires *know* the home ground." Kinnell's irony is that transcendence must be earthbound, grounded in physical reality.

In the first section of *Mortal Acts, Mortal Words* Kinnell introduces a motif central to the entire collection: the "music of grace," his term for that element which sings out of the day-to-day experiences of mortality and affords the only kind of transcendence possible–that which is experienced when one delves deeply into mortal, bodily existence. In "After Making Love We Hear Footsteps" Fergus can sleep through his father's snoring, noisy music, or loud talking, but the "mortal sounds" of his parents' lovemaking awaken him as the "habit of memory propels [him] to the ground of his making,/sleeper only the mortal sounds can sing awake...." The challenge in "Brother of My Heart" is to "sing, even if you cry," for "the bravery/of the crying turns it into the true song...." This music of grace is, at best, temporary, limited, and born out of adversity. Nevertheless, Kinnell's poetry is ultimately optimistic, asserting that "Even sad music/requires an absolute happiness" which becomes the ideal standard against which sadness is measured.

The poems in *Mortal Acts, Mortal Words* repeatedly echo Kinnell's belief that this music of grace can best be sensed through physical acts. It is not the soul that sings in "The Choir"; rather, "eyes, nostrils, mouth strain together in quintal harmony/to sing Joy and Death well." The central catalyst in this volume is the embrace, ranging from a satisfied little boy's hug to the "last embrace the dying give." In "St. Francis and the

Cover for Kinnell's 1983 Pulitzer Prize and American Book Award-winning collection which led to a major critical reappraisal of his poetry

Sow" Kinnell asserts that touching can "reteach a thing its loveliness" and allow it to thrive and "flower, from within, from self-blessing." Kinnell uses as his example a sow, an animal close to the earth and far removed from the artificial trappings of civilization, in order to remind humanity of its close connection with the natural world. Often his poetry implores readers to recognize and accept the "sowness" in themselves, just as the sow feels lovely "all down her long thick length, /from the earthen snout all the way/through the fodder and slops to the spiritual curl of the tail." Such understandings are not reached by looking inward to find the spiritual presence of a universal creative force, for in Kinnell's poems such a search is futile. Rather, burdened with mundane existence, every living creature needs to be reminded of its own loveliness by experiencing the physical touch of another being. The poem "Goodbye" concludes with this pronouncement: "It is written in our hearts, the emptiness is all./

That is how we have learned, the embrace is all."

The second section of *Mortal Acts, Mortal Words* focuses on the poet's perception of life as a series of transitory, ordinary acts–the theme of the entire volume as set forth by the title and by the epigraph from Petrarch: "mortal beauty, acts, and words have put all their burden on my soul." In "On The Tennis Court At Night" the court parallels existence, "an arena where every man grows old/pursuing that repertoire of perfect shots." Like life, tennis is a game of "the double faulter's groans" and the "grunt of overreaching," with only "very occasionally" a "well-hit ball." Dying in a hospital, an aged tennis player waves his arm back and forth, remembering countless hours devoted to the game. But at the time of death his arm becomes useless, "causing/all those bright trophies to slip permanently,/though not in fact much farther, out of reach." All that remains is a single trophy on the windowsill which reads, "Runner-Up, Men's Class B Consolation Doubles/St. Johnsbury Kiwanis Tennis Tournament 1969." Underscoring the insignificance of his accomplishment, the inscription is a reminder that we grow old while pursuing, not achieving. Like the starfish in "Daybreak," who seem to have fallen from heaven and are drawn deeply into the mud by the earthly pull of gravity, humanity is weighed down by earthly existence. "Les Invalides" suggests the routine nature of life with consecutive lines (five in all) beginning with "always": "Always it's the dusk deepening" for these old men playing boules, "always . . . creaking grace, the slow amble, the stillness."

Yet even more difficult than accepting the mundane nature of existence is coming to terms with mortality. The five poems in the third section of *Mortal Acts, Mortal Words* deal with the deaths of the poet's brother and mother. In "The Sadness of Brothers" Kinnell tries to imagine his brother as he might be had he not died twenty-one years earlier. He suggests that love, finding its initial expression through the embrace, can surpass the limitations of time and death to which the flesh must surrender. A certain degree of immortality can be achieved by the individual who lives beyond death in the minds of those who were embraced in life. In the poet's memory–"twenty-one years too late"–the brothers embrace "with sore, well or badly spent/ but spent, hearts," holding each other, "friends to reality, knowing the ordinary sadness of brothers." In his interview with Jack Crocker, Kinnell explains that "the most difficult thing for the

human being is the knowledge that he will die." In an effort to deal with death, he continues, "we develop, one after another, some manner of accounting for death, or of turning it aside or of making it more tolerable." Thus, in "The Last Hiding Places of Snow," he imagines his mother's voice comforting him with "her mother-love" and "telling of goodness of being, of permanence." But in truth she lives only in his memory, her dying having filled him with "dread which comes when what gives life beckons toward death."

Thus *Mortal Acts, Mortal Words* recounts a spiritual journey beginning with the initial awareness of mortality at childhood and then trudging through the acceptance of mortal acts and mortality itself. In the final section of this volume the cycle is complete; the tone implies a positive affirmation of life by one who has discovered that there is "still time,/for those who groan/to sing,/ for those who can sing to heal themselves." "The Rainbow" suggests that rather than seek dreams which vanish, perhaps it would be better to "turn more carefully to what we can/touch and feel, things and creatures."

The publication of *Selected Poems* in 1982 prompted critics to define in retrospect the stages of Kinnell's poetic development. In the *Times Literary Supplement* Jay Parini noted that *What a Kingdom It Was* (1960) and *Flower Herding on Mount Monadnock* (1964) "anticipated the major phase represented by *Body Rags* (1968) and *The Book of Nightmares* (1971)." Most reviewers recognized that *Mortal Acts, Mortal Words* signaled a shift from what Parini referred to as the "ferocity" of Kinnell's earlier collections; Parini added, however, that while the poet's newer work might seem less powerful, it is nevertheless marked by a "luxurious wholeness, a sense of grace." Harold Bloom called the 1980 collection Kinnell's "weakest volume so far," but added that it was written by "a poet who cannot be dismissed, because he seems destined still to accomplish the auguries of his grand beginnings." In a review of *Selected Poems* Morris Dickstein stated that Kinnell is "one of the true master poets of his generation." He continued, "There are few others writing today in whose work we feel so strongly the full human presence."

In addition to *Selected Poems* Kinnell also published in 1982 *How the Alligator Missed Breakfast*, his only prose fiction since his 1966 novel *Black Light*, which was republished in 1980 with revisions. While *How the Alligator Missed Breakfast* was written to entertain children, it reflects themes common to Kinnell's other works. For example, when the animal characters in this story endeavor to be something they are not, by nature, meant to be, Kinnell alludes to his disgust with twentieth-century technological man's false sense of dominion over nature. A rabbit tries to fly; an alligator takes a ride in a bathtub and swallows a car in an effort to avoid the pain and trouble of walking; a porcupine ends up looking like a chair, a shoe, and a hat when he tires of "prickleprackling" his friends and goes to a barber for a haircut. These creatures' antics are amusing, but the charge is far more serious when, in Kinnell's other work, individuals are scoffed at for failing to acknowledge their close affinities with the natural world. This book also makes a subtle statement about the nature and purpose of writing: Miss Hiphop's desire to write a book entitled *Learning How to Fly, by a Rabbit* calls to mind Kinnell's statement in a 1976 interview with Margaret Edwards (*Walking Down the Stairs*) that "writing is a way of trying to understand the incompleteness [of existence] and, if not to heal it, at least to get beyond whatever is merely baffling and oppressive about it."

In 1985 "The Fundamental Project of Technology" appeared in Kinnell's most recent volume, *The Past.* Two years earlier this single poem of 144 lines was published in a limited edition, numbered and signed. (As is often his practice, Kinnell made substantial changes in the text between publications, and the references here are to the revised version collected in *The Past.*) "The Fundamental Project of Technology" is one of the poet's many attempts to heal through writing, this time focusing on the destruction wrought by the bombing of Hiroshima and Nagasaki in 1945. Overcoming the limitations of many political poems whose subject matter soon makes them outdated, Kinnell uses these two catastrophic events as a backdrop for his larger concern: once more he laments humanity's efforts "to de-animalize human mentality, to purge it of obsolete/animal characteristics, in particular of death. . . ." Kinnell asserts that we have evolved into a species obsessed with "pseudologica fantastica's mechanisms" in our desire to dominate nature, and we have reached an ironic impasse: technology has led us to believe that "to establish deathlessness it is necessary to eliminate/those who die." The epigraph to the poem is taken from an inscription at the entrance of the Nagasaki museum which describes the atomic blast: "A Flash! A white flash sparkled!" Each stanza ends with a reference to

this image, suggesting finally that unless our children are taught differently, the senseless preoccupation with conquering nature will be repeated "until the day flashes and no one lives/to look back and say, a flash! a white flash sparkled!"

The Past is an uneven collection, and consequently, reviews have been mixed. As Roger Mitchell points out in the *American Book Review*, certain poems in this collection "are as good as anything we write these days." On the other hand, James Finn Cotter, writing in the *Hudson Review*, believes Kinnell's elegy to James Wright to be a superior poem, although he finds it "too exaggerated," as if Kinnell is "straining for the epic moment while only half-believing it himself." Alice Phillips, in her *Village Voice* review, expresses the valid complaint that Kinnell's "philosophizing, which he seems to be doing a lot of lately, is not his strength, and his poems periodically degenerate into bad mysticism, vague declarations about the nature of existence, or simple cutesiness." Equally true, however, is Cotter's assertion that Kinnell's "real ability lies in describing what is." At its best *The Past* conveys vivid images of the poet's own recollections of his life up to the present and his struggle to come to terms with the possibilities of the future.

Kinnell has returned in *The Past* to favorite subjects, motifs, and techniques. For example, in "The Angel" he rearranges the Platonic chain of being that places angels between humankind on earth and God in heaven. In this poem the angel is a dog "who mediates between us/and the world underneath us." For Kinnell, animals are the angels, understanding that earth is the only plane of existence and that heaven is an imaginative attempt to escape mortality. In *The Past* music is once again a major metaphor; more directly than in *Mortal Acts, Mortal Words* it becomes an analogy for poetry itself. "Last Holy Fragrance," the elegy for James Wright, contends that "poetry sings past even the sadness/that begins it" and that poets "are only seeking that chant of the beginning,/older than any poem. . . ." The first poem in *The Past*, "The Road Between Here and There," makes use of the type of Whitmanesque catalogue successfully employed by Kinnell in his famous poem "The Avenue Bearing the Initial of Christ into the New World." In this newer poem each line is a list of past events, beginning with the word "here," as if references to physical places could somehow revive the past. The word is ambiguous, suggesting both the physical "here"

Dust jacket for Kinnell's latest collection of poems

which is attainable and the temporal "here and now" which is not.

The final and perhaps most ambitious poem in *The Past* is "The Seekonk Woods." This complex poem could easily be referred to as Kinnell's attempt to explore, in his highly individualized voice, the same ideas that Robert Frost probes in "Directive." In both poems the persona must embark on a journey that carries him through a rehearsal of his past and ultimately demands total self-abandonment as he struggles to define the source and meaning of his existence. After exploring his past and examining what he has learned about his relationship to nature—including the animal nature in himself—the speaker in Kinnell's poem comes to accept that in this life he will be forever "slogging for the absolute" but never attaining it because he is inextricably bound to human limitations. Furthermore, although humanity has lost sight of its connections to the rest of nature, the physical body—which is made up of natural elements—repeatedly

compels him to return to his past and discover the source of his existence. The speaker conjectures that perhaps his childhood friend, "lured by bones' memory,/comes back, sometimes, too, to the Seekonk woods/to stand in the past and just look at it." In "modern Seekonkese," as the poem explains, the name of these woods translates as "slob blowing fat nose"—a description that suggests a less-than-desirable picture of the cruder, more animallike side of man. Such a pilgrimage, in other words, might allow the speaker to rediscover his position in the natural world. Early in the poem Kinnell's persona recalls his earliest memory of the railroad tracks in the Seekonk woods. As a boy he was unable "to step naturally" on "ties set too close together," but he thought then that as he grew older his stride would eventually allow him to walk comfortably by skipping every other tie. He believed that maturity would eliminate his having to "hobble," a word suggesting that life is comprised largely of feeble efforts to overcome daily struggles. As an adult, however, the speaker recognizes that he is still unable to walk comfortably along the railroad tracks; his stride, "once/too long to touch every tie," is now "still just too short to reach every other . . . ,/the hobble/of too much replaced with the common limp/of too little." With child-like faith in the ideal, he had once thought he would "walk in time with the way/toward the promised meeting place of rails/in that yellow Lobachevskian haze up ahead." Suggesting that there might in fact be a place where two parallel lines defy Euclidean laws and come together, Kinnell introduces a central motif in this poem: contrasting the geometric principles set forth by Euclid and Lobachevsky, he establishes a contrast between the finite and the infinite, the real world and the ideal.

In the climax of the poem the speaker realizes that not only is man limited by his mortality but the ability to recognize this limitation "is surely/existence's most spectacular feat." In the blackest hours, "in the night's night," death lurks. Yet even "on this ordinary afternoon, in these humblest woods," he can intuitively see his own death and thus come to terms with his human limitations: "this unlikely event happens again—a creature/straggling along the tracks foreknows it" and understands that he is destined "to remain the wanderer/in velocity if not in direction." In an ideal world, Kinnell suggests, time would be cyclical; rather than progressing in a linear fashion from the past into the future, all events would be in the present. But here the railroad tracks are analogous to the forward progression of time which is limited, offering no alternative for direction.

Typical of a Kinnell poem, the journey that delves into the self ideally leads the traveler to a selfless perception of his place in the world. Total self-abandonment is necessary. If the speaker can get far enough outside of himself to achieve selflessness, he will be less preoccupied with mortality and better able to focus on the present moment. The persona realizes that such a state of mind would enable him to "come back from the living and enter/death everlasting—consciousness defeated." But immediately he recognizes the danger in desiring to abandon a linear concept of time in favor of the cyclical view that places all moments in the present: death, too, would become an everlasting state—hardly a viable alternative in Kinnell's philosophy that advocates transcendence through physical, earthly existence. "So what if we groan?" the

speaker asks. One should not seek to rise above groaning, for that is a mark of humanity, one's "noise." Once the individual can achieve—however temporarily—some state of transcendence, "laughter is [his] stuttering/in a language [he] can't speak yet."

In the final lines of "The Seekonk Woods" Kinnell once again alludes to the linear progression of time to which he is bound but with which he must be content if he is to live: "Behind/the world made of wishes goes dark. Ahead,/if not tomorrow then never, shines only what is." The speaker has learned to accept his brokenness and looks ahead—in keeping with a linear view of time—confident that what he will find there will shine. Although recognizing the necessity of delving deep within to regain knowledge of his source, the speaker does not intend to remove himself from the vitality of his world. Rather, the journey prepares him to pursue life more intensely. In keeping with Kinnell's long-held ideas "The Seekonk Woods" offers no permanent solution to the imperfect and limited condition of humanity. Instead, as Robert Frost said, art should provide a "momentary stay against confusion," each poem coming out of its own moment.

Critics disagree about the merits of Kinnell's work after *The Book of Nightmares*. Harold Bloom prefers earlier poems such as "The Bear" and "The River that Is East." Michiko Kakutani of the *New York Times,* however, praises the newer work for its focus, "however tentatively, on the undying spirit, on the possibility that death may mean not mere extinction, but a reconciliation with the universe's great ebb and flow." Jay Parini describes Kinnell's poetry since *The Book of Nightmares* in this manner: "In place of ferocity and narrative acceleration one finds a luxurious wholeness, a sense of grace." Despite the intensity of his earlier work Kinnell has become, in Parini's words, "a poet of consolation." With the publication of *The Past,* Roger Mitchell expressed best the tenor of the overall critical reception: "I am glad now to have poems from *The Past.* They are more human in scale, less committed to being rituals and myths and more to being responses to what—so it feels—is really there in Galway Kinnell's life." James Dickey was correct, then, when he wrote twenty-six years ago that the events in Kinnell's life would determine the direction of his poetry. Increasingly with each volume since *The Book of Nightmares* Galway Kinnell has turned to his own memories of the past to write poetry that fits his own definition: "saying in its own music what matters most."

Interviews:

Philip L. Gerber and Robert J. Gemmet, " 'Deeper than Personality': A Conversation with Galway Kinnell," *Iowa Review,* 1 (Spring 1970): 125-133;

James J. McKenzie, "To the Roots: An Interview with Galway Kinnell," in *Contemporary Poetry in America: Essays and Interviews,* edited by Robert Boyers (New York: Schocken Books, 1973), pp. 240-255;

Walking Down the Stairs: Selections from Interviews (Ann Arbor: University of Michigan Press, 1978);

Thomas Gardner, "An Interview with Galway Kinnell," *Contemporary Literature,* 20 (Autumn 1979): 423-433;

Thomas Hilgers and Michael Molloy, "An Interview with Galway Kinnell," *Modern Poetry Studies,* 11 (1982): 107-112.

References:

Harold Bloom, "Straight Forth Out of the Self: *Mortal Acts, Mortal Words,*" *New York Times Book Review,* 22 June 1980, p. 13;

James Finn Cotter, "Poetry's Need to Name," *Hudson Review,* 39 (Spring 1986): 157;

James Dickey, "Galway Kinnell," in *Babel to Byzantium* (New York: Ecco, 1981), pp. 134-139;

Morris Dickstein, "Intact and Triumphant," *New York Times Book Review,* 19 September 1982, pp. 12, 33;

R. W. Flint, "At Home in the Seventies," *Parnassus,* 8 (Spring-Summer-Fall-Winter 1980): 51-62;

Lorrie Goldensohn, "Approaching Home Ground: Galway Kinnell's *Mortal Acts, Mortal Words,*" *Massachusetts Review,* 25 (Summer 1984): 303-321;

James Guimond, *Seeing and Healing: The Poetry of Galway Kinnell* (Port Washington, N.Y.: Associated Faculty Press, forthcoming);

John Hobbs, "Galway Kinnell's 'The Bear': Dream and Technique," *Modern Poetry Studies,* 5 (Winter 1974): 237-250;

Michiko Kakutani, "Mortality and Love," *New York Times,* 2 November 1985, p. 13;

Robert Langbaum, "Galway Kinnell's *Book of Nightmares,*" *American Poetry Review,* 8 (March-April 1979): 30-31;

Takako Lento, "The Deathwish and the Self in Contemporary American Poetry," *Kyushu American Literature,* 19 (May 1978): 17-27;

Ralph J. Mills, Jr., "A Reading of Galway Kinnell," *Iowa Review,* 1 (Winter 1970): 66-86; 2 (Spring 1970): 102-122;

Roger Mitchell, "That's It," *American Book Review* (March-April 1987): 23;

Howard Nelson, ed., *On the Poetry of Galway Kinnell: The Wages of Dying* (Ann Arbor: University of Michigan Press, 1987);

Arthur Oberg, "The One Flea Which is Laughing," *Shenandoah,* 25 (Fall 1973): 85-91;

Jay Parini, "From Scene to Fiery Scene," *Times Literary Supplement,* 1 March 1985, p. 239;

Alice Phillips, "Past Imperfect," *Village Voice,* 31 (1 April 1985): 56-57;

Andrew Taylor, "The Poetry of Galway Kinnell," *Meanjin,* 36 (1977): 228-241;

Lee Zimmerman, *Intricate and Simple Things: The Poetry of Galway Kinnell* (Urbana & Chicago: University of Illinois Press, 1987).

Larry McMurtry

(3 June 1936-   )

Sarah English
Meredith College

See also the McMurtry entries in *DLB 2, American Novelists Since World War II*, and *DLB Yearbook: 1980*.

NEW BOOKS: *Cadillac Jack* (New York: Simon & Schuster, 1982; London: Allen, 1986);
The Desert Rose (New York: Simon & Schuster, 1983; London: Allen, 1985);
Lonesome Dove (New York: Simon & Schuster, 1985; London: Pan, 1986);
Texasville (New York: Simon & Schuster, 1987);
Film Flam: Essays on Hollywood (New York: Simon & Schuster, 1987).

PERIODICAL PUBLICATIONS: "Bedtime for America," *Rolling Stone* (5 February 1981): 10, 12-13;
"Life is a Foreign Country," *New York Times Book Review*, 8 September 1985, pp. 1, 36.

In the 1980s Larry McMurtry has produced four novels, including a Pulitzer Prize-winner. An earlier novel, *Terms of Endearment* (1975), has been made into a successful film. He has published most recently a collection of engaging, comical essays on Hollywood and the movies. He continues to run his Washington, D.C., rare-book store. But though McMurtry is dazzlingly prolific, he is not repeating himself. In every novel he takes some kind of risk, enters some new territory. And although not all of his ventures have been uniformly well received, he is at long last beginning to be recognized as a serious writer.

Cadillac Jack (1982), McMurtry's first novel of the decade, is his only one set in Washington, D.C., where McMurtry has lived since the early 1970s. The hero, Cadillac Jack–named for his pearl-colored Cadillac–is a one-time rodeo cowboy, now a roving antique dealer, who has arrived in Washington for the first time. The novel follows him closely for a week of his life, during which time he attends three dotty Washington parties, goes to Texas to acquire fifty pairs of cowboy boots, turns down a chance to buy 11,000

Larry McMurtry (photograph by Lee Marmon)

birds' nests, and commences love affairs with three women while keeping in touch with his three ex-wives (primarily through the phone in the Cadillac) and also taking time out to visit two teenagers who give jacuzzi massages (one version is called the Double Bubble Brunch). The novel moves a bit uneasily through two worlds: that of Washington's social/political elite and Jack's world of antique auctions, collectors, and swap meets. What holds it together is the presence and voice of Jack, who tells his own story.

McMurtry's picture of Washington is satire of the broadest kind. In fact, his penchant for satire has been somewhat underrated; in *Film Flam: Essays on Hollywood* (1987) he notes that he had intended *The Last Picture Show* (1966) to be a satire and was surprised by director Peter Bogdanovich's view of the book: "My task, for a while, was to keep the balloon of Bogdanovichian romanticism from lifting us clear off the earth. In rereading the book I realized that, despite my efforts at savage satire, I had still somewhat romanticized the place and the people." It is impossible to miss the satire on Washington in *Cadillac Jack.* To start with, McMurtry has given his Washington characters totally outlandish names, such as Dunscombe Cotswinkle, an aged statesman; his wife Cunard (nicknamed Cunny); Pencil Penrose, a Georgetown hostess; Lilah and Andy Landry, socialites; Oblivia Brown, hostess with the mostest; and Harris Harisse, an heir.

In the preface to the Touchstone paperback edition McMurtry notes that he had been reading Alexander Pope and Evelyn Waugh when he wrote the book, but his satire is broader than Pope's, more on the order of Samuel Butler's. There is a CIA plot to sell off everything in the Smithsonian, and Jack cannot even find a journalist interested in investigating the story. At the first Georgetown dinner party Jack attends a couple of pugs named Wog-ers and Gog-ers are invited onto the table, where they eat one guest's coq au vin and crawl into the bosom of another. At the second dinner party he attends, the guests are served a tablespoon of soup and "the breasts of some very small bird." The book seems to suggest that life in Washington, D.C., is insufficiently nourishing: the guests at an embassy reception descend on the hors d'oeuvres like locusts, and the bureaucrats look pallid and underfed. Texas politician Boog Miller comments that the town is full of "stump-suckin' women"; Jack explains:

> Some horses are called stump-suckers because they have a penchant for chewing wood. Once they get the taste they'll gnaw on stumps, fence posts, boards, and the corners of feed sheds. This neurotic habit is more apt to manifest itself in highly strung, overbred animals than in your common plugs.
>
> Cowboys universally distrust the stump-sucking horse as being a beast with a mental disorder that renders them unfit for the long-term, trust-laden relationships they like to maintain with their mounts.
>
> Boog seemed to hold the women of Washington in much the same distrust.

The novel's reviewers in general were not amused by the satire on Washington. Eden Wash Lipson of the *New York Times* found it "cartoonish" (*New York Times Book Review*, 21 No-

vember 1982), and Peter Prince commented in the *Nation* (20 November 1982) that McMurtry's "wild fantasies about Washington high life . . . give the impression of society observed purely through a keyhole." McMurtry himself, in the preface, suggests a link between his picture of Washington and Jack's activities as a collector: "The city, as the old nest collector observed, is a graveyard of styles. It is also a city of museums, and its defining attitudes are curatorial. Indeed, its ponderous social life is not unlike a museum exhibit, in which a good many of the major canvases have long needed dusting. The book became a kind of exhibit of capitol portraits."

The reviewers were better pleased with the novel's antique dealers and collectors. McMurtry, of course, knows their world from his career as a bookscout and dealer. They are a gallery of eccentrics, most of whom finally seem a bit sad, like Beulah Mahoney, Rudolph Valentino's former secretary, who sold Jack the hubcaps from Valentino's car and died within six months of parting with them. Some collectors end up snowed under by their growing collections. Others, like Jean Arbor, Jack's most interesting lover, who is beginning a new life as a single mother and antique dealer, so love the objects in their stores that they take little pleasure in making a sale. In the preface McMurtry comments on collecting: "As an antique scout, Jack is a student, and a fairly acute one, of the way in which people relate to their objects. He would like to hope, at first, that people are better at loving other people than they are at loving objects, but his bleak conclusion is that human love is unstable, whether directed at another human or at a Sung vase. The people he meets are as fickle in regard to their *objets* as they are with one another; they cling to a fine thing for years and then get rid of it in an hour, much as they might a fine person."

Jack, traveling scout and dealer in objects who refuses to be tied down to a store, seems to have his relationships to objects licked: "One of my firmest principles is that those who sell should not keep. The minute a scout starts keeping his best finds he becomes a collector. All scouts have love affairs with objects, but true scouts have brief intense. passions, not marriages. I didn't want to own something I loved so much I wouldn't sell it." His problem, of course–and one that he is aware of–is that he relates to women just as he relates to objects. He wants a number of them at the same time and is unable to make a commitment to any of them. In the preface McMurtry calls Jack "a very detached man." A couple of reviewers found that detachment a flaw: Peter Prince called it "apathy, depression, and world weariness." Jack's detachment is leavened, though, by genuine if sometimes bewildered kindness; he is like McMurtry's earlier character Joe Percy (*Moving On*, 1970; *Somebody's Darling*, 1978) in that he is willing to make love to a woman out of pure kindness if he thinks that the act will wipe out her unhappiness for a little while. His voice is that of the typical McMurtry male, humorous and wistful and, as Thomas Mallon noted in the 26 November 1982 issue of *National Review,* "just fine with a line." He is like other McMurtry characters–and like McMurtry himself–in his love of travel for its own sake. In bad moods, Jack says, "I usually hit the road . . . trusting that the long roads and blue skies of America will restore me to lucidity and a simple sense of purpose."

Sometimes McMurtry seems to lose control of *Cadillac Jack*; for example, he attempts to put some thematic weight–the point being that even the finest relationships do not last–on the disintegration of Boog and Boss Miller's marriage, but this occurs mostly offstage and for reasons never made clear to the reader. There are more characters than can be easily sorted out and a number of incidents that do not lead to much of anything. These "flaws," though, may be a part of McMurtry's satiric vision of contemporary life.

McMurtry's next novel, *The Desert Rose* (1983), was written in three weeks as a vacation from working on *Lonesome Dove* (1985). McMurtry was asked to write a screenplay about the life of a Las Vegas showgirl; he did some research and began writing, and, he says in the preface to the paperback edition, "before I had written a paragraph I knew I was writing a novel."

Like *Terms of Endearment, The Desert Rose* is a mother-daughter story. The novel alternates between the points of view of Harmony, a showgirl approaching middle age, and her teenage daughter Pepper, a rising star as a dancer. Both women are beautiful, and that is about all they have in common. Here, unlike in *Terms of Endearment,* it is the mother who is endlessly sympathetic and generally willing to make the best of what life deals out to her and the daughter who is egotistical and demanding. In the preface, McMurtry explains that the theme attracted him because showgirls are "a dying breed": "I have always been attracted to dying crafts–cowboying is one

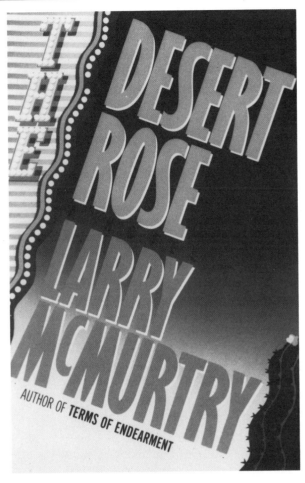

Dust jacket for McMurtry's 1983 novel about a Las Vegas showgirl. McMurtry explained in a 1984 preface to the book that the story was originally planned as a film script and was written during a hiatus in his work on Lonesome Dove, *published in 1985.*

such. It became clear that the showgirls were the cowboys of Las Vegas; there were fewer and fewer jobs and they faced bleak futures, some with grace, and some without it."

Harmony faces her bleak future with optimism. During the week or so of her life that the novel portrays, she suffers setbacks: a boyfriend who has left her after totaling her car steals the insurance check out of her mailbox; a fellow showgirl falls on stage and shatters an ankle; Harmony herself turns thirty-nine and is fired from the Stardust on the same day. At the same time, her daughter Pepper drops out of high school, gets a job as a dancer at the Stardust, and accepts a marriage proposal from a wealthy older man–all without consulting her mother, whom Pepper resents for no good reason. Through it all, Harmony continues to tend to her pet peacocks and sympathize with her friends.

Harmony's resilience is admirable, but the optimism of her narrative voice gets somewhat predictable.

McMurtry himself seems happy with this novel. In the preface to the paperback edition he writes: "Harmony's voice won me at once; I felt I had rarely, if ever, made a happier choice of point of view." Although *The Desert Rose* was not widely reviewed, critical comment was generally favorable, with the exception of D. Keith Mano's comment in the *National Review* (25 November 1983) that the novel was a dull and overly sentimental picture of "women who get used up by the Male System." In the *New York Times Book Review* of 23 October 1983 Steve Tesich called Harmony "a touching, beautiful woman" who "just doesn't get what she deserves." In the *New Leader* of 14 November 1983 Emily Benedek found *The Desert Rose* to be a breakthrough book, the first in which McMurtry proved himself "capable of writing about the modern West without being derailed by ghosts or stylistic artifice."

However, it was McMurtry's next novel that proved to be his real breakthrough into popular and critical success. In *Lonesome Dove*, which won the Pulitzer Prize for Fiction in 1986, McMurtry moves back in time to the post-Civil War West, the West of cattle drives, Indian fighting, saloons, and outlaws, the West that has been turned into myth in thousands of American novels and movies. In the grittiness of its details McMurtry's picture of the old West is realistic and antiromantic (or low mimetic, as Northrop Frye would say), in the manner of Thomas Berger's *Little Big Man* (1964). *Lonesome Dove* lets the reader know that buffalo hunters and their hides smelled awful. One of the two heroines, Lorena, is a whore–of course–but the Dry Bean saloon where she works is no glamorous dance hall but a grubby bar with a hot dusty bedroom upstairs. The other heroine, Clara, raises horses in Nebraska; she has spent much of her life in a sod house and is realistic about its hardships: "Clara had always hated the sod house–hated the dirt that seeped down on her bedclothes, year after year. It was dust that caused her firstborn, Jim, to cough virtually from his birth until he died a year later. In the mornings Clara would walk down and wash her hair in the icy waters of the Platte, and yet by supper time, if she happened to scratch her head, her fingernails would fill with dirt that had seeped down during the day. For some reason, no matter where she moved her bed, the roof would trickle dirt right onto it. She tacked mus-

lin, and finally canvas, on the ceiling over the bed but nothing stopped the dirt for long."

The novel is also realistic about the hardships of a cattle drive. In the main action the heroes drive a herd of cattle (most stolen from below the Mexican border) from Lonesome Dove in south Texas to the northern border of Montana to start a ranch. They endure thunderstorms (where the lightning sometimes glitters on the horns of the cattle), a cloud of grasshoppers, quicksand, a desert, a sandstorm, and, by the end, snow. None of it sounds like fun. A number of the most appealing characters die, killed by savage accidents like being struck by lightning or bumping into a nest of moccasins in a river or being ambushed by the occasional bunch of starving Indians who have enough energy left to fight. It takes courage and endurance–and luck–to survive in McMurtry's old West.

Courage is what McMurtry's main characters have. They emerge as authentic heroes without becoming stereotypes. The leaders of the cattle drive are Captains Woodrow Call and Gus McCrae, former Texas rangers who are fine fighters, little disposed to tolerate insolence from anyone. Woodrow Call is a worker and a planner, tense behind his silences, so embarrassed by his only love affair that he refuses to acknowledge his illegitimate son. Gus McCrae is Call's opposite: a native of Tennessee, a University of Virginia graduate (although he has forgotten his Latin), a constant talker whose voice carries for a hundred yards over the plains. What he has to say is often surprising and funny. It was Gus who composed the sign that advertises their livery stable in Lonesome Dove; it says, among other things:

FOR RENT: HORSES AND RIGS
FOR SALE: CATTLE AND HORSES
GOATS AND DONKEYS NEITHER
  BOUGHT NOR SOLD
WE DON'T RENT PIGS.

Gus also articulates some of the novel's major themes. He recognizes that he and Call and the Texas Rangers in bringing order to Texas have helped to create a civilization where they are no longer needed (Robert Warshow made the same point about the hero of the western movie in "The Westerner," an essay McMurtry knows). Gus makes the point vividly: "We'll be the Indians, if we last another twenty years. The way this place is settling up it'll be nothing but churches and dry-goods stores before

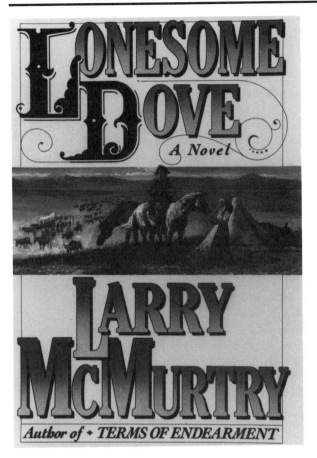

Dust jacket for McMurtry's novel of the American West that depicts a cattle drive from Texas to Montana. It won the 1986 Pulitzer Prize for fiction.

horses, saddles, guns–but the gifts usually make him feel sad and guilty–he spends much of his journey in tears over his lost friends. A small-town sheriff and his deputy are generally ineffectual, incapable of fighting outlaws or even of finding their way to Texas without help. The sheriff's wife, Elmira, is going mad from boredom, missing the old days when she was an outlaw's mistress. The most important outlaw, Jake, a former Texas ranger turned horse thief and killer, is no black-mustached villain but a handsome drifter, a gambler who cannot make strong commitments to other people. Gus comments about Jake: "He wasn't a killer. Jake liked a joke and didn't like to work. I've got exactly the same failings. It's lucky I ain't been hung." Lorena is no stock whore-with-a-heart-of-gold: she is young, beautiful, and vulnerable, yet she knows exactly what the adoration-from-afar of the cowboys means and how little good their affection would do her.

McMurtry also shows an amazing fertility of imagination in creating secondary characters. Po Campo, the Mexican cook who gathers wild birds' eggs for breakfast and fries grasshoppers for dessert, lets it be known rather casually that he killed his wife (and still misses her biscuits). Some of the most vivid characters are animals: the Hell Bitch, Call's aptly named mare; a Texas bull that picks a fight with a bear; the pigs Gus would not rent, who follow the cattle drive all the way to Montana on their own initiative, only to be eaten during the winter. *Lonesome Dove* is a rich book that bears rereading.

By and large the novel won over the reviewers. Whitney Balliett of the *New Yorker* (11 November 1985) found the adventures of the cattle drive facile, but called Clara a "Jamesian heroine," one of the "few full-scale female protagonists" in American fiction. *Newsweek*'s Walter Clemons called *Lonesome Dove* "a marvelous novel," "amply imagined and crisply, lovingly written" and having "just about every symptom of American Epic except pretentiousness" (3 June 1985). In *Time* (10 June 1985) R. Z. Sheppard wrote: "The book's great length and leisurely pace convey the sense of a bygone era, while the author's attachment to misfits and backwaters never goes out of style. Neither does his premise: two aging gunfighters give it one more shot. Gus McCrae and Woodrow Call are descended from the noble buddy system of American literature. Exotically paired males like Natty Bumppo and Chingachgook, Ishmael and Queequeg, Huck

you know it. Next thing you know they'll have to round up us old rowdies and stick us on a reservation to keep us from scaring the ladies." He also recognizes that there is a certain pointlessness in the cattle drive, since he and Call have little desire to be ranchers. The point of the trip, for Gus, is the fun of discovering unsettled country: "This is rare country, this Montana. We're a lucky bunch. There ain't nothing better than this. . . . I wouldn't have missed coming up here. I can't think of nothing better than riding a fine horse into new country. It's exactly what I was meant for, and Woodrow too." Like the classic western hero, Gus chooses the pleasure of discovery over the love of women, but unlike that hero, Gus likes and even understands women; he has experienced love and knows its value.

The other characters are also more than stereotypes. Newt, Call's unacknowledged son, comes of age during the cattle drive (hardships like storms are often narrated from his point of view, making them especially vivid). Newt's growth into manhood is acknowledged by the classic gifts–

and Jim, fling themselves at the wilderness and sooner or later paddle into the mainstream."

Perhaps the most perceptive comment came from Nicholas Lemann in the *New York Times Book Review* of 9 June 1985. He argued that *Lonesome Dove* begins as a realistic "antiwestern" but that the action transforms Gus and Call "from burnt-out cases into–there is no other word– heroes . . . absolutely courageous, tough, strong, loyal, fabulously good fighters." Lemann continued: "All of Mr. McMurtry's antimythic groundwork–his refusal to glorify the West– works to reinforce the strength of the traditionally mythic parts of 'Lonesome Dove' by making it far more credible than the old familiar horse operas. These are real people, and they are still larger than life. The aspects of cowboying that we have found stirring for so long are, inevitably, the aspects that are stirring when given full-dress treatment by a first-rate novelist." Lemann concluded, though, that the novel's heroism precluded its being taken quite seriously: "The potential of the open range as material for fiction seems unavoidably tied to presenting it as fundamentally heroic and mythic, even though not to any real purpose. If there is a novel to be written about trail-driving that will be lasting and deep without being about brave men–and about an endless, harsh, lovely country where life is short but rich–it is still to be written. For now, for the Great Cowboy Novel, 'Lonesome Dove' will have to do."

Nostalgia and realism have been jostling each other in McMurtry's work for some time now. Both attitudes are present in many of his characters, and nostalgia is often an issue in McMurtry's own comments about his fiction. He has said in print, more than once (*In a Narrow Grave*, 1968; *Film Flam*), that he prefers the film *Hud* (1963) to his first novel, *Horseman, Pass By* (1961), because he believes that the novel overidealized Homer Bannion, the aging rancher who adheres to the code of the old West, at the expense of his wild stepson Hud, a more modern character who is perfectly willing to lease the family ranch to oilmen. McMurtry's comments about the 1971 adaptation of *The Last Picture Show* as a film reveal that he had somehow made that novel more romantic and nostalgic than he intended. In 1981 McMurtry called on other Texas writers to stop dwelling on the past and to write about the realities of modern, urban Texas. During the same year, in a *Rolling Stone* article entitled "Bedtime for America," he criticized Ronald Reagan

for capitalizing on "the politics of nostalgia." McMurtry seems to mistrust his own nostalgia. His latest novel, *Texasville* (1987), declares all-out war on that emotion.

Paradoxically, McMurtry breaks into new territory in *Texasville* by returning to Thalia, Texas, the fictional version of his own hometown, Wichita Falls, that was the setting of *The Last Picture Show*. In many ways, *Texasville* seems to show McMurtry commenting on the earlier novel. In *Film Flam* McMurtry reveals that writing the screenplay for *The Last Picture Show* made him dissatisfied with the novel: "I discovered the real reason why writers are ill-advised to script their own books. . . . The real danger is that, in scrutinizing his old text time after time, the writer will suddenly glimpse the book he ought to have written. . . . In the case of *The Last Picture Show*, the better book I discovered had to do with the older couples in the story. While Peter [Bogdanovich] was working out his fascination with youth, I was beginning to develop mine with middle age. I was annoyed that I had wasted so much time in the novel on those uninteresting kids."

Texasville is primarily a novel about the middle-aged. It features some of the central characters from *The Last Picture Show* now in their forties. Moreover, there is a significant change in point of view from *The Last Picture Show*. The earlier novel was written in third person but most often seen through the eyes of Sonny Crawford, who emerged as the most sensitive kid in town. At the end of the novel Sam the Lion, that grand old man of the West, has died and left Sonny his pool hall, along with his memories of an older and more heroic Texas. In *Texasville* Sonny still owns the pool hall (now a video arcade), and he has acquired a hotel, a Laundromat, a convenience store, a car wash, and several other downtown properties; he has also become the mayor. He still has his memories–and they are driving him crazy. More and more frequently, Sonny thinks he is in the 1950s; he wanders into the ruins of the picture show to watch nonexistent movies and drives his car into what once was Ruth Popper's garage and now is another family's television room. At one point he considers suing the whole town for the alienation of his intellect. Once sensitive and nostalgic, Sonny now seems merely pathetic. Ruth says that what is wrong with him is resignation. Jacy (now a sympathetic character, though she was vain and selfcentered in *The Last Picture Show*) elaborates: "I just don't want to see him. Something about him

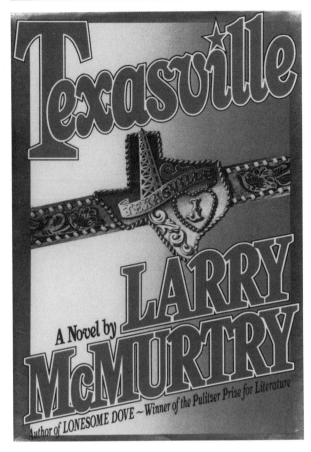

Dust jacket for McMurtry's 1987 novel, a sequel to The Last Picture Show *(1966)*

makes my skin crawl. It happened the day I married him, too. My skin started crawling.... It's his willingness to be unhappy, or something. It gave me the creeps then, and it gives me the creeps now." Sonny himself explains his problem to his friend Duane Moore: "You don't care about the past. But I care about it. I started thinking about it and now I can't stop." Nostalgia has clearly gotten Sonny nowhere, and in *Texasville* the point of view has shifted from him to his tougher friend Duane.

Duane has managed to come home from Korea without getting shot and become an oil millionaire, only to see his wealth evaporate in the oil glut of the 1980s. (The whole town is affected by the oil situation: at one point an oilman suggests bombing OPEC, and when Sonny disappears into the picture show the crowd at the Kwik-Sack becomes convinced he has been kidnapped by Libyan terrorists and round up a posse.) Duane owns four deep oil rigs that cost almost three million dollars each and are now worthless, a twelve-thousand-square-foot mansion that

he mostly finds irritating (he has moments when he can barely make it across the waterbed), a swimming pool and a jacuzzi, and a two-story log doghouse built like "a replica of a frontier fort"–and none of it is paid for. One motif of his quietly desperate life is that he is being smothered by the things he owns; once, in a fit of hostility, he runs his pickup truck over some eighty-five Willie Nelson tapes. His beautiful wife Karla, who is given to wearing T-shirts with slogans like "WOMAN'S PLACE IS IN THE MALL," cannot give up her compulsive shopping now that she and Duane are poor: on the same day when they install a satellite dish she goes to Dallas and buys "a Betamax, a VHS, and four thousand dollars worth of movies."

Duane's family life is as ragged as his financial state. He has four children: Dickie and Nellie, who are more or less grown, and eleven-year-old twins who were born ten years after Karla had her tubes tied. All are problems. Twenty-one-year-old Dickie is the local drug dealer. Engaged to an unstable girl who threatens to shoot him, he nonetheless commences an affair with a married woman in her forties, with whom Duane is also having an affair (the woman ultimately prefers Dickie; in the meanwhile her estranged husband moves into Duane's house). At nineteen Nellie has been married three times and is living at home and neglecting her two babies. The twins have spent most of their childhood in the emergency room because of the wounds they inflict on each other; Karla "learned never to take the twins to the hospital at the same time: there were too many weapons in hospitals." Duane feels helplessly responsible for all of them: "He couldn't tell that he had made any impression on any of his children. It was a haunting feeling, because in many respects he knew he had been a fairly effective man."

In this novel as in *The Last Picture Show* adults who are not the children's parents can have more influence on the children than the parents: at one point Duane's whole family moves in with Jacy and all take turns confiding in her. Even Duane's neurotic dog Shorty transfers his affections. Duane feels as if the center is not holding: "Everything, it seemed, had been washed too many times, had worn too thin. His friendships and his little romances all seemed sad and fragile to him. They had once been the comfortable and reliable fabric that was his life. But the fabric became too old to bear the weight of all the bodies and personalities and needs of the people who

271

tossed and turned on it. At some point a toenail or an elbow had poked through, and now it was all tearing." Even so, Duane is in better shape than most people in Thalia: he and Karla have remained genuine, if argumentative, friends, and he has kept his interest in life and his sense of humor.

Other characters from the earlier novel have also undergone changes. Jacy, now famous for her role as a jungle queen in Italian movies, has come home to pull herself together after losing a son in a freak accident on a movie set. Ruth Popper, now Sonny's secretary and a passionate jogger, is being rewarded for an unhappy youth by a happy old age. Lester Marlow, Jacy's old boyfriend, is now the president of the local bank and soon to face trial for seventy-three counts of fraud. His wife leaves him during the course of the novel; she takes up with Dickie and shows more than a passing interest in Duane. Joe Bob Blanton, who returns for his class reunion, has become a spokesperson for the pedophiliac community in Syracuse, New York. There are a number of new characters, most of them a bit sketchy, and everyone is sleeping with everyone else. Sex is still the main recreational activity in Thalia, and affairs are commenced with fewer romantic illusions than in *The Last Picture Show*. The marriages are generally joyless: as Duane says, "It's hard to stay exciting for a whole lifetime."

Texasville gets such structure as it has from the preparation for and celebration of Thalia's centennial, which also allows McMurtry to poke fun at nostalgia. The title comes from the one-time town of Texasville, originally the Hardtop County seat. In its day the town was a clapboard post office with an attached saloon. Never prosperous, Texasville was deserted when its proprietors drilled for oil and struck rattlesnakes; nothing is left of it but a couple of weathered boards that may well be fakes manufactured for the occasion. The planned events of the centennial celebration include a replica of Texasville, a wagon train (it gets lost), a marathon (Ruth wins), souvenirs (too few are sold), dances, floats, parades, and a pageant that begins the town's history with Adam and Eve (played by Duane and Jacy). The unplanned events include a tumbleweed stampede and the arrival in town of a long-distance trucker hauling 60,000 eggs. When he leaves the truck for a nap, the children find the eggs and throw all 60,000 of them, beginning hostilities against the Byelo-Baptists, teetotalers who have spent the centennial knocking beer out of people's hands with brooms. Their preacher reacts: "It's punishment time! The Lord's raining down egg bombs on this haven of sots."

Texasville is a funny book. Its undertone of melancholy notwithstanding, it is full of satiric comedy. There is nothing romantic/mythic/nostalgic about McMurtry's vision of Texas here. Instead, the novel confirms what McMurtry said as a panelist in a symposium commemorating Texas's sesquicentennial in 1986: "Texas does have to come to grips with the psychological fact that societies are not necessarily and inevitably progressive–that things don't always get better and better." In *Texasville* Duane comes to the same grim realization, musing about himself and his friends: "What *would* they do with the rest of their lives? He had no idea, but whatever it was, it seemed all too likely that they would do it less well than what they had done so far–a depressing prospect."

Texasville has received generally good reviews. John Skow of *Time* admired McMurtry's "wonderfully loose-jointed narrative style" and "the Jamesian restraint of the language" (20 April 1987). Michiko Kakutani of the *New York Times* also praised the sureness of McMurtry's voice and his "feeling for people and place" (8 April 1987). In the *New York Times Book Review* Louise Erdrich compared *Texasville* to *The Last Picture Show* with some reservations about the newer book: "The leisurely, lyrical character development, description and complexity that distinguished the first book are absent from the sequel. . . . 'Texasville' often reads like a movie script, all dialogue and situation. The individual scenes are sharp, spare, full of longhorn humor and color, but motivation is sketchy, rarely described, clued by action rather than reflection" (19 April 1987). Too often it seems to be McMurtry's fate to be accused of sentimentality when he is lyrical, and lack of feeling when he is satiric.

McMurtry's newest book, *Film Flam,* is a collection of essays on the movies, most of which originally appeared in *American Film*. Most of the essays are either meditations on being a screenwriter or discussions of specific movies–in the voice of a man who calls them movies, not films. A self-confessed fan of silly movies, McMurtry can find little to admire in the Hollywood product these days: "With rare exceptions the pictures coming out of Hollywood today are the last resorts of the gutless. In my opinion, a little film

Dust jacket for McMurtry's 1987 collection of previously published essays about movies and the Hollywood attitude toward them

flam is all such an industry deserves." Generally skeptical about European "art" films since he walked out on *L'Avventura,* McMurtry writes penetratingly about movies as audiences experience them in settings like drive-ins and the "fringe theaters" of Times Square; such audiences, he argues, are not seeking "pedestrian realism"–their own lives offer plenty of that–but the illusion of "the heroic–the triumph over circumstance."

McMurtry's comments about movies are direct and unpretentious, most interesting when they illuminate his own work, as does his contention that the "fragmented contexts of modern life" have made love an impossible subject for movies. McMurtry's comments about the film adaptations of his novels are singularly modest. He explains the success of *The Last Picture Show:* "*The Last Picture Show* was exactly the kind of novel from which good pictures are made–that is, a flatly written book with strong characterizations and a sense of period and place. Films like *The*

Blue Angel, Jules and Jim, and *Treasure of Sierra Madre* were made from just such books–books that offer a director no stylistic resistance whatever. Towering classics always have a style, and adapting them is like attempting to translate poetry, only more difficult. . . . True equivalents simply don't exist, and the book that best lends itself to filming, in my view, is the book from which one can abstract a place, a period, and a story for which the director can feel free to develop a style of his own." Thus McMurtry is also modest in his discussion of the screenwriter's craft. He insists that in itself a screenplay is only a "blueprint," useful for budgeting and casting but less a self-sufficient work of art even than an architect's plan or a musical score. And McMurtry is engagingly ready to admit that what has drawn him into screenwriting is the money.

McMurtry's general unpretentiousness as a critic and novelist may have helped to keep his work from being given the type of serious attention it deserves. Again and again reviewers have praised his characters, his readability, his original narrative voice, his mixture of humor and bleakness, and always, when he writes about Texas, his sense of place–only to imply that his novels are popular and somehow not quite serious. The popularity and informality of McMurtry's fiction have encouraged critics to place him somewhere below the first rank of American novelists. In a *New Yorker* review (15 June 1987) of *Texasville* and *The Thanatos Syndrome* by Walker Percy (a writer who has been taken far more seriously than McMurtry), Terrence Rafferty neatly sums up the relative standing of the two writers: "Covering the same span of history, the two novelists form a nearly perfect dialectical pair: the visionary and the realist, the cosmic and the regional, the major and the minor. Percy has squeezed out six ambitious works of fiction in twenty-six years; McMurtry has knocked off eleven of his readable, character-dominated novels in that time. Percy's books rate front-page reviews and all manner of awards and honors; McMurtry's get made into movies. . . . 'The Thanatos Syndrome' is dedicated to the Harvard psychiatrist Robert Coles, 'Texasville' to Cybill Shepherd, who played the beautiful tease Jacy in the film of 'The Last Picture Show.' Both writers are trying to portray what it's been like to live in America for the past two and a half decades, yet the work of each reads almost like a science fiction version of the other's, as if they were describing alternative universes. (And Louisiana isn't even that *far* from Texas.)"

However, there are three recent signs of serious critical regard for McMurtry's work. The first, chronologically, is a short discussion of all of McMurtry's novels through *Lonesome Dove,* published in the December 1986 *English Journal.* Within the confines of two pages, Don Melichar can do little more than tell what each book is about and recommend the novels to other readers; nonetheless, the essay's appearance in an academic journal is encouraging. The second sign of encouragement is Terrence Rafferty's above-quoted review. Having acknowledged McMurtry's place as a "minor regional writer," Rafferty argues that in some ways McMurtry is superior to Walker Percy, less inclined to repeat himself and cannibalize from his own earlier work, gifted with more "comic precision," better able to create a novel that "really *is* about history, at least as Americans live it." Most recently, in the *New York Review of Books* (13 August 1987), no less a scholar/critic than Robert M. Adams made a case for the depth and originality of McMurtry's vision. Confining his discussion to three of the novels, *The Last Picture Show, Lonesome Dove,* and *Texasville,* Adams argues that McMurtry has been under-rated: "As a serious novelist he hasn't received much consideration, probably because his western settings have led eastern critics to confuse him with writers of cowboy melodramas. He can do cowboy melodrama, and do it very well, but even as he does it, there are overtones and nuances of feeling that transcend the formulas. Comparison with classic American writers is probably premature (if one ventured on such comparisons, they might be with Bret Harte, not Mark Twain; Sherwood Anderson, not William Faulkner; Frank Norris, not Stephen Crane), but it is safe to say that Wichita Falls has produced an artist."

References:

Robert M. Adams, "The Bard of Wichita Falls," *New York Review of Books* (13 August 1987): 39-41;

Don Melichar, "Recommended: Larry McMurtry," *English Journal* (December 1986): 49-50;

Terrence Rafferty, "The Last Fiction Show," *New Yorker* (15 June 1987): 91-94;

R. C. Reynolds, "Showdown in the New Old West: The Cowboy Vs. the Oilman," *Lamar Journal of the Humanities,* 6 (Spring 1980): 19-31.

Barbara Pym

(6 June 1913-11 January 1980)

Mason Cooley
College of Staten Island, City University of New York

See also the Barbara Pym entry in *DLB 14, British Novelists Since 1960.*

NEW BOOKS: *An Unsuitable Attachment* (London: Macmillan, 1982; New York: Dutton, 1982);

A Very Private Eye (London: Macmillan, 1984; New York: Dutton, 1984);

Crampton Hodnet (London: Macmillan, 1985; New York: Dutton, 1985);

An Academic Question (London: Macmillan, 1986; New York: Dutton, 1986);

Civil to Strangers and Other Writings (London: Macmillan, 1987; New York: Dutton, 1988).

Many, perhaps most, writers suffer a decline in popularity after their deaths. But since Barbara Pym's death early in 1980 her reputation among both critics and her readership has continued to grow. Pym's literary career can be divided into three distinct periods marked off by dramatic changes in her literary fortunes. The first, a time of steady, modest success, began with the publication of *Some Tame Gazelle* by Jonathan Cape in 1950, when she was in her late thirties. She had worked on the book sporadically since 1934, revising it three times before Cape accepted it. She then established a pace of writing a novel every two years. Five more novels were brought out by Cape in the next ten years: *Excellent Women* (1952), *Jane and Prudence* (1953), *Less Than Angels* (1955), *A Glass of Blessings* (1959), and *No Fond Return of Love* (1961). They were favorably reviewed and won her a following, not large but faithful. She received admiring letters from distinguished literary contemporaries, including Ivy Compton-Burnett, Elizabeth Taylor, Philip Larkin, and Lord David Cecil. She seemed assured of an honorable place in the literature of her generation.

The second period, the time "in the wilderness," began in 1961, when she submitted *An Unsuitable Attachment* to Cape, and the book was summarily refused. From then until the end of 1976, when Barbara Pym was sixty-three years

old, she did not succeed in finding a publisher for her novels, despite many attempts to place her work. Given the boisterous, swinging literary mood of the 1960s and early 1970s, no publisher wanted her mild, understated comedies about such quiet types as genteel spinsters, eccentric clergymen, elderly office workers, antique dealers, and elegantly narcissistic middle-aged women. Though Pym's confidence was very much shaken, she continued to write, encouraged by her friends. Sometimes she felt almost resigned to writing only for herself and them. To this dark period belong the composition (and repeated rewriting) of two of her finest books—*Quartet in Autumn* (1977) and *The Sweet Dove Died* (1978).

The third period began in January of 1977, when something close to a miracle occurred. The *Times Literary Supplement* asked a number of distinguished writers to name the most overrated and underrated writers of the last seventy-five years. Barbara Pym's was the only work named underrated by two respondents: Philip Larkin and Lord David Cecil. The latter said, "Underrated. Barbara Pym, whose unpretentious, subtle, accomplished novels, especially *Excellent Women* and *A Glass of Blessings,* are for me the finest examples of high comedy to have appeared in England during the last seventy-five years." These favorable notices occurred in a literary climate that had become more favorable to Pym's kind of novel; the taste for angry young men and talkative scamps reeling from pub to pub had run its course. The media picked up the *TLS* article. There were a number of interviews in the press as well as an interview on BBC television with Lord David Cecil. Both Jonathan Cape and Macmillan were now eager for her books, and E. P. Dutton quickly became her American publisher.

The last three years of her life were a time of growing fame and critical esteem. She was besieged by invitations to give talks and interviews. Friendly, but shy before groups, she said to someone who asked her to speak, "My 'rediscovery' as

275

Barbara Pym at the International African Institute (copyright © Barbara Pym Estate)

a novelist has not done anything for my gifts as a speaker." Macmillan brought out *Quartet in Autumn* and *The Sweet Dove Died;* the former was short-listed for the Booker Prize, and the latter made the *Sunday Times* best-seller list (two things that had never happened to Pym before). All of her earlier novels were reprinted. Just two months before her death, despite increasing ill health, she completed *A Few Green Leaves* (1980), an elegiac and pastoral work which contains a reprise of many of her central themes and character types. Her comic sense was now muted, but still gently pervasive.

Since Pym's death her work has achieved something very rare in the last hundred years: it is appreciated both by the common reader and by critics. The demand for her books is such that they are all in paperback editions priced so low as to suggest that they are expected to be competitive in sales with popular romances. There is a growing body of secondary work on Pym, including five book-length critical studies now in print, with more announced; Robert Emmet Long's bibliography, printed early in 1986, lists thirteen articles in journals, and the number increases almost

monthly; there is a Barbara Pym newsletter; in the summer of 1986 there was an all-day Barbara Pym Conference at St. Hilda's, Oxford, her old college. All this critical activity surely indicates that a way is being prepared for Pym's work to find a place in the canon of the English novel. The critical account of Pym's work is just now being created, but certain emphases are already clear.

One is the central importance of "excellent women" to her novels. Mildred Lathbury in *Excellent Women* is the prototype for these heroines. A gentlewoman a little over thirty, not beautiful, unmarried, and already thinking of herself as a spinster, Mildred (like most other "excellent women") is very much alone in the world. She is without a husband or a lover, without parents or other close relatives, and with only one or two close friends. Her chief connection with others comes through the church and the life of her parish. She has a part-time job with a charity devoted to the relief of distressed gentlefolk but no "career" to occupy her mind. She is kindhearted but often satirical, shy but curious and observant, easily drawn into the lives of others but also often eager to retreat to the tranquility of her privacy. She is a loyal but unsentimental friend, an ardent church-worker with a streak of skeptical humor about the church. She is both ambivalent and unhopeful about marriage. Mildred and her fictional counterparts are the representatives of a new breed, both in literature and in life: educated women living alone, not as a temporary measure, but as a settled way of life. They are a growing part of modern city life; their hard task is to find a contented mind and a congenial way of life without the traditional supports of family, love relationships, satisfying work, or a close-knit community.

Timid and seemingly defenseless, these heroines are nevertheless agile as mountain goats in keeping their balance in the life of a great city. Their existence may seem narrow and lonely, but they are protected by their intense interest in the trivia of their lives–the meals, the journeys by bus and tube, the church services, the small exchanges of office life. Like Pym herself, they regard the ordinary details of life with respect and affection. Their old-fashioned propriety and overactive consciences suggest the Edwardian world of empire and decorous gentlefolk that vanished after World War II. But their nervous, nervy, alert, observant, and mobile ways of being are in the very spirit of the modern.

A second key theme is unrequited love, with its attendant melancholy, yearning, and living in fantasy. The rather plain heroine is typically in love with a handsome man, who may be a clergyman or at least a member of what Coleridge called the clerisy–the learned professions. She loves silently and devotedly, expecting nothing in return. The man, aside from his looks, has little to recommend him; he is likely to be vain, vague, bumbling, and affected, aware of the devotion he has inspired but responding only with occasional moments of kindness and more frequent moments of exploitation. Though Pym was not a feminist, and indeed appears to have had no political views of any kind, she had an encyclopedic knowledge of the way men exploit women in the office and in ordinary social life. She also knew that women helped create, with their adoration and willingness to serve, the contentedly vain males who almost absentmindedly use their services. The war between men and women is carried on with all the consciousness and sense of responsibility on the side of the women and all the power and obliviousness on the side of the men.

These lonely heroines and the melancholy inspired by their unfulfilled loves account for the note of sadness that runs through Pym's novels. There is the daylight world of ordinary living, humdrum but satisfying, and then there is the inner world of erotic mourning. But this sadness is recuperated and transformed by the fundamentally comic vision which informs Pym's work. Comedy, by one definition, is "tragedy averted." The word "tragedy" is too strong for the events of Pym's world, but the novels certainly can be said to be about "melancholy overcome." The romantic longings of the heroines are not usually fulfilled; indeed, some passages in the novels suggest that these heroines almost prefer yearning to fulfillment, a lover in fantasy to a lover in fact, one who would be always present and making demands. They are not compensated for their devotion in the conventional way of romantic comedy–by wedding rings at the end of the novels. But Pym takes care that, no matter what their emotional state, her heroines never miss a meal and almost never miss a night's sleep. Their sense of humor soon restores their sense of proportion, so that they do not remain long lost in melancholic love. Also, they are rescued from sorrow by their lively sense of the pleasures of ordinary existence. The bread of daily life and the ability of the heroines to appreciate the comedy of existence are what save them from the nullity of depression. It is here if anywhere that Pym comes close to revealing herself as an explicitly Christian writer–one who believes that blessedness does not come from the multiplication of blessings, but from an awareness of the blessings one already has.

Even in her youthful days at Oxford, Barbara Pym had already learned how to use the comic spirit to rescue herself from melancholy, a lesson she was later to turn to great artistic account. In a journal entry written when she was just twenty, in July of 1933, Pym wrote: "After lunch I took some Yeastvite tablets and continued to take them after tea and supper. A slightly unromantic way of curing love-sickness I admit, but certainly I feel a lot better now. (Hilary is playing 'Stormy Weather' incessantly–my theme song I think!) After lunch I read Richard Aldington's new book, *All Men Are Enemies*–it was rather interesting but intensely depressing. After tea I turned to Burton's *Anatomy of Melancholy* and began to read about Love Melancholy–but I haven't yet got to the part where he deals with the cure. Perhaps I'm suffering from the spleen

Pym with poet Philip Larkin, 1977 (copyright © Barbara Pym Estate)

too–in that case I may be completely cured by taking a course of our English poets–which all points to drowning my sorrows in work. I think I shall try to develop a 'Whatever is, is right' attitude of mind–and quite honestly I suppose all this *is* rather good for me–and an affair with Lorenzo probably wouldn't be!"

Pym's art is so seemingly straightforward and lucid that it might seem to leave little for critics to say about it. However, her books keep unfolding with rereading, yielding up new pleasures and layers of implication. Much of her comedy is understated and demure, rendered with a half-smile; and the more one considers her characters, the more twists and turns of complexity they take on. There is still a lot for criticism to do before these books are thoroughly assimilated, their cloak of unassuming domestic realism shown to cover a rich and subtle manifestation of the comic spirit.

More important even than the critical activity that has followed Pym's death is the publication of four more books by her: three novels not published during her lifetime and a volume of autobiographical writings edited by her literary executor, Hazel Holt, and her sister, Hilary Pym. In 1982, after a delay of almost twenty years, *An Unsuitable Attachment* was published with a foreword to the British edition by Philip Larkin. As Larkin

is quick to say, it is not one of Pym's stronger books. Its chief weakness lies in the character of John Challow, the young man to whom Ianthe Broome, the "excellent woman" of the novel, becomes "unsuitably attached." Originally, Pym wrote to Larkin, "John had been intended to be much worse–almost the kind of man who would bigamously marry a spinster, older than himself, for the sake of £50 in the P.O. Savings Bank!" In the published version, however, his unsuitability has much decreased. He is five years younger than the heroine and of a lower social class. His employment record is nondescript: he has spent a couple of years working as an extra in the movies, and meets Ianthe when he is hired as an assistant in the library where she works. Otherwise he is attractive, well-behaved, and very much in love with the heroine. When he and Ianthe announce that they are going to marry, there is a certain amount of grumbling from her relatives and friends, but that is all that is left of the original "unsuitability."

This softening of John Challow's unsuitability can be referred to one of Pym's most consistent characteristics as a novelist: her antimelo-dramatic cast of mind. In her life she tried to avoid exaggerated emotions and scenes (at least after adolescence); in her fiction she either dissolved potential melodrama into laughter, or moderated it to the point where it was no longer recognizable as melodrama. In this novel the melodramatic promise of the title is not kept, and one critic even suggested that the term "unsuitable attachment" might more correctly be applied to the excessive attachment of Sophia, the vicar's wife, for Faustina, her cat. The course of true love between Ianthe and John has too little impediment to afford much dramatic interest. The other romance, between Sophia's sister Penelope, the "pre-Raphaelite beatnik," and a rather prim anthropologist, Rupert Stonebird, is so tentative that there is scarcely any story to tell. There is not quite enough narrative interest to carry the novel steadily forward–and that may have been fatal to the book's publishability in the action-packed 1960s.

Pym believed that the texture of daily life was more important than the great conflicts and crises; therefore exciting plots were never her strong point. Indeed, what Dr. Johnson said of the novels of Samuel Richardson might be said of the novels of Barbara Pym: that anybody who reads them for the story would hang himself. Her genius lies in her comic invention, her wonderful ear and eye for absurdity, her ability to render the texture of middle-class life, her gift for revealing detail. Her books are shaped by her belief that the ordinary is the most important thing in life, not emotional heights and depths. If she does not give us a strong story line, it is because she does not really believe in them. She does give a feast of her typical comic situations and themes.

One of the chief of these themes is the wary, curious relations of men and women, expressed in the first two sentences of the novel: "They are watching me, thought Rupert Stonebird, as he saw the two women walking rather too slowly down the road. But no doubt I am watching them too, he decided, for as an anthropologist he knew that men and women may observe each other as warily as wild animals hidden in long grass." In this novel, courtship is shy and intermittent; women tend to be the hunters and men the hunted; a woman's excellent furniture may be more of an inducement to a proposal than her personal charms or excellent character; a young woman may take being called a "jolly little thing" tragically, as a deathblow to her hopes for romance; a romance may be endangered because a young man forgets for a time to repay the money he borrowed to pay his weekly rent.

More pervasive even than the men and women circling one another is the almost universal taste for inappropriate behavior followed by even more inappropriate moralizing, such as this brilliant moment when a minor character, Lady Selvedge, who is known for her stinginess, stops for a cheap lunch on her way to open the vicarage bazaar:

> Lady Selvedge ate quickly, commenting on the excellence and cheapness of the food as she did so. "Luncheon for only three and ninepence," she declared, reaching out towards a miniature steamed pudding and drawing it towards her, "excellent!"
>
> At this point the young man, who had been reading a folded newspaper, looked up and said in a slightly truculent voice, "Excuse me, madam, but that's *my* pudding you're about to eat."
>
> "Oh no, this is mine," said Lady Selvedge firmly, making a shielding movement with her hands round the pudding in its little dish.
>
> "I think the young man is right," said Mrs. Grandison. "I don't remember seeing you take a pudding. The dishes get rather confused when they're all together on the table," she added, trying to put things right.
>
> "Oh well then, I suppose it is not mine," said Lady Selvedge grudgingly pushing the pudding back toward the young man, who then proceeded to eat it in a kind of defiant confusion.
>
> "These sort of people eat far too much *starch*," said Lady Selvedge to Mrs. Grandison in an audible whisper. "Meat pie, chips, roll and butter, and now this stodgy pudding. A dish of *greens* would be much better for you," raising her voice and turning towards the young man.

An Unsuitable Attachment is the most "churchy" of all Pym's novels. It is set in a North London parish, where the vicarage is located in the one genteel corner of a working-class area with a large black population. The vicar, his wife, and his sister-in-law, as well as their immediate neighbors, make up the cast of characters, and the events of the church year are important events in the story–a bazaar at the end of summer, the Harvest Festival, Christmas, an Easter trip to Rome, and finally a church wedding in summer. Overall, *An Unsuitable Attachment* does not show Pym at her best, but in some of the individual episodes she is working at the top of her form.

A Very Private Eye (1984) is a narrative of Barbara Pym's life put together from her letters and journals, with brief connecting links provided by the editors, Hazel Holt and Hilary Pym. The book was a best-seller in England and the United States. It takes Pym from high-spirited hilarity and reckless seeking of romance in her Oxford days through her period as a WREN officer in Italy during World War II and then to her life as an editor and novelist, published and unpublished, on up to her stoic acceptance of the medical verdict of inoperable cancer. There are gaps in the story, and the unhappy romances seem to follow a pattern, the beloveds to be chosen almost *because* they are unlikely to respond. They all seem to be vain and demanding, expecting much and giving little. If Pym had had the bad luck to marry any one of them, she would probably have had a man who made so many demands that she could never have completed the twelve novels, numerous short stories, drafts of books, and journals and letters that make up her very substantial literary production.

The autobiographical writings bear out the impression made by the novels of a woman witty, kind, intelligent, and often unhappy. But these writings also show that Pym was far more sexually and socially adventurous than her "excellent women," that when she was young she was often emotionally reckless, and even in later life had none of the timidity of many of her heroines. She was interested in good clothes and she liked to eat and drink and smoke. Two months before her death she was able to make a mild witticism about her fondness for an occasional drink. In writing to Philip Larkin she states: "I go to the Churchill regularly and feel I'm getting the best cancer treatment there is. At the moment though I've lost my appetite and don't even like *drink* which is a bore."

Much of the appeal of the book lies in its picture of Pym's hard-won steadfastness in the face of grievous personal and literary disappointments. She never let go of her intelligence and humor for long, and even in the private entries in her journals she always writes like an artist, felicitous and exact in her recording of experience, as exemplified by this entry written in Dublin on 17 July 1968:

> In Molesworth St. why should there be a notice to say "Marmalade For Sale" in the window of the Hibernian Church Missionary Society?
>
> The lone American lady drinking *creme de menthe* on the rocks to match her emerald ring and the other ladies so old and preserved enjoying exotic cocktails in the bar of the Great Southern Hotel Killarney.

Crampton Hodnet (1985) was begun in 1939, in the early months of World War II, and completed by April 1940. Then Pym became involved in war work and did not turn her attention to the novel again until after the war, when she made some alterations and additions, but then decided the story was too dated and never sent it on the rounds to publishers. It remained among her other papers until Hazel Holt rescued it and put it into publishable form. She says at the end of her prefatory note: "Barbara herself hit upon the exact word to describe this book. It is more purely funny than any of her later novels. So far, everyone who has read the manuscript has laughed out loud–even in the Bodleian Library."

The setting is genteel academic and clerical North Oxford society at an unspecified time in the recent past, probably the early 1930s, when Pym attended St. Hilda's College, Oxford. The novel is a romantic comedy, or in part perhaps a burlesque of a romantic comedy. It is written in a mood of high good humor, and it often veers into farce. At this point Pym had a taste for the more blatant forms of absurdity and pretense: there is little of the more subdued and refined nonsense that was to fill her later novels.

The characters divide more or less into two groups–the three pairs of lovers (though the word "lovers" is a little strong) and their allies, and the blocking characters, the censorious snoops and gossips who try to separate the lovers. The amorous party is comparatively youthful and modern, with even a hint of the Jazz Age in one of the character's habit of listening secretly to popular music on Radio Luxembourg. The first couple introduced are the conventional juvenile lovers, Anthea and Simon; the second, Jessie Morrow, a paid lady's companion who is fading into drab spinsterhood, and Mr. Latimer, an extremely handsome but limp curate; the third, Francis Cleveland–a married, middle-aged university lecturer–and his brilliant, beautiful undergraduate student, Barbara Bird.

The blocking characters are older and Victorian-comic. This party is headed by the terrific Miss Doggett, a seventy-year-old Mrs. Grundy who conducts a reign of terror at her tea table and bullies Jessie Morrow without ceasing. She is a fully realized comic monster on the scale of Lady Bracknell in Oscar Wilde's *The Importance of Being Earnest*. Also of her party are old Mrs. Killigrew, "wonderful for her age," and her son, a librarian at the Bodleian who wears crepe-soled shoes so that he can sneak up on library patrons unheard.

In the early chapters the lovers are surrounded by a network of spies, and it seems that the novel is going to be about the various shifts to which the lovers must resort in order to circumvent those who oppose their love. But as it turns out true love is *not* defeated by an oppressive older generation, however much the elders may thunder and threaten. All three pairs of lovers do in fact separate by the end of the novel but for reasons having nothing to do with Miss Doggett and her allies. Anthea and Simon separate because he meets someone else and jilts Anthea, who shortly replaces Simon with one of his friends. Jessie Morrow and Mr. Latimer separate when she refuses to marry him because he only wants a wife to fend off the parish women

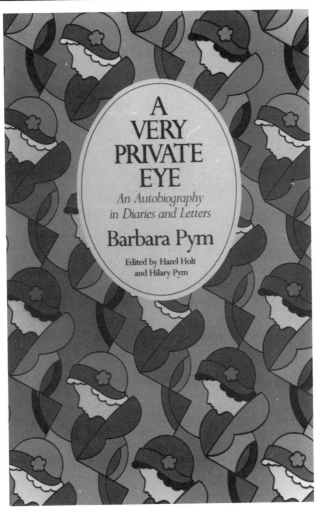

*Dust jacket for Pym's autobiographical best-seller in both England and the
United States*

who buzz around him. Francis Cleveland and
Barbara Bird miss the channel boat as they are
eloping to Paris. In the Dover hotel where they
check in to wait for the next boat, they separately
come to recognize the truth that they do not really want to go to Paris together, and part.
Barbara Bird likes the idea of romance, but she dis-
likes sex; Francis Cleveland likes romance and
sex both, but he longs for the comforts of home
and the attentions of his wife. Both find adultery
too arduous, and each returns home alone.

The romances come apart on their own because the partners are disinclined. Even at this
early stage Pym had a skeptical view of the relations of men and women. Each of the three men
lies to his beloved, and each of the women, finally, has all too clear a picture of what her
suitor is really like. What starts out as a situation
out of romantic comedy as old as Roman comedy–

one in which an impediment from the outside is
the problem–turns into a more modern one in
which the impediment is created by the couples
themselves. Despite the old-fashioned provincial
setting and the heavy-handed Victorian moralizing of the blocking party, the pairs of lovers insist on arriving at separation in their own way
and for their own reasons. The struggle between
young and old dissolves and is replaced by a
story of the vagaries of the erotic sentiment.
Thus, in the earliest of her posthumously published novels to be completed, Pym brilliantly combines love and farce, ancient and modern, a
traditional comic intrigue plot and a modern
story of the unpredictable levity and inconse-
quence of "being in love."

An Academic Question appeared in the summer of 1986 and was on the whole well received
by reviewers, especially considering how skimpily

Dust jacket for a final selection from Pym's unpublished papers which includes the complete title novel, sections from three other novels, stories, and an autobiographical essay

developed and unfinished it is. To bring the book into being, Hazel Holt smoothed together two different versions of the story and also incorporated some of Pym's notes, so that the book is to a considerable extent her creation as well as Pym's. Holt says in the prefatory note, "This [first] draft, written in the first person, was, she felt, too 'cosy' to have any chance of being published in the unsympathetic literary climate of the day, so she wrote another version, this time in the third person, attempting to make the whole thing more 'sharp' and 'swinging.' But she was writing against the grain and was not happy with it, and although still 'tinkering with it' in October 1972, she became absorbed in the novel that was to become *Quartet in Autumn* and abandoned it."

The result is a very entertaining and readable account of life in a provincial university in the late 1960s as seen through the eyes of Caroline (Caro) Grimstone, the young, restless wife of

a lecturer in anthropology. But there is not much of a central idea, and some episodes are merely suggested rather than fully worked out. Pym was trying hard to write something exciting and up-to-the-minute outside her usual manner of working, but everything she touches takes on a thoroughly Pymean caste. For example, Kate, the heroine's four-year-old daughter, is Pym's only effort at a child character, and a thoroughly Pymean child she is. The mother, describing Kate's relations with her grandmother, states, "She spoiled Kate, but only as the kind of little girl she wanted her to be—one who had a great deal in common with children in television commercials—and Kate was cunning enough to go along with her. She would call her 'Nana' to her face and 'Grannie' to me, which made me wonder if she was already showing signs of a brilliant mind that could easily master the subtleties and ramifications of kinship terminology." Three generations are watching one another, mirroring and deflecting messages, unaggressive but self-consciously strategic.

Pym also devised a plot that was intended to have a wealth of melodramatic action: the theft of a manuscript from an old man dying in a nursing home (surely a Dickensian touch), an ugly power struggle among anthropologists, adultery, and a student riot that destroys the part of the library that houses the Stillingfleet collection, from which the manuscript was purloined. These events do take place, more or less, but they are softened by Pym's characteristic mildness and preference for anticlimax to climax. The potential melodrama is subdued into domestic comedy. The theft helps Caro's husband finish his article and establish his reputation, but the old man dies before he misses his manuscript; the student riot dwindles into a Guy Fawkes celebration in which fireworks accidentally damage the library. The heroine hopes that her discovery of her husband's adultery will generate some excitement, but it fails to do so.

Caro suspects that her husband is having an affair with a colleague, Iris Hornblow. When she confronts him, he denies the charge. But he adds that he did, as a matter of fact, recently have intercourse with a young woman named Cressida, the assistant editor (like Pym herself) of an anthropological journal in which he is publishing an article. Afterwards, he violates Caro's sense of propriety by *not* sleeping on the divan in his study but in their shared bed. In the morning she decides not to make up the defiled marriage bed as a sign of its violation. After consulting with a couple of her friends, who seem somewhat inattentive, she decides to go home to her mother. That visit turns out to be rather unsuccessful, and Caro then goes to the office of the learned journal to confront Cressida, who is in the midst of an office crisis. The two women sit and have coffee while Cressida awaits the arrival of the office temp to help her, and Caro leaves without mentioning the original purpose of her visit. Pym's deflation of melodrama is always at the service of comedy, dissolving self-righteous uproar into laughter. Pym was trying to work against her own vision of things in this book, but fortunately she did not succeed, and her wonderful powers of comic invention did not forsake her.

In 1987 *Civil to Strangers and Other Writings*, a collection of unpublished writings and several previously uncollected short stories, was published. Since Barbara Pym's death, her work has grown steadily in reputation. It now seems likely to become a permanent part of the literary heritage.

References:

Diana Benet, *Something to Love: Barbara Pym's Novels* (Columbia: University of Missouri Press, 1986);

Barbara Brothers, "Women Victimized by Fiction: Living and Loving in the Novels of Barbara Pym," in *Twentieth-Century Women Novelists*, edited by Thomas F. Stanley (Totowa, N.J.: Barnes & Noble, 1982), pp. 61-80;

Charles Burkhart, *The Pleasure of Miss Pym* (Austin: University of Texas Press, 1987);

Hortense Calisher, "Enclosures: Barbara Pym," *New Criterion* (September 1982): 53-56;

Lord David Cecil, "Barbara Pym" (obituary), *Journal of the Royal Society of Literature*, Biennial Report,(1980-1981): 25-26;

Isa Kapp, "Reappraisal: Out of the Swim with Barbara Pym," *American Scholar*, 52 (11 March 1977): 237-242;

Philip Larkin, "The World of Barbara Pym," *Required Writing: Miscellaneous Pieces 1955-82* (New York: Farrar, Straus & Giroux, 1984), pp. 240-244;

Robert Liddell, "Two Friends: Barbara Pym and Ivy Compton-Burnett," *London Magazine*, 24 (August-September 1984): 59-69;

Robert Emmet Long, *Barbara Pym* (New York: Ungar, 1986);

Jane Nardin, *Barbara Pym* (Boston: Twayne, 1985);

Lotus Snow, "The Trivial Round, the Common Task: Barbara Pym's Novels," *Research Studies*, 48 (June 1980): 83-93.

Eudora Welty

(13 April 1909-   )

Ruth M. Vande Kieft
Queens College, City University of New York

See also the Welty entry in *DLB 2, American Novelists Since World War II.*

NEW BOOKS: *The Eye of the Story: Selected Essays and Reviews* (New York: Random House, 1978);
The Collected Stories of Eudora Welty (New York & London: Harcourt Brace Jovanovich, 1980);
One Writer's Beginnings (Cambridge, Mass. & London: Harvard University Press, 1984).

The fifth decade of Eudora Welty's career as a writer brought three publishing events: the first, not unexpected; the second, naturally expected; the third, a complete surprise. The first, *The Eye of the Story: Selected Essays and Reviews* (1978), seems "right" for its stage in Eudora Welty's career, a time of ingathering and consolidation. Though the *idea* for the volume may not have been the author's, the execution of it surely was, for everywhere are signs of careful authorial editing, mostly in the way of compression, refinement, clarity. The selection is both wide and representative of some of the author's most distinguished nonfictional writing over the years. Several of the best of the essays were originally lectures; others, occasional pieces in a lighter vein.

The book contains four sections: "On Writers," "On Writing," "Reviews," and "Personal and Occasional Pieces." It is always clearly the fiction writer whose mind is at work, for evident in the essays and reviews is the "willing imagination" enjoined on readers of her own fiction, the celebration of life in others' fiction, the use of a critical language graceful, clear, and discriminating, brightened by metaphor. The dominant tone is one of praise, celebration of these "blessed achievers." Yet the sympathy she brings to her readings does not prevent her from seeing the distinctive features of each writer's work, and articulating them precisely. Her comments, especially in the essays on Jane Austen, Henry Green, and Chekhov and in the reviews of works by Elizabeth Bowen, Virginia Woolf, William Faulk-

ner, Isak Dinesen, and E. M. Forster, show how much of what she finds beautiful and interesting in their fiction is also present in her own: Jane Austen's use of a small world of mostly family relationships as the stage for "the argument of souls"; Henry Green's zestful exploration of outrageous and irrational behavior; Chekhov's genial humanity, his search for a reality often fantastic or incongruous since human vagaries make it so. The essay on Willa Cather provides Welty the occasion for enlarging on her ideas about the relationship between the writer's life and art. Willa Cather's move from Virginia to Nebraska at the vulnerable age of nine, causing a "wrench to the spirit," was metamorphosed into her "technique of juxtaposition," her placing of widely disparate characters, times, and experiences side by side in her novels. Welty generalizes concerning this technique: "Personal history may turn into a fictional pattern without closely reproducing it. . . . Essences are what make patterns. . . . In the novel, relationships, developments of acts and their effects, and any number of oblique, *felt* connections, which are as important and as indispensable as the factual ones in composing the plot, form a structure of revelation. The pattern is the plot opened out, disclosing–this was its purpose–some human truths." These words are actually the germ of her own, then unconceived, autobiography, in which she was to show how the patterns of her life are translated into the patterns of revelation manifested in her fiction.

Of the essays included under the heading "On Writing," the most well known and influential is "Place in Fiction"; a more recent meditation on time ("Some Notes on Time in Fiction") seems to reflect the mature writer's long thoughts on this more abstract component of fiction, the fruits visible in her 1972 novel, *The Optimist's Daughter* (while place is the friend–near, familiar, and lasting–time is the enemy–running out, leading toward death). These essays, together with "Looking at Short Stories," "Writing and Analyzing a Story," and "Words into Fic-

Dust jacket for Welty's 1984 autobiography

tion," form a primer for fiction readers, a guide for critics and analysts, and a credo for Welty's own fictional theory and practice. In "Must the Novelist Crusade?" she asserts the author's right to privacy and independence, the freedom to remain detached, as writer, from specific social and political issues which might rapidly consign a novel to oblivion if it had been no more than propaganda, however honorably intended.

The final section, "Personal and Occasional Pieces," evokes persons and places in or near Welty's Jackson, Mississippi. One piece in particular, "The Little Store," anticipates *One Writer's Beginnings* (1984) in making the events of an "ordinary" kind of errand in an "ordinary" child's life seem extraordinary because of the intense inner life and imagination of the child, who meets life with curiosity, apprehension, excitement, and a generally rapturous embrace. The sketch shows Welty to be both rooted and a traveler, both shy and intrepid, an insatiable reader, a sensitive observer, a joyous adventurer, a survivor of many private ordeals and losses, her own and others'.

The second event of recent years in Welty's career, the expected one, was the publication of her collected stories in 1980, a hefty 622-page volume which includes, in chronological order of publication, and with only minor revisions, all the stories previously collected in *A Curtain of Green* (1941), *The Wide Net* (1943), *The Golden Apples* (1949), and *The Bride of the Innisfallen* (1955). The only previously uncollected stories are the last two in the volume, "Where is the Voice Coming From?" and "The Demonstrators," born out of the civil-rights anguish of Welty's time and place. The first of these stories was the only one to draw special comment from her (as "unique" in its coming about as a response to a specific event, the shooting of civil-rights leader Medgar Evers). The preface is largely given over to a testimonial of love and gratitude to her family and the then "strangers," later friends–important writers, editors, and literary agents–who fostered and supported her career: Robert Penn Warren, Cleanth Brooks, Katherine Anne Porter, John Rood (editor of the "little magazine" *Manuscript*, in which her first story, "Death of a Traveling

Salesman," appeared), John Woodburn, and Diarmuid Russell. *Collected Stories* sold widely and occasioned some general "overviews" of her work in periodicals. Though reviewers were generally favorable, one or two found the famous early stories from *A Curtain of Green* and *The Wide Net* to be her best, forming her most significant contribution to the genre.

The unexpected event in Eudora Welty's career, the publication in 1984 of *One Writer's Beginnings,* a slender 100 pages, was a complete surprise because of her repeated and firm refusals to allow a public look into her private life. She told an interviewer in 1972, "A writer's word should be everything.... That should be read instead of some account of his life.... My own [private life] I don't think would particularly interest anybody, for that matter. But I'd guard it, I feel strongly about that. They'd have a hard time trying to find something about me."

It is possible that the autobiography would never have been written had it not been for the invitation of Harvard University, in April 1983, to inaugurate the William E. Massey lecture series in American Civilization, and her friend Daniel Aaron's suggestion that the lectures be autobiographical. She responded with three intimate lectures given to the warmly appreciative student audience. The three lectures were titled "Listening," "Learning to See," and "Finding a Voice." The book is enchantingly bound and jacketed and contains a small portfolio of photographs of Welty, her family, and grandparents. It was immediately popular and became the first book published by Harvard University Press to make the best-seller list, where it remained for many weeks.

It seems inevitable that the book should have been successful, not only because the grace, wit, and subtlety of the author's style are evident here as in her fiction, but because the book accomplishes so much in a short space. Faithful to the implied purpose of the lecture series, this is Americana of the highest order, swiftly evoking the physical settings, way of life, manners, and morals of three distinct regional types over a period of almost a hundred years in the late nineteenth and early twentieth centuries: the well-educated, independent, story-telling Appalachian "pioneer" (her mother's roots); the saturnine, pious, gentle, midwestern farmer (her father's roots); and the small-town middle-class Mississippian of the "New South," a society very much in transition (her own and her brothers'

roots). Drawing on memories and impressions from visits to her grandparents made when she was a child, as well as family stories and legends told by her mother and her five brothers, Welty recreates the texture of life of these American character types with warmth and sympathy, but always with a comic, lightly satirical eye, undercutting the sentimentality often threatening such a memoir. Her descriptions of her youth in Jackson include portraits of such early-twentieth-century characters as the dedicated and authoritarian teacher, the librarian, the born southern storyteller, the traveling entertainer. In her commentary on the lives and times of the characters described and her experiences of them, she shows a fund of wit and wisdom that makes her a worthy successor to the tradition of American autobiography which includes Benjamin Franklin, Mark Twain, and Mary McCarthy, though her satire is gentler and her view of human nature kinder than that of the others.

Most important, the book is a probing of the sources, development, and practice of the author's art as a fiction writer. In this respect it stands as a recent entry in the tradition which includes Wordsworth's "Prelude" or Joyce's *Portrait of the Artist,* though her work is far more modest in scope and intention, sensitive and personal. And though Welty is clearly and passionately devoted to her art she never takes the grand tone about it, nor displays awestruck attitudes toward her developing powers of imagination and insight. She is too eager to share credit for it all– her loving attitudes toward her characters to the loving nature of her parents, for each other and their children; her gifts as a narrator to the southern penchant for story telling; her love of myth, legend, fantasy, of any and all kinds of books, to their mere and myriad *existence,* consumed by her in an ecstasy of promiscuous reading; her success to the encouragement of her mother and the help of her literary "angels."

She tells the story of her beginnings as a writer not in strict chronological order, but in the order of patterns noted and their perceived significance. For, she says, "time as we know it subjectively is often the chronology that stories and novels follow: it is the continuous thread of revelation." The progression of that revelation is spiraling, with repeated time periods, kinds of experience and themes explored, and an always growing sense of illumination as she makes connections and discovers patterns by the use of memory and hindsight. This could have made the book seem more elegiac than it is (since all of the loved ones whose presence she evokes so compellingly are dead), were it not for the zest with which she re-creates her joyful youth, the free sharing of the tenderness and devotion she feels for her parents, to whom she dedicates her book. In their very different ways, each had given her invaluable gifts. Christian Webb Welty, who had suffered the loss of his mother when he was seven, had looked to the future, to the progress he optimistically thought would follow upon the development of modern science, technology, and business. Cautious and protective of his family, he provided a "frame of regularity" for the life of his high-spirited and romantic though shy and impressionable daughter and inspired in her as well a sense of pride in craftsmanship, of responsibility for the excellence of what she made.

But to her mother, Chestina Andrews Welty, she feels she owes the passion and spirit of her art. "Chessie" Andrews had possessed a strongly independent nature, a devotion to books and learning, a hedonistic pleasure in fiction. Eudora Welty sees the adventuresomeness of her own impulse toward risk-taking in fiction writing as part of the same spirit which drove her mother into her burning house in order to save her precious set of Charles Dickens's works, and, as a girl of fifteen, led her to accompany her dying father by river raft and train to Baltimore in search of medical aid. That independent spirit, matched against her mother's protective and self-sacrificial tendencies, produced a struggle that might have been only guilt-inducing had it not been for the author's strong sense of commitment to her art and (though she does not say so) to her success in its practice.

The first two sections of *One Writer's Beginnings* ("Listening" and "Learning to See") are given over largely to Welty's preparation as a writer; the last ("Finding a Voice") to her performance as one. Her descriptions of what she calls her "sensory education" convey delicately and exuberantly how it feels to be an imaginative, highly absorbing child. She links each sense impression and learning experience to her development as a writer. Ticking clocks throughout the house, kept in perfect working order by her efficient and order-loving father, are linked to her fiction writer's sense of time; his country boy's "weather sense" she links to her "meteorological sensibility," her coupling of inner, psychic mood and atmosphere with external weather. An early awareness of movement, not only in the music

Cover for the paperback edition of Welty's 1978 selection of book reviews and critical essays, her first such collection

which attended every state and stage of her growing up but in the sound of the human voice and words on a page (heard inwardly), informed her own later reading and writing. Words, more than something heard, were experienced visually as letters, and often tactually, the roundness of the moon seeming to fill her mouth "as though fed to me out of a silver spoon," round as "a Concord grape Grandpa took off his vine and gave me to suck out of its skin and swallow whole, in Ohio." She learned to listen *for* stories, rather than merely *to* them, making that act part of the intensity with which she lived, part of her sense of urgency and anticipation, waiting for some nameless joy to come, secrets to be revealed. The excitement gave her a "fast-beating heart," at one point, literally, for she was confined to bed with this malady for a time.

The mature writer whose central preoccupation was with the mysteries of life, of human identity and relationships, the meaning of love and separateness, displayed an ordinary child's appetite for the secrets of adults, but it led to extraordinary revelations, sometimes painful. There is a dark thread of early deaths that appears in the tapestry of Welty's life. She tells of her repeated and unsuccessful attempts to learn from her mother "where babies come from"–but of how two shiny nickels discovered among her mother's treasures had led to her opening another secret door than the one which opened on the mystery of sexual love. The nickels had been placed on the eyes of a baby brother who had died, neglected, her mother said, in attempts made to save her own life. This taught the incipient writer that "one secret is liable to be revealed in the place of another that is harder to tell, and the substitute secret when nakedly exposed is often the more appalling." Such a shock of mortality, deepened by the fact that both of her parents had suffered an early loss of a parent, made them especially cautious and protective of their second-born child.

The shadow of mortality did not fall directly on Welty as a child, but it did on her as a beginning writer. At the age of fifty-two Christian Welty died of leukemia. This loss fell just about the time Eudora Welty was beginning her serious fiction writing. It marked the end of a relatively carefree, protected youth. Can there be any doubt that such a shattering loss deepened her sympathy and awareness of the depths of the human heart, just as her work for the WPA as an itinerant publicity writer and an amateur photographer broadened her awareness of others' lives? The suffering, loneliness, frustration she found wherever she traveled; the courage, endurance, inner freedom, capacity for joy she encountered in whomever she met–all found their way into her fiction. Part of her vision of life and death would always be a sense of the total arbitrariness of death's advent and the finality of its separation. In her fiction there are many unexpected deaths, catastrophes, accidents and near-accidents. The classical mode of tragedy, in which deep-seated flaws in character bring on the tragic fall, is almost entirely missing in her fiction, along with any clear villain. Evil is external, concealed behind the curtain of green (nature); sickness, injury, death are always surprising, and yet inevitable, like other forms of change subject to no human motive, and lacking in any clear sign of divine management.

One Writer's Beginnings tells of other formative influences of Welty's experiences and temperament on her fiction. Family trips in the summer seemed like "wholes unto themselves"–like stories–with change and development, each with its own revelations, an ongoing process as time yielded new perspectives. Traveling by car or train, later usually alone, accustomed her to viewing the outside world through a window frame. This habit of seeing things through a "framing device" (described in "A Memory" as part of her youthful efforts to be a painter), later merged with another kind of seeing eye, that of the photographer, looking from a distance, through a lens, waiting for the right, revealing moment, capturing movement in time and space. Then, in her mind's eye, from her safe position as observer (preferably invisible–"a powerful position"), with her empathetic imagination, she would draw closer, move into the minds of her characters, match her vision to theirs, thus wedding the inside world to the outside. "My work," she says, "in the terms in which I see it, is as dearly matched to the world as its secret sharer."

The autobiography shows both how much Welty did, and did not, draw upon her own experience to write her fiction. Readers of *Losing Battles* (1970) will recognize how often the life of Banner folk in hill country Mississippi resembles that of her mother and her ancestors in the mountains of West Virginia; and the resemblances sometimes become identifications in *The Optimist's Daughter*. But the differences are equally apparent, and the closer we get to the "central problem" of the novel, the less relevant it seems to the author's personal situation. The surviving parent in the novel is the father, a southern gentleman and small-town judge, with some virtues and limitations very different from those of Welty's northern Republican father. In *One Writer's Beginnings* Welty states how she has never invaded the lives of real persons in writing her fiction, being herself private, and knowing that "living people to whom you are close–those known to you in ways too deep, too overflowing, ever to be plumbed outside love–do not yield to, could never fit into, the demands of a story." She never created characters who spoke for her in person. Yet she finds in one character, totally unlike herself in outward identity, the German-speaking music teacher of "June Recital," something like the core of herself as an artist. "What I have put into her is my passion for my own life work, my own art. Exposing yourself to risk is a truth Miss

Eckhart and I had in common. What animates and possesses me is what drives Miss Eckhart, the love of her art and the desire to give it until there is no more left."

Anyone familiar with "June Recital" knows how much the exercise of discipline informs and controls Miss Eckhart's character and gifts as a teacher, and this is true also of Welty's practice of her art. The romantic passion is always kept in check by a classical balance and reserve, as though an inward voice might be warning her, "Nothing too much," teaching her lessons of economy, reticence, understatement. And humor flashes out everywhere, tempering the mood of heroism or high romance or tragedy, bringing human beings back to size. Like Chekhov, the spirit of whose work her own often resembles, she excels in "mixed" forms.

One Writer's Beginnings shows the importance of the lyrical to all her fiction–the impulse to praise a world and life she finds often horrifying, but more often beautiful, funny, amazing, joyful. Her preference for and use of the form of the short story, in which feeling can be sustained at a high level for the relatively brief, concentrated time it takes to read; her imaginative power to penetrate the heart of a character, find and give voice to the strong or tenuous, elusive feelings which well up or linger there; the obvious pleasure she takes in the creative act of writing; the flow and look and feel of those limpid sentences, chunky and bright with metaphor, yet paradoxically dark and dense with mystery–all these virtues of her work show her to be a lyricist in prose fiction.

At a time of much cultural and political instability, if not disintegration and decadence, Welty's affirmation of life, her celebration of its essential goodness, her positive artistic credo, have made her and her work especially honored and cherished in the American "post-modern" world of arts and letters. Yet the unique blend in her ancestral origins, marking it as distinctively American, along with her strong character trait of independence, we also recognize as largely, now, part of our past. Doubtless some of the popular embracing of *One Writer's Beginnings* is nostalgia for a lost innocence–of pioneer and small-town American places and styles of life; of turn-of-the-century and Depression-era struggles, hopes, and

aspirations; of times when values seemed clear and integrity was the hallmark of our national character. That integrity is still vibrant in this author, along with a modesty, a quiet dignity, an immense warmth, graciousness, and overflowing gratitude to her readers. The past few years have brought her much increased exposure to a variety of audiences, from that bastion of academic achievement and enterprise, the Modern Language Association, to the masses who watch television ("prime-time" network as well as several appearances on public television), to the members of P.E.N. (where she joined Saul Bellow in a reading from her work in 1986). The numbers of honorary degrees and sundry other honors and citations have grown: she may possibly be the most "awarded" writer in America. The past few years have seen her win the Commonwealth Award of the Modern Language Association and two Presidential Medals. Her achievement and her manner, her humility and warmth, have won her what few Americans have attained–the affection and respect of all who know her. This applies even to feminists who, while celebrating her triumphs as a woman writer, have looked in vain for the subversive attitudes and actions which so often lie behind the achievements of notable women. Not that hers was a completely charmed career: in her autobiography she tells how hard she worked trying to place her stories, finding a reading public and a market. And for many years that public was small–perhaps it is still smaller than sales might indicate, when the fiction, apart from the familiar comic stories, so often turns out to be difficult and elusive, notably lacking in strong plots or anything dimly sensational. Critics, who have been productive in proportion to her recent growth in fame, are discovering that, for all its surface simplicity, this is a complex, subtle, and often obscure art which quietly resists the heavier critical constructs and vocabularies of our day.

Yet the ideal quality of Welty's literary career cannot be gainsaid, the fulfillment and quiet luster of it. When so many honors and awards are bestowed by professors and presidents (not only college presidents, but national–one a Democrat, the other a Republican), by religious and civic leaders and all sorts of "little people," it is difficult not to feel a sense of "rightness" about the career.

New Entries

Anita Brookner
(16 July 1928-   )

Robert E. Hosmer, Jr.
Mount Holyoke College

BOOKS: *An Iconography of Cecil Rhodes* (N.p., 1956);

J. A. Dominique Ingres (Paulton, U.K.: Purnell, 1965);

Jacques-Louis David (Paulton, U.K.: Purnell, 1967);

Watteau (London: Hamlyn, 1968);

The Genius of the Future: Studies in French Art Criticism (London & New York: Phaidon, 1971);

Greuze: The Rise and Fall of an Eighteenth-Century Phenomenon (London: Elek, 1972; Greenwich, Conn. & New York: Graphic Society, 1974);

Jacques-Louis David: A Personal Interpretation (London: Oxford University Press for the British Academy, 1974);

Jacques-Louis David (London: Chatto & Windus, 1980; New York: Harper & Row, 1980);

A Start in Life (London: Cape, 1981); republished as *The Debut* (New York: Linden, 1981);

Providence (London: Cape, 1982; New York: Pantheon, 1984);

Look At Me (London: Cape, 1983; New York: Pantheon, 1983);

Hotel du Lac (London: Cape, 1984; New York: Pantheon, 1984);

Family and Friends (London: Cape, 1985; New York: Pantheon, 1985);

A Misalliance (London: Cape, 1986); republished as *The Misalliance* (New York: Pantheon, 1986);

A Friend From England (London: Jonathan Cape, 1987; New York: Pantheon, forthcoming).

TRANSLATIONS: Waldemar George, *Utrillo* (London: Oldbourne Press, 1960);

Jean-Paul Crespelle, *The Fauves* (London: Oldbourne Press, 1962);

Maximilien Gauthier, *Gauguin* (London: Oldbourne Press, 1962).

OTHER: "Rigaud: *Portrait of Louis XIV*, 1681," "Delacroix: Scenes from the *Massacres at Chios*, 1824," "Ingres: *The Turkish Bath*,

Anita Brookner (photograph by Mark Gerson)

1862," "Cezanne: *The Bathers*, ca. 1900," in *Great Paintings*, edited by Edwin Mullins (London: British Broadcasting Corporation, 1981; New York: St. Martins, 1981);

Margaret Kennedy, *Troy Chimneys*, introduction by Brookner (London: Virago, 1985; New York: Penguin, 1985);

Edith Templeton, *The Island of Desire*, introduction by Brookner (London: Hogarth, 1985);

Templeton, *Summer in the Country*, introduction by Brookner (London: Hogarth, 1985);

Templeton, *Living on Yesterday*, introduction by Brookner (London: Hogarth, 1986).

In 1981 a serious, scholarly Reader in art history at London's Courtauld Institute of Art published her first novel, *A Start in Life* (better known to American readers as *The Debut*). Within the next three years, three more novels followed, the last a Booker Prize winner. The author herself expressed shock and surprise at the critical and popular success of her fiction. *The Debut* was praised as "a precise and haunting little performance" (Annie Gottlieb, *New York Times Book Review*, 29 March 1981), and its author lauded for her "impeccable prose and sly wit" (Michele Slung, *Washington Post*, 28 April 1981) as well as "her precision and perception and confidence of the telling" (Anne Duchene, *Times Literary Supplement*, 29 May 1981). The appearance of two more novels and the acclaimed television adaptation of *Hotel du Lac* (1984), the Booker McConnell winner, have catapulted Brookner to the forefront of contemporary British writers, making this reserved art historian a literary celebrity.

Anita Brookner was born in London, the only child of Newson and Maude Schiska Brookner, both Polish Jews. Her father had been born in Poland, her mother in England. Brookner has described her parents as "bizarre" and "eccentric," noting that she "loved them painfully, but they were irascible and unreliable people. They should never have had children; they didn't understand children and couldn't be bothered ... they were mismatched, strong-willed, hot-tempered, with a very great residual sadness which I've certainly inherited. We never had much fun." Reflecting on her home life with her parents, whom she cared for until they died, Brookner confessed in a 1985 interview with Ann Kolson: "I was a great disappointment to them as I didn't marry young, have children, fulfill family expectations, conform to family traditions." Childless and single, she describes herself as "this grown-up orphan with what you call success," and as "the world's loneliest, most miserable woman."

Anita Brookner received both informal and formal education. At home her father supervised her reading: "My Polish father, who remained very Polish, thought that the best thing he could do for me was to unveil the mysteries of English life which could be found in the novels of Charles Dickens: he really believed that. So I was set to read Dickens at the age of 7, and I read all the novels." Her formal education took place at James Allen's Girls' School, King's College, Univer-

sity of London, where she read history, and the Courtauld Institute, where she took a Ph.D. in art history. Her English education was supplemented by foreign study; three years' research in Paris made her feel much more at home there than in England. Even today she considers herself an outsider in England, living among people she describes as "high-spirited and ungracious," and "flippant, complacent, ineffable, but never serious."

Brookner's academic career began with her appointment as a visiting lecturer in the history of art at the University of Reading (1959-1964). In 1964 she joined the faculty of the Courtauld Institute, first as a lecturer (1964-1977), then as a Reader in the history of art (1977-). Brookner, a Fellow of New Hall, Cambridge University, was the first woman to be Slade Professor of Art at Cambridge (1967-1968). In the course of her professional career, Brookner has established herself as a gifted teacher, an internationally respected authority on eighteenth- and nineteenth-century French art, and noted author of several major studies in the field.

During the early and mid 1960s Brookner began her career as a published, professional writer in her discipline, translating publications on art historical topics for Oldbourne Press (1960-1963) and contributing two volumes, *J. A. Dominique `Ingres* (1965) and *Jacques Louis-David* (1967), to a series on "The Masters" for Purnell. None of these books offers the opportunity to characterize Brookner's work to the extent that her *Watteau* (1968) does.

A slim volume with more pages of illustration than text, *Watteau* is not a work of her own design, following as it had to, the scheme of "The Colour Library of Art" series issued by Paul Hamlyn. The fourteen-page introduction, a bio-critical essay on the painter, gives a sense of Brookner's scholarship; several features stand out. First, Brookner's concern is to detail the cultural background for Watteau's achievement, emphasizing the role of the commedia dell'arte, asserting that "it might well provide the key to the inspiration of Watteau's art and to its iconography." The material she presents to substantiate her assertion is both evocative and convincing. Second, Brookner is at pains to separate the legend from the facts of Watteau's career: biographical accuracy is important to this art historian. Third, her discussion of Watteau's character as an artist illuminates what Brookner calls his "modernity," "originality," and "spiritual ease." Finally, she focuses her attention on Watteau's "Gilles" and reveals her overriding purpose when she expresses the hope that "the critical spirit of the twentieth century will do him similar justice" to that of the Romantics who "discovered in this very wryness [discernible in the painting] the gravity of a vanished era." Though restricted by the requirements of a series format and the limitations of space, Brookner's *Watteau* is an informative and learned study, appropriate for the general reader; her commentary is incisive, her prose style fluent in this work which is really an outline for a full treatment of that enigmatic French artist.

Watteau was followed by *The Genius of the Future* (1971), a study of French art criticism of the late eighteenth and early nineteenth centuries. Brookner concentrates on six figures (Diderot, Stendhal, Baudelaire, Zola, the brothers Goncourt, and Huysmans), whose work impresses her because of its "prophetic nature" and "its peculiarly strong flavour of personality." She has organized her subjects in approximate chronological order so that her text exhibits a narrative progression; indeed, her narrative fluency is so sustained that *The Genius of the Future* possesses an organic, as well as intellectual, unity. For each figure, Brookner isolates a key theme—for Zola, it is "the heroism of everyday life"—and uses it as a touchstone for her discussion. In effect, her presentations are paradigmatic, as seen in the chapter on Baudelaire. Brookner provides an introduction with theme (Baudelaire exhibits "the withdrawal symptoms of a man of faith who made the choice, perhaps the wrong choice, of operating in the sphere of the beautiful rather than that of the good"); an abbreviated biographical sketch with cultural context illuminated; specific consideration of the aesthetic dimension; and a concluding analytical reflection (Baudelaire is "the great master of aesthetic and moral counterattack"). *The Genius of the Future* is a work of impeccable scholarship, precise, carefully annotated and designed, whose grace and narrative ease enable the discerning reader, whether art historian or layperson, to read it with pleasure and profit.

Brookner undertook her study of the French painter Jean-Baptiste Greuze in response to her perception that "certain aspects of Greuze's work mark him as an historically more important figure than was hitherto accepted." In addition, her discernment of a "close connection between Greuze and a much more important painter, Jacques-Louis David," informs *Greuze:*

Dust jacket for Brookner's 1971 study of French art criticism of the late eighteenth and early nineteenth centuries

The Rise and Fall of an Eighteenth-Century Phenomenon (1972). Three of the book's nine chapters are given over to a discussion of the cult of *sensibilite*, defined by the author as "essentially a fashion in ways of feeling" that extended to philosophy, literature, and painting. Against that backdrop, Brookner recounts Greuze's life before proceeding to discuss his development as an artist and his influence. Her fine attention to a good number of his previously neglected drawings rescues the artist's reputation. Her concluding evaluation, that "Greuze is *sensible*, his faults are those of *sensibilite*, and therefore belong to the wider domains of morals and taste," may be more generous than deserved, but certainly her argument about just how much David learned from the older man is solidly convincing. Throughout, *Greuze* displays the depth of scholarship and the meticulous attention to detail that distinguishes Anita Brookner's art criticism; while this narrative may not be quite as seamless as that of *The Genius of the Future,* and that may well be a result of the academic nature of the exercise as well as the painter's tumultuous career, nonetheless this study in European cultural history is intellectually vital and engagingly written.

Jacques-Louis David: A Personal Interpretation is the published text of Brookner's address to the members of the British Academy on 30 January 1974. Viewed in retrospect, this sixteen-page lecture is clearly a blueprint for her 223-page study, *Jacques-Louis David*, published in 1980. Brookner's major themes and concerns are already present: tracing "a very definite progression from one state of being to another" in David's work; highlighting his paintings done from 1784 to 1787, when "David achieved a style devoid of ambiguity, with complete fusion of formal and emotional intention"; delineating a biographical profile, though here it is necessarily skeletal. Brookner discusses only twelve of David's paintings, dwelling on three, *The Oath of the Horatii, Death of Socrates,* and *The Death of Marat,* before declaring that "David possessed in abundance the necessary weakness and also its indispensable corollary, the endless desire of the heart," and placing him among "the happy few" for whom "art and life are indistinguishable." *Jacques-Louis David: A Personal Interpretation* testifies to Brookner's powers as a critical scholar and her charms as a lecturer: her text displays learning animated by anecdotal wit.

In *Jacques-Louis David,* the major study that follows, Brookner begins her careful, thoughtful analysis of David's career as a painter by sketching the eighteenth-century background before shifting to aesthetic concerns by describing the formative influence of Diderot's theory of composition and the various influences of Winckelmann, Boucher, Fragonard, Chardin, and, of course, Greuze. This is really a reciprocal reading, demonstrating how David was both formed by the sociopolitical/cultural context and how he helped to shape the forces creating that context, particularly when he painted patriotic and emblematic canvases like *The Oath of the Horatii* or staged elaborate festivals and pageants in post-Revolutionary France. From early years in Paris to an Italian sojourn of five years' duration and into the thick of the French Revolution Brookner traces the development of this "very great French artist," whose fortunes rose and fell according to his political connections: up, then down, with Robespierre; up, then down, with Napoleon. Six years after her lecture, Brookner still places David among those "happy few" while she lauds him as an art-

ist with "a power of sensibility, of excitability, of emotional generosity."

Sometime in 1980 Brookner wrote what now appear to be her last essays on art history. For a British Broadcasting Corporation production on painters from Duccio through Picasso, she prepared four essays: "Rigaud: *Portrait of Louis XIV,* 1681"; "Delacroix: Scenes from the *Massacres at Chios,* 1824"; "Ingres: *The Turkish Bath,* 1862"; and "Cezanne: *The Bathers,* ca. 1900." Each is a pungent, knowledgeable analysis of the painting under consideration, informed by sound scholarship and reflection yet written for a lay audience. All four were included in a volume titled *Great Paintings* (1981). Since then, she has published no formal essays on art historical topics. Indeed, her response to Shusha Guppy's recent question "Will you ever write on art history again?" ("No. That particular career is over.") serves notice that she will not return to the field.

Thus, by 1980, Brookner had earned considerable recognition as an art historian. The process began with her appointment as Slade Professor of Art at Cambridge University (1968); the first woman to hold this prestigious chair, she delivered a series of lectures on cultural and intellectual history that earned her professional recognition as well as personal success. With those lectures, an address to the British Academy, and three major studies in art history to her credit, to say nothing of sixteen years' distinguished teaching at the Courtauld Institute, Brookner had become an internationally renowned authority on eighteenth- and nineteenth-century French art. Her writing in the field shows that she had acquired more than sheerly technical command of information: in addition, she had developed a distinctive style. All her published work exhibits the power of invention, schematic design, dramatic pacing, narrative fluency, and a precise sense of audience. In short, Brookner had honed her skills so that her scholarship reveals a consummate rhetorician at work.

Yet in 1980 Brookner turned to the writing of fiction; since then she has written six novels. In that time she has published no more essays on art history, nor is she likely to do so. Asked in 1984 by John Haffenden if she would be writing more art criticism, she responded by saying, "I doubt it. It takes too long: *Jacques-Louis David* took ten years. I think I've lost what I had originally, perhaps the energy and perhaps the belief that I can do it." That energy which she so admires about certain eighteenth-century figures,

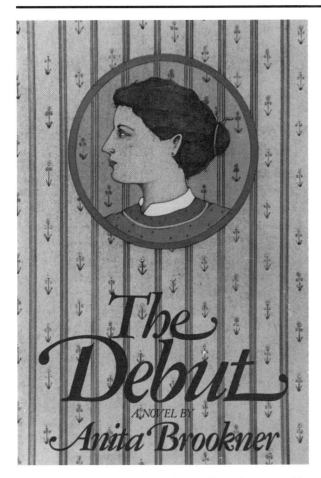

Dust jacket for the American edition of Brookner's autobiographical first novel

David in particular, she has converted to the service of fiction, beginning in 1981 with *The Debut.*

In a *Publishers Weekly* interview Brookner herself has provided some of her motivation for becoming a novelist: "It was most undramatic. . . . I had a long summer vacation in which nothing seemed to be happening, and I could have got very sorry for myself and miserable, but it seemed such a waste of time to do that, and I'd always got a lot of nourishment from fiction. I wondered–it just occurred to me to see whether I could do it. I didn't think I could. I just wrote a page, the first page, and nobody seemed to think it was wrong. An angel with a flaming sword didn't appear and say, 'You shouldn't be doing this.' So I wrote another page, and another, and at the end of the summer, I had a story. That's all I wanted to do–tell a story." She wrote the first draft of *The Debut* (and the first draft is essentially the only draft for all her novels, an efficient distinction she shares with Muriel Spark) in several months, working in her office

at the Courtauld Institute. During each of the following five summers she followed the same practice, thus producing six novels in as many years. Yet Brookner's rather ingenuous explanation ("I never decide to write a book. It somehow happens.") does leave something out.

In 1984 she amplified this comment with remarks of some psychological depth and probity: "Writing novels was a kind of first-aid when I found myself in a disagreeable state of will, paralyzed: it worked momentarily. I felt alone, abandoned, excluded, and it was no good moping. It was a gamble . . . it's a form of editing experience." And she continues, with chilling insight plumbing the depths of her own experience in fiction-making: "when deception is practised on you . . . you write novels out of that sense of injustice . . . or you go under."

Anita Brookner did not "go under," for the novel she wrote during that summer of 1980 was published to substantial critical acclaim in 1981, praised by Nicholas Shrimpton as "a very pungent fable about the sacrifice of daughters to the needs of elderly parents" (*New Statesman*, 22 May 1981). Two more novels followed: *Providence* (1982) and *Look At Me* (1983).

These three novels bear such striking similarities to one another that they can be considered together. Indeed, one way to discuss Brookner's fiction is to divide it into two groups, treating the first three novels as a unit and the remaining three as individual entries, separate but certainly related to the first. Others, Gerda Charles for example, find it convenient to read the first five books together as "different slices of what appears to be largely autobiography," but that does Brookner some disservice. Charles, however, is on target when she isolates the great theme of Brookner's novels as "the plight of the clever, feeling woman of great sensibility who longs all too humanly for love and companionship with a man of particular quality but has neither the beauty to attract him nor the coarseness to grab for him."

In *The Debut* Dr. Ruth Weiss, reared on tales about Cinderella, Anna Karenina, and Emma Bovary, but encouraged to emulate the example of David Copperfield, believes that literature has ruined her life. Only too late does she realize that Cinderella has given her unrealistic expectations, for the prince she fervently awaits will never come. Virtue must be its own reward, since it does not pay off in the real world. What is wanted there is manipulative power. Critical, introspective, and disciplined, Ruth had beheld "the moral universe unveiled" in Dickens; yet, when she reflects on what she has since learned from Balzac, that moral fortitude is irrelevant, she understands that it is better to be "engaging" and "attractive" rather than virtuous, "better [to be] a bad winner than a good loser."

The child of a German-Jewish father and an English mother, perhaps the most narcissistic, childish parents in contemporary fiction, Ruth was brought up in an ancestral, claustrophobic flat by her Jewish grandmother Weiss, for whom she was named. Repulsed by the antics of the coarse Mrs. Cutler who becomes housekeeper on the death of her grandmother, Ruth withdraws to the world of French language and literature, preparing herself for an academic career; the forty-year-old woman who narrates *The Debut* describes her "evening hours in the library as the most satisfying of her life." At university, Ruth makes a friend of Anthea, a vivacious, freewheeling sort with a "modern" philosophy of love ("it is a game only if you win–if you lose, it's far more serious"), but they do not develop a substantial relationship.

Ruth's attempts to do that with a man fall flat: Richard Hirst, a psychologist/social worker, is a spoiled, self-centered brute given to saying things like, "Sometimes, Ruth, I wonder if you're really a caring person." While Ruth achieves a degree of self-knowledge, at one point telling herself, "I have no manipulative powers," admitting that they "constituted the quality which distinguished the villains from the virtuous," she is radically incapable of acting upon her insights. Though a reading of Balzac's *Modeste Mignon* reveals that "all the vices turn out to be virtues," she cannot effect the necessary conversion.

In Paris for research on her dissertation, "Vice and Virtue in Balzac," she lodges with old friends of her parents but spends most of her free time with a handsome couple, Hugh and Jill Dixon. Her perceptions about literature are intensified; she begins "to think of the world in terms of Balzacian opportunism," perceiving "that most tales of morality were wrong, that even Charles Dickens was wrong, and the world is not won by virtue." Insight, yes, but not independent, self-actualized living: falling for a French academic, Prof. Duplessis, Ruth feels that if he loves her, she will be redeemed. Her notion of male-female relationships is unliberated, her longings are thoroughly middle-class, for she would replicate her grandmother's pattern of cosseting the male. The affair with Duplessis never materializes;

Ruth returns to London to care for her father, incapacitated by a stroke; her mother dies; her own rather last-minute marriage lasts but six months, cut short by her husband's death in a motorcar accident. At the end of the novel, Ruth is a widowed assistant lecturer in French literature, left to care for her invalid father, murmuring to herself, "Do you think anyone will notice?"

In *The Debut* Anita Brookner treats five of the major concerns of her fiction: the plight of that sensitive, solitary woman of middle age who achieves a degree of insight but is unable (or unwilling) to act upon it, and remains bitterly disappointed; the depiction of female characters who represent a number of options for womanhood in contemporary society; a concern with what forms of behavior most become a woman; the twin themes of alienation and exile; and the relationship between literature and life.

The first three concerns are clearly and carefully interrelated; the first needs no elaboration, the second may, however. In *The Debut*, as in all subsequent novels, Brookner presents alternative female models, possibilities for different ways to play the game, to borrow Anthea's metaphor. Those options range from grandmother Weiss, the Jewish mother par excellence, to Helen Weiss, a fading coquette-actress of childish ways and hopeless dependence, to Jill Dixon, a golden, charming, social creature, to Anthea and the rough-edged Mrs. Cutler who declares that *she knows* men. Other female characters like Molly Edwards, an aging, single friend of Helen's, Sally Jacobs, Ruth's father's mistress, and Rhoda Wilcox, another old friend of Helen's, round out the cast. In this novel delineating one woman's tortuous passage into something like adulthood, some of these possibilities are recognized, but none is acted upon. When, at the outset of her short-lived affair with Hugh Dixon, Ruth realizes that Dickens was wrong, that the world is not won by virtue, her criteria for determining her own behavior shift: "she had lost her understanding of the world before the fall," and it is no longer a question of whether she should not do something, but whether she would or not. Ruth has chosen, perhaps fallen into, that pattern of behavior which most becomes her; with an almost lethal determinism dictating the course, she will live a circumspect and repressed existence, still hoping for a world in which virtue will merit fulfillment, in which Cinderella will go to the ball and meet her prince.

Integral to these concerns is the theme of alienation/exile, for Ruth feels that she is indeed an alien and she is correct in both literal and metaphorical ways. The child of conflicting heritages, one central European, the other insular, she is really "homeless" once grandmother Weiss dies. Neither London nor Paris is home to her. Metaphorically, she is an existential exile, without roots in time or place; our first glimpse of her tells it all: "Her appearance and character were exactly halfway between the nineteenth and twentieth centuries." For one without spatial or temporal fixed points, what else can life be but perpetual exile?

Finally, this is a novel about the relationship between literature and life, something that might be said of any fiction, but here Brookner has given the theme particular poignancy in several ways. First, she has not only taken her title straight from Balzac (*Un Debut dans la Vie*), but, more important, she has interwoven elements from his *Eugenie Grandet* with the story of Ruth Weiss: Ruth is an academic, a specialist in Balzac, and it is his fiction that grants her insight, for the story of the virtuous but wasted Eugenie prompts Ruth to go to Paris in search of that grand affair. With ironic force, the example of Eugenie becomes an exemplum of Ruth's fate. Second, Brookner isolates literature, or more precisely, certain fictions, as formative for Ruth: tales by the Grimm brothers and Hans Christian Andersen, and novels by Dickens, that taught her that "virtue would surely triumph." Passing through Victor Hugo, Alfred de Vigny, and Emile Zola, she came to Balzac. Despite what she learns from the last ("the supreme effectiveness of bad behavior"), Ruth would not be disabused of her notion of an eminently moral universe. Such is the power of the fictive myth embedded in her psyche. Third, Mrs. Cutler, the dispenser of worldly wisdom and pragmatic advice, offers a summary judgment about one type of literature; when she finds Helen reading a romance, she thunders: "those things don't happen in real life . . . you should know that by now." But Helen does not really know that any more than her daughter; if real knowledge consists not only of perception but of consequent action, mother and daughter partake of the same naiveté, the one dying a physical death from shock, the other an emotional death from perception.

Like Ruth Weiss, Kitty Maule, the heroine of *Providence,* is an academic, a specialist in the Romantic tradition who holds an appointment at a small British college; like Ruth, Kitty is the child of mixed parentage, her deceased father a British military officer, her mother an elegant, spoiled Frenchwoman; like Ruth, Kitty is highly susceptible to literature; and like Ruth she longs for a grand romantic affair that will never be. It is as if all the elements of Ruth's character have been intensified, including the ultimate disillusionment.

Kitty's grandfather, Vadim, a Russian acrobat, met her grandmother Louise, a seamstress, in Paris. They married, and immigrated to London where they established a successful couturier business on Grosvenor Street. Their only child, Marie-Therese, married John Maule; this couple's only child, Therese (Kitty), was brought up by her grandparents, dressed elegantly, and fed romantic notions of life. Kitty embarks on an academic career, much to the chagrin of her family who want her to marry well.

The object of Kitty's romantic longings is Maurice Bishop, a senior colleague and specialist in cathedral architecture, a figure she endows with far greater appeal than is obvious, and to whom she attaches far more importance than he grants her. Like Ruth Weiss, she chooses to coddle a man: Kitty types Maurice's notes, thinks of herself as "useful" to him, all the while recognizing that she is neither "indispensable" nor "necessary" to him. Clearly, this is no grand passion—nor will it ever be, for Kitty and Maurice are worlds apart, particularly in essential matters like spirituality (he is a devout Roman Catholic, she is without religious faith of any sort). Nonetheless, she is willing to accept the relationship for what it is, cherishing the ill-founded hope that it will blossom. Long after the "affair" is over and Maurice has married one of Kitty's students, the fey and fetching Jane, Kitty will say of that afternoon when she first saw Maurice in the college's senior common room, that it was "in retrospect, the best moment of my life." Kitty is indeed a pathetic creature, unable to apply what she teaches to her own life: her seminar on *Adolphe*, Benjamin Constant's novel about failure which portrays a calculating hero who ruins the woman who sacrifices everything for him, tells her nothing of her own existential situation. While Kitty achieves a significant degree of insight ("I function well in one sphere only. . . . Perhaps I will . . . make a unity somehow . . . what I cannot do is reconcile"), she cannot act upon it.

In this novel, too, there are alternative possibilities for womanhood: Louise, Kitty's grandmother who combines the practical and the romantic in the world of fashion; Marie-Therese, her mother, a delicate, "feminine" creature; Caroline, Kitty's neighbor, who waits for another "Mr. Right" to come along; Pauline, Kitty's colleague, tied to a blind mother. Yet none of them suits her. The behavior that becomes her most would be some way of reconciling her life with her grandparents', the world of academic life with the world of things French. Indeed, Kitty is a divided, alienated self, something she herself recognizes; she thinks of herself as "foreign" or as an "orphan" a good deal of the time; painfully divided between two "homes," one her grandparents' house in Dulwich, the other her own flat in Chelsea, she wanders between the two, without orientation or destination. She longs to belong, she searches for personal identity and self-validation from others. She wants to live in and through Maurice Bishop and even when she realizes that this will never be, she persists in that hope. She cannot reconcile disparate elements in her existence; she cannot achieve a healthy psychic integration; she is a neurotic crippled by alienation, inundated by a sense of exilic strangeness she cannot overcome. Too late she realizes that virtue and decorum of the type epitomized by *Adolphe*'s heroine Ellénore are self-destructive; unwilling to internalize that lesson of literature, she rationalizes the unhappy outcome of her affair by taking to herself all responsibility for that failure and declaring, "I lacked the information." If that were true, her "resolution to be more definite, more admirable [and] . . . not allow anyone to dominate her," found after a visit from Maurice, would have achieved different results.

Here literature has provided Kitty with a role model which damages; this woman who can discourse brilliantly on the "Romantic Tradition," can speak of romance in intellectual terms but has no clue about romance in real life; it remains, as it must, for a woman of her solitary sensibilities and uncertainties about standards of behavior, an academic subject, not a lived experience. The emblematic power of her analysis of *Adolphe*, that it is about "the painful astonishment of a deceived soul," resonates through *Providence*.

In this novel, as in *The Debut*, Brookner has succeeded in delineating the character of that deceived soul, interweaving another literary analogue which imparts depth and richness to the portrait. Brookner's fine-line attention to detail, her ability to recapture states of consciousness with precision, and her talent for choosing language that recreates that distinct ambiance of disparate worlds distinguish *Providence*. Such is the power of her artistry that the reader is always acutely aware of seeing everything through the eyes of a narrator who is perched rather precariously just this side of the solipsistic void.

In *Look At Me*, Brookner's third novel, the world becomes darker, more forbidding, the pain of alienation so acute that the protagonist turns into a voracious, vengeful monster in the end. Frances Hinton works as a cataloger in a library devoted to visual representations of illness. She spends her days sorting, labeling, filing, and arranging other people's maladies, observing everything with detachment and distance, everything except melancholy, which she calls "her own disease." It has become that following the experiences that have brought Frances to the "present" situation of chapter one: this present is the filter for the narrative and that means at least two things: Frances tells her own story from the vantage point of having made it through; and, wounded and scarred by her experience, she may be an unreliable narrator. The reader of *Look At Me* needs to evaluate Frances's perceptions carefully, perhaps with some of that distance and detachment she has used in looking at others' lives.

The circularity of the novel's structure gives it an undeniable integrity; this is a work of metafiction, for at novel's end the reader discovers that he has been reading the novel Frances has been writing about her own life. Beginning and end are set in the present; what intervenes is the history of another solitary woman's desperate attempts to be accepted by others, to satisfy her intense hunger for life, experience, and love. The novel chronicles Frances's passage from observer to participant, then back to observer. In chapter one, a kind of prologue, Brookner slashes a psychological profile with extraordinary rapidity and probity; in two sentences she takes us into Frances's psyche: "It is wiser, in every circumstance, to forget, to cultivate the art of forgetting . . . problems of human behaviour continue to baffle us, but at least in the Library we have them properly filed. . . . It is extremely interesting, in a hopeless sort of way."

Frances, an only child left for years with a mother only recently deceased and an ancient Irish housekeeper in a cavernous flat, hungers for life. Her short-lived involvement in the social whirl around a glamorous couple, Nick and Alix Fraser, brings her a relationship with James

Anstey, one of the doctors at the Institute of which her library is a part. Frances has flashes of insight. She knows that she is deficient in those vices needed to survive; she knows what she wants from Nick and Alix, declaring to herself, "I'll try to catch hold of their vulnerability and apply it to myself." She wants to learn all she can about them, knowing that she might not understand it all but hoping that it might be the food of real life. And that is a large part of her problem, which is, at root, cognitive or epistemological as well as moral. Because she wants to understand everything according to reason, to intellectualize all matters, even those of the heart, she cannot abandon herself and become the selfish, greedy, amoral animal she recognizes she must be in order to achieve romantic bliss with a man.

Frances annotates experience, carefully recording each day's activities until her new life with Nick, Alix, and James takes over; writing had been a substitute for experience—now it is no longer needed to witness to her existence or validate her worth. About an evening's walk home with James she writes: "It was then that I saw the business of writing for what it truly was and is to me. It is your penance for not being lucky. It is an attempt to reach others and make them love you." Now, however, she feels worthy and notes, "by the fact of his existence, he James had given validity to my entire future." But, when James spurns her attempt to seduce him ("Not with you, Frances. Not with you," he remonstrates), she retreats, writing herself into a new way of life, "with dread and sadness."

Frances reverts to the role of observer-writer, determined to make "everyone . . . pay for the penalties they exacted" from her. After a final dinner with Nick, Alix, and James, at which James's eyes were fixed on someone else, "his face foolish with desire," she walks home alone, dazed and wandering through labyrinthine park paths, but "still poised, still terrified, still murderous," she resolves that "everything must be converted somehow, into entertainment." Frances will take her final revenge in fiction, of course. The novel closes with her ensconced in her mother's deathbed, resolute in her determination ("I would become subsumed into my head, and into my hand, my writing hand"), and voracious in her desire to consume others. Her despair is extreme.

Thus Frances takes her place alongside Ruth and Kitty: solitary, romantic, disappointed,

Dust jacket for the American edition of Brookner's Booker Prize-winning novel

guileless, an alien in the world of real experience, comfortable only in the world of literature. Though alternative models are presented to her as well—Alix, Olivia, her colleague at the library, Miss Morpeth, her predecessor there, Mrs. Halloran, who, like Mrs. Cutler, "knows men"—none is a real possibility for Frances. Some combination of repression, good manners, and alienation prevents her from becoming the beast who can survive in that jungle, so she retreats to her own lair. Yet Frances differs from Ruth and Kitty in at least two significant ways. First, her relationship to literature is different from theirs, for she is the creator of written fictions rather than just a consumer of them; her resolution to write is a program to set things to right, to create that world in which virtue is rewarded and the good do live happily ever after. And Frances Hinton is a woman to whom images, whether pictorial, photographic, or dream-produced, are important, for as she declares, "I feel the power of images very strongly, even when I do not understand them." In this regard Anita Brookner's own comments are telling; responding to a question from John Haffenden, she said: "What attracted me to art history is the power of images, which act differently from words. Images recur in a way that words don't. Dreams are usually wordless, but they're full of images, and an image can carry over in some mysterious way and generate things. Images are more powerful and primitive than words."

Second, Frances Hinton is a monster, a word monster; between Ruth and Kitty, on the one hand, and herself on the other lies a moral gulf. Frances Hinton becomes a predator; while consumption of this sort is an amoral activity in other areas of the animal kingdom, here it may be seen as immoral. In the end Frances Hinton is a malicious woman bent on revenge at whatever cost. Little does she know that the greatest cost paid has been exacted from her own person.

Look At Me is certainly the darkest of the three novels, for it chronicles one woman's passage through the tunnel of harrowing existential nightmare into a mausoleum. In the author's own words, it is "a very depressing and debilitated novel." Nonetheless, as Julia Epstein has pointed out, "*Look At Me* is a nearly impossible achievement, a novel about emptiness and vacancy . . . a book about language, a *Bouvard et Pecuchet* of the soul."

With *The Debut, Providence,* and *Look At Me,* Anita Brookner succeeded in painting a triptych, not a triple portrait. Ruth Weiss, Kitty Maule, and Frances Hinton, while similar in their sense of decorum, their romantic longings, and their near-repressive control, and while caught in the same existential predicament, respond in different ways. Ruth marries, only to be quickly widowed; Kitty never marries, but pursues a brilliant academic career, reading and teaching the romance of literature rather than living the romance of life; and Frances retreats from life nearly altogether, preferring to collect and order images in the library and in her notebooks, substituting cataloging and writing for living. Brookner has put it well herself in describing the novels as "transcripts from a random passage through life and a rather unsuccessful passage."

On the other hand, Brookner's fourth novel, *Hotel du Lac* (1984), which won England's prestigious Booker Prize and brought her considerable critical praise as well as a larger audience, may be read as the transcript of a somewhat successful passage. This novel reveals its author's consistent preoccupation with the great themes treated in her previous three novels, yet here Brookner has painted a richer canvas with an ending that offers far greater possibility for its heroine; in the end, as Anne Tyler has noted, Edith Hope has arrived at "a nonromantic, wryly realistic appreciation of her single state," and that appreciation leads to acceptance as well as an ability to make life-enhancing choices.

Edith Hope, a thirty-nine-year-old writer of romantic fiction, has been sent by friends to a resort hotel in Switzerland "to forget the unfortunate lapse which had led to this brief exile": she had left her husband-to-be, a man of "mouse-like seemliness," standing on the steps of the registry office, unable to go through with a sensible, "safe" marriage. And so, "doomed for a certain time to walk the earth," Edith spends time at the Hotel du Lac, out of season; the metaphysical aptness of that time reinforces Edith's sense of alienation, for she is doubly dislocated: once geographically, then again psychologically.

At the hotel she meets other women: Iris Pusey, a wealthy widow who spends nearly all her time shopping for clothes, following her motto that "a woman owes it to herself to have pretty things"; her daughter, Jennifer, a sexually charged, aging nymphet given to wearing pink harem pants, seducing bellboys, and exhibiting hysterical behavior; Monica, a young wife unable to conceive and sent to the hotel to prepare for another try; Mme. de Bonneuil, an elderly countess packed off by her son and his second wife. These women are more than emblematic types: as Hermione Lee has observed, they "become exempla in Edith's interior debate about women."

Edith's contact with Iris and Jennifer reopens the "question of what behavior most becomes a woman, the question around which she Edith had written most of her novels." Edith perceives the central principle according to which Mrs. Pusey operates; of her, Edith notes: "she knew from the outset what some unfortunates never learn: she knew the best is there to be taken, although there may not be enough to go around." Edith, the daughter of an English father and an Austrian mother, thinks about her own parents, long since dead; she feels abandoned by that father who died when she was very young but left a lasting impression and that mother who should have taught her the rules of correct behavior with men but never did. Edith knows her own problem: "she could make up characters but she could not decipher those in real

life. For the conduct of life she required an interpreter." Dividing the world into those ultra-
feminine types like Iris and Jennifer, who
"consume men and demand treats" and those
"multi-orgasmic girls with their executive brief-
cases who can go elsewhere" than to her novels
for entertainment, Edith confronts her own alienation, realizing full well she fits comfortably in neither category. She must decide whether to accept
the offer of marriage extended by a fellow guest,
Mr. Neville, who tells her to "assume [her] . . .
own centrality," and enter "a partnership of the
most enlightened kind" realizing that not to do
that means, as he tells her outright, facing "a life
of exile of one sort or another."

Near novel's end Edith feels that she has acquired adult seriousness for the first time; she
has decided to accept Neville's offer. In a most significant moment of insight, Edith perceives an important distinction between literature and life
when she notes, "I believed every word I wrote.
And I still do, even though I realize now that
none of it can ever come true for me." Yet when
she observes Neville emerging from Jennifer's
room the morning after having reached her decision, she sees her father's patient face before her
and hears his oft-repeated admonition, "Think
again, Edith. You have made a false equation." Acting upon that vision, Edith takes charge of her
own life and departs the hotel, not in retreat but
in quest, accepting her solitary state, acknowledging it as the mixed blessing that it is. When she
changes the wording of her telegram from "Coming home" to "Returning," she acknowledges the
fact that there can be no home for her: the domestic propriety of a familial nest will not be hers,
nor can it be, for she will continue to cherish
that romantic ideal. So long as she does that, she
will be dislocated—by choice—from the reality of
husband, children, regular meals, laundry, marketing, and cleaning house. She accepts that
"exile of one sort or another."

Thus, *Hotel du Lac* ends not only with a significant degree of acceptance and optimism, but
with what Barbara Hardy has deemed "Edith's
final affirmation of integrity." This fiction of one
woman's random passage, written with elegance,
cool formality, and wit, is the most satisfying of
Brookner's first four novels not only in terms of
narrative but also in terms of style. Substantial
pleasure derives from reading the well-told tale
of Edith Hope's coming to terms with herself
and life in contemporary society; even greater
pleasure may be derived from the purity and pre-

Dust jacket for Brookner's 1985 novel, her first to focus on several major characters

cision of Anita Brookner's style: haunting descriptions of an anesthetic atmosphere; evocative delin-
eations of landscape, both geographical and
emotional; resonant renderings of shifting states
of consciousness. Brookner's ability to create a
prose that is luminous with metaphor, rich with
reference to Proust, Eliot, James, and Collette,
rhythmic with variety and repetition, and vibrant
with silence as well as absence makes *Hotel du Lac*
a stylistic tour de force.

Some critics have complained that
Brookner's first four novels are essentially and
transparently autobiographical, that these genteel, repressed heroines with their romantic longings are only figures in a four-part roman à clef.
She has called these comparisons "inevitable" and
"a great bore," while admitting, "I have been that
woman at times." Brookner's fifth novel, *Family
and Friends* (1985), is enough of a departure
from the previous four to silence these critics,
should their contentions have merit. Here
Brookner is no longer writing the story of that solitary woman deceived by literature and terribly

concerned with decorum. Instead, she has parceled these concerns out among several major characters, both male and female, while focusing critical attention on the notion of exile. In expanding her canvas and concentrating on five major characters, none of whom displays the rich complexity of her previous protagonists, and greatly enlarging the cast of minor characters as well, Brookner has dissipated some of her energies. But whatever benefits may have been sacrificed in that process have been more than adequately compensated for by the effects she achieves with the cinematic dynamic process *Family and Friends* displays as Brookner chronicles this story of exile without a kingdom.

In her first four novels Brookner has provided portraits of contemporary women who are, in effect, exiles: solitary women overwhelmed when experience in the real world turns out to be not at all like the lives fed to them in literature, whether written by others, as in the cases of Ruth and Kitty, or by themselves, as in the cases of Frances and Edith. Deceived and disappointed, they wander through the maze of contemporary experience, shouldering the burdens of being stranded in a meaningless universe. For them, there is no promised land, no "home."

While all of these novels can be read as "fictions of exile," carefully and fluently nuanced, the first three seem to emphasize exile as psychological dislocation, the last, the psychological intensified by the geographical. In all cases, Brookner's concern is to delineate one central female character. In *Family and Friends* she has continued her exploration of the dimensions of exile while enlarging her canvas considerably.

At the center is Sofka, a pragmatic, widowed matriarch who dominates the lives of her four children: Frederick, the eldest, handsome, rakish, and Oedipal; Mimi, her late father's favorite, beautiful, but depressed; Betty, complicated and precociously sexual; and Alfred, bright, self-sacrificing, and virtuous. Brookner's novel follows the story of all five members of the Dorn clan, and while each evolves in a distinctive way, taken together, the childrens' lives have neither the substance nor the impact of their mother's.

In Sofka's world roles are carefully defined: men are successful entrepreneurs, devoted to family, occasionally straying from the path of virtue with an attractive vitality, for "there is nothing the virtuous Sofka admires so much as a man with a bad reputation." Women are to acquire and practice sophisticated social graces while waiting for marriage and family. With talismanic optimism, Sofka has "named her sons after kings and emperors and her daughters as if they were characters in a musical comedy . . . the boys were to conquer and the girls to flirt."

She knows that sentiment is a luxury that must be discarded in a world where everything is a commodity to be bought, bartered, or consumed, and that "nothing is worth waiting for, not even the ideal partner, not even if that partner exists." Thus, when she has arranged Mimi's marriage to an old family retainer, she crushes her daughter's romantic objections with a scornful rejoinder: "Love! It is marriage we are talking about here." Even Sofka's dealings with God reflect her pragmatic approach to life: she "addresses the Almighty, rather as she would address her bank manager, with the assurance of one who has always been solvent."

Despite all her strategies, Sofka's plans go afoul. Frederick and Betty, her favorites, break away, he to the Riviera, she to Paris, then New York and Hollywood, while Sofka mourns because "handsome Frederick and wicked Betty have taken her heart with them." Both end up living in suspended adolescence, not really escaping their mother after all. Frederick is a child-man in paradise with an earth-mother wife who lets him play all day. Restless and petulant, Betty "sits like a child in her childlike clothes, eating concoctions that might have been devised for a child's party." So much for those whose animal vitality had endeared them to their mother.

Mimi and Alfred remain at home, searching for escape. Marriage merely exacerbates the problem for Mimi; childless and living in the family's London mansion, she realizes, finally, that sentiment is "a lingering illness." Alfred, though he vows to imitate Frederick and "consume hecatombs of women," is burdened by his virtue. He cannot escape, nor does he really want to, in the end. In a novel where good character is a burden, not an asset, and "the good live unhappily ever after," what is the point of living at all? Nowhere is this painful phenomenon seen more clearly than in the person of Alfred who feels that "he must vindicate his buried self . . . walk out of the door and start life again . . . in gardenia-scented exile," something he will never do, of course.

With an unerring narrative sense Brookner follows the fortunes of these four children and their mother, adding dimension and interest to the story by several means. She has created a cast

Denholm Elliott as Philip Neville and Anna Massey as Edith Hope in a scene from the 1985 BBC/Arts & Entertainment Network coproduction of Hotel Du Lac *(courtesy of Arts & Entertainment Network)*

of richly varied major characters, thus offering a panorama of engaging figures. Brookner's scene painting is masterful. Even that most cliché-ridden time of day, sunset, glistens with painterly brilliance: "the sky is now an impenetrable indigo, yet along the horizon there is still a faint smudge of salmon-coloured brilliance. The wind rustles the leathery palm leaves and the oranges and lemons glow on the trees as if lit from within. Amber light gushes from the cafe." Brookner's descriptions of the life and rituals of these central European Jews are often moving. Clearly, she feels a deep bond with these people. Her prose brightens, for example, when she sketches the ritual of Sunday afternoon tea and marzipan cake; the reader feels that she has often been there. Yet this novel is not a sad chronicle. Wry humor and wit frequently humanize the narrative. In sum, Brookner has created a story whose characters, in the fullness of their heritage and lived experience, engage her sensibilities so deeply that she has crafted a resonant, enduring fiction.

With her next novel, *A Misalliance* (1986), Brookner returned to familiar territory, telling the story of Blanche Vernon, a sophisticated woman of early middle age whose husband, Bertie, has left her for a much younger woman. Deserted by the couple's friends, who regard Blanche's behavior as increasingly eccentric, this solitary woman, always elegantly coiffed and fashionably fitted out, takes refuge in rituals: shopping for each day's evening meal, paying meticulous attention to the quality of meat, vegetables, fish, and fruit, selecting fine wines for herself; doing volunteer work at the hospital; visiting the Italian rooms at the National Gallery. She is, however, a different Brookner heroine, not only in her chic lifestyle but also in the extent to which chaos continuously threatens to disrupt her world. Her elaborately schematized life of ritual represents a desperate and propulsively self-willed attempt to ward off that chaos. Blanche Vernon is not a guileless romantic, but an intelligent, cultured woman who reads Greek literature for pleasure, not for role models or moral les-

Draft for a review from Brookner's notebook (courtesy of the author)

sons, and knows how to serve a meal in high style.

Yet without her husband, whom she considers an undeserved "treat, a prize won in a lottery," Blanche finds life meaningless. She had carefully created herself as an appropriate wife to a wealthy real-estate agent, not only as a professional hostess but also as an adoring companion waiting at home each day with a stock of anecdotes ready to accompany drinks before dinner.

Blanche may be more concerned with decorum than any previous Brookner heroine. It is not just that she has schooled herself in all the social graces, the perfect finishing school product living in St. John's Wood. It is also that she is a woman of extraordinary self-control, keeping a perfect figure clothed in elegant tweeds and silks, and never carrying on. As Patricia Craig notes (in the *Times Literary Supplement* of 29 August 1986), "Blanche Vernon ironically laments her inability to throw a tantrum." And the irony is, of course, that she has lost her husband to a woman who would throw a tantrum, an indecorous creature named "Amanda," but known as "Mousie." The disruption wrought by this event has alienated Blanche: she has lost some of her bearings and wanders through the familiar and unfamiliar in an attempt to regain orientation and purpose.

More precisely than Ruth or Kitty or Frances or Edith, Blanche has divided the female kingdom into categories. At the hospital she makes the acquaintance of Sally Beamish and her silent three-year-old stepdaughter, Elinor, hoping to extend the range of her volunteer work to their lives. Contact with them spurs Blanche to considerable reflection. Blanche shares Frances Hinton's plight: she needs to acquire the ability to reconcile elements of her existence: "Moving between her inner and outer worlds as she did . . . Blanche was forced to the conclusion that her previous life had been deficient in every way. Timidly trying to confront reality, she had misjudged the density of reality itself. . . . She saw suddenly and precisely something that had previously only appeared to her in a vague and nebulous light: a great chasm dividing the whole of womanhood."

On the one side of the chasm are the pagan, hedonistic women–greedy, manipulative, without conscience–living happily ever after: women like Sally and Mousie. On the other side are "good" women deemed "evangelical" by Blanche, devoted to caring for others, women like Blanche's neighbor, Phyllis Duff, "that embod-

iment of heavenly duty and obedience," and her own sister-in-law Barbara "with her bridge evenings and her gouty husband." Blanche's visits to the Italian rooms at the National Gallery have granted these types of women emblematic significance: on the one hand, nymphs and goddesses with secret wiles and wanton smiles, on the other, self-sacrificing virgins and martyrs.

Blanche has her flash of insight; on a visit to Sally's rather bohemian basement flat, she finds herself lost in reflection: "And she herself, she further thought, had made the mistake of trying to fashion herself for the better half, assuming the uncomplaining and compliant posture of the Biblical wife when all the time the answer was to be found in the scornful and anarchic posture of the ideal mistress." Like Ruth, Kitty, and Frances, Blanche knows that she lacks the manipulative abilities and greedy, nearly childish animality of the guileful female. And that insight is sharpened by her contemplation of Italian paintings; they enhance her perception: "all those deities carrying on their uninhibited lives. *In full view.* It took me a long time to realize that anyone can do it, if they have a mind to."

Painfully, Blanche extricates herself from the affairs of Sally and Elinor, paying the price of what may well be the most excruciating migraine in fiction, and resolves to close her flat and head south for some sun (" 'The sun is God,' said Turner" she tells herself again and again). Yet, before she leaves, in an ambiguous ending, Bertie bumbles in and announces, "I'm back, Blanche," making this novel, like the previous five, precisely the kind of "moral puzzle" Anita Brookner intends it to be.

And if there is a significant commonality of substance, there is also a significant commonality of style, for certainly the wit, courage, lack of sentimentality, and irony that animate the works of Diderot and Stendhal characterize Brookner's as well. And that style has the morality discernible in the best of David's paintings: the articulate integrity of the earnest heart.

Brookner herself has observed another telling correlation; asked to account for the wit and humor of her novels, she told John Haffenden: "it comes from a lot of reading. Here is the connection between art history . . . and fiction: it's the energy I admire. If you have a cause, you have to propound it with energy. My cause is to tell a story or perhaps to cast a moral puzzle." She has expended that energy in the execution of her own work; few literary artists can approach her in the painterly brilliance of her landscapes or in the efficient architecture of plot or in the draftsmanship of her character delineation.

Interviews:

John Haffenden, "Anita Brookner," in *Novelists In Interview,* edited by Haffenden (London & New York: Methuen, 1985), pp. 57-85;

Ann Kolson, "Exploring the Hearts of Hopeful Romantics," *Philadelphia Inquirer,* 4 March 1985, D1, D4;

Amanda Smith, "Publishers Weekly Interviews: Anita Brookner," *Publishers Weekly* (6 September 1985): 67-68;

Shusha Guppy, "Interview: The Art of Fiction XCVII: Anita Brookner," *Paris Review,* no. 109 (1987): 146-169.

References:

Julia Epstein, "Images of Melancholy," *Washington Post Book World* (24 July 1983): 6;

Barbara Hardy, "A Cinderella's Loneliness," *Times Literary Supplement* (14 September 1984): 1019;

Hermione Lee, "Cleopatra's Way," *Observer* (9 September 1984): 22;

Anne Tyler, "A Solitary Life Is Still Worth Living," *New York Times Book Review* (3 February 1985): 1, 31.

Paul Hemphill

(18 February 1936-   )

Stephen Whited
Lexington, Kentucky

BOOKS: *The Nashville Sound: Bright Lights and Country Music* (New York: Simon & Schuster, 1970);

The Good Old Boys (New York: Simon & Schuster, 1974);

Long Gone (New York: Viking, 1979);

Too Old to Cry (New York: Viking, 1981);

The Sixkiller Chronicles (New York: Macmillan, 1985);

Me and the Boy (New York: Macmillan, 1986).

OTHER: Ivan Allen, *Mayor: Notes on the Sixties*, ghostwritten by Hemphill (New York: Simon & Schuster, 1971).

With two novels, two collections of essays from his daily general-interest newspaper columns and magazine articles, a political autobiography ghosted for Ivan Allen, Jr., an extended essay about a trip up the Appalachian Trail, and what is considered by many to be the best book on country music and Nashville, Paul Hemphill has consistently produced some of the most carefully pictured views of southern American life. Hemphill describes himself as "a committed Southern writer," and indeed his subject matter tends to favor southern locations and concerns; however, his experiences as a traveler and a journalist have offered him a vast panorama of subjects and images that provide a breadth of vision not found among most journalistic commentators.

Paul Hemphill was born 18 February 1936 in Birmingham, Alabama, to Paul and Velma Nelson Hemphill. Playing baseball and serving meals to athletes, he worked his way through Auburn University for a B.A. in 1959; while at Auburn he also served as sports editor of the college newspaper and yearbook. His first full-time work in journalism was as a sportswriter for the *Birmingham News* (1959-1961).

In the early 1960s he worked as sports information director for Florida State University, spent a year in France on active duty in the Ala-

Paul Hemphill (copyright © 1985 by Alan Jones)

bama Air National Guard, and wrote sports (and, later, general interest) columns for such papers as the *Augusta Chronicle*, the *Tampa Times*, the *Atlanta Times*, and the *Atlanta Journal*. In addition to newspaper work he has published articles in the *New York Times Sunday Magazine*, the *Baltimore Sun*, *Newsday*, *Atlantic Monthly*, *Sports Illustrated*, *TV Guide*, *Life*, and *Writer's Digest*. He was selected a Nieman Fellow at Harvard for 1968-1969 where. he completed work on his first book, *The Nashville Sound: Bright Lights and Country Music* (1970). Divorced from his first wife, Susan Milliage Olive, in 1975, Hemphill lived and worked briefly in San Francisco, writing for the *Examiner*. In 1976 he returned to free-lance writing after his marriage to Susan Farran Percy, a writer and editor for *Atlanta* magazine; they have one child, and Hemphill has three children from his first marriage.

In recent years Hemphill has aired commentaries on National Public Radio's "All Things Considered," served as senior editor of *Atlanta* magazine, and lectured and taught in many colleges and universities. He continues to publish commentaries on a free-lance basis, and is now writer in residence at Brenau College in Gainesville, Georgia.

An "urban squatter," as he calls himself, Hemphill has lived for many years in an old neighborhood of east Atlanta. "Yes, right here on this dinky little old street that hardly anybody in Atlanta knows about, I have found it. I'm home," Hemphill told readers in *Goodlife* (June/July 1985). Typically, the statement carries the weight of a journalist's perception, for this once quiet, rundown inner-city neighborhood is now a hotbed of political infighting and urban renewal. But the statement is also of interest to the Hemphill reader who will recognize a familiar theme present in all of his work–the importance of roots and commitment.

Mayor: Notes on the Sixties (1971), an autobiography of Atlanta's Ivan Allen, Jr., ghostwritten by Hemphill, and *The Nashville Sound,* a portrait of the country music capital, bear marked similarities in style and presentation, for in both works Hemphill's journalism background is exhibited in its best light. In stark, matter-of-fact terms, he presents in as few words as possible all the necessary particulars for a clearly delineated picture. Here is one of Allen's anecdotes offered in the first few pages of *Mayor:* "There was a time when a friend of mine and I were challenged to a golf match by two young Negroes who worked around the pro shop at the Capital City Country Club: the club pro finally relented to the match, but said we would have to play at 4 o'clock on a Monday morning, and there were 250 caddies rooting for the two Negroes and only my friend's father rooting for us. The fact that because this was a biracial match we had to play at dawn stirred me a little, but not enough to make a lasting impression, and I honestly can't recall that the racial issue was ever even mentioned while I was a student at Georgia Tech. Even those of us who later were to admire Franklin Delano Roosevelt, my father and myself included, tended to

think of poor whites in the rural South when we heard the term 'social problems.' We had only the vague feeling that the Negro's lot was not good. But, then, that was the system."

The narrative is expository; one feels propelled by a carefully plotted dramatic structure– the facts ordered, the tone set, the setting fully visualized. In strict chronological order the journalist builds around this structure all the necessary details, which accumulate into the "big picture." Allen is presented as liberal, energetic, and gentle. His rise to power, his moderate views of the race issue, his ties with Washington are all subtly presented in the manner of a southern storyteller. The strength of *The Nashville Sound* also lies in Hemphill's journalistic method. Most reviewers praised the book's accuracy but either focused on the humor and character or exposed their distaste for country music. Again, Hemphill, the southern-raised observer, looks carefully at what he holds to be useful in the tradition of the music and the people it reflects, their struggles and their fights. Perhaps the best example of Hemphill's style and purpose is this sketch of Charley Pride:

> It isn't surprising . . . that there is only one black man in country music today worth mentioning: Charley Pride, a strapping, handsome, sufficiently dark young man who grew up listening to the Grand Old Opry every Saturday night in Sledge, Miss. Pride gave professional baseball a shot (two weeks of Spring training with Gene Autry's Los Angeles Angels in 1961) and spent five years singing in clubs in Montana before singer Red Sovine talked him into going to Nashville. It looked like the gimmick to beat all gimmicks ("Come on, you gotta hear my nigger," one A & R man was told) until Chet Atkins heard Pride and put him on record. . . . Now Pride is RCA Victor's hottest property, country or pop. . . . He's promoted as Country Charley Pride, and there might be something to the suspicion that he is Nashville's house nigger (he lives in Dallas, actually) if he didn't sing "Kawliga" better than Hank Williams did. Maybe he's just hanging around to remind everyone where Hank learned to pick the guitar.

The honesty and forthright presentation of the character sketch is typical of all the portraits offered in the book. However, *The Nashville Sound* is more than a collection of star biographies.

*Dust jacket for Hemphill's 1974 collection of
newspaper columns*

not be embarrassed in front of her friends in Birmingham." The essay recalls an incident of Hemphill's eighteenth year in which his father walked out on the family over a dispute with his wife over alcohol.

> He left. She and my sister were hysterical. *It's the son's place to go find him and talk to him.* Bewildered I got into the car and raced into town, to the lot cluttered with tires and rusty engines and oil pans. I could see him sitting all alone in a dark corner of the cab, swigging from a pint, and when I pulled up and parked in the gravel beside the truck we tried not to look at each other.... I heard myself saying, "They're crying...." He sniffed and cleared his throat and then spoke in a frightened, vulnerable voice, a voice I had never heard come out of him before. "I'm not runnin' anywhere, son. There's a lot a boy don't know. I don't mean to make your mother cry, but sometimes a man's, a man's—" His voice had broken and when I dared look up at his face, bleached white by the pale lights on the lot, I saw that my old man, too, was crying.

In this rite of passage, Hemphill plays out a scene he will use in several books in which a younger man sees the humanity that resides beneath the carefully nurtured self-image of the older man. And the rest of the book's essays maintain that interest in the problems of change; Hemphill examines many changing faces–from football to country music stars to traveling evangelists to the changing race relations in the smallest of southern towns.

Hemphill gives the reader an understanding of how the country music business is run, what it had to overcome, who (Chet Atkins) made it what it is today, when it all got started, and where it all came from (it's a delightful irony that the most popular "redneck" form of music is a direct development of black and Appalachian folk music).

Hemphill's other journalistic writing documents his feelings about a variety of subjects, ranging from his relationship with his father's southern politics to his observations of Vietnam. In *The Good Old Boys* (1974), a collection of Hemphill's newspaper columns, the first essay in a section called "Growing Up Redneck" is entitled "Me and My Old Man." The article, appearing originally in the Sunday *New York Times Magazine*, upset his parents; Hemphill says, "I am told, my mother ordered my old man to buy up every copy of the [*Times*] in which it appeared and to burn them in the backyard so she would

In the final section of the book Hemphill collects a series of dispatches from around the southeast–Virginia to Texas. These vignettes demonstrate Hemphill's great strength as a commentator on American culture. He offers a quick view of the area, describes a local character who typifies the setting, and lets the picture tell the story. From Eutaw, Alabama, Hemphill examines "a land of rich black soil and huge cotton crops and cattle and large plantations, and black did not refer only to the color of the soil. It also referred to Negroes. Black people made up well over half the population, and they were bound in the strictest system of slavery known to the South." But times have changed: "Greene County is a monument to all of those people, all of those years, all of those events, all of the sweat and the blood-shed and the sacrifices that took place in the

South in the late 1950's and the early 1960's." Hemphill focuses on Harry Means, elected to the county commission in 1969; he controls an 800-acre farm south of Eutaw "on the road to Demopolis." Hemphill lets Mr. Means do the talking:

> "I guess I started thinking about running when everybody started registering in '65," he was saying Saturday night in the den of his wide brick home. He had attended a commission meeting at the courthouse that morning and then spent the afternoon in the fields. "I started thinking about all those years of slavery, and how every time an appointed job opened up it went to a white man, so I just did it."
>
> "You never thought of leaving, did you?" he was asked.
>
> "Leaving?" he said.
>
> "Going somewhere else to live, to work."
>
> He looked incredulous. "I was born and raised here. We had a little property. Lots of the other ones left, but they didn't have no property. If we can get some industry in here, won't nobody have to go off."
>
> "Your kids want to stay?"
>
> "Sure," Harry Means said. "They got a chance now. Everybody got a chance, including poor white folks. This is a new day we've got here."

Despite the hopefulness this dispatch from 1969 seems to express, Hemphill's *Too Old to Cry* (1981), another collection of newspaper columns, exposes the rootlessness many felt in the late 1960s and early 1970s. The book, like *The Good Old Boys*, offers the same careful look at sports figures, writers, newspapers, and the war in Vietnam, but the last section, entitled "Home Again, Home Again," brings the reader again to that persistent theme of the return to one's roots. In a well-known article (at least among newspaper writers) about quitting the newspaper, Hemphill relates his entry into the instability of the free-lance market. Tired of low pay, high pressure, and ambitious editors, Hemphill says, "with the next column due by dawn, I had run out of gas," and adds, "I don't know why men make dramatic decisions at the age of thirty-three–change jobs, leave families, kill themselves–but they often do. 'You have to remember,' I recalled a friend's saying as he dumped a secure advertising job and ran off to Hollywood to write scripts, 'we are no longer promising young men.' " Besides this essay about

quitting the paper Hemphill offers other essays in this section about decline–loss of family, drinking problems, a move to San Francisco and more newspaper work. But there is hope:

> "There are people," someone recently wrote, "who would kill to be where Paul Hemphill was in the summer and fall of 1976." Mainly they kill themselves, I thought, but I could understand the theory. Last summer I went to San Francisco in order to recover from my various aches–divorce, whiskey, ennui, no money–by writing a daily newspaper column. I went in search of the Promised Land for the same reasons held by all those before me. . . . My lady came out from Tallahassee and we married. The steady money eased other pains. I quit the newspaper job and went back to free-lancing, my briar patch, and a couple of books I was working on. We had fun, each of us getting a fresh start in a new land. . . . There has been too much travelling. In forty-one years I have lived in a lot of places and seen a lot of things, most of the time in search of an elusive Promised Land. I'm not sure anymore that there is such a place. If there is, maybe it was always right there at home, in Birmingham or Atlanta or Tallahassee. . . . It is time to go home now–home to the family and the old friends and the familiar streets and the children and the dogs–and see what is at the beginning of the rainbow.

Hemphill moved back to Atlanta and at forty-three found himself exhilarated at again becoming a father: "the doctor implor[ed] the mother to 'push one more time,' and we sat there and looked up at the mirror and Susan rolled out the words that I will never forget. They were simple words, spoken slowly and evenly, and when I heard them I felt as though I were hearing the Old Testament capsulized into three words. 'Oh, Paul, *look!*' she said. I stood up and threw my arms out like Rocky in the movie and, to the embarrassment of all, shouted, 'That's just about the goddamndest thing I'll ever see in my life.' Susan, the mother, told me to shut up and sit down and don't go around town bragging."

Thus, Hemphill presents the full circle of life, or in this case life renewed. It is a progression that he will return to again. In *Me and the Boy* (1986) he records a trip up 700 miles of the Appalachian Trail with his son, abandoned ironically enough near the Mason-Dixon line because of the father's failing knees. In a recent interview

Dust jacket for Hemphill's 1979 comedy about a minor-league baseball team

Hemphill described the book as "a father and son expedition. I divorced his mamma when he was not quite ten, so here he was nineteen and I was forty-eight; and, boy, that's the ultimate togetherness. Until then I don't know how many times we'd awakened under the same roof." The book recounts their experiences with the elements ("It took me six hours to walk five and half miles through three separate and distinct storms–rain, lightning, hail. All of the sudden sun, and then here comes another one"), encroaching civilization ("I was thinking, my God, ain't this nice because. . . , well, nobody, no telephone, just another world; but it got dark and the whole valley lit up. There was Franklin, there was Clayton, there was Dillard. . . , can't get away from it."), and the relationship between generations ("He says, 'I want to get a bus and go back home. . . . I don't like you anymore.' It killed me,

you can imagine.") *Me and the Boy* re-establishes the bond between generations, between Hemphill and his son, between Hemphill and his father, between Hemphill and his heritage. This tripartite relationship appears over and over in his writing: from his father's tears in "Me and My Old Man" to his own tears in *Me and the Boy*.

In his novels Hemphill takes this three-way relationship to its culmination with *Long Gone* (1979), *The Sixkiller Chronicles* (1985), and a projected novel he describes as being "about a good old boy. I want to say good-bye to all that. It's really about the South, the move from the country to the city. . . . My guy has got to be from a small town; . . . I want him to go to Auburn or Georgia and be a pretty good football player; and all of a sudden he gets caught in the transition, all the rules change."

Long Gone is the story of Stud Cantrell, the baseball player/manager of the Graceville Oilers. The novel is essentially a comedy that commemorates Hemphill's own attempt to play professional baseball ("I failed at baseball. I bottomed out after a five-day tryout in Class D and tucked my tail and ran into seclusion. I didn't come out for two weeks.") and continues his preoccupation with the passing of one's youth and promise– hence the contrasts between Jamie Weeks, an eighteen-year-old hopeful, and Stud, an "alcoholic forty-year-old manager who has learned too much for his own good." Gilbert Millstein reviewed the book in the *New York Times* with this comment: "I found it so good, so true, so funny, so full of tolerant cynicism about palpable villains, so full of love for people who deserve better than they get and so knowing in its delineation of whatever he chooses to delineate." What Hemphill delineates is the day-to-day struggle, its pathos and humor, that make up the southern experience, in this case that of a hard-luck ballplayer.

Having worked his way up through the Yankees farm system, Stud had his whole life organized for success, but in 1942 he "reluctantly enlisted in the Marines."

> First, he was shipped to the South Pacific; second, his wife wrote him to say she was leaving him for a man at the plant where she worked; and third, he took so much shrapnel in his right knee that they were going to amputate until he talked them out of it.

So when he came back to the States, he found he was no longer a promising young man.

Stud is precisely the sort of man generations of southern fathers have warned their daughters about. He is, nevertheless, a most resourceful man: he woos Dixie Lee Box, raised in a trailer camp in Crestview, Florida; he nurtures the immature but cocky Jamie Weeks during his first experiences with pro baseball; and he introduces the first black player into the league. But Stud's ultimate challenge involves a gentleman's wager made by the Dothan bankers and a team owner in which Stud is required to throw the championship to prevent losing the Oilers' financial backing, to prevent a sex scandal among the Dothan elite, and to keep his place (humble as it is) in baseball. Stud does the only thing he can do; he survives.

Stud reappears briefly in Hemphill's second novel, *The Sixkiller Chronicles,* as a Grand Ole Opry fan watching the stars at Tootsie's Orchid Lounge, "a squared fifty-ish man wearing white tasseled loafers and a string tie." Introducing himself to Jaybird Clay, son of Bluejay Clay, a country music star, Stud says, "Well, by God, I finally made it. . . . They call me 'Stud,' actually, for obvious reasons. This here's the little woman. Used to be Dixie Box. Fella wrote a book about us one time when I was still playing ball. Maybe you read it. Got Dixie all pissed off. . . . Any time you're down in Dothan and want to play some golf, let me know. I run the pro shop at the Wiregrass Country Club down there." This survivor has not only endured, he is supported by the power structure that had threatened to ruin him. The exchange between Stud and Jaybird also serves to establish a connection in this scene between endurance and the legacies left by family ties and histories. It is appropriate that Stud, in his enthusiasm to be in Nashville, should be the one to speak to Jaybird, who is attempting to turn his back on his father and the fame that the family name has acquired.

Hemphill says of *The Sixkiller Chronicles* "I wanted to do one on generations, which was very much on my mind. I reckon when you're pushing fifty you start thinking about legacies." However, Hemphill may be too close to the subject. *Kirkus* felt that the book, which focuses on three generations of the Clay family, is "too often delivered in flat journalese–while characterizations and vignette-plotting never rise above predict-

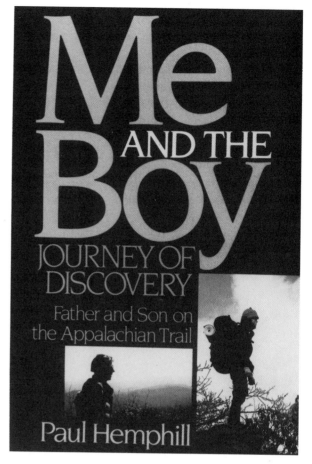

Dust jacket for Hemphill's latest work, an autobiographical account of a 700-mile hike on the Appalachian trail

able, soggy movie level." The review in *Publishers Weekly* was more on track: Hemphill "shows with feeling and humor how both country and music are being hauled into the 1980's, with the resulting loss of an old, settled way of life. Unfortunately, each Clay seems more like an action or reaction to this movement rather than a real, founded human being." The novel is a pastiche of Hemphill's earlier writing, and unfortunately he relies too much on his reporting techniques, telling us more about the Clays than he shows.

In a mixture of fact and fantasy Bluejay Clay lives out his life in Sixkiller Gap, North Carolina, where he presides over a 100-acre farm slowly being surrounded by ski resorts, industry, and condominiums. He is also the legendary "STAR OF THE GRAND OLD OPRY, 'The Longer You're Gone (The Harder it Gets),' Decca Records Recording Artist, Nashville, Tennessee." The novel offers a pastiche of Hemphill's *The Nashville Sound* as background to Bluejay's last forty years, his son Jaybird's youth lost in hopeless marriage and alcohol, and his grandson Robin's rejection of materialism. The three generations struggle to find their commonality, and they do so through the family and the land held in trust by Bluejay. In his usual fashion Hemphill scatters throughout the book various images of popular culture, history, and local color. Much of the country music background can be traced to *The Nashville Sound,* "stealing from myself," as Hemphill puts it. Thus Bluejay becomes a patriarch based on such country music stars as Ernest Tubb and Merle Haggard, and Hemphill says, "There are a lot of lines that belong to my old man."

In part two of the book, "Jaybird," Hemphill presents the second generation of the family. Again Hemphill draws on his own experiences with divorce, alcoholism, and loneliness, better presented in his journalistic work. As Jay and the first wife Becky separate over class and value differences, Jay also falls away from his father and all that "tacky" old music to follow his career as music entrepreneur for rising new rockabilly stars. Hemphill paints a painful picture of divorce as Jay's attempts to see his son Robin are thwarted and his alcohol intake increases. "Jaybird went to the pay phone in the foyer of the rooming house and called person-to-person to Robin Clay in Andrews, NC, and the boy answered but his mother picked up on an extension a split second later and told the operator that Robin Clay wasn't there and the boy started to protest but then the line went dead. Jaybird went to his room and put on his sheepskin coat and boots and cowboy hat and walked four blocks through the snow to a package store and bought a quart of Gordon's vodka . . . ."

In section three, "Robin," the reader is taken with the Clays into the 1980s. Robin has grown up in affluence, studied medicine at Harvard, and must decide what to do with his life in a time when he can read in the paper "about how the Atlanta Braves had not only agreed to pay one of their start sluggers $1 million a year but were also including a 'fat' bonus of some $2000 for every time he showed up for a Friday weigh-in at 215 pounds or less!" He and his wife Meg decide to return to Sixkiller Gap: "Now, as Meg kept saying, came the *real* real world. No longer would they have to explain to their peers, most of them aghast that they were 'throwing away' their training, why they were doing what they were doing. It seemed to them quite enough to live simply and work quietly and honestly at what they did best." This return then marks the completion of a generational cycle so prevalent in Hemphill's work.

Having fought his battles with a failed marriage, alcoholism, the vissicitudes of journalism, writing, and politics, Hemphill can now offer the view from "home":

> . . . after all those years of wandering I have finally found my niche, my outpost, my corner of the world, whence I will send my remaining dispatches. My God, that sounds like I'm retiring before I've turned fifty; and that's not what I mean at all despite even further evidence that I might be prepared to stand aside, as Adlai Stevenson put it when he quit politics, in order to "watch the others dance."

Hemphill is one of the best contemporary southern "watchers." He is still writing, still thinking about the nature of living the good life, raising another family, but most importantly, he is still open to the changes going on around him, yet keenly aware of the value of his heritage.

Owen Johnson

(27 August 1878-27 January 1952)

Samuel Irving Bellman
California State Polytechnic University, Pomona

BOOKS: *Arrows of the Almighty* (New York & London: Macmillan, 1901);

In the Name of Liberty: A Story of the Terror (New York: Century, 1905); republished as *Nicole, or In the Name of Liberty: A Story of the Terror* (London: Macmillan, 1905);

Max Fargus (New York: Baker & Taylor, 1906);

The Eternal Boy: Being the Story of the Prodigious Hickey (New York: Dodd, Mead, 1909); republished as *The Prodigious Hickey* (New York: Baker & Taylor, 1910);

The Humming Bird (New York: Baker & Taylor, 1910);

The Varmint (New York: Baker & Taylor, 1910);

Lawrenceville Stories (New York: Baker & Taylor, 1910);

The Tennessee Shad, Chronicling the Rise and Fall of the Firm of Doc Macnooder and the Tennessee Shad (New York: Baker & Taylor, 1911);

Stover at Yale (New York: Stokes, 1912);

The Sixty-First Second (New York: Stokes, 1913);

Murder in Any Degree (New York: Century, 1913);

The Salamander (Indianapolis: Bobbs-Merrill, 1914);

Making Money (New York: Stokes, 1915);

The Spirit of France (Boston: Little, Brown, 1916);

The Woman Gives: A Story of Regeneration (Boston: Little, Brown, 1916);

Virtuous Wives (Boston: Little, Brown, 1918);

The Wasted Generation (Boston: Little, Brown, 1921);

Skippy Bedelle: His Sentimental Progress from Urchin to the Complete Man of the World (Boston: Little, Brown, 1922);

Blue Blood: A Dramatic Interlude (Boston: Little, Brown, 1924);

Children of Divorce (Boston: Little, Brown, 1927);

Sacrifice (London, New York & Toronto: Longmans, Green, 1929);

The Coming of the Amazons: A Satirical Speculation on the Scientific Future of Civilization (New York & Toronto: Longmans, Green, 1931);

The Lawrenceville Stories (New York: Simon & Schuster, 1967).

(courtesy of the John Dixon Library, Lawrenceville School)

PLAY PRODUCTIONS: *The Comet*, Bijou Theatre, New York, N.Y., 30 December 1907;

The Salamander, Harris Theatre, New York, N.Y., 23 October 1914.

PERIODICAL PUBLICATIONS: "The Social Usurpation of Our Colleges," "I–An Introductory Article to a Series Disclosing the Growth of Snobbery at American Universities," *Collier's*, 49 (18 May 1912): 10-11, 39; "II–Harvard," 49 (25 May 1912): 12-14,

36-37; "III–Yale," 49 (8 June 1912): 12-13, 23-25; "IV–Princeton," 49 (15 June 1912): 17-18, 24; "V–The Fraternity System," 49 (22 June 1912): 21-22;

"The Founding of the Lit," *The Lit,* June 1945, pp. 5-7.

The prolific author Owen McMahon Johnson, an amateur politician in his later years, made a noteworthy contribution to the literature of American youth around the turn of the century. In a high-quality series of novels about a group of youngsters at the Lawrenceville School in New Jersey, and a follow-up novel about campus life at Yale University, Johnson provided realistic narratives rich in social commentary (and satire) as well as in character development, authentic dialogue, and a taut story line. In his other fiction, in which he dealt with subjects such as war and peace, New York bohemians, and marriage and divorce, Johnson failed to display the same degree of literary skill that he did in the Lawrenceville stories and in *Stover at Yale* (1912), the one possible exception being *The Salamander* (1914), an intimate look at Manhattan "girls on the make" in the early 1910s. Though Johnson led other lives after his days at Lawrenceville and Yale were over, an important part of his creative intellect was content to remain young and relive those golden schooldays.

Johnson was born in New York City on 27 August 1878, the son of Katherine McMahon Johnson and Robert Underwood Johnson, a poet and writer who would later become an editor of the *Century* magazine (where he was already a staffer) and considerably later, ambassador to Italy. Owen Johnson's first published work was a little story which appeared in the *St. Nicholas* magazine when he was six. In "The Founding of the Lit," a revealing autobiographical essay written to commemorate the fiftieth anniversary of the literary periodical he had founded at Lawrenceville in 1895, Johnson stated that since that first story had appeared in *St. Nicholas*, "The urge to fill a blank page with creations, often fantastic, of my imagination had been strong...." He recalled that the real beginning of his editorial career took place when he was twelve and became "an associate editor of a remarkable publication called the *Chimney Seat* ..., published for the benefit of the fund being raised for the Washington Memorial Arch...." Though only two issues were printed (copies were placed in the cornerstone of the arch), Johnson and his

friends–using pressure tactics–made $150 for their fund.

The next five years represented a formative period in Johnson's life. During this time he was exposed to the highly congenial, mind-expanding world of the Lawrenceville School, where he completed his four-year college-prep course and then, by special permission, stayed on for an extra year so that he could launch the *Lawrenceville Lit.* This endeavor "was a personal adventure," Johnson recalled half a century later. He had graduated at sixteen, "Class of '95, owing to no outstanding class room distinction but to an uncanny sense of what deviltries were working in the minds of those who prepared the examination papers–almost a gift of telepathy." These cursory confessional remarks give the reader no feel at all for the Lawrenceville School's psychological effect on Johnson and on his creative powers. He later explained that his literary characters really did live in his vicinity when he was a student at the school–the single exception being Dink Stover, who was a blend of several individuals–and that each of his stories had a factual basis. Moreover, the unbelievable-sounding nicknames were real: "the Coffee-Colored Angel, the Triumphant Egghead, the Tennessee Shad, the Gutter Pup, and the Walladoo Bird. Billy Hickok (the 'Prodigious Hickey') and some of his fellow imps of the Dickinson House were the fertile poetic imaginations which produced them." Brian de Boru Finnegan was modeled on a younger schoolmate, Frederick P. Flanagan, and the Tennessee Shad represented Johnson's classmate William Edgar Heron. That very important member of the faculty, "the Old Roman," as Johnson referred to the boys' formidable Latin teacher, was based on the school's redoubtable Latinist, Lawrence Cameron Hall.

Johnson's staying on for a postgraduate year at Lawrenceville in order to start his literary magazine resulted from an "impulsive decision" and was, he felt, "the decisive act" that led to his own stories about Lawrenceville. In his explanation he revealed that what he wrote owed much more to his editorial function than to his artistic inspiration. The fiction pieces submitted to him by the other students were lacking in conviction, as well as being "mushy, lurid, and unintentionally humorous." Depressed by their substandard quality, he "laid down the first law" for potential contributors: "Don't invent–interpret! Write from your own experience." Happily, the students began to do just that, but Johnson felt that he must "set the example," and so he began to write about what went on at Lawrenceville, making use of familiar campus characters. But, he admitted, his stories for the magazine were generally rough-hewn and derivative in style; one of them, however, "Beauty's Sister," was recycled in the *Century Magazine* and was later incorporated in *The Eternal Boy: Being the Story of the Prodigious Hickey* (1909).

After leaving Lawrenceville Johnson attended Yale University. Here began in earnest his complicated battle with social snobbery, secret societies, the fraternity system, and the woefully inadequate and misguided education offered by academia. Though opposed to snob rule in universities and colleges, Johnson seems to have been ambivalent about affiliating with a privileged social organization. Thus he joined a social fraternity, Alpha Delta Phi, but failed to receive a bid to one of the prestigious senior secret societies. Predictably, however, he was made editor of the *Yale Literary Magazine* and continued to store up keen observations of campus types and social relations among various student groups for later use. He graduated from Yale in 1900.

Upon entering the "real world" Johnson continued to write fiction. His first novel, *Arrows of the Almighty* (1901), set in the early nineteenth century, was a fast-paced adventure story about a dashing young man of great promise: John Gaunt, son of a Baltimore belle and the sophisticated, dissolute, self-destructive scion of the "Delaware Gaunts." John is the victim of a strange hereditary taint, a persistent brooding melancholy. Much of the story is concerned with John's trials and tribulations. His childhood is clouded by his father's personality deterioration and by his long-suffering mother's rejection of her compulsive-gambler husband, who is being systematically robbed by a man she despises—his boon companion and household guest, Captain Brace. Grown to manhood, John marries the daughter of a prominent Ohio family (her father is a former senator). When the Civil War breaks out John's father-in-law obtains for him the commission of colonel, his duties to be those of a noncombatant officer in charge of the commissariat. As a result John faces endless difficulties with suppliers and contractors bent on defrauding the government. Harder to cope with than those line-of-duty problems is the psychological effect of the war on his wife, who is having their first child.

What is probably of greatest significance in the novel is its curious foreshadowing of Johnson's most important fiction, his schoolboy stories with their vivid projections of student and teacher personality types, their lively descriptions of campus capers, and their presentation of the wholesome effects of normal boyhood friendships. John Gaunt is supported throughout his young manhood and maturing years by the friendship of one of his first schoolmates, Jack Hazard, a devil-may-care "cut up" disinclined to study or get serious after the fun is over. The twenty-two-year-old Johnson, in describing the early schooldays of the mischief-making Hazard and the sobersided Gaunt (they were later to be nicknamed "Johnnie Gay" and "Johnnie Glum") was apparently writing about experiences very near and dear to him.

Noteworthy in this regard is Johnson's picture of Yale College in the early 1850s (Gaunt is Class of '55), which includes a look at a faculty figure who would assume a somewhat greater role in Johnson's Lawrenceville stories, the Latin teacher called "the Roman." But in describing, in a nutshell, John Gaunt's manner at Yale, Johnson might have been prefiguring his own beau ideal of approximately forty years later: Stover at Yale. Gaunt, though admired and respected, never got to be "A popular favorite"; still, "in the frays with the sophomores, in the conflicts with the police and the fire department,—anywhere, in a word, where blows were to be given and taken,—he was a recognized leader." Gaunt looked "too deep into men, his eyes were too sharp for hypocrisy; and when he had unearthed a toady or a humbug, his dislike was too apparent." It might have been "because he was older in thought than his comrades that many felt not quite at their ease before his searching eyes."

Johnson's next two novels were *In the Name of Liberty: A Story of the Terror* (1905), which dealt with the French Revolution, and *Max Fargus* (1906), a sordid account of several sleazy characters involved in a scramble for the fortune of an elderly moneygrubber (the namesake of the novel). A shabby, "designing" woman, aided and abetted by a dishonest lawyer named Bofinger, gets Fargus to marry her—the idea being that she and Bofinger will, before too long, come into possession of Fargus's wealth. Fargus, an unsavory character like the others in this story, not only foils their plot, but, with the help of Bofinger's law partner, gets his revenge. He goes into hiding—in the house that is opposite the one his wife is liv-

Johnson (top row, second from right) with his fellow residents of Green House, a dormitory on the Lawrenceville campus, circa 1893-1894 (courtesy of the John Dixon Library, Lawrenceville School)

ing in–and the two conspirators incur a number of liabilities, including heavy indebtedness, in order to obtain Fargus's money. Legal complications and other hindrances, including the machinations of Bofinger's partner, Groll, ensure that they will never have access to what they have been seeking so desperately. Now brought to ruin and pitted against each other, they have unwittingly made it possible for the crafty Groll to be the sole inheritor of the Fargus fortune. In a chilling speech to Bofinger, Groll tells of Fargus's determination to wreak *extra*ordinary vengeance, for the ordinary kind would have been meaningless. "I had to find him something that would not only bankrupt you both but crush out of you all youth, ambition, and hope. . . . Fargus wished not only all that made life blotted out, but that life itself should be the most unendurable thing to you both. He succeeded. He knew it–strange man! He died happy."

Following are two quite different opinions–one of them contemporary–of Johnson's first decade out of Yale, when he was not only working at the novelist's craft and trade but also doing a stint as a reporter in the police court. John R.

Tunis, in a 24 September 1967 *New York Times Book Review* critique of a one-volume edition of the Lawrenceville stories, had this retrospective view: "After leaving Yale, Johnson began writing seriously. He was immediately successful. For about a decade he earned $70,000 yearly, in an era when the income tax was nonexistent. . . . When he met [the Russian actress] Alla Nazimova, he helped her learn English, and in 1908 wrote a play, 'The Comet,' for her, which ran two years on Broadway."

Arthur Bartlett Maurice, a Lawrenceville schoolmate of Owen Johnson and a writer for the *Bookman*, obtained an interview with him for an article in the "Personal Portraits" section of the June 1914 issue. Those years before 1909, Maurice explained, "had been years of persistent endeavour, of achievement, but in no more than a small way had they been years of material reward." Then Maurice quoted an imaginary representative of public opinion. "He has written two or three books, and they are not at all bad, but they don't seem to have caught on. He may do something yet. But so far he does not seem quite to have found himself." Actually, Maurice continued, speaking for himself now, Johnson "was just beginning to find himself " (that is, in 1909). As for the early books, they "were all more or less expressions of that early talent which is inevitably imitative." Thus Maurice saw *Arrows of the Almighty* and *In the Name of Liberty* as "The work of a boy who had read and digested much romantic fiction"; and he detected the influence of Balzac's fiction in *Max Fargus* and the influence of Ibsen's dramas in Johnson's play *The Comet.* "Imitation, of course," Maurice decreed, "perhaps not recognized then, but not to be denied now."

In Johnson's later works, when he wrote about high society with its flaming parents and their domestic intrigues and realignments, he seems to have lost some of the literary skill he had been developing throughout his school years. This was odd, considering that Johnson was well acquainted, from extensive personal experience, with the tumultuous high-society lifestyle he portrayed, and also taking into account his earlier advice to potential contributors to the *Lawrenceville Lit*: they should interpret rather than invent, and should write from their own experience. On the subject of the drop in quality of Johnson's novels that followed the Lawrenceville stories, F. Scott Fitzgerald was quite blunt. Writing to H. L. Mencken on 4 May 1925, he had this to say: "There's nothing the matter with some of Johnson's later books, they're just rotten that's all. He was tired and his work is no more writing in the sense that the work [of] Thomas Hardy and Gene Stratton Porter is writing than were Dreiser's dime novels."

What diverted some of Johnson's attention and interest from the problems of campus life to those of domestic life was his changing domestic situation and fast-paced manner of living. Early on he would be torn between two worlds, the one he had irremediably outgrown and the one he would long continue to whirl in, and as a writer he would be more effective in writing about the former. But a greater appreciation of what Johnson brought to all of his writing may be gained if one recognizes that he happened to be an unusually well-rounded man. Tunis described Johnson as having been "a fencer, a tennis player, a golfer . . . , a portrait painter and a musician" as well as "one of the founders of the Berkshire Symphonic Festival." Johnson was also a founder of the Authors League. According to Tunis, he was "a social lion of the early 1900's," an individual who "knew everyone, went everywhere."

It follows then that Johnson's domestic life was neither simple nor narrow. The author's first wife, whom he married in 1901, was Mary Galt Stockly of Lakewood, New Jersey. She died in 1910. In 1912 he married Esther (or Elaine) Cobb, a San Francisco socialite, better known in later years as Cobina Wright; they were divorced in 1917. Around this period–before World War I and after–Johnson traveled about Europe and subsequently remained there for a few years. In 1917 he married a French woman, Cecile Denis de la Garde of Chignens, who died less than a year later. Johnson retained his French contacts; in 1919 the French government honored him by making him a Chevalier of the Legion of Honor. Ten years earlier he had received another signal award from his own country: membership in the National Institute of Arts and Letters. In January 1921 Johnson married Catherine Sayre Burton of New York; she died in March 1923. In 1926 he married the socially prominent Gertrude Bovee Boyce, who survived him.

What may be called Johnson's "major phase" as a writer of fiction spans about three years, 1909 to 1911, and includes four novels and a thin volume of six brief stories. The first of the trilogy that has been referred to as the Lawrenceville stories–*The Eternal Boy: Being the Story of the Prodigious Hickey*–introduces Johnson's little world of school and village in the early 1890s. While much of the novel is concerned with schoolboy pranks, including study-avoidance routines and sports rivalries, especially among the various houses on the Lawrenceville campus, Johnson was not by any means attempting to rival the hackwriting syndicates that were shamelessly grinding out titles like *The Rover Boys at School* and *The Motor Boys at Boxwood Hall.* Lawrenceville life was real, and earnest, not the empty dream of the pulps: things *were* by and large what they seemed in the narrative.

Among the highlights of this amusing book are the great pancake contest of Hungry Smeed; the downward trajectory of William Orville Hicks ("the Prodigious Hickey"), whose riotous and sometimes destructive behavior eventually caused his painful expulsion from the school; an intriguing psychological and physical battle between two nearly compatible roommates: Lovely Mead and the Gutter Pup; the rehabilitation of lonely misfits, like the nondescript and overage Barker Smith–who desperately needed to earn a nickname–and the pipsqueak young orphan known as the Great Big Man; and the disastrous

Johnson (center) in May 1930 with four of his Lawrenceville schoolmates who served as models for characters in his short stories. To his right are J. S. MacNider ("Doc Macnooder") and W. O. Hickok ("The Prodigious Hickey"); to his left W. L. Righter ("Turkey Reiter") and W. H. Dibble ("Flash Condit") (photograph courtesy of the John Dixon Library, Lawrenceville School).

educational philosophy of the new mathematics instructor Mr. Baldwin, who politicizes the entire campus with the application of a pet theory that nearly ruins the Lawrenceville School. Johnson dealt with a number of important issues in this book, as some of the contemporary reviewers noticed–including the critic in the *American Library Association Booklist* (April 1909), who wrote that it was "Hardly a book for children, because of its deplorable attitude toward teachers and study in general, but entertaining and even instructive for adults."

The Humming Bird (1910) is a literary interlude, allowing Dennis de Brian de Boru Finnegan, barely in his teens and too small for team baseball–though an avid student of the game and an aspiring journalist–to show what he could do. The boy becomes the wildest, liveliest baseball reporter ever: "Stevens frisked the lozenge once to the back woods and then unmuzzled a humming bird to the prairies which nested

in Jackson's twigs----"; "Hickey ticked off a slow freight to the pretzel counter and cannon balled to first just ahead of Tyrell's slap." One reviewer of this literary gem felt that Johnson had "become the Homer of the American prep school. True, he speaks in a language as incomprehensible to some as a Chinese dialect, and hence he loses some of the universality of a Homeric appeal" (*The Independent*, 18 August 1910).

The Varmint (1910), the longest and most ambitious of the three Lawrenceville novels, is a complicated opposite number to *The Eternal Boy*, in fact a masterfully written bildungsroman that deserves far more notice than it has ever received. John Humperdink Stover (known as Dink or Young Stover), aged fifteen, begins his career at Lawrenceville just after the spring term gets underway. Fresh and ludicrously overconfident, he soon antagonizes most of the people with whom he comes in contact, from the Roman (the fearsome Latin teacher) to the other schoolboys at his dormitory, the Green House. For his violation of numerous social taboos, the brash, immature "varmint" is forced to undergo a variety of painful ordeals: humiliating encounters with those he has offended by word, manner, and deed; personal recognition of his own cowardice when under threat of attack; bloody schoolyard battles; denunciation and excommunication by the president of the Green House; and ostracism by his housemates. During and after Stover's long-drawn-out initiation trials, he is also being taught harsh lessons in behavior modification and survival strategy, as well as bitter lessons about human nature in challenging situations. Because he is naive and credulous, the campus con artists, Doc Macnooder and the Tennessee Shad, sell him an assortment of worthless trinkets from their warehouse of "sucker supplies"; a schoolboy considerably younger than he instructs him in the art of kidding around and making small talk with the other boys; the coach and football captain help him learn "how to play the game"; and an "older woman" (twenty-four years old) acquaints him with the delights of romance and budding love.

Johnson allowed Stover to emerge triumphant from all of his trials, physical and psychological. He and his sworn enemy, Tough McCarty, somehow wind up close friends, and Stover is able to become a campus hero following a series of gridiron triumphs–despite an earlier angry repudiation of the Lawrenceville student body, and despite his judgment about a disputed football goal, favoring the opposing team. Among the most entertaining parts of this novel are those which concern Doc Macnooder's financial manipulations. In relating Macnooder's astute conniving to that same tendency in America's hard-hearted lords of high finance, Johnson was at his best as a satirist and social commentator. *The Varmint,* a vividly drawn picture of an eastern prep school "About five miles away from anywhere" (actually, the Lawrenceville School is less than five miles from Princeton), is replete with penetrating character studies and educational psychology and philosophy. At the very end it is amusing to observe Stover, now big man on campus, complain to the Roman, his supposed persecutor, about a new little Lawrenceville "varmint" that he cannot stand, only to be made to see–by the Roman's gentle smile–his latest error in judgment.

In his next Lawrenceville novel Johnson abandoned the moralizing instructive approach of *The Varmint* in order to present a more playful scrutinization of campus high jinks. For this pleas-

ant task his creative memory supplied him with the right supporting characters to use as temporary star performers, and also with appropriate low-comedy situations. *The Tennessee Shad, Chronicling the Rise and Fall of the Firm of Doc Macnooder and the Tennessee Shad* (1911) features the campus con artists–the protagonist, a lazy schemer and designer of projects utilizing the resources of others for *his* private benefit, and his cohort, Doc Macnooder, an "amateur practitioner but most professional financier." Among the Shad's schemes, generally concocted with his associate and sometime rival, are the Criminal Club, whose members shave each other's heads and then march lockstep into chapel; a tonsorial parlor specializing in scalp massage, to help repair the damage done by the Criminal Club; and a plot whereby a group of the boys contract the German measles so they can spend some time in the school infirmary under leisurely conditions. The Shad generally manages to avoid harm or inconvenience when his plans misfire.

Much of the story concerns the exploitation of a very wealthy newcomer to Lawrenceville, sixteen-year-old Montague Skinner (soon renamed the Uncooked Beefsteak), who arrives at the school in style, riding in a hackney coach with his valet. One of this dandy's most desirable traits that would enhance a house's reputation was a "money is no object" attitude, combined with an intense desire to please the boys. The firm of Doc Macnooder and the Tennessee Shad, taking an immediate interest in young Skinner (who had to be placed in a much lower form than that of his age group), finds numerous ways to ease him of his capital. One method is by holding a special (and illicit) "event" at his expense: a midnight gourmet feast and smoking contest which ends disastrously. Young Skinner persists in being too fresh with his supposed buddies, no matter how hard they try to get him to stay in his place, and they reduce this foolish "soft touch" to an overburdened personal servant. The book concludes with two low-keyed episodes: the Uncooked Beefsteak's strategy in breaking the shackles of his involuntary servitude, and the final error on the part of Macnooder and the Shad that causes them to dissolve their firm.

A more important book is Johnson's ambitious college novel, *Stover at Yale.* Contemporary reviews were favorable, the *Outlook* for example stating that the book would be of great interest to students as well as graduates who wanted to ponder the problems presented by college life.

Publicity still for "The Prodigious Hickey," an American Playhouse *production broadcast on 26 January 1987. "Hickey" (Zach Galligan) is seen refereeing a boxing match between "The Gutter Pup" (Steve Baldwin) and "Lovely Mead" (Josh Hamilton) (photograph by Anthony Bliss).*

In a way, *Stover at Yale* reads like a reform document of academic muckraking. Johnson, mainly through the use of dialogue, vents assorted criticisms of Yale in particular and college life in general. Moreover, in the middle of chapter twenty-three, in the symposium scene, Johnson gives an overview, provided by a highly articulate student named Brockhurst (who later would *not* be tapped for a senior society), of the cultural and technical matters regrettably lacking in Yale's curriculum. But, as commentators have observed, the novel's accusations are weakened by inconsistencies and sellouts on Stover's part. Johnson, apparently calling for a radical reorganization of Yale, both academically (practical curricula) and socially (elimination of the snobbish secret societies), presents instead bull sessions, preachments, and tokenism, not a method of effecting top-to-bottom correction.

Underlying the author's ambivalent feelings about what was wrong with Yale and what to do about it is his notion that democracy, so greatly to be prized, has its limits when it comes to all-out competition. Winning is the thing, and top-level leadership is the "greatest good." Yet one gathers from reading Johnson that there is an in-definable quality inherent in the real winners in social, political, or campus competition. No matter how vocal these happy few may be in their opposition to the status quo, no matter how much they antagonize all or most of the other group members, if they have a particular background and a certain kind of power and determination to "make it big," not only will their obstacles crumble but their opponents who come to attack them will stay to sing their praises. Stover, in fact, seems to lead a charmed life in spite of all his temporary troubles with the people he encounters at Yale. For example, when he is still a freshman he wins out over a senior in a competition for the position of end on the second-string football team. Given Johnson's depiction of what seem to be natural-born heroes, his attitude toward collegiate athletic competition is ironic if not actually confused. Thus Johnson makes much of Yale football as a "school for character" and "the discipline of the Caesars," where victory was based on a comrade's "broken hopes," and he speaks of "the savage fanaticism" of Americans to succeed in every kind of competition.

In contrast to Stover's ignominious lone stand at Lawrenceville, as depicted in *The Var-*

mint, is his daring, meritorious stand against Yale's sophomore secret societies–a position that brought him powerful enemies and threatened to doom him socially (following Stover's attack on those societies Yale's president abolished them). In "the fall of the junior year, he was the undisputed leader of the class, a force that had brought to it a community of interest and friendly understanding." It was by leading the Saturday night football rallies, where his magnetic personality unified the heterogeneous group, that Stover managed this success; "he had no underlying motive, because he had achieved in himself absolute independence and fearlessness of any outer criticism, and his strength with the crowd was just the consciousness of his own liberty." At the end of the book Stover, though fairly certain he had alienated too many people to be chosen for one of the elite senior societies, was tapped for Skull and Bones, in fact by his old antagonist Le Baron. Stover's "eyes were blurred with tears, and he knew how much he cared, after the long months of rebellion, to be no longer an outsider, but back among his own with the stamp of approval on his record."

Despite its flaws *Stover at Yale* is richly endowed with the elements that made up Yale campus life in the 1890s: a broad range of male types socializing, engaging in sports, clashing or cementing friendships, exchanging confidences, and discussing their college experience. However, the book provides more than a "nostalgia trip" for today's reader. Johnson effectively blends object lessons in social growth (one of Stover's friends is an older student from a lower-class background, married to a woman of doubtful virtue) and self-discipline with his highly entertaining sequences of the *study and strife, fun and frolic* gamesmanship to which the Yale men are so deeply committed. Christian K. Messenger, in *Sport and Play in American Fiction: Hawthorne to Faulkner* (1981), called the book "the finest novel about eastern college life at the turn of the century."

In five important articles in *Collier's* bearing the overall title of "The Social Usurpation of Our Colleges" and appearing between 18 May and 22 June 1912, Johnson revealed his strong interest in improving conditions in academia. The articles, particularly "III–Yale" and "V–The Fraternity System," take up his critical arguments where he left off in *Stover at Yale*. In "I–An Introductory Article to a Series Disclosing the Growth of Snobbery at American Universities," Johnson

complained that America's leading universities had changed over the three preceding decades from "institutions of learning" to "worthy schools for character" providing "a social experience." He suggested rewarding "the men of late development" and bringing into universities "those who could influence [them] for the best." A "graduate Order of Merit" could be established, a kind of social clubhouse, with membership awarded "only to graduates of six years' standing, and that only for the most distinguished achievement." In "V–The Fraternity System" Johnson recommended reformation through a three-step process of "gradual evolution": (1) "the bringing of all students into a dormitory system founded on the class unit"; (2) "the bringing of all students into a common dining hall, divided again by classes"; (3) "the prohibition of the Saturday night exodus and the establishment of Saturday night . . . as the distinctive grouping time of the class." Aside from these "purely democratic forms," Johnson called for proper "standards of education" through "scholarship tests for social success" and the abandoning of "what has been the most harmful single influence for evil–the general, unrestricted elective system."

Johnson's last school novel, *Skippy Bedelle: His Sentimental Progress from Urchin to the Complete Man of the World* (1922), was a piece of literary busy work. Set in 1896 this pale Lawrenceville novel features a budding inventor of futile contrivances such as a foot regulator for bathtubs, a souvenir toothbrush, and mosquito-proof socks. Johnson seems here to have been parodying Tom Swift, hero of the pseudo-scientific pulp novels by Victor Appleton. Skippy "sought diligently among the need of human nature for something on the grand scale. He tried his hand at a perpetual-motion machine. He thought out a combination submarine and airship which would put the navies of the world at the mercy of his country. He even descended to such trivial abstractions as a Reversible Shirt-Front." Much of this fifteen-year-old's story concerns bittersweet "young love," the result of "the intrusion into his still simple scheme of things of that arch-disturber–WOMAN."

Most of Johnson's remaining literary efforts deal with "society": domestic dilemmas, designing women, inconstant men, serial matings, children spilling from broken homes. The most important of these books is *The Salamander*, a novel about bohemian girls in Manhattan, hungry for excitement, preying on wealthy men and holding on to as many generous suitors as possible while offering little in return. The sociology of these gold diggers is explored by Johnson in his highly informative foreword and throughout the story. Some of the Salamanders' terminology is given, such as "prop" (a free-spending, automobile-owning youth from a wealthy family), "orgy" (a superlatively lavish banquet), "tea party" (a dinner or luncheon that is anything short of lavish), and "precipices" (taking extreme risks with male admirers). The Salamanders' "basic strategy . . . [is] acceptance that raises hopes, then an excuse that brings tantalizing disorder, but whets the appetite"; their strict rule, "never allowing business to interfere with pleasure."

Doré Baxter, the heroine of the book–which could have been a serious novel of enduring value if Johnson had not treated her story as a melodrama for unreflective readers–is an extraordinary femme fatale capable of outdoing the wiliest, prettiest Salamander in Manhattan. She manages to juggle eight or more ardent suitors ranging from her country bumpkin fiancé back home in the Midwest, to the evil, unscrupulous tycoon Albert Edward Sassoon, who is driven mad with lust. How the distracted and endangered Doré avoids severe harm and disposes of all suitors but one makes for an interesting if literarily unsophisticated story.

Among Johnson's numerous other works are *The Woman Gives: A Story of Regeneration* (1916), an account of "a queer collection" of bohemian types living on the two upper floors of Teagan's Arcade in Manhattan's Lincoln Square; *The Wasted Generation* (1921), a romantic drama of World War I filled with sentimentality and political argumentation; *Sacrifice* (1929), a novel of divorce avoided for the sake of the children despite a crumbling marriage and newfound lov-

ers for each partner; and *The Coming of the Amazons: A Satiristic Speculation on the Scientific Future of Civilization* (1931), a futuristic flight of fancy about a world dominated by women. Critics frequently acknowledged Johnson's shallowness in his fictional handling of adult problems, and it is hard to avoid the conclusion that he did not devote enough painstaking effort to his craft once he had established himself as a popular writer.

After Johnson left off his literary labors he dabbled in politics. Earlier, having worked for the Republican National Committee, he had become disillusioned with the Republicans and left the party when Warren Harding was nominated for president. Considerably later, as an ardent supporter of Franklin D. Roosevelt, Johnson made two bids for the office of congressman from Massachusetts on the Democratic ticket (1936 and 1938), failing each time. He died early in 1952 at his home in Vineyard Haven, Massachusetts, and was buried in Stockbridge Cemetery.

References:

David Lamoreaux, "*Stover at Yale* and The Gridiron Metaphor," *Journal of Popular Culture*, 11 (Fall 1977): 330-344;

The Lawrenceville Experience 1985-86: The Catalogue of the 176th Year of The Lawrenceville School, Lawrenceville, New Jersey (N.p., n.d.);

John O. Lyons, *The College Novel in America* (Carbondale: Southern Illinois University Press, 1962);

Arthur Bartlett Maurice, "Owen Johnson," *Bookman*, 39 (June 1914): 416-420;

Christian K. Messenger, *Sport and Play in American Fiction: Hawthorne to Faulkner* (New York: Columbia University Press, 1981);

John R. Tunis, "A Man of Distinction," *New York Times Book Review*, 24 September 1967, p. 8.

Garrison Keillor
(7 August 1942-   )

Peter A. Scholl
Luther College

BOOKS: *G. K. the DJ* (St. Paul: Minnesota Public Radio, 1977);
The Selected Verse of Margaret Haskins Durber (St. Paul: Minnesota Public Radio, 1979; London: Faber & Faber, 1987);
Happy to Be Here (New York: Atheneum, 1982);
Lake Wobegon Days (New York: Viking, 1985; London: Faber & Faber, 1986);
Leaving Home (New York: Viking, 1987).

RECORDINGS: *A Prairie Home Companion Anniversary Album* (St. Paul: Minnesota Public Radio, 1980);
The Family Radio (St. Paul: Minnesota Public Radio, 1982);
News from Lake Wobegon (St. Paul: Minnesota Public Radio, 1982);
Prairie Home Companion Tourists (St. Paul: Minnesota Public Radio, 1983);
Ten Years on the Prairie: A Prairie Home Companion 10th Anniversary (St. Paul: Minnesota Public Radio, 1984);
Gospel Birds and Other Stories of Lake Wobegon (St. Paul: Minnesota Public Radio, 1985);
A Prairie Home Companion: The Final Performance (St. Paul: Minnesota Public Radio, 1987).

OTHER: "Has It Been Ten Years Already? He Asked," in *Ten Years: The Official Souvenir Anniversary Program for A Prairie Home Companion* (St. Paul: Minnesota Public Radio, 1984), pp. 11-12.

PERIODICAL PUBLICATIONS: "At the Opry," *New Yorker* (6 May 1974): 46-69;
"After a Fall," *New Yorker* (21 June 1982): 36-39.

As *Lake Wobegon Days* (1985) climbed steadily toward the top of the *New York Times* bestseller list in the fall of 1985, an editorial in the *Des Moines Register* offered "a plea to the editors of People magazine, booking agents for television talk shows and gossip columnists: Please, lay off Garrison Keillor before you do something fool-ish, like turning him into a celebrity." But it went on to make it plain that he already was: "He seemed safe from the ravages of celebrityhood in the age of Sting, Madonna and other single-name superstars. But then he wrote a book that's selling like hotcakes and is getting reviewed everywhere. Time magazine even put his picture on its cover." Similar pleas and mock complaints soon followed as the supposed Keillor "cult," an odd-lot of scattered devotees to his *A Prairie Home Companion* radio show, was revealed to be in fact a broad, national following. The familiar comparisons to Mark Twain, Will Rogers, and James Thurber were now offered with more authority: "He is . . . ," said the London *Observer*'s reviewer of *Lake Wobegon Days*, "the best humorous writer to come out of America since James Thurber." His announcement that *A Prairie Home Companion* would go off the air in June of that year was carried as news nationwide. In the wake of his departure for Denmark shortly after the last show, it became clear that his celebrity status and his success as a performer had not drowned his foremost ambition: to be a writer of distinction.

Gary Edward Keillor was born 7 August 1942 in Anoka, Minnesota, the third of six children in the family of John P. Keillor, a railway mail clerk and carpenter, and Grace Denham Keillor. In the years when Keillor was growing up just north of Minneapolis and south of Anoka in what is now Brooklyn Park, the area was rural enough to provide him with many of the experiences out of which he evolved his fictional town, "Lake Wobegon," in the heart of "Mist County."

While they were not far from the Twin Cities, the Keillors lived an old-fashioned existence by most standards. They had a half-acre garden and a big white house, with "a cornfield across the road, a deep twisting ravine behind the house and dry creek bed with big rocks where we made camps and forts, and just over the hill, the Mississippi to swim in and skate and skip stones." They were members of the Plymouth Brethren, a protestant sect of dissenters from the Anglicans,

Garrison Keillor (photograph by Jim Brandenburg, courtesy of Minnesota Public Radio)

a group without ordained clergy that bears a close resemblance to the "fundamentalists" known to listeners of *A Prairie Home Companion* and readers of *Lake Wobegon Days* as the "Sanctified Brethren." His people were slow talkers and plain livers, family people of Scottish descent, who frowned on drinking and dancing and were "not at all happy when Gary had a poem published in the high school literary magazine."

The countless hours of Bible readings, the elucidations of scripture by traveling evangelists, and the secular storytellings in family gatherings made lasting impressions on Keillor, who has said that becoming a full-time writer has been his ambition since he was "a little kid." He has repeatedly mentioned the influence of his Aunt Ruth (Keillor) Blumer and Great Uncle Lew Powell, both storytellers who held family gatherings spellbound with their "long, meandering talks." "I made up my mind," he says, "that the most wonderful thing in the world would be to be a storyteller."

"Our family believed television was bad for you, like movies or smoking or playing cards," Keillor has written. Radio, apparently, was not considered so worldly. Keillor remembers sitting, at age three, on the lap of his Uncle Jim, their heads together listening to his crystal set "as a

tiny band played and a man said it was true, the war was over." Keillor has said that "The idea for [*A Prairie Home Companion*] . . . came . . . out of things remembered from childhood–in my case, radio, which was a big part of my youth, since we didn't get a television in my house until I was already in high school."

Though very much in the public eye, Keillor is reserved and often remote. His complex, much-celebrated inwardness has a long foreground: "Something happened to me when I was six or seven years old," he told an interviewer. "I have dim memories of it. I became fearful, always looking around, always checking, always alert. You never overcome it. You go on from there." Keillor's high school teacher in Anoka, Deloyd Hochstetter, remembers him as a "tall, thin kid sitting in the back. . . . He never contributed to class discussions, but one time he gave a laid-back satire about what's in the records in the principal's office. He had them rolling in the aisles, but everything was written out–that's how shy he was."

Keillor has said that he was a " 'kid' journalist, having started his own 'paper' while in grade school." According to one account, he took "Garrison" as a pen name in the eighth grade because "it sounded mighty formidable, like someone not

Keillor on the set for his nationally broadcast radio show A Prairie Home Companion *with musicians (left to right) Butch Thompson on piano, Peter Ostroushko on mandolin, Johnny Gimble on fiddle, and Chet Atkins on guitar (photograph by Rusty Gautreaux, courtesy of Minnesota Public Radio)*

to be trifled with." "I didn't have a whole lot going for me in school," Keillor says; by "writing for my teachers I could get back some of the points I lost."

To the shy, small-town boy of fourteen, his first glimpse of the *New Yorker* in the public library "was a fabulous sight, an immense glittering ocean liner off the coast of Minnesota, and I loved to read it." He carried it around in high school as a "sign of class."

Keillor was particularly influenced by the *New Yorker*'s "great infield of Thurber, Liebling, Perelman, and White." "They were my heroes . . . ," he writes; "and in my mind they took the field against the big mazumbos of American Literature, and I cheered for them. . . . I cheer for them now . . . , and still think (as I thought then) that it is more worthy in the eyes of God and better for us as a people if a writer make three pages sharp and funny about the lives of geese than to make three hundred flat and flabby about God or the American people."

Keillor attended the University of Minnesota on and off from 1960 to 1966, graduating with a B.A. in English and journalism. As a student, he edited a literary magazine, *The Ivory Tower*. His brother Philip also remembers a

"noisy, satirical column called 'Broadsides,' in which he slashed at student radicals, the college president and any other targets that seemed pompous and pretentious." After graduation Keillor left Minnesota for Boston and New York, to try to get a job as a writer–an expedition which ended in failure. He returned to the Twin Cities and the University of Minnesota, where for a while he worked on a master's degree in English, but then took a job with KSJR-FM in Collegeville, the first station in the Minnesota Public Radio network. "I had a choice between radio and writing . . . ," he says; "I never got a writing job, so I chose radio."

He was to spend fourteen years on and off, from 1968 to 1982, working as a disk jockey in a morning slot. Keillor started with a classical format and gradually evolved his own eclectic mix of music and talk, *The Prairie Home Morning Show,* which eventually included anecdotes about a place called Lake Wobegon. In 1969 and 1970 Keillor began to invent sponsors, which was to become one of his trademarks. "I dearly love public radio," he explained, "but to me radio isn't radio without commercials." The first of these was "Jack's Auto Repair," but when listeners informed him that there were indeed establishments with that same name, he thought that to avoid complications he'd "better find some place to put these sponsors in."

For most of those years in early-morning radio he was also logging in many hours at the typewriter. There were periods, indeed, when he devoted himself entirely to writing, notably in 1970, on the heels of selling his first story to the *New Yorker* ("Local Family Keeps Son Happy"), when he retired with his first wife, Mary Guntzel, and infant son, Jason, to a farm near Freeport, Minnesota. He had met Mary when they were both students at Minnesota. They were married in 1965 and Jason (who continued to live with his father) was born in 1969. The marriage ended in 1976 and the novel, set in a radio station, was never finished.

While his marriage was "disappearing" in the spring of 1974, Keillor, Mary, and Jason took a trip to California on the train, feeling flush with the $6,000 he had just received from the *New Yorker* for "At the Opry." In that profile he had written about Nashville's Grand Ole Opry: "The best place to see the Opry that night [its last performance in Ryman Auditorium, "the Mother Church of Country Music"] . . . was in the [radio control] booth with my eyes shut, . . . the music coming out of the speaker just like the radio, that good old AM mono sound. The room smelled of hot radio tubes, and, closing my eyes, I could see the stage as clearly as when I was a kid lying in front of our giant Zenith console. I'd seen a photograph of the Opry stage in a magazine back then, and, believe me, one is all you need."

It was in Nashville listening to the Opry that Keillor first thought "of starting up a show like that in Minnesota." He went home and talked to Bill Kling, the head of Minnesota Public Radio, who "took it hook, line, and sinker." Three ninety-minute segments of *A Prairie Home Companion* were taped at the Walker Art Center in Minneapolis, 7 April 1974, and the first live show aired on 6 July, from the Janet Wallace Auditorium at Macalester College in St. Paul. There were twelve persons in the 400-seat hall, and selling tickets was long-term producer of the show, Margaret Moos. Moos was also Keillor's "POSSLQ" (person of the opposite sex sharing living quarters), a government acronym he used to label their relationship. Their breakup excited considerable media attention in the summer of 1985 (Moos returned in January 1987 to produce the last six months of the show).

On 10 August 1985 the *Prairie Home Companion* monologue concerned the 25th Lake Wobegon High School Reunion, where Keillor was supposedly swept off his feet by "Margreta," a Danish foreign exchange student–just as he had been by her real-life counterpart, Ulla Skaerved, whom he had reencountered at his twenty-fifth reunion at Anoka High School, where she had been a foreign exchange student. They were married 29 December 1985 in Holte, Denmark.

A Prairie Home Companion, frequently described as a radio variety show, was broadcast live from 5:00 until 7:00 P.M., CST, and performed before a live audience. Keillor emceed the whole, singing "Hello Love" at the opening of each show, usually doing a commercial for Powdermilk Biscuits (which often became a virtual essay on the needs of "shy persons"), Bob's Bank, Bertha's Kitty Boutique, or (later) Minnesota Language Systems. On each broadcast Keillor read around eighty "messages" sent in from listeners and gathered from the live audience–another feature he borrowed from old-time radio. "Because it's live," Keillor said of the show, "there's an intimacy with a listener and you can draw on people's imaginations." The heart of each show was Keillor's monologue, "The News from Lake Wobegon," which he delivered a little beyond the halfway point.

"Our show down deep in its heart is a gospel show," Keillor has written, and his own singing seems at its best in gospel songs, such as "Sweet Hour of Prayer"–songs which the Plymouth Brethren sang unaccompanied back in Anoka, while the Lutherans down the street performed Bach chorales. Roy Blount, Jr., who has appeared on the show, characterizes the music as "traditional, and what a range of traditions: from Appalachian, by way of Ukrainian, Afro-American and Scottish, to Yiddish." Keillor retained a core of regulars on the show and a number of visiting groups and individual performers. Notable among the regular groups were The Butch Thompson Trio; The Powdermilk Biscuit Band (1975-1979); The New Prairie Ramblers (1979-1981); and Stoney Lonesome, with Peter Ostroushko (1981-1987). Notable vocalists have included Vern Sutton, Philip Brunelle, Jean Redpath, Robin and Linda Williams, and Greg Brown. Albums of many of these performers are available from Minnesota Public Radio, which has also produced three albums of music and Keillor's own songs, commercials, skits, and monologues.

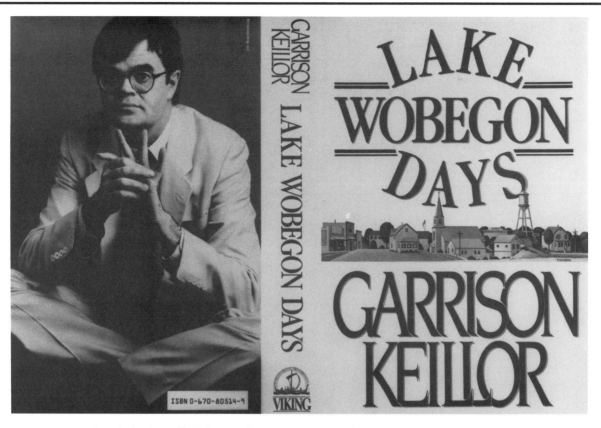

Dust jacket for Keillor's first novel, an evocation of his fictional hometown Lake Wobegon

Keillor himself wrote nearly all the spoken material used on the show in the early years and was often assisted in delivering sketches and commercials by regulars, such as his morning show co-host "Jim-Ed Poole" (Tom Keith) and later by Howard Mohr, who wrote and performed from 1982. Keillor alone was responsible for the monologue, "The News from Lake Wobegon." The "rube jokes" and commercials for Jack's Auto Repair and other Lake Wobegon enterprises, which Keillor had been telling on his morning show, changed on the Saturday evening show, starting out at about three to five minutes and burgeoning around 1979, when they became the "centerpiece of the show." The monologue, said Keillor, "made the transition from being a very short series of small town jokes to being something of a story or an essay." Monologues typically ranged from about ten to thirty minutes, averaging around twenty. Keillor wrote out a first draft of about four or five double-spaced pages. He edited and reviewed it and then went on stage to "do something that is more or less based on the draft." He never read from a script, knowing that the spontaneity of his narrative was one of its essential features, and that a rehearsed speech

has different overtones and nuances than the special, intimate quality he sought: "It's hard, too, to write for voice," he says.

Some of the monologues are on the record albums with music from the show, and many more can be heard on tapes, including four hour-long cassettes on *News from Lake Wobegon* (1982), and two more hours on *Gospel Birds and Other Stories of Lake Wobegon* (1985). Regular listeners will remember many of the tales that are in *Lake Wobegon Days* from their earlier versions narrated on the air.

In the mid 1970s Keillor, who was then bearded, was known to appear in bell-bottoms, a turtleneck sweater, granny glasses, and a floppy leather hat. The beard came off in 1981, and for many years his onstage trademark was a white linen suit (prompting even more comparisons to Twain), worn with suspenders, red socks, and a wild tie. He no longer looks like a member of the counterculture or a gentle lumberjack, but has been described more recently as "a chiseled, professorial man." How a notoriously unhandsome and famously shy person can go onstage without a script to tell stories to millions of radio listeners plus a studio audience is a rich paradox: "I can

Publicity photo of Keillor used to advertise the television broadcasts of the final seventeen episodes of A Prairie Home Companion *(photograph by Mike Habermann, copyright © 1987 by The Walt Disney Company)*

talk into the microphone like this very handsome dude," he told a studio audience during a warm-up once, "and, as you can see, that might not be the case. But the audience at home doesn't know that. . . ." There is, however, his perfect storyteller's voice: "Above all else, Keillor has a marvellous voice, lazy but powerful, deep and wide, full of natural drama," wrote Robbie Brechin, an Australian reviewer.

In its first ten years, *A Prairie Home Companion* produced 477 live broadcasts, of which 20 originated from remote locations, and 25 taped broadcasts plus 86 nonbroadcast road shows. It first moved to the World Theater in St. Paul, an old legitimate theater building which was completely renovated for $3.5 million and rededicated in 1986 after a two-year "Save the World" funding campaign, on 4 March 1978. Minnesota Public Radio arranged for its own nationwide broadcasting of the show in 1980, after being rejected for syndication through National Public Radio. NPR had decided that the "humor was too regional," a decision they had reason to regret, since Minnesota Public Radio subsequently made effective use of the popularity of the show

to organize, with other major public radio stations, a rival noncommercial network, the American Public Radio Associates. By 1985 APR was serving 287 public radio stations, and *A Prairie Home Companion* was estimated to have two million listeners. The show has won two Corporation for Public Broadcasting Awards, as well as the 1980 George Foster Peabody Award. On 26 April 1986, the official reopening of the World Theater, *A Prairie Home Companion* was televised nationally by the Public Broadcasting System.

By 1977 Minnesota Public Radio was aware that Garrison Keillor was their most popular attraction, and they asked him for a book of his writings to dangle before the noses, "as a sort of nightcrawler," of potential contributors during Pledge Week. In his prefatory remarks to *G. K. the DJ* (1977), Keillor says that most of the miscellaneous pieces within the book "were written *against* radio, with a mind towards escaping from the studio and becoming an artist. I considered that my art was good workmanlike art, the carpentry of prose sentences, and no relation to what passed for art on radio. . . ." The burden of his brief against radio was that it was ephemeral: "We think we are wasting our lives feeding words and music into a goat. Radio eats everything, it eats constantly, and when you are done with your shift at the zoo, what do you have to show for it? *Nothing, dear God.*"

The nineteen previously published works that comprise *G. K. the DJ* include doggerel poems and comic or satirical pieces, mostly on matters of local concern to Twin Cities residents, such as his "Ode to the Street System of Southwest Minneapolis." Among the five works which originally appeared in the *New Yorker* are the only three pieces from this book subsequently reprinted in *Happy to Be Here* (1982): "My North Dakota Railway Days," "Drowning, 1954," and "Local Family Keeps Son Happy."

"My North Dakota Railway Days" tells about the narrator's railroad experience in the first quarter of this century. A humorous tale on the tall side, it is undoubtedly grounded on elements of Keillor's father's work as "a Railway Mail Service clerk on the St. Paul-Jamestown run."

"Drowning, 1954" is one of Keillor's few openly autobiographical *New Yorker* stories, a work he chose to read aloud on later promotional tours for *Happy to Be Here.* It tells how the twelve-year-old Keillor, sent to swimming lessons in Minneapolis after his cousin had drowned, used to sneak away from the dreaded YMCA

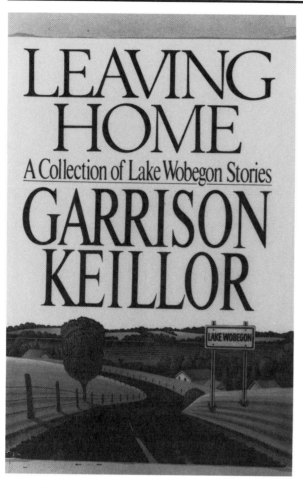

Dust jacket for Keillor's 1987 collection of A Prairie Home
Companion *monologues*

pool and head off "for the WCCO radio studio
to watch 'Good Neighbor Time' "–one of the old-
time radio shows on which he would later model
A Prairie Home Companion. Once he found himself in the same elevator with announcer-
commentator Cedric Adams, who used to
promote the Purity Baking Company: "I wished
that I were like him and the others, but . . . I
began to see clearly that I was more closely related to the bums and winos. . . ." Years later
Keillor would himself do some effective announcing before a live studio audience on behalf of
those "Powdermilk Biscuits, in the big blue box
with the picture of a biscuit on the cover, made
from whole wheat raised in the big bottomlands
by Norwegian bachelor farmers. Whole wheat
gives a shy person the strength to get up and do
what needs to be done."

Leading off this collection is the first piece
he sold to the *New Yorker,* "Local Family Keeps
Son Happy," published first in 1970. "They
bought it off their slush pile," Keillor says, "and
paid me some fantastic sum." It is a short newspaper parody about a suburban couple who "buy a
woman for their 16-year-old son" and are
pleased with the results: "He is more poised and
relaxed." It ends with one of the bought
woman's recipes–Fancy Eggs. The use of the mundane newspaper format and style in relating such
exotica has more in common with the work of
Donald Barthelme than it does with Will Rogers.
And the urban/suburban milieu of this and much
of his other published fiction here and in *Happy
to Be Here* has something in common with Woody
Allen–for its inventive wit and zaniness–and
John Cheever–for its exploration of the white
American middle class in cities and suburbs.

The Selected Verse of Margaret Haskins Durber
(1979) was another Minnesota Public Radio pre-
mium offered to contributors. The title page
bears the crest of Lake Wobegon, with the town
motto, *Sumus quid sumus* (which appears as a chapter title in *Lake Wobegon Days,* grammar corrected,
as *Sumus quod sumus*): We are what we are.
Durber, explains Keillor, is the Poet Laureate of
the town, and her book includes fourteen poems,
including odes in praise of the Minnesota Science
Museum (close to the World Theater), the state
fair, and the Fourth of July. All the poems were
read or sung on the air, and two of them were
put on albums: "The Ballad of the Finn Who
Didn't Like Saunas" on the *Anniversary Album*
(1980) and "The Song of the Exiles (The Lake
Wobegon Anthem)" on *The Family Radio* (1982).

Happy to Be Here, published in hard cover
by Atheneum in 1982 and in paper by Penguin
in 1983, sold 210,000 copies before it was reprinted in August 1986. The hardback collected
twenty-six of Keillor's *New Yorker* pieces and three
from the *Atlantic,* and the paperback edition
added four additional pieces from these two magazines and one from *Twin Cities.* The jacket photo
of a bearded Keillor on the hard cover was replaced with a clean-shaven version on the paperback, who is identified as the "World's Tallest
Radio Comedian" (Keillor is 6 feet 4 inches tall).
Many of these pieces, like some of those in *G. K.
the DJ,* show the witty and urbane Keillor rather
than the wistful, wandering storyteller in exile
from Lake Wobegon, where "smart doesn't count
for very much." Here he shows what is seldom
seen or heard on his radio show–an animus
against high-rolling Republicans, monied cul-
ture-vultures, and professional jargon artists in

government, academia, or down in the shopping centers.

John Hyde's review in the *Des Moines Register* noted that the book has no Lake Wobegon material at all, but in it "Keillor skillfully parodies the gushiness of Life magazine and the overblown music criticism of Rolling Stone. He needles Congressional pomposity, the granola ethic, the 'alternative wedding,' country poets, and those folks determined to build the world's tallest building, and shy people, including himself. . . ." Keillor's stylistic virtuosity and range are evident in his ability to shift from the language of "Literature" ("Ten Stories for Mr. Richard Brautigan, and Other Stories") to executive-suite gobbledygook ("Re the Tower Project"), to the jargon of hype and public relations ("Jack Schmidt, Arts Administrator"), and back to the voice of midwestern old-time radio ("WLT [The Edgar Era]").

Keillor has frequently been criticized for wallowing in nostalgia and sentimentality for the title, format, live messages, and Heartland wholesomeness of *A Prairie Home Companion*. Several stories in *Happy to Be Here*, however, show he was forearmed with ironic awareness as he developed this material. "Friendly Neighbor," for example, is written from the point of view of a fan of Walter "Dad" Benson, who "was a nationally known personality from the days when 'Friendly Neighbor' was carried by the Mutual Network, but the Midwest was always his home." Keillor, who has gained the warm attention of many in the religious press for his "religious sensibility," gently ironizes as a minister says to Dad, "You were a pastor of the flock as much as I . . . for your sermons were in the form of stories . . . and brought home spiritual truths far better than preaching ever could."

Before Powdermilk Biscuits were offered over Minnesota Public Radio, Slim, in "The Slim Graves Show," was said to open by saying, "Good morning, friends and neighbors, it's time for SLIM GRAVES and the Southland Sheikhs for SUNRISE WAFFLES–gosh, they're good!" Slim's wife, Billie Ann, falls for the lead guitarist, Courteous Carl, and listeners help the triangle resolve by purchasing boxes of the waffles with either Slim's or Carl's picture.

Although typically more prone to parody than to satire, at times in *Happy to Be Here* Keillor comes close to sounding Swiftian. He satirizes political figures in seven short pieces, as in the mock-newspaper story, "U.S. Still on Top, Says Rest of World," which opens with an epigraph from Richard Nixon: "America today is Number One in the world. . . ." Keillor reveals the fatuity of such an assertion by elaborating upon it and concludes by noting that the United States was also voted first by the "Association of World Leaders" for Best Credo and Most Telephones, but that while this country had dominated the scene for most of the twentieth century, it still trails the "Roman and British Empires and Mongol Horde in total wins."

Yet satire and dark humor are not characteristic of Keillor even in his urbane and sophisticated phases. "The older you get," says Keillor, "the more you see what you would like to write powerful satire against, and the less impulse you have to do it, because you know what an empty gesture it would be." Comparing him to Ring Lardner and Mark Twain, L. S. Klepp noted that these humorists "sometimes descended into misanthropy; when Keillor lapses, it's into sentimentality. But at his best he, like them, gives us a gallery of shrewdly observed American characters, seen in a comic light but with compelling sympathy and truth." Even when he deals with death, as in "Drowning, 1954," his comedy avoids bitterness: "Any writing that does not have the anticipation of death in it is kind of foolish," Keillor has said, "and I don't think that comedy is foolishness. It's very moral."

When Keillor left his morning radio show in April 1982, much to the dismay of loyal Minnesota Public Radio listeners, the reason given was that he needed more time to work on a novel about Lake Wobegon, which he expected to finish in about a year. It took him longer than he estimated to complete, but when it finally appeared in the fall of 1985, *Lake Wobegon Days* advanced steadily up the *New York Times* best-sellers list to number one during Christmas week, selling a million copies by April. It was a Book-of-the-Month Club selection, the best-selling hardcover book of 1985, and was still on the *New York Times* list in July 1986 when the Penguin paperback edition was published, appearing as number one on the paperback best-sellers list by 3 August.

The delay in the book's first appearance is understandable, even though Keillor had hundreds of radio monologues to draw upon, dozens of characters, a well-defined setting, and plenty of thematic substance. But it is the familiar curse of the American humorist to be a writer of short pieces, and few have succeeded in fusing their short masterpieces into a shapely novel.

7/19/86
3 of 9

Clint Bunsen

Including ~~a guy~~ who listened to Wally's invite and said, "You know what you ought to do? There's a bunch of 24 Lutheran ministers coming through here on a tour on Friday, you ought to give them a boat ride so they get a nice look at town."

It's a long story how 24 Lutheran ministers were on a tour of rural Minnesota and I can't tell you the whole story otherwise I'll be in the fix I was in in Juneau where I talked right up until they turned out the lights and locked the door --- the longest monologue in the history of public radio --- and the reason is that you folks have become so skeptical, you make me spend too much time on the details and not enough on the moral of the story----

"Meeting The Pastoral Needs of Rural America in Crisis

The 24 Lutheran ministers were on a five-day seminar organized by an old seminary pal of Pastor Ingqvist's, the Rev. J. Peter ~~Olesen,~~ *Larson* who called up Pastor Ingqvist in April and said, "You know what the problem with us Lutherans is--- we're so doggone theological we can't see past the principles to the people --- *and the people are hurting,* I'm organizing a tour of a hundred ministers to go around look at rural problems and I want to visit Lake Wobegon in ~~lake~~ mid-July" and Pastor Ingqvist said fine and forgot about it until last Sunday, his wife Judy said, "What's this on the calendar for Friday? Tour ~~and wienie roast~~ */ Larson at house*."

"Oh that," he said. "Well," he said, "I was meaning to discuss that with you," he said. "It's a bunch of Lutheran ministers *coming through town* and I thought we ~~could~~ have them over for a little picnic supper in the backyard."

"How many?" she said. "I don't know," he said, "but certainly no more than a hundred."

"Well," she said, "I *think your best bet would be wieners* ~~hope you get enough buns for all of them~~ *exactly* You probably just want to boil them. Maybe you could get someone to make you some potato salad."

Rural problems was what Pete wanted to see, but how do you take 24 ministers around to ~~people's homes~~ *someone's house* and point to ~~this~~ him and say: "There's one. He's in trouble. I don't give him long. No sir. He's headed down the chute."

~~It seemed a little strange to Pastor Ingqvist.~~

Page from a 1986 radio script for a Prairie Home Companion *monologue that was revised and published as "Pontoon Boat" in* Leaving Home *(courtesy of the author)*

Lake Wobegon Days has a double pattern of development: chronological and seasonal. The first is linear or historical and biographical, and in this movement we read of the founding of the early explorers who discovered the site of what was to become first New Albion and later Lake Wobegon. We read of the forbears, the Unitarian missionaries out from Boston to convert the Ojibway Indians through interpretive dance and of Gunder Muus, the first of the Norwegian bachelor farmers. We hear about, in rough chronological order, the major historical events that have affected the town, such as the founding of New Albion College and the almost-visit of King Haakon VII. And of course there is the personal story of Gary Keillor, the little boy growing up among the Sanctified Brethren, envious of those glorious Catholics and splendid Lutherans; and the restless adolescent, risking death and damnation in the family car after whisky sours with a girl.

The second pattern is cyclical rather than chronological. The turn of the seasons, considered as a structural principle, is a more fitting organizational scheme for a tale about a place or a people–for things that go on and on, without the more obvious linear trajectory of an individual life. Keillor's Saturday radio monologues typically responded to the changes of weather and season, and this practice offered a sense of immediacy to the live audience while it evoked a sense of the timelessness of Lake Wobegon. This cyclical scheme worked well to divide the 1983 tape set of *News from Lake Wobegon* into four hour-long cassettes, one for each of the seasons. And in the book, similarly, there are chapter titles for each of the seasons in consecutive order, though not all four are contiguous.

Insofar as *Lake Wobegon Days* is a novel, it is a kind of bildungsroman, a portrait of the humorist as a young person. But while there is a great deal about the narrator's childhood and coming of age, there is no sustained, accumulating sense of his development over time. The Keillor who has epiphanies in Lake Wobegon is a major character, but the book is not finally about him and his destiny so much as it is about the people who over the years have lived in this place.

The seams still show where Keillor welded these two patterns of development together to make one book. The *Los Angeles Times* reviewer felt that Keillor's "effort to transform the 20-minute monologues of his radio program into a more sustained written form doesn't work entirely. . . . It is a pastiche, and a very talented

one; but there are times when the whimsy frays." More generously, the London *Observer* said, "Keillor writes so beautifully that the book never once gives the impression of Old Scripts revisited."

The location of Lake Wobegon in time and space is given many more particulars in the book than listeners could ever manage to piece together from the radio monologues. It is possible to locate where Lake Wobegon would be: the first English settlers left Anoka and traveled about twenty miles a day; in six days they had passed through St. Cloud (about 100 miles) and on the seventh they had arrived at the site of New Albion. The name was changed when Norwegian immigrants, not sensitive to the connotations of "dismal, unhappy, dilapidated, bedraggled" that so upset the English settlers, gained ascendancy on the town council and chose Lake Wobegon because they liked the lake and the sound of these words, which in Ojibway mean "the place where [we] waited all day in the rain."

The abundance of such detail is one of the main points of difference between the book and the radio tales. "I thought I could put in the historical part," Keillor says of the book, "that you could never do on radio. The parodies of 19th-century correspondence, the memorial prose. . . . You couldn't do this in the frame of a radio narrative," for "it wouldn't sound right." The tales on radio are "starved for detail, in literary terms," Keillor says. "You just can't supply that on radio. The listener supplies it." "Novelists," on the other hand, "create characters who stride across our landscape. But [with radio] it is more likely that we enter into theirs."

In "Home," one of the early *Bildung* chapters, Keillor tells how he has become one of the wanderers in this nation of transients, inhabiting eleven apartments and three houses in the twenty-five years since he put his books and his old dog Buster in the 1956 Ford and drove off to Minneapolis. Set on "redesigning" himself, he hid when he saw an old friend from the hometown, because he "didn't care to be the person he knew" anymore. His return is something in the vein of the Prodigal Son, who is not welcomed by everyone, who knows that he has not been loyal or fully worthy of those who loved him in that place, but who comes knowing that he can still go back. Keillor is no Sinclair Lewis, revolting against a graceless and provincial Zenith, full of narrowminded bores–though Lewis's real Sauk

Center is in the next county, just west of where Lake Wobegon would be if it existed.

The wonderful thing about Keillor's tone in detailing life as it is lived in Lake Wobegon is not derived from his pathos, knowing he can never go home again. He refuses to emphasize his status as exile in the novel. The wonder flows from his understanding that the complicated person he has become in "The Cities" is truly no step up from the guy down in the Sidetrack Tap he might have been had he never left home in the first place. Sitting in a hotel room on Rodeo Drive in 1983 he told Matt Damsker of the *San Diego Union*, "I think it takes a real act of redemption to jump back into the old life, and I look for that redemption. I don't want to just tell funny stories about paradise."

He celebrates, he does not satirize, the Sanctified Brethren and their schismatic history. The young Keillor who almost runs into his Uncle Louie's Fairlane as its reflective sign flashes "The Wages of Sin is Death" at him, is not a youth of finer mettle, destined to fly up and away from humble origins. Keillor's sense of comedy issues from his understanding that while it makes sense to laugh at the foolishness of humankind, this laughter is not satirical, in the interests of changing them. Nor is this laughter hollow, the kind familiar in much contemporary comedy, which begins in the recognition that since life is absurd, we may as well amuse ourselves where we can. Keillor laughs because he knows that no matter how ridiculous our lives can be, no matter how small and mean we are, "life is a comedy" because "God is the author, and God writes an awful lot of comedy"–an idea he offered in the autobiographical *New Yorker* story "After A Fall" (reprinted in the Penguin edition of *Happy to Be Here*) and in a radio monologue which aired 13 February 1982.

Such a comic vision derives from Keillor's theological understanding of the meaning of life, even though there must be considerable truth in L. S. Klepp's observation that, "As a humorist Keillor owes a great deal to the narrow, repressive religious training that he had to throw off to become a humorist." There is rebellion and righteous indignation against a repressive upbringing in the "longest footnote American fiction," the "95 Theses 95." "You have taught me to worship a god who is like you, who shares your thinking exactly, who is going to slap me one if I don't straighten out fast. I am very uneasy every Sunday, which is cloudy and deathly still and filled with silent accusing whispers." This protracted, intemperate complaint, voiced in the fourth thesis, must contain much that Keillor himself has felt and still feels–but which he has apparently mastered. While the exile's complaint does speak for a part of Keillor, so do Brother Bob, Father Emil, and Pastor Ingqvist.

And so it is no surprise that the last, and perhaps the most entertaining chapter in *Lake Wobegon Days* is "Revival," and that the book ends with a tale of a heavy smoker (Keillor himself smoked Camels until the summer of 1985) who nearly gets himself killed after trying to get another carton during a blizzard. As more than one reviewer has noted, his recognition in a snowbound car in the ditch, still smokeless but at least alive, is possibly fitting as the moral for the entire book: "Some luck lies in not getting what you thought you wanted but getting what you have, which once you have it you may be smart enough to see is what you would have wanted had you known." Though he must have "thrown off" a lot, he does not scoff at fundamentalists, and he has no doubt retained what he might consider many of their beliefs, such as the belief that humans are sinful, but that human life is a comedy because God has the power to make all things come to good.

Keillor is perhaps most beloved for his evocations of home, of the ideal American place to come from. Yet one of the attributes of home in Keillor's work is evanescence. Prior to June 1987 Keillor never left his home state for a prolonged period, but he had a history of frequent moves within it. Dozens of his stories concern flight from Lake Wobegon, and the title of his radio show gains ironic force with the realization that it was adapted from the Prairie Home Lutheran cemetery in Moorhead, Minnesota: we are permanently at home only when we are gone. All this may have much to do with his choice of *Leaving Home* as the title for his second book of Lake Wobegon stories, published by Viking in fall 1987 after a summer that saw Keillor end his show, sell his home in St. Paul, and say that he doubted he would ever reside there again.

The period leading up to this latest book had been crowded with momentous events and decisions in his career and personal life, including the enormous success of *Lake Wobegon Days*, his breakup with Margaret Moos, his marriage to Ulla Skaerved, planning sessions with producer Sidney Pollock for a film about Lake Wobegon, the televising of *A Prairie Home Companion,* and his decision to end the show.

The gala dedication of the refurbished World Theater in April 1986 had spoken powerfully of Keillor's ability to attract large amounts of capital and media attention, especially as the dedicatory show was televised and aired nationally. Keillor did a good job at not changing things to suit the cameras, yet longtime fans were no doubt unsettled and left wondering how this man, who had talked long and earnestly about his own and his show's unsuitability for television, could have allowed such an exception to what had seemed firm and high principle.

A crisis was brewing, and it had already come to a head by 30 January 1987, the day Bill Kling, President of Minnesota Public Radio and the man who first gave the go ahead to *A Prairie Home Companion* back in 1974, wrote a letter to the Board of Directors. He told them an agreement had been made with the Walt Disney Company to produce a series of seventeen live television programs of *A Prairie Home Companion* between 14 February and 14 June 1987. He indicated that this would increase the audience for the show and provide a "visual archive," but there were somber overtones to part of his rationale. "Initially," Kling wrote, "I thought it was a medium that would provide some new creative territory to Garrison. . . . If successful, that could reinvigorate his interests in the show." Kling already knew what millions were taken aback to hear on 14 February when, early in the show just after a Powdermilk Biscuit spot, Keillor stepped to the microphone and said: "I'd like to take a minute tonight to announce to all our friends that *A Prairie Home Companion* will be leaving the airwaves on Saturday, June 13, at the end of this season. The show has had a good long run of 13 years in Minnesota, and we're very grateful to all of you who made it seem worthwhile.

"The decision to close is mine–the sort of simple, painful decision that our parents taught us to make cheerfully. It simply is time to go. I want to resume the life of a shy person and enjoy with my affectionate family a more peaceful life, a life in which there are Saturdays. We want to live for a while in my wife's country of Denmark. I want to be a writer again. And it is time to stop."

Though there had been persistent rumblings that the show might be coming to a close since 1984, the announcement still shocked many, though with hindsight it was easy for feature writers to find reasons for his decision in the many stories which publicized it. That he might indeed be weary was readily understandable, and now that he had considerable financial independence, he could certainly do what he most wanted to do. A desire to devote himself more wholeheartedly to writing was nothing new– he had quit early radio shows several times to do the same thing early in his career. And then there was his disenchantment with celebrityhood and his festering irritation with the hometown newspapers. He told Peg Meier of the *Minneapolis Star and Tribune* that he had been "treated in Saint Paul the way Elizabeth Taylor is treated in Hollywood" and that the newspapers were forcing him away: "What makes him angriest," she reported in March 1987, "is that the papers printed the address where he bought a new home a winter ago. . . . They view him as a symbol of excess and unearned wealth, as a distant figure without morals."

Leaving Home collects thirty-six stories originally written for performance on *A Prairie Home Companion* and "A Letter from Copenhagen" dated 13 July 1987. In the letter Keillor discusses his reasons for giving up the show and for leaving Minnesota: "I lost touch with the people who raised corn and with their church and wasn't invited to Sunday dinner and slowly lost my bearings, and felt lost at home." But the changes were not only of his own making. Shopping malls had sprung up "like fungus" where there had been only roadside vegetable stands; in one of them, while autographing copies of one of his books, he "felt its peculiar dementia, low and steadily throbbing from florescent lights, air conditioners, and electronic systems including synthesized violins playing homogenous hymns to the anesthetized people, and knew that somewhere we had gone wrong." The hometown paper's increasing attention made him feel "watched," and it became apparent to him "that life might be better somewhere else."

The collected stories are, for the most part, drawn from those told over the last two years of the show, and the last, titled "Goodbye to the Lake," is adapted from his final monologue. The volume includes several stories about characters who, for one reason or another, left home. There is Darlene, the thirty-eight-year-old waitress from the Chatterbox who finally leaves when her mother stops saying to her, "Why don't you ever do something for yourself?" and one day utters the same sentence in the past tense. There are recollections of David Tollefson, father of Val and a carpenter, who, though married and father of five, left with the wife of a neighbor in 1946 and never came back. There is Dale Uecker, who decided not to go to Saint Cloud State together with his high school sweetheart, but to join the navy. Of his departure, Keillor says, "It's a wonderful thing to push on above toward the horizon and have it be your own horizon and not someone else's. It's a good feeling, lonely and magnificent and frightening and peaceful. . . . "

If Keillor's exit from *A Prairie Home Companion* was not entirely unexpected, his quick return to the United States after one summer as an expatriate certainly was. The fall of 1987 found him speaking to the National Press Club in Washington, D.C., with a new book just out and the news buzzing about that he had a residence in New York City–where many a midwestern writer had come to roost before.

Garrison Keillor is a writer of essays and fiction, a radio performer and singer, who by fall of 1985 was widely heralded as a humorist of the caliber of Twain or Thurber. As a teller of tales, he draws upon some of the longest suits in the tradition of American humor: he is a brilliant vernacular yarn-spinner and an acute local color observer and nostalgic realist of the Upper Midwest. His humor is sustained by his comic faith, which like Powdermilk Biscuits, helps readers

and listeners "get up and do what needs to done."

Interview:

Roy Blount, Jr., "A Conversation With Garrison Keillor," *Minnesota Monthly* (June 1987): 13-24.

References:

John Bordsen, "All the News from Lake Wobegon," *Saturday Review* (May/June 1983): 12, 18-19;

Gracia Grindal, "We Are What He Says We Are," *Lutheran Partners* (May/June 1986): 19-23;

L. S. Klepp, "Cookin' with Small Potatoes," *Village Voice Literary Supplement*, 38 (September 1985): 12-13;

Howard Mohr, "Keillor has had enough of celebrity," *Minnesota Star and Tribune*, 22 March 1987, pp. A1, A6;

Peter A. Scholl, "Garrison Keillor and the News From Lake Wobegon," *Studies in American Humor* (forthcoming);

John Skow, "Lonesome Whistle Blowing," *Time*, 126 (4 November 1985): 68-73;

Amanda Smith, "The Sage of Lake Wobegon," *Boston Phoenix*, 23 March 1982;

James Traub, "The Short and Tall Tales of Garrison Keillor," *Esquire* (May 1982): 108-117;

Mark E. Vander Schaaf, "A Spark from Heaven: Garrison Keillor's *A Prairie Home Companion*," *Another Season*, 2 (Winter 1983): 6-18.

Janet Lewis
(17 August 1899-   )

Donald E. Stanford
Louisiana State University

BOOKS: *The Indians in the Woods* (Bonn, Germany: Monroe Wheeler, 1922); republished, with an introduction by Lewis (Palo Alto, Cal.: Matrix Press, 1980);

The Friendly Adventures of Ollie Ostrich, illustrated by Fay Turpin (Garden City: Doubleday, Page, 1923);

The Wheel in Midsummer (Lynn, Mass.: Lone Gull Press, 1927);

The Invasion: A Narrative of Events concerning the Johnston Family of St. Mary's (New York: Harcourt, Brace, 1932);

The Wife of Martin Guerre (San Francisco: Colt Press, 1941);

Against a Darkening Sky (Garden City: Doubleday, Doran, 1943);

The Earth-Bound, 1924-1944 (Aurora, N.Y.: Wells College Press, 1946);

Good-bye, Son, and Other Stories (Garden City: Doubleday, 1946; revised edition, Athens: Swallow Press/Ohio University Press, 1986);

The Trial of Sören Qvist (Garden City: Doubleday, 1947; London: Gollancz, 1967);

The Hangar at Sunnyvale: 1937 (San Francisco: Book Club of California, 1947);

Poems 1924-1944 (Denver: Alan Swallow, 1950);

The Wife of Martin Guerre: An Opera, libretto by Lewis, music by William Bergsma (Denver: Alan Swallow, 1958);

The Ghost of Monsieur Scarron (Garden City: Doubleday, 1959; London: Gollancz, 1959);

Keiko's Bubble, illustrated by Kazue Mizumura (Garden City: Doubleday, 1961);

The Last of the Mohicans: An Opera, libretto by Lewis, music by Alva Henderson (Wilmington, Del.: Wilmington Opera Society, 1978);

The Birthday of the Infanta: An Opera in One Act, libretto by Lewis and Malcolm Seagrave, music by Seagrave (Los Angeles: Symposium Press, 1979);

The Ancient Ones: Poems, drawings by Daniel M. Mendelowitz (Portola Valley, Cal.: No Dead Lines, 1979);

Janet Lewis, in a portrait by her brother Herbert (Bookman, September 1932)

Poems Old and New, 1918-1978 (Chicago: Swallow Press/Athens: Ohio University Press, 1981);

Mulberry Street: An Opera, libretto by Lewis, music by Alva Henderson (Onset, Mass.: Dermont, 1981);

The Swans: An Opera in Three Acts, libretto by Lewis, music by Alva Henderson (Santa Barbara, Cal.: John Daniel, 1986);

The Legend. The Story of Neengay, an Ojibway War Chief's Daughter, and the Irishman John John-

339

ston: An Opera Oratorio, libretto by Lewis, music by Bain Murray (Santa Barbara, Cal.: John Daniel, 1987).

RECORDINGS: *Poets Reading Their Own Poems,* Library of Congress, Division of Music, Recording Laboratory (Phonodisc PLI2), 1954;
Janet Lewis Reading at Stanford, The Stanford Program for Recordings in Sound (SPRS5), 1975.

PERIODICAL PUBLICATIONS:
POETRY
"Cold Hills," comprises "Austerity," "The End of the Age," "Geology," and "Fossil," *Poetry,* 16 (June 1920): 140-141.
FICTION
"At the Swamp," *Bookman,* 70 (October 1929): 164-167;
"Still Afternoon," *Pagany,* 1 (Spring 1930): 80-82;
"La Pointe Chegoimegon," *Hound and Horn,* 5 (October-December 1931): 80-90;
"A Small Voice Tells Me So," *McCall's,* 71 (April 1944).
NONFICTION
"Isak Dinesen: An Appreciation," *Southern Review,* 2 (April 1966): 297-314;
"Sources of *The Wife of Martin Guerre,*" *Tri-Quarterly,* 55 (Fall 1982): 104-110;
"Elizabeth Madox Roberts: A Memoir," *Southern Review,* 20 (October 1984): 803-816;
"Letters from the Little County: The Summer of 1919 and 1920," *Southern Review,* 20 (October 1984): 829-835.

Janet Lewis, best known today for her *The Wife of Martin Guerre* (1941), which Albert Guerard, in *Contemporary Novelists* (fourth edition, 1986), has called "one of the greatest short novels in American Literature," is the author of five novels, a collection of short stories, a number of volumes of poetry, and six librettos. Among her honors are the Friends of America Literature Award, 1932, for *The Invasion: A Narrative of Events concerning the Johnston Family of St. Mary's* (1932); the Shelley Memorial Award for Poetry, 1948; the Commonwealth Club of California Gold Medal, 1948, for *The Trial of Sören Qvist* (1947); a Guggenheim fellowship, 1950; and the Robert Kirsch Award, 1985.

She was born near Chicago, the second child and only daughter of Edwin Herbert Lewis and Elizabeth Taylor Lewis. Her father, a teacher of English at the University of Chicago and profes-

sor of English at the Lewis Institute, Chicago, was a poet, novelist, and scholar. He encouraged his daughter's early interest in the writing of poetry and fiction, and she credits him with being the first to teach her the rudiments of good prose and poetic style. When Lewis was six years old, she and her family moved to the Chicago suburb of Oak Park where she later became slightly acquainted with Ernest Hemingway. They attended the same high school.

The family spent their summers on the American island of Neebish and the nearby Canadian island of Saint Joseph on the St. Mary's River south of the Sault in northern Michigan. It was here that from childhood on Lewis became acquainted with the Indians, listening to their stories and the stories of her father around the campfire. Especially interesting were the tales told to her by descendants of the Johnston family about their grandmother Neengay, a full-blooded Ojibway Indian, and her husband, John Johnston, an Irish fur trader. From them she acquired material for her first and favorite novel, *The Invasion.* She also drew on her experiences in northern Michigan and in Canada for her earliest poems and for several of her short stories. She has retained a special interest in the Indians throughout her career, and some of her most recent poems are about the Indians of the Southwest.

Lewis had planned to choose Vassar for her college education, but when, in her senior year in high school, she went over to the University of Chicago to hear her father deliver the commencement address, she was so impressed with the campus that she decided to attend that university. After two years at the Lewis Institute, she entered the University of Chicago in 1918 and received her Ph.B. as a major in French in 1920. At Chicago she became a member of the poetry club as a result of submitting her poem "The Freighters," derived from her experiences at the Sault. The official invitation to join was signed by the secretary, Yvor Winters, her future husband, whom she did not meet, however, until 1921, for he had been forced to leave the university because of illness. Among her friends at the club were Maurice Lesemann, Elizabeth Madox Roberts, and Glenway Wescott. Her first publication, "Cold Hills," a sequence of four poems, appeared in *Poetry* magazine in June 1920, the year of her graduation from the university.

In the summer of 1920 Lewis was in Paris. The decade of the famous expatriates was just beginning, but Lewis did not consider herself to be one of their number. She was more interested in exploring the streets of Paris with a historical point of view, noting where the great writers and personalities of the past had lived. She was employed for some months in the passport bureau of the American consulate. She then returned to Chicago to work on the staff of *Redbook* magazine and to teach at the Lewis Institute. Early in 1922 she discovered she had tuberculosis. She entered the Sunmount Sanatorium near Santa Fe, New Mexico, and began a desperate battle against tuberculosis which lasted for several years. She was not pronounced fully cured until 1929. Her determination and her equable disposition helped pull her through. As she told Mitzi Hamovitch in a 1982 interview, there comes a moment when you have "to be cheerful or die. You take your choice." During her stay at the sanatorium she became engaged to Yvor Winters. It was the same sanatorium at which he had been cured. They were married in the summer of 1926 in Santa Fe, and they had two children, Joanna and Daniel.

At the time of his marriage Winters had been teaching French and Spanish for a year at the University of Idaho in Moscow. He returned for another year of teaching at Moscow without his wife for she was not yet well enough to travel. In the summer of 1927 Lewis and her husband went to California, and Winters entered Stanford University as a graduate student in the fall of 1927. He remained as a teacher at Stanford until his retirement in 1966. He died in 1968. Lewis and Winters settled first in Palo Alto and then permanently in Los Altos, a few miles from the Stanford campus.

Lewis's first wish was to be a poet, and, as did her husband, she considers poetry to be superior to prose. In writing of Lewis's first book, entitled *The Indians in the Woods* (1922), as well as of *The Invasion* and of Lewis's more recent Indian poetry, Helen P. Trimpi said, "The Indian habit of mind with its intimate relationship to the natural world, its dependence upon the changing seasons, and with the ordered understanding of the basic experiences of human life, has an affinity with her intelligence." Several qualities are immediately apparent in these verses of her youth: the love of Indian life, past and present; the ability to perceive and record precise details and particulars; and the ability to employ effectively the rhythms and imagery of the then recent free verse movement, and in one instance, "A Song of the Following Gulls," the forms of traditional

verse. This poem is typical of her writing in free verse:

The Indians in the Woods

Ah, the woods, the woods,
Where small things
Are distinct and visible,

The berry plant,
The berry leaf, remembered
Line for line.

There are three figures
Walking in the woods
Whose feet press down
Needle and leaf and vine.

According to Lewis the three Indians walking in the woods are mythical figures–Manibush (the culture hero), his wife, and the Grandmother (Nokomis, the Earth). She had planned to do a series of Manibush poems but never filled out the series.

Lewis's second book of verse, *The Wheel in Midsummer* (1927), contains poems written in the sanatorium near Santa Fe; others, like "The Freighters," were composed before she went to New Mexico. Indian material and the northern Michigan landscape are still present, but there is a movement toward her own subject matter, as distinct from that of the Indian, and a movement also away from free verse toward conventional meters. One of the finest written in conventional rhymed verse is the well-known "Earth-Bound" where, as so often in her poetry and prose, living nature is seen as beneficent and at one with human love:

And healing is a tree whose leaves
Fall round us like the falling sleaves
Of love, that bending down at night,
Covers with them a face alight.

Perhaps the most moving poem in the volume is "During Illness," quoted here in its entirety:

Ah, Landor, if thy page lay clear
For me these uneventful days,
Great courage I might study there,
Even Alcestis' quiet gaze.

As has been mentioned, Janet Lewis's first novel grew out of hearing, as a child, stories around the campfire during summer vacations on Neebish and St. Joseph's islands, stories told by Howard and Molly Johnstone (as they spelled the name) about their Ojibway grandmother Neengay and her Irish husband John Johnston, who spent most of their married life at the Sault. The novel grew out of a sketch Lewis wrote about Molly Johnstone. To do the job properly she began to research Johnstone's early life and that of her ancestors. By the time she finished the task she had enough material for *The Invasion*. The theme of the novel is forcefully stated by an Irish lady of quality, Mrs. Anna Jameson, in her letter written in 1837 to one of the Johnston family, Jane Schoolcraft: "the propinquity of the white man is destruction to the red man; and the farther the Indians are removed from us, the better for them. In their own woods they are a noble race; brought near to us, a degraded and stupid race. We are destroying them off the face of the earth. May God forgive us our tyranny, our avarice, our ignorance, for it is very terrible to think of."

The invasion theme underlies the story, but it does not dominate it, for this is not merely a novel of social protest. It is a dramatic and exciting chronicle of a specific family that actually existed and played a part in the history of what was once called the Northwest, living in a specific time, from 1790 when John Johnston first came to the New World until 1928 when his last grandchild Anna Maria ("Molly") Johnstone died, and in a specific place, the St. Mary's River area and the southern shore of Lake Superior.

The story of the Johnston family begins with the marriage in 1792 of Johnston with the daughter of the famous Ojibway Indian chief Waub-ojeeg, The White Fisher. She is called at first the Woman of the Glade, later Neengay (Mother), and finally, when she is baptized, Susan. The action depicts the eventful lives of Neengay (Lewis's favorite heroine) and her descendants.

As the historical narrative approaches the mid nineteenth century and deals with Neengay's children and grandchildren, the invasion theme becomes more marked and persistent. In 1855 the Treaty of Detroit gave the Indians the coup de grace: "gone [were] the Ojibway and Ottawa nations. Hereafter there were to be only citizens of the United States, having varying ancestry." There follows a fine ironic juxtaposition, a brief but devastating critique of Longfellow's *The Song of Hiawatha* (published in the same year as the signing of the Detroit treaty) which Lewis considers to be a sentimental popularization of Indian life,

a mere "fairy-tale" written in a tiresome, mechanical meter far removed from the subtle rhythms of the Indian languages. Longfellow had access to Henry Rowe Schoolcraft's *Algic [Algonquin] Researches* (1839) as did Lewis in writing *The Invasion*, but Longfellow disregarded or misused his sources.

By 1855 the Indian nations had disappeared. The individual Indians lived on in dwindling circumstances. By the early twentieth century the wilderness which supported Indian life was depleted, and in its place was the powerful machine civilization of the white man. This is the purport of a remarkable description of the locks at the Sault which occurs toward the end of the novel. J. V. Cunningham called it, in 1932, "one of the firmest descriptive passages in modern literature." The civilization obsessed with machinery, with things, has supplanted the living, organic world of nature. The dangers of this obsession will be reexamined in Lewis's second novel, *Against a Darkening Sky* (1943).

Lewis presents the Indians and the white men of all classes realistically and without bias. She does not yield to the temptation to glamorize or sentimentalize the frequently harsh and cruel lives of the Indians of the period. Her characterizations and descriptions of the noble chief, White Fisher, and the beautiful Neengay are convincing, and there are a multitude of other characters precisely and vividly delineated. She is especially responsive to the beauties of the woods, fields, rivers, and lakes of the St. Mary's area, and some of the most remarkable passages in the book are the seasonal descriptions of the natural setting done with the perception of a poet and appropriately integrated into the action. Lewis considers the Indians who live so close to nature to have poetic sensibilities equal or superior to the whites.

For her next novel, written before but published after *The Wife of Martin Guerre*, Lewis turned to a recent time and place and social situation she knew at first hand, the early 1930s in the northwestern end of the Santa Clara valley, near the San Francisco Bay. *Against a Darkening Sky*—the title calls to mind Yvor Winters's poem "Before Disaster," also written in the 1930s—came out of the experiences of the Depression years when democratic capitalism seemed on the verge of extinction.

Mary Knox Perrault, of Scottish ancestry, is one of Lewis's "patriarchal women," hard working, honest, self-sufficient, and resilient in the

Lewis with her late husband, poet and critic Yvor Winters

face of catastrophe. She is devoted to her family, which consists of her husband, three sons, and a daughter. The Perraults live on enough land to grow fruit trees and vegetables, in South Encina, not to be found on any map. Lewis says of it: "South Encina is not a 'real' place. I wish that it may assume for the reader, however, a little of the reality of Barchester, or of Wessex." Mary is interested in and involved with the affairs of her neighbors. The book, with absolute but low-keyed realism, depicts her experiences and her day-to-day concerns including the financial problems and the love affairs of her children. The novel, besides its considerable literary merit, has value as a sociological document of the place and the period. There are certain themes which appear also in *The Invasion* and in the later novels. Charles L. Crow has defined one of them: "The warmth and order of the Johnston home, which radiate from Neengay's kitchen [in *The Invasion*], represent basic civilization.... The theme of the well ordered household ... appears in every one of her novels." And it is a woman, of course, who is always at the center of these well-ordered households.

With reference to the thematic significance and the underlying drama of *Against a Darkening Sky*, Crow refers to the final paragraph of chapter three. Mary is standing in the kitchen looking at her son Jamie soon after hearing of the fatal automobile and train accident which took the lives of a close friend, Agnes Hardy, her two grand-

children, and another woman: "She was overwhelmed by the realization of love lavished upon life which was held so cheap in a world of machines and locomotives. Four lives were gone, suddenly and casually, as if they had never been cherished. This was the tremendous drama in which she moved, life created by tenderness and patience in a world of mindless destruction." The novel opens with mindless accidental destruction and closes with intended, but equally mindless, destruction—a lynching in a city close by.

A corollary theme in the drama of civilization as represented by the struggle of Mary to hold her family together is the penalty man is paying for his obsession with things, especially with machinery, which is the product of highly competent mental activity. There was, for example, the tragedy of the giant dirigible, *Macon*. It was kept in a hangar (so tremendous that it had its own weather system) not far from Lewis's home. Toward the end of the novel, Mary's son, Duncan, and a friend drive out to look at the dirigible. There is a fine description of the airship—its power, beauty, and fragility. The reader is supposed to be aware of its imminent catastrophe, the loss of the airship on 12 February 1935 in a storm. It was a case of misapplied ingenuity. The engineering that went into the building of the *Macon* was brilliant. But those who ordered its construction should have had enough intelligence to realize that it could not survive a severe storm. The thematic and symbolic significance of what

343

at first may seem an irrelevant incident in *Against a Darkening Sky* is obvious. As the boys are leaving the hangar, news is brought to them that the body of a wealthy young man named Terry, who had been kidnapped and murdered, has just been found. Terry was the former boyfriend of Mary's daughter, Melanie. His murder is yet another example of mindless violence. In the concluding chapter, Mary is in the kitchen after having given Duncan a direct order (something she rarely did) prohibiting him from driving over to nearby San Tomás to watch a lynching which he referred to as "fun": "She rinsed three milk bottles in scalding water and set them on the table, ready for the new milk. Battle, murder, and sudden death, she thought, still did not prevent one's having to do the dishes.... behind them all was something to be dreaded for the sake of Melanie, Andrew, Duncan, Jamie, and this was the incoherent civilization, the moral wilderness emerging from the physical wilderness."

The dangers of the moral wilderness, or of what Lewis calls elsewhere moral relativism, are symbolized by "the darkening sky" and are thematic throughout Janet Lewis's fiction. Mary Perrault as the center of a well-ordered household has similarities with other Lewis heroines, but as Ellen Killoh has pointed out, she is faced with a situation different from the heroines of the three historical novels which followed. "In the world of Mary Perrault the family no longer mirrors the state. It has become instead a refuge from the incoherence of the world outside. In such a situation the domestic rule of a woman like Mary Perrault cannot acquire the political resonance of the world outside." She is in an individual, single-minded struggle against an increasingly chaotic society.

On Memorial Day 1933, one year after the publication of *The Invasion*, the body of Allene Lamson, wife of David Lamson, sales manager for the Stanford University Press, was discovered in the bathtub of the Lamson house. Lamson was convicted of murder on purely circumstantial evidence and sentenced to hang. The conviction was reversed by the California Supreme Court. After three retrials resulted in two hung juries and a mistrial, Lamson was released without acquittal. The trials aroused strong emotions on the Stanford campus. Yvor Winters and others were convinced that the death of Mrs. Lamson was caused by an accidental fall in her bathtub. He joined a committee for the defense of Lamson, helped the defense lawyer prepare his brief, coauthored a

book on the case, and published several poems about it. Janet Lewis was equally sure of Lamson's innocence. After the trials, Lamson and his second wife settled in California not far from the home of the Winters family, and they became friends. The plots of three of Lewis's novels written after the trials turn on the correct or incorrect interpretation of circumstantial evidence. It seems likely that the Lamson case had some influence on her choice of subject.

Lewis's third novel, *The Wife of Martin Guerre* (written in 1937 and published in 1941), has as its source *Famous Cases of Circumstantial Evidence with an Introduction on the Theory of Presumptive Guilt* by S. M. Phillips (1873). "Case of Martin Guerre" in fifteen pages briefly summarizes the facts. Martin and Bertrande were united in a childhood marriage (both at the age of eleven) in 1539 in Artigues, France. In the ninth year of their marriage a child, Sanxi, was born. Sometime thereafter Martin appropriated for his own use some seed wheat belonging to his father, and to escape his father's wrath he absented himself from Artigues and from his wife and child who remained in Artigues with the family of Martin Guerre senior. He was absent about seven or eight years and did not communicate with any member of the family. One evening, after Martin Guerre the elder died, the son reappeared and was joyfully accepted by Bertrande and by both families. Two children, one of whom died in infancy, were born of this happy reunion. But eventually, under pressure from Martin's uncle, Pierre, Bertrande was induced to proclaim her supposed husband an imposter. At the trial which immediately followed, the alleged imposter defended himself well, explaining his absence during which he served as a soldier, unable to communicate with his family. However, a majority of witnesses identified him as one Arnaud du Tilh, a soldier who looked very much like Martin. He was convicted and sentenced to suffer decapitation. Upon appeal, he defended himself so well that a verdict was about to be pronounced in his favor when a soldier stumped in on a wooden leg, claiming that he was Bertrande's husband. He was arrested and denounced as an imposter. A severe interrogation of both men followed in an attempt to discover who was the true Martin Guerre. Here is an example of the familiar theme of appearance versus reality. A decision was reached by majority vote of the court, and the reader is left in no doubt, for the imposter confessed just before his execution.

This historical case is made to order for a suspenseful dramatic novel, and Lewis, in retelling it, maintains the suspense until the very end. She does much more, however. By means of extensive research into the history and customs of France in the sixteenth century, she has written a detailed and convincing period piece with characters of depth and individuality, with vivid scenes of farm life (the main characters are well-to-do peasants), with perceptive, poetic descriptions of the landscape, and with memorable incidents such as the child wedding ceremony during which the groom scratched the face of the bride. Lewis has described how she wrote the book: "Without departing otherwise from the facts given in *Famous Cases,* I wrote a first and rather short version of the story, to be told that it was not believable. And in order to make it more believable I extended it with bits from *L'Ancienne Regime* of Frantz Funck-Brentano, and my imagination, memories of Provence, and gossip with an old woman from Auvergne who was my neighbor in Palo Alto."

The most memorable characters are Martin Guerre, the elder, and his daughter-in-law Bertrande de Rols. The elder Martin, as head of family, has complete authority over all its members which is sometimes extended to the point of tyranny. It was from fear of his wrath that his son absented himself for years. He becomes a symbolic patriarchal father figure at the same time he maintains his identity as an individual. Donald Davie has compared him to similar figures in Lewis's other fiction, to parson Sören Qvist in *The Trial of Sören Qvist* and to the bookbinder John Larcher in *The Ghost of Monsieur Scarron* (1959). "Each of these books," he says, "is a fable about authority."

The most successfully delineated character, however, is Bertrande de Rols. Torn between two men, she has to come to a life and death decision, for at the final trial it is her evidence that will be given the most weight. She must decide to whom she owes affection, loyalty, and love. Her inner struggle is masterfully portrayed. Lewis in her foreword states: "The rules of evidence may vary from century to century and country to country, and the morality which compels many of the actions of men and women varies also, but the capacities of the human soul for suffering and for joy remain very much the same." The novel was reprinted several times, translated into several languages, and produced as an opera for which Lewis wrote the libretto.

For her next historical novel, *The Trial of Sören Qvist,* Lewis returned to *Famous Cases* for her source, to the story of parson Qvist of Jutland, Denmark, a saintly man who, early in the seventeenth century, was decapitated for the murder of one Niels Bruus. The evidence was circumstantial–yet so convincing that even Qvist considered himself guilty. The motive for the crime and the reasons for the execution are succinctly summarized in *Famous Cases.* Sören Qvist, pastor of the little village of Vejlby, famous for his moral integrity, had one fatal flaw. He was quick to anger. But he was also quick to suffer remorse and to penalize himself for what he considered to be a sin. When he rejects a suitor of his daughter, the wealthy but evil cattle farmer Morten Bruus, Morten plots revenge. Qvist makes the mistake of hiring Morten's poor brother Niels as a farm hand, not knowing that Morten had committed Niels to accept the job in order to provoke the pastor to uncontrollable outbursts of wrath. His deliberately irresponsible and shiftless behavior causes the good parson to lose his temper more than once, and on the final occasion, when Niels is unusually impertinent, Qvist strikes him so hard with the flat of his spade that he takes off into the woods and is not seen again. Sometime later, Morten charges the pastor with murder and apparently proves it by conducting a search party to a place on the pastor's farm where a corpse is dug up that is identified by everyone present as the corpse of Niels Bruus. Several witnesses testify that they saw Qvist in his nightdress burying the corpse, and the magistrate, well disposed towards the pastor, is forced by the evidence and by Qvist's own testimony to pronounce the pastor guilty and to order his execution. The tense drama of this bizarre yet terrible situation and its eventual denouement lose nothing in Lewis's retelling.

As in *The Wife of Martin Guerre,* Lewis beautifully re-creates the pastoral life of a remote age– this time in Denmark in the first half of the seventeenth century. It is the life of hardworking men and women living peacefully in an established society with occasional rumblings from the Thirty Years War. Lewis brings to life the saintly character Sören Qvist and the villainous Morten Bruus. She invents a love affair not even hinted at in the story as told in *Famous Cases*– the love between Anna, the lovely innocent daughter of Qvist, and the gallant honest magistrate, Tryg Thorwaldsen, who is forced to pronounce the death penalty on his fiancée's father. The capacity of the two lovers for anguish and ecstasy is considerably greater than that of Bertrande de Rols in *The Wife of Martin Guerre*. Qvist is physically destroyed although spiritually triumphant. "He is," says Lewis in her foreword, "one of a great company of men and women who have preferred to lose their lives rather than accept a universe without plan or without meaning." The love of Anna and Tryg is perhaps blighted forever. What was a bizarre and unique legal case in *Famous Cases* has been made into a somber tale which has the quality of classical tragedy. The book was enthusiastically reviewed and almost every reviewer commented on the limpid quality of the prose style.

Lewis began writing short stories as early as 1922. The best of them appear in *Good-bye, Son, and Other Stories* (1946). The tone of her short fiction is similar to that of *Against a Darkening Sky*, quiet and meditative on the surface, with little violence or overt physical action, but with psychological and philosophical significance for those who look for it. The first story in the collection, "Proserpina," is typical. Johnnie Plows is obsessed by the thought of his own death, and after his doctor diagnoses a failing heart, he starts shopping around for his coffin while with troubled spirit he awaits the arrival of Proserpina, goddess of death and the underworld but also goddess of rebirth. He finds her in the kind, serene eyes of an old friend while eating her cake and drinking her wine. Death for Johnnie comes peacefully and naturally.

The theme of death, mutability, and rebirth is constant in these stories, of which "Proserpina," "River," "Summer Parties," and "Nell" (in part) take place in the Sault area familiar to Lewis since childhood. "River" is a detailed fictional account of an incident which occurred near Neebish island. The father, called the Dominie, takes his children on a fishing trip as he was accustomed to do every summer. They catch no fish, but on the return trip the boat encounters a "deadhead" which turns out to be the body of a village character drowned about a week ago. The Dominie inserts the stringer, empty of fish, into the collar of the corpse and slowly rows to the post office dock where the body is turned over to the son of the postmaster for official disposition. The postmaster says, "Just moor the old boy to the dock, Perfesser, and I'll take care of him." "You can keep the stringer," replies the Dominie. The story ends with the father asking his daughter, "Afraid of the river this morning?" "No," she

answers, looking up in surprise. "Ought I to be?" "No," he says, "I think not." The daughter has learned to accept death as not frightening, but as inevitable and natural. The Lewis family frequently referred to their father as "the Dominie," that is, teacher and master. He is the prototype of authoritarian heads of families in Lewis's fiction.

In the later stories the scene shifts to the midwest and the far west. The most remarkable of these is "Good-bye, Son," a "ghost" story with a decided difference. Sara McDermott's son dies at birth. Four times he appears to her, as a child, as a boy, as a student of high school age, and as a young man of college age, each time under circumstances in which he probably would have died. His final appearance is in uniform, and when immediately thereafter she hears of the bombing of Pearl Harbor, she knows "that this was the last time she would have lost him, and that this time, as at all other times, except the very first, she would have not been alone." The story is a meditation on love, death, and rebirth, and on the death of the beloved as both an individual and a communal experience, to be shared and accepted as inevitable and perennial.

During the 1930s and 1940s Lewis had been primarily occupied with writing and researching her four novels and her stories. But she had other literary commitments as well. She and Winters and Howard Baker edited a little magazine, *The Gyroscope*, which ran for four issues, May 1929 to February 1930. It published early work by writers who later became famous, including Lewis (two stories), Winters, Caroline Gordon, and Katherine Anne Porter. Lewis was also writing poetry. In *The Earth-Bound, 1924-1944* (1946), she republished the best of her early verse together with new poems which reveal an advance in technique and a mature depth of feeling and subject matter. One of the very best is the frequently admired "In the Egyptian Museum." In the first stanzas, artifacts from an Egyptian burial, arranged under the glare of electric lights in a glass case, are precisely and beautifully described. They were originally made to console the mourner "through the orderly beautification of the dead" to quote Helen Trimpi's phrase in her critique of the poem. Yet, paradoxically, for the poet-observer, they do not console, as evidenced in the last two powerful stanzas:

Such pain is garnered here
In every close-locked case,

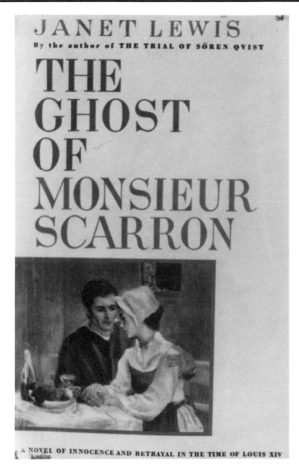

*Dust jacket for Lewis's 1959 historical novel set in Paris
during the 1690s*

Concentrate in this place
Year after fading year,

That, while I wait, a cry,
As from beneath the glass,
Pierces me with "Alas
That the beloved must die!"

"Child in the Garden III" characteristically combines significant nature imagery with appropriate
rhythms. The lines "The hummingbird in thin
air standing–/Motion and quiet reconciled" represent to Kenneth Fields Lewis's abiding concern
with what she has called "the variant principles
of life" and also, as Fields says, "the embodiment
of opposites." One of the loveliest poems, "Lines
with a Gift of Herbs," is reminiscent of Lewis's earliest American Indian poems with its loving attention to the small and the beautiful. As Yvor
Winters wrote in *Forms of Discovery* (1967), each
herb, preserving its identity, represents "the permanent and reassuring beauties of the world
around us." *Poems 1924-1944* (1950) republished

all of the poems in *The Earth-Bound* and added a
few others.

Before she wrote *The Ghost of Monsieur Scarron,* a long novel that takes place in seventeenth-
century Paris, Lewis, as she explained to Roger
Hofheins and Dan Tooker, engaged in a great
deal of preparation. She had maps of seventeenth-
century Paris, six by three feet, "fresh ones from
the originals. . . . When I got to Paris, I knew the
Paris of 1690 better than the Paris of 1951." In
Paris, her first visit there since 1920, she examined at first hand the locale of her story and continued to read memoirs of the period. The result
was a detailed picture of Parisian life of the
1690s at all levels of society together with another tale of suspense, derived from the "Case of
the Bookbinder" in *Famous Cases,* involving circumstantial evidence.

At the head of this hierarchical society is
the Sun King himself, Louis XIV, his mistress,
the celebrated Madame de Maintenon, and his numerous courtiers, churchmen, and government officials. Much lower down is the protagonist, Jean
Larcher, the bookbinder, and his family who belong to the relatively successful petite bourgeoi-
sie, and below them are the rabble of the great
city–human, passionate, volatile, oppressed, and
dangerous. The daily life of the king is described
in detail. There is a scene at the beginning of the
book that presents the *lever,* the morning awaken-
ing of the king, in vivid, meticulous detail. He is
one of the principal characters of the story, a
kind of deus ex machina in reverse, for he brings
about the final catastrophe rather than preventing it.

The dingy street life of prerevolutionary
Paris is also carefully presented. The story, like
that of the previous novel, involves circumstantial
evidence wrongly interpreted and resulting in a
miscarriage of justice. It is also a dramatic and suspenseful tale of adulterous passion and bloody revenge. Recondite knowledge, such as the barbaric
dentistry practiced in the period, is skillfully
worked into the action and gives the story verisi-
militude. The novel begins with a depiction of
the settled and contented life of Jean Larcher,
his wife, Marianne, much younger than Jean, the
restless son Nicolas who wishes to see the world before settling into his father's business, and the arrival of Paul Damas, who will be taken into the
shop by Larcher during his son's absence and
who will eventually become Marianne's lover.
The scene then shifts to the king and his court
and to the incident that brings about the catastro-

phe. The king is irritated and the entire court upset by a malicious pamphlet satirizing the king's mistress, Madame de Maintenon, the widow of the satiric poet Paul Scarron. In the pamphlet Scarron's ghost reproaches Maintenon for her amorous relationship with Louis XIV. The king orders a search for the author, printer, and distributors of the pamphlet and commands that when found they be hanged. After Damas and Marianne become lovers, Damas persuades Marianne to flee with him, and to secure their comfort and safety, Damas with the help of Marianne, robs Larcher of his life savings in gold and plants a bundle of the scurrilous Scarron pamphlets (which he had accidently come by) in Larcher's shop. Execution and bloody revenge follow.

Most remarkable in this novel is the portrayal of Marianne who was only briefly mentioned in "Case of the Bookbinder." This relatively innocent and religious young woman undergoes a complete moral transformation (not without eventual suffering and bitterness) from being a contented housewife taking orders from her authoritarian husband (reminiscent of Martin Guerre, the elder) to the passion-ridden lover of Damas, so dominated by her love that she is bound to him even after she becomes aware that he not only brought financial ruin to her husband but his death as well. It should be noted, however, that there is an extra dimension that makes the novel more than a tale of illicit love. It is the criticism of a society that is under the sway of an absolute monarch, supported by the church, who flaunts his wealth in the face of the starving populace and who carelessly snuffs out the lives of innocent people.

Though Lewis continued to write poetry throughout this period it was not until 1979 that her next book of verse appeared. In writing *The Ancient Ones* (1979) she returned to the poetic form employed in her youth, free verse, and to the early subject matter, American Indians. The free verse is different, however, and so are the Indians. In 1977 she visited what is perhaps the most awe-inspiring area in the Southwest, the cliff dwellings of Navaho National Monument in Northeast Arizona, riding a horse to Keet Seel and walking to Betátaken and out again. The result was a series of poems about the Navajo and Hopi Indians and their ancestors written, for the most part, in a free flowing unrhymed verse with long lines which, as Suzanne J. Doyle has pointed out, gave Lewis the opportunity for meditative

comment lacking in the early poems which simply presented the imagistic material. "Awátobi" links the holy war that was waged between the village of Awátobi and the tribe of The Three Mesas with events from French history that occurred about the same time. In "The Ancient Ones: Water" we meet Manibush, the one in changing shapes, who appears in the form of water. He is present also in the moving poem "the Anasazi Woman" observed as a sun-dried mummy in a museum in Tucson, who ages ago "unconfused . . . met the morning sun . . . /Knowing no land beyond the great horizons," knowing also in "her own language. . . . The gods of life/Who are the One in many changing forms." The poem ends on a personal note:

Oh, unconfused and bless'd,
In a strange sepulchre your body lies,
Most beautiful, most unconcerned, and small,
My sister, my friend.

In *Poems Old and New, 1918-1978* (1981) Lewis brings together the very best of previous collections and adds a few more recent poems including the notable "For the Father of Sandro Gulotta," written on the request of an Italian father (personally unknown to the poet) whose son, aged seven, was dying of leukemia. It is a philosophical meditation on the theme of the possibility of fulfillment in a brief time. There is also a tribute to John Muir and "Words for a Song," written on the occasion of the poet's eightieth birthday.

Janet Lewis is by talent and temperament primarily a lyric poet. It is not surprising therefore that as her career as a novelist drew to a close, she should find herself equipped to write compositions to be set to music. Since 1956 she has written the librettos for six operas. The first, an adaptation of *The Wife of Martin Guerre*, with music by William Bergsma, was first produced at the Juilliard School of Music in 1956. Richard F. Goldman, writing in that same year, said that it is "probably the most distinguished libretto in the annals of American opera." Lewis's next libretto was for an opera by Alva Henderson, *The Last of the Mohicans*, adapted from James Fenimore Cooper's novel. It was produced at Wilmington, Delaware, in June 1976 and at Lake George Opera Festival in 1977.

A tale by Oscar Wilde was adapted by Lewis for her next libretto, cowritten by Malcolm Seagrave. *The Birthday of the Infanta: An Opera in*

Lewis with her friend, English poet Donald Davie (photograph by Doreen Davie)

One Act was produced by the Hidden Valley Opera Ensemble on 2 April 1977, with music by Seagrave. It was beautifully printed by Charles Gullans's Symposium Press in 1979. This small opera presents the tale of a dwarf who falls violently in love with the Infanta when her highness tosses him a rose as a reward for his excruciatingly funny dancing. The dwarf, thinking the Infanta must be in love with him, seeks her throughout the palace, comes to the hall of mirrors and, seeing himself as he really is, collapses with a broken heart. Dying, he attempts to struggle to his feet when the Infanta reappears and orders him to amuse her once more. As he falls dead she comments that in the future she should be brought entertainers with no hearts. Lewis's limpid free verse is quite adequate for the action and music. It rises to genuine poetry in the words sung by the dwarf in the final scene.

The Swans (1986), an opera in three acts, with music by Alva Henderson and a libretto by Lewis adapted from a fairy tale taken from the Grimm collection, presents a dramatic confrontation between pure evil in the form of Gundala who goes from old hag to a beautiful queen and back to old hag again, and the innocent princess Lore. Gundula weaves a magic web by which she transforms the six sons of the king to six golden-crowned swans. To enable the swans to return to their human forms the princess Lore is forced to

weave six shirts from nettles, working in complete silence for six years. Her successful fulfillment of her task, the victory of good over evil, of life over death, is celebrated at the end with lines characteristic of Lewis's entire career:

> What joy to tread in mortal form
> The earth where each may play a part. . . .
> How good to speak with mortal tongue
> The love that overflows the heart.

Lewis returned to her first novel, *The Invasion,* for the libretto of *The Legend,* an opera-oratorio with music by Bain Murray. It was first performed at Cleveland State University, 8 May 1987, with William Parker singing the role of John Johnston and Daisy Newman the role of Neengay. Of all Lewis's librettos, *The Legend* is probably the most successful from a literary point of view—that is, it can stand on its own as a dramatic poem. There is an easy-to-follow story line, Indian material thoroughly familiar but freshly treated, and a cadenced free verse as an effective medium. In act one Johnston, after severe trials in the wilderness in which he gives and receives life-giving help to and from the Ojibways, meets Neengay, the beautiful young daughter of the Ojibway war chief. There follows her apowa retreat, a traditional Indian custom for maidens before marriage, her dreams of the future, and her marriage, flight, and forced return to Johnston.

She is foreseen in later years as the mediator between her people and the whites, and as the founder of a dynasty which produces "makers of treaties,/Averting bloodshed." Act two consists of a series of episodes presenting the building of the Johnston home at the Sault, the organization of the raid on Mackinaw, the burning of the home by the Americans in the war of 1812, the death of Neengay's father, a confrontation between General Cass and the militant Ojibway warrior Sassaba, and two final incidents showing George, Neengay's son, and Neengay as peacemakers between Indians and whites. The epilogue presents the final outcome–the ecological destruction by Americans and Canadians of the Indian hunting grounds and of the Ojibway and Ottawa nations.

Interviews:

Roger Hofheins and Dan Tooker, "A Conversation with Janet Lewis," *Southern Review* (April 1974): 329-341;

Mitzi Berger Hamovitch, "My Life I Will Not Let Thee Go Except Thou Bless Me: an Interview with Janet Lewis," *Southern Review*, 18 (April 1982): 299-313.

References:

Dorothea Brande, Review of *The Invasion, Bookman,* 75 (September 1932): 518-519;

Brigitte Hoy Carnochan, "Janet Lewis," in *Women Writers of the West Coast: Speaking of their Lives and Careers,* edited by Marilyn Yalom (Santa Barbara, Cal.: Copra, 1983);

Carnochan, *The Strength of Art: Poets and Poetry in the Lives of Yvor Winters and Janet Lewis. An Exhibition of Books and Manuscripts with an Introduction by N. Scott Momaday* (Stanford, Cal.: Stanford University Libraries, 1984);

Evan S. Connell, Jr., "Genius Unobserved," *Atlantic Monthly,* 224 (December 1969): 152-156;

Charles L. Crow, *Janet Lewis* (Boise, Idaho: Boise State University, 1980);

J. V. Cunningham, "The Gyroscope Group," *Bookman,* 75 (November 1932): 703-708;

Donald Davie, "The Historical Novels of Janet Lewis," *Southern Review,* 2 (January 1966): 40-60;

Davie, "The Legacy of Fenimore Cooper," *Essays in Criticism*, 9 (July 1959): 222-238;

Millicent Dillon, "Without Living, There's Nothing to My Writing," *Stanford Observer,* March 1976, p. 4;

Suzanne J. Doyle, "Janet Lewis's The Ancient Ones," *Southern Review,* 16 (April 1980): 531-537;

Kenneth Fields, "Motion and Quiet Reconciled," Jacket Essay for *Janet Lewis Reading at Stanford,* The Stanford Program for Recordings in Sound (SPRS5), 1975;

Richard F. Goldman, Review of *The Wife of Martin Guerre: An Opera,* in "Current Chronicle," *Musical Quarterly,* 42 (July 1956): 390-394;

Fred Ingles, "The Novels of Janet Lewis," *Critique: Studies in Modern Fiction,* 7 (1964-1965): 47-64;

Ellen Killoh, "Patriarchal Women: A Study of Three Novels by Janet Lewis," *Southern Review,* 10 (April 1974): 342-364;

Thomas Parkinson, *Hart Crane and Yvor Winters* (Berkeley: University of California Press, 1978);

S. M. Phillips, *Famous Cases of Circumstantial Evidence. With an Introduction on the Theory of Presumptive Proof* (Jersey City, N. J.: Frederick D. Linn, 1879);

Theodore Roethke, "Integrity of Spirit," *Poetry,* 69 (January 1947): 220-223;

Timothy Steele, "Janet Lewis and the Untranslatable Heart," *Los Angeles Times Book Review,* 3 November 1985, p. 2;

Helen P. Trimpi, "The Poetry of Janet Lewis," *Southern Review,* 18 (April 1982): 251-258;

A. Thomas Trusky, ed., *Women Poets of the West, 1850-1950,* (Boise, Idaho: Ahsahta Press of Boise State University, 1978).

Papers:

The Janet Lewis papers are in the Yvor Winters/ Janet Lewis Collection, Stanford University Library, Stanford, California.

Bobbie Ann Mason

(1 May 1940-   )

Nancy G. Anderson
Auburn University at Montgomery

BOOKS: *Nabokov's Garden: A Guide to Ada* (Ann Arbor: Ardis, 1974);

The Girl Sleuth: A Feminist Guide to the Bobbsey Twins, Nancy Drew, and Their Sisters (Old Westbury, N.Y.: Feminist Press, 1975);

Shiloh and Other Stories (New York: Harper & Row, 1982);

In Country (New York: Harper & Row, 1985).

PERIODICAL PUBLICATIONS: "The Elements of E. B. White's Style," *Language Arts,* 56 (September 1979): 692-696;

"Fan City," *Redbook,* 155 (September 1980): 31, 132, 136, 138-139, 141;

"Kath Walker, Aboriginal Poet," *Denver Quarterly,* 15 (Winter 1981): 63-75;

"Underground," *Virginia Quarterly Review,* 58 (Spring 1982): 291-299;

"Gooseberry Winter," *Redbook,* 160 (November 1982): 28, 30, 142-143, 146-147;

"Private Lies," *Atlantic Monthly,* 251 (March 1983): 62-67;

"New Ground," *North American Review,* 268 (June 1983): 30-32;

"Airwaves," *Atlantic Monthly,* 252 (August 1983): 40-46;

"Trexlertown," *Vanity Fair,* 46 (September 1983): 135-136;

"Art of Darkness," *Vanity Fair,* 46 (October 1983): 30, 32, 34;

"Hunktown," *Atlantic Monthly,* 253 (January 1984): 56-64; reprinted in *Landscapes* (Frankfort, Ky.: Frankfort Arts Foundation, 1984);

"The Foreign Traveler, Jamaica, Listen to the Music. It Sings Jamaica," *Esquire,* 101 (April 1984): 50-59;

"Do You Know What It Means To Miss New Orleans?," *Paris Review,* 26 (Fall 1984): 79-92;

"Love Life," *New Yorker,* 60 (29 October 1984): 42-50;

"Big Bertha Stories," *Mother Jones,* 10 (April 1985): 10-12, 14, 16-17, 26;

"Reaching the Stars: My Life As A Fifties Groupie," *New Yorker* (26 May 1985): 30-38;

"State Champions," *Harper's,* 274 (February 1987): 68-74;

"Bumblebees," *New Yorker,* 63 (9 March 1987): 32-40;

"Midnight Magic," *New Yorker,* 63 (24 August 1987): 26-33;

"La Bamba Hot Line," *New Yorker,* 63 (7 September 1987): 27.

Rural Kentucky and the changes caused by urban development have provided Bobbie Ann Mason with many of her subjects, characters, and themes. Mason was born on 1 May 1940 to Wilburn A. and Christie Lee Mason, who owned a dairy farm outside Mayfield, Kentucky. In this rural setting Mason spent her childhood doing her chores, listening to rock and roll music on the radio, reading about her favorite performers, and reading Nancy Drew mysteries. The lives of the pop stars and the Nancy Drew stories provided distractions from the daily routine of her life. She became a serious fan of the Hilltoppers, a quartet that earned national fame with its renditions of "Only You" and "P.S. I Love You," after its origin in the 1950s at Western Kentucky University in Bowling Green. Her admiration and work for the Hilltoppers, which resulted in her appointment as the national president of the Hilltoppers Fan Club, gave her some contact with the world outside rural Kentucky. She wrote the organization's newsletter, coordinated request campaigns, and, accompanied by her mother, attended concerts throughout the Midwest, where she became acquainted with dance halls, ballrooms, hotels, big cars (the Hilltoppers had a blue 1954 Fleetwood), and the limelight—the Hilltoppers always introduced their president when she was in the audience.

In the fall of 1958 Bobbie Ann Mason entered the University of Kentucky, where she discovered the works of Hemingway, Fitzgerald, Salinger, and Wolfe. She began to chart her route to the big time: "It was a romantic dream to be a writer. It seemed like a calling. . . . It was

Dust jacket for Bobbie Ann Mason's first novel, inspired by a trip to the Vietnam Memorial in Washington, D.C.

a way of getting out and escaping the limited possibilities of here." One summer, while in college, Mason wrote for the *Mayfield Messenger;* immediately after receiving her B.A. in 1962, she moved to New York City, where she drew on her youthful interest in popular music and movie stars, writing for such fan magazines as *Movie Stars, Movie Life,* and *T.V. Star Parade.* In 1966 she graduated from the State University of New York at Binghamton with an M.A.; she then entered the English graduate program at the University of Connecticut. In 1969 Mason married Roger B. Rawlings, a fellow graduate student, and in 1972 she received her Ph.D. after completing a dissertation on Vladimir Nabokov. She was assistant professor of English at Mansfield State College in Pennsylvania from 1972 through 1979.

Soon after receiving her doctorate, Mason turned her dissertation into her first published book, *Nabokov's Garden: A Guide to Ada* (1974). This 196-page book provides a careful reading and detailed analysis of nature imagery and symbolism in *Ada.* Mason's thesis in this study is that "Nabokov's interpretation of the Garden of Eden story emphasizes not only the misplaced importance of the sin of sensuality (not a new contention), but also the results of human solipsism–the loss of nature, the alienation from our world, the despair arising from imprisonment in our minds. But triumphantly he shows the way out of the labyrinth Van Veen is trapped in–through the imagination of the artist."

In immediate reaction to her work on the literary dissertation, according to the preface to *The Girl Sleuth: A Feminist Guide to the Bobbsey Twins, Nancy Drew, and Their Sisters* (1975), Mason returned to the series books she loved in her childhood. Drawing on her background of literary criticism and her interest in popular culture, she discusses these works, both from the memories of her childhood enthrallment and her adult maturity, even skepticism, in order "to give some critical attention to the form and substance of the series books which girls read, to comment on their quality and their possible impact on young girls' imaginations, and to examine the stereotypes which have been popularized by the books." Mason traces the readership of several series, from the Honey Bunch books, which appeal to girls from age four to eight, the Bobbsey Twins chronicles, for girls age eight to twelve, and the Nancy Drew series, intended for teenagers. Mason does not believe juvenile readers today will view Nancy Drew and her "sisters" in the same way earlier readers did: "Once Nancy was a brilliant symbol of almost liberation. Now she is establishment–not a leader or pathfinder, but a cliché." Although she criticizes the series for their sexual stereotyping, racism, and idyllic portrayal of family life and suggests that modern readers will find "Nancy's exploits too superficial

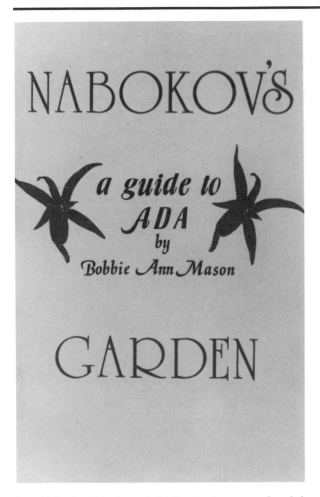

Dust jacket for Mason's analysis of nature imagery and symbolism in Vladimir Nabokov's Ada, *based on her dissertation*

and her character too thin," she recalls their important influence: "for girls deprived of stimulating, accomplished role models, the girl detectives have held out a rare promise."

Even as she presents her adult insights into these books and knowledge about the "authors" (many are written by syndicates; there is, for example, neither a "Laura Lee Hope" of the Bobbsey Twins series, nor a "Carolyn Keene" of the Nancy Drew and Dana Girls series), Mason plays with language and descriptions in *The Girl Sleuth*, foreshadowing characteristics of her fiction and essays. She creates a "Great Chain of Bobbsey," with the twins just below angels in the hierarchy. The humor pervades the imagery as well: sexual stereotyping is "as plain as pink and blue," and the Bobbsey Twins are "cookie cutters on my imagination." In an interview published in 1986, Mason stated her attitudes about *Nabokov's Garden* and *The Girl Sleuth* and about writing nonfiction: "Through both of those books I was kind

of letting loose a little bit. I had fun working on them, but they weren't fiction. . . . I'm really not very good at non-fiction. . . . I don't have that kind of logical mind you need to work out essays." Mason's statement that she is not very good at nonfiction is contradicted by her capturing of life and landscape in travelogues, autobiography, and "reporting," as she classifies essays such as "Art of Darkness" and "Trexlertown."

In the late 1970s, after working on a novel, Mason began writing short stories and sending them to the *New Yorker:* "I was in my mid-thirties, although I'd gravitated toward it [serious pursuit of fiction writing] for three or four years, trying to get up the courage to do it. I had never gotten any encouragement to speak of along the way, and then didn't have time to write during graduate school. So after graduate school I very, very slowly got focused on it. And then just from sheer act of will–because I thought I had to do it or else–I sat down one summer and wrote a novel. That was about 1976. Then in 1978 I started writing stories and sending them to the *New Yorker*–without an agent, on my own. Probably the second story I wrote I sent to the *New Yorker*, which seems like a pretty naive thing to do."

The editors, Roger Angell in particular, responded with encouraging comments, and in 1980 the magazine accepted her twentieth submission, "Offerings," a short story about rural Kentucky, family relationships, and change. This story was published in the 18 February 1980 issue of the *New Yorker* and was later included along with fifteen other pieces in *Shiloh and Other Stories* (1982). Fourteen of the selections in this collection ("Shiloh," "Detroit Skyline, 1949," "Offerings," "Still Life with Watermelon," "Old Things," "Drawing Names," "The Climber," "Residents and Transients," "The Retreat," "The Ocean," "Graveyard Day," "Nancy Culpepper," "A New-Wave Format," and "Third Monday") had been previously published; the other two–"The Rookers" and "Lying Doggo"–had not. Mason first planned to be a novelist: "I tried to write a couple [of novels], but then I discovered that short stories were more suited to my style and inclinations. . . ." Since 1980 Mason's stories have appeared in such magazines as the *New Yorker*, the *Atlantic Monthly, Redbook, Washington Post Magazine, New Boston Review, Bloodroot*, and *Ascent;* she has also become a frequent contributor to "The Talk of the Town" in the *New Yorker*. Her stories–those in the collection and the others published before and since its release–as well as her essays and journalistic works share many of the same stylistic characteristics.

Clearly, Mason's childhood and youthful experiences have provided the subject matter, the people, and the language for her fiction and some of her nonfiction. As she looks back on the rural Kentucky in which she grew up, she sees her home as a place that is changing: "a world invaded by four-lane highways, K marts, 'Shrimp Night' at the Holiday Inn and the shopping mall in nearby Paducah." Into this setting of a changing Kentucky, Mason places her characters, whom she divides into two groups: "Some people will stay at home and be content there. Others are born to run. It's that conflict that fascinates me." Mason expounds on this thematic difference through Mary Sue, the first-person narrator of "Residents and Transients," who applies the classifications to cats: "In the wild, there are two kinds of cat populations. . . . Residents and transients. Some stay put, in their fixed home ranges, and others are on the move. They don't have real homes. Everybody always thought that the ones who establish the territories are the most successful–like the capitalists who get ahold of Park Place. . . . They are the strongest, while the transients are the bums, the losers."

Mary Sue, who has stayed in her parents' old farmhouse while her husband finds a new home for them in Louisville, is living by this dualistic philosophy and having trouble facing the move to the city. One night she sees her life reflected in a rabbit that has been run over, but not killed: "It is hopping in place, the way runners will run in place. Its forelegs are frantically working, but its rear end has been smashed and it cannot get out of the road." In the paradoxical desire for change but fear of it, the monotony but security of roots, lie the plots and themes of Mason's stories: the past versus the present or history versus progress, the influence of mass culture, the disintegration of the family, and the changing roles of males and females.

Mason's characters are working-class people in a once-rural society being overrun by fast food outlets, superhighways, shopping malls, and television. They drive trucks or work at K Mart, Rexall, Kroger, J. C. Penney; they go to shopping malls or watch *All in the Family*, *M*A*S*H*, *WKRP in Cincinnati*, and *The Waltons* as they eat Kentucky Fried Chicken and Big Macs. They try to pay their bills and to make their marriages (or relationships) survive and to find some happi-

ness, but something is usually missing. David Quammen, in the *New York Times Book Review*, describes these people with their "pathetically modest hopes" as having "the dawning recognition–in some cases only a vague worry–of having missed something, something important, some alternate life more fruitful than the one that's been led." And these "small-town folk who itch to get out but rarely do so" continue the search for that thing missing from their everyday lives in an assortment of ways: Louise Milsap ("Still Life with Watermelon") gets fired from Kroger and begins to paint only watermelons; Sabrina Jones ("A New-Wave Format") performs in *Oklahoma* at a local Little Theatre, uses fennel toothpaste, and cooks "odd things"–eggplant and vegetarian lasagna; Norma Jean Moffitt ("Shiloh") works out with dumbbells before going to work at Rexall while her husband constructs a log cabin of Popsicle sticks and dreams of building a real cabin from a kit. Even when they "escape" from these small towns, something pulls them back: the title character in "Nancy Culpepper" (who also appears in "Lying Doggo") convinces her husband "to think about relocating his photography business" from near Philadelphia back to her home state of Kentucky, and she returns to help move her aging grandmother and to search for the original Nancy Culpepper; Darlene, the first-person narrator of "Fan City," returns to Lexington for graduate school after a summer of writing for a fan magazine in New York City. According to Anatole Broyard, in his *New York Times Book Review* article about regional fiction, Mason's characters, for the most part, "live, without history or politics, a life more like a linoleum than a tapestry."

Bobbie Ann Mason treats all of her characters–male and female–with sensitivity, regardless of the extremes to which the characters go. She describes them "as kind of naive and optimistic for the most part: they think better times are coming and most of them embrace progress. But I think they reflect that tension that's in culture between hanging onto the past and racing toward the future." But Mason does not believe that progress will solve their problems any more than the past, their own history and heritage, did: "I don't want to be nostalgic and romantic about the [rural] past, because I think it's very hard [as a way of life]. On the other hand, I don't think they're going to find answers in a K Mart." In a conversation with her husband (in "Lying Doggo"), Nancy Culpepper recognizes the abrupt changes in her life, even as she seems to question whether there is progress or improvement: "One day I was listening to Hank Williams and shelling corn for the chickens and the next day I was expected to know what wines went with what."

Some of Mason's characters believe that history holds the hope for the future. Just as Sherry Williams ("Do You Know What It Means To Miss New Orleans?") studies archaeology, so Norma Jean and Leroy ("Shiloh") visit the famous Civil War battleground, where Leroy realizes that "He is leaving out the insides of history. History was always just names and dates to him. . . . And the real inner workings of a marriage, like most of history, have escaped him." Edwin drives a bus for the mentally retarded ("A New-Wave Format") and plays "new-wave" music: "It makes Edwin sad to think how history passes them [his passengers] by, but sometimes he feels the same way about his own life."

The change, regardless of whether it is progress, is reflected in innumerable ways: families separated or broken up, parents and children divided by generation gaps, a middle-aged man not knowing the world of his youthful lover, middle-aged women still hiding their cigarettes from their mothers, a father becoming more agoraphobic as he reads college texts to keep up with his daughter, a wife sickened by the power she has over her husband, and families facing relocation for work or retirement. The stories of these people have vague, unresolved, openended conclusions as individuals request (or announce) divorce, propose marriage, demand moves, face putting the beloved dog to sleep, reach the ocean. The unsettling endings are somewhat countered by the naiveté and hesitant optimism of the characters as they anticipate better times. R. Z. Sheppard, in *Time*, however, stresses the unsettling quality of the stories: "when the cult of life-styles and celebrity junk-think crack the rectitude of western Kentucky, there must be a lot of people everywhere who are having a hard time feeling at home at home."

According to Wendy Smith, in her *Publishers Weekly* interview, Bobbie Ann Mason uses "decidedly and deliberately plain" prose to capture the lives and times of these people: "I've always written that way, just kind of bluntly. . . . I think it's a way of being realistic rather than trying to dress something up, which I never learned to do." One characteristic of this simple style is the frequent use of the present tense. Related to this

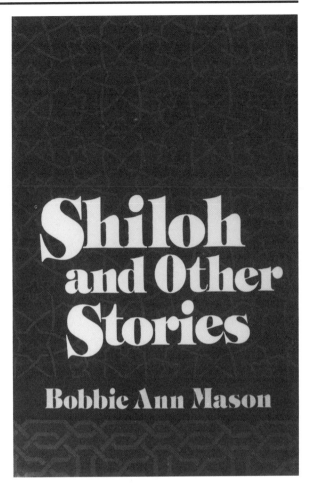

Dust jacket for Mason's first collection of short stories, which received the Hemingway Foundation Award in 1983

use of the present tense is the short opening sentence, as if the reader has started in the middle of an action perpetually taking place: "Leroy Moffitt's wife, Norma Jean, is working on her pectorals"; "For several weeks now, Louise Milsap has been painting pictures of watermelons"; "Mary Lou Skaggs ['The Rookers'] runs errands for her husband"; "Opal ['Love Life'] lolls in her recliner, wearing the Coors cap her niece brought her from Colorado." In a *New York Times Book Review* article about the use of present tense in modern fiction, including works by Bobbie Ann Mason, Ann Beattie, and Tom Wolfe, Ben Yagoda describes an effect of that tense, an effect Mason uses meaningfully: "On one hand, he [the writer] implies that the events represent a pattern that the characters are endlessly repeating. At the same time, we are frequently given to understand that beneath the surface is something that cannot be said—a trauma, perhaps, like an incipient divorce, or a more general sense of desperation–and is all the more palpable for being unstated."

Through a deceptive simplicity, Mason's style suggests a certain sadness about the inability of the individual to express that thing beneath the surface, rather than a palpability in the silence. These reticent characters frequently listen to rock and roll music, an important component of Mason's fiction, because "it expresses the aspirations and emotions of people who don't always reveal them more openly."

The dialogue and imagery in these stories also reflect Mason's blunt style. She does not try to capture the "polite, social" southern talk; rather she wants to convey the expressions and rhythm of her characters' speech: "I like to died when the jailer woke 'em up . . ."; "I reckon" and "golly-Bill"; "If that don't beat all"; "I'm the one that showed out." The humor slips into these expressions as someone has misunderstood words but tries to use them: "datsun dog" or "stacking up" (instead of "shacking up"). The images, frequently similes, are as apt as they are humorous: women's curls "resemble pencil trimmings" or are "like the coils of a new pad of steel wool." Leroy's wrecked truck "sits in the backyard, like a gigantic bird that has flown home to roost." Often a juxtaposition of details or events provides the irony: just as a woman tells a friend of her husband's infidelity ("Love Life"), the waitress asks, "Is everything all right?"; the immediate response is, "No, but it's not your fault." Nancy Culpepper's graduation picture hangs on her grandmother's bedroom wall next to a picture of Jesus: "Nancy looks sassy; her graduation hat resembles a tilted lid. Jesus has a halo, set about the same angle." Often a cliché takes a new turn, as when Mary Sue almost has "to swear on a stack of cats," an appropriate oath since she says that "One day I was counting the cats and I absent-mindedly counted myself."

Bobbie Ann Mason's particular blending of characters, settings, themes, and style is effective, and her stories have been successful. *Shiloh and Other Stories* was nominated for the National Book Critics Circle Award, the American Book Award, and the P.E.N./Faulkner Award for fiction; it received the Hemingway Foundation Award in 1983. For this collection she also received an award from the American Academy and Institute of Arts and Letters to encourage new writers. Individual stories had additional recognition: "Shiloh" was selected for *Best American Short Stories, 1981*, and "Graveyard Day" was re-

printed in *Best American Short Stories, 1983*, and *The Pushcart Prize VIII, Best of the Small Presses* (1983). A more recent story, "Big Bertha Stories," was selected for *Prize Stories 1986: The O. Henry Awards*. Her stories are also appearing in anthologies such as *New Women and New Fiction: Short Stories Since the Sixties*, edited by Susan Cahill (1986), *Soldiers and Civilians: Americans at War and at Home*, edited by Tom Jenks (1986), and *The New Writers of the South: A Fiction Anthology*, edited by Charles East (1987). In 1983 and 1984 Mason was also awarded a fellowship from the National Endowment for the Arts, a grant from the Pennsylvania Arts Council, and a Guggenheim Fellowship. David Quammen, in the *New York Times Book Review*, perhaps best summarizes the excellence of *Shiloh and Other Stories*: " 'Shiloh and Other Stories' . . . shows not only how good she can be but how consistently good she remains. The most improbable thing about this volume is that not a single page lags, hardly a paragraph fails, not one among 16 stories is less than impressive." Quammen suggests that "All the bad portents, all the sickening changes seem somehow connected, uniting 'Shiloh and Other Stories' as tightly as a good novel."

With the success of her first collection of fiction behind her, Bobbie Ann Mason returned to novel writing even as she continued to produce short stories. In 1985 she published *In Country*. Using her emphasis on characters with her "Shopping Mall Realism"–to use Joel Conarroe's phrase from his review in the *New York Times Book Review*–Mason began writing. She "had the characters first, in various situations I was exploring. . . ." She was still using the blue-collar workers, struggling farm families living in houses with old linoleum, and people who have moved to the city, but, to this combination, Mason has added a seventeen-year-old protagonist and a supporting cast of Vietnam veterans. Mason insists that a statement about Vietnam was not the motivation: after thinking about the characters and situations, "I think it came out of my unconscious the same way it's coming out of America's." But Mason further insists: "I think that in fiction I'm just concerned with portraying the experience; the textures of the experiences are more important than any one-sided vision of things. I don't think fiction should be didactic."

In the tradition of the initiation novel, Mason conveys the Vietnam experience through Samantha Hughes. Sam, as she is called, graduates from high school in Hopewell, Kentucky, in the summer of 1984 and spends that summer listening to popular music, watching *M*A*S*H* reruns with her mother's brother, Emmett Smith, and outgrowing her high-school sweetheart, a Kroger bagboy. As she thinks about a job at Burger Boy and possibly going to college in the fall, she begins her quest to get to know her father, who was killed in Vietnam before she was born. Sam's mother, Irene, has remarried, moved to Lexington with her successful husband, and had another baby. Sam has stayed in Hopewell with Emmett, a psychological victim of Vietnam whose physical problems—a rash and head and stomach pains—have become so serious that Sam fears Agent Orange poisoning. Sam's search takes her to Emmett and his Vietnam buddies, her mother's old Beatle records, both sets of grandparents, her father's war diary which no one has read, and finally a night in a snake-infested swamp where, alone, she tries to recapture the "in-country" feeling of being in Vietnam. The summer's search ends with a trip to Washington, in her newly acquired VW, with her father's mother and Emmett. The climax of the book is their visit to the Vietnam Veterans Memorial, where they read—and touch—the name of "Dwayne E. Hughes" and place a pot of geraniums in his memory. When Sam discovers her own name, "SAM A. HUGHES," she comes to an understanding of her father, Emmett, herself—an understanding of Americans in general: "She touches her own name. How odd it feels, as though all the names in America have been used to decorate this wall." Sam has sought for her father so hard that her developing understanding is a resolution, but a resolution overcast with the realization of the losses involved in the Vietnam experience.

Although Mason had characters and events for the novel in mind before she "had any knowledge that any of it had to do with Vietnam," her first visit to the Vietnam Memorial had a powerful influence on her, and thus on her novel: "I looked at everyone at the Memorial reading for names, parents crying and people bringing flowers and letters. When I saw all those people there, I knew that was my subject, that it was every American's story in some way or another." This influence is reflected in Sam's dramatic, emotional visit to the Memorial. Thus, Mason makes the Vietnam experience part of the tapestry of her characters' lives and avoids didacticism. The statements in the novel about Vietnam are her characters' opinions, not thematic denunciations.

One veteran says, "The war would have been fine if they'd let us win it." When Emmett tries to explain the childish reaction of running away to get revenge, Sam suggests, "That explains what the whole country was doing over there. The least little threat and America's got to put on its cowboy boots and stomp around and show somebody a thing or two."

Like characters in Mason's short stories, Sam seeks answers in history, specifically history books, but "The books didn't say what it was like to be at war over there." She even tries to tell her father's photograph how many important historical events, like Watergate and men on the moon, he missed. Finally she sets out to re-create her father's past in her own present by going to the "jungle," spending the night at Cawood's Pond: "She had to walk carefully. She was walking point. The cypress knees were like land mines. There would be an invisible thread spread across the path to trigger the mine. She waded through elephant grass, and in the distance there was a rice paddy."

When Emmett finds her the next day, he tells her, in a hysterical outburst: "You can't learn from the past. The main thing you learn from history is that you can't learn from history. That's what history *is*." Again Mason is stating that answers are not in the past, but perhaps not in the present either.

The stylistic characteristics of *In Country* are the same ones used in Mason's short stories: present tense, realism in a simple style, vivid descriptions, humor. The trip to Washington, covered in the opening and closing chapters that frame the basic story of the novel, is told in present tense; the summer's events that lead to the journey are in the past tense. The brand-name realism is ubiquitous. The descriptions are detailed, vivid, humorous—even if ironical to complement the searching and suffering. Sam listens to her boyfriend's parents discuss plans for a "theme wedding": "Everybody's coming in a jeep." Emmett's friend Pete has a tattoo on his chest: "a map . . . showing the location of his car." Like Mary Sue in "Residents and Transients," Sam, out in the swamp, imagines herself a cat, "small and fragile and very alert to movement, her whiskers flicking and her pupils widening in the dark." So Mason's characters change, adapt, even learn a few things—from their own experiences and perhaps a little from the past.

Like *Shiloh and Other Stories*, *In Country* was immediately successful: 40,000 copies in the first

Bobbie Ann Mason, Talk of the Town

ASBURY PARK, ~~1985~~

Three ladies of our acquaintance motored recently across Maryland and Pennsylvania to the New Jersey shore. The ladies, in summer dresses and ~~Dr. Scholl's~~ sandals, drove down the Garden State Parkway, a pleasant, tree-lined drive, to Exit ~~117~~ /05 and down Route 71 through Asbury Park, Ocean Grove, Belmar, Avon-by-the Sea, and other attractive towns, stopping at a quaint hotel in Spring Lake. The ladies noted how clean and nice the New Jersey shore was. "This is much more tasteful than Ocean City, Maryland," they said.

They were on a pilgrimage. One of the ladies had left her husband *for the weekend* once and flown to Houston ~~just~~ to see a Bruce Springsteen concert. Another one had fainted ~~once~~ at a "Born in the U.S.A." stadium concert in Washington, D.C. And the third ~~one~~ had stood in line all night for Springsteen tickets once, despite chicken pox.

"We're really in New Jersey!" cried the one who had been to Houston. "He has probably been on this highway. His car has no doubt stopped at this stop light!"

A guy behind them was combing his hair in the mirror of his beat-up old Chevy. It looked like him, but it wasn't ~~him.~~

Asbury Park's boardwalk is crumbling, the old Victorian-Art Deco-Colonial splendor, ~~in ruin,~~ *and* some of the shops boarded up. The casino is still alive*ly*, though, its brick building boldly framed by a ~~line~~*chorus*~~up~~ of green tarnished-copper sea monsters (winged horses with flippers and mermaid/tails). After visiting Olympic Bob's Palace ~~of Fun~~ (claustrophobic indoor rides with loud noises and *flashing* lights), the ladies sauntered down the boardwalk in the bright sun. They saw Sandy's Arcade, the convention hall, Ho-Jo's by-the-sea, the nut shops, the

Revised typescript page for a "Talk of the Town" contribution by Mason which appeared in the 15 September 1986 New Yorker

printing, a $40,000 advertising campaign, a Warner Bros. option for a movie, five foreign publishers, and Book-of-the-Month Club adoption. The reviewers praised the same things they had praised in *Shiloh and Other Stories:* intriguing characters, realism, simple style, and humor. Joel Conarroe, in the *New York Times Book Review,* commented on the danger in Mason's "deciding to devote not a short story but a novel to so frugally educated a character," but praised the book for its "disarming simplicity" and "exceptional achievement." In his review in *Time,* Paul Gray was more reserved in his assessment: he thought Sam's search "a bit predictable and repetitious" and the novel "a short story that almost outstays its welcome." But Gray joined other reviewers of this work and the short story collection in praising Mason as a "chronicler of vanishing American enclaves."

Bobbie Ann Mason has certainly realized one of her childhood determinations: "to hit the big time." Like her fictional creation Nancy Culpepper, Mason thinks of a move back to Kentucky, "but it just never worked out. I'd like to, though; I don't want to lose touch with my material." Her interest in the people in her home state persists because "their lives are changing, and they're doing different things, so I think I'll see where they go." Regardless of the move, Mason says, "I plan to be writing stories for a while."

Interviews:

Wendy Smith, "PW Interviews Bobbie Ann Mason," *Publishers Weekly,* 228 (30 August 1985): 424-425;

Enid Shomer, "An Interview with Bobbie Ann Mason," *Black Warrior Review,* 12 (Spring 1986): 87-102.

References:

Nancy Anderson, "Four from the South," *Washington Book Review,* 3 (Spring-Summer 1983): 17, 22;

Edwin T. Arnold, "Falling Apart and Staying Together: Bobbie Ann Mason and Leon Driskell Explore the State of the Modern Family," *Appalachian Journal,* 12 (Winter 1985): 135-141;

R. H. Brinkmeyer, "Finding One's History: Bobbie Ann Mason and Contemporary Southern Literature," *Southern Literary Journal,* 19 (Spring 1987): 20-33;

Anatole Broyard, "Country Fiction," *New York Times Book Review,* 19 December 1982, p. 31;

Andrea Chambers, "Pages Bobbie Ann Mason's *In Country* Evokes the Soul of Kentucky and the Sadness of Vietnam," *People Weekly,* 24 (28 October 1985): 127-129;

Joel Conarroe, "Winning Her Father's War," *New York Times Book Review,* 15 September 1985, p. 7;

Hilary DeVries, "Mining the vagaries of rural America: Bobbie Ann Mason's characters are 'just plain folks' like herself," *Christian Science Monitor,* 20 November 1985, p. 28;

Paul Gray, "Enclaves," *Time,* 126 (16 September 1985): 81;

Tom Jenks, "How Writers Live Today," *Esquire,* 104 (August 1985): 123-124;

David Quammen, "Plain Folk and Puzzling Changes," *New York Times Book Review,* 21 November 1982, pp. 7, 33;

J. D. Reed, "Postfeminism: Playing for Keeps," *Time,* 121 (10 January 1983): 60-61;

Maureen Ryan, "Stopping Places: Bobbie Ann Mason's Short Stories," in *Women Writers of the Contemporary South,* edited by Peggy Whitman Prenshaw (Jackson: University Press of Mississippi, 1984), pp. 283-294;

R. Z. Sheppard, "Neighbors," *Time,* 121 (3 January 1983): 88;

Anne Tyler, "Kentucky Cameos," *New Republic,* 187 (1 November 1982): 36, 38;

A. E. Wilhelm, "Private Rituals: Coping with Change in the Fiction of Bobbie Ann Mason," *Midwest Quarterly,* 28 (Winter 1987): 271-282;

"A Writer's Desk: Bobbie Ann Mason," *Saturday Review,* 11 (November/December 1985): 80;

Ben Yagoda, "No Tense Like the Present," *New York Times Book Review,* 10 August 1986, pp. 1, 30.

Michael A. McCollum

(25 August 1946-   )

William J. Scheick
University of Texas at Austin

BOOKS: *A Greater Infinity* (New York: Ballantine, 1982);
Life Probe (New York: Ballantine, 1983);
Procyon's Promise (New York: Ballantine, 1985);
Antares Dawn (New York: Ballantine, 1986);
Antares Passage (New York: Ballantine, 1987).

PERIODICAL PUBLICATIONS:
FICTION
"Duty, Honor, Planet," *Analog*, 99 (April 1979): 10-35;
"Scoop," *Isaac Asimov's Science Fiction Magazine*, 3 (June 1979): 116-139;
"Beer Run," *Analog*, 99 (July 1979): 112-132;
"A Greater Infinity," *Analog*, 100 (November 1980): 10-54;
"Gift," *Analog*, 100 (December 1980): 106-123;
"The Shroud," *Analog*, 101 (2 March 1981): 90-100;
"Which Way to the Ends of Time?," *Analog*, 101 (17 August 1981): 14-64;
"Who Will Guard the Guardians?," with Catherine McCollum, *Analog*, 102 (14 October 1982): 150-162;
"Life Probe," *Amazing Stories*, 56 (January 1983): 104-115.
NONFICTION
"The Disposal of Nuclear Waste in Space: Will It Ever Be Feasible?," *Analog*, 98 (March 1978): 35-49.

Michael McCollum

Born and raised in Phoenix, Arizona, Michael McCollum is a graduate of Arizona State University, from which he received a Bachelor of Science degree in engineering in 1969, with a concentration in aerospace propulsion and in nuclear engineering. An avid science fiction reader, he had become interested in the aerospace industry before attending college, and after graduation he was employed as an aerospace engineer by Pratt and Whitney Aircraft at the Florida Research and Development Center.

He resided for three years in Florida and took a few graduate courses at the University of Florida Extension Center in West Palm Beach. On a trip home to Phoenix he met and married Catharine Cannon, whom he describes as "a hometown girl," on 4 March 1972. He returned with his wife to Arizona to work for the AiResearch Manufacturing Company, now known as Garrett Fluid Systems Division, where he is currently employed as a third level engineering supervisor. In the course of his career as an engineer he has worked on most military and civilian aircraft in production today, including the classified Air Force rocket engine on which the Space Shuttle main engine design is based.

Residing in Tempe, Arizona, Michael and Catherine McCollum have three children: Robert, Michael, and Elizabeth. Although in the past McCollum has vigorously pursued flying, skydiving, and scuba diving, he has recently, as an adjunct to his writing, become interested in microcomputing. He now principally concentrates on engineering and on writing science fiction.

McCollum believes that his fiction participates in the "hard science" tradition of Robert Heinlein and Larry Niven; that is, he prefers to center his stories around a scientifically technical lynchpin and then to be rigorous in the extrapolation of whatever scientific assumption he makes. For example, in *Life Probe* (1983) he postulated an intelligent machine waking up one light-month from Earth. Since faster-than-light communication is not possible, he was forced to plot the novel so that the probe and the humans do not have to talk directly to each other until the probe actually takes up an orbit around the sun. The reason for this is the difficulty of holding a conversation with a lag of thirty days between comments. As the probe gets closer to the solar system the time for a round-trip message decreases. Consequently, in the dates given for various events in the book the proper time delay has been taken into account. McCollum used a computer printout showing the probe's position on each day, how long it would take a message to get from the probe to Earth, and how long it would take for the return message to reach the probe.

In 1979 McCollum published his first story, which provided the basis for the cover of the April issue of *Analog* and which still remains the author's favorite work. This story, "Duty, Honor, Planet," is set in the future, when Mexico tries to provoke concessions from an environmentally sensitive United States by using nuclear weapons to destroy several national parks. The head of the United Nations, which has become more determined to enforce peace in the world, fears that the breakout of war between America and Mexico would lead to worldwide devastation. The Secretary General of the United Nations and the President of the United States covertly plot to have the central character, Frederich Stassel, stationed in a patrolling satellite. They predict that if Stassel were faced with a Mexican attempt to destroy Havasu Falls in the Grand Canyon (which

Stassel associates with sad memories of his deceased lover), he would, and in fact does, disobey an order to refrain from interfering; and they predict, correctly, that Stassel's unsanctioned, independent action would break a deadlock in the United Nations and would preserve world peace by insuring an end to Mexican aggression against the United States.

The secretary general and the president believe that Stassel is like his father, "who did his duty as he saw it and worried about following orders later." This self-reliant independence of mind is the chief attribute generally of McCollum's protagonists. Stassel and his later avatars in McCollum's fiction are mythic American prototypes, antinomian heroes who possess a freedom of mind and an internal conviction necessary to the health and development of the human race.

This individualist type appears as well in *A Greater Infinity* (1982), a novel based on three stories: "Beer Run" (1979), "A Greater Infinity" (1980), and "Which Way to the Ends of Time?" (1981), and first published in *Analog*. This book concerns the adventures of Duncan MacElroy, the narrator, whose role in the future causes him to be pursued by the Dalgiri, a race of warriors who, in another timeline, descended from the Neanderthals and who have, for one thousand years, been trying to dominate the humans of other timelines, of which they have added twelve to their empire. Discovering that his life is at stake, MacElroy decides to join the humans of the Talador timeline, where there is a confederation of thirty-two alternate universes in resistance to the Dalgiri and where he is trained at the Time Watch Academy. MacElroy's destiny, so feared by the Dalgiri, is fulfilled when he leads the Taladorans to a new gateway to another cluster of timelines that the Dalgiri had wanted for themselves.

MacElroy possesses an autonomy of mind that makes him a special, driving force among the Taladorans. This attribute differentiates the many timeline variants of humanity from the Homo sapiens of MacElroy's and the reader's world. Although in all its alternate versions "the human mind is a wondrous machine," MacElroy is certain that the human race of his and our timeline has "something unique": an autarchic quality greater in degree than in any other version of mankind.

To the advantage of the human race of MacElroy's alternate universe is the fact that it

Cover for McCollum's second work, built upon the theme that mankind does not always use its richness of mind in meeting the challenges posed by the frontier of space

has never been handicapped by the discovery of gateways and timelines; and MacElroy is relentless in his resistance to the Taladorans' wish to add his world to their confederation. MacElroy realizes that the knowledge of crosstime travel has short-circuited any thought of space exploration in the other timelines; and the exploration of infinite space as a way to resolve the problem of diminishing resources, provides a crucial stimulus to evoke the independence of mind characteristic of humanity in MacElroy's world. He explains to the Taladorans, "You talk so blithely of the endlessness of Paratime. You have no true concept of infinity until you've spent a cold winter's night staring into the eyepiece of a telescope. . . . Alternate universes may be infinite in number, but space . . . that is the greater infinity."

This greater infinity stimulates "something unique" in the self-reliance of the humanity of MacElroy's timeline because it serves as a challenging frontier. "Spreading into space, pushing back a frontier which [the Taladorans] never realized existed," the humanity of MacElroy's universe evinces a special ingenuity in its new ideas. It is this uniqueness that MacElroy both evidences in himself and preserves by protecting his world from exposure to the knowledge of Paratime.

A Greater Infinity did not receive very much critical attention. One complaint did surface: that MacElroy is too adolescent in his thinking and behavior to be a successful protagonist. On the positive side, however, there was agreement among some critics that MacElroy's narrative is a satisfying thriller.

The fear in *A Greater Infinity*, that something could happen to the humanity of MacElroy's timeline so that it might lose its uniqueness of self-sufficiently generating new ideas in response to frontier challenges, informs "Gift" (1980), a story somewhat propagandistic in its argument against solar energy. This story concerns R. J. Cowen, a business tycoon who got rich by helping an apparently stranded alien in exchange for the secret of how to use solar energy as a resource for power. Thirty years later he again meets this alien, who is now on a pilgrimage of atonement and who tells Cowen that when they first met he had not been stranded but had been sent to keep humanity bound to its solar system. Because of the sheer efficiency of solar power the people of earth stopped all nuclear research, with the result that the human race is bound to the sun as a source of power, and therefore has never been able to explore more than the inner planets of the solar system. Humanity has thus never become a problem for the aliens. Realizing now what the absence of the frontier of infinite space has meant, Cowen resolves to spend his fortune in an effort to reclaim this frontier and to stimulate again the uniqueness of the human mind. "The honor of the human race is at stake," Cowen says; at stake is "our innate knowledge that we are the best people in the whole damned universe."

Cowen's sentiment about mankind is identical to that of Fria in "Who Will Guard the Guardians?" (1982), a story written by McCollum in collaboration with his wife, Catherine. Having lived alone for more than four centuries, Fria is one of fifty overseers at command centers on earth; she and the others watch for the possible return of aliens who long ago devastated human civilization. She is lonely and depressed, but in her eventual replacement, Amber, she discovers energizing maternal feelings and a renewed hope in the ability of mankind to use its uniqueness of mind to spring back in response to the frontier-like challenge of the aliens: "Humanity was down, but not out."

That mankind does not always use its richness of mind in meeting such challenges is a theme of *Life Probe*. In this novel Eric Stassel (the grandson of the protagonist in "Duty, Honor, Planet") is a member of the United Nations Peace Enforcement Directorate, an international military force dedicated to the prevention of global war. The likeliness of this war increases with the arrival of an alien-crafted probe moving toward the solar system. Stassel hopes that in the long run the probe will aid in the maintenance of world peace, but in the short run it causes the Pan-Africans to fear that the white races will use the probe to subjugate them and, consequently, causes the Pan-Africans to engage their illegal warships in a battle with Stassel's forces. Aided by the probe, Stassel defeats the Pan-African ships, but the probe is also destroyed.

The probe, however, had constructed an electronic surrogate human brain, and this surrogate survives the destruction of the probe. At first the surrogate wants to self-destruct, because without the probe it cannot complete its and the probe's mission: to find for the Makers, who built the probe, a race which has discovered faster-than-light flight. The Makers need this knowledge because their stellar system is running low on the raw materials needed to sustain their civilization. Stassel convinces the surrogate that humans can aid it in completing its search. Together they oversee the construction of *Pathfinder*, a slower-than-light starship to be sent to Procyon, where the probe suspected an answer would be found.

Stassel is as much an individualist as his grandfather, the protagonist of McCollum's first story. He combines a sense of duty to society with an independence of mind. He is like the Makers, "a race that has learned the advantages of peace, yet still retains a healthy competitive spirit." Ideally, McCollum suggests, mankind, in spite of its heritage of a violent nature, will one day manage to combine racial duty and individual competitiveness; indeed, as a sign that humanity is headed in the right direction, McCollum emphasizes the importance of the United Nations

as an organization benefiting the human race (social duty), but headed by people like Stassel (independent, competitive spirit). For McCollum, world peace is not (like fear) an impediment to individual self-reliance, but rather an empowering matrix enabling the human mind to realize the rewards of a "healthy self-interest, driving curiosity, and . . . competitiveness."

If world peace nourishes these qualities, a sense of frontier stimulates them into expression. The Makers need faster-than-light flight in order to benefit (in raw materials and in spirit) from a sense of a frontier; having exhausted its stellar system, the Makers' race "gazes outward with longing." Faster-than-light flight will open up the greater infinity of the universe, without access to which humanity will become like the Makers, a people "locked into a vast cage," the cage of "Einstein's barrier." As Stassel says, "Our only real chance for survival is to get out among the stars"; "if we stay in this one system we will surely destroy ourselves." Stassel refers not only to the eventual exhaustion of resources but also to the ways in which human self-interest, curiosity, and competitiveness are unhealthily and destructively turned inward upon mankind itself when no challenging frontier exists to turn these attributes creatively outward. Stassel is interested in "what the race can accomplish when faced with a worthwhile challenge," with the sort of new starry frontier to be entered by *Pathfinder* in search of other life.

Although Roland Green complained in *Booklist* (August 1983) that *Life Probe* is unoriginal in plot and characterization, most critics agreed with Jeff Clark in the *Library Journal* (15 June 1983) that the story is competent, even clever, and that it holds the reader's interest. Tom Easton thought that the threads of the plot are enjoyably interwoven and the characters are interestingly developed. Whereas another critic thought that the novel evidenced scientific savvy, Easton doubted that small black holes could power spacecraft, though he conceded that the future depicted in the novel might well come to pass.

Whereas *Life Probe* fared rather well with critics, *Procyon's Promise* (1985) was somewhat less fortunate. For some reviewers, like the anonymous evaluator for *Publishers Weekly* (28 June 1985), the later novel told a rousing and clever story as good as its predecessor. Nevertheless complaints against the book included thin characterization and weakness in plot as two chief defects. In Tom Easton's opinion *Procyon's Promise* is not only

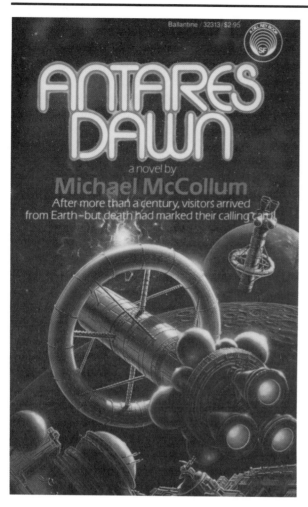

Cover for McCollum's 1986 novel about the attempts of the inhabitants of a colonized planet, cut off from fellow human contact, to reestablish ties to Earth

anticlimatic, with an unsurprising conclusion, but it is also a work which cannot be appreciated independently from *Life Probe*.

Set about three hundred years later than *Life Probe*, *Procyon's Promise* concerns humanity's discovery that Procyon had been only an outpost for a race with faster-than-light flight and that these visitors have departed. A discarded message is found, however, and from its information a faster-than-light starship, *Procyon's Promise*, is built. This vessel returns to earth, where unrest subsequently develops among some who fear what might happen if the Makers were to be given mankind's knowledge of interstellar flight. An attempt to capture *Procyon's Promise* by the ruling political body (the Communion) on earth is foiled by the starship's sentient computer, which later guides the vessel to the stellar system of the Makers. The Makers, having already found the secret, have left their system for new starry hori-

zons, and in fact, were themselves visitors to Procyon.

These horizons are important, as Chryse Haller (McCollum's self-reliant individualist) knows. Early in the novel she remarks how the "human race is suffering from claustrophobia"; "we're bored with life. The sense of adventure has left us. There aren't any frontiers left." At the end of the novel she explains to Captain Robert Braedon, who is depressed over the absence of the Makers, "Far from being wasted, your struggle has succeeded beyond your wildest dreams! You've undergone a test of strength, passed gloriously, and will now reap the rewards of victory." Not only has Braedon evinced a self-sufficient individualism in overcoming frontierlike obstacles, but he has liberated "starbound" humanity by making available "the sort of challenge the human race needed." As Haller uses "one hand to sweep the horizon," she tells Braedon that the earth now has "an entire universe to explore," a new frontier of "unlimited expansion" where human self-interest, curiosity, and competitiveness can be directed away from mankind, who experience these attributes as destructive detriments when the race lacks a sense of adventure among new possibilities.

For McCollum, and as the computer of *Procyon's Promise* warns, these human attributes should ideally be balanced with a social concern for the race, with a quest for integration through peace both within mankind and, later, between star civilizations. With peace at home and infinity abroad, human attributes should be directed away from mankind and outwardly toward distant starry horizons, where these same attributes can be creatively stimulated into expressing frontierlike new ideas, which (for McCollum) embody the wonderful uniqueness of the autonomous human mind.

This creative kind of peace is absent in *Antares Dawn* (1986). In this novel a claustrophobic tranquillity exists on Alta, a colonized planet of the star Valeria whose inhabitants have been cut off from fellow human contact because its foldpoint–the means of travel between the stars–disappeared 125 years ago when Antares exploded. Suddenly, in 2637, a large military spaceship (ironically named *Conqueror*) appears in the Altan system, but it is a battered hulk containing several dead Earthmen. On the one hand the Altans are pleased by the arrival of this wreck because it means that once again they have a foldpoint and so should be able to regain contact with Earth; on the other hand the Altans are worried by the possibility that whatever destroyed the mystery ship might at any time flash into their system and easily destroy the colony.

The colony sends Richard Drake, commanding officer of the Altan Space Navy Cruiser *Discovery*, to lead an expedition through the foldpoint back to Earth. During his journey Drake finds that New Providence, the planet of the star Napier, is totally dead, devastated by nuclear weapons. From data found in a university library on this world, Drake learns of attacks on the colony by the Ryall, competitive reptilian aliens obsessed with the destruction of humanity, which have gained access to human space as a result of new foldspace interconnections after Antares went supernova. Drake pushes on, in spite of some resistance from several of his passengers, and arrives at Sandarson's World, a colony of the star Hellsgate that, like Alta, has been cut off from Earth. This colony is locked in a century-long, losing battle with the Ryall, but with Drake's help the Sandarians repulse the worst assault on them to date. Drake now plans to return to Alta, where a ship will be built that can pass through the highly radiated foldpoint in the Antares Nebula, a foldpoint which Drake believes the mystery ship used and he too can use in reaching Earth.

Richard Drake is a typical McCollum protagonist, an individualist whose self-reliance makes him a strong leader. His personal attributes were nurtured on Alta, "a frontier world"; as is evident in other of McCollum's stories, such frontier settings provide challenging conditions that stimulate the best qualities of the human mind. Something vital to this frontier status of Alta is threatened by the colony's "long isolation" following the explosion of Antares, but the reopening of its single foldpoint means that "Altan society, in near stasis for more than a century, would come alive again." This potential restoration of a frontier sensibility lies at the heart of Drake's rejec-

tion of arguments that he should retreat from contact with the Ryall and "return to [Alta's] pre-*Conqueror* isolation." As Drake's lover pertinently remarks, "human beings weren't meant to be cooped-up in a single star system"; they need "the freedom of the stars," a frontier freedom eliciting humanity's best characteristics.

Here as elsewhere McCollum indicates that the interaction between a frontier and the human mind can lead humanity to a salutary peace quite different from a cooped up stasis, a peace informing the creative management of inquisitiveness, self-interest, and rivalry. The ideal of this sort of peace counters the Ryall's perversion of such features of the mind as self-interest and competitiveness in their unquestioned, paranoid "assumption that conflict between . . . species is inevitable." Drake's quest for this fulfillment of human destiny continues in *Antares Passage*, a sequel published in December 1987.

References:

Tom Easton, "The Reference Library," *Analog*, 103 (December 1983): 162; 106 (February 1986): 181;

Jay Kay Klein, "Biolog," *Analog*, 100 (November 1980): 53.

Author's Note: The philosophy of my books, if any, is that the human race must either expand or die. If peace among humans results from this expansion, it's because we will be too busy fighting nature (or aliens) to squabble with one another. Furthermore, as noted in the essay, we are the best damned people in the universe!

It should be noted, however, that both of these ideas are the result of my personal taste in fiction. I enjoy stories that end on an optimistic, looking-to-the-future note. Also, stories in which human beings do not triumph eventually over the aliens are not particularly popular. The readers are, after all, only human!

Jill McCorkle

(7 July 1958-   )

Ann DeWitt Moss
Algonquin Books of Chapel Hill

BOOKS: *The Cheer Leader* (Chapel Hill, N.C.: Algonquin Books, 1984);

July 7th (Chapel Hill, N.C.: Algonquin Books, 1984);

Tending to Virginia (Chapel Hill, N.C.: Algonquin Books, 1987).

The beginning of Jill McCorkle's career as a fiction writer is unusual, probably unparalleled by any other young writer. In what is believed to be a "first" in book-publishing history, Algonquin Books of Chapel Hill brought out two novels by this hitherto unpublished novelist in the fall of 1984. McCorkle began to receive attention in 1980, when she won the Jessie Rehder Award for a short story published in the Spring 1980 issue of *Cellar Door*, a magazine produced by undergraduate writing students at the University of North Carolina at Chapel Hill. McCorkle graduated from UNC with highest honors in creative writing in 1980. At Hollins College, where she earned a Master of Arts degree in creative writing in 1981, she was awarded the Andrew James Purdy Fiction Prize for her graduate work.

Jill Collins McCorkle was born in Lumberton, North Carolina, to Melba Collins McCorkle and John Wesley McCorkle, Jr. After completing her studies, she moved to New York and worked as an office receptionist. While in New York she wrote *The Cheer Leader* (1984). She completed *July 7th* (1984) in Florida, where she worked as an acquisitions librarian from 1982 to 1984, when she returned to Chapel Hill and took a job as a secretary at the university medical school. In 1986 she accepted a lectureship in creative writing at UNC Chapel Hill. McCorkle has also taught at Duke University in the continuing education program, and she is currently teaching creative writing at Tufts University.

McCorkle had always "liked to write, wanted to write, and, in fact, did write." She was seven when she wrote her first short story and she remembers writing what she describes as "some pretty embarrassing poems," but she really "got hooked" on writing when she was a sophomore in college. In her first formal writing class under the guidance of Max Steele, her efforts were exposed to others as they had not been before. Professor Steele's encouragement became the inspiration McCorkle never anticipated, the push she needed to get started. At the same time, however, he made her very aware that she may never publish, that writing was a very competitive business. His admonishments, she felt, were positive; he always reminded her that she had to love the process enough to see it through without regard for editorial criticism. The most important aspect of Steele's introduction to "being a writer" was his insistence that she write for herself first. McCorkle says that he gave her "the sense that it was mine, and that stuck with me. I think, having grasped that idea, I got going. I knew I could do it. At least I wanted to try."

Others in the English department at UNC heightened McCorkle's awareness of what she could do; they strengthened the confidence she needed to write "for herself." Among them was Lee Smith, now a professor at North Carolina State University. McCorkle remembers becoming aware that "Lee wrote about the kinds of things I was interested in anyway. Lee was normal in terms of her life and the way she acted. From her I learned that what I knew was important, that I could write about what I knew and make it interesting. I guess I began to realize that I had something to say. She taught me that."

When McCorkle was admitted to Professor Louis Rubin's honors class in the creative writing program, she admits that she was terrified (Rubin has edited and written a number of books, both fiction and nonfiction). McCorkle says, "Dr. Rubin was different. I never felt he made it easy for me; therefore, when I got his attention and his affirmation, it was a major accomplishment."

People have often asked McCorkle, as they do all authors, when she first thought of herself as a writer, and she quickly replies, "When I pub-

Jill McCorkle

lished. Before that I didn't feel that I deserved to call myself a writer." Her first piece of published fiction, a short story, appeared in the Fall 1979 issue of *Cellar Door*. "Mrs. Lela's Fig Tree" concerns the innocence and sensitivity of a young girl whose relationship with her next door neighbor forces her to respect the responsibilities of growing up at the same time she experiences the whimsical romances of youth. McCorkle's depictions of both the young girl and older woman are overwhelming in their accuracy. Later, in October 1984, *Seventeen* magazine republished the story as "The Spell of the Beautiful Garden."

McCorkle's second published story, "Bare Facts," earned her the Jesse Rehder Prize for Fiction. In this story are perhaps the origins of character types that reappear in McCorkle's later, more mature fiction. Here it is already evident that McCorkle is an acute observer as she presents predicaments of ordinary people.

The first issue of the *Crescent Review* (Fall 1983), a magazine begun by writers and devotees in Winston-Salem, North Carolina, included McCorkle's story "Carson," which drew favorable responses from readers. Carson's limited intelligence allows him only a confused memory, yet he has strong feelings, the source of which he does not comprehend. His inability to understand the world he lives in and the reader's ability to do so develop into a compassionate, touching tale of human frailty. "Carson" was previously published in the 1981 issue of *Cargoes* at Hollins College.

Having two novels published simultaneously caused a considerable amount of attention to be focused on McCorkle, including a prominent review by Annie Gottlieb in the 7 October 1984 *New York Times Book Review*. *The Cheer Leader*, McCorkle's "first" novel, is about Jo Spencer, a young woman who grows up bright, happy, pretty, and popular in a small town in North Carolina. Jo Spencer is the kind of girl who knows just what to be and what to do. Cheerleader, May Queen, straight-A student, popular and cute and virginal and in perfect control of her life, she is, in her own words, "fit." However, one summer at Moon Lake, Red Williams enters her controlled world. He has "Been Places" and "Done Things." Red is older, more experienced, utterly different from all that Jo Spencer has known. Loving Red, or wanting to, she begins to lose that "perfect control." The swirl of the changes that the lazy-starting North Carolina summer brings, the accelerating pace and intensifying pressure to be what Red desires as well as what her family and friends expect of her, ultimately spin Jo out of "fitness" altogether, until halfway through her first year at college her careful, normal life explodes.

Gottlieb, in her *New York Times Book Review* piece, described the novel thus: "Angst is what *The Cheer Leader* is all about. . . . Jo's first love affair, with a 'wild' older boy whom she naively believes loves her, leads to a horrified sense of betrayal, an anorexic breakdown in her first year of college and finally a tentative recovery." Gottlieb, like other reviewers, noted that the plot is familiar, that Jo Spencer's story recalls that of nineteen-year-old Esther Greenwood in Sylvia Plath's *The Bell Jar* (1963), which McCorkle acknowledges in the novel. But McCorkle's skill moves her work beyond the familiar plot.

A gifted storyteller, Jill McCorkle reveals in *The Cheer Leader* what it means to have grown up in years so recently gone by that their dynamics and patterns have not yet been fully explored. Slumber parties and dope parties, the age of songs such as "Dizzy" by Tommy Roe and television comedies like "I Dream of Jeannie," the coming-of-age rituals of a town in the late 1960s and early 1970s–the seemingly trite made suddenly startling–take on a memorable clarity of definition in this remarkable work.

In *July 7th* McCorkle portrays another teenager suffering from adolescent angst. This novel, like *The Cheer Leader*, revolves around young people. However, Sam Swett, a young writer-hitchhiker, offers a more satisfying artistic solution. He lands in Marshboro, North Carolina, after having courted madness and alcoholism in New York, where he failed "to find out what it is I want to do with my life." Sam Swett resembles Jo in being a child of relative privilege, without genuine problems, yet, as Madison Smartt Bell pointed out in the Summer 1985 issue of *Quarterly West*, "he has a crushing burden of unjusti-

Dust jacket for McCorkle's 1984 novel about a girl coming of age in the late 1960s

fied *angst*." Bell further noted that "*July 7th* is strikingly different from *The Cheer Leader* in structure." He calls *July 7th* a "technical *tour de force*." In the short span of twenty-four hours the reader is introduced to at least twenty different residents of Marshboro. Just after midnight, beginning at the Quik Pik, a convenience store near the interstate, the seventh of July began turning into the kind of day that the town of Marshboro would long remember.

Charlie Husky, the late-night clerk, was found facedown next to the Slurpee machine, suffocated with saran wrap. The murder and the ensuing events of the next twenty-four hours involve the reader in the life of this small North Carolina town in a delightful novel of zany comedy and abrupt pathos.

Pure chance has dumped twenty-one-year-old Sam Swett in the Quik Pik at the time of the murder. Sam has shaved his head, given away everything he owns except his typewriter, is drunker than he has ever been in his life, and is running away as fast as he can from his family and upper-middle-class upbringing. Chance, too, deposits Harold Weeks in the back room, passed out from the effects of another bad night after leaving his wife Juanita. Soon the reader meets Juanita Suggs Weeks, the unforgettable, sexy electrologist who loves Harold passionately; Ernie Stubbs, who has "Made It" into the most expensive subdivision in town, though he is not as far from his upbringing on Injun Street as he imagines; and Corky Revels, the strange, timid waitress at the Coffee Shop whose sorrowful past keeps her from present happiness–until, maybe, this unusual summer day.

Two of the most remarkable presences in Jill McCorkle's fine novel are Granner Weeks and Fannie McNair. These women, holding their families together with tough persistence, know instinctively what the others have still to learn–that people learn to live by living with each other. McCorkle has an extraordinary skill for detailing individual lives and showing how they join to form the collective life of Marshboro, North Carolina.

It is at Granner Weeks's birthday party, on the seventh of July, that events begin to unfold which solve the murder mystery and bring the characters to recognize what human beings should be and what they sometimes are. Sam Swett wonders how he can write it all down as he has planned to do without really knowing and understanding, but he *has* learned from what happened and from the people he has met. This novel shows that McCorkle does know and understand. She sees and hears clearly; she captures the exact tone; she provides the right detail. Unlike Sam, McCorkle has written it all down.

Novelist Elizabeth Spencer has commented that "Jill McCorkle emerges as a strong new Southern writer, with the gratifying gift of both seeing and telling it like it is. She is up to dealing with a rich range of characters, whom she knows both inside and outside, and who come across as living people." According to Lee Smith, "Jill McCorkle has left the old stereotypes dead under the magnolias as she stakes out her own territory: the New South with its subdivisions and Winn Dixies and country music, lovesick electrolysists and dope-smoking cheerleaders and swinging town cops, its tricky new racial and social balances. It's scary the way she invades her characters, writing so closely to them that the books seem to happen inside your head."

Both *The Cheer Leader* and *July 7th* received positive reviews in major newspapers across the United States. When asked how she handled the

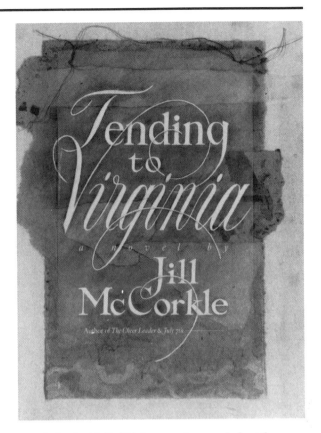

Dust jacket for McCorkle's latest work, a novel about three generations of a family whose lives have been centered in a small town undergoing change and growth as part of the New South

excitement of achieving a place on the national literary scene, McCorkle replied, "I was out of my mind happy, but also scared. I decided the best way to keep my composure was to pretend that it hadn't happened, so I just kept on writing."

McCorkle's third novel, *Tending to Virginia*, was published in the fall of 1987. It is a novel about heritage, about three generations of a family whose lives have been centered in a small town that undergoes change and growth as part of the New South. It is a novel about female secrets and female bonds, laced with humor, mystery, and insight.

Tending to Virginia is primarily the story of Virginia Turner Ballard, known to her North Carolina relatives as Ginny Sue. It is also the story of her mother, her grandmother, her great aunts, her closest cousin–three generations of women who gather around Virginia to help her at the end of a hard pregnancy, to tend to her, to help her prepare for the fourth generation.

This kind of family attendance offers the occasion for reviving and trading entwined family stories. *Tending to Virginia* is a novel of one family's most important stories—how they happened, how they were perceived, how remembered, how their truth is revealed.

Virginia asks her grandmother if her marriage was always happy. She asks her mother if she has been content with her life in this tiny town. She asks her aunt if a childless marriage was her choice. She asks her cousin if sex is all that matters. She asks herself if she loves her young husband.

The answers evolve. The automatic "Yes, always" is elaborated and embroidered upon as old truths, packed away in memory for decades, are uncovered. In a remarkable final scene, an eruption of family confessions becomes revelation— revelation as legacy, passed down among a family's women. In her characterizations of these vivid women playing out their generational roles in the contemporary South, Jill McCorkle presents powerful insight—that the strongest family bonds are, for better or for worse, as often created by what has been held back as by what has been spoken.

Tending to Virginia received front-page attention in the *New York Times Book Review* (1 October 1987). Alice McDermott wrote that "it is the talking—the perfect dialogue, the vivid recollections, the memories and emotions that in the end will not fit neatly into the shape of its plot—that make *Tending to Virginia* so rewarding. And it is Jill McCorkle's skillful use of voice . . . that distinguishes the work of this young chronicler of the new South." A reviewer for the *San Francisco Chronicle* (22 November 1987) describes McCorkle's third novel as one "to be remembered and celebrated."

McCorkle married Dr. Daniel Shapiro on 23 May 1987, and the couple recently moved to Boston where Shapiro is performing his residency. McCorkle is working on the beginnings of two novels and a collection of short stories. No doubt, she will continue to move beyond her own expectations and maintain her acclaim. Readers will continue to hear the voices of her fiction long into the future.

Richard Stern

(25 February 1928-   )

James Schiffer
Hampden-Sydney College

BOOKS: *Golk* (New York: Criterion, 1960; London: MacGibbon & Kee, 1960);

Europe: Or Up and Down with Schreiber and Baggish (New York: McGraw-Hill, 1961); republished as *Europe: Or Up and Down with Baggish and Schreiber* (London: MacGibbon & Kee, 1962);

In Any Case (New York: McGraw-Hill, 1962; London: MacGibbon & Kee, 1963); republished as *The Chaleur Network* (New York: Second Chance Press, 1981; London: Sidgewick & Jackson, 1981);

Teeth, Dying and Other Matters (New York: Harper & Row, 1964; London: MacGibbon & Kee, 1964);

Stitch (New York: Harper & Row, 1965; London: Hodder & Stoughton, 1967);

1968: A Short Novel, An Urban Idyll, Five Stories, and Two Trade Notes (New York: Holt, Rinehart & Winston, 1970; London: Gollancz, 1971);

The Books in Fred Hampton's Apartment (New York: Dutton, 1973; London: Hamish Hamilton, 1974);

Other Men's Daughters (New York: Dutton, 1973; London: Hamish Hamilton, 1974);

Natural Shocks (New York: Coward, McCann & Geoghegan, 1978; London: Sidgewick & Jackson, 1978);

Packages (New York: Coward, McCann & Geoghegan, 1980; London: Sidgewick & Jackson, 1980);

The Invention of the Real (Athens: University of Georgia Press, 1982);

A Father's Words (New York: Arbor House, 1986);

The Position of the Body (Evanston, Ill.: Northwestern University Press, 1986).

OTHER: "American Poetry of the Fifties," edited by Stern, *Western Review*, 21 (Spring 1957): 164-238;

Honey and Wax: Pleasures and Powers of Narrative, edited by Stern, illustrated by Joan Fitzgerald

Richard Stern (photograph by Layle Silbert)

(Chicago & London: University of Chicago Press, 1966).

PERIODICAL PUBLICATIONS:
FICTION
"In the Dock," *Triquarterly*, 60 (Spring/Summer 1984): 177-192;

"Losing Color," *Antioch Review*, 44 (Winter 1986): 40-41.

NONFICTION
"Hip, Hell and the Navigator," *Western Review*, 23 (Spring 1959): 101-109; republished in *Ad-*

vertisements for Myself, by Norman Mailer (New York: Putnam's, 1959);

"Lillian Hellman on her Plays," *Contact,* 3 (1959): 113-119;

"That Same Pain, That Same Pleasure: An Interview with Ralph Ellison," *December,* 3 (Winter 1961): 30-46; republished in *Shadow and Act,* by Ellison (New York: Random House, 1963);

"Penned In," *Critical Inquiry,* 13 (Fall 1986): 1-32.

In a recent essay in *Critical Inquiry* on the forty-eighth P.E.N conference Richard Stern remarks parenthetically that he has been "for twenty years almost celebrated for being uncelebrated." The comment, sadly, is more than a little true. Since 1960 Stern has published an impressive list of novels, short story collections, and "orderly miscellanies"; yet his work has not to date brought him the kind of following that has greeted his closest literary friends, Saul Bellow and Philip Roth. With the exception of *Other Men's Daughters* (1973) none of his books has reached a wide audience, or at least as wide an audience as Stern would like. "I wish my books were distributed in the A & P," he said in a 1978 interview. "I wish millions of people would like them." There is still hope. All of Stern's novels published in the 1960s and 1970s (except *Europe: Or Up and Down with Schreiber and Baggish,* 1961) have been republished in paperback editions over the last six years, and in 1988 Grove Press will bring out his collected stories. Given the complexity of Stern's vision, however, his work is likely to remain unsung in the homes of most average American readers.

If Stern has not exactly wooed the masses, he has at least often delighted many of the best writers and critics of our time. Indeed, the authors quoted on the dust jackets of his books constitute a virtual Who's Who of twentieth-century letters: first and foremost, of course, Bellow and Roth and Bernard Malamud (what Bellow has jokingly called the "Hart, Schaffner, and Marx" of contemporary literature–Malamud was Schaffner), but also Flannery O'Connor, Anthony Burgess, Richard Ellmann, George P. Elliot, Joan Didion, Thomas Berger, Norman Mailer, Hugh Kenner, and John Cheever, to name just a few. In addition, Stern has held Fulbright, Guggenheim, and Rockefeller fellowships, and his fiction has won numerous awards, including those from the Longwood Foundation, the American Library Association, the Illinois Arts Council, and the Na-

tional Council on Arts and Humanities. His novel *Natural Shocks* (1978) won the Carl Sandburg Award for Fiction in 1979, and in 1985 Stern was awarded the Medal of Merit for the Novel by the American Academy and Institute of Arts and Letters. Not bad for a writer who once described himself as a "has-been without ever having been a been."

Stern was born and raised in New York City, the son of Marion Veit and Henry George Stern, both assimilated children of immigrant German Jews. According to his son, Henry Stern was a "natural storyteller" as well as a moderately prosperous dentist (among his patients were Isadora Duncan and Catherine Cushing, author of the play *Pollyanna*); there was also money, evidently, on the Veit side of the family. It was a comfortable childhood. "My parents," Stern writes, "were large-minded and puzzled enough to permit their hard-nosed little *Wunderkind* to set up his cave of books and records amidst the aunts and roasts, suffering a temper which sent him at six under the bed for days, at twelve into occasional weeks of silence." Life outside the cave of books included walks in Central Park with world-renowned pianist Artur Schnabel, whom young Stern pestered because Schnabel claimed that only Germans could play Beethoven correctly.

At sixteen, rejected by Harvard and Yale, Stern entered the University of North Carolina at Chapel Hill, where he continued to read deeply and where he nurtured his childhood dream of becoming an author. He became good friends with fellow student-poets Donald Justice and Edgar Bowers. "I wasn't in their class," Stern says, "but they treated me as a fellow poet, and I went on for years writing some poetry. But I made a decision. Or an internal decision was made by my small talent. So I've written only one or two poems a year since then. . . . The little poetry I write is totally different from my fiction. It's more conspicuously formal, as if I'm tying up some loose ends, shaving some stray hairs from my expressive life."

In 1947 Stern received his B.A. and was inducted into Phi Beta Kappa. Bowers and Justice headed west to study with Yvor Winters at Stanford, while Stern stayed east and "proved incompetent" at three jobs, one of them with Paramount International Films in New York. A year in the work-a-day world was enough to send him back to school, this time to Harvard, where he received his M.A. in English in 1949 and also won a Bowdoin Prize for criticism. Harvard and

Stern's mother, Marion Veit Stern (courtesy of the author)

Cambridge would later be the setting for *Other Men's Daughters.*

Stern spent the next three years in Europe, an experience that provided the physical, cultural, and literary background for three of his first four novels and a number of his early short stories. Living in postwar Europe was "consistently pleasurable," he has written, because he enjoyed being "that least penalized of outsiders of the early 1950s, the American Abroad." His first European year he taught at the Collège Jules Ferry in Versailles. The next fall Stern held an appointment as *Lektor* at the University of Heidelberg and moonlighted evenings as a cable clerk for the occupation army. During the final year in Europe Stern worked in Frankfurt as a U.S. Army Educational Adviser, teaching illiterate soldiers to read and write (a fictionalized account of a similar job turns up in the story "Wissler Remembers" in *Packages*, 1980).

On 14 March 1950 Stern married Gay Clark in France. Their first child, Christopher, was born the next year in Heidelberg; three more children–Kate, Nicholas, and Andrew–were to follow, all of them born in the United States. From the start of Stern's career the pleasures and heartcrushing strains of family life have been important motifs in his fiction.

With wife and son Stern came back to America in 1952 to pursue a Ph.D. in creative writing at the University of Iowa. The family lived "on the second floor of the uggggliest house west of the Mississippi, a shingled cube that listed in the breeze." According to Stern, writing in *The Invention of the Real* (1982), it was a "big time for poets" at Iowa (Robert Lowell was one of his teachers there), but that did not stop Stern and his pals from deciding "that the James-Lubbock-Brooks-Warren-Tate notion of the perfected story was finished.... *We* knew it was time to take off Flaubert's corset. And to throw away Joyce's glue, shears, and colored markers." That first September in Iowa he received a letter from John Crowe Ransom (the subject of his Bowdoin Prize essay at Harvard) accepting his story "Cooley's Version" for *Kenyon Review.*

While at Iowa Stern worked on the staff of *Western Review,* and he continued to contribute stories, translations, articles, and reviews to the journal even after he left in 1954. "The Sorrows of Captain Schreiber" was published in *Western Review* in 1953 and was later reprinted in *Prize Stories of 1954: The O. Henry Collection.* For the Spring 1957 issue of *Western Review* Stern edited "American Poetry of the Fifties," an important collection that included "new" poets like Bowers, Justice, and Don Peterson, as well as Galway Kinnell, James Merrill, W. S. Merwin, Robert Pack, Adrienne Rich, May Swensen, and James Wright. In 1959 Stern published his interview with Norman Mailer, "Hip, Hell, and the Navigator," in *Western Review;* the interview was included the same year in Mailer's *Advertisements for Myself,* a book that served as one of the models for Stern's three miscellanies.

The 1950s saw the proliferation of new openings in the academy for creative writers. For Stern the "MLA bazaar" brought a position as instructor at Connecticut College in 1954, starting salary $3,500. The next year he moved to the University of Chicago. Except for brief stints to teach in Italy on a Fulbright and to lecture at different times in South America, Africa, and Asia, Stern has remained at Chicago for the last thirty-two years. This professional stability in an age of scholar gypsies has allowed him to go his own way as an author, writing to please himself. "My whole life," he once said, "has been planned so that I could make a living at the university, so that I don't have to live on my writing." Not that Stern's relationship with the university lacks reciprocity. In 1966 he "affectionately and gratefully" dedicated his anthology, *Honey and Wax: Pleasures and Powers of Narrative,* to the university.

And Stern takes his job as a teacher of writing seriously. He has a reputation as a demanding but very perceptive and helpful reader of student work. Novelist Douglas Unger, who worked with Stern in the early 1970s, recalls being lifted from despair about his future when he received from his mentor a helpful check for $100, a copy of *Natural Shocks* (1978), and a note encouraging him to keep writing. "Richard Stern," Unger observes, "was and still is the kind of teacher who keeps track of his students, who writes to them, helps them stay alive with encouragement and in other ways, a man who cares more about what follows the classroom than anything that might happen in it."

Stern's views about living in Chicago are beautifully rendered in "Chicago: Mostly a Love Letter," an essay he wrote for *Harper's* in 1961 (included with revisionist footnotes in his 1973 miscellany, *The Books in Fred Hampton's Apartment*). After living in Chicago six years the transplanted New Yorker wrote that he loves Chicago ("the unresponding thing") for its variety, its openness, its "powerful suggestion of human possibilities." The essay includes praise for Mayor Daley, his "essential highmindedness," an opinion that was partially retracted by 1973. There are also complex passages that blend poetic and realistic effects: "Chicago outlines the lake with question-mark-shaped beaches pointed at the tip with clumps of handsome museums and apartment houses whose glass skin reflects the out-lying factory fires whose profits are their source." Stern is proudly conscious of being part of the city's realist tradition, and several of his stories and novels are set in Chicago, most of them in the Hyde Park neighborhood where he has lived since the mid 1950s.

"Chicago is what happens to you here," Stern remarks in his *Harper's* essay. What happened to Stern in Chicago is that he became a writer of books. From 1960 to 1965 he published four novels and one collection of short stories, a pace that led friend Flannery O'Connor to call him "One-a-year Stern" and to warn in jest that he was not "helping the Brotherhood" by being so prolific. *Golk* (1960), Stern's first published novel, was rejected by eighteen houses before it found its way into print with Criterion Books, a small company that went bankrupt the same week the book appeared. Despite this misfortune *Golk* was nominated for a Pulitzer Prize in 1960 and received a warm critical reception. Inspired by the popular 1950s television show *Candid Camera*, *Golk* is among other things a brilliant satire on the television industry and its effects on the American public, especially the way television has created a nation of absurd exhibitionists and passive voyeurs. As Bernard F. Rodgers, Jr., states in his foreword to the 1987 Phoenix edition: "Twenty-seven years after its initial publication, *Golk* remains noteworthy as one of the first–and, with Kosinski's *Being There*, still one of the few–treatments of the character and impact of television in serious American fiction. Its moving and hilarious portrait of Poppa Hondorp, mesmerized in front of the screen; its black comic treatment of the world of rating battles, middle-level media managers, and god-like network moguls . . . ; its witty demonstration of how this powerful new medium quickly began to create its own language; its exploration of Golk's and Hondorp's Faustian bargains with the medium–all retain their freshness."

But the satire on television is not, in fact, the main interest of the novel; instead, the book dramatizes the betrayal of genius by mediocrity. The nominal hero, Herbert Hondorp, is a thirty-seven-year-old New Yorker who has never worked a day in his life. Dependent on his affectionate but domineering physician father (who has a growing lipoma on his neck), Hondorp loves to read and to wander the streets of Manhattan. One day while browsing in a bookstore Hondorp is "golked," that is, captured on camera talking to a bookshelf; before he knows it, he is helping the hidden camera crew to snare its next victim, who is tricked into believing he has found a sheet of paper with Shakespeare's handwriting on it. As with most golks, the scheme reveals not just the victim's stupidity, but his deeper flaws as well–in this case, mendacity and greed. Moments later Hondorp is invited to join the staff of *You're on Camera* by Sydney Golk, the program's brilliant, dome-headed creator. All the crew members, it turns out, are victims of earlier "golks," including Elaine, a black bombshell whose sexual favors Hondorp soon enjoys (earning the book a "strong meat" warning from the reviewer for the 1 April 1960 *Library Journal*), and Jenny Hendricks, a twenty-three-year-old ex-jet-setter whom Golk has salvaged from a destructive marriage to a sadistic millionaire.

Golk is probably Stern's most tightly plotted novel. Flushed with success and unwilling to repeat himself, Golk overreaches: he designs, films, and airs three skits that expose the corruption of important public officials, including a presiden-

Stern, age ten (courtesy of the author)

tial adviser and a union official with ties to the Mafia. *You're on Camera* becomes even more popular, but also too troublesome for the network executives, who ask Hondorp and Hendricks to replace Golk. The two underlings agree to supplant their mentor, rationalizing their betrayal as being "for the good of the show" and consummating their unholy alliance by living together. Without Golk's genius, however, the program falters, and soon everyone is unemployed. By that time Hondorp and Hendricks have separated, and Hondorp finds himself with "all trace of his ambition, all desire for change gone absolutely and forever."

Writing in the *Nation* (7 May 1960), Terry Southern hailed *Golk* as "a book . . . to be recommended on many levels, and to be enjoyed by all—except, no doubt, those very ones in whose laments its author so lyrically sings." In *Commonweal* (13 May 1960) Charles Monaghan compared Stern with Bellow, Vladimir Nabokov, William Gaddis, and J. P. Donleavy, and praised the book

"for a consistent and pleasant lightness of tone that never degenerates into frivolousness, for intriguing characterization and plotting, and for an efficient and clear prose style."

Europe: Or Up and Down with Schreiber and Baggish, Stern's second novel to be published, was actually written before *Golk* and then revised after the latter appeared. Built on the Nietzschean theme that "Every man of character has a typical experience which recurs over and over again," the novel traces the mostly comic fortunes of the two American title characters (and of a third American, Robert Ward, who is far less important) as they zigzag their way across Europe, occasionally intersecting. Max Schreiber is a middle-aged lawyer who has left a failed marriage and young daughter in the States. He has the repeated unhappy experience of being disappointed in love: first (in flashback) with Micheline, who runs off with his wartime army driver, a black corporal named Tiberius; then with Traudis Bretzka, a young German girl whom Schreiber also loses—this time in Beirut and once again to his old nemesis Tiberius, who has become rich transporting Middle Eastern oil.

Former dry-goods clerk Theodore Baggish goes to Europe to make his fortune and succeeds by cleverly and callously manipulating those at hand, including poor Schreiber. As John P. Sisk commented in the *New York Times Book Review* (12 November 1961), "Baggish is a superb creation. . . . The graph of his ascent from rags in America to riches in the family of a German industrialist, the neat opposite of the historical pattern, is traced with splendid irony."

Stern has called *Europe* his most "literary" novel: "It plays with other treatments of Europe by American writers," especially by Henry James. In terms of its deliberately loose structure the book is also one of his more innovative works. Stern even introduces a character (Juliette) for the single purpose of defending the book's form against Baggish, who unwittingly attacks it. Juliette claims that whenever she faces a blank page, she says to herself " 'write me something new, something different, something which displaces this single-situation tyranny . . . , something which knocks the reader on the head by bringing in characters who don't recur, situations which work only in roundabout ways of contrast and comparison.' I never let the reader take hold. When he thinks he has me, I'm not there. Ha, ha, ha, ha, ha. . . ." The passage is for Stern a rare excursion into metafiction.

In general, reactions to *Europe* tended to be less favorable than those for *Golk*. A reviewer for the *Times Literary Supplement* (13 April 1962) said that "There are many good pages in *Europe*, but the novel as a whole is too episodic and purposeless–and is a rather disappointing successor to Mr. Stern's mordant first novel *Golk*." Flannery O'Connor, however, praised the character of Baggish and said she preferred *Europe* to *Golk*. And in his *New York Times Book Review* piece Sisk wrote: "The story may appear to be a picaresque ramble that gets by on its witty and stylish observance of exotic scenes. Actually, it is effectively and unobtrusively controlled by theme and tone. Mr. Stern's comic vision lights up a venal world."

While *Golk* and *Europe* are both comic novels that veer at times toward satire, *In Any Case* (first published in 1962 and published in 1981 as *The Chaleur Network*) seems to be everything but comic, though it too has its moments of humor. Billed by McGraw-Hill as "a novel of suspense and self-discovery," *In Any Case* has also been described as a spy novel, a mystery, a confession, and a novel of ideas. In this first-person narrative, American expatriate Samuel Curry receives a book claiming that his son Bobbie, who was killed in World War II, betrayed the French underground organization to which he belonged. Certain that his son is innocent and anxious to clear his name, Curry tracks down the surviving members of the network. In what Peter Buitenhuis (*New York Times Book Review*, 14 October 1962) called a "reverse Oedipal twist," the fifty-seven-year-old Curry becomes romantically involved with Jacqueline, Bobbie's former lover and a member of the network. Eventually, Curry finds and confronts Robert Arastignac, the double agent who betrayed Bobbie and his comrades to the Nazis, ostensibly to protect a second, more important underground organization.

As he gradually discovers the truth about Bobbie's role in the network and about his death, Curry also begins to face up to his own many failures as a husband and father. For most of his life Curry has been a narcissist and a loner–in the war he also proved a physical coward when he refused to allow a local resistance group to use his house as a meeting place. But during the novel Curry comes to acknowledge the painful truth about his selfish past. In one scene he is confronted by a former girlfriend whom he has just accused of betraying his son: "Was I to kill Bobbie? Are you telling me I killed Bobbie?

Look at yourself, you, famous all over Paris for your disregard of him. Your women–me, brought and flaunted in front of him. It's you who knocked him down. You couldn't stand anyone in your way. You were made to be alone. Lying with me, moaning over me, you were always by yourself, loving nothing but Sam." A similarly bitter public quarrel years before with his wife Hélène led to her passive suicide from a thigh wound which she concealed until it was too late to cure.

Whatever Curry's sins against his son and against women, he is made to suffer in his relationship with Jacqueline. For the first time in his life he is able to love unselfishly; yet, ironically, he can never be certain that she loves him. At the end of the novel he and Jacqueline are married, and she is pregnant. But he is not sure the child is his: he even suspects that the child might be Arastignac's. Yet Curry seems content to allow Jacqueline as much freedom as she desires. "What else is there to do?" asks the subtly transformed Curry. "Shoot her?"

In exploring the psychology of love in the context of the morally ambiguous world of espionage, *In Any Case* recalls the serious spy fiction of Joseph Conrad and Graham Greene and looks forward to the novels of John LeCarré. Curry's journey toward painful self-knowledge and regeneration also anticipates the pattern of several of Stern's later novels. In addition, the book echoes a number of themes that are sounded in *Golk* and in *Europe* and that will recur in later books: the relationship between father and son, especially as that relationship is colored by parental guilt; the love between an older man and a younger woman; the American in European exile; the distinction between amateurs and professionals; and what Stern has called "the division between men of action and contemplative men."

In Any Case sold only about 5,000 copies, even though it won the Friends of Literature Award and was nominated for the National Book Award, and though most reviews were enthusiastic. In *Saturday Review* (17 November 1962) Joan Bostwick found the book "subtle and fresh," and Richard Ellmann proclaimed that *In Any Case* "takes in more of life than *Golk*, and does so with the same talent and daring. One must read it to find out what the American novel is up to." Peter Buitenhuis also preferred *In Any Case* to Stern's earlier novels. In the *New York Times Book Review* he wrote that the book "seldom flags in its narrative pace and excitement. Mr. Stern has the skill

Stern with friends aboard the Queen Mary *en route to Europe in September of 1949 (courtesy of the author)*

of a born storyteller as well as a highly literate, allusive mind."

In 1964 Stern published *Teeth, Dying and Other Matters,* a collection of stories written between 1949 and 1962. Also included in the volume–against the wishes of his editor at Harper and Row–were "The Pursuit of Washington," an amusing and politically astute essay about Stern's unsuccessful attempts to interview Kennedy and Nixon in 1959, and *The Gamesman's Island,* a three-act play that Stern concocted with a little help from Donald Justice about an inventor of games and his husband-swapping daughters. Like Stern's two other plays (*Reparations,* written for television, and *Dossier Earth: Twenty-Four Blackouts from the Middle of the Electric Age*), *The Gamesman's Island* has never been professionally performed.

All the stories in *Teeth, Dying and Other Matters* (except "The Good European") were previously published in journals ranging from *Western Review* and *Epoch* to *Harper's* and *Partisan Review,* and as a group they stand for, in Stern's words, "a certain variety of interest in different sorts of people, different sorts of activity and different ways of writing stories. A collection of stories is a

family reunion, not a birth." In other words, there is little unity to the volume. Several of the stories (especially the early ones) reflect Stern's European experiences, as does "The Assessment of an Amateur," which won the Longwood Prize in 1959 after it was published in *Kenyon Review.* In that story a young American living in Paris on a Fulbright loses his "small interest in the arts" as a result of his association with boorish American pianist and champion moocher Dave Higgins. "The Good European" recounts the return to Europe of Harry (Heinz) Pfeiffer, a German-Jewish refugee from the Nazis who has become an American citizen. Pfeiffer, who has never truly adjusted to life in America, is also understandably ambivalent about postwar Germany: "he saw in her looseness and silly posturing the awkward attempt to atone for the misery she had madly inflicted in her fifteen-year exile from the European tradition." Nevertheless, he and his wife are disappointed when he receives orders from his company supervisor to return to New York.

Several of the later stories are comedies of urban loneliness and failed communication that produce delightful mixtures of pathos and laughter. In "Teeth," tall, homely Ethel Wilmotte, a Uni-

377

versity of Chicago history instructor, sets her sights on her dentist, Dr. Hobbie, a "gentle fool" of a man who is separated from his "expert dancer" wife (she has run off to live with the florist in the bank building where he has his office). At the end of the story Miss Wilmotte's abscess is relieved but not the ache in her heart–having inherited money from his father, Dr. Hobbie has become reconciled with his wife. Poor Miss Wilmotte is left alone to rewrite her article on opium use in nineteenth-century England.

In "Wanderers" Stern presents the story of Miss Swindleman, a cashier at the Hotel Winthrop in New York. Her mission in life is to impose order on the "avaricious disorder" of the wandering Jews who fill the hotel lobby and who send her postcards from every corner of the world. But the pattern of the story, like several others in the collection, is to move the protagonist from self-righteous isolation toward confrontation with others, which in turn sparks a moment of self-revelation. When Lepidus (a friend of hotel tenant Harvey Mendel) calls her a "piss-cold, anti-semitischer virgin-whore" because she refuses to change a fifty, a transformation occurs within her. Later, when the same Lepidus is pushed out a window by Mendel and falls to his death, Miss Swindleman protects the assailant. "An opening had been made," states the narrator, but a few lines later he adds: "The opening was a wound in Miss Swindleman. Days passed, and embarrassment at defending Mendel was all she could stuff in to stop the raw ache. She was altered, but alteration had nowhere to go." The ending of the story recalls the powerful conclusions of Flannery O'Connor's fictions, but it lacks their images of possible salvation. The best Miss Swindleman can accomplish–and this she does achieve–is to acknowledge that she too is a wanderer.

"Dying," the last story in the volume, concerns Professor Bly, a young plant physiologist and minor poet who is invited by Chicago businessman F. Dorfman Dreben to enter a contest to write a brief inscription for Dreben's mother's gravestone. The story is a darkly ironic parable on filial devotion, life and death, artistic integrity and compromise.

Some reviewers of *Teeth, Dying and Other Matters* found the collection uneven, and more than one complained about the inclusion of the essay and the play. Though he liked "The Pursuit of Washington" and found much of *The Gamesman's Island* "bright and amusing," Saul Maloff stated

in the *New York Times Book Review* (27 October 1964) that "no book . . . is an opportunity for desk clearing." Stephen Donadio, in *Partisan Review* (Spring 1965), also declared the essay and play "expendable." For Donadio "the stories are what count, and they are, generally, fine examples of economy, intelligence, and literary tact." In the *New York Review of Books* (22 October 1964) Frederick Crews wrote that " 'Teeth,' 'Wanderers,' and 'Dying' would be the envy of any contemporary writer," though he also observed that the memorable stories deal with "insignificant little people from whom Stern is intellectually detached." Granville Hicks, in *Saturday Review* (12 December 1964), praised Stern's obvious talent as a writer but worried that Stern "seems to lack a center" and was "either unwilling or unable to show us where he really lives."

In 1962 and 1963 Stern resided with his family in Italy on a Fulbright fellowship. During this time he made the acquaintance of Ezra Pound in Venice and visited him once a week from November to March. Pound was a writer of great importance to Stern (his second published critical article, "Pound as Translator," appeared in *Accent* in 1953). During one of his visits to the aging poet Stern repeated a story he had heard from Peggy Guggenheim about Pound playing tennis in Paris. Suddenly Pound sat up in bed and accused Stern of fabricating the story. Embarrassed and angered, Stern sat silent for a while, then went to Pound's side to say farewell–probably, thought Stern, for the last time–and to apologize for upsetting the old man. To Stern's surprise Pound gripped his hand and said, "Wrong, wrong, wrong. I've always been wrong. Eighty-seven percent wrong. I never recognize benevolence." Stern offered words of encouragement, but Pound added, "You don't know what it's like to get off on the wrong path. Not to remember." Again Stern tried to console him by speaking of Pound's artistic successes, only to hear Pound say, "No. I've only left scattered notes. Haven't made anything clear."

According to Stern, "the emotional aftermath" of this experience led him to write *Stitch*. Published in 1965, the novel transforms poet Pound into octogenarian sculptor Thaddeus Stitch, who has been given his own island near Venice where the artist occasionally works on his magnum opus (corresponding, of course, to Pound's *Cantos*): "He descended, down by the fishwall, by a minaret-pyramid, by shelves of figures, plowshapes, an aluminum river, heads he knew,

Manuscript page for Golk, Stern's first book (courtesy of the author)

half-heads he half-knew, nonheads that were heads, bodies and bodylike nonbodies, scenes, stone events, a fair of blazing rocks, a Last Supper of eyes. An endless maze of solids conjured out of colored earth stuff." Stitch repudiates his life's work ("Wrong, wrong, wrong") to Edward Gunther after treating his American guest rudely, just as Pound treated Stern. Thirty-five-year-old Gunther has quit his ad-writing job in Chicago and taken his family abroad to explore Europe and to find himself, dissipating the family savings in the process. Edward has a brief, frustrating affair with American Nina Callahan, who is writing an epic poem on women, an effort that Stitch tells her will not succeed because it is "without love."

Stitch is the culmination of many themes and techniques from earlier works. Like Golk it is deeply concerned with the nature of genius. Other resemblances to earlier works include the use of multiple points of view, which Stern deploys in Golk and Europe. In this novel the fragmentation of perspectives creates a cubistic effect entirely appropriate to Stitch's own island of unfinished, counterpoised forms. Nina Callahan has her forerunners in the strong women of the earlier novels: Jenny Hendricks of Golk, Traudis of Europe, and Jacqueline of In Any Case. In addition, the book returns to the American in Europe motif, so important in Europe, In Any Case, and several stories in Teeth, Dying and Other Matters. Edward believes it is "best to be American and live in Europe." His wife Cressida, however, has a different view of his European transformation: "Europe had brought out the worst in him, culture-hunting, church-licking, you'd think he was on the verge of conversion to see him eating up Madonnas, lecturing the kids on their inadequate grasp of Europe's greatness, then exhibiting a behavior that had about as much to do with civilization and culture as a tiger vomiting the remains of a jackal. Adultery, negligence, sloth. . . ." The inevitable separation, with Edward living unhappily alone in California at the close of the novel, is poignantly rendered. For all his faults, Gunther loves his children.

In a review for the New York Review of Books (9 December 1965) titled "Herzog in Europe," Bernard Bergonzi recognized Stitch as Pound "in the most transparent of guises" and also praised the passages from Stitch's point of view as a "skillful and accurate pastiche of Pound's own writings." However, he felt Stitch has too little to do with the action. "Possibly," Bergonzi speculated,

"Mr. Stern wanted to make him the center of his novel, but found he couldn't do it, as the obtrusive figure of Edward kept getting in the way." In Chicago Review (Winter/Spring 1966) Hugh Kenner took issue with Bergonzi and others. Stern's originality, he wrote, is to contrast Stitch "with another failure," Edward Gunther, "who fails without style." The strength of the novel, Kenner asserted, is that "before our eyes Edward shrinks from the human norm to the International Standard centimeter, while Stitch comes to incarnate what there is to take heart by . . . his dedication to getting something right, out there on the island." Poet Karl Shapiro shared Kenner's judgment; he called Stitch "the best, most decent thing ever written about Pound."

1968: A Short Novel, An Urban Idyll, Five Stories, and Two Trade Notes was published in 1970. As its long title suggests, the volume is a gathering of fictions of varying lengths and kinds. The novella "Veni, Vedi . . . Wendt," first published in Paris Review in 1970, offers a fierce satire on the hollowness of American academic life and a withering portrait of a failed marriage. Composer Jeffrey Wendt, on a summer teaching assignment at the University of California at Santa Barbara, is the narrator. Wendt is writing an opera on Horace Walpole and having a freeway-motel affair with the bounteous Patricia Davidov, the "yeast" of Wendt's imagination and also the wife of the chairman of the music department. Meanwhile, Wendt's own bitter wife, Velia, keeps a careful catalogue of "all his deformities" in her notebook and runs the vacuum cleaner outside his study door while he is trying to compose. After losing his temper with his son, Wendt can feel a moment of disgust at his "violent failure as a father." But he resists the burden of marital guilt. "Hold off," Wendt tells himself, "from that puritan, judaic, masochistic analysis which will show me as tyrant, betrayer and brute, and will see Velia as Ariel calabanized by me."

1968 also contains "The Idylls of Dugan and Strunk," which traces two University of Chicago functionaries who topple with their younger girlfriends out of their ivory tower onto riot-torn South 63rd Street in Chicago on the night of Martin Luther King, Jr.'s assassination. The final scene presents a tableau confrontation between the library and the ghetto. The twin ironic stories "Gaps" and "Gifts" are about sexually restless men and their relationships with a daughter in one story and a son in the other. There is also "Storymaking," a fictionalized, affectionate, but not entirely flattering portrait of Philip Roth shortly after the death of Roth's ex-wife and right before the publication of *Portnoy's Complaint* (1969). At the end of the sketch, the narrator says of his own departure from New York: "The minor, low-living burgher, with difficulty still married to the same wife, deprived of fifty-dollar-an-hour self-revelations, never penis-threatened with a knife, never easing the needy wand in the family steak, fantasist but no solipsist, story-searcher but, usually, smalltime inventor, flies back with daughter to Chicago." Stern wrote a more complimentary piece on Roth for *Saturday Review* in 1981, a portrait of the artist and actress Claire Bloom in their home in western Connecticut.

Critical responses to *1968* were sharply divided. At the negative extreme Martin Levin, writing in the *New York Times Book Review* (12 July 1970), felt that the "parts were greater than the whole." And D. A. N. Jones complained in the *New York Review of Books* (13 August 1970) that Stern's English was "allusive and exclusive, mingling a studied demotic with a little learning, none too lightly worn." But these critics were countered by a number of readers who loved the collection. Philip Roth, for example, expressed outrage at the "thoroughgoing regularity" and "dedication" with which Stern's work had been neglected. He said *1968* was "as deeply comic, as quirky and intelligent and elegant, as anything Stern has ever written." A reviewer for the *Times Literary Supplement* (21 May 1971) concurred, stating that Stern's prose is "as dazzling as early sunshine in cloudless winter: it makes you blink." And in *Book Week* Floyd Lawrence called *1968* a "remarkable prose cadenza" that "through its shifting syntax, its blend of slapstick and social tragedy and its detached wit and deeply felt terror, evokes a response much like the one we give to the conclusion of Pope's 'Dunciad.' "

The portrayal of the Wendts' volatile marriage in "Veni, Vidi . . . Wendt" recalls the mutually destructive pairing of the Gunthers in *Stitch*. The repetition of the "troubles of the marriage bed" theme suggests a personal source. Certainly, the vigorous depiction of spousal rancor in both novels has the shrill ring of authenticity, though the details are different in each book and though Edward Gunther and Jeffrey Wendt come across as no better—and often much worse—than the women they marry and betray. When asked at various times if he is an autobiographical writer, Stern has been candid. "In the first ten or fifteen years of my writing life," he said in an interview

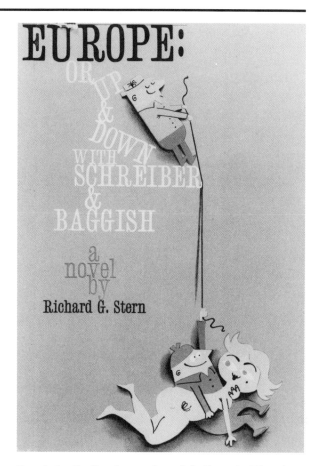

Dust jacket for Stern's second novel, built on the Nietzschean theme that "Every man of character has a typical experience which recurs over and over again"

published in *Chicago Review* in 1980, "I was always gripped by stories which were 'out there.' I could see them more or less complete even though I might not know the end of one I began. In the last ten or twelve years, I've begun to use a version of a character whom I can recognize as myself. The reason for that, I think, has something to do with the desire not to restrict myself, restrict my intellect or my emotional capacities."

The goal is never an exact "xeroxing of events," Stern explains in "Inside Narcissus," his important essay on autobiographical fiction (first published in the Spring 1978 issue of *Yale Review* and later collected in *The Invention of the Real*). "The fiction writer's story," he states, "even when it originates in actuality, comes to be dominated not by it as much as by the writer's feeling of coherence, amplitude, pace. . . ." Thoughts such as these are not usually enough to console those who get exhibited along with the author. To protect the innocent Stern often tries to "dislocate" himself and the situation. "Every dislocation," he states, "frees me from that easy memory which resembles memoir or reporting." Just as Stern changes the location, the car, the hair color, the number and sexes of the children, he also changes the professions of his protagonists, a practice that he says "not only opens up a technical vocabulary that is probably rich in metaphor and unforced symbolism, it can even suggest story lines and characters."

One can see the process of dislocation at work in Stern's next novel, *Other Men's Daughters*. Instead of Hyde Park and the University of Chicago, we have Cambridge and Harvard; instead of writer/English professor Stern, we have Robert Merriwether, a professor of physiology who also works nine hours a week as a physician at Harvard's Holyoke Center. At the clinic the over-forty, unhappily married Merriwether meets young Cynthia Ryder, a beautiful, twenty-year-old summer-school student from Swarthmore. "You were thirsty, and you went to the well," says a friend. Merriwether, a dipsologist who has published a "semi-popular" book on thirst, responds, "I was thirsty and someone delivered a case of champagne to the door. I hardly knew I was thirsty till it came."

The business of the novel is to chart with great beauty, intelligence, irony, and compassion the process of Merriwether's rebirth and the painful dissolution of his marriage. The "low-keyed, middle-aged prof softened by American life and Harvard cream" is transformed by love into "the Burgher Outlaw gripped by passion for a girl a year older than his son." Though Merriwether gets the girl, nothing is easy in Stern's universe, especially not the course of Merriwether's love. The protagonist oscillates between fear of losing Cynthia (he tries for a while to stash her in an apartment building for elderly women), guilt about his wife and four children, and fear of ending the affair because, the reader is told, Cynthia is unstable and might harm herself. His wife, Sarah, meanwhile, angrily wonders if the affair is his compensation for a flagging career. But Merriwether's passion is more than mid-life crisis: "I feel about her," he says, "the way Galileo did about the telescope. My feelings for her enlarge my feelings for other things."

Still, Merriwether is comically, agonizingly slow in his retreat from the family home. He stays through the divorce proceedings, and even for six weeks after the divorce, living on the third floor, eating the meals Sarah prepares while he watches *The Dick Van Dyke Show*.

Merriwether says he remains in the house for the sake of the children. "You can't keep using the children to kill ME," Sarah responds, finally evicting him. The novel ends with Cynthia joining Merriwether for a brief retreat in the Colorado Rockies. The mountain setting may seem like the backdrop of a "true romance" conclusion, but Stern strongly implies that Cynthia's and Robert's struggles have not ended.

There exists a general parallel between events in the novel and events in Stern's life. In 1972 Richard and Gay Stern were divorced after twenty-two years of marriage. Since the early 1970s Stern's more or less constant companion has been Alane Rollings, whom he married in 1985. Rollings, a gifted poet, earned a master's degree in Far Eastern Literature and Languages at the University of Chicago in 1975. In 1984 she published a highly praised volume of poems, *Transparent Landscapes*. Stern's relationship with his first wife, Gay, has over the years settled into something approaching mutually supportive concern. Through the divorce and after Stern has never lost contact with his children.

That Stern's fictions since the early 1970s often spring from the materials of his life may be relevant to a literary biography, but knowledge of Stern's life is never necessary to an appreciation of his books. No doubt awareness of the similarities and differences between the life and the art influences (and not always in a positive way) how some readers view his work. But there is no effort on Stern's part to rewrite his own history to make his fictional counterparts look better than Stern might in real life. On the other hand, what distinguishes Merriwether from earlier Stern protagonists like Edward Gunther and Jeffrey Wendt is the obvious sympathy and acceptance–as well as ironic distance–with which Merriwether is portrayed. The same generosity is also extended to Sarah Merriwether, to Cynthia, and even to Cynthia's father, who comes to challenge the August-May couple in France. Everyone's point of view matters, is part of the truth.

Other Men's Daughters has sold better than any other book that Stern has written, and the response from most critics has also been excellent. *Time* (31 December 1973) named it one of the ten best works of fiction of the year, and Jonathan Yardley wrote in the *Washington Post* (28 October 1973): "It is a pleasure to find a novel written with such intelligence and feeling, a novel that judges none of its people but holds them up to calm and affectionate scrutiny." In the *New*

York Times Book Review (18 November 1973) James R. Frakes stated that Stern "executes wonders with his apparently hopelessly melodramatic subject" and renders his characters "unsentimentally persuasive by ... uncompromising honesty and unblinking comprehensiveness." And, Frakes adds, "One of the miracles of this novel is how such comprehensiveness is achieved with so much economy, so many ellipses."

Although Stern is primarily a writer of stories and novels he has also published dozens of poems and translations, some forty pieces of reportage and criticism, and more than seventy reviews in a host of literary journals, magazines, and newspapers. Most of these pieces, as well as excerpts from one of his plays, *Dossier Earth*, are gathered in Stern's three "orderly miscellanies," a genre Stern compares to a "bouillabaisse, the Plaza, and such collections of odd pieces as the *Arabian Nights*, the Greek and Confucian anthologies, the *Mahabarata*, and, God help us, the Bible." The first of the miscellanies, *The Books in Fred Hampton's Apartment*, appeared in 1973, a few months before *Other Men's Daughters*. Stern's other two collections, *The Invention of the Real* and *The Position of the Body*, were published in 1982 and 1986 respectively.

The title essay in *The Books in Fred Hampton's Apartment*, about the Black Panther leader killed by Chicago police, is a masterpiece of subtle contrast and implied tragedy. Stern also reprints "The Pursuit of Washington"; this essay, the Fred Hampton piece, and others in the miscellany explore the relationship between men of action and the books they read, continuing Stern's interest in the contrast between active-public and contemplative-private lives. In addition, the volume contains autobiographical sketches, Stern's 1961 response to a *Commentary* questionnaire about being a Jewish writer, a packet of delightful letters from Flannery O'Connor, and a satirist's squint-eyed view of a Modern Language Association convention. *The Invention of the Real* and *The Position of the Body* display a comparable variety. The former has vivid portraits of Pound, Bellow, Borges, Beckett, and Mailer. The latter collection has essays about Stern's tour of Africa, portraits of Robert Lowell and Lillian Hellman, and notes on the "debris" of his latest novel, *A Father's Words* (1986).

All three collections also contain a number of thoughtful, independent-minded essays and reviews. The first miscellany has early pieces on Proust and Joyce and Pound, as well as his notori-

ous 1961 bombing of Joseph Heller's *Catch-22* (1961) in the *New York Times Book Review*. Stern also pans Nabokov's *Pnin* (1957) and Updike's *Couples* (1968), cautiously praises Malamud's *The Tenants* (1971), and hails Bellow's *Henderson the Rain King* (1959). There are kind words too for an experimental novel, Ivan Gold's *Sick Friends* (1969), and for Capote's *In Cold Blood* (1965). Books reviewed in the later two miscellanies range from *RN: The Memoirs of Richard Nixon* (1978) and Henry Kissinger's *The White House Years* (1979) to Suzanne Langer's *Mind: An Essay on Human Feeling* (volume 3, 1984) and Mary Robison's *Days* (1979).

Stern's next novel after *Other Men's Daughters*, *Natural Shocks*, was published in 1978. It is to date Stern's darkest and also his most complex novel. Protagonist Fred Wursup is a successful journalist, the author of *Down the American Drain*, a best-selling book on government inefficiency. From the roof of his New York apartment Wursup uses field glasses to watch the movements of his ex-wife, Susannah, and his two sons in the apartment where he once lived across the street. As in *Other Men's Daughters*, the protagonist also has a young girlfriend, geologist Sookie Gumpert, who keeps a separate apartment and travels frequently to read papers at professional meetings. Unlike Stern's previous novel, however, *Natural Shocks* does not focus on the protagonist's relationships with ex-wife and girlfriend. Instead, Stern uses Wursup to explore the phenomena of celebrity, journalism, friendship, and death.

Death is everywhere in *Natural Shocks*, even within protagonist Wursup. As a world-traveled journalist he has seen just about every glory and every horror of the modern age. Understanding everything, committed to nothing, he has trouble feeling: "There were glacial rifts in Wursup, times when he was as unfeeling as the chemicals which made him."

Wursup, the professional voyeur, the exposer, the pryer into shells, the creator of celebrities, finds himself getting transformed into a celebrity. He doesn't like the experience, especially when hack journalist Ollie Fenchal writes a feature that describes Wursup as a "genial mollusc." The death implicit in becoming a celebrity–a character, a public mask–is emphasized again when playwright Hamish Blick commits suicide, an event that forces Wursup to recall his crass intrusion into Blick's life a few years before for the sake of a story.

Between major projects Wursup accepts an assignment to write a magazine article on death, but gets nowhere reading the countless books on the subject that have recently been published. Ironically, one result of the Fenchal story is that it leads to a letter from a nurse at St. Vincent's Hospital inviting Wursup to "get in touch with death." At the hospital Wursup meets eighteen-year-old Cicia Buell, who is dying of cancer. As he gets to know her, he falls in love, if not with her, then with the pathos of a young girl's dying. The relationship with Cicia shakes the world-hardened Wursup. Three times he tries to escape his feelings for her, traveling to Rome, to Bruges, and to Maine, but finally he returns to witness her death in the hospital.

Just as it is Wursup's nature to flee from emotional involvement, so the structure of *Natural Shocks* is correspondingly digressive. One line of action, for example, traces Susannah and the small newsletter where she works. Through most of the novel her life seems "constructed to arouse pity," and she feels "herself stranded in the shallowest part of her nature." We learn that while she was married she had a long and secret affair with Wursup's best friend, Will Eddy. "She got away with it," the narrator informs us, "so she paid through the nose and kept paying." Things turn out well for her, however; she marries Kevin Miyako, the editor of *Chouinard's Newsletter*. Another cluster of characters and actions centers on Wursup's friend, senatorial candidate Jim Doyle, whom Wursup tries unsuccessfully to save from political ruin. On another front Wursup's father and the woman he lived with in Chicago commit suicide together. At the apartment where Cicia lives when she is not in the hospital the reader is introduced to several other characters: for example, Tina, a lesbian poet who has loved Cicia longer than Wursup and who also feels guilty writing about ("cannibalizing") her death; and Tommy, Cicia's autodidact father, who must endure "the terrible reversal ... the younger breaking up while the older was intact."

Not everyone appreciated so many pockets of interest, so many loosely connected characters and events. In the *New York Times Book Review* (1 January 1978) Anatole Broyard wrote that the novel "fails to cohere," a view echoed later by Benjamin DeMott in *Atlantic* (1 March 1978). In a review in the *Nation* (11 February 1978), however, Patricia Meyer Spacks praised the very "looseness" Broyard faulted; "the force of the novel," Spacks wrote, "derives partly from its curious

lack of emphasis." Stern himself has described the novel as "a kind of Jackson Pollock painting. The book seems a constant agitation, nothing is quite let go. Every time you think a story line will be resolved, it isn't. Something else opens up." He has also conceded that the book "may be a failure in that it doesn't hold hard to one thing." This was not the opinion of R. L. Schwartz, who wrote in the *Minnesota Daily* (27 February 1978) that "*Natural Shocks* is a near-masterpiece. Put Richard Stern high on any list of writers who count."

As Stern was writing *Natural Shocks*, his meditation on death, some of the people closest to him began to die. The novel, in fact, is dedicated to dear friend and colleague Arthur Heiserman, who died of cancer at the age of forty-six in 1975. In 1978, after *Natural Shocks* was published, Stern's mother died, and her death was followed six months later in January 1979 by the death of his father. The loss of both parents to death and senility is rendered in "Packages" and "Dr. Cahn's Visit," two very different yet complementary stories included in *Packages*, published in 1980. Robert Boyd, writing in the *St. Louis Post Dispatch*, observed that reading the two stories in sequence "creates an extraordinary illusion of depth.... Between the two stories, the complex set of relationships among the narrator, his dying mother and his senile father is illuminated with a depth of sensitivity and clarity rare even in novels." Mark Harris, meanwhile, praised "Dr. Cahn's Visit" as one of the "very best very short stories in the English language" (*New Republic*, 15 November 1980). The characters in the two stories are probably the same people, Harris observed, but they are transformed to serve different aesthetic needs. Harris continued: "each story proclaims its own conditions, and Stern always respects the demand of fiction to serve itself before it serves his own private needs or memories."

Other stories in *Packages* return to concerns of earlier books. "Double Charlie," about a once successful, now inactive songwriting team, humorously explores rivalry and betrayal in friendship, an issue in *Golk, Europe, In Any Case,* and *Natural Shocks.* "Riordan's Fiftieth" depicts a Chicago bus driver who maintains his dignity and cheerfulness even though his soured wife and television-gazing children have forgotten his birthday; the story has the urban realism of "Teeth" and "Wanderers," but Stern's sympathy for Riordan is not mixed with the ironic ice of the earlier stories. "A

Stern with Inca children in Peru in 1979 (courtesy of the author)

Recital for the Pope" not only returns to the young American in Europe motif but also reintroduces (somewhat altered) two main characters from *Stitch*, Nina Callahan and Edward Gunther. This story, as well as "Troubles" (about the blossoming wife of a selfish graduate student) and "The Ideal Address," show Stern's continuing interest in and ability to depict strong, sensitive, appealing female protagonists.

As with Stern's earlier collections, *Packages* displays its author's skills at a variety of short-story forms. "Wissler Remembers," Stern's gentle reverie on teaching, and "Mail," about a cartographer cum minor poet and his many correspondences, are structured by association of memories. Other stories in the volume are more conventionally plotted. "Lesson for the Day," for example, follows the hilarious attempt of Kiest, an unemployed Ph.D. (his incompetent wife has the academic job), to seduce his neighbor's wife.

Critical reaction to *Packages* was more uniformly enthusiastic than that for *Teeth* and *1968*. Saul Bellow declared that "Richard Stern has always had a wonderful way with short stories, and in his new collection is more wonderful than ever." Alice Shukalo marveled at Stern's range of characters, his ability to comprehend the lives of people as diverse as a Chicago bus driver and an

American teenage girl in Rome. In *Hudson Review* (Autumn 1981) David Kubal stated: "Mr. Stern's lucidity, together with his capacity for affection and the comic, are very rare qualities, shortages in contemporary fiction. The informed reading public, at least, wants its fictive realities uncontaminated by an author's suggestion that human character is greater than its circumstances, or that the condition itself has its goodness, or that anyone should be forgiven or tolerated. That Mr. Stern continues to offer these consolations in a body of work, which now contains nine major fictions, tells us of his artistic integrity."

Stern's tenth and most recent work of fiction, *A Father's Words*, presents the first-person saga of Cy Riemer, the father of four grown children and a son whose mother and father die within eight weeks of one another (leaving Riemer with the comically rendered dilemma of sudden wealth). Riemer has for years been the editor of a very small but highly respected science newsletter. After a period of bitterness and tension, he and ex-wife Agnes live near each other in Chicago in a state of amicable divorce. The other figure in Stern's now-familiar triad is Emma, Riemer's younger girlfriend, who wants the legitimacy of marriage as well as a child of her own. Riemer is reluctant.

For one thing, Cy already has four grown children, and he's not sure he can endure another twenty years of fathering. Furthermore, he has doubts about his capabilities as a parent, or, at least, he's disturbed by some things he sees in the lives of his children. When Agnes, whose home has been the center of the family, enters the Peace Corps, Cy feels he must be the one who holds the family together. Thus, he sets off on a cross-country odyssey to embrace and encourage each child. The first stop is St. Louis to see his youngest child, Livy, who has just joined the FBI. Though proud of her spunk and pleased that she is realizing her professional goals, Riemer is concerned that she is still unmarried and worries that her life is "moving from a.m. to p.m. before she knew it."

In Washington he visits Ben and Jenny, both married (Ben's wife is pregnant with Riemer's first grandchild), both authors of books. However, their respective books offer a grim view of family life (Jenny's is *The Wobbling Nucleus: The Family in Literature from Medea to Finnegans Wake*, while Ben's "fetal history of mankind" is titled *The Need to Hurt*). Riemer is disturbed that Jenny is reluctant to have children. "I'm frightened of the barrenness in you . . . ," he tells her. "And I wonder if it comes from some deep resentment at me."

The final stop, Manhattan, is also the most important to the novel, for it is there that Riemer visits his oldest son, Jack. In his mid thirties, unable to stay with any job or woman for more than a few months (the novel chronicles Jack's very brief marriage to Maria Robusto, the daughter of a pornographic filmmaker), Jack is a major worry and disappointment and source of guilt to his father. "If I'm unfair to Jack," Riemer says early in the novel, "it's because I know I'm both his model and his despair; he's the dye which shows up my inadequacy. Every fault I think I've overcome–or hidden–shows up in Jack; in spades." Riemer visits Jack in his barren tenement apartment where he lives on Wonder Bread and peanut butter ("a cave was better furnished," thinks the father) and takes his wayward son out for an expensive Italian meal, which Jack wolfs down along with a forty-dollar bottle of Bordeaux. Outside the restaurant on Broadway, Riemer offers to pay Jack's debts and to help set him up for yet another job search or perhaps pay for psychotherapy. But Jack refuses the offer: "Face it, Dad. I'm finished. I'm never going to be what you want me to be. You can't buy it for me. I can't get it my own way either. . . . We missed the train." The novel is built around this *gran refiuto*.

But *A Father's Words* does not end with Jack's refusal. Instead, Riemer returns to Chicago to learn that Emma is pregnant. At last Riemer is forced to decide about marrying a second time; his choice is a measure of his growth through the events of the novel. Meanwhile, in a reversal of fortune that recalls Hondorp's sudden leap into Golkian fame, Jack becomes the creator of a new television series. Riemer flies back to New York (Jack has sent plane tickets to everyone in the family) to watch the pilot. The only interesting character in the show, Riemer realizes with a shock of recognition, is the detective-hero's doctor father, a philandering "addled intellectual" whose "high-falutin' carelessness" makes trouble for everyone and propels the plot of every episode. Riemer is shaken by the resemblance between himself and the father on the screen, but he is forgiving, or at least he says to Jack: "where else should you draw characters from but people you know, people you feel strongly about? I just wish you didn't feel about me the way it shows up." The idea of

Dust jacket for Stern's most popular book, the story of a married middle-aged professor who falls in love with a twenty-year-old summer-school student

Stern the autobiographical novelist making his hero Riemer the victim of his son's caricature is wonderfully ironic.

A Father's Words is in some respects uncannily similar to *In Any Case*. Both novels are explicitly about father-son relationships; both are first-person narrations from the father's point of view. In each the father comes to realize he shares or is even the cause of his son's faults or crimes (in Bobbie's case, his alleged crimes). Sam Curry owns up to his many treasons, his betrayals of himself and of those he claims he loved. Emma confronts Riemer with the same fear of commitment in himself that he loathes in Jack. Both novels depict love relationships between older men and younger women which end in marriage and pregnancy.

The differences between *In Any Case* and *A Father's Words* are also instructive; they are in a sense one way to measure Stern's development over a period of twenty-four years. The later novel is more economical, more accessible, more humorous, more deeply felt, more tolerant of the protagonist, more natural in its dialogue, and more convincing in its depiction of other characters. *A Father's Words* is "an excellent novel," said John Gross in the *New York Times* (11 April 1986), and Doris Grumbach wrote in the *Chicago Tribune* that Stern's most recent novel produced in her "an apostolic desire to convince a wider audience to try Stern, especially this vintage Stern."

Although *A Father's Words* was well received by critics, Stern's own comments indicate that it was a difficult book for him to write. He has expressed regret about the lost time, the "cemetery" of wasted pages, his failure to recognize that the heart of *A Father's Words* "was—is—a transfiguration and projection of the author's relationships to two wives and four children." Since the book was published, furthermore, he has had to deal with the pain and anger of those who served as models for characters in the novel. "I think I'm finished now with family novels," he writes in "The Debris of a Novel" in *The Position of the Body*. "I've hurt everyone I can hurt. Not—as far as I know—trying to hurt, but there it is."

Despite such gloomy thoughts the 1980s have been a decade of substantial accomplishment and recognition for Stern. In addition to *Packages* and *A Father's Words*, Stern's second and third miscellanies were published, and several of his earlier novels were reissued. In 1981 Second Chance Press republished *In Any Case* as *The Chaleur Network*. Since that time, Arbor House has printed new editions of *Stitch*, *Other Men's Daughters*, and *Natural Shocks*; in the fall of 1987 Phoenix Books reissued *Golk*. Not having these books in print for so long had been for Stern "a form of death"; their reissue, on the other hand, has been cause for celebration, as is the anticipated publication in 1988 of his collected stories. Stern was also greatly cheered by the Medal of Merit for the Novel from the American Academy and Institute of Arts and Letters. "Totally unexpected," he wrote in his acceptance speech. "Out of the unblue blue. Strange, beautiful, heartrending, disturbing. The last because you'd settled into a version of yourself which excluded such acknowledgment."

At present, Stern is at work on a new novel, one which he says avoids "the domestic subject matter and sedate prose which have been my stock-in-trade." Instead, he would like the new book to reflect his recent interest in the work of T. Coraghessan Boyle, Barry Hannah, and Thomas Pynchon, writers whose "energy, allusiveness, obliquity, obscenity," and linguistic range Stern admires.

Stern's own admirers—the number is growing—are ready for anything, either a radical departure, or more of the delightful same. Whatever Stern writes next, they are confident that it will be the carefully wrought, deeply satisfying work of a dedicated master.

Interviews:

Robert L. Raeder, "An Interview with Richard Stern," *Chicago Review*, 18 (Winter/Spring 1966): 170-175;

Larry Rima, "An Interview with Richard Stern," *Chicago Review*, 28 (Winter 1977): 145-148;

Bonnie Birtwistle and James Schiffer, "Stern Talks about Writing," *Chicago* (June 1978): 184-190;

Elliott Anderson and Milton Rosenberg, "A Conversation with Richard Stern," *Chicago Review*, 31 (Winter 1980): 98-108;

Birtwistle, Schiffer, Anderson, Rosenberg, G. E. Murray, and Mary Anne Tapp, "Q-*and*-A," in Stern's *The Invention of the Real* (Athens: University of Georgia Press, 1982), pp. 219-233;

Marcia Froelke Coburn, "Writer Takes Hard Look at Brick Wall," *Chicago Sun-Times*, 20 November 1983, p. 3.

References:

Hugh Kenner, "Stitch: The Master's Voice," *Chicago Review*, 18 (Winter-Spring 1966): 176-180;

Bernard F. Rodgers, Jr., Foreword to *Golk* (Chicago: Phoenix, 1987), pp. vii-xii;

Douglas Unger, Introduction to *Natural Shocks* (New York: Arbor House, 1986), pp. 1-5.

Elie Wiesel

(30 September 1928-   )

John K. Roth
Claremont McKenna College

See also the Nobel Peace Prize entry in *DLB Yearbook: 1986*.

BOOKS: *Un di Velt Hot Geshvign* (Buenos Aires: Central Farbond Fun Poylishe Yidn in Argentina, 1956); revised and abridged as *La Nuit* (Paris: Editions de Minuit, 1958); *La Nuit* translated by Stella Rodway as *Night* (New York: Hill & Wang, 1960; London: MacGibbon & Kee, 1960);

L'Aube (Paris: Editions du Seuil, 1960); translated by Anne Borchardt as *Dawn* (New York: Hill & Wang, 1961); translated by Frances Frenaye (London: MacGibbon & Kee, 1961);

Le Jour (Paris: Editions du Seuil, 1961); translated by Borchardt as *The Accident* (New York: Hill & Wang, 1962);

La Ville de la chance (Paris: Editions du Seuil, 1962); translated by Stephen Becker as *The Town Beyond the Wall* (New York: Holt, Rinehart & Winston, 1964; London: Robson, 1975);

Les Portes de la forêt (Paris: Editions du Seuil, 1964); translated by Frenaye as *The Gates of the Forest* (New York: Holt, Rinehart & Winston, 1966; London: Heinemann, 1967);

Les Chants des morts (Paris: Editions du Seuil, 1966); translated by Steven Donadio as *Legends of Our Time* (New York: Holt, Rinehart & Winston, 1968);

Les Juifs de silence (Paris: Editions du Seuil, 1966); translated from the original Hebrew by Neal Kozodoy as *The Jews of Silence: A Personal Report on Soviet Jewry* (New York: Holt, Rinehart & Winston, 1966; London: Valentine Mitchell, 1968);

Zalmen ou la folie de Dieu (Paris: Editions du Seuil, 1968); translated by Nathan Edelman as *Zalmen, or the Madness of God* and adapted for the stage by Marion Wiesel (New York: Random House, 1974);

Le Mendiant de Jérusalem (Paris: Editions du Seuil, 1968); translated by Lily Edelman and Wiesel as *A Beggar in Jerusalem* (New York: Random House, 1970; London: Weidenfeld & Nicolson, 1970);

Entre deux soleils (Paris: Editions du Seuil, 1970); translated by Lily Edelman and Wiesel as *One Generation After* (New York: Random House, 1970; London: Weidenfeld & Nicolson, 1971);

Célébration hassidique: Portraits et légendes (Paris: Editions du Seuil, 1972); translated by Marion Wiesel as *Souls on Fire: Portraits and Legends of Hasidic Masters* (New York: Random House, 1972; London: Weidenfeld & Nicolson, 1972);

Le Serment de Kolvillàg (Paris: Editions du Seuil, 1973); translated by Marion Wiesel as *The Oath* (New York: Random House, 1973);

Ani maamin: un chant perdu et retrouvé (Paris: Editions du Seuil, 1973); translated by Marion Wiesel as *Ani Maamin: A Song Lost and Found Again* (New York: Random House, 1973);

Célébration biblique: Portraits et légendes (Paris: Editions du Seuil, 1975); translated by Marion Wiesel as *Messengers of God: Biblical Portraits and Legends* (New York: Random House, 1976);

Un Juif aujourd'hui (Paris: Editions du Seuil, 1977); translated by Marion Wiesel as *A Jew Today* (New York: Random House, 1978);

Four Hasidic Masters and Their Struggle Against Melancholy (Notre Dame, Ind.: University of Notre Dame Press, 1978);

Le Procès de Shamgorod (tel qu'il se déroula le 25 février 1649): Pièce en trois actes (Paris: Editions du Seuil, 1979); translated by Marion Wiesel as *The Trial of God (as it was held on February 25, 1649, in Shamgorod): A Play in Three Acts* (New York: Random House, 1979);

Images from the Bible (Woodstock, N.Y.: Overlook Press, 1980);

Le Testament d'un poète juif assassiné (Paris: Editions
　　du Seuil, 1980); translated by Marion
　　Wiesel as *The Testament* (New York: Summit,
　　1981; London: Allen Lane, 1981);
Five Biblical Portraits (Nore Dame, Ind.: Univer-
　　sity of Notre Dame Press, 1981);
Contre la mélancolie: Célébration hassidique II (Paris:
　　Editions du Seuil, 1981); translated by Mar-
　　ion Wiesel as *Somewhere a Master: Further Ha-
　　sidic Portraits and Legends* (New York:
　　Summit, 1982);
Paroles d'etranger (Paris: Editions du Seuil, 1982);
*The Golem: The Story of a Legend as Told By Elie
　　Wiesel* (New York: Summit, 1983);
Le Cinquième Fils (Paris: Editions Grasset, 1983);
　　translated by Marion Wiesel as *The Fifth Son*
　　(New York: Summit, 1985);
Against Silence: The Voice and Vision of Elie Wiesel, 3
　　volumes, edited by Irving Abrahamson
　　(New York: Holocaust Library, 1985);
Signes d'Exode (Paris: Grasset et Fasquelle, 1985);
Job ou Dieu dans la tempête (Paris: Grasset et
　　Fasquelle, 1986);
The Night Trilogy: Night, Dawn, The Accident (New
　　York: Farrar, Straus & Giroux, 1987);
Le Crépuscule, au loin (Paris: Grasset et Fasquelle,
　　1987).

In Elie Wiesel's autobiographical *La Nuit*
(1958; translated as *Night*, 1960), a transport arrives at Auschwitz-Birkenau. Bewildered Jews
from Sighet and other Transylvanian towns
emerge from train-car prisons into midnight air
fouled by burning flesh. Elie Wiesel, fifteen, his father, mother, and little sister, Tzipora, are
among them. Separated by the SS, the boy loses
sight of his mother and sister, not fully aware
that the parting is forever. Father and son stick together. In the commotion they hear a voice snarl,
"What have you come here for, you sons of
bitches? What are you doing here? . . . You'd
have done better to have hanged yourselves
where you were than to come here. Didn't you
know what was in store for you at Auschwitz?
Haven't you heard about it? In 1944?"

Caught in the Holocaust, the Nazi attempt
to exterminate the Jews of Europe, Wiesel and
his father learned soon enough what was in store
for them. They were sent "left" by Dr. Mengele,
the SS doctor whose baton directed life and
death. Headed toward a pit of flaming bodies,
they were steps from the edge when ordered to
the barracks.

From April 1944 until January 1945 Wiesel
and his father endured Auschwitz's brutal regi-
men. As Soviet troops approached the camp the
two were evacuated to Germany. Severely weakened by the death march to Buchenwald,
Wiesel's father perished there, but the son was liberated on 11 April 1945 and eventually reunited
with his older sisters, Hilda and Beatrice.

Wiesel remembers the consuming fire that
destroyed his pre-Holocaust Jewish world. Intensified and honed in silence, his memories have
found expression in a remarkable life of service
and authorship. On 14 October 1986 his words
and deeds were recognized by the announcement
that he had won the Nobel Peace Prize.

Speaking shortly after that announcement,
Wiesel said of the Holocaust, "I'm afraid that the
horror of that period is so dark, people are incapable of understanding, incapable of listening." Yet
Wiesel's writing, indeed all his work, testifies that
he does not despair. Hatred, indifference, history
itself, may do their worst, but Wiesel protests
against that outcome. By remembering the particularity of what happened to his people under Nazi
domination, and by acting on the imperatives
that such memory enjoins, he believes there is a
chance to mend the world. Wiesel's survival embodies that philosophy.

"The only role I sought," insists Wiesel,
"was that of witness. I believed that, having survived by chance, I was duty-bound to give meaning to my survival, to justify each moment of my
life." He has done so by leading the United
States Holocaust Memorial Council, by protesting
on behalf of oppressed people everywhere–
Soviet Jews and peoples in Cambodia, Biafra, Ban-
gladesh, and Latin America among them–by
interceding with world leaders such as Ronald Reagan and Mikhail S. Gorbachev, and by teaching
and lecturing throughout the world. But the foundation for these actions is Wiesel's writing desk in
New York City. There he composes in French his
novels, plays, essays, dialogues, and historical studies. Assisted by his wife, Marion Rose Wiesel,
who translates his recent work into English,
Wiesel has an especially receptive audience
among American readers, including large numbers of college and university students.

Wiesel received the Nobel Peace Prize in ceremonies held in Oslo, Norway, on 10 December
1986. Reflecting on that honor, Wiesel said: "I
have always felt that words mean responsibility. I
try to use them not against the human condition
but for humankind; never to create anger but to

Dust jacket for the American edition of Wiesel's 1973 novel Le Serment de Kolvillàg, *the story of a village that disappears except for one surviving witness who has sworn himself to silence*

attenuate anger, not to separate people but to bring them together." On previous occasions he has also remarked, "I write in order to understand as much as to be understood." All of these efforts have compelled him "to wrench [the Holocaust's] victims from oblivion. To help the dead vanquish death."

Wiesel does not see himself primarily as a philosopher, theologian, or political theorist. Instead his methods are usually those of the storyteller. Storytellers can deal with ultimate questions, but they do not always answer them directly. That style attracts Wiesel, because his Holocaust experiences make him suspicious of answers that put questions to rest. Such answers oversimplify. They falsify by settling what deserves to remain unsettled and unsettling.

In October 1986, shortly after the Nobel Peace Prize announcement, a reporter for *Le Monde* quizzed Wiesel about the religious implications of the Holocaust. "Did theodicy die in Auschwitz?" he wondered. "Can one still speak of providence today?" The title for the article in which these questions appeared–"My Protest is Within Faith"–drew on one of Wiesel's fundamen-

tal commitments. Thus Wiesel, who says "I am sometimes for God, often against God, but never without Him," replied as follows: "I have always thought that all questions were valid but that all answers were not necessarily so. . . . I believe that theodicy still exists, even after Auschwitz, but after Auschwitz it exists as a question, not as answer. Of course, you are asking me if one can still believe in providence after what happened. There again, I understand your question, but there is no answer. You know very well there is no answer. One must live with the answer, sometimes in opposition to the answer, or sometimes with the question but in opposition to the question. But to give the answer, and the answer alone without the question, this I cannot do."

The journey that took Elie Wiesel to Auschwitz and beyond began in his native Rumania, where he was born in 1928 on 30 September, the Jewish holiday of Simchat Torah, which celebrates the yearly completion-and-beginning of reading from the Law. His hometown, Sighet, was a border community in the Carpathian mountains. Once a part of the Austrian Empire, it was ceded to Rumania after World War I and subse-

Cover for the 1987 republication in a single volume of Wiesel's first three books

adopted language, he plunged into literature and philosophy at the Sorbonne from 1948 to 1951. Camus, Kierkegaard, and Kafka were among the writers who influenced him most. "All I wanted," he says of himself at the time, "was to study." He spent time in India, too, hoping to write a dissertation on asceticism in the Jewish, Christian, and Hindu traditions. He wrote at length on the subject but was unable to complete all of his university work because he had to support himself as a journalist. In that capacity Wiesel reported for *Yediot Ahronot,* Tel Aviv; *L'Archiv,* Paris; and *Jewish Daily Forward,* New York. These assignments took him to Israel in 1949 and then to New York in 1956 to cover the United Nations. That same year he was struck by a taxicab in Times Square. When a long convalescence prevented him from making a required return to France to renew expired papers, Wiesel, a "stateless person" at the time, was persuaded to apply for U.S. citizenship. He was naturalized in 1963.

During the first postwar decade, writing of more than a scholarly or journalistic kind had also been on Wiesel's mind. But he had vowed to be silent about his Holocaust experiences for ten years, and thus it was only in 1956 that he published his first book. Written in Yiddish, *Un di Velt Hot Geshvign* (And the World Remained Silent) was an 800-page account of his life in Auschwitz. Two years later he pared the manuscript to little more than 100 pages, translated the book into French, and published it as *La Nuit.* Of this memoir–it is Wiesel's best-known work and certainly the place to begin for any reader unacquainted with his writings–Wiesel observes that "all my subsequent books are built around it."

Wiesel also claims that "I have never spoken about the Holocaust except in one book, *Night*– the very first–where I tried to tell a tale directly, as though face to face with the experience." That self-appraisal is correct but only to a degree, for if the Holocaust is not often placed center stage in his writings, it nonetheless shadows every word he writes. Ever conscious of the particularity of his Jewish identity and of the Holocaust's impact upon it, Wiesel underscores that "not all victims were Jewish. But all Jews were victims. The universality of the Holocaust lies in its uniqueness."

More than twenty-five of Wiesel's books have been published since *Night* appeared. As of this writing, they include four works that are yet to be published in English translations: two collections of essays and stories, *Paroles d'etranger*

quently came under Hungarian control during World War II. Its Jewish people were deported after the Nazis occupied the territory of their faltering Hungarian allies in 1944. In addition to his yeshiva schooling, the young Wiesel was encouraged by his father, Shlomo, a grocer and shopkeeper, to study modern Hebrew language and literature. His mother, Sarah Feig, ensured that her son knew the stories and teachings of the Hasidic masters, as well as the traditions of Torah, Talmud, and Kabbala. Early in the war Wiesel's father was jailed for several months because he helped rescue Polish Jews who had found their way to Hungary. Nevertheless, the boy's worlds of study, faith, and Jewish tradition remained relatively undisturbed. Then his experience was shattered by entry into what Wiesel calls the Kingdom of Night.

Liberated at the war's end, Wiesel was assisted by French relief agencies and eventually took up residence in Paris. With French as his

Dust jacket for the American edition of Wiesel's 1964 novel Les Portes de la forêt, *the story of a young man's reconciliation to living in a world that his god has abandoned*

(1982) and *Signes d'Exode* (1985); a dialogue and commentary with Josy Eisenberg, *Job ou Dieu dans la tempête* (1986); and a novel entitled *Le Crépuscule, au loin* (1987). There are also three large volumes of his reviews, forewords, commentaries, and other occasional pieces that have been carefully compiled by Irving Abrahamson as *Against Silence: The Voice and Vision of Elie Wiesel* (1985).

Critics have called Wiesel's prose "charged, so subtle, so superb" (John Leonard, reviewing *A Beggar in Jerusalem* in the *New York Times*, 27 January 1970) but also "pretentious, stylistically self-indulgent and didactic to the point of sanctimony" (Robert Kirsch, reviewing *The Oath* in the *Los Angeles Times*, 2 January 1974). In *Legacy of Night: The Literary Universe of Elie Wiesel* (along with Molly Abramowitz's *Elie Wiesel: A Bibliography*, it identifies many reviews of Wiesel's work) Ellen S. Fine points out that his "style is unique because of the way it fuses aspects of the French novel with Jewish lore." She adds, how-

ever, that "the thrust of his writing does not lie in his literary techniques and he has openly rejected the notion of art for art's sake. He is basically a storyteller with something to say."

Wiesel has hundreds of tales to tell. Yet in one way or another they all trace back to a biblical tradition in which Moses, speaking in God's name, commanded his people to choose life. With the Holocaust as the background, Wiesel's writings set before the reader life and death and urge him or her to choose life.

What life-choosing means in a world scarred by the Holocaust is not, however, a story easily told. The task involves what Robert McAfee Brown calls a tortuous "journey from the reality of nihilism toward the possibility of affirmation." Wiesel still wonders whether the task can be accomplished. Too often words are "inadequate, worn, foolish, lifeless." The problem is compounded, he believes, because "a novel on Majdanek is either not a novel or not about Majdanek. Between the dead and the rest of us there exists an abyss that no talent can bridge." And yet Wiesel's talent finds ways to communicate. He raises disturbing, life-intensifying questions about the relationship between God and man. "A Jew," asserts Wiesel, "defines himself more by what troubles him than by what reassures him. . . . To me, the Jew and his questioning are one." To be touched by Wiesel's instructive words–at once concrete and richly symbolic–is to be moved toward that identity. Thus, it is Wiesel's gift to draw on the singularity of his Jewish experience and tradition in such a way as to touch profoundly anyone who follows him with sensitivity.

Night begins with a boy who "believed profoundly." It ends with a reflection: "From the depths of the mirror, a corpse gazed back at me. The look in his eyes, as they stared into mine, has never left me." In *l'univers concentrationnaire*, as another survivor, David Rousset, names it, assumptions treasured and persons loved were stripped away. But the dead left Wiesel behind to encounter the living.

In Wiesel's next work, *L'Aube* (1960; translated as *Dawn*, 1961), a young Holocaust survivor, Elisha, strives to free Palestine from British rule so that a people and a nation can find new life. But Elisha finds this is easier said than done. Once the possible victim of an executioner, he must execute a British captain, John Dawson, in retribution for the slaying of an Israeli freedom fighter. "That's it," Elisha says to himself. "It's

done. I've killed. I've killed Elisha." Insofar as
choosing life requires choosing death as well,
dawn may be difficult to distinguish from the "tattered fragment of darkness" that reflects Elisha's
face as he gazes through a window at the breaking of a not-so-new day.

Hitler's Final Solution seemed to mock
every search for a healing resolution; thus, the
title *Dawn* is ironic. In *Le Jour* (1961; translated
not literally, as Day, but as *The Accident*, 1962), despite the fact that he has friends, and even a
woman who loves him, another survivor, Eliezer,
steps in front of a moving car. The "accident" is
no accident, and yet life returns to be chosen
again. "The problem," Wiesel proposes, "is not:
to be or not to be. But rather: to be and not to
be." But how to do so? Wiesel returns to that question again and again.

In *The Accident* the victim's artist-friend,
Gyula, whose name means redemption, urges
Eliezer to choose life and put the past behind
him. He paints Eliezer's portrait. The eyes are
searing, for "they belonged to a man who had
seen God commit the most unforgivable crime:
to kill without a reason." After showing Eliezer
the portrait, Gyula symbolizes the end of the past
by setting fire to the canvas. Though he is moved
by Gyula's testimony, Eliezer will not be fully
healed by it, for the novel's final line states that
Gyula departed and forgot "to take along the
ashes."

Wiesel's first works travel through the destruction of a supportive universe into a post-
Holocaust world of ambiguity, despair, and
nothingness in which life almost succeeds in fulfilling a desire to cancel itself. The depths of despair had to be plumbed as a prelude to Wiesel's
hard-won insistence that the essence of being Jewish is "never to give up—never to yield to despair." That affirmation is one of his categorical
imperatives, but to form and keep it is anything
but easy.

Wiesel's initial trilogy (reissued as such in
The Night Trilogy: Night, Dawn, The Accident, 1987)
was followed by *La Ville de la chance* (1962; translated as *The Town Beyond the Wall*, 1964). Once
Michael's home, Szerencseváros is now in the vise
of Communist victors over Nazi tyrants. Secretly
returning to see whether anyone can be found, Michael stands before his former home. Ages ago a
face watched silently there while Jews were sent
away. The face, seeking a hatred from Michael to
match its own hidden guilt, informs the police. Michael finds himself imprisoned in walls within his

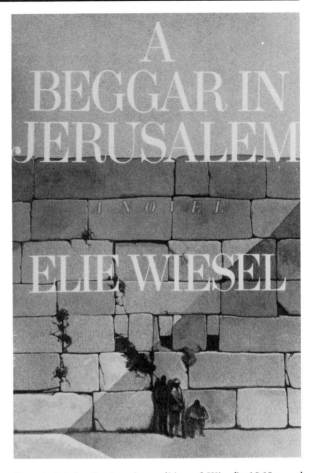

Dust jacket for the American edition of Wiesel's 1968 novel
Le Mendiant de Jérusalem, *which won the*
Prix Médicis

past, tortured to tell a story that cannot be told:
there is no political plot to reveal; his captors
would never accept the simple truth of his desire
to see his hometown once more; his friend,
Pedro, who returned with him, must be protected. Michael holds out. He resists an escape
into madness and tries his best to rescue his cell
mate from a catatonic silence.

The Town Beyond the Wall is one of Wiesel's
most eloquent protests against indifference. It is
also an affirmation of Gyula's insight from *The Accident*: "Maybe God is dead, but man is alive. The
proof: he is capable of friendship." Gregor, another Jew spared alone in the destruction of a universe and now a resident of Brooklyn, is the
protagonist in Wiesel's 1964 novel, *Les Portes de la
forêt* (translated as *The Gates of the Forest*, 1966).
The struggle is long, but he also resists his own suffering by taking heart from friends who were left
behind. Married to Clara, whom he met in the forest Resistance, Gregor finds that their life together focuses on the missing, the absent, the

dead–Gavriel, Leib, Yehuda–all of whom taught worthy visions of life only to have those visions end violently. Love cannot grow in those surroundings–at least not love for the living–and Gregor decides to leave Clara in the hope that the past, present, and future can separate themselves more clearly. But the book ends with Gregor's renewed determination to breathe life into his relationship with Clara, with his taking of Gavriel's name, and with his honoring Leib by joining a synagogue community to pray the *Kaddish*, "the solemn affirmation, filled with grandeur and serenity, by which man returns God his crown and scepter." One of the keys to this change is the message of Yehuda: "It's inhuman to wall yourself up in pain and memories as if in a prison. Suffering must open us to others. It must not cause us to reject them."

Wiesel introduces *The Gates of the Forest* with a Hasidic tale. Its ending includes this thought: "All I can do is to tell the story." Wiesel's story is an interrogation of life that, to cite Brown once again, moves "from solitude to solidarity, from looking into the visible face of death to looking into the invisible face of God, and . . . from being alone in a forest to being surrounded by others in a city. . . ." The message that builds as Wiesel's career proceeds is that good reasons for choosing life can indeed be found, even in a world turned upside down by the Holocaust. Choose life because suffering and indifference are real, because friendship exists, love is possible, and responsibility is put upon us. Such reasons are largely those of refusal, resistance, and rebellion against every power that yields needless, senseless waste. Learn the links between suffering and indifference, between friendship and responsibility. Respond to suffering with love. Respond to indifference with protest. Constituting Wiesel's story, these responses provide reasons enough to live hard and well.

By 1965 Wiesel's literary prowess was winning book awards such as the French Prix Rivarol and the National Jewish Book Council Literary Award. His credits were enhanced further in the next year with the appearance of *Les Juifs de silence* (1966; translated as *The Jews of Silence: A Personal Report on Soviet Jewry*, 1966) and *Les Chants des morts* (1966; translated as *Legends of Our Time*, 1968). Originally a series of articles for *Yediot Ahronot*, the former describes the first of Wiesel's many visits to the Soviet Union on behalf of persecuted Jews, whose cause he has championed for more than twenty years. The latter

brings together fifteen short pieces by Wiesel– many of them autobiographical–on a wide range of pre- and post-Auschwitz themes, including recollections of his father's death, Yom Kippur in Auschwitz, a meeting with a Spanish Jew, and "A Plea for the Dead," which contains some of Wiesel's most frequently quoted words: "At Auschwitz, not only man died, but also the idea of man. . . . It was its own heart the world incinerated at Auschwitz."

That Wieselian counterpoint continues to make the battle against despair one that lacks victory as a foregone conclusion. Memories, losses, lack of progress in humanity's moral condition still gnaw away. Nothing guarantees that life chosen will be life left to live. "Et pourtant, et pourtant . . . " (And yet, and yet . . .): frequently those words intrude in Wiesel's writings. Experiences and ideas seem to be moving inexorably to one conclusion, but then Wiesel signals that there is more to say and inquiry must be sustained. Thus, another of Wiesel's characters insists that "God requires of man not that he live, but that he choose to live. What matters is to choose–at the risk of being defeated."

Those lines belong to an old Russian rabbi in Wiesel's first play, *Zalmen ou la folie de Dieu* (1968; translated as *Zalmen, or the Madness of God*, 1974), which has been produced in Israel, Germany, and Canada, as well as in the United States and France. Provoked by his assistant, Zalmen (or by the madness of God), the rabbi risks Soviet wrath by telling a troupe of visiting actors from the West about the suffering of his people. It remains unclear whether the rabbi's protest changes anything, but Wiesel's protest between the lines is that we must not leave the rabbi alone, we must not allow his sacrifice to be in vain.

Le Mendiant de Jérusalem (translated as *A Beggar in Jerusalem*, 1970), arguably Wiesel's most complex and brilliant novel, also appeared in 1968, but in a sense he had not planned on writing it. Wiesel thought *The Gates of the Forest* could conclude a cycle of novels reflecting on the Holocaust and its aftermath. After its completion he had turned to work on a book about the plight of Soviet Jews, *Le Testament d'un poète juif assassiné* (1980; translated as *The Testament*, 1981), which would be delayed for over a decade due to the Six Day War that broke out suddenly in 1967. Under threat again, this time the Jews were victorious. A divided Jerusalem, including the western wall of the ancient temple, was restored to their

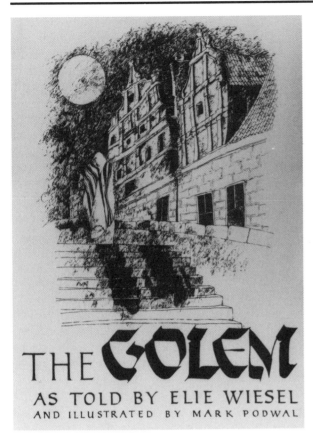

Dust jacket for Wiesel's 1983 recounting of the many legends concerning Rabbi Yehuda Lowe's creature of clay, told through the character of gravedigger Reuven

keeping. *A Beggar in Jerusalem* was Wiesel's response to this moving event.

Apparently the lone survivor of a Nazi massacre, David, the novel's narrator, is in Jerusalem. Although the city has been secured by Israeli troops, that result creates no simple satisfaction. The prices paid for the repeated "destructions of Jerusalem elsewhere than in Jerusalem" remain too high for that. In both joy and sadness, David finds companionship with Shlomo, Dan, Menashe, Yakov, Moshe, Zalmen–spirits who gather at the Wall. They wait–some for understanding, others for lost friends–all in their own ways for God. They also swap stories and thereby roam the world restlessly. David watches for his friend Katriel, but this man, whose name in Hebrew means "the crown of God," is missing in action. David tells Katriel's story. In doing so he tells his own as well. David has fallen in love with Malka, but she is Katriel's widow. "Do you understand," Wiesel writes, "that love, no matter how personal or universal, is not a solution? And that outside of love there is no solution?"

David and Malka marry. As they bear witness to the past, their marriage suggests that despite what has happened, even because of it, life must be loved. Wiesel dedicated *A Beggar in Jerusalem* to his future wife, whom he married a year after its publication. Marion Wiesel–her French and English, says her husband, are "perfect" and thus "she is the ideal translator"–is a native of Vienna and also a survivor. She has a daughter, Jennifer, from a previous marriage. In 1972, again bearing witness that life must be loved, Marion and Elie Wiesel became the parents of Shlomo Elisha, who is named for Elie Wiesel's father.

Meanwhile, Wiesel continued to write. *Entre deux soleils* (translated as *One Generation After*, 1970) appeared in 1970, twenty-five years after the liberation of Auschwitz. Akin to *Legends of Our Time*, it recollects some snapshots, a watch, a violin, the death of a teacher, and excerpts from a diary. Wiesel, increasingly successful and honored as an author, also remembers that "my first royalties were two bowls of soup, awarded me for a creative work never set to paper." In his Auschwitz block Wiesel used words to re-create a Shabbat meal. The taste of the soup he won that night, says Wiesel, "still lingers in my mouth."

In 1972 Wiesel was appointed Distinguished Professor in the Department of Jewish Studies at City College of the City University of New York, a position he held until 1976, when he became Andrew Mellon Professor in the Humanities at Boston University. In 1972 he also published one of his best-loved books, *Célébration hassidique: Portraits et légendes* (translated as *Souls on Fire: Portraits and Legends of Hasidic Masters*, 1972). Along with *Four Hasidic Masters and Their Struggle Against Melancholy* (1978) and *Contre la mélancolie: Célébration hassidique II* (1981; translated as *Somewhere a Master: Further Hasidic Portraits and Legends*, 1982), *Souls on Fire* is Wiesel's tribute to a Jewish spirituality that found ways to celebrate life, even "in the shadow of the executioner."

Born out of Jewish suffering, plus a passionate love for life and tradition that could not find adequate expression in eighteenth-century Europe, Hasidism renewed the old and found ways to celebrate. Nourished by its examples and stories, succeeding generations kept Hasidism alive, even in Auschwitz. Thanks to writers such as Wiesel, this tradition lives on–perhaps stronger than anyone might have guessed–even though the eastern European communities in which it emerged are gone. Introducing Israel Baal Shem Tov, the movement's founder, and his many disciples, Wiesel describes Hasidism as fiercely human-istic. Its aim was always to affirm the world of life-here-and-now, to make life better here-and-now. Therefore, life must be lived so it can be cele-brated; it must be celebrated so that it can be lived.

Characters and stories from the Bible capti-vate Wiesel no less than his Hasidic teachers and their tales. In 1973, for example, Wiesel penned *Ani maamin: un chant perdu et retrouvé* (translated as *Ani Maamin: A Song Lost and Found Again*, 1973), the text for a cantata with music by Darius Milhaud which premiered at Carnegie Hall, New York City, 11 November 1973. The title comes from a Jewish song of faith that Wiesel learned in Sighet. He heard it in the camps, too. "Ani maamin . . . I believe. I believe in the coming of the Messiah, and even if he tarries I shall wait for him. . . . I believe."

Wiesel's text imagines a meeting between God and three biblical figures: Abraham, Isaac, and Jacob. These patriarchs work to gather "the echoes of Jewish suffering in the world, and make them known in heaven." When history be-comes Nazi slaughter, the observers return from earth to challenge God with Holocaust reports. Urging intercession, they have mixed success at best, but they refuse either to abandon their peo-ple or to let God alone. Three other works fo-cused on the Bible—*Célébration biblique: Portraits et légendes* (1975; translated as *Messengers of God: Bibli-cal Portraits and Legends*, 1976), *Images from the Bible* (1980; a volume containing reproductions of the paintings of Shalom of Safed), and *Five Bibli-cal Portraits* (1981)—make similar points. Included in these books are reflections on Joseph, Job, Joshua, Jeremiah, plus others before and after them. Collectively, one of their most challenging messages is that "it is given to man to transform di-vine injustice into human justice and com-passion."

That message is also Azriel's, the main char-acter in Wiesel's 1973 novel, *Le Serment de Kolvillàg* (translated as *The Oath*, 1973). Like many of Wiesel's leading men, Azriel has a name that contains the Hebrew *El*, which refers to God. Michael in *The Town Beyond the Wall* is "who is like God"; Gavriel is "man of God" in *The Gates of the Forest;* and even Wiesel's own name, Eliezer, means "help of God." Azriel is "whom God helps." If that meaning is valid, the fact is not im-mediately apparent because *The Oath* tells of a community that disappeared except for one sur-viving witness.

A long record of testimony against violence had seemed to do little to restrain men and women—and even God—from further vengeance. And so, besieged in a pogrom in Kolvillàg, Azriel and other Jews were inspired by Moshe to try a dif-ferent life-saving strategy: "By ceasing to refer to the events of the present, we would forestall or-deals in the future." Only Azriel survives. He bears the chronicles of Kolvillàg—one created with his eyes, the other in a book entrusted to him for safekeeping by his father, the community's historian. Azriel bears the oath of Kolvillàg as well, torn between speech and si-lence but true to his promise.

Many years later, Azriel meets a young man who is about to kill himself in a desperate at-tempt to give his life significance by refusing to live it. Azriel decides to intervene, to find a way to make the waste of suicide impossible for his new friend. He succeeds by breaking his oath and relating his own experience. His young friend's testimony is that "by allowing me to enter his life, [Azriel] gave meaning to mine." Si-lence has its virtues, but it must also be broken to ensure that no executioner kills twice, the second by failures to tell the tale.

Still other ways to recount his story and its variations on the theme of life-choosing appear in Wiesel's 1977 work, *Un Juif aujourd'hui* (trans-lated as *A Jew Today*, 1978). Pondering further what it means to be Jewish, one of Wiesel's affirma-tions is that the Jew's "mission was never to make the world Jewish, but, rather, to make it more human." Part of Wiesel's attempt to do so in this book involves a series of distinctive dialogues. The dialogue in Wiesel's novels is always remark-able, but in *A Jew Today* and in his earlier book *One Generation After* he crafts a dialogue form that becomes a genre distinctively his own. The words and lines of these dialogues are spare and lean. They are utterly, yet deceptively, simple. "Every word," as Robert McAfee Brown con-tends, "points to things that can never be seen, to complexities beyond our ability to grasp. The sim-pler the sentence, the more complex the idea." Al-though the settings are unidentified and the characters unnamed, these conversations commu-nicate the particularity of Wiesel's experience, memory, and concern in powerfully moving ways.

One example from *A Jew Today* is a dialogue between "A Man and His Little Sister." She asks: "Will you remember me too?" He reassures her; he has "forgotten nothing." He will tell that she was only eight when she died, that she had never seen the sea or been to a real wedding, and that she never hurt anyone. She wants him to remember how she loved her new winter coat, Shabbat, and God. He shall; he will speak, too. But the little sister worries about her brother, now a man alone and cold. She grieves for herself, for him, for them all. She also asks two more questions and her brother answers:

> "When you speak of your little sister leaving you like that, without a hug, without a goodbye, without wishing you a good journey, will you say that it was not her fault?"
> *"It was not your fault."*
> "Then whose fault was it?"
> *"I shall find out. And I shall tell. I swear to you, little sister. I shall."*

This dialogue never happened. It could not have happened. And yet it did. In the introduction to *Legends of Our Time* Wiesel tells a tale about meeting an old teacher who had known his grandfather. The teacher wanted to know what his friend's grandson was doing. When Wiesel answered that he was a writer of stories, the teacher asked, "What kind?" Specifically, he wanted to know, were these stories about things that happened or could have happened? Yes, replied Wiesel, his stories were of that kind. The old teacher, sensing ambiguity in the response, pressed on: Well, did the stories happen or didn't they? No, Wiesel admitted, not all of the things in his stories did happen; some of them, in fact, were invented from start to finish. Disappointment came over the old man. That means, he said, that you are writing lies. Taken aback, Wiesel paused, then responded: "Things are not that simple, Rebbe. Some events do take place but are not true; others are—although they never occurred." Wiesel adds that he does not know whether his answer was sufficient, but it is also true that he has not stopped re-creating the dialogues that are such an important part of "legends of our time."

Awarded honorary degrees by Wesleyan University (1979), Brandeis University (1980), and Yale University (1981), to name only a few, plus literary prizes such as France's 1980 Prix Livre-Inter (for *The Testament*), Wiesel took on new responsibilities when President Jimmy Carter appointed him to chair the United States Holocaust Memorial Council, which is charged to honor the dead, remember the past, and educate for the fu-

ture. Wiesel served in this position from 1980 to 1986. Meanwhile he commutes weekly to Boston University to meet his students. Within that busy schedule, which also includes many trips abroad, time is saved for writing in his New York study—specifically the hours between 6:00 and 10:00 A.M. There his present pattern is to work concurrently on three kinds of writing: a novel, reflections on Hasidism and Talmud, plus studies of biblical characters.

Wiesel also finds time to write essays, reviews, and plays. Rarely has he written dialogue more powerful than that in his drama, *Le Procès de Shamgorod (tel qu'il se déroula le 25 février 1649): Pièce en trois actes* (1979; translated as *The Trial of God (as it was held on February 25, 1649, in Shamgorod): A Play in Three Acts*, 1979). Wiesel is not inclined to be a systematic theologian, but he takes religious questions with the utmost seriousness. In *Night* he spoke of the flames that destroyed his faith forever. And yet that is not inconsistent with his continuing dialogue with God. For if Auschwitz made it no longer possible to trust God simply, it made wrestling with God all the more important. Wiesel remains at odds with God, because the only way he can be for God after Auschwitz is by being against God, too. To accept God without protest would do too much to vindicate God and legitimize evil. Nowhere does Wiesel argue for that point more effectively than in *The Trial of God*, which has been performed in France, Norway, and Italy, and whose stage instructions indicate that it should be played as a tragic farce.

The play is set in the village of Shamgorod at the season of Purim, a joyous festival replete with masks and reenactments that celebrates a moment in Jewish history when oppressors were outmaneuvered and Jews were saved. Three Jewish actors have lost their way, and they arrive at the village. Here they discover that Shamgorod is hardly a place for festivity. Two years before, a murderous pogrom had ravaged the town. Only two Jews survived. Berish the innkeeper escaped, but he had to watch while his daughter was unspeakably abused on her wedding night. She now lives mercifully out of touch with the world.

In the region of Shamgorod, anti-Jewish hatred festers once again, and it is not unthinkable that a new pogrom may break out to finish the work left undone. Purim, however, cannot be Purim without a play, and so a *Purimspiel* will be given, but with a difference urged by Berish. This time the play will enact the trial of God. As the characters in Wiesel's drama begin to organize their play-within-a-play, one problem looms large. The defendant, God, is silent, and on this Purim night no one in Shamgorod wants to speak for God. Unnoticed, however, a stranger has entered the inn, and just when it seems that the defense attorney's role will go unfilled, the newcomer–his name is Sam–volunteers to act the part. Apparently Berish's Gentile housekeeper Maria has seen this man before, and she advises the others to have nothing to do with him. However, her warning goes unheeded.

Berish prosecutes. God, he charges, "could use His might to save the victims, but He doesn't! So–on whose side is He? Could the killer kill without His blessing–without His complicity?" Apologies for God do not sit well with this Jewish patriarch. "If I am given the choice of feeling sorry for Him or for human beings," he exclaims, "I choose the latter anytime. He is big enough, strong enough to take care of Himself; man is not." Berish's protest is as real as his despair. Neither deny God's reality; both affirm it by calling God to account.

Sam's style is different. He has an answer for every charge, and he cautions that emotion is no substitute for evidence. In short, he defends God brilliantly. Sam's performance dazzles the visiting actors who have formed the court. Despite their curiosity, Sam will not tell them who he is, but his identity and the verdict implicit in *The Trial of God* do not remain moot. As the play's final scene unfolds, a mob approaches to pillage the inn at Shamgorod once more. Sensing that the end is near, the Jewish actors choose to die with their Purim masks in place. Sam dons one, too, and as he does so, Maria's premonitions are corroborated. Sam's mask is worthy of his namesake, Samael. Both signify Satan. As a final candle is extinguished and the inn's doors open to the sound of deafening and murderous roars, Satan's laughter is among them.

Set nearly three centuries before the rise of the Third Reich, this play is not about the Holocaust. And yet it is, because Wiesel introduces the script by reporting that he witnessed a trial of God in Auschwitz. What he does not mention in that foreword is that when the rabbis who conducted the Auschwitz trial had finished and found God guilty, those men–each "erudite and pious"–noted that it was time for their customary religious observances. So they bowed their heads and prayed.

Wiesel has observed that many of those freed from the Nazi camps believed that the world must not have known about them. Disabused of that naiveté, some still clung to the idea that if they told what had happened to them, the effect would be sobering and transforming. That hope, too, proved illusory, for the story has been told, responsibility has been assessed, and if anything the Holocaust is more widely a part of human memory today than at any time before. Such labor, however, has not been sufficient to check the violence, suffering, and indifference that waste life away. Not even anti-Semitism has been eclipsed. At times Wiesel hints that eventual self-destruction is the price humankind will pay for Auschwitz, but that counsel of doom will not be his last word, as evidenced by his 1980 novel *Le Testament d'un poète juif assassiné* (translated as *The Testament*, 1981), which Wiesel began more than ten years earlier. It traces the odyssey of Paltiel Kossover, a character who represents hundreds of Jewish intellectuals condemned to death in 1952 by Joseph Stalin, whose contribution to mass murder rivaled Hitler's. In this novel the Holocaust stands not center stage but, as usual, casts its shadows before and after all the action. This book, moreover, contains Wiesel's most fundamental answer to the question he must face repeatedly: have things gone so far that memory and protest rooted in the Holocaust are essentially futile?

Arrested and questioned, Paltiel, whose name means "God is my refuge," expects to disappear without a trace. He is encouraged by his KGB interrogater to write an autobiography in which, the official hopes, the prisoner will confess more than he does by direct questioning. Kossover can sustain his life by writing about it, but he has no reason to think his testament will ever reach anyone he loves. Even less can he assume that his telling the tale of his own experience will in any way influence history. Still, he tries his best, and what his best amounts to involves an ancient story–often repeated by Wiesel– that serves as the prologue for *The Testament*.

It speaks of a Just Man who came to Sodom to save that place from sin and destruction. Observing the Just Man's care, a child approached him compassionately:

"Poor stranger, you shout, you
scream, don't you see it's hopeless?"
"Yes, I see."
"Then why do you go on?"

"I'll tell you why. In the beginning, I thought I could change man. Today, I know I cannot. If I still shout today, if I still scream, it is to prevent man from ultimately changing me."

Kossover does not escape the Soviet prison, but his testament finds a way out. It reaches and touches the poet's son, and thus Wiesel insists again by way of analogy that the enormous loss of the Holocaust is not all that remains.

A future still awaits our determination. That theme, carried forward from *The Testament,* informs two of Wiesel's most recent books, one set in sixteenth-century Prague, the other in twentieth-century America. In *The Golem: The Story of a Legend as Told by Elie Wiesel* (1983), Wiesel re-creates legends about "the 'Golem made of clay,' created in the year 1580 by the great and famous Rabbi Yehuda Lowe of Prague, known as the Maharal." Wiesel's storyteller, a wizened gravedigger named Reuven who claims to have witnessed as a child the numerous miracles attributed to the Golem, recounts how the Maharal, seeking to defend his people from suffering, was granted wisdom to create from clay a "servant and ally" whose mission would be to "protect the people of Israel from their enemies." This the Golem did for ten years. Then the Maharal and his two favorite disciples apparently determined it was time "the Golem returned to dust." With tears in their eyes, they took the Golem to the attic of their synagogue. As the appropriate ritual was enacted, "the Golem fell into a deep, endless sleep."

After a few days, Reuven testifies, most people forgot the Golem. Nevertheless, threatening excommunication to any who disobeyed, the Maharal forbade further access to the attic. Eventually the Maharal died and circumstances changed. Much later a few persons ventured into the attic. One went mad, another perished, a third lost his soul. Why this happened, no one was sure, but the explanation given to Reuven by a wandering beggar is that "the Maharal had forbidden access to the attic because, in truth, the Golem had remained alive. And he is waiting to be called."

As for himself, Reuven adds, "I wish I knew." The reader wonders, too. Why the Maharal's tears, for example? Were they shed for a friend who was needed no longer because things would be better—or were they anticipations of destruction that even the Golem could not fore-

stall? Other questions are equally disturbing: Why the Maharal's prohibition against entering the attic? Was it because he wanted people to draw not from his inspiration but from their own to create protection against "fire and death"? Have those resources been there all along but forgotten? If so, when one looks, so to speak, into the attic and finds them, what will the reaction be to the unjustifiable and unnecessary power of injustice? Wiesel gives his readers work to do. The task, however, is not only to wrestle with the meaning of his texts but also, like the Maharal, "to improve the lot of [their] brothers and sisters."

That assignment is taken seriously by Ariel, who narrates Wiesel's 1983 novel *Le Cinquième Fils* (translated as *The Fifth Son,* 1985), which is dedicated to his son "Elisha and all the other children of survivors." At the outset the reader is reminded of the Passover ritual that refers to "four sons: one who is wise and one who is contrary; one who is simple and one who does not even know how to ask a question." After Auschwitz additions need to be made. They should include a son who is not here and also a son who was not there. Ariel, the fifth son, is both—one son and yet two. Ariel, born in 1949, is today a professor "in a small university in Connecticut." He has a brother, but that fact was long hidden from him by his parents. His brother, also named Ariel, was hunted down and killed by the SS in Davarowsk when he was a child.

His parents, Rachel and Reuven Tamiroff, survived, chose life in New York, even gave Ariel a second birth to affirm it, and yet they found that a second Ariel might double their sadness more than their joy. For what identity could they give him, and what identity did they give him by naming him Ariel? No one is better equipped than Elie Wiesel to probe such issues. The two Ariels, their father, and the encounters they have had—all are encompassed by his own experience. In the words of Ariel, who in this case may well speak for Wiesel himself, "I have said 'I' in their stead. Alternately, I have been one or the other."

The second Ariel discovers neither his brother's story nor his own until he finds the letters that his father has written to his deceased son. He also learns that Reuven Tamiroff's melancholy derives in part from the conviction that he and Simha Zeligson made good their attempt to assassinate Davarowsk's SS leader, the *Angel,* in 1946. For years they meet weekly to study and debate, seeking to determine in retrospect whether their action was indeed just. But Ariel learns that the *Angel* lives, prosperous and happy, as a German businessman. He decides, too, that unfinished business must remain so no longer.

However, Ariel does not kill, and the reason has everything to do with Ariel's being Jewish, with his being the fifth son, with his being human. Wiesel hints about how that works. Ariel, for example, receives advice from his neighbor and friend, Rebbe Zvi-Hersh, who says, "To punish a guilty man, to punish him with death, means linking yourself to him forever: is that what you wish?" In this case, however, the question is just as important as the traditional counsel that precedes it. If "yes" is not the best answer, "no" does not follow without pain. For anyone who cares, as Ariel's "sad summing up" implies, the truth is that a life lived after Auschwitz–not only by the first generation but also by the second–cannot be one's own alone but instead will be permeated by "the memory of the living and the dreams of the dead."

That fact may account for the name Wiesel bestowed on the two fifth sons. Ariel is a biblical name. It appears more than once in Scripture, and its meanings are diverse. The name can mean "lion of God" and also "light of God," which could explain why a later tradition thought of Ariel as an angel altogether different from the *Angel*. Unfortunately, a darker side haunts the name as well. In Isaiah's prophecy, for instance, the following words can be found: "Yet I will distress Ariel, and there shall be moaning and lamentation, and she shall be to me like an Ariel" (Isaiah 29:2). The first Ariel signifies Jerusalem; the second suggests that Ariel will become like an altar, a scene of holocaust. But the oracle sees more. In time, "the nations that fight against Ariel" will themselves be quelled by "the flame of devouring fire" (Isaiah 29:5-8). Perhaps that is true–or will be–but having met the *Angel*, Ariel Tamiroff remembers another old saying: "The Lord may wish to chastise, that is His prerogative; but it is mine to refuse to be his whip." For both his brother's sake and his own, Ariel will identify with his people, with Jerusalem even though he chooses to live in the Diaspora, and thereby with the well-being of humankind. Thus, he seems most like his namesake in the book of Ezra, where Ariel is called a "leading" man (Ezra 8:16). His leadership urges remembrance and return from exile. It seems to respond to devastation and sadness by acts of restoration that rebuild Jerusalem and mend the world.

As the title of Irving Abrahamson's 1985 three-volume compilation of Wiesel's miscellaneous writings suggests, this survivor ultimately takes his stand "against silence." Thus, in April 1985, when Wiesel received the Congressional Gold Medal of Achievement from President Reagan, he used the occasion to contend that the president ought not visit a cemetery in Bitburg, West Germany, where members of the SS are buried. "That place, Mr. President, is not your place," Wiesel argued. "Your place is with the victims of the SS." Those words did not deter the visit, but Wiesel's testimony created tension that deserved to be felt.

"You cannot live without tension," Wiesel reckons. Anguish and sorrow, anger and sadness, impassion his writing, but so do action and satisfaction, affirmation and solidarity. Never is one strand present without the others. "The Holocaust experience," he insists, "requires an attitude of total honesty. . . . Our future depends on our testimony. . . . This is why survivors often overcome their fear and trembling and speak up. For the sake of our children and yours, we invoke the past so as to save the future. We recall ultimate violence in order to prevent its reoccurrence. Ours then is a twofold commitment: to life and truth."

Interviews:

Gene Koppel and Henry Kaufman, *Elie Wiesel: A Small Measure of Victory* (Tucson: University of Arizona Press, 1974);

Harry James Cargas, *Harry James Cargas in Conversation with Elie Wiesel* (New York: Paulist Press, 1976).

Bibliographies:

Molly Abramowitz, *Elie Wiesel: A Bibliography* (Metuchen, N.J.: Scarecrow Press, 1974);

Irving Abrahamson, "Elie Wiesel: A Selected Bibliography," in *Confronting the Holocaust: The Impact of Elie Wiesel*, edited by Alvin H. Rosenfeld and Irving Greenberg (Bloomington: Indiana University Press, 1978).

References:

Edward Alexander, *The Resonance of Dust: Essays on Holocaust Literature and Jewish Fate* (Columbus: Ohio State University Press, 1979);

Michael G. Berenbaum, *The Vision of the Void: Theological Reflections on the Works of Elie Wiesel* (Middletown, Conn.: Wesleyan University Press, 1979);

Alan L. Berger, *Crisis and Covenant: The Holocaust in American Jewish Fiction* (Albany: State University of New York Press, 1985);

Robert McAfee Brown, *Elie Wiesel: Messenger to All Humanity* (Notre Dame, Ind.: University of Notre Dame Press, 1983);

Harry James Cargas, ed., *Responses to Elie Wiesel: Critical Essays by Major Jewish and Christian Scholars* (New York: Persea Books, 1978);

Ted L. Estess, *Elie Wiesel* (New York: Frederick Ungar, 1980);

Sidra DeKoven Ezrahi, *By Words Alone: The Holocaust in Literature* (Chicago: University of Chicago Press, 1980);

Ellen S. Fine, *Legacy of Night: The Literary Universe of Elie Wiesel* (Albany: State University of New York Press, 1982);

Christopher J. Frost, *Religious Melancholy or Psychological Depression?: Some Issues Involved in Relating Psychology and Religion as Illustrated in a Study of Elie Wiesel* (Lanham, Md.: University Press of America, 1985);

Irving Halperin, *Messengers from the Dead* (Philadelphia: Westminster Press, 1970);

Josephine Z. Knopp, *The Trial of Judaism in Contemporary Jewish Writing* (Urbana: University of Illinois Press, 1975);

Lawrence L. Langer, *The Holocaust and the Literary Imagination* (New Haven: Yale University Press, 1975);

Alvin H. Rosenfeld, *A Double Dying: Reflections on Holocaust Literature* (Bloomington: Indiana University Press, 1980);

Rosenfeld and Irving Greenberg, eds., *Confronting the Holocaust: The Impact of Elie Wiesel* (Bloomington: Indiana University Press, 1978);

John K. Roth, *A Consuming Fire: Encounters with Elie Wiesel and the Holocaust* (Atlanta: John Knox Press, 1979);

Byron L. Sherwin and Susan G. Ament, eds., *Encountering the Holocaust: An Interdisciplinary Survey* (Chicago: Impact Press, 1979).

Wole Soyinka: A Correction

In the 1986 *DLB Yearbook* entry on the Nobel Prize in Literature it was incorrectly reported that Wole Soyinka was a member of the class at the University College in Ibadan that also included Chinua Achebe and John Pepper Clark; that he studied under George Wilson Knight at the University of Leeds from 1954 to 1960 (he left the university in 1958); that he took a doctorate at the University of Leeds in 1973; that in the early 1960s he taught at the Universities of Lagos and Ife; and that in 1965 he was imprisoned for one month, when in fact he spent three months in jail accused of the theft of a tape containing a bogus "election victory" broadcast. We regret these errors.

Literary Awards and Honors Announced in 1987

ACADEMY OF AMERICAN POETS AWARDS

ACADEMY OF AMERICAN POETS FELLOWSHIP
Josephine Jacobsen.

LAMONT SELECTION
Garrett Kaoru Hongo, for *The River of Heaven* (Knopf).

IVAN YOUNGER POETS AWARD
Jon Davis, Debora Greger, Norman Williams.

WHITMAN AWARD
Judith Baumel, for *The Weight of Numbers* (Wesleyan University Press).

LANDON TRANSLATION AWARD
Mark Anderson, for *In the Storm of Roses,* by Ingeborg Bachmann (Princeton University Press).

AMERICAN ACADEMY AND INSTITUTE OF ARTS AND LETTERS AWARDS

AWARDS IN LITERATURE
Evan S. Connell, Ernest J. Gaines, Ralph Manheim, Sandra McPherson, Steven Millhauser, Robert Phillips, and Roger Shattuck.

AWARD OF MERIT FOR DRAMA
A. R. Gurney, Jr.

HAROLD D. VURSELL MEMORIAL AWARD
Stephen Jay Gould.

JEAN STEIN AWARD
Wendell Berry.

MORTON DAUWEN ZABEL AWARD
Paul Metcalf.

MILDRED AND HAROLD STRAUSS LIVINGS
Diane Johnson and Robert Stone.

RICHARD AND HINDA ROSENTHAL FOUNDATION AWARD
Norman Rush, for *Whites* (Knopf).

ROME FELLOWSHIP IN LITERATURE
Padgett Powell.

SUE KAUFMAN PRIZE FOR FIRST FICTION
Jeannette Haien, for *The All of It* (Harper & Row).

WITTER BYNNER PRIZE FOR POETRY
Antler.

BANCROFT PRIZES

Thomas M. Doerflinger, for *A Vigorous Spirit of Enterprise: Merchants and Economic Development in Revolutionary Philadelphia* (University of North Carolina Press).

Roger Lane, for *Roots of Violence In Black Philadelphia, 1860-1900* (Harvard University Press).

BOLLINGEN PRIZE IN POETRY

Stanley Kunitz.

BOOKER PRIZE

Penelope Lively, for *Moon Tiger* (Deutsch).

BOSTON GLOBE LITERARY PRESS COMPETITION

GRAND PRIZE
D. R. Godine Publishers, Inc., Boston, Mass.

NONFICTION PROSE
Graywolf Press, for *The Delicacy and Strength of Lace,* by Leslie Marmon Silko and James Wright, edited by Anne Wright.

FICTION
University of Georgia Press, for *Rough Translations,* by Molly Giles.

POETRY
Ecco Press, for *The Triumph of Achilles*, by Louise Gluck, and *Poems of Fernando Pessoa*, translated and edited by Edwin Honig and Susan M. Brown.

MOST VALUABLE REPRINT
North Point Press, for *Between Meals*, by A. J. Liebling, and *The Sleepwalker*, by Herman Broch.

DESIGN, GRAPHICS AND REPRODUCTION
North Point Press, for *Around the Day in 80 Worlds*, by Julio Cortazar.

CALDECOTT MEDAL

Richard Egielski, illustrator of *Hey, Al*, written by Arthur Yorinks (Farrar, Straus & Giroux).

HONOR BOOKS
Paul O. Zelinski, for *Rumpelstiltskin* (Dutton); Ann Grifalconi, for *The Village of Round and Square Houses* (Little, Brown); and Suse MacDonald, for *Alphabetics* (Bradbury).

CAREY-THOMAS PUBLISHING AWARD

Elisabeth Sifton.

HONORS CITATIONS
Carl Bodner's America (University of Nebraska Press) and *Fra Angelico* (Clarkson Potter).

SPECIAL CITATION
Daniel Halpern, Ecco Press.

COMMON WEALTH AWARD

John Ashbery.

CURTIS G. BENJAMIN AWARD

Herbert S. Bailey, Jr.

DELMORE SCHWARTZ MEMORIAL POETRY AWARD

Lee Young.

DRUE HEINZ LITERATURE PRIZE

Ellen Hunnicut, for *In the Music Library* (University of Pittsburgh Press).

EDGAR ALLAN POE AWARDS

GRAND MASTER AWARD
Michael Gilbert.

NOVEL
Barbara Vine, for *A Dark-Adapted Eye* (Bantam).

FIRST NOVEL
Larry Beinhart, for *No One Rides for Free* (Morrow).

FACT CRIME
Carlton Stowers, for *Careless Whispers: The True Story of a Triple Murder and the Determined Lawman Who Wouldn't Give Up* (Taylor).

CRITICAL/BIOGRAPHICAL STUDY
Eric Ambler, for *Here Lies: An Autobiography* (Farrar, Straus & Giroux).

ORIGINAL SOFTCOVER NOVEL
Robert Campbell, for *The Junkyard Dog* (Signet).

JUVENILE NOVEL
Joan Lowery Nixon, for *The Other Side of the Dark* (Delacorte).

SHORT STORY
Robert Sampson, for "Rain in Pinton County," in *New Black Mask* number 5.

TELEVISION EPISODE
David Jackson, for "The Cup," an episode of *The Equalizer*, from a story by Andrew Sipes and Carleton Eastlake (CBS).

TELEVISION FEATURE
Phil Penningroth, for *When the Bough Breaks*, from the novel by Jonathan Kellerman (NBC).

MOTION PICTURE
E. Max Frye, for *Something Wild*.

ELLERY QUEEN AWARD
Eleanor Sullivan.

ROBERT L. FISH MEMORIAL AWARD
Mary Kittredge, for "Father to the Man," in *Alfred Hitchcock's Mystery Magazine)*

ELMER HOLMES BOBST AWARDS

NONFICTION
Flora Lewis.

FICTION
John Updike.

POETRY
Louis Simpson.

SPECIAL AWARD FOR LIFELONG CONTRIBUTION TO ARTS AND LETTERS
Sir Harold Acton.

GOVERNOR GENERAL'S LITERARY AWARDS (ENGLISH LANGUAGE)

FICTION
Alice Monroe, for *The Progress of Love* (McClelland & Stewart).

POETRY
Al Purdy, for *The Collected Poems of Al Purdy* (McClelland & Stewart).

DRAMA
Sharon Pollock, for *Doc* (Playwrights Canada).

NONFICTION
Northrop Frye, for *Northrop Frye on Shakespeare* (Fitzhenry and Whiteside).

INGERSOLL PRIZES

T. S. ELIOT AWARD FOR CREATIVE WRITING
Octavio Paz.

RICHARD M. WEAVER AWARD FOR SCHOLARLY LETTERS
Josef Pieper.

IOWA SCHOOL OF LETTERS AWARD FOR SHORT FICTION

Abby Frucht, for *Fruit of the Month*.
Lucia Nevai, for *Stargame*.

IRMA SIMONTON BLACK AWARD

Joanna Cole, for *Dr. Change* (Morrow).

JANET HEIDINGER KAFKA PRIZE FOR FICTION

Hortense Calisher, for *The Bobby-Soxer* (Doubleday).

JOHN D. AND CATHERINE T. MACARTHUR FOUNDATION AWARDS

POETRY
Douglas Crase, Richard L. Kenney, Mark Strand, May Swenson.

FICTION
Walter Abish.

JOHN DOS PASSOS PRIZE FOR LITERATURE

John Wideman.

LOS ANGELES TIMES BOOK AWARDS

BIOGRAPHY
Kenneth S. Lynn, for *Hemingway* (Simon & Schuster).

CURRENT INTEREST
Richard Dawkins, for *The Blind Watchmaker* (Norton).

FICTION
James Welch, for *Fools Crow* (Viking).

HISTORY
Robert J. Lifton, for *The Nazi Doctors: Medical Killing and the Psychology of Genocide* (Basic Books).

POETRY
William Meredith, for *Partial Accounts: New and Selected Poems* (Simon & Schuster).

ROBERT KIRSCH AWARD FOR BODY OF
WORK
Paul Horgan.

NATIONAL BOOK AWARDS

FICTION
Larry Heinemann, for *Paco's Story* (Farrar, Straus
& Giroux).

NONFICTION
Richard Rhodes, for *The Making of the
Atomic Bomb* (Simon & Schuster).

NATIONAL BOOK CRITICS
CIRCLE AWARDS

FICTION
Reynolds Price, for *Kate Vaiden* (Atheneum).

GENERAL NONFICTION
John W. Dower, for *War Without Mercy: Race
and Power in the Pacific War* (Pantheon).

BIOGRAPHY/AUTOBIOGRAPHY
Theodore Rosengarten, for *Tombee: Portrait
of a Cotton Planter* (Morrow).

POETRY
Edward Hirsch, for *Wild Gratitude* (Knopf).

CRITICISM
Joseph Brodsky, for *Less Than One: Selected Essays* (Farrar, Straus & Giroux).

CITATION FOR EXCELLENCE IN
REVIEWING
Richard Eder, *Los Angeles Times*.

NATIONAL JEWISH BOOK AWARDS

HOLOCAUST
Robert J. Lifton, for *Nazi Doctors: Medical Kill-
ing and the Psychology of Genocide* (Basic
Books).

ILLUSTRATED CHILDREN'S BOOKS
Myra C. Livingston, author, and Lloyd
Bloom, illustrator, for *Poems for Jewish Holi-
days* (Holiday House).

ISRAEL
Samuel Heilman, for *A Walker in Jerusalem*
(Summit Books).

JEWISH THOUGHT
Arnold M. Eisen, for *Galut: Modern Jewish Reflections on Homelessness and Homecoming* (Indiana University Press).

JEWISH HISTORY
David Biale, for *Power and Powerlessness in Jewish History* (Schocken).

SCHOLARSHIP
Reuven Hammer, for *Sifre: A Tannaitic Commentary on the Book of Deuteronomy* (Yale University Press).

VISUAL ARTS
Joy Ungerleider-Mayerson, for *Jewish Folk
Art From Biblical Days to Modern Times*
(Summit).

YIDDISH CITATION
Berlkagan, compiler of the *Lexicon of Yiddish
Writers* (Workman's Circle).

SPECIAL CITATION
Lucius N. Littauer Foundation.

NATIONAL MEDAL FOR LITERATURE

Robert Penn Warren.

NEWBERY MEDAL

Sid Fleischman, for *The Whipping Boy* (Green-
willow).

HONOR BOOKS
Cynthia Rylant, for *A Fine White Dust* (Bradbury); Patricia Lauber, for *Volcano* (Bradbury); and Marion Dane Bauer, for *On My
Honor* (Clarion).

NOBEL PRIZE IN LITERATURE

Joseph Brodsky.

O. HENRY AWARDS

Louise Erdrich, for "Fleur" (*Esquire*, August
1986); and Joyce Johnson, for "The
Children's Wing" (*Harper's*, July 1986).

PEN AWARDS

PEN/BOOK-OF-THE-MONTH-CLUB TRANS-LATION PRIZE
> John E. Woods, for *Perfume: The Story of a Murderer*, by Patrick Süskind (Knopf).

ERNEST HEMINGWAY FOUNDATION AWARD
> Mary Ward Brown, for *Tongues of Flame* (Dutton/Seymour Lawrence).

RENATO POGGIOLI TRANSLATION AWARD FOR A WORK IN PROGRESS
> Linda Lappin, for *Fratelli* and *Il Custode*, by Carmelo Samonà.

ALGREN FICTION AWARD FOR WORK IN PROGRESS
> Karl Evans, for *Diamonds of the First Water*.

SHEAFFER-PEN NEW ENGLAND AWARD FOR LITERARY DISTINCTION
> Andre Dubus.

PRESENT TENSE/JOEL H. CAVIOR LITERARY AWARDS

FICTION
> Art Spiegelman, for *Maus: A Survivor's Tale* (Pantheon).

HISTORY
> Bernard Lewis, for *Semites and Anti-Semites: An Inquiry into Conflict and Prejudice* (Norton).

BIOGRAPHY/AUTOBIOGRAPHY
> Victor Perera, for *Rites: A Guatemalan Boyhood* (Harcourt Brace Jovanovich).

JEWISH RELIGIOUS THOUGHT
> David Weiss Halivni, for *Midrash, Mishnah, and Gamara: The Jewish Predeliction for Justified Law* (Harvard University Press).

GENERAL NONFICTION
> Lesley Hazelton, for *Jerusalem, Jerusalem* (Atlantic Monthly Press).

PULITZER PRIZES

FICTION
> Peter Taylor, for *A Summons to Memphis* (Knopf).

GENERAL NONFICTION
> David K. Shipler, for *Arab and Jew: Wounded Spirits in a Promised Land* (Times Books).

HISTORY
> Bernard Bailyn, for *Voyagers to the West: A Passage in the Peopling of America on the Eve of the Revolution* (Knopf).

BIOGRAPHY
> David J. Garrow, for *Bearing the Cross: Martin Luther King, Jr. and the Southern Christian Leadership Conference* (Morrow).

POETRY
> Rita Dove, for *Thomas and Beulah* (Carnegie Mellon).

DRAMA
> August Wilson, for *Fences* (NAL).

REA AWARD FOR THE SHORT STORY

Robert Coover.

REGINA MEDAL

Betsy Byars.

RITZ PARIS HEMINGWAY AWARD

Peter Taylor, for *A Summons to Memphis* (Knopf).

ROBERT F. KENNEDY MEMORIAL BOOK AWARDS

RUTH LILLY POETRY PRIZE
Phillip Levine.

HONORABLE MENTION
> David J. Garrow, for *Bearing the Cross: Martin Luther King, Jr. and the Southern Christian Leadership Conference* (Morrow).
> Robert Coles, for *The Political Life of Children* (Atlantic Monthly Press).
> Elizabeth Becker, for *When the War was Over;*

DLB Yearbook 1987

The Voices of Cambodia's Revolution and Its People (Simon & Schuster).

SCOTT O'DELL AWARD FOR HISTORICAL FICTION

Patricia Beatty, for *Charley Skedadde* (Morrow).

WHITBREAD AWARD

Kazuo Ishiguro, for *An Artist of the Floating World* (Faber).

WHITING AWARDS

Mindy Aloff, Joan Chase, Mark Cox, Pam Durban, Gretel Ehrlich, Deborah Eisenberg, Alice McDermott, Reinaldo Povod, Michael Ryan, and David Foster Wallace.

W. H. SMITH AWARD

Elizabeth Jennings, for *Collected Poems* (Carcanet).

Checklist: Contributions to Literary History and Biography, 1987

This checklist is a selection of new books on various aspects and periods of literary and cultural history; biographies, memoirs, and correspondence of literary people and their associates; and primary bibliographies. Not included are volumes in general reference series, literary criticism, and bibliographies of criticism.

Alcott, Louisa May. *The Selected Letters of Louisa May Alcott*. Edited by Joel Myerson and Daniel Shealy with Madeleine B. Stern. Boston: Little, Brown, 1987.

Baker, Houston A. *Modernism and the Harlem Renaissance*. Chicago: University of Chicago Press, 1987.

Barbera, Jack, and William McBrien. *Stevie: A Biography of Stevie Smith*. New York: Oxford University Press, 1987.

Burgess, Anthony. *Little Wilson and Big God*. New York: Weidenfeld & Nicolson, 1987.

Caldwell, Erskine. *With All My Might: An Autobiography*. Atlanta: Peachtree, 1987.

Camus, Albert. *American Journals*. New York: Paragon House, 1987.

Chitham, Edward. *A Life of Emily Brontë*. New York: Basil Blackwell, 1987.

Cohen-Solal, Annie. *Sartre: A Life*. Edited by Norman MacAfee. Translated by Anna Cancogri. New York: Pantheon, 1987.

Davis, Linda H. *Onward and Upward: A Biography of Katharine S. White*. New York: Harper & Row, 1987.

Delany, Paul. *The Neo-Pagans: Rupert Brooke and the Ordeal*. New York: Free Press, 1987.

Dillard, Annie. *An American Childhood*. New York: Harper & Row, 1987.

Donald, David Herbert. *Look Homeward: A Life of Thomas Wolfe*. Boston: Little, Brown, 1987.

Drake, William. *The First Wave: Women Poets in America 1915-1945*. New York: Macmillan, 1987.

Ellmann, Richard. *Oscar Wilde*. London: Hamish Hamilton, 1987.

Emerson, Lidian Jackson. *The Selected Letters of Lidian Jackson Emerson*. Edited by Delores Bird Carpenter. Columbia: University of Missouri Press, 1987.

Gallagher, Brian. *Anything Goes: The Jazz Age Adventures of Neysa McMein and Her Extravagant Circle of Friends*. New York: Times Books, 1987.

Gindin, James. *John Galsworthy's Life and Art: An Alien's Fortress*. New York: Macmillan, 1987.

Glendinning, Victoria. *Rebecca West: A Life*. New York: Knopf, 1987.

Graves, Richard Perceval. *Robert Graves: The Assault Heroic 1895-1926*. New York: Viking, 1986.

Hardy, Thomas. *The Collected Letters of Thomas Hardy, Volume Six: 1920-1925*. Edited by Richard Little Purdy and Michael Millgate. New York: Oxford University Press, 1987.

Harris, Mary Emma. *The Arts at Black Mountain College*. Cambridge, Mass.: MIT Press, 1987.

Howard, Donald. *Chaucer: His Life, His Works, His World*. New York: Dutton, 1987.

James, Henry. *The Complete Notebooks of Henry James*. Edited by Leon Edel and Lyall H. Powers. New York: Oxford University Press, 1987.

Joyce, James. *James Joyce's Letter to Sylvia Beach, 1921-1940*. Edited by Melissa Banta and Oscar A. Silverman. Bloomington & Indianapolis: Indiana University Press, 1987.

Kerman, Cynthia Earl, and Richard Eldridge. *The Lives of Jean Toomer: A Hunger for Wholeness*. Baton Rouge: Louisiana State University Press, 1987.

Lovell, Mary S. *Straight on till Morning: The Biography of Beryl Markham*. New York: St. Martin's, 1986.

Lynn, Kenneth S. *Hemingway*. New York: Simon & Schuster, 1987.

McCarthy, Mary. *How I Grew*. New York & San Diego: Harcourt Brace Jovanovich, 1987.

McCormick, John. *George Santayana*. New York: Knopf, 1987.

Miller, Arthur. *Timebends*. New York: Grove Press, 1987.

Oates, Stephen B. *William Faulkner: The Man and the Artist*. New York: Harper & Row, 1987.

O'Brien, Sharon. *Willa Cather: The Emerging Years*. New York: Oxford University Press, 1986.

Perelman, S. J. *Don't Tread On Me: The Selected Letters of S. J. Perelman*. Edited by Prudence Crowther. New York: Viking, 1987.

Rodgers, Marion Elizabeth, ed. *Mencken and Sara: A Life in Letters*. New York: McGraw-Hill, 1987.

Seldes, George. *Witness to a Century*. New York: Ballantine, 1987.

Simpson, Eileen. *Orphans: Real and Imaginary*. New York: Weidenfeld & Nicolson, 1987.

Smith, Meredith Etherington, and Jeremy Pilcher. *The "It" Girls: Elinor Glyn, Novelist, and her Sister Lucille, Couturière*. New York & San Diego: Harcourt Brace Jovanovich, 1987.

Stannard, Martin. *Evelyn Waugh: The Early Years 1903-1939*. New York: Norton, 1987.

Thomas, Caitland, with George Tremlett. *Caitland: Life with Dylan Thomas*. New York: Holt, 1987.

Townsend, Kim. *Sherwood Anderson*. Boston: Houghton Mifflin, 1987.

Tytell, John. *Ezra Pound: The Solitary Volcano*. Garden City: Doubleday, 1987.

Wagner-Martin, Linda. *Sylvia Plath: A Biography*. New York: Simon & Schuster, 1987.

Washington, Mary Helen. *Invented Lives: Narratives of Black Women 1860-1960*. Garden City: Anchor/ Doubleday, 1987.

Woodress, James. *Willa Cather: A Literary Life*. Lincoln: University of Nebraska Press, 1987.

Necrology

Jean Anouilh–3 October 1987
Peggy Bacon–4 January 1987
Carlos Baker–18 April 1987
James Baldwin–1 December 1987
Franklin Bandy–11 April 1987
Jim Bishop–26 July 1987
William Bowers–27 March 1987
Hob Broun–16 December 1987
Fanny Butcher–14 May 1987
Erskine Caldwell–11 April 1987
Joseph Campbell–31 October 1987
Vera Caspary–13 June 1987
Beatrice Chute–6 September 1987
George Dennison–8 October 1987
Lovat Dickson–2 January 1987
Talbot Donaldson–13 April 1987
Richard Ellmann–13 May 1987
William Fifield–14 December 1987
John F. Fleming–20 December 1987
Robert Francis–13 July 1987
John Huston–28 August 1987
Maria Jolas–4 March 1987
John Oliver Killens–27 October 1987

Joseph P. Lash–22 August 1987
Margaret Laurence–5 January 1987
Primo Levi–11 April 1987
Richard Levinson–12 March 1987
Arnold Lobel–4 December 1987
John Logan–6 November 1987
Alistair MacLean–2 February 1987
John Bartlow Martin–3 January 1987
Hildegarde Flanner Monhoff–27 May 1987
Howard Moss–16 September 1987
Charles George Muller–14 December 1987
Charles Murphy–29 December 1987
Arch Oboler–19 March 1987
Frederick A. Pottle–16 May 1987
Waldo Salt–7 March 1987
Daniel Sargent–24 January 1987
Alice Sheldon–19 May 1987
Monroe M. Stearns–17 December 1987
Michael Stewart–20 September 1987
Howard M. Teichmann–7 July 1987
Glenway Wescott–22 February 1987
Anthony West–27 December 1987
Hugh Wheeler–27 July 1987
Marguerite Yourcenar–17 December 1987

Contributors

Nancy G. Anderson ....*Auburn University at Montgomery*
Samuel Irving Bellman ....*California State Polytechnic University, Pomona*
Richard R. Centing ....*Ohio State University*
Kimberly Rae Chambers ....*University of Virginia*
Mason Cooley ....*College of Staten Island, City University of New York*
Sarah English ....*Meredith College*
George Garrett ....*University of Virginia*
D. C. Greetham ....*City University of New York*
R. S. Gwynn ....*Lamar University*
Mark Heberle ....*University of Hawaii*
Bill Henderson ....*Wainscott, New York*
Robert E. Hosmer, Jr. ....*Mount Holyoke College*
Howard Kissel ....*New York Daily News*
George L. Kline ....*Bryn Mawr College*
Kenneth A. Lohf ....*Butler Library, Columbia University*
Irma S. Lustig ....*University of Pennsylvania*
Charles W. Mann ....*Pennsylvania State University Libraries*
Ann DeWitt Moss ....*Algonquin Books of Chapel Hill*
Charles M. Oliver ....*Ohio Northern University*
Michael Pinkston ....*Louisiana State University Press*
Anne Posega ....*Washington University Libraries, Special Collections*
Walter W. Ross ....*Columbia, South Carolina*
John K. Roth ....*Claremont McKenna College*
William J. Scheick ....*University of Texas at Austin*
James Schiffer ....*Hampden-Sydney College*
Peter A. Scholl ....*Luther College*
Steven Serafin ....*Hunter College of the City University of New York*
David R. Slavitt ....*Philadelphia, Pennsylvania*
Fred L. Standley ....*Florida State University*
Donald E. Stanford ....*Louisiana State University*
Dawn Trouard ....*University of Akron*
Nancy Lewis Tuten ....*University of South Carolina*
Ruth M. Vande Kieft ....*Queens College, City University of New York*
Stephen Whited ....*Lexington, Kentucky*
Rhonda Zangwill ....*Elmer Holmes Bobst Library*

413

Cumulative Index

Dictionary of Literary Biography, Volumes 1-67
Dictionary of Literary Biography Yearbook, 1980-1987
Dictionary of Literary Biography Documentary Series, Volumes 1-4

Cumulative Index

DLB before number: *Dictionary of Literary Biography,* Volumes 1-67
Y before number: *Dictionary of Literary Biography Yearbook,* 1980-1987
DS before number: *Dictionary of Literary Biography Documentary Series,* Volumes 1-4

B

Cumulative Index

E

F

I

J

L

M

N

Q

Cumulative Index

T

W

Y

Z

Dictionary of Literary Biography